# THE SCIMITAR FILE

ERIC MORGAN

and

JOHN STEVENS

AN AIR-BRITAIN PUBLICATION

Copyright © 2000
Eric Morgan, John Stevens and
Air-Britain (Historians) Ltd.

First published 2000, reprinted 2002

Published in the United Kingdom by

Air-Britain (Historians) Ltd,
12 Lonsdale Gardens,
Tunbridge Wells, Kent TN1 1PA

Sales Dept:
41 Penshurst Road, Leigh,
Tonbridge, Kent TN11 8HL

Correspondence to:

R.C.Sturtivant, 26 Monks Horton Way,
St.Albans, Herts, AL1 4HA
and not to the Tunbridge Wells address

ISBN 0 85130 323 4

All rights reserved.    No part of the contents of this
publication may be reproduced, stored in a retrieval system
or transmitted in any form or by any means electronic,
mechanical, photocopying, recording or otherwise without
the prior written permission of Air-Britain (Historians) Ltd.

Printed in the United Kingdom by
Cromwell Printers Ltd
Aintree Avenue
White Horse Business Park
Trowbridge, Somerset BA14 0XB

Front cover painting by Professor Dugald Cameron OBE:
Scimitar F.1 XD322 '109/R' leading a trio of No.800
Squadron aircraft over HMS Ark Royal.

Rear cover drawing by David Howley:
Scimitar F.1 XD235 '149/R' of No.803 Squadron in 1964.

# CONTENTS

| | |
|---|---|
| Roll of Honour | 5 |
| Acknowledgements | 6 |
| Glossary of Terms and Abbreviations | 8 |
| Introduction | 11 |
| Origins, Ancestry and Development | 12 |
|     Type 505 - The 'Carpet Interceptor' | 13 |
|     Type 508 | 15 |
|     Type 529 | 21 |
|     Type 508 – Specification 500/R | 21 |
|     Type 525 | 21 |
|     Type 529 | 21 |
| Type 544 | 26 |
| The Scimitar | 36 |
| Daily Mail Bleriot Air Race | 53 |
| Pilot's Observations | 55 |
| Squadron and Unit Histories | 96 |
| Individual Aircraft Histories | 161 |
| A Description | 184 |
| Variations on a Theme | 192 |
|     Type 511 | 192 |
|     Type 522 | 192 |
|     Type 523 | 192 |
|     Type 526 | 194 |
|     Type 537 | 194 |
|     Type 539 | 194 |
|     Type 543 | 196 |
|     Type 556 | 200 |
|     Type 558 | 202 |
|     Type 560 | 202 |
|     Type 561 | 202 |
|     Type 562 | 204 |
|     Type 563 | 205 |
|     Type 564 | 205 |
|     Type 565 | 207 |
|     Type 566 | 207 |
|     Type 567 | 207 |
|     Type 572 | 207 |
|     Type 576 | 209 |
| Index of Names | 215 |
| Photo Miscellany | 219 |

## Dedication

To the men who designed, built, flew and maintained "the beast".

*XD243 '190/R', XD267 '193/R', XD248 '195/R' and XD250 '197/R' of No.807 Squadron in 'Box' formation during a looping manoeuvre in June 1959. (via M.J.Hooks)*

# ROLL OF HONOUR

| | | |
|---|---|---|
| Lt Cdr Tony Alan Rickell | Royal Navy | 5 July 1955 |
| Cdr John Desmond Russell | Royal Navy | 25 September 1958 |
| Sub Lt Colin Richard Cresswell | Royal Navy | 19 November 1958 |
| Lt Richard William David Westlake | Royal Navy | 7 February 1960 |
| Lt Nicholas John Norris | Royal Navy | 16 November 1960 |
| Lt George Coryton Edwardes | Royal Navy | 3 May 1961 |
| Flt Lt M.Farmer | Royal Air Force | 22 June 1961 |
| Lt Thomas Mark Horace Laister | Royal Navy | 20 September 1961 |
| Lt Andrew Gordon MacFie | Royal Navy | 31 July 1963 |
| Mr Terence E. Hill | Airwork | 26 June 1968 |

# ACKNOWLEDGEMENTS

To compile enough information to complete a book of this nature one needs the help of a great many people. To all those who so kindly gave their help and time, we express our grateful thanks:

Anne Adie (late of *Vickers News*); C.F.Andrews; Chris Ashworth; Ivor Barnes; David Brown (Naval Historical Branch MoD); Charles Burnet; Mick Burrow; Mrs E.Cawdron (ex RAE Bedford); Derby Childehouse (photographic help); W.R.Chorley; L.R.Colquhoun DFC GM DFM (log books and advice); Kim A.Collinson; David Coombs (ex PO AH1); Graham Cooper (DARA Fleetlands); John Coughlan; RNAS Culdrose photo section; Ray Deacon; C.J.Diamato; David Dorrell (ex 'Air Pictorial'); Norman Eames (ex POEL); P.J.V.Elliot (RAE Farnborough); D.W.Good (RAE Farnborough); Mike Groth; James J.Halley (Air-Britain); David Hicks; Denis Higton; Major Tony Hill (P&EE Shoeburyness); Ron Holbrow; Lee Howard (DARA Fleetlands); John Jeffs; Brian Keeble (ex AH3); Tony Leigh (ex L/A AE); M.J.Lithgow OBE (log books); Len Lovell (ex Head of Research at the Fleet Air Arm Museum); FCA(AH)ATC J.McCallum (of RNAS Culdrose); FCA(AH)ATC Eric McVeigh (for his hospitality at Yeovilton); K.J.Meadows (PRO Farnborough); David Mondey FRHistS AMRAeS; D.W.Morgan MBE MRAeS (log books and advice); Lt C.F.Motley RN (Rtd); Nick Parker; J.K.Quill OBE AFC (log books and advice); Richard Riding (ex *'Aeroplane Monthly'*); Roy Rolland (ex AH3); John Spencer (photographs); A.Taylor (ATC); John Tipp (BARG); Denis Webb; W.P.Welsh (FEI Paris); Brian Wexham ARPS (Vickers PLC).

Also the many ex-squadron pilots who were kind enough to sit down and recall their memories of long ago:

Vice Admiral Sir Edward Anson KCB FRAeS; Commander T.V.G.Binney OBE RN (Rtd); Lt Cdr A.R.Campbell RN (Rtd); Lt Cdr P.Cardew RN (Rtd); Commander A.M.D.de Labilliere RN; Lt Cdr P.G.de Souza RN (Rtd); Commander T.C.Evans AFC RN (Rtd); Commander C.C.Giles RN (Rtd); Lt Cdr A.J.Goodenough RN (Rtd); Captain F.Hefford OBE DSC AFC MRAeS RN (Rtd); Commander G.R.Higgs AFC RN (Rtd); Lt Cdr G.B.Hoddinott RN (Rtd); Commander J.D.H.B.Howard RN (Rtd); Lt Cdr M.T.Hynett RN (Rtd); Captain A.J.Leahy CBE DSC RN (Rtd); Lt Cdr T.C.S.Leece RN (Rtd); Rear Admiral L.E.Middleton DSO FRaeS FBIM; Commander N.J.P.Mills RN (Rtd); British Airways Captain C.Morris; Commander D.P.Norman AFC RN (Rtd); Commander S.G.Orr DSC AFC RN (Rtd); Lt K.B.Owen RN (Rtd); Commodore D.Pentreath DSO RN; Lt Cdr J.W.H.Purvis RN (Rtd); Captain D.F.Robbins RN (Rtd); Lt Cdr J.G.L.Smith RN (Rtd); Commander P.M.Stevenson RN; Captain W.A.Tofts CBE AFC RN (Rtd); Lt Cdr N.M.Tristram RN (Rtd); Mr P.A.Waring; Captain J.L.Williams RN (Rtd); Captain J.Worth RN.

Special thanks to Ray Sturtivant and Theo Ballance for the help so generously given and dates extracted from their excellent book "*The Squadrons of the Fleet Air Arm*". Also to Dave Morgan for his considerable help and support in explaining the intricacies of some of the aircraft's systems and details surrounding the trials programmes; to Lee Howard for his great help in transforming our original manuscript into its present form, and for providing the majority of the excellent information on RNAY Fleetlands and various other miscellaneous units; to Denis Webb for allowing us to extract information about the Type 525 from his forthcoming memoirs "*Never a Dull Moment*"; and to Terry Heffernan, the unpaid Public Relations Officer of Boscombe Down who gave the encouragement to see it through!

Our thanks also go to Air-Britain for their expansion of our serial number listing into an extensive individual aircraft history file. The society has been in existence since 1948, and if you are an aviation enthusiast you should join their ranks and be counted.

It is some years since I sent the manuscript for this book, in an unfinished state due to mediocre health, to Air-Britain. Its members have accomplished a transformation, both in the wordage and in the amount of additional material they have managed to obtain. In effect they have converted my efforts and those of John Stevens into a 'real' book and a much more comprehensive history of one of Britain's major seaborne fighters.

I had prepared my own list of detailed histories of the individual aircraft, but this has been surpassed by the additional information that Air-Britain's members have produced. One person who has been at the forefront of this is Ray Sturtivant, who through his fortitude and despite his own ill health has achieved an excellent result.

In his efforts to get the ultimate he accumulated more than a thousand photographs, from which about a quarter were eventually chosen as being the best for this purpose.

The main company information came from the Supemarine Archives, which I was able to view and study first hand. As a consequence there are drawings of all the various projects which never materialised.

I served in the Civil Service from 1943 to 1946 on Radar, and then twenty years in the Royal Air Force, followed by another twenty years with Vickers Armstrongs (Aircraft) Ltd. As can be seen, my life has been in aviation, and I know about organisation and methods, but I must say that Air-Britain's organisation must be on a par with the best.

E.B.Morgan
August 2000

# GLOSSARY OF TERMS AND ABBREVIATIONS

| | |
|---|---|
| A&AEE | Aeroplane and Armament Experimental Establishment (Boscombe Down) |
| AAM | Air-to-air Missile |
| A/c | Aircraft |
| AC | Alternating current |
| Acft | Aircraft |
| ACRB | Aircrew Refreshment Bar |
| ADA | Action Data Automation [part of ships' radar system - automatic feed of information into Operations Room] |
| ADA | Assistant Director Aircraft |
| ADD | Airstream Direction Detector |
| Addl | Additional |
| ADDL | Aerodrome Dummy Deck Landings |
| A/E | Airframe/Engine trade |
| AEO | Air Engineering Officer |
| AES | Air Engineering School |
| a/f | Airfield |
| AFC | Air Force Cross |
| AFM | Air Force Medal |
| AFT | Advanced Flying Training |
| AH | Aircraft Handler |
| AH1 | Aircraft Handler 1st Class |
| AHU | Aircraft Holding Unit |
| AII | Audio Incidence Indicator |
| AIU | Accident Investigation Unit |
| ALO | Air Electrical Officer |
| AMIEE | Associate Member of the Institute of Electrical Engineers |
| AMRAeS | Associate Member of the Royal Aeronautical Society |
| arr | Arrived |
| ASI | Air speed indicator |
| ASM | Air-to-surface Missile |
| Asst | Assistant |
| ASSU | Air Speed Sensing Unit [or Aircraft Servicing & Support Unit - depending on context] |
| ASV | Air-to-surface-vessel [radar] |
| ATC | Air Traffic Control/Air Training Corps |
| AUW | All-up weight |
| AVM | Air Vice Marshal |
| AVPIN | Starter Fuel (Isoprophylnitrate). |
| AVCAT | Gas turbine fuel (high flash point kerosene, used on RN ships to reduce fire risk while in bulk storage for aircraft) |
| AVTAG | Gas turbine fuel (volatile gasoline product for gas turbines, mainly used by U.S. forces ashore and some civil aircraft as JP4) |
| AVTUR | Gas turbine fuel (the most widely-used kerosene for gas turbines and the cheapest to produce. Used by UK military and civil operators) |
| AWI | Air Warfare Instructor |
| AWRE | Atomic Weapons Research Establishment |
| BFT | Basic Flying Training |
| BLC | Boundary layer control (air blown over wing from engine) |
| BHS | Type of accelerator |
| Bolter | To miss the arrester wire, accelerate and fly off |
| BSC | Basic Servicing Card |
| BU | Broke Up (in flight)/Broken Up (for scrap) |
| CA/C(A) | Controller (Aircraft) |
| CAP | Combat Air Patrol |
| Catwalk | Walkway around the flight deck, below flight deck level |
| Cat H | Heavy damage (sub-category not recorded) |
| Cat HX | Heavy damage repairable by ship or station |
| Cat HC | Heavy damage repairable on ship or station but requiring contractors working party |
| Cat HY | Heavy damage not repairable by ship or station |
| Cat L | Light damage (sub-category not recorded) |
| Cat LQ | Light damage repairable by squadron resources |
| Cat LX | Light damage repairable by ship or station |
| Cat LC | Light damage repairable on ship or station but requiring contractors working party |
| Cat LY | Light damage not repairable by ship or station resources |
| Cat SS | No damage to aircraft |
| Cat ZZ | Lost, unrepairable or beyond economical repair |
| CB | Companion of the Order of the Bath |
| CdeC | Capitaine de Corvette [French Navy] |
| Cdr | Commander |
| CEA | Chief Electrical Artificer |
| CG/CofG | Centre of gravity |
| $C_L$ | Coefficient of Lift |
| CNR | Chief of Naval Research |
| CO | Commanding Officer |
| Condition 1 | Ship closed up for combat, fighter aircraft manned and catapults loaded for immediate launch |
| Condition 2 etc | Ship at lower states of readiness |
| Cont | Contract |
| CPO | Chief Petty Officer |
| CRT | Crash Rescue Training |
| c/s | Call Sign (Radio) |
| CWP | Centralised Warning Panel/Contractors Working Party |
| DACR | Director Aircraft Carrier Research |
| DAEO | Deputy Air Engineering Officer |
| DANav | Director Air Navigation |
| DARD | Directorate of Aircraft Research and Development |
| DarmD | Directorate of Armament Development |
| DAW | Department of Air Warfare |
| DAX | Direct action arresting wires |
| Deg | Degree(s) |
| DegC | Degrees Centigrade |
| DegK | Degrees Kelvin |
| Deld | Delivered [to] |
| Detd | Detached |
| Dett | Detachment |
| Desynn | Instrument system for indicating rotational movement |
| DFC | Distinguished Flying Cross |
| DFM | Distinguished Flying Medal |
| DH | de Havilland |
| DL | Deck landing |
| DLP | Deck landing practice |
| DNAW | Director of Naval Air Warfare |
| DoI | Died of Injury |
| Doppler | Navigational aid |
| DOR | Director of Operational Research |
| DSC | Distinguished Service Cross |
| DSM | Distinguished Service Medal |
| DSO | Distinguished Service Order |
| Dt | Detachment |
| DT | Drop tank |
| DTD | Director General of Technical Development |

| | | | |
|---|---|---|---|
| E | East | IMN | Indicated Mach Number |
| (E) | Engineering [Officer] | IP | Identification Point |
| EAS | Equivalent Air Speed (IAS corrected for instrument and position error) | IR | Instrument Rating |
| | | JPT | Jet Pipe Temperature |
| ECU | Engine Change Unit | | |
| EF | Engine Failure | KCB | Knight Commander of the Order of the Bath |
| E.L. | Electrician | Kt | Knot(s) |
| EMC | Electromagnetic Compatibility | kW | Kilowatt(s) |
| ENE | East north east | | |
| EngL | Engineering Electrical | (L) | Electrical [Officer] |
| EngM | Engineering Mechanical | LABS | Low Altitude Bombing System |
| ERU | Ejector Release Unit [on Armament Carrier] | Lb | Pound(s) (weight) |
| ETPS | Empire Test Pilots School | L/C | Lieutenant Commander |
| | | LCN | Load Classification Number [runway] |
| FAA | Fleet Air Arm | LP | Low Pressure [cock] |
| Fam 1 | First familiarisation flight | Lt | Lieutenant |
| FBIM | Fellow of the British Institute of Metallurgy | Lt Cdr | Lieutenant Commander |
| FCA | Fleet Chief Airman | LTS | Long term storage |
| FDO | Flight Deck Officer | MA | Master of Arts |
| FF | First Flight | MADDL | Mirror Aerodrome Dummy Deck Landing (i.e. an ADDL with a mirror sight) |
| Finals | Final approach to land | | |
| FL | Force Landed | MAP | Military Aircraft Photographs |
| Flameout | Flame in combustion chamber extinguished | MARTSU | Mobile Aircraft Repair, Transport and Salvage Unit |
| FLYCO | Flying Control (usually aboard a ship) | | |
| Flyex | Flying exercise | Maxaret | Dunlop Anti-skid brake unit/system |
| FN | French Navy [Aeronavale] | MBE | Member of the Order of the British Empire |
| FOAC | Flag Officer Aircraft Carriers | MC | Medium Capacity (bomb) |
| FOD | Foreign object damage | MinTech | Ministry of Technology |
| Fpm | Feet per minute | MoA | Ministry of Aviation |
| FR | Flight refuelling | MoD | Ministry of Defence |
| FRAeS | Fellow of the Royal Aeronautical Society | Mod 494 | Modification to enable fuel tanks to be cross-connected, allowing the recovery of fuel which would otherwise have been lost, and stabilising the aircraft around its centre of gravity |
| FRHistS | Fellow of the Royal Historical Society | | |
| FRU | Fleet Requirements Unit | | |
| | | | |
| GCA | Ground Controlled Approach | MoS | Ministry of Supply |
| GEV | Ground Engineering Vehicle | Mpa | MegaPascal [measurement of pressure] |
| GGS | Gyro Gun Sight | MRAeS | Member of the Royal Aeronautical Society |
| GI | Ground Instruction (Ground Instructional Airframe) | MRCA | Multi Role Combat Aircraft [became the Tornado] |
| | | MRG | Master Reference Gyro |
| GM | George Medal | MTP | Maintenance Test Pilot |
| Goofers | People watching the flying on a ship | MTPS | Maintenance Test Pilot's School |
| GP | General purpose | MVO | Member of the Victorian Order |
| | | | |
| Hangar Queen | Aircraft continuously used for spares and not flown | N | North |
| | | NACA | National Advisory Committee for Aeronautics |
| HE | High explosive | NAD | Naval Air Department (RAE Farnborough and later RAE Bedford) |
| HiCap | High Level Combat Air Patrol | | |
| Howdah | Catapult control position which could be raised or lowered from flight deck | NAMM | Naval Aircraft Maintenance Manual |
| | | NARIU | Naval Air Radio Installation Unit |
| hp | Horse power | NASU | Naval Air Support Unit |
| HP | High Pressure [cock] | Nav-aid | Navigation aid(s) |
| HRH | His/Her Royal Highness | Navex | Navigational exercise |
| HUD | Head Up Display | NE | North-east |
| Hussenot | Type of aircraft data recorder plotting data against time on roll of paper | NILO | Type of pen nib fairing behind the jet pipes |
| | | Nm | Nautical mile(s) |
| HV | High Velocity | NPL | National Physical Laboratory |
| HVAR | High Velocity Aircraft Rocket ? | NSR | Naval Staff Requirement |
| Hyd 1/2 | Combination of number 1 and 2 hydraulic systems which together operated the flying controls, and other such systems such as undercarriage, hook, flaps | NTU | Not taken up |
| | | OBE | Officer of the Order of the British Empire |
| | | OFS | Operational Flying School |
| | | OK | Crew member survived accident |
| IAS | Indicated air speed | | |
| ICAN | International Commission for Air Navigation | PBC | Polyurethane Barrier Coating (sealants) |
| IDF | Interceptor Day Fighter | P/DTD | ? /Directorate of Technical Development |
| IF | Instrument Flying | P&EE | Proof and Experimental Establishment |
| IFF | Identification friend or foe | PFS | Preparation for service |
| IFR | In-Flight Refuelling/Instrument Flight Rules | PIO | Pilot Induced Oscillation |
| ILS | Instrument Landing System | PO | Petty Officer |

| | | | |
|---|---|---|---|
| POEL | Petty Officer (Electrical) | SHAPE | Code name for 2,000lb atomic bomb |
| PR | Photographic Reconnaissance | Shp | Shaft Horse Power |
| PRC | Sealant compound | S/L | Sub-Lieutenant |
| Psi | Pounds per square inch | SOC | Struck Off Charge |
| PUP | Pull-up Point | SP | Senior Pilot |
| | | Sqn | Squadron |
| QFI | Qualified Flying Instructor | s.t. | Static thrust |
| QGH | Descent controlled using bearings on radio transmissions from aircraft | SSE | South south-east |
| | | STS | Short term storage |
| QNH | Barometric air pressure at sea level | | |
| | | TACAN | Tactical Air Navigator homing beacon |
| RAAF | Royal Australian Air Force | TAS | True Air Speed |
| RATOG | Rocket-assisted take-off gear | TER | Triple Ejector Rack (bomb) |
| RAF | Royal Air Force | Temp | Temporary/Temporarily |
| RCL | Recoilless [gun] | TFH | Total Flying Hours |
| RD | Research & Development (Branch) | TI | Trial installation/Tactical Instructor/Technical Instruction [depending on context] |
| RDN | Research & Development (Navy) | | |
| Retd | Returned | TIR | Temporary In-use Reserve [aircraft] |
| RFA | Royal Fleet Auxiliary | TMB | Target Marker Bomb - nuclear device |
| RN | Royal Navy | TO | Take-off |
| RNAS | Royal Naval Air Station | TOC | Taken on charge |
| RNAY | Royal Naval Aircraft Yard | Trail | To make a condensation trail |
| RP | Rocket Projectile | | |
| Rpg | Rounds per gun | U/c | Undercarriage |
| Rpm | Revolutions per minute | U/s | Unserviceable |
| RSP | Reduced to spares and produce | USMC | United States Marine Corps |
| R/T | Radio Telephone | USN | United States Navy |
| Rtd | Retired | USS | United States Ship |
| RTO | Resident Technical Officer | | |
| RY | Ready for collection | VA | Vickers-Armstrong |
| | | VHF | Very high frequency (radio) |
| S | South | VIP | Very Important Person |
| SAR | Search and Rescue | VIT | Variable Incidence Tail? |
| SAH | School of Aircraft Handling | VT | Variable Time |
| SBAC | Society of British Aircraft/Aerospace Constructors | W | West |
| Sec | Second | wef | With effect from |
| SF | Station Flight | Wfu | Withdrawn From Use |
| SFC | Specific fuel consumption | WOC | Written Off Charge |

*Three aircraft of No.807 Squadron with everything down flying over another with wings folded at the SBAC Show at Farnborough in September 1959.*

*Front view of Type 544 prototype WT859 with noise suppresser supports underneath. (Vickers-Armstrongs)*

# INTRODUCTION

For those Fleet Air Arm pilots and groundcrew of the 1950s, who were familiar with the diminutive Hawker Sea Hawk and its friendly high-pitched whistle, benign handling qualities and (relative) ease of maintenance, the first sight and sound of its intended replacement, the new Supermarine Scimitar, must surely have been both an exciting and fairly daunting experience.

Evolving from an original undercarriage-less Naval aircraft concept devised by the Admiralty towards the end of the Second World War, the Scimitar was the last in a long line of fighter aircraft designed and built by the Supermarine Division of Vickers-Armstrongs (Aircraft) Ltd and its predecessors that stretched back as far as 1914. Its introduction into service in 1958 was an important milestone in Naval aviation. It was the first swept-wing, twin-engined, single-seat jet aircraft to serve with the Fleet and, as far as the latter was concerned, was to be the last until the advent of the Sea Harrier; it was the largest and heaviest aircraft that had yet landed aboard a British aircraft carrier and, perhaps more importantly, it finally made the Royal Navy a nuclear-capable force.

Possibly remembered best by those who came into contact with it on the ground for its ability to leak fuel from every seam imaginable, and by those who flew it for its apparently unlimited power, the Scimitar would serve the Fleet Air Arm for less than a decade in five front-line squadrons and a further five training and trials units.

With retirement from the front-line in 1966, the Scimitar began an unexpectedly long and gentle swansong in civilian hands with the Fleet Requirements Unit at Hurn. This would see it remaining in service until 1970, though ironically still being almost outlived by its predecessor, the Sea Hawk.

Sadly the initial order for one hundred airframes was cut back to just seventy six, out of which only three complete examples of this elegant second-generation Naval jet still exist, though a handful of cockpit sections survive in private hands around the United Kingdom.

In putting together this book, which may hopefully go some way to prevent the Scimitar from becoming another of the forgotten types, the authors have endeavoured to use as many personal accounts of the men who flew and maintained the aircraft, as well as using and quoting from much hitherto unseen original Vickers documentation.

*de Havilland Vampire F.1 TG426 during flexible deck landing trials at the Royal Aircraft Establishment, Farnborough in December 1947. (via P.S.Wilson)*

# ORIGINS, ANCESTRY AND DEVELOPMENT

As with the vast majority of British post-war military aircraft designs, the Vickers-Supermarine Scimitar suffered from a protracted gestation period brought about by radical and quite often inept official plans which sought to give the industry a definite World-lead, but which sadly saw it lose its place to other countries.

At a meeting held at RAE Farnborough on 11 January 1945 a series of experiments to investigate the practicability of one such idea was discussed: landing aircraft without undercarriages on a flexible aircraft carrier deck. The concept was radical, but one which would, it was intended, result in an much lighter aircraft with an increased payload/range and climb performance for the same size.

In the autumn of 1945, Supermarine proffered its Type 505 to utilise such a facility. Even before their first venture into jet-propelled aircraft, the Attacker, had flown, Supermarine had embarked on a new aircraft design based around two of the proposed new Rolls-Royce AJ.65 (Axial Jet 6,500lb; later to be named Avon) axial turbine engines. The Attacker, with its single Nene centrifugal engine, had some 5,000lb of static thrust; the AJ.65 promised to deliver an initial 6,500lb each.

It was not until April 1946, however, that the decision to build the rubber 'carpet' above the runway at Farnborough was made. The initial design and construction of the flexible deck was settled by early model experiments, followed by further tests in which a pilot-less glider was catapulted on to a full scale 'carpet'.

On 29 December 1947, with its undercarriage retracted, an arrester hook fitted and fuselage suitably strengthened, de Havilland Vampire F.1 TG426, made a less than desirable first landing on the flexible deck at Farnborough, in the hands of eminent RAE test pilot Lt Cdr Eric 'Winkle' Brown OBE, DSC, AFC. Encountering turbulence on the approach, which was made at too slow a speed, the arrester hook struck the ground, pitching the aircraft forward on to its nose which penetrated the carpet. The aircraft suffered considerable damage and was subsequently written off, though Brown emerged unscathed.

*Lt Cdr Eric ('Winkle') Brown landing de Havilland Sea Vampire F.21 VT803 on the flexible deck rigged on the light fleet carrier HMS Warrior in November 1948. (via P.S.Wilson)*

*de Havilland Vampire F.1 TG286 after landing on the flexible deck rigged on HMS Warrior c.1948/9. (RAE Farnborough)*

Not disheartened by this the programme continued and, three months later on 17 March 1948, the first of some fifty successful landings at Farnborough was executed using replacement Vampire F.1 TG286. On 3 November 1948 sea trials of the flexible deck began aboard the light fleet carrier HMS *Warrior*, during the course of which a total of two hundred landings were carried out using TG286, along with F.21's VG701, VT795, VT802, VT803 and VT805 piloted by Lt Cdr Brown, Lt B.H.Harris, F/Lt G.E.C.Genders AFC DFM, Lt Cdr P.S.Wilson, Lt W.N.Plews, Lt G.J.Horne, Lt Cdr J.E.Thomas (USN) and Lt W.Andon. Only minor incidents were reported and the trials were considered successful.

## TYPE 505 – THE 'CARPET INTERCEPTOR'

With the Type 505, drawn up in Supermarine's own specification No.495 for an undercarriage-less fighter to be operated off aircraft carriers and aerodromes, thoughts were given to the use of bi-fuel rocket units to boost climb performance, but were quickly ruled out on the grounds that such power plants had yet to be perfected together with the problems associated with the storage of such volatile substances aboard ships.

The 505 was to be a single-seat, mid-wing monoplane with a 'V' type (or 'butterfly') tail, and straight thin, tapered wings. This radical configuration was chosen to save weight and gain speed. Following a discussion with DACR Department Admiralty on 21 February 1946, and having given due consideration to all the factors involved, it was concluded that the aircraft ought to be designed initially to limits on overall length of 47'6", on folded width 27'0", and on weight 20,000lb. Positioned diagonally, an aircraft of these dimensions would pass down a 45' x 33' lift with approximately a foot to spare all round and could be accommodated on the majority of existing and projected carriers. The maximum number which could be carried on each class of ship was as follows, the lower figure being a certainty and the higher a figure which could be achieved by careful stowage; *Ark Royal* 50-54 aircraft, *Implacable* 44-49 aircraft, *Hermes* 18-20 aircraft, and *Majestic/Colossus* 12-14 aircraft.

### CONSTRUCTION DETAILS

#### Wing

The NPL 7% transonic wing, proposed for the Type 505 with 15% leading edge and 25% plain trailing edge flaps, was manufactured of 5ft span and 2ft chord and tested in the closed return wind tunnel at the University College, Southampton during May and June 1946.

The wing was divided into two semi-cantilevers mounted on an approximately rectangular sectioned fuselage, the roots of the mid wing being bent upwards to meet the top of the fuselage while struts were carried from the kink to the lower fuselage longerons, the whole being faired in by the engine covers. The exceptionally small thickness/chord ratio of 7% made it necessary to employ steel spar flanges and an unusually thick light alloy skin for the torsion box. The construction was therefore extremely robust.

A nose flap extended throughout the complete span. A plain flap of 25% mean chord was fitted at the trailing edge over the inner part of the span and could be deflected to 40 degrees. The possibility of boundary layer control as an alternative to the nose flap was also explored.

Spoilers, for use during the landing approach, were fitted. This control was designed to give the pilot a direct mean of adjusting the path of the aeroplane during his approach which was of particular importance in carrying out a satisfactory landing.

Dive recovery flaps were fitted to the under surface of the wing, the purpose of which was to restore both the wing lift and downwash over the tailplane, which reduced at high Mach numbers tending to make recovery from a dive difficult if not impossible.

#### Propulsion

Power would come from two Rolls-Royce AJ.65 axial turbojets, located side by side in the fuselage. This configuration, with the two air intakes required, resulted in a saving of 20% in body frontal and skin areas. In addition the aircraft would not suffer from the adverse effects of asymmetric handling in the event of engine failure and would allow for cruising on one engine without trimming difficulties. Moreover, the resultant flat-bottomed fuselage shape in cross-section made the aircraft more laterally stable when landing on the carpet.

#### Armament

Though the preferred armament fit for the Type 505 had been a choice between the internally-housed 5.9 inch rocket gun or the 4.5 inch recoil-less gun, the 30mm MG 213/30 gun appeared to have reached a more advanced stage of development. It was therefore decided to utilise a pair of these with housing for 200 rounds of ammunition per gun. Provision was made, however, for the subsequent installation of either of the alternative armaments.

#### Performance

It was noted that a further improvement in performance could be achieved by employing a swept-back wing, but this was not included as it would result in a larger aeroplane with the consequent shipboard stowage problems.

Great stress had been laid upon the design of a wing having a conventional plan from, but on which the compressibility effects were delayed to the highest possible Mach number. It was by then well known that thickness/chord ratio was the overriding parameter in this respect. Consequently the thinnest practical aerofoil section was used, namely a thickness/chord ratio of 7%. However, sweep-back was regarded as a refinement to be introduced as a further stage in development when the specific characteristics of the configuration were fully understood.

#### Longitudinal and Directional Controls

Fore and Aft (longitudinal) trimming was provided by altering the incidence of the tail; the rear fuselage being hinged and moved by an electric actuator.

Longitudinal control was by elevators moving symmetrically when the stick was moved fore and aft. Directional control, via the rudder pedals, moved the elevators differentially.

*The completed mock-up of the Type 508, with one of the proposed AJ.65 engines suspended above it, at the Hursley Park experimental hangar, near Winchester, Hampshire (Vickers-Armstrongs)*

Fuselage

The fuselage was of light alloy construction; armour protection, being largely built-in, resulted in an extremely robust structure. The cockpit layout would be practically identical to that of the 'Jet Spiteful' (this became the Attacker).

Experience on the Spiteful and Seafang aircraft had shown that these aircraft were very inaccessible at the tail end, the situation being finally met with a number of screw-down stressed doors. These were most unsatisfactory to work with, and much of the maintenance work was done by crawling down the fuselage. Thus in the Type 505 it was proposed that the fuselage plating aft of the elevator spar would be removable as a single fairing held by a few fasteners and other panels would be provided.

Following on from the wind tunnel tests a further series of sixteen tests was decided upon on 6 August by the Supermarine Chief Aerodynamicist Sammy Hughes and Assistant Chief Designer and Head of Technical Office Alan Clifton. Some were to be carried out in the NPL 9ft x 7ft wind tunnel and others at the RAE in their spinning and high and low speed tunnels. One of these tests was to ensure that the Type 505 with its Vee-type tail could recover from a spin, on the subject of which the RAE stated that: *"Broadly speaking, we consider the Vee tail promising for spinning"*.

On 2 August 1946, Supermarine issued TOR.4767 in reference to design work on the Type 505, to state the problems involved in the construction of the type, define the stage reached at present and suggest programmes of design work.

Three of the design problems were:
(1) Drop tanks. It would ease design problems and reduce structure weight if these were moved inboard from their position on the wing tips.
(2) ilerons. Design and operation affected the whole of the outer wing and the control system. A decision was required on size and type, and also aerodynamic data for operating loads.
(3) Tail unit. Design had not yet settled. This affected the rear end of the fuselage, control system and aircraft CofG.

Another of the problems requiring clarification was in relation to main skin access doors. In the Seafang there were 27, and since doors weighed two to three times as much as plain skin, it was required that there would not be so many on the Type 505. Other items requiring scheming were dive recovery flaps, lift spoilers and engine covers.

In the Type 505 the fitting of 75mm recoil-less guns needed a special structure. It was noted that the fitting of these units would considerably influence the design of the forebody bottom and large doors would probably have been required for their removal. The effect on the forward tank suggested that two tank installations would be required. Since the guns were mounted near the aircraft centre-line, it would also interfere with pilot's controls. There was also a danger of damage to guns during carpet landing. Mounting of 30mm cannons, it was decided, would be less complicated. The ammunition tanks would be part of the structure if possible, as on the Spiteful wing.

The gun initially selected was the 4.5in RCL recoil-less gun being developed by Fort Halstead. When a round was fired, it simultaneously ejected backwards a counterweight of equal mass so that no recoil reaction was felt on the airframe, so called the swinging chamber cannon.

Even though a full scale mock-up was made of this installation, it was dropped and the decision made that the first design would incorporate the 30mm cannon installation.

The jury undercarriage was a new requirement necessary for the initial flights before carpet landing could be considered. The design was such that long stroke oleos would be fitted and also, as it would be Supermarine's first tricycle-arrangement layout, a considerable amount of design effort would be required.

Even the drop tanks had to be designed into the initial requirements, due to the profound effect they had on the aircraft structure (strengthening of the wing spars at tip and root in the case of tip tanks). It was at this stage that Supermarine recommended that the drop tanks be fitted inboard to help to save weight, and this was later approved.

In 1947, however, the Admiralty and Air Ministry finally admitted that a landing carpet was not a practical proposition. This was due to the extra ground equipment necessary for service use, but mainly because of the extensive and expensive modifications required to its aircraft carriers to enable them to operate this type of aircraft. Such a modification programme would entail the vessels being out of commission for lengthy periods of time – something which was completely unacceptable for strategic reasons – and would probably not be ready at the same time as the aircraft themselves. As a result, the requirement was promptly cancelled and all work on undercarriage-less aircraft ground to a halt.

DIMENSIONS

Span 35ft; Length 46.75ft; folded width approx 25.0ft, folded height approx 9.0ft. Wing T/C at root and tip 7%. Incidence of wing 2 degrees, tail dihedral 35 degrees.

WEIGHTS

Basic 12,220lb (11,760lb RAF). Loaded 15,500lb (13,500lb RAF). Fuel 405 gallons (215 gallons RAF).

PERFORMANCE

Maximum speed; 680mph at sea level, 630mph at 20,000ft, 590mph at 45,000ft. Rate of climb; 27,250ft/min at sea level. Climb to 25,000ft in 1.2min, 45,000ft in 3.0min.

**TYPE 508**

The requirement having been revised and re-issued under Specification N.9/47, Supermarine were asked to re-examine the project with a view to incorporating an undercarriage into the design. The only limitation placed upon the design was that the approach speed should not exceed 105 knots. The decision was also taken that the design should make provision for ready conversion to undercarriage-less type as, when or if the Royal Navy ever reverted to the rubber deck concept.

The wing had to accommodate part of the undercarriage, and therefore had to be enlarged. This new design was basically a scaled-up Type 505 with a tricycle undercarriage, the main wheels retracting into the underside of the fuselage.

The effect of the addition of an undercarriage, plus the increase in wing area required to meet approach speed requirements, increased the weight of the redesign very appreciably; a stark contrast with the original idea which had been to reduce the weight considerably. The wing was thickened from 7% to 9% in order to reduce structure weight and also the size, the length remaining unchanged, but the retraction of the wheels into the underside of the fuselage resulted in a deeper body. To save weight in the centre section, the wing spars were run under the fuselage to serve additionally as undercarriage mountings, resulting in a modified engine mounting.

With these modifications the speed was reduced by 20mph to 660mph at sea level; the difference between the RAF version and the RN version was only 3mph at 45,000ft. However, the requirements regarding fuel were at variance as follows:

|  | R.N. | R.A.F. |
|---|---|---|
| All-up weight (lb) | 17,500 | 15,300 |
| Cruising height (ft) | 45,000 | 45,000 |
| Fuel for take-off (gallons) | 47.5 | 47.5 |
| Fuel for climb (gallons) | 60.5 | 52.5 |
| Fuel for 10 minutes combat (gallons) | 70.0 |  |
| Fuel for 3 minutes combat (gallons) |  | 22.0 |
| Fuel for 45 minutes cruising (gallons) | 146.0 |  |
| Fuel for 30 minutes cruising (gallons) |  | 36.0 |
| Fuel for 15 minutes loitering (gallons) | 91.0 |  |
| Total fuel for sortie (gallons) | 415.0 | 218.0 |

Also, the RN version was fitted with an arrester hook, catapulting gear, folding wings and a heavier radio installation, all of which helped to increase the all-up weight by 2,200lb. The resultant aircraft dimensions and performance had to suffer; the increase in span was 5ft, wing area increase 45sq ft and tail area by 13sq ft.

DIMENSIONS

Span 40.0ft. Length 46.75ft. Folded width approx. 26.0ft. Folded height approx. 13.0ft. Wetted area of fuselage 315sq ft. Wing area gross 310sq ft. Wing T/C at root and tip 9%. Incidence of wing 2 degrees. Tail area true, gross 86sq ft, dihedral angle 34 degrees.

WEIGHTS

Basic 14,140lb (13,534lb RAF). Loaded 17,500lb (15,300lb RAF).

PERFORMANCE

Top speed 650mph at sea level; 625mph at 25,000ft; 575mph at 45,000ft.
Rate of climb 18,500ft/min (21,200 RAF) at sea level; 12,000ft/min (13,500 RAF) at 25,000ft; 3,500ft/min (4,500 RAF) at 45,000ft. Climb to 25,000ft in 1.75 mins (1.5 RAF); 49,000ft in 4.5 mins (3.85 RAF).

As with the Type 505, the armament selected for the Type 508 was the 30mm MG213/30, due to its advanced stage of development over the 4.5 inch swinging chamber gun. Again structural and space provision would be made for the subsequent installation of the alternative armament. Power plants too were the same Rolls-Royce AJ.65s.

Although the pilot was provided with an ejector seat, Supermarine had given some thought to the use of a jettisonable cabin and an 'ultimate requirement from the point of view of the pilot's safety'. However the idea was not proceeded with as the sheer complexity of this one system was deemed to be too much to cope with on what was, after all, an experimental aircraft which itself required testing first.

The V-tail configuration of the Type 505 was retained. Dive recovery flaps of 3.1sq ft would be fitted to the under surface of the wing, air brakes operable up to the maximum diving speed in the form of spoilers on the upper surface of the wing.

The raising of the fuel pumps above the engine centre line by rotating the engine through 45 degrees about its fore and aft axis was necessitated by the wing joint fouling the pump drive and Rolls-Royce agreed that this could be done. To make room for the chassis operating jack the oil tank had to be removed with agreement of Rolls-Royce, who also agreed that the forward engine attachments be moved aft to pick up on the front spar frame and be bolted down on rubber pads.

*The cockpit layout of Type 508 VX133. (Vickers-Armstrongs)*

As design progressed, so the size of the aircraft changed. On 28 November the dimensions were: span 40ft, length 46.75ft, gross area 307.8sq ft, aspect ratio 5.2.

The possibility of fitting a 3.7in recoil-less gun resulted in a series of tests having to be carried out to ensure that when fired it would not damage the airframe. A Mosquito fuselage was obtained, and a specially erected gantry was arranged at Woolwich to allow a 3.7in RCL gun to be positioned approximately 2ft above the fuselage, with the nose of the aircraft some 6ft forward of the gun muzzle. When the first round was fired on 28 November 1946, a row of rivets 2ft forward of the muzzle pulled out of the special alloy panel that had been fitted approx. 0.5in in depth for an area of 9in diameter centred 6in forward of the muzzle. A door in the side of the fuselage, about 14in x 10in and fastened at the four corners by Dzus fasteners approximately 13ft aft of the gun muzzle, was blown off and the plywood skin of the fuselage cracked. On the second round, with the gun in the same position, flash from the efflux tubes extended more than 8ft aft of the tube exit. An extensive area of slight damage showed on the internal structure of the fuselage and another panel approximately 18ft aft of the gun muzzle blew off. On the third round, with the gun 7.5in above fuselage and the muzzle 4ft aft of the nose of aircraft, a major portion of the fuselage was internally damaged. On the fourth round, the nose of the fuselage split diagonally downward from in front of the muzzle. Finally, on the fifth round, the fuselage disintegrated and was described as a write-off!

A Beaufighter fuselage was next used, with the gun mounted 13.5in above and 12ft aft of the nose. On firing the first round, 20 gauge stringers and frames about 2" depth collapsed from 8in to 60in forward of the gun muzzle and many rivets were pulled out. For the second round the fuselage was reversed to note blast effect of efflux gases; rivets were loosened and local buckling occurred. Another round was fired in this position, at which point the fuselage frame about 12in aft of the efflux tube mouths was fractured and adjacent stringers badly buckled.

No further tests were carried out, but Mr Ackers of RAE Farnborough considered that the blast tube should be at least 8in diameter to permit reduction of gas pressure, the estimated gas velocity being 6,000ft per second at the efflux tube exit and 2,000ft per second at the muzzle. The conclusions of the tests were that normal joints in the vicinity of the blast area on standard fuselages were impracticable and points of entry for blast should be eliminated. The blast pressure and reactionary impulses could seriously affect control surfaces.

Rolls-Royce was visited on 9 January 1947 by Supermarine's Chief Designer Joe Smith and Head of Project Office Arthur Shirvall. Rolls-Royce explained that, as too many versions of the AJ.65 were emerging due to various alterations, they wanted to see a more or less standard engine. They argued that a major alteration to the engine carcass was involved in the rotation through 45 degrees, and they preferred a single central gearbox for auxiliaries, although they fully realised the difficulties lying in the way of its achievement. The armament position was still not settled, however, so Supermarine could not say whether the parallel engine arrangement was suitable. It had several structural and installational advantages, however, and might have conceivably allowed the return to the centrally placed gearbox in the top of fuselage. The main disadvantage of the scheme was that the air intakes to the engines became more curved, and it seemed probable that their efficiency would be appreciably decreased.

Another meeting on 6 February revealed that the RAE were content to waive tests on the mainplanes on the prototypes, but would ask for a single wing test in the event of production. But the main spar frame, being regarded as of unusual design, and a mid-portion of fuselage, would have to be tested. As little testing had been done on forward fuselages with nose wheels, an evaluation of that would be required too. The rear section contained the dual novel features in the form of the Vee-tail and the region of the turbine exits, so the RAE concluded that a complete fuselage with tail surface would be required for a series of destruction tests.

During a visit on 5 May 1947 to Supermarine, Rear Admiral Matthew Slattery, then Chief of Naval Research, requested Supermarine to investigate the possibility of reducing the folded width to 20ft. The original project included jettisonable tanks on the wing tips, but reducing the folded width rendered it practically impossible to meet the requirement to fold with tanks full. Thus, in Supermarine Report No.4944, it was decided to locate them inboard of the fold below the wing, which also gave easier filling and draining facilities, but when carried it was agreed that they would probably introduce compressibility effects at a lower Mach Number when jettisoned, though this was not considered to be a handicap. The alternative proposal that was arrived at involved the aircraft having an internal fuel of 510 gallons and external jettisonable fuel tankage of 420 gallons.

On 4 June, Report No.4953 prepared by Sammy Hughes, Chief Aerodynamicist of Supermarine, listed the current requirements of the Type 508, amongst which were:

(a) Maximum level speed not less than 640mph at sea level, 610mph at 20,000ft.
(b) Time to 40,000ft must not exceed 6.0 minutes.
(c) Approach speed with 185 gallons fuel and all ammunition shall not exceed 105kts.
(d) All up weight not to exceed 23,000lb.
(e) Dimensions. Length 50'6". Height (folded) 17'6", Span (spread) 45'0", (folded) 19'6".
(f) Armament: four 20mm with 200 rpg.
(g) Ejection seat and pressurisation also required.

Around this Supermarine Specification, the Air Ministry issued Draft Specification N.9/47 for a naval fighter, and Supermarine was asked to tender in accordance a letter from the Ministry of Supply, ref. 6/Acft/1508/CB.7(b), dated 10 July 1947.

Two other firms, Hawker with their P.1063 and Westland, did some initial project drawings to this Specification, but neither was followed up. Supermarine submitted their revised Specification 500 Issue 2, which included Technical Office Report No.4953 and drawing No.50800 Sheet 17. The revised dimensions were: Span 41ft. Length 50ft. Folded width 19ft 6in. Folded height 15ft 5in.

A further appraisal of the performance in T.O.R.4977 dated 21 July at an all-up weight of 17,900lb and now with two Rolls-Royce Avon Mk.2 engines of 6,500lb st, gave a performance of 569kts at sea level and 511kts at 40,000ft, rate of climb 18,700ft/min at sea level and 5,300ft/min at 40,000ft, the service ceiling being given as 50,000ft. The fuel was now listed at 510 gallons internal and 430 gallons external.

Specification N.9/47 and naval fighter aircraft to NR/A.17, to Air Staff Requirement OR.254 dated 16 September 1947, was issued on 22 September 1947 to Supermarine, presumably after their tender had been accepted. It was to be "Suitable for economic production of at least 250 aircraft, have a speed of not less than 500kts at 30,000ft, service ceiling not less than 45,000ft and have a support range of 400nm". The armament had now changed, this time comprising four 20mm Mk.V Hispano or Aden HV cannon.

At the beginning of 1948 the requirements were changed yet again. The armament required was now four 20/30mm guns instead of four 20mm, resulting in a weight increase of 864lb, pushing the all up weight to 18,249lb with only 437 gallons of internal fuel. At this point Rolls-Royce informed Supermarine of a weight increase of 400lb per engine. This sudden increase in weight gave great cause for concern as the design was rapidly becoming too heavy for the existing arrester gears. This meant that the Specification requirement of an entry speed into the wires of only 75kts in a 28 knot wind was not feasible.

Wind tunnel trials were conducted during 1949 on the installation and release of 215 gallon drop tanks on pylons. Other tests included catapulting the aircraft in nose and tail down attitudes to find the optimum condition. Rolls-Royce also carried out some work in association with Supermarine during 1950/51 to find improvements in the engine intake design.

A major study was carried out in accelerating methods being carried out by Supermarine. In their report of 15 December 1949 they had investigated the different methods and came up with figures of added weight to the N.9/47 as follows:

| | |
|---|---|
| Catapulting | 115lb |
| Catapulting with reduced acceleration | 50lb |
| Jettisonable RATOG with cordite motors | 25lb |
| Jettisonable RATOG with liquid-fuel motors | 40lb |
| Built in RATOG with cordite motors | 400lb |
| Built in RATOG with liquid-fuel motors | 800lb |

In the case of the cordite motors a total of eight would be required, and only two of the liquid-fuel motors giving 5,000lb st each with fuel for 7.8 seconds. The weight penalty of the built-in units made them a non-starter. It was concluded that catapulting was best, as it used less of the deck space and obviated the need to provision for the rocket motors and expendable fittings. Following a discussion in December, between Messrs Boddington and Noble of the RAE and Clifton, Shirvall and H.C.Smith of Supermarine on the merits of tail-up and tail-down launching, it was agreed that this was more promising and should therefore be developed.

A contract for three prototypes, allocated the serial numbers VX133, VX136 and VX138, was placed to Specification N.9/47 as Type 508s under contract 6/Acft/1508/CB.7(b).

A further review at the RAE on 5 December 1950, on the effects of gun blast on stressed skin structures, elicited the fact that six Meteor noses sustained damage during 20mm gun firing trials at speeds above 350 knots, and it was therefore decided to use 14 gauge thick alloy for local strengthening. It was also stated that there was not enough evidence to show that 30mm guns would have any worse blast effects.

At an Advisory Design Conference at Millbank on 22 February 1951 attended by 38 people from Supermarine, RAE, Royal Navy and the Air Ministry, the requirements of Draft Specification N.113 (for the production version of the Type 508) were gone into, discussed and formulated. This resulted in the aircraft all-up weight limit being 28,000lb. A speed of 528kts was not possible but DAW insisted that 560kts was a firm requirement, though reheat could be used in order to reach it. Drop tanks would not be fitted. As requirements were still changing, some of which would have been advantageous to try out on VX133, investigative tests would now have to be carried out on production or pre-production aircraft.

Before the Type 508 was first flown, experiments were carried out in the wind tunnel which showed that the wake patterns due to the lift spoilers on the wings were unsatisfactory. In configurations appropriate to their use as airbrakes, there was an extensive disturbance at the tailplane which was likely to cause buffeting. A number of configurations and types of spoiler were tested, and the best compromise appeared to be to reduce the inboard spoiler to the size of the outboard one and to reverse the direction of the venting slots.

On 20 June the first engine runs were carried out on VX133 at Hursley Park, the Avon RA.3 engines being numbered 66 and 67, following which, on 29 July, the aircraft was weighed giving a True Tare weight of 16,274lb.

VX133 was then transported by road to the A&AEE airfield at Boscombe Down, Wiltshire, from where Mike Lithgow, the Supermarine Chief Test Pilot, first flew it on 31 August 1951.

Having returned the aircraft to the main Flight Test airfield at nearby Chilbolton, the minimum of 10 hours flying time was quickly achieved in time for the SBAC show at Farnborough on 11 September, qualifying the aircraft to be able to take part. The display was kept to minimum as it was such a new aircraft and had flown so few hours.

The Type 508 was fitted with full span leading edge flaps, as well as conventional trailing edge flaps inboard of the ailerons in order to achieve high lift for deck landings. In addition, lowering the leading edge flaps drooped the ailerons to some extent. Between 12th and 28th November, tests were carried out to determine the stalling speeds under a number of combinations of leading edge and trailing edge flap settings. With the exception of one very unnerving incident while being flown from Chilbolton with Mike Lithgow at the controls in December of the same year, the aircraft achieved its design targets.

The incident referred to was on 5 December when VX133 experienced violent accelerations and sustained what was classified as category 3 damage. The aircraft was thus grounded and an investigation set up to discover the cause. Supermarine called a meeting at Hursley Park on 12 March 1952 between themselves and Air Ministry representatives to discuss the matter, which could have been serious in service aircraft if allowed to continue. Various tests had been carried out already on the servodyne controls, because the pilot had been flying at speeds up to 450 knots doing stick-thumping tests, the speed at which the incident occurred, but no persistent oscillations had been noticed then. Lithgow had experienced a large uncontrollable nose-up attitude, he disengaged the elevator power system, which made the situation worse and the aircraft went into an vertical upward roll to 11,000ft causing Lithgow to black out. He regained control when the 'g' force diminished from its peak of 11g. In these manoeuvres the aircraft had suffered slight damage including the loss of both wingtip pitot heads with the result that no airspeed indication was available to the pilot.

After the incident Lithgow flew back to Chilbolton at a somewhat reduced speed and made a successful landing. It was decided that the servodyne was not at fault, though there had been a loss of ten pints of fluid from the hydraulic system by the time the aircraft had landed, this being put down to a leaking joint. Subsequent rig tests only proved the slow operation of the undercarriage on landing. In the end it was thought that the initial cause of the incident was the failure of a stirrup fitting supporting the port wheel fairing, this being in the form of a light alloy casting, and was cracked prior to the incident. The remedy was to manufacture the new one in welded steel, strengthen the attachment of the fairing to the axle, change the spring-and-cable operation of the belts connecting the wheel fairing to the leg fairing to push-pull operation and fit a different lock to the chassis door. Time, however, would prove that the cause of the chassis door being sprung open remained.

The aircraft was flown from Chilbolton to the RAE at Bedford on 29 April 1952 to resume its trials before returning on 2 May.

For deck landing trials the Type 508 was fitted with two cameras on the underside of the fuselage, together with a mirror assembly and a rear timing light to enable a cine record to be taken of the oleo landing system in operation. The cameras were two 16mm GSAP units with half-inch inverted telephoto lenses, and operated at a speed of 32 frames per second. The forward camera photographed the nose wheel and by means of the mirror assembly the main undercarriage wheels. The rear camera photographed the arrester hook motion. Both cameras were operated simultaneously and remotely from the deck of the aircraft carrier by radio; in the event of this failing, the pilot could manually override by a switch in his cockpit. Previous trials had been spoiled because of foreign matter (hydraulic fluid) being deposited on the camera lenses and mirrors, so this time the cameras were mounted in steel boxes with perspex windows, and the results were excellent.

*A front view of Supermarine Type 508 prototype VX133 about to start up at Chilbolton, with a very period-looking fireman standing by. (Vickers-Armstrongs)*

*Three views of Supermarine Type 508 VX133 during deck trials on HMS Eagle in May 1952. (Crown copyright)*

*A fine view of Supermarine Type 508 prototype VX133 as it swoops low in front of the control tower at Supermarine's test airfield at Chilbolton. (Vickers-Armstrongs)*

On 24 May 1952 VX133 was flown back again to the RAE for arresting trials, returning to Chilbolton on 27th. Having been checked over it was then flown to RNAS Ford, from where it continued to HMS *Eagle* for carrier trials. Seven deck landings were carried out, of which six were successful. The second was deemed a failure due to the camera master switch having been left in the off condition.

Upon completion of the trials VX133 returned to Chilbolton, where the cameras and test gear were removed before continuing its contractors trials. It was whilst Mike Lithgow was carrying out a flying demonstration at the RNAS Lee-on-Solent 'At Home' air display on 12 July 1952 that severe vibration occurred, similar to that previously experienced. This was later found to be caused by oscillation of the ailerons, which has spring tab balancing, and was seen clearly by people on the ground. The amplitude was such that one observer described the ailerons as appearing to be a foot thick at the trailing edge!

The fact that the second incident occurred when it did was fortuitous as there were no indications to the pilots that aileron oscillation was the cause of the vibration.

The next visit to a service establishment was not until the aircraft returned to the RAE on 15 April 1953 for the measurement of loads during arrested landings.

Another problem arising from the flight test programme was the tendency for directional oscillation (snaking) at medium and high speeds. This was cured by adding large aerodynamic strakes to the rear fuselage in front of the tailplane leading edges which modified the air flow over the tail unit.

VX133 was finally accepted by the RAE on 13 July 1953, being eventually transferred to RAE Bedford on 22 August 1955. It carried out some trials on HMS *Bulwark* from 31 October 1955, returning to Bedford on 14 November.

The 508's days of flying were almost over when it was despatched by road to HM Dockyard Devonport on 24 September 1956 for trials on board HMS *Centaur* to test the hangar deck strength. This carrier was later have a complement of approximately sixteen Sea Vixen and Scimitar aircraft, four AEW aircraft and up to eight helicopters. VX133 returned to Bedford on 28 November to continue its arrester gear development trials.

*Supermarine Type 508 prototype VX133 in company with Supermarine Type 535 VV119 during SBAC Show Farnborough week September 1951. (via R.C.Sturtivant)*

On 29 March 1963 the aircraft was finally released by NAD/RAE Bedford as being of no further use, and in June was allotted to RNAS Culdrose for ground instructional purposes, being officially transferred to them on 31 October 1963 and transported by road via Lee-on-Solent two months later.

Having been used for many years by the School of Aircraft Handling for tractor driver training for deck handling techniques, this unique prototype aircraft was finally retired from use and finally taken to Predannack circa 1970 for use in fire practice. Sadly, by the time it's historical importance was realised, VX133 had been burnt beyond repair.

*The remains of Supermarine Type 508 prototype VX133 on the dump at Predannack in 1970. (MAP)*

## TYPE 529

The second Type 508, VX136, first flew from Boscombe Down on 29 August 1952. By that time the aircraft had many interior modifications and the fitting of the cannon, so it was decided to allot it a new type number and it became the Type 529. Externally there was little difference in appearance: a white fibre glass nose cap and a 6-inch extension to the tail cone to house radar-ranging and tail warning radar respectively. However these incorporations were never proceeded with due to supply problems and the whole requirement was officially dropped on 18th February 1953. Deck trials were also carried out on board HMS *Eagle* in October and November of 1953. It then went to RAE Bedford for use by the RN Test Squadron.

Unfortunately, during development flying from Chilbolton on 2 December 1953, the aircraft carried out an emergency landing with only the port undercarriage down. The starboard wingtip, flaps, chassis door and aileron distorted and buckled and port chassis door torn from its hinges. Such was the damage inflicted that the aircraft was struck off charge eleven months later, following a period of storage, with the majority of the remnants being transferred to the P&EE at Shoeburyness where they finally expired in September 1961.

## TYPE 508 - SPECIFICATION 500/R

In 1946 the Air Ministry raised specification F.43/46 for a single-seat day fighter for destruction of single high-speed, high-altitude enemy targets. For this very rapid starting was required, a time to height of 45,000ft in six minutes to be attained with a service ceiling of 50,000ft and a maximum speed of 547kts at 45,000ft. The specification was issued to the industry, including Vickers, Supermarine, Hawker and Gloster, on 24 January 1947 as a Gloster Meteor replacement. Supermarine's interpretation of the Air Ministry requirement was to produce an aircraft that would get the heaviest possible armament up to 45,000ft in the shortest possible time. With this in mind they endeavoured to design the smallest and lightest aircraft which would satisfactorily house the 4.5in RCL gun, whilst providing the greatest possible power.

There were to be two versions, one for the RAF and one for the Royal Navy. The RAF version was 2,200lb lighter and had improved performance figures, these being listed in Supermarine specification No.500 and shown in Drawings 50800 Sheets 1 to 6. As shown in sheet 2, the nose wheel had to be offset because of the installation of the RCL gun.

The undercarriage was of orthodox tricycle form, the main wheels retracting inwards into the underside of the fuselage. The nose wheel retracted rearwards, the leg lying below the pilot and alongside the RCL gun barrel housing wheel, the wheel itself tucking in at the back of the pilot.

## TYPE 525

In late 1948 Supermarine reacted to the recent Ministry of Supply Specifications, which called for land-based fighter aircraft of extremely high performances obtainable only by the employment of back-swept wings, by issuing its own specification No. 525 (Type 525). Until this point it had been generally assumed that the special limitation imposed on aircraft to be operated from ships - dimensions and approach speed, in particular - would prevent the employment of swept-wing aircraft by the Navy. Projected developments in Carrier Arresting and Catapulting Equipment, and recent developments in high lift devices for back-swept wings, coupled with the envisaged success of the experimental back-swept wing aircraft (E.41/46 Type 510 VV106) at approach speeds, encouraged Supermarine to begin investigations into the possibility of converting the N.9/47 to a swept wing type for Naval use.

In converting the N.9/47, Supermarine made provision for the wing to fit into the existing fuselage recess, with little alteration. However the high sweep-back of the wing, without dihedral, would result in the tips being much closer to the ground, thus necessitating oleos which were lengthened by 15 inches. The distinctive butterfly tail unit would also be replaced by a more conventional swept-back unit.

The endurance with 630 gallons internal and 430 gallons in drop tanks met the N.9/47 requirements of 2.5 hours at 30,000ft, with the normal reserves.

Following the performance of the Supermarine Type 510 (VV106) during deck trials aboard HMS *Illustrious* in November 1950, the Royal Navy via the Air Ministry requested that the third prototype 508, VX138, be changed from a straight wing to a swept back wing.

The assumption was also that the Type 525's landing performance would be improved with a larger wing area, two engines and double slotted wing trailing edge flaps provided inboard of the ailerons and leading edge flaps over the full wing span.

*Supermarine Type 529 VX136 parked on the airfield at Chilbolton c.1952/3. (Vickers-Armstrongs)*

*Supermarine Type 529 VX136 landing during the SBAC Show at Farnborough in September 1952. Note the extended tailcone fairing. (Vickers-Armstrongs)*

*Supermarine Type 529 VX136 on HMS Eagle during deck trials in November 1953. (MAP)*

Air brakes were fitted to the forward underside of the fuselage and also to the upper and lower surfaces of the wings. During the course of the flight test programme the wing brakes were locked and consequently only those under the fuselage were then operative.

The variable incidence tailplane with its elevator was mounted on the fin and swept back at an angle of 45 degrees at the quarter-chord line. For normal flight, with the flaps up, the range of the tailplane angle was +1.25 to -4 degrees. Operation of the trailing edge flaps however made available a maximum negative incidence of 9.5 degrees through the medium of a flap actuated micro-switch connected in the tailplane electrical operating circuit.

However it was not until 1952 that impetus was given to the project to convert the intended third prototype Type 508 to what would become the Type 525. The bare fuselage of the aircraft had lain in the Experimental Hangar at Hursley Park whilst the main bulk of the department's efforts were expended on other projects.

With a minimum number of the workforce diverted to the 525 project, progress was surprisingly quick. By late 1953 the aircraft appeared substantially complete, but three or four months of work still remained whilst the coppersmiths and electricians carried out the arduous tasks of routing the miles of pipes and electrical looms through the structure. The largest single-seat fighter being produced by the British aircraft industry at that time, the all-up weight had risen from 22,769lb on 1 November 1950 to 28,169lb on 1 March 1954.

With such a seemingly complete airframe, the temptation would normally have been to move the aircraft to Boscombe Down as soon as possible to appease the budget holders and politicians concerned with the project. However the Assistant Experimental Department Manager, Denis Webb, successfully argued that, should this happen and anything go wrong once at Boscombe, the delays incurred by having to transport various components, men and tools back and forth would be huge. The 525 would remain until complete.

In order for the aircraft to be delivered in a complete state by road from Hursley Park to Boscombe Down, a carefully planned route would have to be sought out. To this end a specially-made wooden framework, with telescopic ends to represent the extremities of the tail fin and stub wings, was constructed and fitted to the back of a truck and driven around the suggested routes. Where obstructions were encountered, the framework was extended and checked for sufficient clearances.

*Type 525 VX138 on a Vickers Viscount fuselage trailer on loan from Weybridge, en route from Hursley Park to Boscombe Down. With "Tiller" steering on the rear wheels, this was ideal for taking the sharp bend out of Chilbolton Avenue in Winchester into the Stockbridge Road as seen here. The structure on the back of the tractor was a platform the width of the 525 fuselage and was used for checking clearances and pushing up low wires etc whilst en route. (D.Webb)*

Eventually a suitable route was chosen, with only two potentially tight spots at Stockbridge and the tiny Hampshire/Wiltshire border village of Ford.

Meanwhile at Hursley, VX138 was finally rolled out for its first engine ground runs. It had been feared that the noise created during such tests might result in numerous complaints from the villagers, but the potential consequences of encountering problems once at Boscombe far outweighed those of upsetting the local inhabitants.

Webb's decision was to be proved right. Rolls-Royce representative Freddie Ballington was called in to carry out the ground-runs and as he pushed the throttles forward the engines refused to advance beyond half-throttle. The aerodynamicists were called in and, by using wool tufts, concluded that the airflow inside the air intakes was being disturbed and was thus preventing a smooth flow to the engines. The intakes would have to be redesigned, a job which would take the next two weeks.

To cause as little disruption to traffic on the route to Boscombe Down, the move was planned to begin in the early morning of Sunday 25th April 1954. The fuselage, with the undercarriage retracted and the outer wings removed, was lifted on to a special low-loader normally used for transporting Viscount fuselages which had been brought over from Weybridge. With an escort of three police cars and armed with a long insulated pole to lift up any overhead power or telephone lines en-route, the procession began.

*Type 525 VX138 being unloaded on arrival at Boscombe Down, about to be connected to a hydraulic rig to allow the undercarriage to be lowered. (D.Webb)*

After some ten hours the 525 arrived at the gates of the A&AEE. With no single crane large enough to lift the aircraft, three were put to use whilst a hydraulic rig was hooked up and the undercarriage lowered. Having safely stowed the aircraft in the hangar, the team set off back to Hursley.

The following day they were back. During the morning the outer wings were attached, hydraulic functions completed, engine runs and compass swings carried out and the aircraft pronounced fit to fly. Shortly after lunch Mike Lithgow, in company with Joe Smith, arrived from Chilbolton in the company 'hack' Dominie. Taxying trials were carried out during the afternoon and the following day, Tuesday 27th April, Lithgow made VX138's first flight lasting 20 minutes shepherded by Dave Morgan in Swift WK215.

Two days later this was followed by flights of 40 and 25 minutes. Lithgow made another handling flight on 6 May before flying it to Chilbolton the same day. Later that year he flew VX138 at the 1954 SBAC show at Farnborough between 7th and 12th September in its newly-applied cream livery, following which it was then flown back to Chilbolton on 13th.

After only eleven hours and ten minutes flying time, which had highlighted some other problems with the fuel transfer and

*Mike Lithgow brings Supermarine Type 525 VX138 in on final approach to land at A&AEE Boscombe Down following an early test flight. (via M.J.Hooks)*

stability, VX138 was grounded for modifications.

In line with the fuel system tests, measurements of pressure error (PE) corrections were also carried out in the period from August to October 1954 with longitudinal stability and control measurements continuing to January 1955. For the latter part of the tests the wing configuration was modified by the fitting of a wooden extended wing leading edge; this reduced the thickness chord ratio in order to increase the high Mach number manoeuvring potential and also to reduce pitch up.

At the time of the first flight of the Type 525, a great deal of interest was being shown in Boundary Layer Control, otherwise known as flap-blowing, or "Super Circulation". This was where air would be tapped or taken from each engine and ducted along long narrow nozzles, then blown at supersonic speed across the upper surfaces of the flaps. This air taken from such a powerful engine would not make any reduction in performance unless one engine was shut down (single-engined landings with flap blow on were eventually prohibited for this reason). Flap-blowing would have the benefit of giving the aircraft a lower landing speed and also improve control on the approach to deck landing. It was therefore decided to incorporate this in the Type 525 for trials.

Following the fuel system tests, at which point the aircraft had flown only 41 hours 10 minutes, the aircraft was grounded for modifications yet again; firstly to incorporate the supercirculation system to increase the maximum coefficient of lift by blowing air over the trailing edge flaps, and secondly by increasing the elevator feel ratio to 10:1 to reduce the high stick force per g.

*VX138 in its recently-acquired Naval colour scheme of dark sea grey upper and sky lower surfaces, flown by Mike Lithgow from Chilbolton on 20 June 1955, photographed by Supermarine flight test engineer Charles Burnet from a de Havilland Dominie flown by G.J. ('Chunky') Horne using a 16mm GSAP cine-camera.*

*Supermarine Type 525 VX138 in company with Supermarine Swift F.4 WK273 during SBAC week, September 1954. (Vickers-Armstrongs)*

The work was carried out at the Hursley Park experimental hangar and in June 1955 the aircraft emerged equipped with the new flap-blowing system plus a new-look wing, now officially redesignated the Type 555. The leading edge of the outboard portion had been extended, giving it the distinctive saw-tooth look; also the double slotted flaps had been replaced by plain trailing edge assemblies. The full span leading edge flaps would now move to fully down as the trailing edge flaps started to move. A number of other minor

*Type 525 VX138 resplendent in its new cream colour scheme, taxying along the runway during the SBAC Show at Farnborough in September 1954. (via Philip Jarrett)*

modifications had also been incorporated and, as soon as the weather allowed, extensive flying trials were conducted throughout the month of June from Chilbolton. Lithgow took VX138 on a "*Shop Window*" exercise to demonstrate the effect of the flap-blowing. It was found that the approach speed was reduced by as much as 10 knots and with the other modifications the aircraft was much more stable.

Initial flights of the Type 525 led to adverse criticism of the directional characteristics. The damping in yaw was low, the aircraft performing a steady directional oscillation with associated roll. This effect became more pronounced with increase in I.A.S. and in fact was the limiting factor preventing flight at high indicated air speeds during early test flights. Tests were carried out to determine quantitatively the directional damping characteristics and to investigate the improvement resulting from various modifications made. Photographs of VX138 show the rudder in two parts, one above and one below the tailplane. The rudder operated through a system of rods without power assistance. For all the tests the bottom rudder was locked. Modifications made to the fin, rudder and control circuit were as follows:

(1) Angle (1.0" width overall) was added to the rudder trailing edge. Initially this was 18" in length but was subsequently increased to 27".
(2) The area of the fin was increased by means of an extension on the leading edge.
(3) A friction damping device was fitted to the rudder.

The pilots' impressions of the relative effects of the introduction of the larger fin and of the introduction of the friction damping were that while the former produced some improvement (in particular the directional characteristics) the latter made a considerable improvement and in fact made flight to much higher indicated airspeeds practicable.

As a result of these tests on the 525, the production version Type 544 would have a fully-powered rudder which would reproduce the characteristics of the damping devices without the attendant disadvantage of high friction. The longer engine nacelles of the Type 544, it was thought, would improve the basic directional characteristics and in addition autostabilisation in yaw would be incorporated.

On 4 July VX138 was transferred from Chilbolton to nearby A&AEE Boscombe Down. Its stay was to be all too brief. The following day, 5 July 1955, all work on VX138 came to an untimely and tragic end. Having completed the initial trials programme successfully with no notable problems, and whilst awaiting an available aircraft carrier on which to carry out the deck landing trials in the English Channel, Lt Cdr Tony Rickell, RN of the Aeroplane & Armament Experimental Establishment who was scheduled to be involved in the trials, was given the opportunity to carry out what was termed a 'preview handling' flight which, in view of the nature of the forthcoming trials, would concentrate on low speed flight in the landing configuration.

During his second 'practice approach' which was done at an altitude normally considered safe for such a test, the aircraft stalled and spun. In a desperate attempt to recover[a] Rickell delayed his ejection until it was too late for the system to function properly and he subsequently died of his injuries.

The loss of VX138 dealt a devastating blow to the programme, and effectively set the N.113 programme back by two years.

As the fatal flight had involved the use of the flap-blowing system, an inquiry was soon held. It was found, however, that there was nothing to suggest that flap-blow had anything to do with the accident. Therefore, as all previous flights had shown that the system worked as well, if not better, than expected, it was decided to go ahead and incorporate flap blowing in the new N.113.

## DIMENSIONS

Length 53.0ft; Span 37.17ft, folded 20.0ft; Tailplane 14.04ft: Height 15.1ft, wings folded 15.6ft; Fuselage length 49.1ft; Thickness/Chord ratio 8%.

*A striking rear view of Type 544 WT859 fitted with noise suppressers. (Vickers-Armstrongs)*

*Access to some parts of the aircraft was cramped, to say the least, as can be seen from this close-up view of WT859 on 30 May 1957. (Vickers-Armstrongs)*

*Starboard side view of first prototype WT854 at Boscombe Down. (via Philip Jarrett)*

# TYPE 544

Under contract 7/Aircraft/7784 dated May 1953 was issued Aircraft Specification N.113P for production of the Vickers Supermarine naval swept wing fighter based on Operational Requirement NR/A.17. This called for a single-seat fighter to carry out day interception, day combat air patrol, day-long range and strike support and be able to operate from aircraft carriers by day or night and shore bases around the world.

Dimensions were not to exceed length 50ft, span 55ft (folded 20ft), height 17ft, all up weight 24,000lb. The rate of climb at sea level was to be not less than 18,000ft/min and at 45,000ft not less than 2,000ft/min. Speed 625kts at sea level (without reheat), 530kts (without reheat) or 560kts (with reheat) at 45,000ft. The service ceiling (in initial climb and using reheat) was to be 1,000ft/min to 49,000ft.

Sufficient fuel was required to allow the aircraft to take off and climb to 45,000ft, carry out combat air patrol for 2 hours (more if possible) at economic speed, followed by 5 minutes combat at 20,000ft without reheat and a further 20 minutes loiter at 2,000ft.

## Armament

The whole question of armament at this period of time was so fluid that the only certain fit was the four 30mm Aden cannon. However, guided weapons was a definite requirement with air-to-air rockets also being required, the fittings to be installed during production. Though the information on the weapons under development was at this point not sufficient to allow any firm choice to be made, it was recognised that either *Blue Sky* or *Blue Jay* would be required. It had already been decided that the aircraft should have four wing strong points which could accept bombs, rockets or guided weapons and two of which would accept the external standard fuel tanks. Change of armament roles would be an important factor and the ease of interchangeability on board ship was highlighted as a crucial point.

## Arresting

The maximum approach speed would be 138kts and with a limiting entry speed of 112kts the minimum wind speed would have to be 26kts. At 25,800lb landing weight the aircraft could meet the requirement as originally written (except for the entry speed of over 105kts) but the limiting factor in the development of the aircraft was the arrester gear.

## Construction Begins

Construction of all three of the Type 544 prototypes was carried out in the Experimental Hangar at the Hursley Park design centre. With the premature demise of the Type 525 and the subsequent loss of a valuable research tool which would otherwise have yielded a large amount of valuable development data to speed up the production aircraft, the construction of the first of the N.113D (Development) aircraft, WT854, was rapidly carried out.

As with its forebears, WT854 was roaded from Hursley to Boscombe Down on 14 January 1956 in preparation for its first flight and on 20 January the aircraft took to the air in the hands of Mike Lithgow. During the brief 10 minute general handling flight, Lithgow was joined in the circuit by Dave Morgan in Swift FR.5 WK277 who was carrying out an autostabilisation flight from Chilbolton.

The following day Morgan flew WK277 from Chilbolton to Boscombe Down and from there shepherded Lithgow in WT854 on its second flight of 45 minutes duration. Just over a week later the aircraft was transferred to Chilbolton. It was now a race against time to prepare the aircraft for deck trials and begin to regain some of the lost ground.

With the first prototype 544 now airborne, no time was wasted in preparing for the initial deck landing trials. In consequence the aircraft was unrepresentative of the proposed production version in various respects; in particular it was fitted with double slotted flaps instead of trailing edge flaps with supercirculation, and had a non-standard vertical tail incorporating a smaller rudder. As ground resonance tests had not yet been made, the aircraft's maximum speed was limited to 350 kts. The air intake for engine bay ventilation was positioned at the forward end of the dorsal fin; in later aircraft this was moved further forward, so lengthening the forward part of the dorsal fin along the spine of the aircraft. During the early flight trials a large nose boom was fitted carrying a pitot head and yaw vanes (though by the time of the deck trials this had been replaced by the original rounded version); the fuselage gun barrel ports were sealed, the tail skid was locked in the down position and no hook frame doors were fitted.

## Joe Smith CBE, FRAeS, MIMechE

Sadly on 20th February 1956, just a month after WT854's first flight, Supermarine's Chief Designer Joe Smith died at his home in

*First prototype WT854 surrounded by well-clad technicians at the Aeroplane and Armament Experimental Establishment, Boscombe Down on 21 January 1956. Behind it is Supermarine Swift FR.5 WK277 which had been flown over from nearby Chilbolton by Dave Morgan and which shepherded WT854 on its second flight. (The aircraft is now preserved in the Newark Air Museum).*

Chandlers Ford, Hampshire. He was just 58 years of age.

Smith had taken over upon the death of R.J.Mitchell in 1937, and in addition to his remarkable achievements with the Spitfire during World War II, he was responsible for the Spiteful, Seafang, Attacker and Swift fighter aircraft, together with the Types 508 and 525 which had eventually led to the Type 544.

Following a brief career in the Royal Navy during the First World War, Smith had joined Supermarine in 1921 and then risen to become Chief Draughtsman by 1926. Although Mitchell will be forever credited with the creation of the Spitfire, it was the team led by the lesser-known Smith who turned that creation into a practical realisation for mass production and made it the success that it was.

Succeeding Smith as Chief Designer was his former deputy, Alan Clifton, with George Henson becoming his assistant.

**Return to Boscombe Down**

On Thursday 22 March 1956, just over two months after making its first flight from Boscombe Down, WT854 returned to the Wiltshire base to begin Aerodrome Dummy Deck Landings (ADDLs). The following day, on the eve of the preparations planned for the forthcoming weekend at Boscombe, Mike Lithgow sat down at home and scripted a hand-written note to the Supermarine Assistant Chief Designer George Henson, expressing his serious misgivings about the performance of the aircraft.
In the letter Lithgow stated that, in his opinion, the aircraft was *'..just useable at 35,000 ft in a fighter role..'*, and that although the Navy had recognised this, and had subsequently revised its intended role to that of strike with a hope of matching the performance of the Hunter F.6, they would still be disappointed by its manoeuvring qualities.

Rudder power, Lithgow continued, was *'deplorable'*. The problem had originally been identified on the 525, but even so WT854 had been fitted with an even smaller control surface. The result was that the aircraft became almost uncontrollable during take-offs with any degree of crosswind component. The requirement for nosewheel steering, it was argued, was seen to be a must in this instance and also to aid general ground handling.

But it was on the subject of flap blowing that Lithgow felt most strongly. *'I achieved considerable popularity some time ago,'* he wrote, *'by stating that there was no evidence to show that blowing gave us anything speedwise on the approach and we should be better off without the cost, complication and additional hazard (I think of the single-engined landing with blow & overshoot, or rather I try not to).'*

Nonetheless the ADDL programme at Boscombe got underway, and by 5 April some thirtyeight such sorties had been completed, using a reduced fuel load in order to approximate the intended deck landing weight, with the all-up weight at take-off being 29,000lbs.

During these and previous ADDLs carried out by Vickers-Armstrongs, a final approach speed of 135 to 138 knots was established as comfortable, with a touchdown speed of 130-132 knots. In this case the limit was undoubtedly proximity to the minimum drag speed. It was very evident that any attempt to flare out on the approach merely resulted in a sharp increase of rate of descent unless power was applied simultaneously. This feature was most noticeable also when watching ADDLs. The aircraft, when at about 20ft or so would sink rapidly due to either an intentional or 'subconscious' flare out, or an inadvertent air speed reduction. The tail-down attitude of the aircraft was extremely marked on the approach, but since the view was satisfactory it did not unduly concern the pilot once accustomed to it - and probably caused more concern to the onlooker!

As a result of a large number of measured take-offs it became evident that a reduction in weight for the deck would be necessary, at least until actual experience had been gained. It was therefore decided that the first carrier take-off would be at 27,800lbs, thus leaving sufficient fuel for two landings. As it transpired, this figure was adhered to throughout the trials, except for the final departure when the all-up weight was increased to 28,200lbs.

It was found that the behaviour of the air speed indicator during ADDLs in turbulent air was most unsatisfactory in that fluctuations as high as 5 knots either side of the approach speed were not uncommon. Under these conditions the audio-approach system was unusable and an improvement was desired.

*First prototype WT854 whilst undergoing trials at the Royal Aircraft Establishment, Bedford. Technicians are making readings from the decelerometer carried in the aircraft during the trials. (via Philip Jarrett)*

*First prototype WT854 touching down into the barrier during land-based trials at the Royal Aircraft Establishment Bedford. (E.B.Morgan archives)*

*First prototype WT854 spotted as far aft as possible, with its tail over the rounddown, being prepared for a free take-off from HMS Ark Royal on 5 April 1956. (Vickers-Armstrongs)*

*First prototype WT854 about to touch down on HMS Ark Royal on 5 April 1956. (via Philip Jarrett)*

*First prototype WT854 touching down on HMS Ark Royal on 5 April 1956. (via N.Parker)*

*A pleasing three-quarter front view of first prototype WT854 about to catch the first arrester wire as Mike Lithgow touches down on HMS Ark Royal on 5 April 1956. (Vickers-Armstrongs)*

*First prototype WT854 is struck down on HMS Ark Royal's for'ard lift. As can be seen, it was a rather tight fit. Lt Cdr Little's tyre marks can still be seen on the deck. (Vickers-Armstrongs)*

*Mike Lithgow seated in the cockpit of WT854 as it goes down below on HMS Ark Royal's lift. The nose is folded back to avoid being snagged on the edge of the deck well. (via John Stevens)*

*HMS Ark Royal's deck sporting two black tyre marks left by first prototype WT854 on 9 April 1956 when Lt Cdr C.M.Little inadvertently took off with the parking brake still on. He re-landed successfully and the aircraft had a wheel change before further testing. (Vickers-Armstrongs)*

**Initial Deck Landing Trials**

On 3 April the main party of representatives from Vickers and the Admiralty embarked in HMS *Ark Royal* at Portsmouth, with Mike Lithgow remaining at Boscombe Down to fly WT854 out to the ship the following day. However the British climate had other plans, and unfortunately the ship was unable to sail due to strong winds, forcing the first deck landing of the N.113 to be delayed for 24 hours. It was therefore during the early afternoon of Thursday 5 April 1956 that WT854 appeared in *Ark Royal*'s circuit. Though the visual impression was that the approach was high, the hook struck the base of the round-down some four feet below deck level, much to the surprise of the onlookers, before successfully engaging the arrester wire. Lithgow had found some difficulty in seeing the mirror and this, with possible failure to appreciate the unusually great distance between pilots eye and arrester hook, was accepted as the reason for the low strike. Luckily no significant damage had been done to either aircraft or ship.

During subsequent landings it became obvious that the mirror setting was incorrect for this aircraft, and that a landing with the reflected light in line with the datum lights resulted in the hook striking the round-down. Unfortunately it was not possible to rectify this most unsatisfactory state of affairs (which could, and nearly did, result in the abandonment of the trial) because the mirror was already at its maximum height. For the remaining landings, the reflected light was placed at the top of the mirror. Even so, the first wire was almost invariably engaged.

In all, by the end of the trials, twenty-nine deck landings had been made: seven by Mike Lithgow and twenty-two by A&AEE pilots, comprising nine each by Lt Cdr Colin Little and Lt Cdr Derek Whitehead, and four by Cdr Stan Orr.

As the aircraft had not yet been cleared for catapult launches by RAE Bedford, all take-offs were free and unassisted. A chance was taken, however, during a quiet moment to carry out trial manoeuvring of the aircraft onto the catapult to assess the effectiveness of the non-steerable nosewheel. Directional control by brakes alone was found adequate but it was felt that some improvement could be made.

The aircraft was clear of the deck before reaching the bows with a wind speed of 40kts over the deck, measured by an anemometer at deck level, the take-off distance being between 650 and 700ft. Later, the maximum available was raised to 785ft, allowing the aircraft to be spotted near the round-down. Little or no sink occurred as the aircraft became airborne, provided the wind speed was maintained at 40kts at deck level, and take-off performance during the deck trials showed reasonable agreement with predictions from the tests at Boscombe Down. Satisfactory take-offs were made from the deck with a wind speed between 40 and 42kts and, on those occasions early in the trials where an attempt was made to achieve an optimum take-off, the aircraft unstuck within the last 200ft of deck in such conditions. On many occasions, however, the pilots allowed the aircraft to roll off the end of the deck.

On 9 April, Lt Cdr Colin Little of the A&AEE caused consternation when he inadvertently left the parking brake on during launch. At a weight of 27,700lb, with the wheels locked by the full 4000lb system pressure for the full length of the dry deck, take-off was achieved with an end-speed of approximately 100kts, followed by a considerable amount of sink over the bows and an all pervading smell of burning rubber!

WT854 crawled back into the air and, after a quick circuit, landed safely back on board with distinctly misshapen wheels which were subsequently changed. For several months afterwards *Ark Royal* sported two parallel black tracks on her flight deck. However the incident was not a one-off, and on at least one other occasion the wheels were locked for nearly half the length of the deck due to the same reason. It was found that the 'T'-shaped parking brake handle, positioned centrally below the instrument panel and directly behind the control column, was difficult to reach once the pilot was fully strapped in and the shoulder harness locked. Following the trials a number of minor modifications were embodied to prevent any repetition, including the repositioning of the handle to the top of the instrument panel.

In a Press Release on Monday 30 April 1956, Vickers-Armstrongs (Aircraft) Ltd announced the completion of the deck trials with the N.113, the statement detailing the work carried out leading up to and during the trials, and concluding by quoting the Parliamentary Secretary to the Admiralty who had announced that the aircraft could, '..carry the atom bomb..' and that, '..the possibilities of equipping later models with guided missiles are being investigated'. A 'substantial order' for the N.113 placed by the Royal Navy was also disclosed.

Early tests had revealed that the aircraft suffered badly from Pitch-Up. This phenomenon occurred at high subsonic Mach numbers when g was applied up to the point of the stall. Airflow over the outer wing surface broke away and the resultant nose-up pitch could not be restrained. The purpose of the leading edge extensions subsequently fitted was to reduce the flow separation.

A critical factor effecting this form of instability was the tail height in relation to the wing. Since the tail had 10 degrees dihedral, a simple way to reduce the height was, literally, to fit the tail upside down. These two modifications reduced the pitch-up to an acceptable level.

It therefore only remained to check whether jet blast and noise effects on the tail were still acceptable and this was carried out on a specially-constructed rig set up at Chilbolton, where the local residents were less intolerant to noise than those at Wisley.

*First prototype WT854 after being landed by Mike Lithgow at Wisley with the nose wheel retracted on 20 August 1956. (E.B.Morgan archives)*

*A worms-eye port side view of second prototype WT859 at Wisley in mid-1956. (via Philip Jarrett)*

*Second prototype WT859 on an early flight without its nose probe. Note the dihedral tailplane. (Vickers-Armstrongs)*

*Second prototype WT859 being flown by Dave Morgan over the south coast, complete with nose probe. (via M.J.Hooks)*

*Third prototype WW134 on jacks outside the flight test hangar at Wisley. (Vickers-Armstrongs)*

The tailplane was instrumented to measure pressures, temperatures and noise levels. These tests confirmed that there were no unacceptable consequences of lowering the tail.

On 20 August 1956, Mike Lithgow found on returning to Wisley in WT854 and preparing to land that he could not lock the nose wheel in the down position. The entire undercarriage would lock up satisfactorily, the nose wheel would, however, only release from the lock up and stop at approximately half travel even though full hydraulic pressure was indicated in the cockpit.

The circuit was joined at 230 knots with 1,300lbs of fuel and the wheels selected down. The main wheels showed green lights, but the nose wheel red unlocked light remained on the indicator. The throttles were opened to obviate the possibility of the red light indicating throttles closed/wheels up. Air Traffic Control confirmed visually that the nose wheel appeared to be half way down.

Reducing his speed to 170 knots and making further selections, Lithgow met with identical results. He then increased his speed to 250 knots and applied 'g'. This had no result and, in all, twelve selections were made with no improvement. By this time his fuel was down to 700lbs and it became necessary to land. Accordingly the master emergency lever was pulled, 4,000 psi was noted on the emergency pressure gauge, the nose wheel and arrester hook emergency lever was pulled, but still there was no effect on the cockpit light indication.

Air Traffic Control once again checked the nose wheel position visually and reported it still appeared rather less than half way down. An approach was made at 130 knots and the nose wheel held off with full tail down to 75 knots. Full brakes were applied as the aircraft rocked forward onto its nose, coming to rest at the side of the runway just past the control tower. Lithgow was unharmed and the aircraft was nowhere near as badly damaged as had been feared.

Since the nose leg operating jack attachment and the nose wheel door with its attendant sequence valve operating linkage were broken in the emergency landing, it was not possible to check the functioning of the complete nose wheel system. However, by testing the individual components and part of the system and introducing defects on the test-rig it was established that the trouble was caused by insufficient travel on the nose wheel sequence valve operating mechanism. The failure could be reproduced exactly on the test rig by adjustments of the sequence valve operating link and modification to the valve adjustment procedure was put in hand to prevent any future repetition.

It was established that the emergency system failed to lower the nose wheel because the identification of the nose and the main undercarriage emergency operating levers was transposed. When the lever labelled 'Nose U/C' was operated, it was found that this had in fact operated the main undercarriage emergency systems. Since the first prototype was the only aircraft with separate emergency levers for nose and main undercarriage, the problem was deemed to be a one-off that could not affect the other prototypes.

Repairs were quickly effected and in September 1956, with the tail and wing modifications incorporated, Mike Lithgow displayed WT854 at the (then) annual SBAC Show at Farnborough. Meanwhile the second of the Type 544 prototypes had joined the flight test programme. Unlike the first aircraft, WT859, which Mike Lithgow first flew from Boscombe Down on 22 June 1956, was fitted with single slotted trailing edge flaps and provisioning for supercirculation from the outset, though the non-availability of the Avon 202 engines prevented the system from initially being put to use. On the second day of the SBAC Show WT854 went unserviceable and Dave Morgan took over for the last three days with WT859.

Returning WT854 to the A&AEE at Boscombe Down for handling and assessment trials that were carried out between 17th and 27th October 1956, it was again concluded that the anhedral tailplane and wing modification had greatly improved the behaviour and handling at high Mach numbers and also at low speeds, though a saw-tooth leading edge to the wing, it was felt, would possibly remove the pitch-up altogether.

From August until October 1956, WT859 was engaged in flight flutter tests which were carried out whilst concurrently involved in other development work. Fitted with twin Rolls-Royce Avon RA.28 engines, the aircraft was flown to the Vickers flight test centre at Wisley on 8 October for the fitment of Avon 202 units, prior to being dismantled and roaded back to Hursley Park where the flap-blowing system was connected up. On completion the aircraft was roaded back to Boscombe Down to begin flight trials of the flap blowing system.

**Deck catapult and arrester trials, January 1957**

That same month (October 1956) the testing programme was given an extra boost following the first flight from Boscombe Down of WW134, the third and last of the Type 544 prototypes. WW134 was representative of the proposed production state in most matters aerodynamically relevant to deck operations, with all of the design alterations made to the first two aircraft, including the anhedral tailplane and wing fences, having been incorporated during construction. Differences, however, included the fitment of a fully operational supercirculation system, RA.24 engines, an improved and strengthened undercarriage suitable for greater vertical velocities, and the addition of a cockpit instrument, sensitive to incidence, which gave the pilot an aural indication of his approach speed at any weight.

*Third prototype WW134 about to undergo its first catapult launch, from HMS Ark Royal on 2 January 1957. Note the "Goofers" crowding around the top of the ship's bridge. (Royal Navy)*

This was the first opportunity to fully test the effectiveness of flap blowing on carrier landings. WW134 was therefore put through a similar series of ADDLs and arrester trials as WT854 at Boscombe Down and RAE Bedford between November and December 1956, prior to carrying out the next set of deck trials scheduled for January 1957.

Departing Plymouth on the morning of 3 January, HMS *Ark Royal* sailed for the Channel in increasingly bad weather. This failed to improve, and eventually resulted in just five landings and five catapult take-offs being made, all of which were on 6 January. The pilots involved in these trials were Cdr Pat Chilton RN and Lt Cdr Derek Whitehead RN of A&AEE's 'C' Squadron, and Mike Lithgow.

During the trials the aircraft's weight was controlled by varying the fuel carried, with landings being made at weights between 28,800lbs and 34,400lbs and catapult launches at weights between 29,600lbs and 30,900lbs, except for the final launch which was made at 34,250lbs.

On completion of the trials on *Ark Royal* in January 1957 a report by the Officer in charge of the trials, Commander C.F.Hargreaves RN, was circulated. Dated 23 January 1957, some six days after Vickers had announced the results of the trials to press, the report claimed that it would be unwise to draw any positive conclusions from such meagre evidence as five launches and landings, but Commander Chilton (who carried out 2 launches and 3 landings) was pleased with the handling qualities of the aircraft. He was not impressed by the view from the cockpit, as he found almost the whole flight deck 'hooded' in the final approach, and it appeared that the effects of the enlarged flap area and 'blow' were offset by the slower approach speed then possible. Handling on the deck appeared to present no problems, and all present agreed that it was refreshing to see an aircraft without nosewheel steering approaching the catapult with such obvious ease. At first the securing of the holdback gear was thought to need one engine cut, with the attendant delay in restarting, but later it was found acceptable (perhaps due to the wind speed over the deck) to carry out the operation with both engines idling. This avoided the unpleasant kerosene spillage from the vent almost immediately in front of the tail bumper to which the holdback gear was attached.

Commander Hargreaves completed his report by complimenting the ship and Vickers for their co-operation shown to the trials team, and particularly the assistance given by the Vickers Service Liaison Officer, Mr V.D.Trim.

During March and April of 1957 temperatures of the jet exit pen-nib fairings were measured throughout the speed range. Above Mach One there was a rapid rise in temperature, well above the value acceptable. There was no way of preventing this and some modification had to be considered.

On 17 June, Dave Morgan was carrying out resonance tests on WT859 over the south coast of England, which entailed several dives in excess of Mach One. As the aircraft passed south of Selsey Bill he felt a bang which seemed to come from the port side of the aircraft. He called up 'Pee Wee' Judge, who was also airborne in the area at the time, to give a visual inspection. As he took up position alongside the aircraft, Judge informed Morgan that the port engine jet efflux fairing had disappeared and, with a fuel tank directly behind the exposed skin which was now being blasted by hot gasses, quickly suggested that the port engine should be shut down.

As he examined the damage for himself once on the ground back at Wisley, Morgan was joined by the Chief Designer, Alan Clifton. Musing over the possible causes of the failure, Clifton calmly uttered, "We weren't expecting that to happen"!

**Inertia Cross-Coupling**

The configuration of the Type 544 and the Scimitar was such that inertia cross-coupling effects in rolling manoeuvres had to be considered. Trials were carried out following initial simulator and flight work by Vickers, to determine the magnitude of any such effects and the implication on the Service use of the aircraft.

The phenomenon usually referred to as inertia coupling occurs at high rates of roll when inertia forces become comparable in magnitude with aerodynamic stabilising forces, and the resulting interaction produces coupling of the longitudinal and lateral motions and can result in instability, although marked changes in incidence and side-slip can occur without actual instability.

A thorough study was made of the inertia-coupling problem, which had been highlighted by a series of accidents to Super Sabres in the USAF, and also by the loss of the Bell X-2 on the 27th September 1956, where the NACA test pilot Millburn Apt had lost his life. The problem had become more pronounced with more modern aircraft which tended to have most of their weight concentrated in a lengthy fuselage and low weight short span wings.

Vickers made a thorough investigation of the problem. Computer calculations indicated that the critical angles of sideslip likely to have been produced would have overloaded the fin and rear fuselage. However, this was outweighed by the structural tests carried out, these proving that the strength of those areas was adequate.

After discussion with the A&AEE, the limitation in rolling manoeuvres (which had been applied earlier) were relaxed to: "normal rolling is limited to 360° and rolling pull-outs to 5.0g/full aileron (as a guide it was recommended that full aileron at 5g should progressively be reduced to quarter aileron at 7.5g)". Such a limitation was not likely to restrict normal rolling manoeuvres unduly.

**Handling Trials**

During May 1957 Mike Lithgow carried out a number of handling tests on WT859 and WW134 at the Vickers flight test centre, Wisley. WT859 was used in the lateral and directional tests and the handling with asymmetric power, with WW134 being used to test the behaviour at the stall.

The tests revealed that the take-off could safely be continued in the event of failure of one engine at 135 knots when operating from a 2,000 yard runway. Several flapless take-offs were made, during which the increase in take-off run in this configuration was estimated to be not more than 200 yards. The nosewheel-off and unstick speeds were 130 and 155-160 knots respectively.

The maximum crosswind in which take-offs were made was wind strength 25 knots gusting 27 knots at 90° to the runway. Considerable braking of the lee wheel was required until the rudder became effective at about 70 knots, and it was considered that a steerable nosewheel would make the crosswind take-off a much more comfortable procedure, though in the end this never came to fruition.

On the completion of these tests it was concluded that the all-up stalling characteristics were satisfactory, with ample warning in the form of intense airframe buffet. The all-down stalling characteristics were also considered to be acceptable, although marked longitudinal instability was present. However, this instability was well defined and easy to control.

On 14 June 1957, Lithgow presented a report on his findings following the handling tests. Once again the poor visibility over the nose below the minimum approach speed of between 125 and 120 knots at 29,500lbs, due to the aircraft's increased attitude, was highlighted. A cut-down version of the nose had been flown on WW134 a month earlier, and though early production machines still sported the rather bulky-looking original version, eventually all aircraft were fitted with the revised contour cone, which improved the view considerably.

With regard to landing the aircraft, height control was governed entirely by the throttles, but engine power was never to be removed until touchdown. High, fast approaches with low power settings were to be avoided.

**Audio Incidence Indicator (AII)**

As originally set up the output from the AII sensor was too sensitive to the effect of bumpy air. In smooth air it was not as easy to use as on the approach.

## WW134 Rough runway measurements, October 1959

WW134 was instrumented for rough runway trials in connection with the TSR-2 contract. It was proposed to make accelerated stops, take-off and landings on Wisley grass and also the runway at Turweston, by then a disused airfield in a poor state of repair.

Several runs were made from east to west on the grass alongside the main runway at Wisley. The speeds achieved were rather different to those intended, as it was found that the ASI increased by 15 knots after both engines were cut, and correct stabilisation of the intended speed was therefore impossible. However, this was not material to the result.

After three runs up to a maximum of 85-90 knots the aircraft was taken off the grass by pilot Mike Lithgow, at an all-up weight of 30,000lbs, tyre pressures were 100psi. Although the grass area used was by no means smooth, no difficulty whatsoever was encountered. The ride was a rough one, due entirely to the nosewheel being in contact with the ground (the pressure in the nosewheel tyre was normal at 210psi). When this was raised at 115-120 knots, all noise and vibration and bumping ceased and the aircraft unstuck at 130-135 knots.

Braking action on the grass was much worse than anticipated, and was likened to a very wet runway. There was a constant tendency to wander off to starboard, possibly due to a slight fall away of the surface in this direction. After two runs it was necessary to reload the recorders and it was found that the temperature of the starboard tyre was 135° and the port tyre 115°. Consequently, on the Dunlop representatives advice, the tyres were cooled some 20° before the take-off.

### Final Fates

At the end of May 1958, having been deemed to be at the end of its useful career with Vickers, WT854 was put into storage at Wisley pending disposal instructions. Initially the Empire Test Pilot's School at RAE Farnborough expressed an interest in taking on the aircraft, but this fell through just two months later. The aircraft was subsequently dispatched to RAE Bedford where from the end of 1958 until the start of 1960 it was engaged in the non-flying trials of both arrester and bridle catching gear. Though the aircraft was originally destined to go to the Royal Navy's Air Engineering School at RNAS Arbroath, this allocation was cancelled before the aircraft left Bedford. In late 1964 WT854 was moved by road to the School of Aircraft Handling at RNAS Culdrose, where it was used to train aircraft handlers in the art of manoeuvring large aircraft around the confines of an aircraft carrier deck and hangar area. Finally, in 1967, WT854 was relinquished by the SAH and transported to P&EE Shoeburyness where it eventually expired.

*Two photographs of Supermarine Type 544 one-fifth scale model in the wind tunnel. It has its chassis down, but no nose wheel. (Vickers-Armstrongs)*

A series of tests on WW134 were made during March 1958 to determine the optimum damping for the probe sensing unit. This was checked by carrying out simulated deck landings on the mirror landing sight at Wisley.

When set up correctly the system provided an accurate indication of aircraft incidence which could be used to achieve the correct approach speed for the weight of the aircraft at the time.

The value of this was apparent when considering that the correct Indicated Airspeed for landing varied by at least 10 knots over the normal range of landing weight.

The pilot was provided with a lighted indicator, close to his line of vision, as well as audio tones. The former consisted on a circle (the target incidence) and two arrow heads which indicated the need to increase or decrease incidence. The latter were high pitched bleeps for too low an incidence (speed too fast) and low pitched for too high an incidence (speed too slow). The interval between bleeps reduced as the correct incidence was approached. At the correct incidence/speed the note became steady.

*Front view of second prototype WT859 (by then allocated Ground Instructional serial A2499) poses with some young Naval Airmen at the School of Aircraft Handling, in 1963. The nose section is now in the Brooklands Museum. (Royal Navy)*

*A rather sorry-looking second prototype WT859 nearing the end of its useful days at the School of Aircraft Handling, Culdrose. (via Lee Howard)*

*Third prototype WW134 during underwater ejection trials in the Mediterranean off southern France in June 1962. (Martin Baker via N.Parker)*

The story of WT859 follows a very similar path to its predecessor. It too spent its last days both at Bedford on arrester trials and with the SAH at Culdrose. However, although it too ended up being used for ballistics trials at Shoeburyness, the fuselage managed to remain substantially complete, though rather battered and bruised, until a mass purge of airframes began in 1991. Having recognised the significance of the aircraft, though still having to take into consideration the sheer bulk of what remained, the cockpit section was removed from the rest of the fuselage and is now preserved at the Brooklands Museum in Surrey.

Sadly this was to be the only relatively happy ending to the story of the three Type 544 airframes. The rough runway trials carried out at Wisley and Turweston in October 1959 were destined to be one of WW134's last duties as a test and research vehicle for Vickers. In March 1962 she was flown to South Marston to be prepared for the forthcoming Anglo-French Underwater Sink-Rate Trials, which were to be carried out in the Mediterranean. Having been flown to Toulon, both engines were removed and she was lightered aboard HMS *Centaur*. The exact sequence of events has not yet been determined, but a recently discovered batch of photographs, one of which is reproduced here, shows the aircraft apparently being repeatedly raised and lowered in the sea whilst tests were carried out on underwater ejections by Martin-Baker.

In October 1962, with the trials at an end, and with the whole ship's company lined up in front of the ship's bridge and island to watch, WW134 was boosted off the catapult. HMS *Centaur*'s third commission line-book states that, *'..in fact we enjoyed a series of interesting Flight Deck novelties culminating with the silent launch of a de-engined Scimitar. It was rather like the beginning of a "Tom and Jerry" without the sound – but this Fred did not do his stuff altogether successfully and we felt robbed of the climax'.*

*XD212, the first production Scimitar, shows its beautiful lines during an early test flight in the hands of David Morgan. (Vickers-Armstrongs)*

## THE SCIMITAR

Standing outside on the flight line at South Marston on a clear and cold Friday 11th January 1957, XD212 - the first production Scimitar F.1 - was prepared for its first flight. As he climbed aboard, Mike Lithgow may have lamented that this occasion heralded the beginning of the end of Supermarine's long history of aircraft production. Indeed the rationalisation and subsequent break-up of the vast Vickers organisation had already begun, starting with the recent closure of Chilbolton and transferral of all development test flying to Wisley in Surrey.

Also just twenty-four hours had elapsed since the surprise succession of Harold Macmillan to become Prime Minister following the premature resignation of Anthony Eden. Eden had suffered greatly from the strain of the previous year's disastrous Suez conflict and had stepped down due to ill health. Succeeding Macmillan as Secretary of State for Defence was Duncan Sandys who, just three months later, would produce the White Paper which will forever be linked with the demise of the British aircraft industry.

As XD212 roared off the runway and flew over nearby Swindon, few would have realised that the future of fighter aircraft would soon to be thrown into turmoil.

The construction of the early production Scimitars appears to have been less than straightforward. It has always been assumed that all of the production aircraft were built from start to finish at South Marston. However, it was at Supermarine's Itchen works in Southampton, rebuilt after the war, that the fuselage shells were constructed with the wings being built at nearby Eastleigh, possibly under contract to Saro. Research has also shown that parts of the stern-ends were produced at one of the company's former wartime dispersal units at Bradley Road, Trowbridge, Wiltshire.

The various sections of these early aircraft were then roaded to the Experimental Department at Hursley Park where, as with the early Swifts, they were assembled prior to being again roaded to Supermarine's main factory and airfield site at South Marston. Here they were reassembled and test flown. Later, with the closure of Hursley Park, the assembly line was transferred entirely to South Marston.

From XD213, which first flew at South Marston in May 1957, production proceeded apace with an average of two aircraft rolling off the production line every month. The gap between the first and second aircraft may have been due to the desire to get XD212 onto

*The instrument panel of XD212 in May 1957.
(Vickers-Armstrongs)*

the Controller (Aircraft) books as early as possible, in order to start recouping some of the costs of flight testing.

Most of the test flying of the production machines was carried out by Les Colquhoun. A distinguished former wartime RAF photographic reconnaissance Spitfire pilot, having already earned the DFC and DFM, he had joined Supermarine in 1946. In 1950 he was awarded the George Medal after managing against the odds to successfully land the first production Attacker at Chilbolton when the starboard wingtip folded in flight, jamming the ailerons.

Although Colquhoun was the only permanent production test pilot in residence at South Marston during the Scimitar era, occasionally some of the development test pilots would fly across from their main base at Wisley (the flight test centre having moved from Chilbolton earlier in the year). As well as Mike Lithgow and Dave Morgan there was 'Pee-Wee' Judge. Having joined Supermarines in 1951 to assist in ferrying Attackers to Pakistan, Judge was also involved in some of the production test flying. During his wartime service in the Royal Air Force he had been a fighter pilot in North Africa and was twice shot down in the desert. He flew rocket-firing Typhoons in France and Germany until the end of the war in Europe, after which he served in India and became a Test Pilot at Drigh Road, Karachi. After the war he became a civilian ferry pilot and joined No.615 Squadron of the Royal Auxiliary Air Force flying Spitfires and then Meteors, holding the rank of Flight Lieutenant and leading the squadron aerobatic team. For his service in the RAuxAF he was awarded a Mention in Despatches. Sadly he was to lose his life, having left Vickers, whilst demonstrating the Wallis WA.117 Autogyro G-AXAR at Farnborough on 11 September 1970.

**Gunnery acceptance trials**

Gunnery acceptance trials were called for the Scimitar in Ministry of Supply pro-forma AV/191/01 dated 4 June 1957.

The object of the trial was to clear the gunnery installation, excluding the gun sight, and sighting system, for Service use by day under operational conditions as laid down in aircraft Specification NR/A.17 issue 5.

Preparing the aircraft for ground firing trials was very extensive: positioned on a hard-standing facing the butts at a distance of 50 yards, the undercarriage was kept in the down position and all the wheels chocked fore and aft. Jump cards were placed at 1,000 inches from the gun muzzles for bullet group tests. Using nose, tail, and wingtip trestles, the weight of the aircraft was taken with the wheels still on the ground (and undercarriage locks fitted). No lifting jacks were used.

Using 1-inch hemp rope the nose oleo structure and tail skid were secured to the eye bolts in the hard-standing.

At the completion of the trials it was concluded that the guns functioned satisfactorily and, subject to a list of minor modifications, firing could take place between 200-640 knots, with a restriction of 600 knots when air brakes were used, and an altitude not exceeding 45,000 feet. Temperature restrictions limited the HE ammunition load to 125 rounds, but a full load of practice ammunition could be carried.

Between 9 May and 13 June 1957, a total of seventeen flights in a series of trials were carried out using XD212 to determine whether engine surge could be induced by firing of the Scimitar's four-gun armament.

To bring about a substantial reduction in the number of flights required for the tests, gun switching was introduced, which enabled the port and starboard pair of guns to be fired independently.

The only modification to later aircraft, which could influence the results, was the fitting of intake bulges to cure the banging, this occurring in the intake under certain flight conditions with an engine flamed out. Subsequent to the report into the tests, these bulges were trial fitted to XD212, though it was not thought that they would have any adverse effect, and check firings carried out shortly after on this aircraft by both Vickers and A&AEE pilots confirmed this.

The conditions covered by these tests followed a programme agreed with the A&AEE with the addition of one more severe case as requested by Rolls-Royce Ltd. This was a condition which detailed the two gun firing carried out to save flying time and give preliminary indication of any trouble. Some of the conditions were repeated when gun stoppages occurred with less than 80% of the ammunition load for the pair guns having been fired.

Test firings were made at heights between 30,000ft and 48,000ft, from speeds ranging from 150 knots up to 0.95 IMN. In continuous firing, the guns were given one uninterrupted burst; in ripple this was changed to 0.5, 0.25 and 0.5 second bursts.

After the tests it was concluded that firing of the four-gun armament of the Scimitar under the most severe conditions would not cause engine surge.

**Further deck trials**

Between 18th and 25th July 1957 it was back to HMS *Ark Royal* once again for more deck trials, this time to measure the take-off performance and assess deck landing characteristics.

The two aircraft employed in these trials were WW134 and XD215, respectively the third prototype and the fourth production aircraft. On both, the shape of the top of the fuselage forward of the cockpit had been modified to provide an improvement in the view over the nose.

Again the pilot's were Cdr Pat Chilton, Lt Cdr Derek Whitehead and Mike Lithgow, though now with Lt Cdr H.G.Julian and Lt Cdr Danny Norman of the A&AEE, and Lt Cdr Geoff Higgs of RAE Bedford in addition.

Both aircraft were fitted with the improved view nose, XD215 having a dummy refuelling probe as well. Though it was not possible to fit all the radar into the improved view nose, the ranging unit was fitted into the nose of XD215. Airframe hours at the commencement of trials were WW134 75 hours 40 minutes and XD215 12 hours 20 minutes.

RNAS Ford was used as the diversion airfield, except for one day when Hurn was used due to the ship moving westward because of weather conditions.

On XD215 in particular, large quantities of debris were found lodged on the wing fold bottom skin access panels after folding. This was removed, but on each subsequent wing folding operation after flight, further debris comprising service nuts and bolts, split pins, washers, locking wire, rivet mandrels etc., were found. These obviously came from the outer wing and passed through the various apertures in the fold rib whenever wings were folded.

*Scimitar wings being completed out of the jig at Eastleigh. The jigs can be seen at the top right hand and top left of the photograph. (Vickers-Armstrongs)*

*Scimitar wings being finished after being taken out of the jig at Eastleigh. (Vickers-Armstrongs)*

*Scimitars under construction at Supermarine's Itchen Works, Southampton. A hydraulic test rig for testing folding wings and lowering the undercarriage is being used on the components destined for XD325. (Vickers-Armstrongs)*

*Scimitar fuselages out of the jig in the left foreground, at the Itchen factory. The fuselage assembly rigs are at the top right. The fuselage to the left is being worked on in the inverted position. (Vickers-Armstrongs)*

*Inverted Scimitar fuselages after being taken out of the jig at Itchen around January 1960. (Vickers-Armstrongs)*

*The Scimitar production line at South Marston. Here the fuselages and wings were mated together and systems installed. (Vickers-Armstrongs)*

*The static test airframe (XD233). (Vickers-Armstrongs)*

*The aft engine mounting trimming being fitted to XD232 at South Marston in December 1957. (Vickers-Armstrongs)*

It was pointed out that when the Scimitar was fitted with external stores, and the wings folded, the minimum width of one aircraft was increased by the depth of the two pylons and their associated stores. Most naval aircraft had wings that folded beyond the vertical, which automatically overcame this problem. With the aircraft clean it was hoped to range them three abreast across the hangar, but it was noted that this would not be possible when external stores were fitted. As a compromise the rows would be staggered, but the total number of aircraft per hangar would inevitably be reduced.

By the end of the trials a total of 148 landings and catapult take-offs had been achieved by the six pilots. Blowing over the flaps was used in all cases except for thirteen of the landings. The ninety-four dummy landings achieved by XD215 was in excess of the expected number during a squadron embarkation period. On the basis of an arrester gear limit of 108 knots at 28,000lb, a minimum of 24 knots of wind over the deck was required, but this increased to 30 knots without flap 'blow'.

Considerable satisfaction in the aircraft was generally expressed. Mike Lithgow's demonstration was particularly impressive to the ship's men and non-aeronautical officers. Beyond the unserviceability and atrocious access to some parts of the fuel system, the ship's company was horrified by the amount of fuel spilt onto the deck. On two occasions several gallons were discharged and it was only by rushing about with buckets and dustbins that most of it was put over the side – a taste of things to come.

During the trials, Lt Cdr Whitehead handsomely demonstrated that nose wheel steering was not required for manoeuvring on the deck. It was thought that tail towing would be required as positioning eight Scimitars in the forward deck park and three beside the island could only be done only if the long tail instead of the short nose was pulled out. A bar clamping instantly onto the tail skid shoe was suggested, but the idea was never put into practice.

On completion of the launch and arresting trials, the pilots spent two days carrying out overshoots and touch and go landings to assess the aircraft's behaviour with and without flap blowing. These dummy landings were not recorded in the total of 148 landings.

In all it was thought that it had been a very successful trial period both by the aircraft personnel and the ship. WW134 returned to the A&AEE and XD215 to Vickers at South Marston, both to continue with various further trials.

**Fin Failure and Control Jamming Incidents**

On 18 September 1957, XD217 was flown from Boscombe Down by US Marine Corps test pilot Captain Debencourt to assess supersonic flight and handling at high Mach numbers. Having climbed to 45,000ft and carried out two supersonic dives, Debencourt levelled out at 4,000ft and 600 kts. Suddenly there was a thump and the aircraft developed a noticeable tendency to

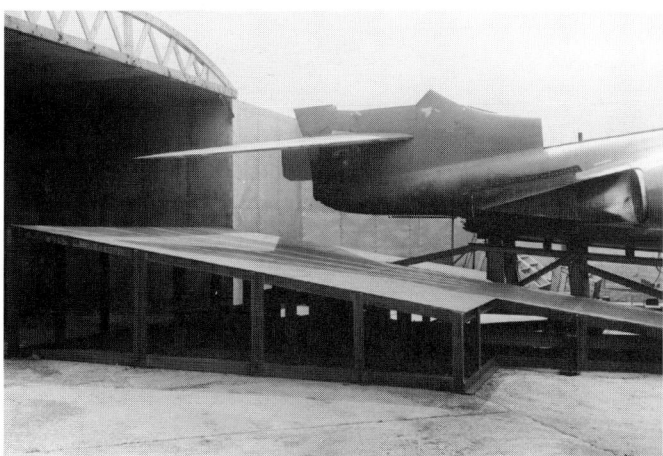

*Noise test specimen showing the position in relation to the carrier deck. (E.B.Morgan archives)*

*A general view of the noise test rig with an RA.28 engine fitted to a Scimitar tail unit at Chilbolton. (E.B.Morgan archives)*

*Aerial view of HMS Ark Royal under way with its radio aerials extended at both sides and XD215 on deck. Also visible is XJ474, the first production de Havilland Sea Vixen, with its wings folded. (Vickers-Armstrongs)*

*XD215 of 'C' Squadron (the Naval Test Squadron) of the Aeroplane & Experimental Establishment on deck landing trials aboard HMS Ark Royal in July 1957. (via Philip Jarrett)*

*XD215 of the Royal Navy Test Squadron, Boscombe Down, being launched from HMS Ark Royal during trials in July 1957. (via Philip Jarrett)*

sideslip. Observation from another aircraft showed that the fin was bent about a line running from about two-thirds height at the leading edge to about one-third height at the rear spar, the portion above this line being bent several degrees to port. The rudder trailing edge was also kinked. Debencourt turned the aircraft around and made a successful emergency landing back at base.

Subsequent investigation revealed no firm cause of the failure; strength tests did not shown the fin to be under strength, but a modification was introduced to make the strength more uniform along the spar. A report issued later concluded the most probable cause was some form of oscillation.

On an air test on 21 October 1957, when attempting to ease the aircraft out of a shallow dive at 0.95 IMN at 35,000ft, the stick appeared to be solid. It could not be freed with one hand but eventually a two-handed pull (estimated at 30lbs) was effective. Subsequently the control appeared to stick if left in any steady position but the break out force was only about 5lbs. The aircraft was difficult to control but successfully returned to Wisley. The lateral control was poor and the rudder appeared to be heavier in one direction than in the other. As a result of this incident all Scimitars were grounded. The primary cause was found to be contamination of the hydraulic system which, it was later shown, could lead to a very high valve loading. Reconditioning of all valves, cleansing of systems and steps to prevent any recurrence of the contamination were in hand by the end of October.

As a follow-on to the hydraulic fluid contamination, another incident took place seven days previously to XD212, whilst being flown by Lt Cdr Abraham, seconded to Vickers from the A&AEE. On 14 October, at a late stage in the take-off from Wisley on the second flight of the day, the pilot considered the longitudinal control to be unsatisfactory and abandoned the take-off run at the point of rotation. In an attempt to stop the aircraft at this high speed, the engines were cut but the wheel brakes burnt out before reaching the end of the runway. Careering across the airfield boundary road, the nose wheel was ripped off as XD212 ran into the adjacent field before hitting a lighting pole, damaging the leading edge of one wing. Some trace recordings were obtained from the aircraft and showed that the speed at which braking commenced was such that the maximum energy absorption of the brakes would not be expected to be sufficient to bring the aircraft to rest. It was concluded that it was probable that the peculiar control feel reported by the pilot was associated with the hydraulic fluid contamination which was found on all aircraft when investigating the incident which later occurred on XD217.

**Foreign Interest**

At a meeting at Weybridge on 10 September 1957 it was announced that the Armament Department at the company's London office had received an enquiry from the Venezuelan Government for the construction of an aircraft carrier to carry 22 fighter aircraft. Vickers had been invited to advise on the design of the carrier based around the possibility of exporting Scimitars, or developments of the type, as strike aircraft to go with the new vessel.

As the Venezuelan Fleet Air Arm at that time did not exist, it was felt that an interim type would be required in order to give adequate operational and deck landing training for the prospective crews prior to getting their hands on a machine as potent as the Scimitar. As with the British Fleet Air Arm, the Sea Hawk was suggested as being the best available aircraft for this purpose, an idea given the full support of Admiral Couchman.

The earliest predicted delivery date of the envisaged carrier was given as 1963 by which stage, it was felt, the Scimitar would be considerably out of date. There were, too, other factors to consider. George Henson scribbled on the bottom of a note to Jeffrey Quill, "*Unless the Venezuelans have a couple of uranium mines spare, surely they are due for a shock about the cost of all this? A lot more is needed than a few aeroplanes to keep a carrier at sea*".

However by October 1957 the decision not to proceed with the Scimitar strike aircraft effectively put an end to this potential export plan and any possible previous interest shown by the German Navy, Swiss and Canadian air forces and any serious development of the type was dropped.

**Performance Trials**

During November 1957 further tests were carried out with WT859 and XD216 to determine the aircraft's handling characteristics during which a speed of IMN 1.25 (1.32 true), ASI 682 knots was achieved.

The subsequent report found that, "*The highest indicated Mach Number and airspeed achieved were thought to be very close to the maximum obtainable on this aircraft. Although the Mach Number achieved above 15,000ft was 0.02 above the design limit, at low altitude the highest values of both Mach Number and IAS were well within the maximum permitted.*"

The report concluded that, "*In view of the flying necessary to achieve these speeds there is thought to be a strong case for recommending 'No Limit' as regards IAS and Mach Number.*"

*17th production aircraft XD228 just after take-off from Wisley. (via Philip Jarrett)*

*Brand new Scimitar XD279 at South Marston in 1959, now with the revised nose cone profile. (Vickers-Armstrongs)*

The climb performance of the Scimitar (without external stores) in ICAN conditions was determined from four climbs to over 45,000ft carried out by WW134 and XD212. The climbs were deliberately selected to give mean temperatures throughout the height range approximating closely to ICAN conditions. To avoid the necessity for temperature corrections, small allowances for wind gradient were applied.

Under those conditions, the rate of climb decreased linearly with altitude from 20,700 ft/min at 5,000ft to 6,000 ft/min at 36,000ft. Above the tropopause the rate of climb decreased linearly to 1,000 ft/min at 46,000ft (47,600ft indicated height). The absolute ceiling, obtained by extrapolation of this line, was 48,000ft (49,850ft indicated).

The time taken to reach 45,000ft was 6.65 minutes from 'wheels roll', 1.3 minutes being the time required to reach 5,000ft, which was the lowest altitude at which the climb could be considered to be stabilised. The ground distance covered during the climb to 45,000ft was 52.5 nautical miles.

Towards the end of 1957 brief tests were made on XD214, to determine the improvement of rate of descent when using 30° wing flap to augment the airbrakes.

The method of the tests was to time the rate of descent from 30,000ft to 2,000ft, the pilot first having carefully stabilised the descent condition at 35-40,000ft, using 75% r.p.m.

The limitations imposed were that the selection of 30° wing flap was restricted to 310 knots and/or 0.8 IMN whichever was the lower. The descents were therefore made at 0.8 IMN until the IAS showed 300 knots.

The result of the timed descents from 20,000ft to 2,000ft were:

(a) 30 degrees wing flap and airbrake 3 minutes 08 seconds
(b) Airbrakes only 4 minutes 23 seconds
(c) 30 degrees wing flap only 6 minutes 00 seconds

**Inboard and Outboard Drop Tank Jettison Tests**

In January 1958 Mike Lithgow, Dave Morgan and 'Pee Wee' Judge flew a series of tests on the seventh production machine, XD218, in order to prove the explosive drop tank jettison system, and to ascertain whether the tanks would clear the aircraft satisfactorily. The aircraft was fitted with standard 200-gallon pattern tanks without fins which were jettisoned from the port inboard station. A similar unjettisonable tank was fitted with a camera and carried at the starboard inboard station, along with a downward pointing camera mounted under the port mainplane and another outward facing camera under the fuselage, to film the sequence for later analysis. The A&AEE supplied a chase aircraft in the form of a Meteor NF.13 and Venom NF.2 carrying a photographer, but were only of use at the lower speeds; at the higher speeds the chase aircraft had difficulty tracking the Scimitar. Several jettisons were carried out, most using the 'Jettison External Stores' button, though on one occasion it was effected by pulling the trigger on the control column with the master armament selector set to 'bombs'. Jettisons were all carried out in straight and level flight at speeds ranging from 180 to 525 knots and at heights between 5,000 and 35,000 ft.

*XD212 and other development aircraft in the flight test hangar at Wisley. (Vickers-Armstrongs)*

It was found that the action of the jettison gun caused a slight roll away from the tank being jettisoned; this was of little consequence, as tanks would normally be jettisoned in pairs which would cancel out the force. At the higher indicated air speeds, the aircraft was left with a slight nose to port directional trim change after jettison. This again applied to the asymmetric release of the tanks and was well within the capability of the rudder trim to deal with. It was therefore concluded that in straight and level flight over the speed range the inboard 200-gallon finless drop tank jettisoned and cleared the aircraft satisfactorily.

These tests were made with new 'swept-forward' pylons which together with the 'finless' drop tanks were the outcome of the initial flying with four tanks.

For the 1957 Farnborough Air Show it was decided to show the aircraft with four drop tanks; the left inboard tank was painted red to indicate that something else was normally carried there (to show 'The Bomb' was not permitted).

On the way to Farnborough, Dave Morgan posed XD218 for the customary air-to-air photographs and took time to do some practice. It was alarmingly apparent that Mike Lithgow's description '*a bit light fore and aft*' after flying it for the first time with four tanks was no exaggeration and Morgan considered it quite unsatisfactory for a vigorous flying display.

Under the direction of the Technical Office engineer Ron McFie, who was overseeing the aircraft at Farnborough, it was calculated that if only the forward fuselage tanks were topped up a useful forward movement of the centre of gravity would be achieved. The aircraft was thus flown in this condition the next day and the stick forces were light but acceptable.

During the course of the week the fins were lost from some drop tanks and it was decided to remove the remainder. This also increased the stick force per g, which was now quite acceptable. As Dave Morgan remarked, "*..the quickest bit of development work we ever did!*".

The problem arose because of the de-stabilising effect of stores carried on the outer pylons, and the cure took some time to arrive at as it entailed the redesign of all four pylons. At the same time the famous Mod 494 was put in hand which completely reconfigured the fuel system following the shocking unreliability experienced with the tank level float switches on which the original scheme depended. This was first fitted in XD215.

The swept-forward pylons were successful. Various configurations of stores were carried and these included: 2 x 220 and 2 x 150 gallon tanks; 2 x 220 gallon tanks and 2 x 1,000lb bombs; 4 x 1,000lb bombs; 8 practice bombs; and 24 rockets.

### Simulated Cold Weather Trials

XD222 had completed 209 hours flying when it arrived at Wisley on 7 May 1958 for winterisation trials in the special stratosphere chamber. An acceptance survey was carried out which showed a number of defects that later deteriorated when subjected to cold and tended to confuse the rational assessment of the winterisation effects. A number of aircraft modifications were introduced, mainly those effecting servicing.

The stratosphere chamber test section consisted of a steel cylinder approximately 50ft long by 25ft in diameter and in order to reduce the aircraft envelope within these dimensions it was necessary to fold the wings and nose, and to crop a portion of the trailing edges of the rudder, tailplane and tail fairing.

To obtain the maximum benefit from the trials Lt Read, a Royal Navy project officer with the cold weather trials group in Canada, conducted the cold chamber trials, supported by a small naval personnel servicing group from A&AEE.

The basic facility was capable of subjecting the aircraft to temperatures down to -60°C and it seemed possible that functioning the various aircraft services, using external power supplies, would provide an indication of their behaviour in an arctic climate. In addition a naval crew would be able to assess the servicing aspects of the aircraft using the appropriate ground equipment and wearing arctic clothing.

The aircraft was allowed to soak in a temperature of -35°C for 16 days. A number of aircraft and servicing equipment defects were brought to light, some of which could have seriously delayed the trials programme of a Scimitar undergoing the winterisation trials in Canada.

Daily inspection and servicing checks experienced no particular access difficulty due to the low temperature, but the equipment supplied was not suitable for low temperature work, with several items freezing up and charging connections failing to seal. However the poor access to items of equipment which were removed for the fault investigation made it necessary to remove the outer gloves, causing great discomfort to the rating concerned. No one managed to reach the upper sets in the radio bay when wearing cold weather dress.

It was concluded that the stratosphere chamber low temperature tests carried out on XD222 brought to light a number of aircraft and servicing equipment defects. If not rectified, these could result in damage to the aircraft during operations in a low temperature region, and also showed that this form of testing was valuable in giving advance warning of engineering defects, being complementary to operational flight trials.

*Supermarine Chief Designer Alan Clifton and Mike Lithgow examining a Scimitar at Wisley. (Vickers-Armstrongs via D.W.Morgan)*

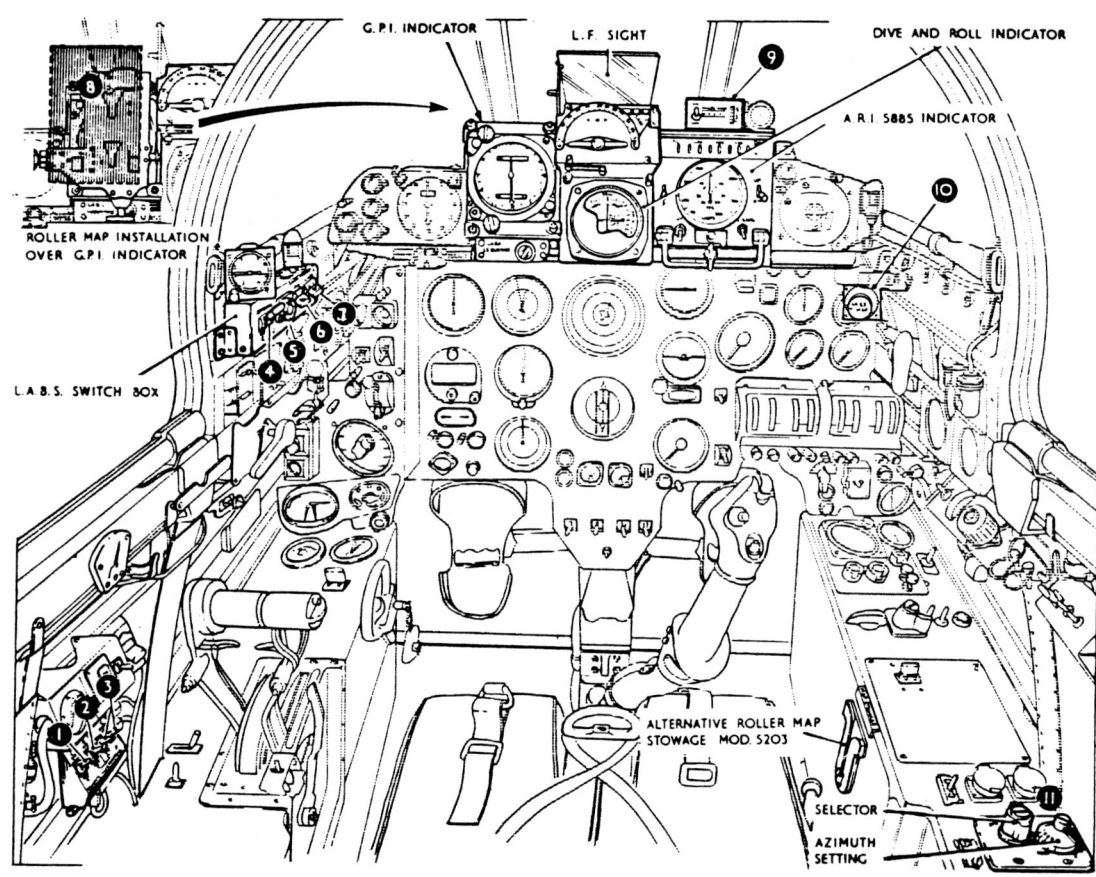

*Drawing of the cockpit showing the equipment installed for LAB configuration. Note the heavily obstructed view through the windscreen.*

KEY: *1 GPI Mk.5 counters switch. 2 GPI Mk.5 lights switch. 3 ARI.5885 inverter switches. 4 Angle selector switch. 5 Manual yaw/roll push button. 6 LABS start switch. 7 LABS sight switch. 8 Roller map. 9 Miles-gone indicator. 10 LABS timer control unit. 11 LF sight control unit.*

The advantages associated with carrying out a low temperature test in Britain and at any season stood out in comparison with a typical season in Canada.

At the other end of the spectrum, the tropical trials were begun by the A&AEE in Bahrain during July 1958 using XD214 *(see the account of Captain D.F. 'Sharky' Robbins later in this book)*, though they were not completed at this stage.

**L.A.B.S. trials**

The system devised to provide a means of delivering a bomb without over-flying the target was known as the Low Altitude Bombing System (LABS).

By releasing the bomb during a looping manoeuvre at 4g it would travel some 30,000 feet from the point of pull-up. An IP, or identification point, which had to be of known bearing and distance from the target, was where the pilot initiated the attack; the delay in the pull-up signal was preset.

The maximum 'throw' was obtained when the bomb released at 45 degrees; a release at 60 degrees was only 3,000 feet shorter but the time of flight in this case was about 11 seconds longer with the obvious advantage in separation from the burst during the escape manoeuvre.

This was the phase after bomb release when the loop was continued and a half-roll made when the nose was about 40 degrees below the horizon, followed by a rapid descent 'to the deck'. Speed reached 620 knots at 50 feet at a distance of 24,000 feet from the point of pull-up; the elapsed time from pull-up being 60 seconds.

When no IP was available the 'Alternate' release method at 100 degrees could be used. In this case the target was the pull-up point. The trajectory of the bomb peaked at 18,000 feet before it started its descent to the target. Separation at burst was somewhat reduced but, allegedly, still sufficient to avoid 'getting your arse fried'! The cockpit would, of course, be blacked out during the entire operation against the nuclear flash. The blast would be no problem as it travelled at the speed of sound, overtaking the aircraft at only 35 knots.

When the aircraft had been lined up on the IP on the correct heading at 600 knots IAS, the whole manoeuvre was flown with reference to one instrument mounted in place of the gun sight – the LABS indicator. This had a vertical and a horizontal needle. The former, pivoted at '6 o'clock' was calibrated in degrees of bank, left and right; the latter, pivoted at '3 o'clock' indicated pitch, nose up and down, also in degrees.

The moment to pull up was indicated by the horizontal needle dropping to the bottom of the scale; 4 g was pulled to return it to and keep it as the 'zero' position. At this stage a heading input was supplied to the vertical needle which would then demand corrections to keep heading constant. The bomb was released automatically at a preset angle of pitch.

The sequence was initiated by pressing the firing trigger when crossing the IP and holding it, throughout the pull-up, or until the bomb released. With the trigger pressed the system would

*Fourth production aircraft XD215 flying from 'C') Squadron (the Naval Test Squadron) of the Aeroplane & Armament Experimental Establishment at Boscombe Down around 1957/8. (via L.Howard)*

*18th production aircraft XD229 at Wisley around 1960. It has the early type of nose cone and polished metal, air intakes. (Air-Britain)*

continue to demand 4 g and it was customary to release it when approaching the top of the loop. The horizontal needle then returned to indicating pitch attitude and as this approached 40 degrees nose down, the half-roll was executed. Some interpretation of the bank indication was required as, initially, the needle moved in the wrong sense. However, before the aircraft was upright it flicked and read normally. In any case reference could be made to the 'roller blind' all-attitude display at this stage.

All LABS trials were done in XD218 and began in July 1958. Initial flights were mainly for familiarisation and at first the g indications were found to be much too sensitive and one could fly a smoother loop on the cockpit accelerometer. It transpired that the damping setting recommended for the LABS accelerometer had been derived from tests in a Canberra so it was not surprising that some adjustment was needed.

Tracked runs were made on the range at Orfordness, but trials there had to be abandoned because of serious complaints about noise. The proximity of a bird sanctuary to the range caused further problems.

Initial carriage trials of the bomb, and vibration measurements, had been completed the previous month with releases being made in straight and level flight, with a 220 gallon drop tank on the opposite pylon. The approach speed for delivery was 600 knots and as speed increased there was a progressively increasing directional trim change towards the bomb, which could be held or trimmed out. However before 600 knots was reached the trim change began to reverse, so it was better to let things settle and then trim out.

Before beginning the actual ballistic trials on the instrumented range at West Freugh, a number of releases had to be made and these were done over the English Channel. This was an approved procedure for the release of inert stores but the pilot was required to clear the area for the release.

As the bomb would travel about six miles from the pull-up point, Dave Morgan used to pick a ship as the IP. From here he would fly on a selected heading for 45 seconds before turning on to the reciprocal to locate the ship and, if nothing had been seen in the area searched, line up on the outbound heading again and start the pull-up after passing the ship. No complaints were received from the maritime fraternity, who probably enjoyed the show!

On the range at West Freugh both the aircraft and the bomb were tracked by kine-theodolites. The bombing line ran North-West/South-East up the centre of Luce Bay, Wigtownshire. For LABS releases the northwesterly heading was used. The run was started at Point of Ayre, the northern-most tip of the Isle of Man. A cluster of rocks provided a useful reference and reporting point, and from there on the bombing line was marked by coloured buoys.

Trials began at West Freugh in the first week of June 1959 and the first drop on the range was on 15 June; a 45 degree release. A further drop was made before returning to Wisley.

By 10 July 1959, after another seven sessions on the range, a total of 17 releases had been tracked at 45, 60 and 100 degrees – a tribute to the efficiency of the range organisation, the serviceability of the aircraft and the dedication of the Supermarine team at West Freugh.

Although this was an end-point ballistic trial, not basically one of system accuracy, it was gratifying to see 'grouping' improve with experience. Because of the proximity of the airfield to the range and the short duration of most of the sorties the ground crew enjoyed being 'part of it all'. The flight test engineer, Chick Manley, managed the trials and the on-board instrumentation as well as co-ordination with the range.

The bomb used during the LABS trials was the length of a drop tank and of considerably greater girth. It was painted in large black and white checks to facilitate tracking and was clearly visible from vantage points on the ground.

When it was not necessary to fly a full escape manoeuvre after a 110 degree release, it was possible to roll off at the top of the loop, turn tightly and watch the bomb climbing for another 7,000 feet or so, before beginning its descent to splash down in the bay. This was a unique spectacle, albeit of no technical significance, which Dave Morgan felt was worth taking a moment or two to watch; being, as it were, the only spectator in the 'upper circle'.

In January 1960 Dave Morgan suffered a neck injury when the car he was a passenger in crashed. Unable to continue flying for the next six months due to his condition, Lt Cdr Paul Millett of the RAE was draughted in as his temporary replacement on the LABS and TMB programme.

**Trials on HMS *Victorious*, 29 August to 4 September 1958**

These trials were a continuation of the those commenced in June 1958 to prove the newly-rebuilt and recommissioned HMS *Victorious*'s catapulting and arrester gear.

The new series included the catapulting of Scimitars at weights up to 37,500lbs and arresting at 34,500lbs, which was the maximum emergency landing weight of the aircraft. The launching weight of 37,500lbs was achieved with full internal fuel plus two full 200-gallon drop tanks on the inboard station.

Combined with the ships trial, Boscombe Down carried out an assessment of AII (Audio Incidence Indicator) and ASSU (Air Speed Sensing Unit) under carrier conditions. Vickers-Armstrongs technical engineers were Messrs Trim, Ron MacFie along with test pilot Dave Morgan who flew aboard in a Sea Balliol on 31 August in company with Lt Cdr Reynolds.

The three Scimitars used were XD220, XD221 and XD226. The first was maintained by No.700 Squadron, and the latter two by Boscombe Down. XD221 was fitted with AII and XD226 with ASSU. Two inboard drop tanks were fitted to XD226 halfway

*Vickers-Supermarine test pilot Dave Morgan flying fifth production XD216 in 1957. (Vickers-Armstrongs)*

through the trials, whilst XD220 carried inboard drop tanks throughout. Fifty one launches were made with the three Scimitars, being 15 by XD221, 14 by XD226 and 22 by XD220.

All of the launches, at 142 knots, were some 15 knots above the minimum launch speed at the high weight. With the exception of one launch in which the aircraft dropped considerably (5 ft or more), the Scimitars climbed away immediately after launching.

*XD226 '510/FD' of No.700 Squadron immediately after being launched from HMS Victorious around August-September 1958. (via J.H.Munday)*

Landings were made up to a maximum weight of 33,990lbs. Ten of these were at weights above the normal landing weight of 31,000lbs. Fifteen landings were made using AII and twelve using ASSU, plus several dummy approaches which were carried out with the ASSU aircraft.

The ship's deck-landing mirror was found to be set 0.25° too low giving 0.5° shallower flight path than required. As a result the first day's landings were made at 3.5° but thereafter landings below 31,000lbs were done at 4°, anything over this weight being at 3.5°. Two landings were made by XD226 with the aircraft well off centre, 14ft to starboard and 9ft to starboard. On both occasions the aircraft landed aft of the rear lift (once with the hook on the round-down), and the pilot did not switch on the accelerometer. From catapult pressure curves the maximum 'g' was estimated to be less than 3.5g.

On each occasion the A-frame was found damaged, the starboard leg of the A-frame being severely bent with a maximum bow of about 1.5 inches in one case. The possibility of a compression failure under combined aft and side loads due to the arrester wire was considerable and thought to be highly improbable. Considerable anxiety was expressed by the trials and engineering officers and an urgent defect signal was considered.

However, examination of the hook marks at the touch down point showed that the hook had struck the starboard edge of the after lift. The lift was tilted up at the forward end to prevent hooks catching on the aft edge, but the side edge of the lift projected 1.5in above the deck where the Scimitar's hook had struck. Further detailed examination of one of the bent frames showed signs of a hammer blow on the port side of the hook. A proposed solution was for a fairing on the deck at the starboard edge of the lift well.

The following defects occurred: XD221, No.5 tank fuel pump failed to transfer and was changed; XD220, port intake suffered a split in the skin, and was subsequently patched; XD226, developed a hydraulic leak in the port brake and had the unit changed. On examination it was noticed that the pad wear was not around the circumference of the unit but showed more wear at the top of the unit. The unit was not stripped, so the state of the inner pads could not be seen. XD226 also experienced a hydraulic leak in the A-frame door sequence valve. The A-frame hydraulic circuit was blanked off for the delivery flight ashore. A slight dent was made in the tailplane tip of XD220 when the tailplane hit a Gannet wing-fold bolt.

It was noticed during the trials that the sharp edges on the deck holdback block caused several severe cuts in nosewheel tyres. A catapult loading technique was eventually adopted which stopped the nosewheel riding over the holdback block and the block edges were chamfered to reduce the risk of further damage.

The aircraft also carried out ten landings under wet emergency landing conditions. After each landing the undercarriage was closely examined for signs of damage from the oleo, and a series of measurements made to determine whether bending of the stub axles occurred. No such damage was observed.

It was concluded from the trials that, from the aircraft point of view, the Scimitar was successfully launched at weights up to 37,150lbs with two full drop tanks, and recovered at weights up to 34,000lbs, 500lbs below the maximum emergency landing weight. Serviceability of the aircraft was good and little time was lost to aircraft defects.

**Type 560**

After the production of fifty aircraft, the design of the Scimitar from XD275 onwards was changed to include *Blue Silk* – an improved airspeed and height version of *Green Salad* with a reduced weight. With the added introduction of UHF radio, TACAN and other modifications the aircraft became redesignated Type 560.

The *Blue Silk* installation necessitated alterations to the cockpit including the loss of the turn and slip indicator; a larger total fuel contents gauge was also fitted and was a great improvement, though still prone to a 250 lb error throughout its range and never read full when in fact the aircraft had a maximum fuel load.

The standby artificial horizon was not fitted due to a shortage in supply, and as a result the use of angles of bank between 5 and 55 degrees in sustained turns was prohibited. Slave artificial horizons were fitted to enable the flight testing to proceed.

The first aircraft to fly with the heavier feel units was XD276 (the 52nd aircraft) and test flights showed it to be a much more pleasant aircraft to fly. Fitting the aircraft with four drop tanks on standard pylons, however, increased the marked instability characteristics to those of previous aircraft. The recovery from pitch-up at 40,000 feet required the use of full forward stick and the response to this was less than rapid. The stick forces at 450 knots during low-level flying were light and accurate turns were found to be difficult.

The updated radio and navigational aids brought about their own problem. The direction finding facilities at South Marston were not available on UHF and those existing at the nearby American bases of Fairford and Brize Norton had been tried with varying degrees of success. With no standard QGH procedure and the standard of direction finding lower than that provided by VHF, it thus came down to the fact that a UHF set was required at Wisley.

On the first test flight of XD276, Les Colquhoun reported that the wing-fold warning had sounded off when pulling 4 g. Problems persisted and on flight number 7, whilst carrying out a supersonic dive with four drop tanks fitted, the cabin pressure fluctuated violently followed by the air conditioning going to fully hot. The aircraft would eventually require nine test flights before being signed off. At roughly £700 per hour, the total test flying bill for this particular machine would have been quite high.

**Continuation of Tropical Trials**

In June 1959 the first Type 560, XD275, was selected to take part in the continuation of the tropical trials to be carried out at RAF Idris, Libya. Among the modifications embodied to this aircraft, provision was made to allow an air-conditioned vent suit to be worn by the pilot. The instrumentation nose from XD215, housing an auto-observer, was removed and fitted to the aircraft, with *Blue Silk*, LABS and VHF packs fitted in a cooled port gun bay, the guns not being installed. UHF was fitted along with inboard 2,000lb pylons and 200 gallon drop tanks.

The aircraft was tested from South Marston by Les Colquhoun who encountered, on approach to land after the first flight, a serious hydraulic problem. The wheels were selected down and locked, the flaps were selected down and the flap blow light was on. At about 170-180 knots the hook was selected up and down twice. During the second operation the aeroplane began to feel unduly left wing heavy and almost immediately the audio warning sounded off. A quick glance at the centralised warning panel revealed the No.1 hydraulic system to be the cause and a look at the pressure gauge which seemed to be fluctuating around 1,000 – 2000lbs confirmed the fault.

The aircraft felt decidedly unpleasant to fly, lateral control

*XD222 with its tailplane cut away to enable it to fit neatly into the climatic chamber for the cold weather trials at Wisley. (Vickers-Armstrongs)*

*Ice-covered XD222 in the climatic chamber during cold weather trials. (Vickers-Armstrongs)*

*Scimitars XD212 and XD227 piloted by Les Colquhoun and Dave Morgan taking off from South Marston during flight refuelling trials in April 1961. (Vickers-Armstrongs via D.W.Morgan)*

especially being very difficult. A further glance around the cockpit revealed the cause for this. It was found that the trailing edge flaps according to the indicator were in the fully up position. As there was no fuel available for an overshoot it was decided to carry on with the approach and land with the flaps up. This was done at an approach speed of 160 knots touching down at 145 knots.

The after-flight examination revealed that a Dunlop hose connection on the flap jack had blown off, thus allowing the flaps to be blown into the up position by the airflow. Had this occurred slightly later in the approach when the speed was down to 130 knots, and the height much lower, the aircraft could have seriously undershot the runway before the pilot realised what was happening.

Nonetheless XD275 was despatched and duly arrived at the Operational Evaluation Unit at RAF Idris on 25 July 1959 with the servicing crew arriving two days later. Stage one of the tests began on 28 July with the functioning of the cabin, *Blue Silk*, master reference gyro and battery bay equipment, to be followed the next day by a 14 minute low-altitude shake-down flight.

The trials involved thirty seven sorties totalling some twenty four hours of flying and covered engineering, armament and photographic assessments. The temperatures experienced during the trials period approached the specification requirement of 45°C, though during the twelve flights required to successfully complete the five sorties for the A&AEE, ground temperatures were up to 43°C and at one point even rose to 48°C in the shade – the hottest there for five years.

Some of the early flights were partly aborted due to mishandling of camera magazines by A&AEE technicians, and three sorties were ruined due to the incorrect operation of the radio and battery bay cooling system. It appeared that the heat soak into the aircraft piping after a high speed flight had reached 65-70°C, sufficient to make the sensing element think that the cooling packs had failed. A hood sun-blind of lightweight fabric and alloy framing was made by the Vickers Apprentice School for assessment under tropical conditions and was found to be extremely useful, keeping the sun off the pilot's head and reducing the glare in the cockpit under conditions of bright sunlight, though it was felt that there was some loss in vision and the ability to eject through the canopy was questioned. Nonetheless the pilot, with head and feet temperatures of around 45°C was fairly comfortable and Stage 1 was completed by 4 August.

The photographic trial consisted of only three sorties carried out on 23 August, 1 and 2 September. Misting of the lenses was found to be a problem, along with the serious sand damage of the forward-facing lens window during high speed low level runs.

**Incident on first flight of XD281, 21 August 1959**

Shortly after take-off on the first flight of XD281, piloted by Les Colquhoun, a turbine blade failure on the starboard engine was experienced. After 1 minute 40 seconds from wheels roll and climbing at full throttle, a loud bang was heard followed by a very severe high frequency vibration on the aircraft. The aircraft was then at 11,000ft almost immediately over the airfield. Both engines were fully throttled back and the aircraft put into a glide towards the aerodrome. Tentative movements of both throttles did not alleviate the very severe vibration nor prove which engine was causing the trouble. However at about 7,000ft with both engines fully throttled the vibration ceased. The emergency landing was continued, but the engines were used without trouble up to about 80% rpm during the final stages of the approach. On the run down of the starboard engine after the HP cock had been closed, very severe vibration was again experienced on the aircraft.

After-flight examination revealed that half of one of the rear

*Scimitar flight refuelling trials on 13 April 1961 with XD227 approaching XD212. The majority of these trials were carried out by David Morgan and Les Colquhoun. (Vickers-Armstrongs)*

turbine blades was missing, two slits had been made in the inner skin of the jet tube presumably by the missing blade and there was obvious damage to the turbine shroud ring. Once the engine had stopped it could not be moved until after it had cooled down.

With the engine changed, XD281 flew again on 24 August and was signed off as acceptable four flights later.

**Engine Problems**

It did seem fairly obvious that the standard of performance on the Avon engines fitted to the Scimitar had deteriorated and, perhaps, what was most disturbing, some of the troubles were of a random nature. Adjustments had effected a cure for two or three flights, but thereafter it had been known for them to reappear. It was thought that snags of this nature must have been caused by defective components and it was hoped that the urgent investigations being carried out by Rolls-Royce on equipment rejected from Scimitars would reveal the cause.

Increasing the engine tolerance did undoubtedly improve the situation with regard to the rpm creep difficulties and not so many adjustments were necessary. However the engine acceleration snags still had to be overcome as it was those that were causing the major component changes.

From the engine re-lighting point of view, experience on the Scimitar fitted with Mod 1585 engines dictated that the maximum relighting altitude should be reduced to 25,000ft. Under any conditions at this height a light-up could almost be guaranteed. Nothing was more certain than that the engine would not light at 35,000ft under any conditions so far tested. At 30,000ft the chance of success was increased by using the Rolls-Royce technique of having the throttle three-quarters open during the light up sequence. However it was thought that before this could be recommended to Service pilots, Rolls-Royce should confirm in writing that it was a desirable practice.

By the end of October 1959 a great deal of flying had been carried out by the Vickers test pilots to eliminate all of the engine problems. The Avon 202 engines were fitted with slotted shroud mini-cage burners (R.R. Mod 1990) to improve the relighting problems. After discussion with Rolls-Royce Service Department, it was thought that the results did not justify any change in the relight drill. For engines fitted with the mini-cage burners the recommended relight altitude should remain at 30,000ft and 0.85 IMN.

There could be no doubt that Mod 1990 had effected a considerable improvement in the relighting characteristics. The results from the tests carried out provided recommendation for the early inclusion of the mini-cage burners into Service aircraft.

**Ground Test of Seat Ejection Through the Canopy, October 1959**

A series of tests was carried out at South Marston from a stationary aircraft (XD213) to investigate the effects of ejecting a pilot and seat from an aircraft without prior jettison of the canopy.

The first ejection was a free shot with the canopy off to provide measurements as a basis for subsequent ejections through the canopy. Both the free shot and the first ejection with the hood in position were carried out using a standard ejection seat with no modifications to provide protection for the pilot. For the final two ejections however, modifications to the seat were introduced to provide a redesigned head box and thigh guards, the head box being supplied and fitted by Martin-Baker Ltd.

For each of the ejections, suitable instrumentation was included on the pilot's person in order that impact loads and accelerations of the pilot and seat could be measured. In addition, cine films were taken of the trajectory and of the progress of the pilot through the canopy.

The aircraft was positioned in front of a rectangular straw mat in order that the damage to the dummy pilot and seat on landing was kept a minimum.

The seat ejection system was to the latest standard and an additional modification was embodied to enable the seat to be fired externally from a distant position by means a cable connected to the main ejector gun. Immediately prior to the assembly of the canopy its interior was painted in a distinctive colour to provide a means of determining the points of contact between the dummy and canopy. After painting, the canopy was assembled to the aircraft and locked electrically, the hood jettison gun being rendered ineffective by removal of the cartridge.

The thickness of the perspex canopy used for each of the ejections was 9/32".

A dummy pilot type R.A.E. Mk 5 was obtained and cavities were provided in the head and trunk to house instruments. For each ejection the dummy wore standard flying clothing and equipment.

In addition an attempt was made to determine the impact loads on the pilots head, shoulders and knees. This was done by strapping pads to the pilot at these positions.

After the first free ejection was completed the second one was carried out through the canopy. This was done satisfactorily and subsequent examination of the dummy pilot and seat indicated that contact with the canopy had occurred on the screen over the pilot's head, the pilot's left shoulder and left knee, the oxygen bottle on the seat and drogue box.

For the second ejection the seat was modified to include thigh guards and canopy breakers. All other conditions were the same as the previous ejection. In this instant traces of paint on the dummy pilot and seat gave evidence of contact with the canopy on the pilot's left and right shoulders and knees, drogue box and thigh guards. Light smears were also evident on the screen over the pilot's head, also over his left forearm and left thigh. The presence of paint at these positions was judged to have been caused by flying perspex.

Due to a tendency for the thigh guards to bend in the previous test, further stiffening was introduced for the third ejection through the canopy. Unfortunately, no loads due to contact with the canopy could be determined for this ejection, since the pilot and seat missed the straw mat and considerable damage was incurred on contact with the ground. However, examination of the dummy revealed no evidence of contact with the canopy on the head, shoulders or knees.

After lengthy discussions and reruns of the cine films it was concluded that provision of the canopy breakers and thigh guards were instrumental in reducing the direct effects of the body striking canopy to very small amounts, and it was felt that these could well be incorporated as a permanent feature of ejection seats, if ejection through the canopy was recognised as a drill.

**Test Findings**

In October 1959, Test Pilot Reports Nos.29 & 30 were completed, covering the recently completed trials of the Specialities Airstream Direction Detector, assessed on ADDLs using a mirror landing sight and later on HMS *Victorious*. The trials also cleared the Scimitar for maximum weight launches and landings with swept-forward pylons and the large tailplane using AII.

During the ADDLs, the performance of the equipment was not affected by the carriage of pylons and four drop tanks and was found much easier to use than Audio Incidence Indication alone. Of the two Vickers-Supermarine pilots engaged on these trials, Dave Morgan, flying XD216, preferred to use the audio facility in addition to the Index and Dial Incidence Indicator, but Mike Lithgow preferred to use the visual indicator only.

After the deck trials on *Victorious* had been completed, it was concluded that the equipment made deck landing very much easier, and safer, by completely eliminating any need to refer to the ASI, thus enabling the pilot to give his undivided attention to the deck and mirror. Handling the aircraft immediately after a catapult launch, particularly at minimum launching speeds, was greatly assisted by the dial incidence indicator which enabled corrections to attitude to be made before sink developed and over-correction to be avoided. The fact that the aircraft was launched 5 knots below the prescribed minimum launching speed (which was not premeditated) without incurring any marked sink could undoubtedly be attributed to use of this indicator. It was also of considerable use during approaches and it was recommended that it be positioned where it could be seen with the minimum of eye movement. However it was stressed that nothing should delay the incorporation of the equipment in squadron aircraft.

It might appear that the second prototype 544, WT859, had led a much more sedate life than the other two (WT854 & WW134), as it has not been mentioned as much. This is not really so, though it is a fact WT859 did not take part in any of the major deck trials. The aircraft was standby for WW134 on occasions and, had anything gone wrong, WT859 was ready to take its place. The aircraft was flown quite extensively by the A&AEE and Vickers being used for trials which included Lateral and Directional Handling Tests and Tests under Asymmetric Power, Roll/Yaw Coupling Flight Tests on the Clean Aircraft, as well as Extension of Longitudinal Handling Tests on the Clean Aircraft at Low Altitude.

**Modernisation Programme**

By late 1959 a number of the earlier aircraft had started to re-appear at South Marston for modernisation. The Royal Navy Aircraft Yard at Fleetlands was already busy converting squadron aircraft from VHF to UHF radio standard with the work being mainly carried out at RNAS Lee-on-Solent.

Following his first post-modernisation flight in XD225 from South Marston on 29 January 1960, Les Colquhoun voiced his concerns over the content of the work contract. *"It seems a pity"*, he wrote in the flight test report *"that whoever decided the mod. standard for these aircraft did not decide to aim for the 51st [aircraft] standard. With the aircraft in their present state it is thought that the first thing the Navy will have to do is to carry out further modification work before the aircraft can enter squadron service"*.

Colquhoun went on to highlight the differences between these older aircraft and the newer machines coming out of South Marston including the positioning of the airbrake selector switch which had been turned down on almost the first aircraft to fly with 700X Sqn at Ford, and which had been modified in all current squadron aircraft but not in those modernised by Vickers. The out-dated VHF radio installations also remained, thus prompting his comment about the Navy having to carry out further work upon receipt.

**Loss of four drop tanks from XD216 in flight**

On 3 March 1960 XD216 was being flown by A&AEE pilot Lt Peter Barber. After a normal take-off on internal fuel with four full drop tanks the aircraft was climbed to 30,000ft for longitudinal handling investigations. Due to an oversight, drop tank fuel was not selected until the aircraft had reached 25,000ft. A turn was first made at an initial IMN of 0.95, following which a second turn was commenced to starboard at 0.9 IMN. The g was increased to approximately 2.5 at which moderate buffet occurred. The stick was then pulled further back and the g started to increase. Without any warning the aircraft rolled rapidly to port; the subsequent motions confused Barber, but he was aware of the occurrence of starboard sideslip. Having released all controls the aircraft eventually emerged in a dive and it was subsequently discovered that during the manoeuvre all pylons and drop tanks except for the starboard inner pylon had become detached from the aircraft, that the nose of the port wing fence was bent, and that the pitot head had been lost.

*XD212 engaged on flight refuelling trials at South Marston on 13 April 1961. (Vickers-Armstrongs)*

The pylons, pylon fairings and drop tanks were subsequently discovered in a field near Dorchester. The latter were shattered but it was evident that in all three cases both the tanks and pylons had remained together until the ground impact.

From a study of the structural failures which occurred, it was concluded that aileron had been used (deliberately or inadvertently) to correct wing-drop when the aircraft was well into the pre-stall buffet, resulting in the aircraft yawing violently and flick rolling. This rate of roll was in excess of 260 degrees per second, and the resulting centrifugal force was the prime reason for the loss of the drop tanks. The Scimitar was an immensely strong aircraft and was hard to break; Dave Morgan had carried out clearance flights on the type during which rolls with full aileron at 6 g were carried out with four 1,000lb bombs fitted. They did not come off. The figure in the case of XD216 was well in excess of the design limitations for carriage of full 200-gallon tanks. As a result of this incident it was recommended that the C(A) release be amended to restrict Service pilots to the onset of buffet in g-stalls when carrying any external stores weighing 500lbs or more.

**Spinning Trials**

The introduction of swept wing aircraft was followed by a number of spinning accidents; sadly, many of them were fatal. As experience was gained it was possible to attribute some of the incidents to the inadvertent application of 'out-spin' aileron when holding the stick forward to recover.

The effect of aileron on the nature of a spin and particularly on spin recovery of straight-winged aircraft was of more interest in the field of specialist aerobatics than in normal flying. And without powered flying there was little or no tendency for the ailerons to be other than central when taking recovery action.

The number of incidents when swept-wing aircraft recovered from a spin after the pilot ejected prompted Dave Morgan to suggest fitting handles painted with black and yellow stripes to each side of the windscreen arch with the instruction "Grasp simultaneously to recover" painted on them!

For the spinning tests of the Swift Mk.5, Morgan had insisted on having a chase-plane; this was flown by 'Pee Wee' Judge. There had been at least two cases of Swifts being abandoned successfully when recovery action failed, but nothing was learned as to the cause. For the spinning trials of the Scimitar a telemetry system was used. A ground station, manned by flight test technician Brian Randall, an ex-Fleet Air Arm Sea Hawk pilot himself, had instruments showing the most important parameters: height and airspeed, tail, rudder and aileron angles, rates of yaw, roll and pitch. The inputs were recorded on the ground as well as in the aircraft. Before starting each spin a two-way system of R/T was selected, enabling the ground 'pilot' to interrupt the actual pilot's commentary if he thought it was necessary to do so.

Because of the vital importance of roll direction (the use of 'in-roll' aileron being a powerful aid to recovery), lights were installed either side of the windscreen arch which indicated this. In the case of a normal, erect spin, yaw and roll are in the same sense; in the case of an inverted spin they are in the opposite sense. In both instances the Turn needle will indicate the direction of yaw and hence which rudder to apply to recover.

As a result of wind tunnel and dropped model tests, along with the results of the Swift tests in mind, the recovery action was 'stick central and fully forward with full opposite rudder, held until rotation ceased'.

The plan was to do six spins, three in each direction, in a sortie starting at 35,000ft and initiating recovery after one turn. The first spin was reluctant to start and it continued in a hesitant way with the nose rising and falling during one turn. Recovery action was effective almost immediately.

The second spin almost stopped when recovery action was taken but then continued rolling at an increased rate. Momentary reduction in g and yaw appearing to follow the rudder combined to provide a completely strange situation and Dave Morgan began to feel disorientated. He released the rudder and applied aileron towards the illuminated roll light. The spin stopped at once.

This situation repeated itself once during the four remaining spins. The disturbing fact was that normal recovery action had no effect. It was decided to discuss the results with Aero Flight at RAE Bedford. After hearing Morgan's description of the then inexplicable results, Peter Bisgood of Aero Flight, who had good reason to suspect what had happened, showed a film of some drop model tests of the Buccaneer. Among these was a recovery which resembled exactly the gyrations of the two 'rogue' spins experienced on WW134. It was not expected to happen on the Scimitar but it was a classic example of a transition to an inverted spin.

A further five sorties were made and it was found that recovery from one- and two-turn spins could be made on rudder alone with the stick released. It was of interest to see that if 'normal' recovery action was taken (full forward stick and full opposite rudder), then at least one in three spins would transfer into inverted ones. Of greater practical importance, it was established that if all controls were released before the spin had completed one turn then the aircraft would recover by itself. This, then, became the action recommended in the Pilot's Notes for the type.

In the last week of March 1960, the results of the tests Mike Lithgow had been carrying out on spinning with the large tailplane and swept-forward pylons was issued. The purpose of that series of spinning trials was to prove the recovery action recommended in a previous report on an aircraft fully modified to carry four external stores both in the clean condition and also when fitted with four empty swept forward pylons. The aircraft used for those trials was XD216, now fully modified with the increased area tailplane, altered feel units, and longitudinal inertia weights. After spinning tests in the clean condition the aircraft was fitted with four production-type swept-forward pylons. No stores were fitted to the pylons, to represent the case following jettison of all stores.

The recovery action used throughout was that found to be most effective during initial spinning test - releasing the stick (which centred automatically due to feel system forces) followed by full rudder until the spin ceased. When the spin was entered off turns, the aircraft was banked 45 degrees and trimmed to 180 knots, which required 85% rpm. The stick was then pulled back gently to full travel and full bottom rudder was applied at about 150 knots. The power was in most cases removed when the aircraft entered the spin. The development of such recovery action no doubt contributed to saving many lives and aircraft during Service use.

The total number of spins in this programme was twenty, with all but the first two being of two turns duration. Nine were with pylons fitted, of which five were off straight stalls and four off turns, and eleven were in the clean configuration of which six were straight and five off turns. All spins were entered with under-

*Vickers-Supermarine Test Pilot Les Colquhoun climbs aboard the final production aircraft XD333 at South Marston in late 1960. (Vickers-Armstrongs via L.R.Colquhoun)*

carriage and flaps up and airbrakes in.

In general it was concluded that the characteristics were very similar to WW134 on which the initial spinning tests had been done, with the exception that the majority were considerably smoother in that very little variation in rate of yaw was noticed.

The height loss was, on average, 15,000ft from entry into a two-turn spin to level flight. By far the major proportion of this height loss was due to pull-out from the ensuing dive. Most recoveries occurred in a vertical or over-the-vertical attitude and in some cases it was not possible to avoid becoming supersonic in these steep dives. However, on three of the twenty spins, recovery occurred with the nose 20 degrees below the horizon, and on these occasions the aircraft was in straight and level flight above 30,000ft.

The turn-and-bank indicator was found to be invaluable in determining the exact point of recovery from a spin. Removal of this from post-51st (XD275) production Scimitars was a matter for renewed concern, especially when considering spin recovery in cloud. It was recommended that consideration be given to its reintroduction, although it could be argued that the Scimitar would not spin without extreme provocation.

It was concluded that neither the introduction of the larger tailplane, nor the presence of four swept-forward pylons, materially affected the spin recovery technique at that time recommended in the Pilot's Notes for the Scimitar.

### The last of the line

Finally, at the end of 1960, the last Supermarine aircraft rolled off the production line at South Marston, thus ending the story of an illustrious company stretching back as far as 1914.

However all did not go smoothly. As XD333 approached completion it became evident that certain vital components were missing from the main stores. Investigation revealed that an overzealous storekeeper, assuming that the parts were no longer required, had sold them to local scrap merchants near Swindon!

It was therefore a very red-faced storekeeper who was despatched, cap in hand, to the scrap merchant to retrieve the parts at an exorbitant price. The resultant delay in delivery of the aircraft to the Navy of some two months led to Supermarine receiving a 'rap on the knuckles' from an official level.

As an aside to this, in late 1999 Fowler's scrap yard in Chippenham, Wiltshire, (most probably the same one) auctioned off a huge amount of its inventory prior to closure. In amongst the various odds and ends were no fewer than *fifteen* brand-new Scimitar canopies still in their original wrappings! Sadly though they were all acquired by an individual who, even after being approached by one Scimitar cockpit-section owner, refused to part with even one. When asked what exactly he intended to do with fifteen Scimitar canopies, he claimed that he wanted to cut them up and turn them into designer chairs!

*Cdr I.H.F Martin hurriedly signs Customs clearance forms at Wisley during the Daily Mail Bleriot Paris-London Air Race. Note the canvas slide arrangement attached to the side of the aircraft, designed specially for the occasion to allow the pilot to vacate the cockpit quickly. (Vickers-Armstrongs)*

# DAILY MAIL BLERIOT AIR RACE, PARIS TO LONDON 15th to 19th JULY 1959

While doing 70 mph on the pillion of a motorcycle in Paris traffic through successive crossroads of equal priority without slackening speed, it is probably best to close ones eyes and meditate on how one arrived in such an unfortunate predicament. This is not easy but could come with practice.

The Royal Navy entered two high speed teams for the Bleriot Air Race, a Sea Vixen with the observer, Lieutenant Commander W.J.Carter as competitor, and a Scimitar (XD268) with the pilot, Commander I.H.F.Martin, as competitor. Because Commander Martin was the only high speed competitor to pilot himself, this is the tale of the Scimitar.

We realised at the outset that there would inevitably be time lost in the Scimitar as the pilot had to strap in before taking off, but this loss was counteracted by the decided speed and acceleration advantage which the Scimitar had over other aircraft in the race. Furthermore the distance suited the Scimitar as it was the only fighter which could race without drop tanks and still have a reasonable fuel reserve.

We decided that it was best to race only from Paris to London to avoid language problems on the R/T and so that proven homing aids would be available in the event of poor visibility. Wisley was selected as the best airfield for several reasons, firstly being to the south-west of London the prevailing winds (which with typical contrariness did not blow) would assist the helicopter and give better visibility than Biggin Hill; secondly, the MTCA-approved route from Wisley to Chelsea was almost straight and one mile shorter than the MTCA-approved route from Biggin Hill via Greenwich Reach which was very doglegged; finally Vickers' valuable support would be readily available.

Assuming a 10 second helicopter-to-Hunter rolling time from Villacoublay to Biggin Hill, and a 45 second Scimitar rolling time via Wisley, we calculated that in still air we still had at least one minute in hand at Chelsea due to the Scimitar's speed advantage. The mythical prevailing south-westerlies would of course improve this by increasing the ground speed of the Wisley helicopter.

It was obvious that we had to devise a method of entering the cockpit with both engines running, so we modified a gantry ladder so that we could avoid the intakes which lie either side of the cockpit. With practice and careful arrangement of the cockpit we achieved a time of 24 seconds for running 15 yards, climbing the ladder and strapping in. A further 10 seconds was required to accelerate to full power. What we had not allowed for in practice was the state of breathlessness and mental dullness with which the pilot arrived for this evolution, and in fact our best helicopter-to-rolling time was 38 seconds.

The Scimitar cockpit is too high to jump from so we designed a canvas slide which enabled the pilot to be on the ground, running, within 4 seconds of wheel stop. On the first attempt this was rather badly bent due to the pilot's over exuberance in jumping on to it. However Vickers design team greased their slide rules and some rapid modifications stressed it to an adequate *G* margin.

On Monday, 13th July, the team moved to Paris, basing themselves on the Champs Elysée. We immediately encountered communications problems and if it had not been for the voluntary trojan efforts of Commander and Mrs Pearson (Assistant Naval Attaché, Paris) and Mr Monty Norman (de Havillands, Paris) the Naval entry would have ground to a halt.

The first attempt was scheduled for Wednesday, 15th July, and accordingly a trial run from the control point in Avenue D'iena to the heliport at Issy, a distance of approximately 4 miles, was arranged with M. Jean Gobar, a young French evening newspaper distributor. A route was agreed which avoided all but four traffic lights, and with some trepidation Commander Martin climbed on to the pillion of Gobar's Gold Flash BSA. Mrs Pearson having impressed upon M. Gobar the advantages of delivering his passenger in a fit state to fly a Scimitar, they set off on what later transpired to be a casual joyride, covering the 4 miles in a heavyish traffic, with two traffic lights against them, in 4 minutes 31 seconds.

Wednesday in Paris dawned fine and hot and the team left Paris by train for Villacoublay. The forecast for London was not particularly good for high speed navigation but we decided to go ahead. It was essential that we now tied together the loose ends of the various units down the route which had not yet functioned as a whole.

This then was the route and the provisionally calculated times:

| From | To | Method | Time |
| --- | --- | --- | --- |
| Arc de Triomphe | Issy | French motorcycle | 05 00 |
| Motorcycle | Helicopter | 80 yards sprint | 00 15 |
| Issy | Villacoublay | Whirlwind | 03 30 |
| Helicopter | Scimitar | Strapping-in and customs | 00 45 |
| Villacoublay | Wisley | Scimitar rolling to stop | 20 00 |
| Scimitar | Helicopter | Slide via Customs | 00 15 |
| Wisley | Lighter off Cadogan Pier | Whirlwind | 10 00 |
| Lighter | Cadogan Pier | Launch | 02 00 |
| Launch | Motorcycle | Sprint up Cadogan Pier | 00 15 |
| Cadogan Pier | Marble Arch | Royal Marines Motorcycle | 05 00 |
|  |  | TOTAL | 47 00 |

Watches were synchronised and H-hour passed to Admiralty who alerted Cadogan Pier and Wisley. Sub Lieutenant Aitchison who was to start up the Scimitar, make the take-off checks and obtain take-off clearance, had a final dress rehearsal with Commander Martin who was then taken to Issy by helicopter where he was met by Gobar and taken to the starting point.

This arrangement of meeting Gobar at Issy had an unfortunate sequel, for next day Lieutenant Commander Carter (Sea Vixen competitor) was to be met at the starting point, as there was no need for him as a passenger, to check his aircraft at Villacoublay. Back at the starting point, on completion of his practice run with Lieutenant Commander Carter, it was explained to Gobar that he was to be *"ici pas Issy"* on the next day. This little pun was greeted with roars of laughter and all left content that the point had been driven home. Unfortunately it was understood by Gobar as *"Issy pas ici"* and as a result the first Vixen run had to be abandoned.

At the starting point there were crowds of photographers and pro-Naval well wishers, including one lady who on the last day most charmingly presented a posy of flowers *"pour la femme"*.

To avoid unnecessary fuel wastage in the Scimitar, which started up at H-hour, we decided that regardless of traffic the race must start at H-hour ± 30 seconds; and so with one eye on the clock, the other on the traffic, and a fist poised above the time clock the moment was selected to punch the card, cram it into a pre-selected pocket and leap on to the back of the motor-cycle.

For the final and fastest run on Sunday 19th, Georges Houels, the French motorcycle champion, was jockey. This run was most exhilarating, as due to his organisation and popularity with the police, all the traffic lights were changed while bands of his friends guarded every cross-roads. As a result of this, and light traffic, Issy was reached in 3 minutes.

The helicopter, piloted by Lieutenant Fournel, was a welcome sight as it quivered at take-off rpm 80 yards away, but an 80 yards sprint in a *G* suit on a hot day leaves one gasping for breath and after a rolling dive into the cabin the 3 minutes before Villacoublay hove into sight was insufficient time to recover before it was "on oxygen mask" and poised for the next stage. Regardless of the physical distress caused by attempting to gasp through the oxygen tube it was essential to put it on at this stage otherwise it became entangled and obstructed the view when strapping in.

Followed by Lieutenant Stanley, the Whirlwind observer, who presented the passport for stamping, Martin climbed the ladder, muttering to himself "Left leg, right leg strap, right garter, left garter, right shoulder, left shoulder strap" past Sun Lieutenant Aitchison who was crouched on the top. At pre-determined times during this drill Aitchison made the R/T and G-suit connections, handed in the passport, then removed the ejection seat pin which he threw over his shoulder as a signal to the ground crew to rush away the ladder, with himself clinging to the top while being battered by the slam acceleration of the jet blast.

For the next few minutes all actions had to be mechanical as the ability to reason was poor, probably due to the brain swinging wide on the Parisian corners. The Scimitar's acceleration is normally more than adequate, but the feeling of urgency is so great in these circumstances that a volley of imprecations were invariably hurled at the sluggish brute which required 1 minute 10 seconds to achieve its racing speed of 720 mph from standstill.

At 2,000 feet and M 0.965 France slid rapidly beneath, and after the first run it was obvious that the D.R. positions had to be marked every minute as the speed allowed no time for a casual comparison of the countryside with the map. As Dieppe shot under the starboard wing it was possible for the first time to sit back and note with interest that dense condensation enveloped the wings and fuselage, and an accidental touch of the cockpit wall confirmed that the "thermal barrier" was no myth.

At Beachy Head the first position report was made to Wisley, and from Haywards Heath onwards they passed steers and ranges. As Gatwick was passed the leg restraint garters were released, the G-suit checked and height reduced to arrive at 1,000 feet ½ mile short of the airfield. At this point the throttles were closed, airbrakes extended, and the aircraft rolled into a 7 *G* 270° port turn which proved to be the fastest way of reducing speed for landing, being some 30 seconds faster than a straight in approach.

On finals the canopy was opened and at touch down the port engine stopped, so that the rpm would have reduced sufficiently to allow a safe slide past the intake. To a cacophony of alarm bells and attention lights as the Centralised Warning System flashed the failure of ancillaries driven by the unwinding port engine, maxarets were applied and harness released. As the aircraft squealed to a halt at the 1,400 yard mark the slide was hooked on to the port side of the cockpit, and with passport and Customs declaration form in hand, a very dehydrated competitor hurled himself onto the slide and, via the Customs Officer, into the waiting Whirlwind, where a most welcome Thermos Flask of lime juice greeted him.

Touching 118 knots the Whirlwind, piloted by Lieutenant Wailes, thrashed across Barnes Common at 1,000 feet and down the river to Albert Bridge, where he put it into a steep autorotational turn for a rapid flare on the lighter. On the first run we could only get a mooring on the south bank so a motor boat was used to cross the river, at what seemed a pathetically slow speed due to the fast current. This was unacceptable and while heavy guns were brought to bear to obtain a berth as close as possible to Cadogan Pier, the Gunnery School at Whale Island was asked to rig a jackstay to save the time previously wasted running up the pier.

A leap from the helicopter to the lighter, a second leap to the bows of the boat, 3 seconds to gather himself and then a leap to the trapeze, found Martin whipping across the water to the invigorating roar of what sounded like 40 Gunnery Instructors inviting a brawny team of sailors to get their so-and-so backs into it.

From a crumpled heap on the pavement it was a mere two paces to the pillion of Marine Hands' motorcycle and so via a carefully selected route, with only Hyde Park Corner traffic lights, we arrived at Marble Arch where with shaking hands the card was fumbled into the clock and stamped. The times for the three runs improved progressively from 46 mins 58 secs to 43 mins 58 secs and finally 43 mins 11 secs when we had to withdraw as the helicopters, their crews and the Royal Marines were otherwise committed.

Much later, when the body's priority demand for adrenalin had ceased, a Senior Officer asked if the race had been enjoyable. The reply was "Yes sir, but mostly to look back on".

*[This account is reproduced from 'Flight Deck' magazine for Autumn/Winter 1959 by kind permission of The Editor]*

*Pilots of No.800 Squadron in September 1961. Left to right Sub Lt Colin Morris, Lt John Carver, Lt John Manley, Lt Cdr 'Bill' Fairhead (AEO), Lt 'Chuck' Giles, Lt Cdr John Ford (Senior Pilot), Lt Cdr 'Danny' Norman AFC (CO), Lt 'Johnny' Johnston, Lt Alan Goodenough, Lt 'Tom' Skead and Lt Peter Banfield. (via Lt Cdr A Goodenough)*

## PILOT'S OBSERVATIONS

To gain a certain degree of insight into what a Scimitar was like to fly and maintain, a number of former pilots and groundcrew very kindly agreed to answer a range of specific questions about the aircraft as they recalled it, and to give their general thoughts and impressions. The resulting different views and opinions make for interesting, informative and often amusing reading.

**Vice Admiral Sir Edward Anson KCB**

Flew the Scimitar from January 1958 until June 1958 in No.700X Squadron; and from June 1958 until August 1959 in No.803 Squadron. He was the Senior Pilot as from September of that year. He logged 300 hours flying the aircraft.

My thoughts on my first take-off were of the enormous acceleration, though I was not too fussed about exceeding the undercarriage limits because it was surprisingly high at 300 knots. Seemed to reach climbing speed very quickly. It climbed like a dingbat. The acceleration did come as a surprise.

I did fly the Scimitar with Boundary Layer Control off. The landing was about 10 knots faster, but aileron control was not quite as good with BLC off.

I don't agree that landing the Scimitar was almost a controlled crash. It had a very good undercarriage. One needed to get used to the fact that you did not flare the aircraft before touch down - it flared itself slightly in the ground effect.

By comparison with other jet aircraft I have flown, up to that time it was an airborne sports car up to 25,000ft, but had a disappointing turning performance above that - this was much better and stiffer at sea level. It was not a patch on the Buccaneer.

I had two dangerous moments while flying the Scimitar, both at Ford in the IFTU.

First, Air Traffic at Ford gave a let down to Pete Barber and I as two independent units. They then set about engineering a collision. They nearly succeeded. Everything went darker in the cockpit, and on looking up I saw the bottom of Pete Barber's aircraft only about ten feet above me.

Second, again Pete Barber and I were airborne at the same time. The weather was pretty bad on take-off and deteriorated markedly. Pete Barber was diverted to Tangmere. I declared that I was getting fairly low on fuel and asked for a GCA. I started down and was told to overshoot at 300 feet (whilst still in cloud) because a Sea Hawk was lining up to take-off. I overshot and was then taken round towards Brighton. GCA then went off the air with radar failure. Air Traffic Control invited me to let down to 1,000 feet - I refused, turned out to sea, let myself down over the sea and broke cloud at 150 feet, did my own homing using time bearings from Ford, did a visual circuit round the back of the control tower at 150 feet and landed with practically no fuel. Air Traffic were no longer my best friends.

I never flew the Scimitar at night.

Regarding developments the Scimitar could have benefited from, the wing needed re-designing because it would not go around corners at altitude. It was too draggy.

If the clock could be put back, I would certainly do it all again. I enjoyed it all.

### Lt Cdr P.E.H.Banfield RN (Rtd)

As a 'flying plumber' (Air Engineer) usually limited to one front line squadron tour, I was lucky to have two: 804 Sea Hawks and then 800 Scimitars - September 1959 to September 1961. I flew 329 hours in the 12 years from 1959 to 1970.

I don't remember it being called the "Beast", but as a young Sea Hawk driver operating at Lossiemouth next to the first new Scimitar squadron (803) it appeared awesome - in a different league - which it was. Awe enhanced by the 600 knot low level loss of Colin Cresswell in an apparent explosion (nobody had flown THAT fast before...)

Acceleration a surprise? You bet! Although well briefed, I was through 5,000 before I got the gear up. It was a combination of the acceleration, disconcertingly noisy pressurisation, and beautiful but light controls, that was so different.

Dangerous moments? - several. Possibly the barrier on *Ark Royal* (no main gear) or ejecting off Lossiemouth (one main gear unlocked). This last caused me a huge fright as I ejected at 1 OK without closing the throttles; descending in cloud I could hear the aircraft coming round again, and having just read *'Into the Silk - the story of Irving parachutes'* where a bail-outer is nearly run over by the aeroplane he just left - I feared for the worst.

One of many best moments - 800 Squadron *'Red Blades'* Danny Norman's aero team; as solo, honking right down Fareham High Street at roof-top level and 500+ knots during a Portsmouth Navy Days routine (the subsequent public outcry ensured that was a unique event).

In comparison to other aircraft - possibly the purest fun aeroplane ever.

Developments? Well the design evolution had to be frozen at some point, i.e., as the N.113 - but goodness was that the best wing available? And where was it supposed to go with two 11,500 lb Avons and only 8,500 lbs fuel?

Taking 1959 as datum it was inferior (well it couldn't DO anything!). As I recall, USN was operating F-4s, F-8s, A-4s, with full air refuelling capability. The F-4s and F-8s with afterburners had Mach 2 capability; all could carry substantial weapon loads, and I've flown them.

'Controlled crash' - certainly not! As with all deck landing aeroplanes, they fly the glide slope onto the deck with no flare. Standard arrival.

Perhaps delivering the last Scimitar (XD220) and doing aerobatics en route to Lee was my best moment; just knowing no one would ever do this again in this aircraft. Loops over Somerset, rolls over the Solent, and of course a low level tight circuit at Lee for a couple of touch and goes (public outcry again) before the LAST landing.

I would absolutely do it all again - one of the best times of my life. So many memories of flying such a fun aircraft with such a bunch of great guys.

### Commander T.V.G.Binney OBE

Commanding Officer No.804 Squadron, February 1960 until September 1961. Logged 260 hours.

I remember my first Scimitar take-off very well indeed. We were having the Squadron Commissioning ceremony in the afternoon and as yet nobody had actually flown the thing. I just managed to get them to agree to let me take the one aeroplane that was serviceable up, to lend an air of legality to the afternoons proceedings. It was a new aeroplane and nothing like as rough and shaky as I had been led to believe. Take-off and climb were of course memorable and it was quite difficult to sort things out so that I had some sort of charge of it by a height of around 15,000 feet. As for the acceleration, it didn't take me by surprise as I had been well prepared.

In comparison with other jet aircraft I have flown, I found it bigger, more powerful, vibrating and the first aircraft I had flown with fully hydraulic control systems. I think I can really say I was never bored in a Scimitar. There was always a degree of anxiety though this was usually subdued by exhilaration.

The tendency to pitch up was not any real problem, but you certainly had to watch it. It was lovely at low level and indeed at medium level, but not much good at high level. It depended what you were using it for. I suppose we had fallen into the old trap of trying to produce an aeroplane that did too many things and so inevitably some of them not very well, but in *Fallex 60* I reckon the three Royal Navy Scimitar Squadrons, Nos.800, 807 and 804, ran rings round the US Navy strike squadrons with our success rate in deep penetration low level, simulated strikes in Northern Norway under atrocious weather conditions.

I had my share of hair-raising moments but I recall one particular incident when it was others who were in danger. On 5 June 1961 we carried out the first of a series of *Shop Window* exercises. No.804's centre-piece consisted of a dive bombing attack by four aircraft, each carrying four VT fuse 1,000lb bombs whilst a helicopter dropped smoke-floats just over a mile on the port bow. This had gone very well in rehearsal, but on the day the smoke float failed to materialise and I was told by FLYCO, "just drop them well away". Well I thought I had, but on pulling round with the familiar backward look over the shoulder I was horrified to see the most awful sight down below. HMS *Hermes*, with the frigate HMS *Puma* about a cable on the starboard bow, was just approaching the froth and foam left behind by our sixteen 1,000 pounders and I could tell by a series of somewhat abrupt messages that the exercise had not gone down very well. Indeed, not only was *Hermes* packed with Staff College observers etc, but worse, the upper deck of *Puma* was covered in Sea Cadets. Nobody was hurt, but the Captain of *Puma* later sent on board two large sacks of splinters dug out of his ship, including a nasty thing about 18 inches long which had skewered the funnel. *Hermes* herself was also hit by a number of splinters. Captain David Pippit's reaction was, from my point of view, superb. "What you want to do is to get ashore and call on the Captain of *Puma* before he calls on me, you might even get a gin", he said. Commander Air (Ian Campbell) chimed in with "Do drop them a bit farther away tomorrow". I was quite extraordinarily lucky to be serving with two such very remarkable men on that occasion and will always be very grateful.

My other worst moment was orbiting at height some 100 miles east of Hong Kong with cloud base at about 150 feet over 'Mother', very low on fuel, with Kai Tak out, and knowing that at the rate aircraft were getting back aboard, I had no chance whatsoever of making it. Eventually we did so just, and the memory of the subsequent landing remains as vivid to me as when in similar circumstances I came in on a closed Thorney Island and the engines cut through fuel starvation just as we braked to a halt.

If the clock could be put back, of course I would do it all again. At that age and in those days I was still in the state where I used to consciously to wonder at my good fortune for being paid for a way of life which I so thoroughly enjoyed.

One further point I would like to make is that although No.804 was a very small squadron, varying between six and eight aircraft, we had one achievement with which I was particularly pleased. This was to take our aircraft and aircrew through from commissioning day and eighteen months of operational flying ashore and in HMS *Hermes*, back to Lossiemouth to decommission with the same aircrew and the same aeroplanes.

### Lt Cdr Philip Cardew

Squadron QFI with No.803 in *Hermes* from March 1962 to September 1963 and Senior Pilot with No.736 from September 1963 to December 1964. Total Hours in Scimitar, 490 day and 10 hours at night.

I enjoyed my first take-off enormously. Compared to other aircraft I have flown it was quite definitely the most exciting.

I would say my best moments were when flying low-level strikes with Doppler Navigation. The permitted IAS gave one the essential thrill.

For deck landing the arrival was precise and easily controlled. The Vixen could easily float over the wires but it would flare beautifully on the runway. The strong point with the Scimitar was its cross wind limitation. Not many, if any, could match that. The weak point was in allowing the nose to drop on deck landing; that would cause a wire miss every time, if not worse.

High up it was a dog, but it certainly arrived there quickly. 530 knots converting to Mach 0.83. I seem to remember that down low it was sensational. Surrounded by its attendant puffball of condensation it looked good too.

There were several incidents that caused both embarrassment and a few breathless moments. Of these, I choose 1962 when engaged in exercises with the 6th Fleet. My mission was HiCap and the enemy were as I recollect, Vigilante's from USS *Forrestal*. I was leading a section at 40,000 feet being vectored in to a quarter attack. We were bounced and in my enthusiasm to obtain camera gun footage 'overcooked' both the Scimitars and my own capabilities. I spun from 40,000 to 20,000 feet. Reminding myself that as the Squadron QFI I had carried out Hunter spinning a year previously with a well known test pilot, I tried most of the tricks he had taught me and happily it worked out and I rejoined the fray. My No.2 was most impressed and unhappily expressed his comments in the hearing of Freddy Mills the CO. Freddy promptly assembled the squadron pilots and stated that 'It was all very well for Philip to spin since he was the QFI' but he, Freddy, 'would not tolerate another of us doing the same.' Exit left one astonished QFI.

While embarked in *Hermes* in 1963 near Penang in the Malacca Strait, I was launched at maximum catapult weight with a light wind on a hot day. My wing blow failed and the aircraft pitched up dramatically and then rolled right. Fortunately those big engines pushed me out of trouble. FLYCO were very impressed and thought I had lost it; they were not alone in that thought!

A further wing blow incident occurred later at Tengah. My left engine flamed out on the way back from live firing up country. I made a careful single engine approach, fortunately with height in hand. This time the blow was on, despite being selected off. I landed OK but breathing heavily with full power plus on the good engine.

In 1962 No.803 Squadron commenced flight refuelling (buddy/buddy) practice off of the Italian coast. I believe we left three hoses and drogues on Mount Etna whilst practising the art and being issued with the more flexible hose. I however managed to bring back one drogue firmly attached to my probe for the subsequent deck landing. It was embarrassing, and Tommy Leece, our CO, summoned the Squadron for a short and very sharp talk about our skill or lack of it!

Comparing with USN aircraft, they were much more advanced year for year, but their operations and direction were not a patch on ours. They preferred to be directed by the RN in cross- operations.

Developments? Reducing parasite and form drag.

I would do it all over again - but only on post Mod-494 aircraft.

Finally I always liked the story about J.W.Beard who, strapped into one of the early Scimitars, was asked to write his impressions on his knee pad. On landing he showed his only comment: "35,000 feet - regained control".

**Commander A.M.D. de Labilliere**

My first Scimitar Squadron was No.807 in February 1959, commanded by Keith Leppard. I stayed there, as it was in the nature of a holding and training squadron for other front line squadrons, until June 1959. From there I went on to the first of the operational Scimitar Squadrons, which was No.803, and r'mained with it until December 1960. In No.803 I was a 'Junior Joe" having only done one front line squadron before, which was in Sea Hawks; therefore I was at the bottom of the professional ladder in this particular outfit.

On leaving No.803, I left the Scimitar, went to sea and then did the AWI (Air Warfare Instructor) course. My next Scimitar Squadron was No.736, commanded by Lt Cdr Peter Newman, based at Lossiemouth. This was the shore-side training squadron that had taken over the task from No.807. I stayed with No.736 until August 1962 before joining No.803 squadron once again; this time commanded by Lt Cdr 'Spiv' Leahy, which was destined for HMS *Hermes*. I was with No.803 then from August through to October 1962. During this appointment I was temporarily attached to 'C' Squadron at Boscombe Down to carry out the early trials on the 'Buddy/Buddy' air-to-air refuelling system and the M990 multi-function bomb fuse which was destined for the 1,000lb bomb. This subsequently never entered service due to the emerging problems of 'Rad-Haz'.

Having left 'C' Squadron I then went back to 803 in September 1963, now commanded by Lt Cdr 'Freddy' Mills; staying with it whilst we served in *Hermes*, *Ark Royal* and at Lossiemouth until February 1965. That was the last time I was actively concerned with the Scimitar, although I think I may have been one of the last uniformed members of the service to fly one as I subsequently flew XD220 while I was at Brawdy; the date of this flight being January 28th 1969.

Give or take about 20, I would say I logged something in the order of 650 hours in the Scimitar. I had no hours in the simulator beforehand. In those days pre-flight briefings were carried out in the cockpit.

I can well remember my first take-off, principally the intrigued crowd of 'goofers' sitting in Air Traffic Control at Lossiemouth. The main thing was (I can remember being briefed on this very carefully) the very stimulating acceleration. I recall well the kick up the backside as you opened up both engines and the speed at which the aircraft shot into the air; also the speed at which one had to react subsequently in order to get the wheels up before you exceeded the appropriate airframe limitations.

It was undoubtedly the sort of aeroplane where the inquisitive pilot at low-level could satisfy his curiosity over con-trails at 40,000ft in a matter of two to three minutes. This was always remarkable fun. Having said that, when one got to 40,000ft there wasn't much you could do about it if you wanted to turn in the opposite direction. If I remember rightly, in the early days one did not use any flap for take-off, subsequently we then generally used a certain amount of flap particularly if the aircraft was carrying drop tanks.

Landing in the single engine configuration was carried out without Boundary Layer Control on. This was fairly frequent in those days. It was necessary to have BLC off as the residual thrust on the remaining engine was inadequate to sustain level flight in the event of having to overshoot.

I would not say that the landing was a controlled crash. It certainly wasn't an elegant operation and it was always rather positive. This was the way the aircraft was designed to arrive. The undercarriage was stressed, (if I remember correctly) to a vertical velocity of 16ft per second, per second. One could undoubtedly put the aircraft down precisely where you wanted to, once you were fully conscious that you were riding the aircraft on the reverse side of the drag curve. This, in the early days of the Scimitar, was a novel experience for those of us whom had come from straight wing aircraft where you were on the other side of the drag curve.

The hydraulic system for the Scimitar certainly was a matter for concern, indeed records show many aircraft were lost due to the problems that were thrown up by a very high pressure system which operated at 4,000 psi. This again was breaking new boundaries in aircraft technology at that time. As for myself, it did not give me any cause for concern simply because pilots in those

*No.736 Squadron's 1962 Farnborough Display team on 'Tina' mounts provided by the Triumph motor cycle company. Left to right Lt Alan Anderson, Lt P.G.De Souza, Lt R.W.Edward, Lt J.F.Kennett (Senior Pilot) and Lt Cdr P.G.Newman (CO). (via M.J.Hooks)*

days made jolly sure that they were completely aware of the emergency drills that had to be carried out. The problems that did occur depended upon whether you were able to lower the wheels, (again never concerning me). Any other situation was controllable. There was a lot of conjecture over what one should do in such an aircraft because of its high angle of attack when it comes into land. This necessitated serious thought being given to whether it could be safely landed in the wheels up configuration, or worse, with two wheels down such as a main and nose. In those circumstances certainly it was reckoned to be unlandable, as far as I am aware authority was never given. In the case of the nose wheel not coming down it was perfectly controllable, you simply put it down on the runway, generally on foam provided you had been given time, and brought it to a gentle halt.

Inertia Coupling was not a thing I personally experienced. This was because we were limited to one 360 degree roll, therefore that problem had been sorted out by the Test Squadron at Boscombe Down. It was something we were very aware of, so the average squadron pilot was not prepared to intrude into those particular forbidden areas. The point that was actually much more significant was the risk of what was called PIO (Pilot Induced Oscillation). This could happen to the aircraft at high speed particularly if in close formation where many minor control inputs were being put in.

My most dangerous moment flying the Scimitar was an incident which I would say could be attributed to a certain amount of incompetence on my part. We used to have *Blue Silk*, a Doppler navigation aid which was used with the LABS (Low Altitude Bombing System) aircraft with which the early squadrons were equipped. Generally there were up to four aircraft with specialist aircrew flying these tactical nuclear bombing aircraft. These aircrew trained separately from the others, and I was one. The reliability of this equipment (which involved a formidable amount of finger work and manual dexterity in a very short period of time to get it to react accurately) was such that it was very easy for it to mislead you. I very nearly flew myself into a mountain which fortunately appeared through cloud just as I was about to descend into it.

My best memory was knowing that it was a fascinating, new aeroplane. We felt that we were undoubtedly on the frontiers of aeronautical development, just reaching the end of the 1950s, where an awful lot of progress had been made and where pilot skill was much more to the fore than maybe it is nowadays where computers tend to enact many functions. All I can say is that I thoroughly enjoyed my time in the Scimitar.

Probably one of the major disadvantages of the aircraft, though not from my point of view, was the formidable problem of maintenance. It had not been designed for easy accessibility; things like fuel flow proportioners were extremely hard to get at and caused long hours of work. Therefore we were very much a manpower conscious organisation. This was the aircraft which forced the FAA to introduce a three watch system, which is still with us today, albeit in a diluted form. The difficulties in getting a reasonable degree of serviceability were onerous, indeed for the ground crews.

The Scimitar was the Royal Navy's most exciting aircraft to have flown; principally because it was the first RN high powered, supersonic aeroplane, and in that sense it was marvellous fun and we tended to have very good 'esprit de corps' in the squadrons we were in.

I have, of course, flown in aircraft such as the Buccaneer and Sea Vixen. The Buccaneer, I would say, was a much more satisfying aeroplane in the sense that one could do so much more that was just frustratingly beyond the capability of the Scimitar. The principal disadvantage of the Scimitar as far as its operational abilities were concerned, was its inability to launch at sea carrying adequate fuel and weapon loads from the steam catapults fitted to carriers such as *Victorious*. The two were just not matched up. We deluded ourselves that we had an operational role, particularly in the Far East when the aircraft was patently not capable of it.

The Buccaneer was another matter, particularly in the case of the Mk.2. In that sense therefore it was a much more satisfying aircraft, you could go a long way and do a lot more with it. It had the second generation avionics and engines, which of course one would naturally expect advantages from. That is not to belittle the Scimitar as, of course, it was not designed to carry out the roles it subsequently was given by the Navy, who were notorious for taking a fighter and turning it into a heavy bomber at a stroke with intermediate development through to tanker, photo reconnaissance, low altitude bomber, nuclear attack and so forth.

To talk about developments the Scimitar could have benefited from, in my case must be conjectural. The most effective, as far as I was concerned, was the two seat version. This in fact was scuttled by the DNAW in the late 50s in favour of the D.H.110, which was taken on in the All Weather role. It had been planned to have an AW Scimitar. I now think therefore that in a practical sense, the development it would have most benefited from was a redesigned wing, which would have enabled it to perform supersonically, preferably with some form of compensating low speed design to enable it to get on and off the deck at adequate speeds with sufficient fuel and weapons on board (without activity tempting one's Maker on every conceivable occasion).

'Pitch-up' was never a problem as far as I can remember. It was one of those things that sound training ensured you were well aware of. Indeed on the occasions that the aircraft did pitch up with me, it was readily controllable.

My personal knowledge of USN aircraft was purely limited to having seen them operate from a ship, but I think the Scimitar used to surprise the Americans with the amount of power it had and its somewhat limited speed performance due to the unfavourable design of the wing. Whereas the USN design philosophy has always been to design aircraft very much closer to the tolerances at which it is to operate, we have always built in a much greater safety factor. Having said that, I think it probably had a similar capability.

I do not think that it would have served any useful purpose for the aircraft to have gone on, even if fitted with more advanced navigation aids and weapons, or despite maybe the fitting of a refined wing. By that stage the design penalties that were manifesting themselves in excessive quantities of manpower being required to maintain it, were being self evidently removed by the arrival of the second generation of swept wing aircraft such as the Buccaneer. This was progress; normal, natural, healthy progress.

Low and high speed handling was of course different. It was an aeroplane that required a positive knowledge of the effects of the three controls, and provided that you were satisfied with that, it was perfectly safe. At low speed you undoubtedly did not get very low and slow because you could end up in a high drag situation, which was difficult to recover from without letting the nose down. High speed handling in my opinion was perfectly satisfactory, provided one was aware of my previous remarks about the tendency toward PIO. It had a very high speed in the order of 630 knots. It was not a good manoeuvring aircraft at low speed or indeed low altitude. In a tactical sense its principal advantage was its ability to come 'down hill' very fast, then slow up whilst still descending by the use of its air-brakes; and of course its formidable acceleration and power/weight ratio, which enabled it to do loops of a radius that other aircraft could not emulate. Having said that, it was the sort of aircraft that was going to lose out every time to aircraft such as the Hunter as soon as it was down to a co-speed manoeuvring situation and in that sense of course it was not satisfactory. Once again we come back to the inadequacies of the wing and the inability, because of the leading edge flap, to use flap in any other situation other than the landing mode.

I would say that the principal changes in handling were caused, not so much by different weapon configurations, but by the fitting of drop tanks. The aircraft's limited range and high fuel consumption meant that for the majority of sorties, the aircraft generally carried drop tanks, sometimes four. In those circumstances it was quite sensitive. As far as weapons were concerned, probably the heaviest load it was designed to carry was the 2,000lb bomb, which was always counter balanced by a drop tank on the other inboard station. Generally, because of the nature of the range of such sorties, you would carry two further drop tanks on the outboard station; assuming that the aircraft could be shot off the deck. Normally the answer to that was no. In this role it handled perfectly adequately. It was, like all other swept wing aircraft where the c of g is moving back, just that little more sensitive than it could be in the normal role. It was a comparative pleasure to fly the aircraft clean because of the increased manoeuvrability, but it was not perfect.

An incident that probably received a certain amount of notoriety was when I was seconded to 'C' Squadron in June 1960. We went out to El Adem in Libya for trials. The purpose of these trials was to test the new VT 907 airburst fuse, which is still in service today (albeit a different Mk), and trials with the in-flight refuelling. At the end of these trials one would come back full of 'Joie de Vivre'. Because the wings were clean, having dropped the bombs on the range a matter of five minutes away, the aircraft could slip through the sound barrier with astonishing ease, particularly in those hot weather conditions. It was my habit to normally climb up to about 12,000ft put the nose down vertically and go supersonic at about 8,000ft, which resulted in a very concentrated supersonic bang arriving on the airfield, provided it was aimed properly. On this particular day unfortunately, we had a lunch time sortie and most of my maintenance team from Boscombe Down had disappeared into the Sergeants Mess. I arrived overhead the airfield and ranged to drop quite a good bang at 7 or 8,000ft, then subsequently landed. One was used to seeing admiring crowds of people gathered around the hardstanding to see this curious aeroplane with folding wings and hook. On this day there were rather more than usual. I paid no heed and as I closed down my engines CPO Tallock, who was our Maintenance Chief, came up the ladder and said, "If I was you Sir, I would push off quick. This lot ain't friendly". It was at this particular moment that I glanced with greater curiosity toward the crowd and noticed that a number of them were covered in bandages and plaster, and seemed to be in a rather dishevelled state. I was then told that the supersonic bang had demolished the entire roof of the Sergeants Mess Bar, in which 80% of the members were imbibing the first beer of the day. After that I rather cut down on my programme of gratuitous supersonic bangs.

The only other incident that happened of note while at El Adem occurred on a low-level navigation sortie with the air-to-air refuelling pod on board. We had decided to have a banyan (Naval jargon for barbecue) somewhere down near the Egyptian border. Unfortunately on my recce, I followed the wrong turn of the desert railway and ended up firmly inside Egypt, which resulted in quite a major diplomatic incident due to the fact that this nuclear bomber (so called) was circling one of their frontier garrison towns. What I thought could be a happy banyan base subsequently turned out not to be so. The Station Commander, one Group Captain Bell, who was a friendly, well disposed chap, suggested that as a high powered team were coming out to investigate the incident it might suit our purposes if I concluded the trials within the next half day and got the Hell out of it back to Boscombe Down. I duly did so, taking his good advice and thereby saved myself a lot of problems.

Another incident or incidents took place on *Victorious* in the English Channel when the First Sea Lord was on board. We had a modification called Mod 494, whereby the fuel tanks were connected up using electrically operated catches. The booster props in the tanks previous to this were notoriously unreliable, being totally immersed and electrically driven. The net result was that the Scimitar had the habit of going to the maximum extreme of its flight profile when you would then get a little green light coming on telling you that you had lost 2,000lb worth of fuel from one of your main tanks, and there was no way that you were going to get home because you could not retrieve the fuel. Mod 494 enabled us to cross connect the fuel tanks and thereby recover fuel which otherwise would have been lost. Nevertheless there were many instances, particularly due to the aircraft's high landing speed and high fuel consumption, which resulted in recoveries requiring something close to crisis management. Not the least of these was in poor weather conditions. I particularly remember one such occasion in the Channel where it was almost impossible to see anything in front of me at all. The front windscreen was very prone, particularly in drizzle, to smearing which totally obliterated one's forward vision. What vestigial vision one had was achieved by looking through the left or right side quarter lights of the front windscreen. Several of my more stimulating arrivals back on board ship were generally in rainy conditions.

The Scimitar was not an aircraft that had been cleared effectively for night flying. It might have been by Boscombe Down, but we did not generally fly it by night.

As for my time flying the Scimitar. Would I do it all over again? Yes please, but preferably with post-Mod 494.

❖❖❖❖❖❖❖❖❖❖❖❖❖❖❖❖❖❖❖❖❖❖❖❖

### Lt Cdr P.G. De Souza

My association with the Supermarine N.113 began in 1959 and was to last nearly ten years, both as a military and civilian pilot. In that year I was given a new lease of life when their Lordships permitted me to change operational roles from anti-submarine to fighters. At that time two or three from each OFS course were being selected to convert to the Scimitar, and I was lucky enough to be given one of the slots. Prior to the actual course, students were sent across the airfield at Lossiemouth to No.764 Squadron to carry out a Hunter conversion, designed to give exposure on a swept wing aircraft and practise some instrument flying using the Interim Dynamic Reference system, as fitted in one of the T.8s and all Scimitars. All subsequent instrument flying practice and ratings were carried out on this specially fitted aircraft.

The Scimitar conversion started with the usual classroom technical lectures and emergency procedure training and then advanced to the simulator phase. The simulator, located in two blue caravans, comprised a static mock-up and an instructor's console, where he could monitor fairly realistic in-flight conditions and inject a wide selection of systems failures and emergencies. It wasn't a bad piece of kit for its day, it gave the student a pretty good insight as to what to expect of the 'beast'. Each student was given five sessions in the box amounting, in my case, to 4 hours 45 minutes of absolute purgatory. The actual aircraft was a very large and intimidating piece of machinery compared with the likes of the Sea Hawk and Venom, and was by far the largest single-seater ever built for the Royal Navy.

A magnificent sight in flight, impressively fast and noisy for its day, the prospect of making my first flight was very appealing, even though the aircraft was already getting a dubious reputation for reliability. My enthusiasm was tempered but not curbed by the fact that the aircraft had claimed two lives in recent months, one of those a close colleague from my original intake to the Royal Navy (a second would be lost shortly after). However, the time at last arrived, and on a nice clear winter's day, 25 November 1959, girt in 'g' suit, immersion suit and all the paraphernalia of the day, I waddled out to the flight line and cautiously climbed the ample ladder of XD226. Even for a fairly large lad, the cockpit seemed very roomy and nicely laid out. The seating position was rather erect for a fighter when the seat was fully raised (necessary for landing) but otherwise visibility and general environment was good. The pilot's mate stowed the two safety pins for the ejector seat and those for the explosive canopy release, gave me a rather unsettling smirk and descended to Terra Firma.

Starting the two Avons was simple enough using the ground electrical supply and a Palouste L.P. air starter. The various check lists were carried out with the aid of flip cards and functional checks were completed prior to taxi. One then moved forward to spread the wings and check the locking pins fully engaged. Taxying was very pleasant due to the high eye-level and good all-round visibility. The footbrakes were effective and responsive. The take-off roll was as stimulating as briefed, and little help was required to get the aircraft to unstick. In fact, having recovered from the surprise of being airborne so quickly, positive forward stick pressure and trim were necessary to dispel the very real sensation of doing a premature loop. Acceleration was very rapid and much fumbling for the gear button ensued to raise the wheels before the 300 kt limiting speed was grossly exceeded. I was fascinated to see the ASI building up in hundreds of knots and only just remembered the transition to Mach numbers as 500 knots corresponded to 0.93M at about 3,000ft. A very firm rotation was made to achieve the necessary climbing attitude and pin the desired climb speed of 0.93m. A quick scan of the cockpit revealed the correct configuration and all the read-outs steady, except for the altimeter, which was winding up at an alarming rate. As if to confirm this, I glanced into the very good rear view mirror and looking back across the aircraft's whale-like back, noted with great satisfaction a plan view of the airfield getting significantly smaller by the second. My brief was to level off at 30,000 feet and this was accomplished with a substantial bunting manoeuvre, and some three minutes after brake release.

The Scimitar was a beautiful aircraft to fly, powerful and responsive, with nicely harmonised power controls and a good roll rate (280 deg/sec). Although good in a straight line its high level performance was very limited to turning, with the onset of buffet occurring at low bank angles and low 'g' above 30 to 35,000 feet, any determination to turn at 45,000ft would result in heavy buffet, longitudinal instability and a rapid arrival back at 30,000ft. The straight line performance was certainly not bad, and if you couldn't out-fight your opposition, you could always out accelerate and outrun him.

Despite its awesome power, the aircraft could never be described as anything more than trans-sonic. As previously mentioned, the acceleration was quite bewildering, but at about Mach 0.98 an enormous drag rise prevented any increase in speed in level flight. With just a small rate of descent the aircraft would penetrate the sound barrier and show a much better turning performance, but the inherent drag rise never permitted much of an increase unless high decent rates were involved. I once got one up to about Mach 1.5 true, but the world was approaching very rapidly. A favourite trick was to cycle the petal airbrakes when just supersonic and bring the aircraft in and out of sonic flight thus dropping several sonic booms on your target. A fair amount of havoc was wreaked this way over the years, especially amongst mink farmers and market gardeners.

Overall, both low speed and high speed handling were remarkably good. Low speed handling was very different to previous generations of fighters, and took a little getting used to, but once the high attitude landing configuration became familiar, one gained plenty of confidence that the aircraft wasn't going to do anything horrid to you on finals. Circuit and landing procedure commenced with a run in and break to down-wind. The aircraft was remarkably strong, stressed to at least 9g for normal operations, so the speed of the run in and the g pulled on the break were more often limited by the previous night's party rather than operational constraints. Having emerged from the grey-out into some semblance of conscious control downwind, the gear was lowered at 300 knots, and increments of flap extended and speed reduced. The aircraft was positively rotated with trim into the classic Scimitar landing attitude. Boundary layer control was selected to prevent separation from the trailing edge flaps and leading edge droop helped the airflow negotiate the high angle of attack. To provide the necessary engine bleed air for the flap blow system, engine power was kept high by increasing profile drag with fully extended petal airbrakes and lowered fuselage flap. Final approach speed was weight related but was generally around 135 knots, very low for a performance aircraft of its size but good for deck landings. It was necessary to raise the seat when downwind to

*Lt P.G.De Souza climbing into his No.803 Squadron Scimitar on board HMS Ark Royal in 1966. The plane captain is standing by to hand him his flying helmet once safely seated. (P.G.De Souza)*

obtain better forward vision, especially on later *Blue Silk* equipped aircraft, where all the gubbins raised the level of the cockpit coaming. Once used to the attitude and the very marked effect power played in controlling the glideslope angle, landing the aircraft was a pleasant experience. It was, indeed, a form of controlled crash, but the substantial oleos were designed for just such a no-cut, no-flare technique.

Ashore, it was usual practice to arrest the normal 600 to 700 FPM descent rate by a judicious application of power just before touchdown. However for deck landing you just drove it in.

Operationally, the aircraft's shortcomings at altitude were quickly appreciated so the Navy lost no time in re-designating its primary role to that of ground attack and strike. At low level its inherent strength and fatigue life put it head and shoulders above most of the competition of the day. It was truly magnificently stable at low level and I know everyone enjoyed howling around at 600 knots IAS at 100 feet, which was possible in those days. Most low level exercises were flown at either 420 or 480 knots, multiples of 60 being easiest for mental dead reckoning. At 600 knots plus, one was wise to put in a bit of nose up trim, since an inadvertent sneeze at a hundred feet could result in picking up some unwelcome flora.

Some aircraft were fitted for LABS attacks (Low Altitude Bombing System). This technique involved a pre-calculated high speed low level run in, from a pre-determined IP speed and height (usually 400 feet) which had to be very accurately flown and the run in to the target area was determined by a timer, started by the armament trigger at the IP, whilst the aircraft was flown on a particular heading for which drift had supposedly been allowed. At the end of this hair-raising episode the pilot followed the indications provided by an instrument like a zero reader, which called for a 4g, wings-level pull up. The bomb was then released at a pre-determined angle of climb and tossed some four to five miles whilst the aircraft made good its escape. One can imagine the multitude of errors that could be compounded in such a manoeuvre by a manually flown single seater. The results were often riotous, (providing international incidents or major property damage were not involved). The aircraft was quite a stable platform for conventional armament and pretty good results were achieved with bombs, rockets and strafing with the four 30mm Aden cannon.

Air-to-Air firing was not easy for some reason, and the introduction of early guided missiles (Sidewinder) negated much interest in that direction. The use of the F95 camera provided the aircraft with a very useful PR role, and the Scimitar took a fairly large part in the development of the in-flight refuelling pod. The latter provided a considerable benefit to Scimitar deck operations in later days, and most squadrons had one or two aircraft equipped for in-flight refuelling.

With regard to carrier operations, the aircraft was actually very pleasant to operate from the deck despite looking very hairy from the 'Goofers'. The high angle of attack and the prominent effect power application had on the flight path, gave the effect that a round-down strike was always on the cards. It never looked quite so bad from the other side of the windscreen, but one never let your guard drop since there never was much ramp clearance, and to land short of the wires usually resulted in a hell of a fright and a summons to the bridge. There was a special setting for the projector sight, the whole being jacked up about six feet to give that little extra clearance over the back end. Since this clearance was reasonably critical, in rough weather, the ship's angle of pitch could curtail Scimitar operations.

The other main problem affecting Scimitar deck operations was wind over the deck. The steam catapult would give an average end speed of about 107 knots for a fully laden aircraft, so the shortfall had to be made up by a wind over the deck created either by natural wind speed, or artificially by the carrier's speed through the water.

The old *Ark Royal* was often subject to mechanical problems which reduced its maximum performance and the smaller light fleet carriers were a little limited in top speed, so light natural wind or totally calm conditions resulted in either reduced payload/ fuel load or curtailed operations altogether. I recall a launch period when just such a situation necessitated the Captain desperately manoeuvring the ship to find wind, chasing the slightest catspaw seen on a glassy sea. Meanwhile I had been tensioned, then lowered from the launch position on the catapult several times, as the minimum wind over the deck rose then died away. Each time I was prepared to launch I switched on the 'blow', switching it off again as the aircraft was lowered to keep engine temperatures down. After several such false starts I must have got out of phase with the blow, because when I was finally fired off, the aircraft had a great desire to want to pitch up. Fortunately it didn't but I remember seeing the ship's bows flare up in the rear view mirror as the aircraft settled on its ground cushion and half a mile of jet wake spray preceded full flight.

Similar problems could be encountered on recoveries, since too high an entry speed into the wires at too great a weight could cause the arrester gear to bottom out and the wire to break. At times we would find ourselves in the carrier circuit burning off fuel down to rather alarming levels before being able to recover. This was quite often accompanied with frenzied instructions to conserve fuel when the after lift got stuck down or the last wire had to be guillotined. It was a standing joke to conserve fuel on one engine and burn off on the other. Enough fuel for a couple of passes and an ejection was about standard, so it paid to do it right first time.

Bolters in a Scimitar were not uncommon due to bouncing the hook over the wires or letting the nose drop on impact with the deck. Loss of attitude would cause the hook to ride over the wires, and unless full power was maintained a very undignified departure over the side would ensue.

In February 1961, whilst serving with No.807 Sqn in *Ark*

*Royal*, we did some Arctic trials up close to the ice pack in the Davies Strait, between Canada and Greenland. It proved that the Scimitar was well capable of operating in sub-zero temperatures and on an ice-coated deck. It wasn't much fun for the operators though, there being few worse feelings than sliding uncontrolled towards the deck edge as the ship heeled in a turn. The aircraft would take charge of the tractor as well and only some pretty fast work by the deck crews averted very expensive accidents. On the rare days that Arctic sea smoke didn't seriously reduce viability by merging with the low stratus, it was interesting to see aircraft con-trailing in the circuit at 400 feet. I think we were very lucky not to lose any aircraft in those conditions since deterioration in visibility occurred very rapidly and it was only some very good CCA controlling and the help of a new 'high/low' visual lighting aid that saved the day. I remember the last Gannet recovered in the trials arrived in the wires, to everyone's surprise, unseen until over the round-down.

Regarding night operations, we did some trials in No.807 in November 1960 whilst in *Ark* off Malta. I don't think any of those who had a go were very impressed with the Scimitar in this role. Personally, I found that the very high body angle in the circuit and the absence of suitable visual cues would readily lead to a high degree of disorientation. The introduction of the then new airflow direction detector went some way in assisting, but it was very much in its infancy and lack of confidence in its calibration did nothing to change our opinion that the Scimitar was a good aircraft, but for day operations only.

The greatest problem with the aircraft was its systems, especially the fuel and hydraulic systems. The fuel system was a nightmare for both operator and maintainer. Internal fuel, about 8,000lb, was scattered among five flexible fuselage tanks and four integral wing tanks. Overload fuel was carried in either 200 or 150 gallon drop tanks. (Four external tanks meant no external armament). Fuel usage and balance was controlled by eight booster pumps which operated in three speed bands, which were further controlled in two height/speed bands. Post Mod.494, the pilot could manually interconnect adjacent tanks in the event of booster pump failures, and to some extent control longitudinal balance by a high degree of manual dexterity and a great deal of luck. Quite often you would end up with some unusable fuel if not quite a lot, and the balance gauges looking like a cross-section elevation of the Alps.

Leaks were the rule rather than the exception, and an aircraft left to sit in the hangar overnight would partially fill the mandatory drip tray with a mixture of fuel and hydraulic fluid. Several aircraft were lost due to in-flight fires caused by the small collector tank, which was strategically sited between the jet pipes, fracturing and disgorging its contents over the readily-available source of ignition.

This was the prime cause of me leaving a Scimitar in flight off Changi, Singapore (XD277, 6th April 1966). Regarding my own little association with Martin-Baker, there is little to add to the original write-up other than my own thoughts at the time. The prospects of having to use the seat was initially not too attractive in view of my previous history of back problems. That is why I was pretty determined to land if possible. When the situation became inevitable, my main thoughts were to make it as copy book as possible so whilst waiting to clear the airfield at Changi and get over the sea, I made several adjustments to the seat height and strap tension. I was quite surprised how clearly one thinks and how beneficial became all those drills one practised in the past. I pushed my bottom as firmly back into the seat as possible and straightened my spine as much as the straps would allow. I pulled the top blind and apart from feeling an enormous kick up the backside remembered nothing until becoming aware of being in a jack-knifed position, looking down at the sea and seeing maps and debris floating away beneath me. My next reaction was of horror when I was convinced that the chute had failed to open since there was no sign of the canopy. My drills immediately made me try for a manual separation from the seat but a quick grope in the right place revealed neither handles nor seat. I remember wondering what I had done to deserve this when it dawned on me that my descent rate was not consistent with a free fall. Craning my neck up and around I eventually saw the periphery of the small main canopy and with exquisite relief reached up and grabbed the webbing, which had had me suspended from the middle of my back, thus pitching me forward. The euphoria of realising that everything had indeed worked as it should, encouraged me to be more adventuresome, and I could now enjoy the silent view of the nearby beach and try and induce some drift to get closer in to land. What I had not realised was that several of the panels of the chute had been ripped during the ejection sequence and as a result, aided by my unnecessary drift inducement, my arrival into the briny was both high speed and undignified.

However, years of wet dinghy drill practice soon had me comfortably settled into my little dinghy, chute and all. I would almost certainly have broken out the emergency rations for a snack had not two young swimmers arrived on the scene and enquired after my welfare. The rescue helicopter from Changi very soon arrived and I rejected a double lift due to feeling some back pain, and accepted the swimmers kind offer of a tow to the beach instead. Once on the beach the chopper eventually gathered me up and dropped me off at the sick bay where they promptly incarcerated me having discovered a broken coccyx and several compressed vertebrae.

The aircraft landed in shallow water with the fire fully developed so it was decided to salvage the remains. When the Navy finally got round to it a few days later, most of the aircraft had been removed by the locals and several sampan loads had to be repossessed from nearly Kampongs.

Incidentally, on that particular flight which was the result of a late programme change I had to borrow a set of leg restraint garters from 'Bush' Skrodski, who had already ejected from Scimitars on previous occasions. I now have that original garter which has seen three Scimitar ejections hanging in my bar at home. I was sorry to learn that Bush was later killed during his third ejection attempt from a Hunter.

Another incident I remember well was the Senior Pilot of No.803 Sqn just failing to make Lossiemouth when disembarking one time. We were all alerted that someone was in trouble and, as always, stood outside the hangars to watch the developments. Regrettably the engine flamed out over the golf course. The pilot ejected safely and the aircraft arrived in a heap in the undershoot. Since, in this particular instance, the aircraft was completely devoid of fuel, there was no fire, and because spares were always at a premium, the various AEOs descended on the wreckage and could be seen carting off deck hook, wheels or anything salvageable. The pilot, who was unhurt, was taken straight home to the married patch by the chopper since he had been at sea some months.

With regard to my own personal experiences, I must say I loved every minute (perhaps just a few moments of terror) of my time on the Scimitar. I served in No.807 Sqn from February 1960 to June 1961 in *Ark Royal* and later in *Centaur*. In November 1961, after CFS, I returned to No.736 Sqn at Lossiemouth as the QFI until August 1963. During this time I did most of the Scimitar conversions of that period, flew solo aerobatics and was a member of the formation aerobatic team at Farnborough in 1962. That was interesting, it being the first time we looped two types in the same formation - Vixens and Scimitars. Because the Vixen took about 4,500ft to loop and the Scimitar about 7,000ft, practices were a bit of a hoot, the two types parting company early in the pull up. It was an eventual compromise by which the Vixen primarily utilised speed and the Scimitar power, that we got the act together.

In September 1965, I joined No.764B Sqn for Scimitar refresher flying prior to joining No.803 Sqn in *Ark* in the Far East, once again as the QFI. It was in No.803 that we probably had the most problems with the aircraft. It was the last operational squadron and some of the aircraft were a little tired. Mind you, we must have also received the last of the reserves as well, since at least nine were written off for one reason or another. Apart from the fires mentioned, the hydraulic system was equally troublesome. Two independent systems operating at 4,000 psi were always springing leaks. No.1 system, which supplied all the main services as primary source, was particularly vulnerable and the cause of most precautionary landings.

There was no manual reversion of controls, so failure of both systems was terminal.

My most worrying moment was probably some time after recovering from the ejection and when *Ark* had returned to the North Sea prior to us finally paying off. We were operating off the North East coast of England and trying to take part in a co-operation exercise with the Army in Yorkshire. It was one of those September days when all of the East coast goes out in low cloud and fog and the North Sea is equally inhospitable. In true 'Press on' fashion, we launched two pairs of Scimitars (Master Greens only) to go and have a look in the exercise area. Needless to say, the weather was too bad to take part in the exercise so we headed back to the ship, where they were getting concerned about the fog banks. The first three aircraft recovered safely off CCAs, but on my final approach I could only get two greens and a red on my undercarriage indicator. The left main gear was locked up and this was confirmed as I overshot the approach. Meantime the fog was getting worse and the carrier kept disappearing into the murk. There followed a rather harrowing period while I tried to get the gear down, operating the emergency system unsuccessfully, whilst doing timed circuits at 400ft in IMC with the stick between my knees, and taking evasive manoeuvres each time the dark shape of the ship loomed out of the fog. For good reasons, I was unhappy about the prospects of another ejection, and wondered if they would ever find me if I did. The thought of a recovery into the barrier was unappealing and potentially messy but as fate would have it at the same moment as the order was given to rig the barrier there was a gentle clunk, and three glorious greens shone out of the instrument panel. One more timed circuit on instruments and I thankfully saw the carrier again and bounced into the wires. For a while I just sat there in the aircraft whilst my right knee shook uncontrollably, the first time I'd experienced that since I first read the lesson at school assembly as a kid.

Soon after that the carrier finally disembarked the air group, and I remember being close to the front for launching. True to form, I developed a huge fuel leak from the drop tank, so I was ignored whilst the rest of the air group was launched. Sitting in isolation on deck, still belching fuel, I was approached by one of our engineers, a lovely character named John Chicken, who viewed life from behind bottle bottomed spectacles, and whose tools of the trade comprised primarily of a hide-faced hammer and an oily rag. He stepped smartly up, gave the drop tank a lusty belt with the hide face, and the leak promptly ceased, so, on 1 October 1966, in XD276, I made by default the very last Scimitar operational flight from *Ark Royal* to Yeovilton, and after a couple of loops over the field, landed to see the 'beast' pass into history.

Strangely enough it was not to be my last Scimitar flight. After resigning from the Navy in 1968, I joined Airwork at Hurn, my home town of Bournemouth's local airport, and flew the Scimitar for quite a few more hours as a civilian on Fleet Requirement duties. Funnily enough the serviceability rate was surprisingly good at Airwork and we had very few problems. They obviously enjoyed their retirement with gentle handling in mainly straight and level flight. My last Scimitar flight was in XD232 for Airwork on March 7th 1969 - nearly a decade after my first. Altogether I completed about 800 hours on the type, with over 330 deck landings.

## Commander T.C.Evans AFC

My experience of flying the Scimitar was gained during the three years I spent in The Naval Test Pilot Squadron at Boscombe Down, Wiltshire, and the three years plus as Commanding Officer, Experimental Flying at RAE Bedford.

I completed over 80 hours of actual airborne time (a few at night) and many more driving XD228 into the DAX Arrester Gear at RAE Bedford. I would guess I have been 'arrested' more times in a Scimitar than any other pilot who flew the aeroplane.

The Scimitar was a well built, tough machine which unfortunately never met the original specification. I did my first familiarisation flight in January 1958 after a thorough briefing and cockpit check from Lt Cdr Danny Norman; no simulators at that time. With less than ten hours in the aeroplane I found myself doing Tropical Trials in Bahrain.

Regarding the acceleration, it certainly got out of the blocks very quickly. Not surprising remembering the power to weight ratio.

My most dangerous moment was spinning; initiating a spin to the left - stick hard back and full left rudder - the aircraft spinning very rapidly to the right. My best moment was recovering from this!

I have flown a lot of different aeroplanes from biplanes to V-bombers. The Scimitar was a straightforward power machine, a bit crude really, but quite delightful below 25,000ft. Above that height the manoeuvre boundary started to get very 'thin' and had virtually disappeared by 30,000ft.

Regarding possible developments, one could suggest lower profile drag, a thinner wing, improved intakes etc, but it was what it was and to achieve the original specification one would really need to start again.

It did a good job in the low-level strike role and also provided much useful data on boundary layer control.

I think one aeroplane was fitted with HUD (head-up display) - I never flew it, but I always felt that such a fit would improve the IF and night flying characteristics (particularly off the catapult - and during a bolter).

An abiding memory is not of an 'in-flight' incident but one on the ground. I was on my way back from Bahrain to Boscombe Down after the hot weather trials. I landed at Diyarbakier (Turkey) with a partial hydraulic failure and a brake problem. On the roll out I applied brake to slow the aeroplane and promptly shot off the runway to starboard. The aircraft came to a gentle halt in the soft sand with the wheels buried to the rims. There was no tractor or suitable towing vehicle available, so they gave me about twenty tough little Turk soldiers, all beef, smiles and little else. My Turkish was non-existent, and trying to explain to these very eager young men what was required was very difficult. Eventually we managed to push and pull the aeroplane back along its inward tracks. The men didn't understand the word 'push' but the judicious use of another four-letter word brought forth shrieks of mirth and Herculean feats of strength.

The service owes a great deal to Mike Lithgow and the Supermarine Test Pilot team for the outstanding work they did in the development of the aircraft. I would also mention Dennis Higton in this respect, he was the boffin responsible for the C(A) clearance programme at Boscombe, and my old friend and colleague, Danny Norman, who could make the aeroplane 'talk'.

Perhaps the best thing about the Scimitar was that it brought together a fine bunch of men, and it was a privilege to know and work with them. I can only hope that I might be remembered as one of them.

Would I do it all again? Absolutely.

**Commander C.C. 'Chuck' Giles**

The Scimitar squadrons I served in were No.700X Flight (March - May 1958), No.803 Squadron (May 1958 to September 1959), No.736 Squadron (October 1959 - March 1961) and No.800 Squadron (April - December 1961), logging a total of 747 hours flying hours.

Coming straight from the Sea Hawk, the Scimitar was certainly an awe-inspiring aircraft to look at - and climb into.

My thought's on my first take-off? I had been told to release the brakes at the end of the runway and regain control at 40,000 feet. They were right! The acceleration was quite fantastic and I had to get the wheels up pretty smartly before reaching their 300 knot limiting speed. It was indeed an exhilarating ride and hugely enjoyable. Later of course came the challenge of getting the machine back onto Ford's comparatively short (2,000 yard) runway, but I had been briefed about speed and height control in an aircraft flying at the bottom of (or possibly on the wrong side of) the speed/drag curve, a new technique for Sea Hawk pilots. So the approach and landing seemed quite straightforward. I had, incidentally, been advised not to look over my shoulder on finals since the very pronounced nose up attitude of the aircraft might prove unduly scary, even disorienting; but I did it anyway and as the aircraft seemed to be flying quite nicely in that ridiculous attitude, it turned out to be just another interesting experience.

My most dangerous moment flying the Scimitar was on 15 July 1959. No.803 Squadron, embarked in HMS *Victorious*, were off the East coast of the United States. Four Scimitars were scheduled to 'cross operate' to the USS *Saratoga*. I was flying No 2 to the CO, Lt Cdr Geoff Higgs, in XD266. We entered the recovery pattern with the Boss leading, but at the last moment he was given a foul deck wave-off - so I became the first on board the 'Big S', and thus found I had carried out the first deck landing of a British swept-wing aircraft on an American carrier.

On the return journey to *Victorious* the four Scimitars did a high speed fly-past over *Saratoga*. I was in the box position and as the speed increased to over 500 knots I experienced, very suddenly, a most violent attack of PIO (pilot induced oscillation). For a few seconds the aircraft behaved like a Bucking Bronco, totally out of control, with very high 'g' forces recorded on the accelerometer: 7 positive g, 5 negative g. My head hit the top of the canopy two or three times and I was surprised the Scimitar did not break up. We were right over the *Saratoga* when this happened and later, back in harbour, US Navy pilots who saw the incident told me they were certain any of their aircraft would have collapsed under such stress. But the Scimitar was very strong: on return to *Victorious* XD266 was assessed as serviceable and flew again the next day. I had never suffered from PIO before, and never have since, despite a great deal of flying in the box position. The causes of this very scary incident were almost certainly twofold; the aircraft was carrying underwing drop tanks, which were partially empty at the time. The acceleration during the fly-past would have pushed the fuel to the back of each tank, which in turn would have moved the centre of gravity backwards: not a good thing, as an 'aft cg' reduces longitudinal stability and can make an aircraft difficult to control. Furthermore, the underwing pylons were of the 'straight down' variety, undesirable in a swept wing aircraft as again this moves the centre of gravity backwards if there is anything heavy (like fuel) attached to them. Shortly afterwards we were equipped with swept forward pylons, which solved the potentially dangerous aft cg problem.

Probably my best and most enjoyable moments in the Scimitar were formation and solo aerobatics during the 1961 Display season, when No.800 Squadron formed a nine Scimitar team called the *Red Blades*. We appeared at Paris, Farnborough and various other shows around the country and our CO, the late Danny Norman, devised a number of different routines for various weather conditions, each of which made sure that the crowd had something in front of them at all times (unlike the formation of 22 RAF Hunters, which took several minutes to turn around and reappear after each manoeuvre). My particular job was flying box in the nine-ship formation, then breaking off to do solo aerobatics. The Scimitar was a big heavy aircraft for nine-ship rolls and loops but it proved excellent in this role. It was hard work but most rewarding.

Comparing the aircraft to others I have flown, a squadron mate of mine who went on to achieve Flag rank, used to remark that the Scimitar was an expensive way to knock someone off a camel. He was absolutely right. In the ground attack role, although range and payload were greatly superior to the Sea Hawk, and the aircraft could carry a nuclear bomb, its weapon system was rudimentary. It was, however, an excellent photo reconnaissance machine, equipped with the new F95 high speed camera. As a fighter it had terrific rate of climb and speed, but failed badly because of its poor turning performance at high altitude. I should add however that when supersonic at high altitude the aircraft could pull 4g without difficulty, though this involved a steady loss of height.

Regarding developments it could have benefited from, the Scimitar had too thick a wing for good high altitude performance. But that wing, used in conjunction with 'blown' flaps, did allow this large, heavy aircraft to operate from our small carriers. A thin-wing Scimitar would undoubtedly have had a higher approach speed, which would have prevented it from operating on carriers in no wind or light wind condition. A more comprehensive boundary layer control arrangement (as came later in the Buccaneer) might have enabled a thinner wing to be used whilst keeping the approach speed sufficiently low, but this would have involved a major redesign and might have proved impracticable for any number of reasons.

Compared to USN aircraft of the day, the Americans couldn't believe that an aircraft with as much thrust as the Scimitar was not supersonic in level flight. Of course this was due to the comparatively thick wing, which enabled it to fly at a speed low enough to operate from our small carriers. Contemporary USN aircraft of similar roles were generally underpowered in comparison, but they invariably had much greater range and endurance.

I do not think that a Scimitar landing could be described as a controlled crash. The pilot set up a constant rate of decent, like any aircraft making a deck landing, and flew the machine into the deck - where it stayed, without any tendency to bounce like say, a Gannet or a Firefly. The same technique was generally used ashore and was good since the aircraft was often (depending on the stores configuration) on the wrong side of the speed/drag curve and any attempt to flare would simply have increased the rate of descent. The Scimitar had an enormously strong undercarriage. It was designed, of course, for high rates of decent during deck landing. Perhaps it is not surprising that onlookers thought of each arrival as a controlled crash.

It is worth noting that on one occasion in *Victorious* a No.803 Scimitar landed with such a high rate of descent that although the undercarriage stood up to the extra punishment, both tyres blew out and the intense heat caused the wheel brakes to fuse to the metal deck. The aircraft was immobile and had to be cut free! Luckily this Scimitar was the last aircraft to land on in that recovery. Perhaps this particular landing was indeed something of a controlled crash!

Finally another incident I will relate. It was 1961 and I was taking part in a display by No.800's *Red Blades* team at the SBAC Show, Farnborough. One of my tasks was to do a high speed inverted fly-past while another group of Scimitars were turning around to come back to the airfield. The Scimitar was a superbly controllable aircraft and this manoeuvre presented no particular difficulty; you just turned the machine on its back and pushed the stick forward to stop it flying into the ground. But on the Thursday of Farnborough Week, I didn't get it right: maybe I should have raised the nose a bit more before inverting the aircraft. Anyway all seemed well as I passed the crowd at 500 knots, 200 feet, but as I crossed the airfield boundary I noticed that the ground was getting closer. Despite full forward stick we were going downhill! Things happen fast at that speed, but the Scimitar had an extremely fast rate of roll and by applying full aileron for a fraction of a second I was able to roll to the upright position in no time at all and then climbed away.

This incident didn't worry me personally, because the Scimitar was such a brilliant performer at low level, but years later I met a Naval doctor who had been watching from the RAF Officers Mess and he thought the worst was about to happen.

Interestingly, the Scimitar was equipped shortly afterwards with a larger tailplane. This of course would have prevented the nose from dropping with full forward stick, indeed the aircraft would probably have been able to climb away inverted.

Would I do it all again? I'd be delighted to fly a Scimitar again, even for one sortie. Maybe I was lucky, but it never let me down and so my memories are happy ones.

### Lt Cdr A.J.Goodenough

I joined No.736 Squadron under training in the OFS at Lossiemouth in August 1959, flying Sea Hawks. I believe that Nos.75 and 76 Courses merged due to the large number of trainees who did not complete BFT/AFT at No.1 Flying Training School, RAF Linton-on-Ouse. In December that year I was given an introduction to swept-wing flying in Hunter T.8s of No.764 Squadron and in January 1960 returned to No.736 for Scimitar conversion.

I joined No.800 Squadron in May 1960 and spent 18 months as a "Squadron Joe", leaving in November 1961. I flew a total of 260 hours in the Scimitar and made 120 deck landings (and one bolter!).

I was relatively inexperienced when I first flew the Scimitar, but on my first take-off, just as my first catapult launch and deck landing (both in the Scimitar), I had been so well briefed that it all seem to go like clockwork. The only real surprise was the rate of climb.

Familiarisation 1 was on Runway 23 at Lossiemouth. "Go up to 90 knots and brake to a halt", was the brief. The acceleration was far greater than I had anticipated and it provided quite a good introduction to my first take-off, but nothing could have prepared me for the amazing rate of climb once airborne. I hardly had time to draw breath after rotating before I was through 10,000 feet and going up like a rocket.

From Lossiemouth I joined No.800 Squadron, who were already embarked in HMS *Ark Royal* in the Mediterranean. I flew onto the ship from Hal Far, Malta, and spent the next 18 months doing a whole lot of different things: LABS, including hurtling a 2,000lb. 'Shape' in the general direction of Filfla, In-flight refuelling, beginning with a short course at Tarrant Rushton in Dorset flying Canberras with the quite recently-formed Flight Refuelling Ltd, Roller Map, *Blue Silk* and Sidewinder trials etc.

I think the greatest fun was being disembarked at Hal Far. In a previous existence I had been in a Coastal Minesweeper plodding around the Mediterranean at 15 knots. Now I could hurtle about at 600 knots over the clear blue sea, dropping bombs, firing rockets, and then back to Hal Far for a run ashore at J.D's or the White Horse in the evenings. It was all a marvellous experience.

One thing I can recall very well was when we went north in *Ark Royal* and were doing cold weather trials off of Greenland and looking down on the ship steaming through the Arctic sea smoke with pack ice on the horizon.

The Scimitar was certainly the most exciting aircraft I have flown. Flying solo is always more fun (with due respect to Observers); this aircraft was so strongly built and powerful that you could really lose your inhibitions in it - but you could not afford to lose your concentration.

In July 1961 I was sent from Lossiemouth to RAF North Front at Gibraltar. I was loaned to No.804 Squadron and joined *Hermes* as she sailed off Gib. I was invited to do a 20° dive-bombing sortie on *Hermes'* splash target. In one dive I had a classic case of target fixation and knew that I had come pretty close to the water during the pull-out. It was not until I had landed back on board that I was shown just how close - the drain pipe on the belly of the aircraft was not missing, as reported elsewhere, but stripped clean of paint by the sea. This had a distinct sobering effect on me, and the CO of No.804 Sqn was not amused!

The turning performance at 30,000ft plus was very poor. If time had permitted, some thinning of the wing might have been useful. An internal starter would have saved carting a Palouste around on a valuable wing station when ground starting was not available.

Low speed handling was good. You set up the approach to land with everything hanging down, hence a lot of drag and engine RPM. You could make corrections to the rate of descent using very small throttle movements. There was so much power available it was easy to overcorrect, and you drove it down the glidepath until the wheels hit the deck. The undercarriage, made by Dowty, was an amazingly strong piece of kit.

High speed control was also good, very responsive controls, terrific rate of roll - you just had to watch out for PIO at low altitude. If you carried wing tanks and/or bombs there was a lot more drag, but you needed tanks if you were going to fly a reasonable sortie. I think the deck cycle (launch to recovery) was only 35 minutes for a clean aircraft.

For deck landings you had to get used to the large hook-eye distance and trust the mirror-projector sight absolutely; it always looked as though you were too high to catch a wire. Single engine approaches were OK provided you remembered: No blow, No airbrake, No fuselage flap (it's still there after 37 years).

Another incident which I still remember clearly was when the squadron launched from *Ark Royal* to fly ashore. I was the last off. Halfway through the catapult stroke I heard the starboard engine power decrease (yes, both throttles were fully open), and once off the deck I had to get onto the ground cushion to keep flying. I struggled near the water with the starboard engine registering about 80% power for what seemed a very long time. Meanwhile the rest of the outfit were circling overhead waiting for me to join, and since I hadn't said anything over the radio - although I was talking to myself a fair bit - the CO (Danny Norman) had no idea what was going on below. "Buck up Red Seven", he said. I told him I was doing my best.

I gradually eased my way up to a more acceptable height, and the engine slowly regained power. The report on the engine check following the flight read: 'Investigated, no fault found.' Does that sound familiar? I just wish that the clock could be put back to when I was 24 and having the time of my life flying this great machine. It was of course a serious and very professional business, but the performance of the aircraft, the camaraderie of the squadrons, and the remarkable understanding of our seniors when complaints about low flying, sonic bangs dropped over grouse moors, etc filtered back to base made it a great pleasure.

### Captain F.Hefford OBE DSC AFC

I was Senior Pilot of No.807 Squadron from December 1959 until July 1961, and logged 295 hours 45 min.

I can remember my first take-off. I had flown a good variety of jets, but I had never experienced such fantastic acceleration before, and I was quite sure I would never get the undercarriage up before I had reached the limiting speed. The aircraft was clean and attained climbing speed very quickly. I think it was 10,000 feet before I caught up with the aircraft.

I would not agree that landing a Scimitar was almost a controlled crash. The hook to pilot's eye distance was as I remember 19ft, which made the runway look far away at touchdown, but the landing was not a crash. You could however get a nice rate of sink on if you let the aircraft slip to the wrong side of the drag curve. It was the shape of the drag curve in the approach configuration that made the Scimitar a real challenge during deck landing. Speed control was not easy.

Compared to other jet aircraft I have flown, the Scimitar was, in its day, a very good interceptor and strike aircraft. It was sufficiently challenging to fly to make the pilot feel good when he had mastered it. The aircraft was very powerful but unfortunately had a big drag rise with speed. It was not as nice to fly as the Hawker products, but it could out climb most aircraft and was difficult to catch at low level.

There is a story that the pitch-up problem was cured by accident during wind tunnel testing. A lunch break was taken, the model was removed for minor adjustment and a young apprentice, when re-assembling the model, put the tailplane on upside down. It had always had dihedral, it now had anhedral. No-one noticed his error and the tunnel was again run. The results were better than ever before and when investigated the upside down tailplane was found. From then on the Scimitar flew with an anhedral tailplane.

Compared with USN aircraft of the time, the Scimitar lacked range, endurance and payload.

My most dangerous moment while flying the Scimitar was a deck landing accident aboard *Ark Royal*. Because of the lack of speed stability (the flat-bottomed drag curve), I had decided to try a single throttle approach technique, it was based on the system used by the auto-throttle in the Sea Vixen. The idea was to set one throttle at the mean approach power, then control speed with the other throttle. This gave very fine adjustment and worked well until the day of the accident. On that day, *Ark* had about 45 knots of wind over the deck and this sometimes produced a downdraught astern of the ship on the approach path. I entered the downdraught, saw the speed dropping and a sink develop, pushed the inboard throttle to full power but as the quarter deck appeared in my windscreen it became apparent that I needed everything there was. With full power on both, my hook tore out the sodium light on the round-down. The aircraft hit the deck hard and all the hydraulic power was lost but fortunately the hook caught a wire and I was able to walk away. The aircraft XD318 was not repairable on board. We had a splendid team in *Ark*, led by Captain Hill-Norton who visited the Wardroom that night to meet us all. Jock Tofts introduced me to the Captain who said, "Hefford! Don't mention that name to me, it's imprinted on my memory for ever" and I replied, rather cheekily "and on the back end of your ship too, Sir". It was about two years later that Alan 'Spiv' Leahy, Captain of another Scimitar outfit, said to me, "You know, I cursed you when as a result of your Deck Landing accident, single throttle technique was banned, it was the best way to get aboard".

My best moment was the day Jock Tofts and I were launched from *Ark* whilst she was moored in Grand Harbour, Malta. It was, I believe, the first time a jet had been launched in harbour. *Victorious* was moored very close to us but her catapults were shorter than ours, and she was unable to launch her aircraft.

The amount of hydraulic failures the Scimitar suffered from did not give me cause for concern. We ensured we all knew our drills. I only experienced two Hydraulic 1 and one Hydraulic 2 failure during my time in the aircraft. One of these was a bit hairy since it occurred at very low level over the sea on a pitch black night.

There was a memorable night when Jock Tofts and I were tasked with a night strike against *Hermes*. Jock, I believe, was the only Scimitar C.O. to take night strikes seriously and to his credit the whole Squadron was night qualified, but in the event the flying fell to us both. We were launched with two Vixens, which were to lead us into the strike using their radar. We hadn't been airborne long when we were recalled as our target was still in harbour. Jock asked me if I would like to join up with him and return as a pair, it seemed like a good idea at the time. The join up turned out to be rather hairy, as when I asked Jock to switch his Nav lights to steady dim, they went out altogether, leaving me staring into a black void. The next I heard was Jock saying "Can you see me?". I replied "No", whereupon Jock said "I can see you - I'm looking right up your jet pipes". Two very shattered Scimitar pilots eventually landed onboard. Not for long though, since we were asked to go again by Dickie Reynolds, Commander (Air). I was most reluctant and I don't think Jock was all that keen. No Vixens were available, one of the aircraft we had used was unserviceable and its replacement was a shocker for night flying since it had a vibrating instrument panel, which was extremely difficult to read under red cockpit lighting. We did our duty though in spite of it being a dark and cloudy, moonless night. I see from my log book I had a Hydraulic 1 failure and needed two GCAs to get aboard. As a result of our efforts we were able to write a paper on night operations and the Scimitar in particular, which resulted in better deck lighting and put a stop to Scimitar night deck ops., until Audio ASI or Angle of Attack had been fitted. Perhaps our sister squadron, No.800 led by Danny Norman, were sharper than we, as they never quite got to night ops from the Carrier. The problem with the Scimitar was the speed instability on the approach. As I've mentioned, this could be coped with by day when there were plenty of visual cues, but at night it required a great deal of concentration. If Audio Airspeed or Angle of Attack had been fitted the task would have been greatly simplified.

The Scimitar could have benefited from higher reliability, a better fuel system and a Navigation/Attack System. Also a small Intercept radar and an Air-to-Air missile.

If the clock could be put back, would you do it all again? Yes - but I would like to miss out the hairy episodes, thanks!

### Commander G.R.Higgs AFC

Commanding Officer Naval Test Flight, RAE Bedford 1955 until 1957. No.700X Squadron 1958. No.803 Squadron Senior Pilot 3 June 1958 until 25 September 1958. Commanding Officer 25 September 1958 until 18 December 1959. Logged 14 hours in the N.113 prototype, and 250 hours day, 10 hours night in the Scimitar.

I can recall my first take-off, it was one of considerable 'poke', but I had already flown the DH.110 (Sea Vixen prototype) and the N.113 and was well used to aircraft of the Hunter/Swift type and research aircraft with high performance. Nevertheless the Scimitar was very stimulating and certainly took you along with it. Mind you, the acceleration during flight at low level to its maximum permitted IAS was second to none and very exhilarating even when well accustomed to it.

I flew the Scimitar many times with BLC off as part of the test programme including carrying out the initial catapult clearance trials ashore and in *Ark Royal*, unblown free take-offs and unblown landings. The catapult trials consisted of gradually reducing launch (end) speeds to the minimum possible in that particular configuration both blown and unblown. The aircraft was very sensitive longitudinally in the unblown case and relatively small stick movements could generate quite exciting aircraft pitching moments. On one occasion, incorrect calculations from the boffins determining tailplane trim angle for the predicted catapult end speed resulted in an uncontrolled pitch-up at the end of the launch even with full forward stick applied to correct. Only the high acceleration of the aircraft (particularly in its unblown state) prevented a catastrophic outcome. At this time too, the head-rest was totally inadequate for catapulting, being too far back, and this coupled with the very high incidence achieved on that particular launch, gave an excellent impression of a vertical launch.

I disagree that landing the Scimitar was almost a controlled crash, most certainly not. Landing the Scimitar was an acceptable and satisfying challenge and touch down on airfields could be cushioned by judicious increase in power with slight increase in incidence just prior to touch down. The same technique could be employed - and I invariably did - in carrier landings but considerable care was necessary, and the practice required experience and precise knowledge of the handling of the aircraft.

The greatest mistake was any attempt to reduce power prior to touch down, or indeed in the latter stages of the approach, since this would almost certainly induce an unacceptably high rate of descent which would be difficult to correct.

How would I compare the Scimitar to other jet aircraft I have flown? At the time it was one of the liveliest aircraft around with better acceleration than any other in service with the possible exception of the Lightning. Its forte was low and medium altitude but at high altitude it displayed its shortcomings and its low "g" threshold was distinctly embarrassing if the direction officer required a late large alteration of course during an intercept.

I never unintentionally experienced Inertia Coupling while flying the Scimitar. The aircraft was not prone to any great degree of coupling unless grossly mishandled and the warning signs ignored.

*Lt Cdr G.R.Higgs the CO of No.803 Squadron during 1958/9 in the cockpit of Scimitar '145/V', probably XD238. (via N.Parker)*

The tendency to pitch up was not a real problem. Unlike some other aircraft of this time, it was unusable since once you reached the onset of buffet, the resulting pitching movements became uncontrollable in a manoeuvring sense. With some aircraft, manoeuvre in the buffet zone could be used to tactical advantage.

In comparison with US Navy aircraft of the time, on the whole it compared very favourably in performance although the Crusader had been in service with a realistic Mach 1 plus performance and basic radar, and the A4D in the strike role, although lacking the performance at lower altitudes of the Scimitar, was better equipped with Navaids. The USN had a broader inventory of aircraft for Naval tasks and guided weapons had long been in service. One must remember too that the F4H Phantom began to replace the F3H in USN service within a year or so of the Scimitar's introduction to the Fleet and this marked a new era altogether in carrier-borne aircraft.

My most dangerous moment while flying the Scimitar? This is easy. During a demonstration off the east coast of the United States in front of a large number of Congressmen, Senators and Senior Service Chiefs from the US armed forces, I carried out a low level high speed attack on the ship culminating in a high (about 7g) 'g' pull up at close to 700 knots. Soon after the rotation, the hood parted company with the aircraft and my visor parted company with my helmet, The sensation was of a tornado swirling around inside the cockpit and I remember trying to keep my hands inside the cockpit and my eyeballs in their sockets. The completion of the manoeuvre with a roll out the top was more by instinct and feel since I could see nothing until the speed reduced, my eyes stopped watering and the maps and other loose articles, such as my briefing pad which had torn loose, either settled inside the cockpit or were lost for ever over the side. The initial decompression inside the cockpit was literally quite breathtaking and I would strongly recommend the experience to anyone who believes he has had the ultimate thrill in an open top sports car. After we had sorted ourselves out, it was really quite pleasant flying around at low speed, reminiscent of former days of yore, and the landing back on board was uneventful. Another first.

I would consider my best moment was the completion of Night Deck Landing Trials in *Victorious* in 1959. Although these would normally have been the responsibility of the Naval Test Squadron at Boscombe Down, they pleaded lack of current experience in night deck landings. We didn't have any either but Charles Evans, FOAC in *Victorious,* thought he might take a slice of notoriety and volunteered me. I, in turn, nominated Lt John Beard as back-up (in the event, time did not permit him to work up and take part). After a number of catapult launches at RAE Bedford, a series of trials were completed in *Victorious* including 19 arrested landings and about 6 rollers to check the missed wire procedure. The Scimitar was not an ideal night carrier aircraft; in fact it was b....y unpleasant primarily because of the very nose high attitude on the approach and resultant considerable 'hook to eye' distance. In addition a strong tendency of the aircraft to pitch forward on touch down was difficult to counteract in the 'missed wire' case. This meant that the fairly large rotation required to regain the flying attitude was difficult to achieve on a dark night with no reference points in the very short time before you ran out of deck. The initial loss of height over the bow on one or two occasions gave those in the 'goofers' their money's worth I was told, although to be perfectly honest, inside the cockpit, it wasn't in the least bit alarming. I couldn't see much value in Scimitar night carrier operations and I doubted whether the risk element involved in continuation training could be justified against the rare occasion of operational need bearing in mind particularly the lack of radar or all weather Navigation Aids.

I suffered several hydraulic failures but only one caused real concern. This occurred when the tail skid ran off the reinforced tracking during a cross wind catapult launch in the Mediterranean. The catapult track in *Victorious* was then quite narrow before it was later modified and would not contend with any slewing of the aircraft longitudinally during the launch due to cross winds. It was of course necessary to launch out of wind for tactical (ships) purpose from time to time, and on this particular launch the wind was about 35 degrees on the bow when the launch commenced, causing the aircraft to slew to the point where the down force on the tail skid caused corrugation of the deck eventually leading to fracture of the tail skid about two thirds the way down the launch. This in turn led to Hydraulic 1 failure. All this during the 2 seconds or so of the launch was quite exciting but it had its good points since I had an unscheduled trip ashore in North Africa for an emergency landing, where the Squadron maintenance team performed magnificently in repairing it under conditions which were far from ideal with little support equipment.

The Scimitar could have benefited from a new wing for improved manoeuvrability at altitude (which of course would have impaired its low altitude strike role for which it later became more useful). Realistically, for its period, it should have been equipped with better Nav/Attack systems. Its equipment was scarcely an improvement on Second World War systems from a practical fighting point of view although the instruments for all weather flying were obviously more advanced.

If the clock could be put back, would I do it all again? With the greatest of pleasure.

❖❖❖❖❖❖❖❖❖❖❖❖❖❖❖❖❖❖❖❖❖

### Lt Cdr G.B.Hoddinott

No.700X Squadron for Scimitar conversion, September 1958. No.807 Squadron September 1958 until March 1960. Logged 422 hours 15 min, including 21 hours and 45 minutes night flying with 4 night deck landings.

On my first take-off, I remember thinking: "This is a piece of p***!". I had flown the Swift Mk.5 for 15 months whilst on

*No.807 Squadron pilots and maintenance heads of departments at Farnborough in September 1959. Left to right – standing unknown; back row, unidentified, Lt Paul Perks, Sub-Lt Ian Aitchison and Lt Cdr T.C.Leece (Senior Pilot); front row Lt G.B.Hoddinott, Lt Cdr K.A.Leppard (CO) and Lt David Pentreath. (via Mike Hooks)*

exchange with the RAF in No.2 Squadron in Germany, so high speed and high rate of climb aircraft were familiar.

I disagree that landing the Scimitar was almost a controlled crash, because the aircraft was flown on the "backside of the drag curve" during an approach to landing. The aircraft's speed and height were controlled by the throttle. In the landing configuration the aircraft was extremely stable and speed and height could be very accurately controlled by finite movement of the throttle. it was an extremely good aircraft to deck land.

Comparing the Scimitar to other jet aircraft I have flown, it was not as satisfying as the Buccaneer but at the time exhilarating and exciting

I cannot say that I ever really experienced a dangerous moment. However after a close formation flypast it was discovered on landing that a shock wave had caused considerable damage to my tailplane - this was not apparent whilst flying.

Due to the amount of hydraulic failures the Scimitar suffered from, did this ever give you cause for concern? No, I do not consider hydraulic failure occurred that frequently.

I consider that the aircraft had reached its design limits. As an American once said: "Only the British could build an aircraft with all that power and still remain sub-sonic".

❖❖❖❖❖❖❖❖❖❖❖❖❖❖❖❖❖❖❖❖❖❖❖❖

**Commander David Howard**

My only Scimitar squadron was No.800. I joined in September 1961, as the squadron Air Warfare Instructor, and left exactly two years later as the acting Senior Pilot. Jock Mancais relieved Danny Norman shortly after I joined but my first flight in the squadron, with all of 5 hours of familiarisation under my belt, was low level formation with Danny. He spent most of the sortie at about 100ft over the Moray Firth in steep turns with me on the inside, below him with nowhere to go, so I had to stay with it. Danny's debriefing was simply "That was OK, Dave" plus the memorable Norman grin - I'd lost about half a stone but assumed I was accepted.

I think I logged about 500 hours in the Scimitar and, before my first flight, had the standard simulator runs amounting to about 5.30 hrs.

My first take-off in the Scimitar impressed me. You had this gorgeous acceleration from those two darned great engines you were strapped to and, relative to all my previous aircraft (all single engined) you felt you were being pressed back into your seat. This was no surprise as briefings had warned you about it. It was just very enjoyable.

I don't think I ever had to fly the Scimitar with BLC off. I can't remember the implications but guess it was one of those experiences to avoid. I must have been lucky.

I don't agree that landing the Scimitar was almost a controlled crash (bear in mind that I flew the Buccaneer afterwards, with the same landing technique). Perhaps it could be considered to be after previous aircraft when a flare out was necessary - and trying to flare a Scimitar produced an uncontrolled crash!

What was different, in my opinion, was the importance of the vertical component of thrust. We'd always been taught to ride the glidepath on the throttle. In the Scimitar this was vital and if you tried to 'pole it down the glidepath' you really got into trouble, especially coming to the deck.

Hydraulics were rarely a problem for me except for one catastrophic failure when I lost the lot (covered later).

If I ever experienced Inertia Coupling it must have been minimal. I'm not aware it was ever a problem and I did a lot of aerobatics including the sort of manoeuvres that might have induced cross coupling.

My most dangerous moment flying the Scimitar was when a bomb I'd dropped cooked off early. We were attacking some old landing craft off Malta and our bombs were fused with an obsolescent fuse that relied on barometric pressure for its activation. One of my bombs exploded way above the surface and suddenly I was flying a pepper-pot with hydraulic fluid leaking away fast and alarm warnings saying so. Fortunately Luqa was fairly close and I got in there safely.

Meanwhile back at the ranch Jock Mancais was certain his AWI had released the bomb too low and collected his own shrapnel that way. I was only saved by the Range Safety Officer - Jake Arbuthnott, Gunnery Officer and a pilot too - who witnessed the attack and came up on the R/T immediately - even before my hydraulic warning sounded - and reported that the bomb had gone off early. Jock is sceptical even to this day.

My best time with the Scimitar was out in the Far East in *Ark* in 1962. We gave a *Showboat* exercise - a demonstration of carrier operations - two days running. On both days the carrier ran like a Swiss watch, the launches and recoveries were immaculate, landing intervals slick, and the weapon attacks on the splash target impressive. For two days that aircraft carrier did exactly what its name implied - it flew aircraft and it flew them darned well, and every man in the ship knew and was proud of it.

Compared with other aircraft I'd flown, the Scimitar was a whole new generation for me. It was my first twin-engined aircraft and something special in acceleration both on take-off and in the air, particularly at low level - if you opened those throttles at low level you really got up and went - with a fuel consumption that was awesome. Something else that was new for me was the fuel flowmeter, which might have been mechanically linked to the throttles judging by the way it wound up when you pushed them forward. At low level the aircraft was enormous fun; obviously not as manoeuvrable as the Hunter or Sea Hawk, and using a tremendous amount of sky, but a joy-ride - for as long as your fuel lasted! At high level it was totally different and your ability to turn almost non-existent. The only aircraft I know that was worse at high level was the F-3 Demon - a misnomer if ever there was one. Against the Demon a Scimitar felt almost high performance at 35,000ft but only because, at that height, the Demon could barely deviate from straight and level. Even so, the Scimitar was still fun – but you've got to come down some time! Overall a most enjoyable aircraft to fly - with an element of fun about it that perhaps there wasn't in other aircraft.

Without doubt the Scimitar could have done with some sort of reliable navigation system. The amount of ground you covered at the speeds available involved too much wrestling with a map. As I was a 'thumbnail' navigator this could end up in me being lost all too often. It wasn't all my own fault though - in 1963 I got hopelessly lost in southern Italy trying to find my way in a Scimitar using a chart based on an Italian AA map dated 1933. I was 30 minutes late for Charlie time but the Captain was extremely nice about the whole affair. Jock Mancais was rather less so. It would be easy but unrealistic to say the Scimitar would have been better off with more sophisticated weapons. Weapons were coming along but, in the Scimitar's time, it was still steam bombs, rockets and guns plus, latterly, Bullpup which was already obsolescent when the Scimitar finally got it. I think the main improvements I would have appreciated would have been that Nav. system and perhaps something - anything - to have improved its high level handling qualities.

Pitch-up was never a problem for me. I was aware of the possibilities but was lucky enough to avoid them.

Comparing the Scimitar with US Navy contemporary aircraft - I've already mentioned the Demon which, unusually for the US, was a disaster. I suppose the contemporary USN equivalent was the A-4. It didn't have the speed of the Scimitar but, in every other respect, was far superior - better range, a handier aircraft, more compact, and with a staggering weapon carrying capability for what was a fairly small aircraft. Additionally the A-4 was extremely versatile in the number of different marks that were developed, and this stemmed from the very sound basic airframe design. Generally, I would say that the USN contemporary Scimitar equivalents were better. The Scimitar, as I remember, was an interim aircraft designed to span the gap between the Sea Hawk and the Buccaneer. As such it had no development stretch (as did the A-4) and I don't think it could have stayed in service any longer, even with more advanced navigation aids and weapon delivery systems. In fact it stayed in service much too long - as many of the last front line squadron, No.803, will testify since many of them had to eject, and some more than once. You also have to remember that it wasn't only dated in its in-flight characteristics and performance.

On the ground it was a nightmare to maintain and, the older it got, the worse it got. And to exacerbate this, the aircraft was extended into a new era of technology; maintenance procedures and concepts that had completely overtaken the principles applying when the Scimitar went to the drawing board. I think my recollections of the aircraft are strongest, not in the air or on the deck, but down in the hangar in the evenings at sea after we had stopped flying. The lower hangar in the *Ark* was directly over the boiler-rooms and many of the lads' messes were at the same level so, in the Far East, it was like living and working in a sauna. Add to that - drip-trays! The Scimitar used to drip fuel and hydraulic fluid from every seam and orifice and had to have trays under the wings as well as the fuselage. All had to be emptied regularly and generally made life even more uncomfortable for the maintainers who frequently were sloshing around as they struggled to produce a full house of aircraft for the next day's operations. And they usually achieved it. Perhaps one positive outcome from the Scimitar was a grittier, 'won't be beaten' generation of maintainers.

Low speed and high speed (at low level) handling was good. Coming to the deck was a delight and great fun because you could wind the Scimitar up into quite a tight circuit. This often alarmed Donald Gibson, when he was Captain, because he once removed his pipe from his mouth (alarm warning for a humble little pilot), to explain in the nicest possible way, that he would have a problem getting a new landing sight in the Far East if I wrote it off on one of my deck landings. High level handling was ponderous. I once did a quarter attack on a Vulcan at 35,000ft which, just outside Sidewinder range, applied all of 20 degrees of bank into the curve of pursuit which left me on that all too familiar 'burble' of the high speed stall and powerless to follow. About the only thing you could compete with at high level was another Scimitar - or the Demon.

Low level handling was fun all round although, at high speed, you covered a lot of sky.

With different weapon configurations the handling could change. Hanging four 1,000lb bombs on what was already a dragmaster made you think a bit, especially launching in the Far East in low wind conditions. There was noticeably more drag and the acceleration, normally good - was badly degraded.

An incident which I'd rather hadn't happened but is amusing to look back on now, involved the boss - Jock Mancais and his box 4 plus me as the singleton fill-in when Jock was off-stage. Our aeros routine ended in a grand finale of the foursome bomb- bursting as I shot up through the middle of them. This particular show was for another crowd of embarked VIPs out in the Far East - lots of humidity and impressive vaporisation in the low pressure areas over the wings and fuselage of the Scimitars at high speed. Calculation of how I got to the middle of the bomb-burst at the right time was pure, Mark 1 eyeball guesstimation, not my long suit at any time. As I raced past the stern of *Ark* at about 50ft and 620 kts in a white cloud of vapour, I knew I'd 'overcooked' it and was early. Closing speed was about 1,000 kts and, in that split-second reaction that stark terror induces, I radioed, "Break early please, boss", and Jock came back with, "Say again". There's not a lot you can do in that situation except go where the others think you're going to go - so I did - and they all peeled away around me. This was perhaps our most impressive bomb-burst finale. I think it was also our last. At the debriefing I asked Jock why, totally uncharacteristically, he'd gone deaf. But he wasn't deaf it was simply that he'd seen me vaporising, knew I was early, and had seized up. But he'd also done what I'd done - gone where the others expected him to go - but rather earlier than normal, which is what the other three had done. The other three were in no doubt - as they impressed on me during the debriefing.

Next to the most exhilarating and satisfying period of my Scimitar flying - *Showboat* - was Bullpup, the US air-to-ground pilot command missile. For Peter Marshall and myself, the two squadron AWIs, this was totally new ground. We'd used our Bullpup simulator as best we could but knew that it was, supposedly, not too realistic. Our target was a rock somewhere off the Philippines. So we launched, found our rock and fired - with quite some success for first-timers. I'm not a fan for the principle of Bullpup - follow it on down while you guide it - and much prefer the 'fire and forget' principle, but this was something different, new and, perhaps, the natural lot of an interim aircraft which, essentially, spanned a time of change not only in basic airframes, but in technology and principles, including weapons.

One incident I'd definitely decline to repeat was a failure of the cabin air-conditioning, as usual on full hot. A chum of mine - a cabin mate, Geoff Ellis - had had to be wheeled down to sick-bay after landing back on in this condition. My failure occurred during a flypast over Hong Kong in which I was the box number in the Scimitar element of a mass flypast group from *Ark* prior to her arrival in Hong Kong. With the ambient air temperature warm, and hot air pumping into the cockpit from whatever stage of the engine compressors, everything in the cockpit gets unbearably hot - not least because most of it is metal. You can just get by flying formation with an occasional nudge of the throttle and then - hands off because it's too hot. But you can't let go of the stick - or at least, I couldn't. I eventually solved the problem by inching a handkerchief out of my flying overalls pocket and tying it around the top of the stick (all this in formation). By holding the two ends I achieved quite reasonable control (in Jock's opinion better than usual!) and got through the flypast and the recovery to the deck, and a long, cold shower.

Another significant occasion was an embarkation flying from Lossiemouth to *Ark Royal* somewhere off Majorca. Because of the Scimitar's range limitations this extended passage necessitated in-flight refuelling over France. At the time, and in typical naval fashion, we were fitted 'for, but not with' the flight refuelling capability. We therefore asked for, and got, the heavy metal to enable us, and off we went - to mayhem. We had been fitted with straight - as in horizontal - probes, but, because the Scimitar, at the low in-flight refuelling speed, was 'sitting up' at a high angle of attack, the straight probe could not lock into the drogue of the tanker. But it did half open the fuel flow, and the result was kerosene all over the place - down the intakes, over the cockpit canopy, through the cabin air-conditioning. We even had flame-outs - a bit alarming since the Scimitar didn't glide at all well. Our alert AEO quickly diagnosed that this time it wasn't pilot problems - fair assumption albeit subjective and ordered, and fitted droop snoot probes. Problem solved. Off we went across France and, apart from one lad who had to divert, probably on pleasure bent, to a French airfield, we landed on in *Ark* somewhere off Majorca - sore but satisfied; it was a very long sortie. This was something of an achievement for the Scimitar.

Finally, if I could put the clock back, I would do it all over again. I thoroughly enjoyed every moment of that period of my flying career, and I look back on the Scimitar with a great deal of affection and happy memories.

## Lt Cdr Maurice T. Hynett

No.736 Squadron, student November 1959 until February 1960. No.804 Squadron March 1960 until September 1961. No.736 Squadron i/c Scimitar Simulator and Tactical Instructor October 1961 until April 1963. No.803 Squadron Assistant AWI November 1963 until December 1963. No.736 Squadron Assistant AWI. ETPS (Scimitar in fleet), Test Pilot student February 1964 until December 1964. Weapon Flight, RAE Farnborough. Experimental Flying Department (Scimitar in fleet) January 1965 until April 1968. Logged 510.05 hours.

Can I remember my thoughts on my first take-off, and did the acceleration surprise me? Yes! A real aircraft at last. How would I compare the Scimitar to other jet aircraft I have flown? Total types flown: 156. The one for which I had the greatest affection, the most memorable, and the one I would pay a lot to fly again: The Scimitar.

What developments do I think the Scimitar could have benefited from? After-burners.

My most memorable flight?: I had a terrible cold one morning but it would never have occurred to me to lie warm in a bed and let a respectable indisposition overtake me. The suffocating regime of my job had so stifled my imagination that even a fully justified day off was beyond my conception. I knew that four students were booked at half-hourly intervals from 0900 onwards; and knew that my morning would be spent without break in the air-conditioned, artificially lit caravan I had learned to refer to as 'the office. I ate my breakfast without enthusiasm, unable to taste the porridge which my wife had prepared in an attempt to keep out the December cold. I put on my uniform cap and snuffily pecked her cheek, promising vaguely and nasally to be back for lunch, and at least to consider the idea of staying at home for the afternoon.

The car was sluggish as the cold, thick oil fought the battery almost to the death. The coldness of the driving seat penetrated the doeskin of my uniform; the heater churned out the ambient iciness of the northern Scottish air, beginning to warm only when I was halfway between Elgin and Lossiemouth.

An Admiralty policeman blocked my entrance at the main gate of HMS *Fulmar*, the Royal Naval Air Station, Lossiemouth. A naval ritual was incongruously in progress; white-gaitered sailors, with silver chains and bosun's pipes, stood rigidly to attention in the Scottish countryside as the white ensign was raised self-consciously in the cold, blue air.

Inside the huge caravan which housed the flight simulator, the servos of the analogue computer were warm and functioning, watched with loving care by the four Chief Petty Officer technicians who made up his staff. 'Heart of oak are our ships'! By 0900 I was seated at my control console, ready to start the daily routine.

The boredom of the job was overwhelming. Each day, unfortunate student pilots were instructed in flight procedures, and exposed to mock emergency situations, as obscure and severe as only a desperately bored man could devise. I knew the job pretty much backwards: I had flown in a carrier-borne Scimitar squadron, and knew the aircraft's systems as well as any engineer. Now, I was halfway through a 'ground tour,' and had not seen an aircraft carrier for over a year. My appointment to this ground job had been a great disappointment.

At 1130 the morning's schedule had been completed. From then on, throughout the day, squadron senior pilots would attempt to send their junior pilots my way for routine training. I was determined to go home early for lunch and to take my wife's advice for the afternoon. The senior pilots would telephone in vain.

As I was telling the technicians of my intentions, the telephone rang; I was inclined to ignore it. My conscience beat me, and I recognised the voice of the station's Lieutenant Commander Flying. An invitation to deliver a Hunter jet trainer to Yeovilton in Somerset was not to be refused. No pilot on a ground tour ever refuses a chance to fly. I had not flown a Hunter for some time, and my sinuses were fully blocked, but no one was asking any questions. Anyway, the Hunter was only a lady's shopping sort of aircraft. I knew it would be all right once I was in the cockpit: the Hunter's switches and instruments would still be where they always were, and the aircraft's pure oxygen was a panacea for all ills.

I struggled into a rubberised immersion suit and grabbed the remainder of my flying gear. The inner helmet with its built-in radio earphones, the hard outer helmet the 'bone dome' still painted in the colours of my former squadron, the black 'P' type oxygen mask, the Mae West with its electronic survival attachments, the leg restraint garters with which I would tie my legs to the aircraft's ejection seat, and finally the ubiquitous cape leather flying gloves. Although I felt like the Dauphin going to war in full armour, I knew that they had all hung far too long in the locker, souvenirs of my former self.

The flight from Lossiemouth to Yeovilton was more than four hundred and fifty miles and took fifty minutes. I parked the Hunter outside Yeovilton's control tower at 1255; my sinuses ached.

Summoned over the radio by the Air Traffic Controller to report to Commander Air's office, I wondered what infringement of the local rules I had made. These night fighter people followed rules of their own. Strike fighter pilots like myself prided themselves on following no rules at all. I confronted the Commander in his control tower office. Although feeling shabby in the dull, grey immersion suit, and although I was two ranks junior to the immaculately groomed Naval commander, the defiance in my attitude was unmistakable.

I was surprised, therefore, at the friendliness of the greeting from this man, hardly known to me and fifteen years my senior. I began to recognise that I was about to be asked to volunteer; I had not served in the Navy so long without being able to recognise the symptoms.

"Heard you were on the way," said the Commander, choosing his monosyllables carefully. "Fly those?". He pointed across the acres of concrete to a Scimitar parked among its nocturnal cousins.

"Used to," I replied, falling naturally into his senior's speech pattern, "but not now".

"One of No.803 Squadron's," continued the Commander, apparently missing the point, "Left here 'u/s'. Take it to Malta now, will you". It was not a question.

I was airborne from Yeovilton at 1410 on a non-stop flight to Malta. My wife, in the north of Scotland, was still waiting for me to come to lunch; I had forgotten to telephone her.

The planned time for the delivery flight was exactly two hours. This fact had caused a flurry of excitement in the flight planning office. Some years previously, RAF Javelins had established the London-Valetta record in two hours fifteen minutes. Now, here was a chance for the Navy to beat this time, flying a marginally greater distance in a quarter of an hour less. The meteorological office was forecasting seventy knot tail winds at forty five thousand feet. Suggestions were made about asking the Royal Aero Club to observe the record attempt officially, but time did not allow it. I had discovered with some alarm that time did not allow for formal applications for diplomatic clearances, either. No technical or refuelling stops could be made en route. I was required to fly this single seat fighter for two hours, knowing its safe endurance to be half an hour less than that. I was being asked to refuel in flight, which I had never done before. I knew, of course, of the introduction of the 'probe and drogue' system of flight refuelling, but this had been introduced since my squadron days had ended. A tanker pilot briefed me quickly.

"Each fighter is equipped with a nozzle on the end of a probe, positioned on the nose of the aircraft or the leading edge of the wing. The pilot's task is to stick the nozzle into a funnel shaped drogue on the end of a pipe, which is trailed behind the fuel tanker aircraft. When the connection is achieved and the relevant switchery activated, the fighter sucks fuel from the tanker and tops up its tanks in mid-air."

The procedure called for some skill in formation flying and much determination on the part of the fighter pilot. Normally, the art of flight refuelling was practised until skill was achieved, at low altitude, where the denser air gave better aerodynamic control. The tanker pilot's briefing ended by arranging a rendezvous over Paris at forty thousand feet, with a view to carrying out the 'top up'. The tanker would then return to base, and the fighter would be clear all the way to Malta. Well, there was always a first time.

At 1409 I was lined up on Runway 27 at Yeovilton and cleared for take-off by Air Traffic Control. I completed my checks and pushed the throttles forward to full power. The twenty three thousand pounds of thrust of the two Rolls Royce engines took effect, and the aircraft leapt into the air at 1410.

I climbed steeply, allowing the speed in the climb to build up to five hundred knots, and then set course for Paris and the rendezvous with the airborne fuelling station. The ground radar station monitored my progress across the Channel and advised me of a course for the rendezvous position. At the same time, I heard instructions being passed to the tanker pilot. Soon I had the other aircraft in sight.

The bat-like form of the Sea Vixen tanker, with its twin boomed fuselage and near delta wings, was spoilt by an appendage I had never seen before. A long hose trailed from the rear edge of its starboard wing, on the end of which was a funnel, gyrating gently, defying penetration. The tanker was poised in the familiar airscape of forty thousand feet: the sky above, black (no air there to diffract the blue of the sun's light); the horizon, distant and indistinct and in places totally obscured by cloud formations some three or four miles below; the air still, and the apparent lack of motion of the other aircraft in spite of the fact that it was covering the ground at eight miles a minute.

The tanker began to decelerate to the required speed for refuelling to begin: a reduction which was imperceptible at first, then the fighter began to overtake the other aircraft. I closed the throttles slightly to maintain position at the rear. As the tanker pilot's instructions came over the radio, I began my approach to the funnel. The probe extended from the front of my own aircraft, solid and still, looking larger in diameter than the funnel into the centre of which it was supposed to fit. As I closed on the tanker, the funnel, oscillating tantalisingly not too far ahead, became progressively bigger. I began to discern the ribs of it and the padding on the circumference. If only it would keep still I might stand a chance of inserting the probe into the centre of it. Suddenly I realised that it would be necessary to stab the funnel by using a short burst of throttle, and then immediately close the throttle slightly so that the speed would match that of the tanker. I remembered being told specifically not to do this, but I intended to try it all the same.

In spite of all my instructions, I hated the thought of touching another aircraft in flight. Throughout my training, instructors had impressed on me the cardinal error of touching another aircraft with one's own during close formation flying, during low flying, or even while taxying on the ground. Now I was required to disregard this basic principle eight miles high and at four hundred miles an hour.

I made the first attempt, and failed to enter. Instead, I clouted the side of the funnel with the probe. I tried and failed again. At this altitude the speed and inertia of the aircraft were high, but control effectiveness, due to the rarefied air, was low. The aircraft was sluggish to respond to my demands and slow to stabilise when I wanted it to be still. If only I could have practised at low altitude, but the fuel situation had not permitted it.

Now the fuel state was becoming critical. If I did not succeed on the next attempt, I must return to Yeovilton. I went in for my third and final go. The probe connected easily and swiftly: Lights flashed magically on the instrument panel and, for the first time in my life, I witnessed fuel gauges registering an increase whilst flying along. After all the strain and effort that had gone into the refuelling, it was over quickly. I found myself one hundred and fifty miles or so south-east of Paris, flying along comfortably with brimming tanks. Next stop Malta.

I contacted various military radar stations as I cruised

effortlessly above the European civil air traffic. The radar stations monitored my progress and gave me advice from time to time. The controllers spoke fractured English, the international language of aviation, but the content of their messages, specialised, factual, numerical information, was difficult to catch. Settling back as comfortably as the Martin-Baker ejection seat would allow, I realised that all I had to do was to point and wait.

Much of aviation amounted to that, I suddenly thought. Flying from a shore base was ninety five percent boredom, during which one pointed the aircraft in the required direction, and then waited until sufficient time had elapsed to achieve an arrival at the required destination.

How different on board a carrier! Three weeks at sea, flying your backside off, then four or five days ashore in some foreign port, spending your month's pay as quickly as possible. Consume as much booze as time and money would permit, then back to sea. Boosting off the catapult before dawn, back for breakfast after an hour's bombing, rocketing or strafing. Another sortie and land back on again by 0800. Another breakfast if you felt like it. Deck-landing had become almost second nature, but never quite. Perhaps it was that one accepted it as a fact of life: the inevitable end of a sortie.

Often there was nowhere else to go but this pitching, tossing hunk of metal, always looking too small, never stable, always obscured by the smoke from its own funnel, always alone with nothing in sight but infinite acres of ocean. This was home, airfield, radar station, arsenal and haven all in one.

No, deck landing never became second nature, merely accepted. Sometimes a pilot would go sick or some other circumstance would break his deck landing continuity. After two weeks off if he had not carried out a deck landing, he would be removed from the flying programme. He would then be required to retrain as if from scratch during the next period close to land, until he had once more proved his proficiency in the art. Those days were gone now.

The voice of the Italian Air Force controller over the UHF interrupted my reverie; I was being handed over to Malta Control. I changed frequency and listened with relief to the English voice of the RAF controller from the Malta base. Soon I saw the yellow islands, Gozo, Comino and Malta in the heat haze far below me. They were smaller than I remembered, and somehow more foreign looking. To return from Hong Kong or the Philippines and to arrive in Malta was just like coming home, like arriving in the United Kingdom itself. To arrive now, after a year in the Scottish Highlands, was to arrive on a strange, sub-tropical island. I looked at my watch: It was 1605. I had flown from Somerset to Malta in one hour fifty five minutes, a new record.

Changing frequency again to call the control tower at Hal Far, the Naval air base in Malta, to which the fighter was being delivered, I was given instructions to descend fast and, as I did so, with air brakes out and throttles closed, the cockpit canopy steamed up. The aircraft was entering the warm air of the Mediterranean after its 'cold soak' at altitude. I checked the fuel gauges: Two thousand five hundred pounds remaining: A safe flying time of twenty minutes. I would be on the ground in five or so. As I descended through ten thousand feet, a new voice broke in on the radio frequency. It was an aircraft carrier, who proceeded to ask if I was an No.803 Squadron aircraft. I duly confirmed the fact.

"Come to Mother," said the voice.

"Say again," I said, with disbelief.

"Land on the carrier," was the firm instruction. "Our position is thirty-two miles east of Delamara Point."

"My fuel state is chicken plus ten minutes," I replied.

"Roger," was the only acknowledgement.

It would take less than four minutes to cover the distance to the carrier, and so I advised Hal Far of my intentions and turned seawards.

The carrier's own Air Traffic Controller was plotting me on the ship's radar, and vectored the aircraft into the correct position to start the approach to landing. I spotted the ship first by its wake, foaming white as the three huge screws drove the enormous tonnage through the water at the speed of a motor car. Then, through the haze, the greyness of the ship, with the 'Dayglo' orange stripe running down the centre of its angled deck.

Plunging down onto the deck, I caught number three wire. It was all so familiar: the intense relief as the hook engaged the hydraulically sprung wire; the violent deceleration as my body was thrown forward, the seat straps biting into the shoulders; the business of the flight-deck crews; the gesticulating aircraft handler in his 'Andy Pandy' suit, signalling to raise the hook and fold the wings. I carried out both instructions with one deft movement, though I had not done so for some time. Had it become second nature? This had been my first deck-landing for over a year. The time was 1620; another five minutes and I would have run out of fuel.

A helicopter took me ashore to Hal Far, where I realised that my head cold had cleared up; I wondered what my wife had done with my lunch.

### Captain A.J.Leahy CBE DSC

Commanding Officer No.803 Squadron 16 December 1959 until 18 December 1960. Logged 198 hours.

My first take-off was on 23 October 1959 in XD279. I had no special thoughts - just terror! The acceleration was not a surprise, as I had been well briefed by No.800 Sqn and no aircraft can match the ship's catapult. The best description of the Scimitar - a three dimensional sports car.

Would I agree that landing the Scimitar was almost a controlled crash? No, the Scimitar was a "no round-out" lander, but it did not used to be a heavy landing. One way of smoothing out an airfield landing was to quickly and smoothly open and shut one throttle to about 1/3-1/2 power but not give the engine time to fully respond.

In comparison with other jet aircraft I have flown, at its time the Scimitar was the fastest fighter in UK service. It may have been more difficult to fly than the Hunter but it could do more and go faster. Single engine performance was streets ahead of and more easy to control than the Meteor or Canberra.

I never experienced Inertia Coupling while flying the Scimitar. I do not think that it could or would roll-couple.

The tendency to pitch up was never any real problem - except only on the catapult with four drop tanks half full (J.W.H. Purvis can elaborate!).

Compared with US Navy aircraft of the time, I think it was better. The combination of the Scimitar and the Type 984 radar in *Victorious* was unbeatable in clear/day conditions. Admiral Noel Gaylor, USN, once remarked that only the Brits could build an aircraft with all that thrust and still be sub-sonic in level flight.

The moment that I felt the most dangerous whilst flying a Scimitar was when directed into Fly 1 right in the bows. The only thing one could see, apart from the Director's hands, was the sea. *[Authors note. No comment on this as I used to be one of those directors!]*.

What would I consider my best moment? All good. Perhaps the first deck landing with under 20 hours on the type, or perhaps cruising at low-level and seeing a contrail high above and knowing that the Scimitar could, and often did, climb faster to a position alongside than that aircraft, whatever it was, could fly straight and level.

The Scimitar might have benefited from further development, but with the Buccaneer on its way as a strike aircraft and with the Sea Vixen and its all weather capability, it would have been pointless.

If the clock could be put back, would you do it all again? No problem, it would be a pleasure.

**Lt Cdr T.C.S. Leece**

No.700X Squadron, Air Weapon Instructor and development September 1957 to July 1958. No.807 as Senior Pilot September 1958 to October 1959. No.803 as Commanding Officer December 1960 to July 1962. Total Hours - day 425.10, deck landings 181. Night 13.10, deck landings, 8 rollers and two landings.

My first Scimitar flight was on 26 September 1957, straight from Sea Hawks with no simulator experience (it did not exist) and with no previous swept-wing experience. I had a good verbal briefing from Tom Innes, the CO of 'X' Flight, and charged off down the runway. I still remember the tremendous power and acceleration on take-off and subsequent climb out and was more than a little relieved to get the beast back down on Ford runway after a 50 minute flight.

*Some No.803 Squadron pilots around 1960/1. Left to right – standing Lt Cdr Colin Casperd (Senior Pilot), Lt Cdr Tom Leece (CO), Sub Lt Paddy Anderson and Lt Jim Purvis; kneeling Lt Eddy Cope and Sub Lt "Curly" Wood. (Royal Navy)*

Pitch-up was never a real problem as it was a simple matter to ease off stick pressure when buffet and pitch-up tendency eased off. The problem was probably worst during high altitude gunnery at subsonic speed when it was difficult to carry out a decent quarter attack due to the 'G' one had to pull and the resultant buffet and possible pitch-up problem. We developed a supersonic high-altitude quarter attack, when of course there were no such problems. During trials I was required to allow a slow speed pitch-up to develop. The aircraft dropped its right wing (I may be wrong but I don't think so) and ended up upside down in what was the initial stage of a spin, but recovery was immediate.

It was a really good aircraft to fly and had singularly few vices. The power was always available to get one out of trouble, as for instance the day I was boosted with full drop tanks but the Flight Deck engineers had the wrong message and only supplied sufficient steam pressure for internal fuel. As we were operating with nil natural wind I did not have near enough speed at the end of the catapult and the aircraft dropped like a stone. I was saved from disaster by the ground cushion effect and the power of those engines.

Hydraulic failures were a problem, as I think we were the first British aircraft with a 4,000psi system. However the stand-by systems were always available, and I never had any real qualms about the hydraulics.

Basic design: The Americans were always astonished that with so much power the aircraft was not supersonic in level flight. The reason for this was the design of the air intakes, the thick wing and the fuselage shape. I believe that a development was considered that would have had a second seat, a 'coke bottle' fuselage and a new wing. By that time, however, we had the Buccaneer coming along and the idea was dropped.

Navigation equipment: There were a number of aircraft fitted with Doppler navigation, In-Flight refuelling etc. for the long range nuclear strike role. One of the troubles with all the extra instrument fixtures was that it took up room on the cockpit coaming and restricted forward visibility somewhat. The smaller pilots had a little difficulty on this score but they all coped.

Engineering: The curse of the Scimitar was its poor serviceability. The reason is not hard to find. It was the first of a new generation, it was built in small numbers, and was in a constant state of development. However the worst feature was lack of accessibility which sometimes required the engines to be taken out in order to rectify some small fault in other equipment that happened to be sited in the bottom of the engine bay. The end result was a constant shortage of operational aircraft with serviceability well below the 50% mark for most of the time.

There were tragic press pictures at the time of a Scimitar sinking with the pilot trapped in the cockpit. This was Des Russell who went over the side on his first landing on *Victorious*. When salvage operations were carried out, it was discovered that he had been trapped by his leg restraint which for some reason he had failed to release prior to landing on the deck. The possibility of such an occurrence had been considered when we in 'X' Flight carried out the initial deck landing trials, as not only was the aircraft new but so also was the associated equipment. One of our principal recommendations was that leg restraints should be released before landing at sea.

High-speed low-level: In the initial stage of its development there was no restriction on speed. Low level close formation was regularly undertaken at speeds of around Mach 0.96 until one day we discovered cracks in the vertical stabiliser. This was put down to severe overloading due to the shock wave off the wing of the formatting aircraft striking the tail of the lead aircraft. Thereafter all close formation was restricted to Mach 0.9.

I was the singleton member of the 1959 RN display team which included Farnborough that year. We had decided that the object would be for the team to do the formation work while the single aircraft made maximum noise at maximum speed at very low level to take advantage of the structural strength of the aircraft and power available. The routine included a high speed run right on the deck at maximum power and speed. The aircraft would accelerate to Mach 0.98 with an IAS of something like 620 knots. It would then try to go faster but the compressibility drag rise would take effect and the aeroplane would slow down a few knots only for the whole thing to start over again. As a matter of interest the routine also included a 9G turn in front of the crowd. It was only possible to sustain 9G for a short time, as although the turn was started from a high speed run, the engines just did not have the power required to keep it up and it was necessary for G to be reduced during the turn. Needless to say, 9G is also quite a load on the pilot.

This high G decelerating effect was put to good use by the late Cdr Ian H.F Martin who flew the Scimitar as the official RN entry for the Daily Mail London to Paris Air Race in July 1959, this being part of the fiftieth anniversary celebrations for Louis Bleriot's first flight across the English Channel. The idea was to get from the centre of Paris to the centre of London and included a motor bike ride behind a Royal Marine dispatch rider, a helicopter ride to the airport where the Scimitar was all ready for flight with all checks done by another pilot and a mad dash across the Channel. Ian discovered that the best way to kill the excess speed was to approach the runway at maximum speed, chop the throttles put out the airbrakes and pull maximum G. This way he arrived at the correct point downwind to turn onto finals with the speed reduced enough for him to lower his wheels etc. We still think we should have won that race but the RAF used the dubious device of routing their helicopter over what we considered to be restricted routing in order to save precious time. They knew they had no aircraft in service that could match the speed of the Scimitar, hence the need for them to 'bend' the helicopter rule.

Spurious fire warnings were quite a problem and caused a number of anxious moments. The usual routine was to shut down the affected engine. I believe that such a spurious warning was the cause of at least one ejection.

Use of blown flaps. The standard procedure was to use blow for all landings. This reduced the approach speed by some 5 knots or so (I forget the exact figure). We all carried out unblown landings as part of the familiarisation course. I think I am right in saying that blow was not used during single-engined deck landings as too much power would be leaked off in the event of an overshoot.

Overall impressions: As a fighter it suffered from lack of radar. It was always Mark One eyeball work after being put into an intercept position by ground control. Once the enemy was seen, however, the aircraft could generally be manoeuvred into firing position for Sidewinder and guns, except at high level when buffet caused difficulties.

As a strike aircraft, the necessity to carry all weapons externally obviously affected performance. As a weapon delivery platform we thought it to be a good aeroplane, the standard conventional loads being the usual bombs, rockets and Bullpup. Navigation to distant targets was hampered by the lack of radar and the Mark One eyeball was the prime aid. This of course meant meticulous pre-flight planning and constant attention en route as the available aids (e.g. *Blue Silk* Doppler) were in an early stage of development and not very reliable.

As a night deck lander, very twitch-making. Although my log book records eight roller and two night landings, they were not in pitch dark but recorded as dark dusk, which was quite dark enough.

As a pilot's aeroplane it was superb. The rate of climb for those days was astonishing. During trials from a standing start we regularly hit 40,000 in 3 minutes 40 seconds. One look at the rivets gave a feeling of confidence in the strength (but it did not do much for performance!). The aeroplane could be thrown round the sky as much as one wished and the rate of role was exceptional. I liked the Scimitar (which was nicknamed 'The Beast') and am proud to have been associated with its development and use.

*The following was taken from the Lossiemouth internal newspaper 'Fulminator' dated Saturday, 1 August 1959 (Kindly sent by Lt Cdr Leece).*

*FLIGHT SAFETY NEAR MISS REPORT*
*'What happened? I was standing at the end of Runway 23 when two Scimitars landed on the far end. As they taxied up the runway folding their wings, another one landed between them in the opposite direction. Immediately afterwards three more landed over the top. I think this is very dangerous and must have been a mistake. Why did it happen: Anoxia? (symptoms are apathy and unconcern). Slight mental lapse of all aircrew involved, or, a deliberate attempt to scare the living daylights out of anyone watching. What did you do? I fell off my bike.'*

**Rear Admiral L.E. Middleton CB DSO**

I was with No.700X Squadron, where I was the AWI, and then in No.803 Squadron, and logged a total of 296 hours in the aircraft.

I can remember my first take-off quite clearly. Everything seemed to be running away, and I was astonished at the phenomenal performance of the aircraft. The acceleration was a surprise. Although I was briefed to start the climb when the speed reached Mach 0.92, the aircraft was on the buffet and howling like a dog (Mach 0.98) before I had realised that I had overshot the speed.

All single engine operations were done with the BLC off. Naturally the aircraft did not handle as well.

I cannot agree that landing the Scimitar was almost a controlled crash. It had a very good undercarriage. One had to get used to the fact that you did not flare the aircraft before touch down, it flared slightly in ground effect.

The Scimitar was well ahead of its time, compared to other jet aircraft, and if we had persevered with later marks and updated the weapon system I am sure it would have been as successful an aircraft as our modern day jets. If one considers that it was the first sophisticated aircraft, it was quite outstanding. At sea level it was capable of Mach 0.95 on one engine, which the Phantom was barely capable of achieving with two engines without after-burner.

My most dangerous moment while flying the Scimitar was when doing LABS trials on the range at West Freugh at 640 knots. I had an engine break up, which was quite exciting, but I got the aircraft into West Freugh.

My best moment was when the Commanding Officer of No.803 Squadron's aircraft went unserviceable at Hyères in the south of France when we were disembarked from *Victorious*, and I was left behind to wait for the aircraft to become serviceable. Unfortunately it took three weeks to repair and I was stuck in the south of France all this time. It was hard to take.

Due to the amount of hydraulic failures the Scimitar suffered from, did this ever give you cause for concern? Yes. Indeed my aircraft in No.803 Squadron, namely XD234, had a history of No 1 hydraulic failures and on one occasion (non diversion, in mid Atlantic) my hook failed to lower when attempting to return to the ship with a No 1 hydraulic failure. I eventually got the hook down by bouncing the aircraft on the deck with only the wheels down. The hook came down on my third attempt. I was bouncing the aircraft without flaps because the remainder of the air group was airborne and I needed to conserve fuel in order to give them time to get back so that a barrier could be rigged, or to bide time before it was necessary to eject if the hook did not come down. It was most difficult to get the aircraft onto the deck at 160 knots. I believe that most of the Squadron pilots treated hydraulic failures as a mundane occurrence, but on this occasion in my heart my knees were shaking.

If the clock could be put back, would you do it all again? Without question, it was great fun.

**Commander N.J.P.Mills**

No.800 Squadron, Senior Pilot/AWI July 1959 until August 1960. No.803 Squadron, Commanding Officer July 1962 until May 1964. Logged about 550 hours with 6 at night.

My thoughts on my first take-off were of impressive acceleration and much easier to fly than one would have guessed from the simulator.

Would I agree that landing the Scimitar was almost a controlled crash? I think some used to refer to it that way but a lot of modern aircraft land using constant attitude e.g. Concorde, I would imagine.

Comparing the Scimitar to other jet aircraft I have flown, at low level it was somewhat similar to the Buccaneer S.2, but at high level it had poor manoeuvrability.

Was the tendency to pitch up any real problem? No more than other swept wing aircraft.

In comparison with US Navy aircraft of the time, it was slow compared with the F8U and F-4.

My most dangerous moment while flying the Scimitar was when an arrester wire failed after landing on *Hermes*. After catching No.1 wire, and at its maximum pullout, it parted way down in the machinery room. Luckily I stopped the aircraft on my brakes. The aircraft suffered complete electrical failure due to the operation of inertia switches, the fire extinguishers also operated. Unfortunately there were some injuries to flight deck personnel caused by the flaying wire.

Did I ever night fly the Scimitar? Yes, but not from a carrier deck except for a pre dawn take-off.

I cannot remember any special incident, but I enjoyed flying the aeroplane and I must have fired, dropped, or just carried almost every possible combination of underwing store available.

The aircraft had a good single engine performance and initially No.800 Sqn did a lot of low level single engine flying until it was found that on re-lighting we were getting fires in the area around the tail pipe. I am not sure if the full single engine clearance was ever restored even after modification.

If the clock could be put back, would I do it all again? Yes.

❖❖❖❖❖❖❖❖❖❖❖❖❖❖❖❖❖❖❖❖❖❖❖

**Lieutenant Colin C.Morris**

Lieutenant Morris, now a British Airways Concorde Captain, flew the Scimitar with No.736 Sqn under training from March 1961 until July the same year. He then joined No.800 Sqn and flew the aircraft from HMS *Ark Royal* from August 1961 until May 1963.

I did just over 8 hours in the simulator and my thoughts on my first take-off were: "How the hell am I going to get the gear up before I reach the 300kt limit speed?". The acceleration was quite a surprise.

Would I agree that landing the Scimitar was almost a controlled crash? Inasmuch that a flare was impossible. Yes. My most dangerous moment I find difficult to be objective about. Never having broken one, it is reasonable to look back on it as all bloody dangerous, but as a young man one was not greatly affected by it.

My best moment, though, is clear: Watching the Vixens night flying. Mind you, low level bombing in the Scimitar was always exhilarating.

The Scimitar had wonderfully harmonised controls, was a superb stable weapons platform, particularly at high speed, (Mach 0.98+), but was totally unsuitable for deck operations. Nonetheless I am proud to have flown it and if the clock could be put back I would do it all over again.

With regard to developments from which the aircraft would have benefited, a sophisticated map display for high-speed low-level flights would have been good. We did trials with a clockwork one, but nothing came of it.

The tendency to 'pitch-up' could cause problems at heights above 30,000ft; it's manoeuvrability limitations made 'pitch-up' a not uncommon experience. The low speed handling was lousy, but the high speed was excellent.

*XD269 going over the port side of the angled deck of HMS Victorious off Kuwait on 9 July 1961 after being unable to stop due to starboard brake failure. The pilot, Lt D.S.McIntyre escaped unharmed. (Royal Navy)*

In comparison with US Navy types at that time, the Scimitar didn't fare well in dog fights, but was good at running away. I don't think that the aircraft would have remained in service any longer even if fitted with a more advanced Nav-Aid and Weapon delivery system. In my opinion it needed a two-seater variant for further development.

After flying Sea Vixens from HMS *Eagle* for some time, I was invited to re-familiarise myself with the Scimitars of No.800B flight, with a view to flying both types from *Eagle* as there was a shortage of Scimitar pilots. On either 17th or 18th February 1966, after three years away from the Scimitar, I took to the air again from RAF Changi. Although I had some 310 hours of Scimitar flying under my belt by that stage, my experience in the circuit convinced me that I would need an awful lot of practice before I went anywhere near a flight deck, and probably that the different techniques of the two types made simultaneous deck operations an unnecessarily dangerous exercise. I fear I would not have lived to fly Concorde.

❖❖❖❖❖❖❖❖❖❖❖❖❖❖❖❖❖❖❖❖❖❖❖

**Commander D.P.Norman**

Royal Naval Test Squadron, Boscombe Down 1956-57. Senior Pilot in 1958. No.800 Squadron as Commanding Officer 1959-61. RAE Farnborough 1961-63 as Commander (Flying). Logged seven hours in the Supermarine N.113, 417.30 day in the Scimitar, 5.25 at night.

The first time I flew the N.113, I was also flying the Seamew, Gannet and Sea Balliol at Boscombe Down. However, I had also flown the Hunter Mk.6 before, which had a comparable thrust to weight ratio and take-off acceleration.

We carried out handling trials with BLC off for C(A) release. For landing the approach speed had to be put up by, I think, 5kts. As the weight of the system contributed about 5kt to the approach speed one wondered whether it was actually a benefit. Lateral control during the approach was excellent with it on, but satisfactory with it off. I seem to remember that BLC off approach was always made with airbrake in and/or fuselage flap up.

Would I agree that landing the Scimitar was almost a controlled crash? Emphatically, No. Firm, positive and controlled - yes; but a crash - never. Seriously, we (Vickers Supermarine and Boscombe) took a lot of trouble to get good handling for the approach, and landing. Speed control was good in spite of the approach speeds being on a very flat portion of the drag curve and the throttles/thrust control being pretty sensitive. The ADD helped a lot in this respect too - I think it may have been the first aircraft fitted with ADD along with the Sea Vixen. Lateral control for line-up was excellent as was the forward view until the *Blue Silk* Doppler navigation system was fitted in the coaming (after my time at Boscombe).

It could not be compared seriously with the Vampire, Meteor or Sea Hawk as it was a generation later and consequently enjoyed much improved performance and handling qualities. These were comparable however with the Swift and Hunter Mk.6. Whereas the Scimitar suffered the snags that arose from twin engines with hydraulic and electrical generation system, it enjoyed twin hydraulic flying controls systems which were preferable to the manual reversion philosophy of the other aircraft. It was much a simpler system than the Vixen, and the lateral controls and forward view were better making it easier to deck land. The main drawback with the Scimitar was lack of level turning ability at altitude, which was less than any of its contemporaries. It was as strong as a horse and 'built like the Forth Bridge'. Consequently it was able to deck land at maximum all up weight, which was a good feature if one needed to recover immediately after launch. The hook-to-eye distance in the landing attitude was very large for an aircraft at that time. The resulting mirror settings to catch the optimum wire gave the impression that one must be bolting when one looked at the deck rather than concentrating on the mirror. It was imperative to keep on the mirror (or its successors) to avoid the hook hitting on the round-down. The Sea Vixen on the other hand had only a low maximum land-on weight which left it with very little fuel for diversion.

I never experienced Inertia Coupling while flying the Scimitar, even though we ran a programme to look for it at Boscombe Down in 1957.

Of those 'dangerous' moments that I was aware of perhaps the following was outstanding. I was doing a slow speed handling test with the blowing off in the landing configuration at about 8,000ft to simulate landing conditions as near as practical. I progressively reduced speed during the test and finally suffered a mild pitch-up. This was checked only by full forward stick but which did not lower the nose. We remained in this stabilised situation for a few seconds before the nose very, very slowly dropped and the angle of attack reduced while I concentrated on avoiding a spin. I was caught unawares and had not planned what to do in this event. I should have switched on the blowing immediately which would have reduced the incidence in less than a second.

I do not recall having more than one hydraulic failure plus a few hydraulic malfunctions and these were certainly less in number than fuel system and electrical system malfunctions. However I was obliged to abandon one aircraft (XD264) on 27 July 1961 on the occasion of a hydraulic failure when one main leg would not lower. The aircraft did not pitch up, stall and crash into the sea due to trim change after the pre-planned ejection over the Moray Firth as had been expected, but quietly turned south and landed in a wood near Banff. Shortly after arriving at the site the air engineers found the particular hydraulic shuttle valve which had malfunctioned and precluded the leg lowering. There was at least one other similar incident in the early '60s.

Did I ever night fly the Scimitar? Yes; 17 hours including 6 night deck landings. The Scimitar had no real night operational capability as it didn't have a radar. Consequently the only purpose in getting night deck qualified was in order to do a pre-dawn launch or a post-dusk recovery. I don't suppose a night deck landing in a Scimitar was any worse than in any other aircraft. The night catapult launch was made more exciting than in many other aircraft because of the shower of sparks from the tail skid on the deck which reflected in the rear view mirror during the catapult stroke.

I think the Scimitar picked up most if not all of the developments that were relevant and available to it at the time e.g. Doppler Nav radar, Sidewinder air-to-air missile, LABS bombing system, UHF radio. It would have benefited undoubtedly from having an air-to-air and/or air-to-ground radar and thus more of an all weather/night capability - but then its contemporary the Sea Vixen undertook this role in those far off days when we could apparently afford specialised aircraft. A very useful development would have been a built-in starter system. The Palouste starter rig was dreadfully cumbersome.

A variety of fence shapes, positions and arrangements were tested in the early days of the N.113 as part of the handling trials programme. There was considerable variety of opinion on the qualitative merits of some configurations. It was alleged that the late Mike Lithgow, then the Chief Test Pilot on the N.113/Scimitar, settled the argument in favour of the final selection by claiming that "it was more aesthetically pleasing" than the almost identical alternative. The trials programme required flying up to some high speed with the canopy off simulating its jettison. It was noisy and draughty, but acceptable even at 550 kts IAS provided one kept the seat well down. The top ejection seat pin was left in in case the breeze pulled the firing blind out. The cockpit lighting in the Scimitar was not particularly good even for a day fighter and was notoriously unreliable (probably because it wasn't used enough). A torch was always carried at night of course and on one occasion saved the aircraft. The main lights failed at the top of the descent and the standby system driven off a separate system started fading. By the bottom of the descent all cockpit lights were out, but I had fitted the torch into the thigh pocket of the immersion suit, and by dint of some fancy knee work, managed to scan the main instruments during the approach and landing.

During No.800 Sqn work up as the 1961 RN formation aerobatic team, it was decided to install smoke generation equipment to further dramatise the show. It was also decided to produce it in red and blue in addition to white. The latter was produced by introducing diesel oil into the jet pipe and the colours by adding the appropriate aniline dye to the diesel. The effect wasn't bad in the air but was most spectacular on the ground and particularly on the maintenance crews handling the dye. This got onto everything it possibly could and was very difficult to remove. The handling parties were eventually divided into red and blue crews in order to make their appearance less terrifying. A trial to see if there might be a tactical application of smoke generation was negative and the system was abandoned at the end of the air show season. During trials of the Scimitar systems it was required to confirm that one of the two engine driven pumps could provide sufficient hydraulic power to the flying control jacks with that engine idling. To do this the plumbers arranged that one system could be totally isolated in the air by an electrical switch. The engine driving the other system was reduced to idle and the controls thrashed around simulating extremely violent evasive manoeuvring. The hydraulic flying control accumulators could be exhausted this way causing the controls to 'freeze' and for a short time the aircraft was like a brick. Within two or three seconds the pressure would build up and normal flight could be resumed. It was nice to know that the system could have coped with this highly unlikely set of circumstances.

**Lieutenant K.B.Owen**

I was a pilot on Nos.736 and 803 Squadrons flying the Scimitar at Lossiemouth and HMS *Ark Royal* before I left the Navy in 1965. I was subsequently fortunate enough to be hired by Short Bros of Rochester, who had an Admiralty contract to ferry new aircraft to the various squadrons, and time expired or aircraft damaged too badly for local repair back to the various manufacturers, frequently on a one time ferry permit. This occasionally challenged our faith in the judgement of the maintenance personnel, who obviously preferred to have the aircraft flown out rather than being dismantled, and transported by road. I always felt it a tribute to the squadron's maintenance departments, that I never heard of any of our pilots having a serious problem with any of the squadron's discards, whereas the factory new aircraft sometimes gave one pause for thought. However, the point is that I was able to continue to fly the Scimitar until I left Shorts at the end of December 1965 when I came over to the USA to fly with one of the major airlines here.

The Scimitar always seemed to me to be an aircraft that could have used a little more development, such as the Hunter benefited from. As an example it had a wet wing, constantly seeped fuel, not much, just enough to keep the hardstanding messy, and the carrier decks like skating rinks.

The hydraulic systems were susceptible to failure due to vibration - this was really terrific for an aircraft with four 30mm cannon, and no manual control reversion. In fairness, I don't remember being concerned about it at the time, but hydraulic failures were more common than they should have been.

I had some experiences which at the time I would have much preferred were happening to someone else. I was fooling around a few feet above the ground one beautiful Scottish morning, admittedly at 600kt, when my canopy departed with a mighty commotion. The next thing I knew, I was at 10,000ft wondering what had happened to my beautiful day. The wind blast at that speed did some strange things; I remember hearing a sound something like a high speed flag, and when I finally located the noise it turned out to be the blind from the ejection seat which had pulled out from its housing and was folded back on top of the seat and rippling ferociously. You can imagine one sits very quietly and straight during the rest of the flight, until very gingerly unstrapping and crawling out of the seat to allow the armourers to re-stow the blind and replace the safety pins. That was enough to be removed from flying status for a few days until the eyeballs, which had been rattled around a bit, re-caged themselves.

My log book also records that a few days later, while turning tightly to finals, (remember we all thought we were "Tigers") the wing flaps retracted themselves, causing immediate and complete loss of control. We rolled about a bit at low altitude, and eventually, the nose rose high above the horizon and we started on up, still with the stick hard against the panel, and a confused and subdued young pilot holding it there. Finally, basic training re-asserted itself, and power was reduced to lower the nose. Once this measure of pitch control had been re-established, a flapless landing was made, still with the stick hard against the panel, doing about 200kts. I seem to remember that the tyre limiting speed was 174kts, but they held together fine, and a very relieved Sub Lt wandered away for a quick nervous pee. The Admiralty were apparently quite pleased to get their Scimitar back, but not nearly as pleased as I was to be able to give it back to them.

The acceleration and initial climb performance was very impressive: brakes release to 40,000ft, took 4.5 minutes, I think. The roll rate was sparkling to say the least, which enabled the 'twinkle' roll to be invented.

**Commodore D.Pentreath DSO**

No.807 Squadron 21 October 1958 until 21 June 1960. Logged 280 hours, with 3 hours 40 min at night.

Did I ever night fly the Scimitar? Yes, I carried out a total of 14 hours and 50 minutes of night flying on type.

My thoughts on my first take-off were of tremendous acceleration, a rapid take-off and climb with the wheels still down necessitating a reduction in power to remain below the 300 knots undercarriage limiting speed before resuming the climb. In the fairly noisy cockpit there was an excellent rear-view mirror in which I could clearly see Lossiemouth's No.23 runway from considerable altitude owing to the climb angle.

Would I agree that landing the Scimitar was almost a controlled crash? No! The aircraft could be landed very smoothly, although this was not due to flare or round-out. The oleos were splendid.

Compared to other jet aircraft I have flown, the Scimitar handled very well at low altitude, that is below 25,000ft, and outperformed most contemporary aircraft. It was very sturdy on the approach and the controls were well harmonised. Not as smooth as the Hunter but a fine pilot's aircraft. It was a noisy cockpit though which detracted somewhat.

I only experienced Inertia Coupling once or twice when rolling fast at high speed, but it was not a problem.

My most dangerous moment was when flying in formation over Farnborough on 7 September 1959. The formation was pulling up after take-off for a loop when we ran out of speed on the way up owing to lack of thrust due to very hot weather and high ambient air temperature. All four aircraft flopped out of control in a disorganised fashion. Not a very auspicious start on Day One of the display. Amazingly we didn't hit each other. The Leader was Keith Leppard, I was his No.2.

I was once flying on a high level interception exercise from *Ark Royal* in the murk off Scandinavia in May 1960 as one of a pair. My R/T failed, so I switched to emergency VHF and continued the exercise on the alternative channel (243.8 MHz I believe), but unknown to me there was a 20 minute limit on this set's use owing to poor cooling in the radio bay. Thus the emergency set soon failed and as I was above 8/8ths cloud and TACAN in the *Ark* was u/s I was going to be a bit pushed to find the ship again. However, after flying left hand triangles for some minutes I spotted another Scimitar 20,000ft below me just joining the CCA pattern. I dived down to join him and returned safely. A close shave.

It was an immensely strong aircraft and gave great confidence at all times. It was also a reasonably forgiving aircraft if handled within the flight envelope with sense and good airmanship.

**Lt Cdr J.W.H.Purvis**

No.736 Squadron 5 October until 11 December 1959. Scimitar Training Course. No.803 Squadron 5 January 1960 until 16 June 1961. No.736 Squadron 4 January 1965 as Senior Pilot, becoming No.764 Squadron 26 March 1965 until 7 May 1965. No.803 Squadron 20 May 1965 until 30 September 1966 as Senior Pilot. Logged 455 hours with 5 at night.

Then a Lieutenant, he was a squadron pilot with No.803 Sqn in HMS *Victorious* in 1960. At that time No.803's Scimitars were still fitted with non-swept forward stores pylons. The incident related here involved XD329. Lt Purvis was launched off *Victorious* at 0630 on the morning of 9 December 1960, and as his aircraft became airborne it pitched up and seemed to stagger in the air. In Lt Purvis's own words: "I believe there was a centre of gravity problem and we were flying with quarter-full drop tanks and bombs outboard, which pushed the CofG as far aft as any configuration. After this swept forward pylons were introduced moving the CofG forward. I had long enough to find out that (a) I could not control the aircraft at all and, (b) my indicated airspeed was 110 knots (about 40 knots below the minimum possible fully loaded). Not being the fastest of thinkers, I can only thank God that there was time for me to realise I had only one choice of action - to pull the blind. Only the powerful Rolls-Royce engines gave me that thinking time. After the ejection I can remember seeing the parachute deploy as if watching someone else. I was actually in the chute for about one second before hitting the sea. Then I was so tied up in rigging lines, and the chopper rescue was so swift, that I can't remember anything but the business of survival until I got out of the chopper and onto the flight deck (probably about three minutes after the ejection). My own thoughts were - what the hell went wrong?".

My thoughts on the first take-off were a sense of great pleasure and I can remember a marvellous feeling.

Would I agree that landing the Scimitar was almost a controlled crash? Not altogether. It did not feel like a crash, except on one occasion when I fell like a brick. You flew straight down without flare, but the immense undercarriage took the impact well.

By comparison with other jet aircraft I have flown, it was another generation. The Sea Hawk was a lovely aircraft to fly, but the Scimitar was great. Far more powerful, versatile, very light to handle, adaptable. Probably the most enjoyable aircraft the Fleet Air Arm ever had - when you got it in the air.

In comparison with US Navy aircraft of the time, they had Phantoms - another generation ahead. But the US Navy went on flying older aircraft while they were any use. We would have competed well with some of them, and probably our weapon accuracy would have compared well with any in the US Navy.

A vivid memory was while doing some strike exercises in Malaya. We were attacked (by arrangement) by our sister squadron in Sea Vixens. A major dog-fight ensued and I was chasing a Vixen in a 5g turn, when another Vixen passed in front of me, just missing a mid-air collision. The airstream caused me to flip so hard I thought we had hit. The pilot was one Blackwood, who was as shattered as I was.

If the clock could be put back, would I do it all again? Yes, of course. Flying Scimitars was a great experience with an excellent crowd of pilots, it was a close well-knit world and the enthusiasm was unlimited. I considered it a privilege to fly in the FAA, to work with such great pilots and maintenance ratings and the Scimitar was the best of the aircraft. We were very lucky. (Time dims the problems, basically the aircraft took so much maintenance that we never really got a lot of flying; the fuel system seldom worked as it should have done; it was a beast to maintain).

**Captain D.F. 'Sharky' Robbins**

RN Test Squadron, Boscombe Down 1957-1958. 100 hours logged on the Scimitar.

One of the development trials on the Scimitar that could not be carried out satisfactorily in the UK was hot weather trials. It was decided, therefore, to send one aircraft to Bahrain for this task. The aircraft would be XD214 and the pilot was to be Lt Cdr D.F. 'Sharky' Robbins RN (now Captain Rtd). It was also decided that while en route for Bahrain Lt Cdr Robbins would have a shot at the London to Malta air-speed record, held by RN Sea Furies since 1949 with a time of 3 hours 20 minutes and 49 seconds.

XD214 was moved to Farnborough as this was to be the departure point. Captain Robbins' account of the flight is as follows:

"My time to Valletta was 2 hours 12 minutes and 27.3 seconds, covering a distance of 1,298 miles at an average speed of 588 mph. Of course the aircraft was capable of quite a bit better than that. The main problem was that it was not a record attempt for its own sake but only a bash while en route on a pre-ordained and immutable date, regardless of weather.

It was in the days before the outboard pylons had been developed, so I only had two drop tanks. Vickers design office said the distance couldn't be made without a 15-20 knot tail wind. I proved to myself that I could stay airborne in XD214 for over 2.25 hours at a healthy cruising speed by flying down to Nice and back (just about half way) to prove it to my satisfaction, without the knowledge of French Traffic Control - what you could get away with in those days!

*Lt Cdr D.F. "Sharkey" Robbins standing by XD214 at Farnborough before his record breaking flight to Malta on 17 June 1958. (Vickers-Armstrongs)*

On 17 June 1958 there was an adverse headwind of 15-20 knots. I departed from Farnborough and shortly after take-off the fuel flowmeter failed. The Scimitar fuel tank gauges were impossible to read better than an accuracy of plus or minus 10%. I pressed on, thinking that if I could get a definite fix on top of Nice in less than one hour I would continue the attempt. I climbed to 28,000 feet, set up an I.M.N. of 0.91 and continued in a cruise climb. The south coast of France was clear and I was overhead Nice at around 39,000 feet after just over an hour, so I levelled out and increased speed to 0.93 I.M.N. North of Sicily my anxiety about fuel increased and I thought it prudent to shut down one engine and start a very shallow descent. I arrived at RAF Luqa without enough fuel to go around again if required. It would have been a different story with functioning flowmeters, four drop tanks, or even better a tail wind - 650 mph at least or, on the right day, even 700mph."

The record was ratified and Captain Robbins has a certificate signed by Lord Brabazon of Tara to prove it. He was also awarded the Geoffrey De Havilland Trophy for 1958 in recognition. However the record did not last long, being outdone by a very mere RAF Hunter (Captain Robbins description) within the next year or two. Of course the subsequent Hunter record was made on the right day.

The trials in Bahrain were started but cut short because of the situation in the Middle East at the time. Tragically, while in Bahrain, Captain Robbins was involved in a very bad road accident and suffered severe injuries to his head and face, as a result of which his test flying career was terminated abruptly. He did however return to flying after a spell of about three years, though regrettably, he says, never to active test flying.

Asked if he could remember his thoughts on his first take-off: "Regretfully I was not built like an ape with arms down to the knees - I had strapped in tightly and could not reach the undercarriage selector. The limiting IAS was approaching rapidly and I had to climb steeply while loosening my harness. As for acceleration, it was not a surprise to me. The Swift in afterburn was comparable.

Relative to other aircraft I have had flown, the Scimitar was a battleship built to resemble an aeroplane. For well known reasons the Royal Navy was late into the operation of transonic jet aircraft from carriers. The Scimitar was a hasty order from a family of development aircraft (508, 529) which were stressed for landing on a rubber deck. The result was the battleship-like construction and the undue size and weight. It was a big boy's aeroplane, yet remarkably free from any major vices. I think most pilots will look back on it with some affection.

I never experienced Inertia Coupling while flying the Scimitar. I did a lot of the coupling trials, involving rolling pullouts with full aileron at g and never noted any symptoms, although the trace recordings did show some tendency.

It was extremely difficult to manoeuvre above 35,000ft. It was quicker to drop down to 25,000ft, go about and then climb up again.

My most dangerous moment while flying the Scimitar was when I experienced rudder damper failure. While flying low level at 0.95 I.M.N., I experienced rudder buzz which cracked the fin post. Since the aircraft was built like a battleship it did not fail or break up and I subsequently landed safely.

I consider my best moment was achieving an IAS of 728 knots, subsequently verified from a trace recorder. Even in these days, still quite an IAS.

What developments do I think the Scimitar could have benefited from? A drawing board and a clean sheet of paper!

If the clock could be put back, would I do it all again? Yes, of course".

**Lieutenant W.P. 'Bill' Ryce**

I served with No.800 Squadron from its formation on 1 July 1959 until I left eighteen months later in December 1960 to return to Lossiemouth and join 700Z Flight, the Buccaneer IFTU when it formed in early 1961. I was the squadron photographic officer. We spent the first nine months at Lossiemouth, and embarked in HMS *Ark Royal* on 3 March 1960.

I flew the Scimitar 306 times but this only amounted to 235.45 hours. On this type I made 113 deck landings of which 4 were at night. I flew only nine Scimitars and their serials were XD265, XD273, XD276, XD277, XD278, XD279, XD280, XD282 and XD321.

I well remember my first Scimitar take-off: 14 July 1959 was the date and it was a lovely morning at Lossiemouth. Runway 23 was the duty runway. I remember thinking, I'd better not cock this up. I was surprised at the high cockpit noise level on the take-off run having been used to the fairly quiet Sea Hawk and Hunter. I was not, however, surprised at the acceleration as I had watched several take-offs and had mentally flown the take-off profile many times. It was however a truly exhilarating experience and when I landed forty minutes later I felt a real sense of pride and achievement.

I was very keen to fly the Scimitar and was delighted to get the chance after only nine months of front line service on the Sea Hawk. I always maintained a healthy respect for it however but at age 23, cause (or pause) for thought was not at the front of the mind.

My most dangerous moments were:-

(a) A wing folding / flap sequencing problem arose as I was manoeuvred on to the starboard catapult in *Ark Royal*. The result was that my flaps retracted as I was being launched and I left the deck fully stalled. I pushed the stick forward and recovered - just. Observers said my wheels touched the water. After that we were not allowed to fold wings when the flaps were extended.

(b) During a launch from the port catapult in *Ark Royal* the camera mounting came loose and hit me very hard. I had turned my head a bit and the impact was on the side of my bone-dome where it made a big hole. I saw stars.

(c) I was the only aircraft airborne and was returning to *Ark Royal* from a low level strike north of Norway when I was advised that the ship had run into a heavy swell and was pitching more than usual, albeit slowly. I was told, after being recovered, that the stern was moving +/-28 feet and that the projector sight gyros were about to topple. Needless to say the deck looked awesome from the cockpit when on the approach.

The best moments were undoubtedly when flying low-level through the Scottish Highlands on a sunny morning.

Comparing the aircraft with other types flown, the Scimitar has always been my favourite aircraft even after 41 years of flying umpteen types. In 1959 it had an impressive performance, was new, single seat, swept-wing and was used for many interesting roles. What more could a 23-year old ask for?

Regarding developments, I think it was a wonderful aircraft for its time and it provided a very useful learning experience for the Royal Navy but its shelf life was limited when viewed from the Buccaneer perspective and the Fleet Air Arm's role. A re-designed thinner wing would have given it better high altitude performance and effectiveness.

In comparison with US Navy Aircraft, we seemed to cope pretty well when we encountered them, but I don't feel qualified to give a definitive answer.

Handling, I would say depended on the altitude and that big fat wing. I also recall that we were on the wrong side of the drag curve when on the approach so this required a certain amount of care, especially on carrier landings.

It always coped with different weapon loads if treated with respect. I made quite a lot of LABS runs at Tain range and although this was mainly with 25lb practice bombs I made some with large, heavy, nuclear dummies. To release them from the port wing, pulling about 4.5g and at about 45-50 degrees of pitch, inevitably in cloud and then complete the pull over the top was always an interesting manoeuvre. Hands and feet were going everywhere! The Buccaneer, with its bomb bay storage definitely had the edge in this area.

Flying out of Abbotsinch down to West Freugh meant flying at low-level to keep out of controlled airspace. After four LABS runs on the range and a return up the Clyde, again low-level (taking care to miss Ailsa Craig) the fuel state was inevitably low. When I was doing this it was always hazy and there was always a sense of relief to find the railway line from Greenock that led back to Abbotsinch. On this occasion the relief had just been experienced when the controller told me that the runway at Abbotsinch was blocked by a Sea Hawk with a wheel problem. I was invited to go to Renfrew, the civilian field, as I certainly did not have the fuel to go anywhere else. This course of action appealed to me as I was trying to make my number with a girl working in the terminal there. Fighter pilot arriving with Scimitar attached seemed to be a good way of impressing her but when I was on very short finals - mentally making plans - I was told that the runway was now clear. So near yet so far! However as I made my frustrated departure I pulled a few 'g' and without thinking pointed my rear and therefore two Avon 202s at the terminal. Many windows were shattered. They were very good about it and invited me back - preferably without my Scimitar. If you are interested, no, she was not impressed!

The early Scimitar days were exciting times. There was still a confidence and belief in the fixed-wing future of the Fleet Air Arm and for me the Scimitar epitomised that confidence. I feel very privileged to have flown the Sea Hawk, Scimitar and Buccaneer with the Royal Navy, especially from the carriers, but most of all I feel very lucky to have enjoyed the 'Scimitar experience'.

### Lieutenant J.G.L.Smith

Scimitar Squadrons: No.736 for conversion training, January and February 1960; No.804 March 1960 - September 1961, as Staff Officer for latter part; No.800 October 1961 - April 1962. I then flew back to the UK to do the AWI's course and spent the rest of my 8 years on Hunters and Buccaneer Mk.1s. I logged 394 hours in the Scimitar.

I don't recall the Scimitar being called "The Beast" when I started to fly it, but I did approach my first flight with great trepidation. My thoughts and feelings on my first take off were absolute exhilaration and the acceleration at Lossiemouth on a cold winter's day was awesome.

My most dangerous moment: When one is 20 years old one does not really think of danger, but probably one of the most stupid things that I ever did was during a low level strike led by Hunters in the North of Scotland. I was part of a group of Scimitars that were to bounce students on the AWI's course. They were proceeding low level to do a strike on a range on the very North Coast of Scotland. I took off early to in-flight refuel so that I could wait for them with full tanks. I was in the middle of refuelling when the word came that they were off early and were almost in my position. I broke off the refuelling but in my haste forgot to put the switches back to normal, which meant feeding both engines from the one tank. I caught the strike doing about 400 knots and was lining up for the interception when both engines flamed out! It really speaks wonders for those Avon engines because I just pulled around a convenient mountain, put the switches back to normal, hit the relight buttons, got an immediate relight, slammed the throttles back to full power and caught the strike on the other side of the mountain. I thought nothing about it at the time, but just thinking about it now brings me out in sweat.

My best moment: On No.804 we ferried some Scimitars to Singapore for the Far East reserve. I had to test fly one clean, nothing hanging below the wings. I stuck it low level at full power up the Straits of Malacca. I did get some longitudinal instability which did frighten me a little.

Compared to other jet aircraft I have flown, it is in my top three, along with the Hunter and Tristar.

Was landing a controlled crash? Yes, the technique was different and I had quite a lot of trouble with it at first.

Developments? Something to make it turn better at attitude.

An incident I will relate is as follows: (Extract from the *South China Morning Post* published in Hong Kong, January 28th 1961): *"The split-second twin explosions of two Royal Navy Scimitar jet fighters crashing through the sound barrier shattered the show windows of five shops along Waterloo Road and caused a near panic in the area. The incident also caused the metal frames of another show window to buckle and bottles and other objects in homes in the area to topple. Bewildered people rushed into the streets from shops and homes. Newspaper offices were flooded with telephone calls enquiring as to the cause of the supersonic blasts. An official Royal Naval statement said the two planes, attached to the aircraft carrier HMS Hermes, exceeded the speed of sound while flying over Kai Tak airport at about 30,000ft during a routine training mission. A spokesman for an insurance company said he did not think that damage brought about in such a matter was recoverable under any insurance policy here."*

The background to this is that one of the officers on the RAF Squadron at Kai Tak when we disembarked there had instructed both Maurice Hynett's and myself at flying school. As we left to go flying one day he taunted us with the challenge of, "You young ***** think you're so good, lets hear you drop a sonic bang on the airfield". Fortunately we had a very switched-on RAF exchange officer, Mike Webb, who said, "Would you mind authorising that?" - and he did! So the authorisation book showed: 'Low Level bombing at Port Shelter and Sonic Boom on Kai Tak'. As they say, the rest is history, but we did a very good job.

Incidentally I did drop a practice bomb on a tent on Tarhuna range, but that story would take another chapter.

### Commander P.M.Stevenson

Cdr Stevenson was the Production Maintenance Test Pilot at RNAY Fleetlands from November 1961 until December 1963, the Station Test Pilot at Yeovilton from 1964 until 1965 and then the Commanding Officer of the Royal Navy's Maintenance Test Pilot School at RNAS Brawdy from 1966 until 1968.

Having started flying training with the RAF in 1958, he then went to Operational Flying Training School at Lossiemouth with No.736 Sqn, which had Sea Hawks. After this he joined No.806 front-line Sqn, again with Sea Hawks, and on to HMS *Albion* and out to the Far East. Paul returned to the Test Flying School at Abbotsinch, then up to Lossiemouth again to No.764 Sqn for flying training on Hunters. Following this he converted to Scimitars, on No.736 Sqn, with about five trips in the simulator before his first flight in September 1961.

"The most powerful aircraft I had flown previously was the Hunter, on which I had done my swept wing conversion. On my first Scimitar flight I really felt as if everything had been left behind when I had taken off: mind, body, guts as well, and didn't really feel that I was totally in control. However, I soon caught up and then was overtaken by the exhilaration of the power of the aircraft, being able to wham the throttle forward and just be pinned into the back of the seat. By the time I had really latched on to it, I found on the short runway at Lee that I could actually take off and be recording the RPM and temperatures on my kneepad as the aircraft went down the runway, and still be in charge.

Having qualified at the MTP School, I went to Fleetlands as the Maintenance Test Pilot. It was almost a part time appointment, as the hours I flew in the Scimitar were very few. The programme comprised first test-flights or full test flights, check test-flights, acceptance test flights and the occasional delivery (to Lossiemouth). During those two years I probably did not get more than 100 hours in the Scimitar. But because of the odd failure some of the sorties were less than 10 minutes in duration. I flew other aircraft such as the Vampire, Devons and green Sea Hawk of 781 Sqdn as well, and I also did an engineering job at Fleetlands. I also did an "apprenticeship" on the Fleetlands helicopters with a few hours as second pilot.

During a test flight one had to do a 'creep climb' on the engine, setting the power at 92% at 2,000ft, and checking the increase or decrease on the rpm, which should ideally have been +3% up to 40,000ft. From take-off, and doing the reduced power climb, a Scimitar would reach 40,000ft in just under 4 minutes in the clean configuration.

Of course most squadron pilots only flew it with tanks on, when it's performance would deteriorate considerably. But I had the privilege to fly it clean, particularly during air-day demonstrations for instance. With 20 knots of headwind I could hold the nose down once airborne and stay level with the runway with the undercarriage up. At 180 knots one rotated to a 55 degrees climb holding it to about 3,000 to 3,500ft. At this height you cut to a wingover, diving to the runway to do horizontal flick rolls. Its rate of roll was impressive, something like 540 degrees a second. As a result you were restricted to only one rotation before stabilising and carrying out another. Failure to do this could result in Inertia Roll Coupling and divergence, which could have disastrous results.

On 17 April 1962 I took off from RNAS Lee-on-Solent in XD239 on a routine test flight. Pressurisation was on, of course, and with the undercarriage now up I started a gentle turn from Runway 05. It was at this point that the stick jammed on the right hand side of the cockpit, even though I had not moved it very far for this slight turn to starboard to do a climb out down the Solent. I began to roll in towards the Engineering School at *Daedalus* and, with both hands on the stick, I struggled to pull it across the cockpit to gain control. I recovered at 300ft with the wings past the vertical. Flying with crossed controls to keep the stick away from the jamming position, I then flew up to 20,000ft and lowered the undercarriage to see if it was going to be landable, or if I would have to eject. With the gear down I found the stick was absolutely free, so I retained the configuration and began a 40 mile straight in approach from beyond the Needles followed by a relatively comfortable emergency landing on the runway back at Lee, taxied back to dispersal and shut down.

The aircraft was checked initially with a hydraulic rig and no problem was found. I was told that I would have to fly it again to see if I could reproduce the defect, but I refused to do so until they had found an actual problem. The aircraft ended up on jacks, undercarriage up, all hydraulics on, pressurisation on, and it was at this point that we reproduced the defect. In the external panel just forward of the undercarriage, one of the securing screws was found to be about an inch too long. As this was screwed up, it had gone through the captive nut on the airframe and pushed on to a Tufnol block which held some of the hydraulic lines. At the top end of the loop of the hydraulics was another Tufnol block situated just underneath the control column. When the pressurisation was on, the cockpit floor moved down a very small amount. With the undercarriage up, the pipe acted like a 'Bourdon' tube and expanded slightly. Because the screw was too long it had pushed the block up. So the screw, the undercarriage-up selection and the cockpit pressure, all combined to cause an interference between the Tufnol block and the bottom of the control column. I had taken off with about 8,000lb of fuel on board with a clean aircraft, and if I had crashed the Tufnol blocks would have burnt leaving no evidence and no witness marks, and consequently the cause of the crash would probably never have been determined.

At one time at Fleetlands I had a cold and had to get a squadron pilot, who had been off Scimitars for a while, to stand in for me. He was sent down to do the test flights that were needed following maintenance, and I briefed him. He had not flown from *Daedalus* before; there were not many aircrew, big jet aircrew, who had experience of flying from Lee. Most naval airfield runways were then 2,000 yds and subsequently 2,500+ was the norm. Lee-on-Solent only had 1,430 yds at its maximum length on Runway 23/05. As a result, techniques there had to be adapted. For instance we had to reduce the tyre pressure, as the LCN for the runway was less than normal. Generally you came at 5 knots below your normal datum speed. Although the aircraft would fly slower than that, you could not afford to do so because the tail bumper would hit first. There was also the rule that you had to have a 5-knot head-wind component before you would be cleared to land. This squadron pilot, after his first take-off from *Daedalus*, told me he hadn't actually got any readings down by the time he had got to 10,000ft, he was thinking more of the aircraft going up and controlling it than actually getting the test flight readings done. He had to come down to 2,000ft and start again.

Take-offs from *Daedalus* were not too much of a problem, the abundance of power leaving you in no doubt that you were going to get off the ground. The real problem was the landing, coming in at 127 knots and stopping before you reached the end of the runway. In the two years that I was there, however, I only put my hook down three times. Once I engaged the wire due to a wet runway and a cross wind, the other times I was able to stop with the brakes,

The Rolls-Royce Avon 202 was a fine engine. An engine check test flight consisted of recording your take-off rpm and temperatures, accelerations on the ground from ground idle and also from a higher rpm setting. I think I used to accelerate from either 60 or 70%, from which you would get an acceleration of 3 seconds to maximum power. I believe you were allowed up to 13 seconds from ground idle. Once airborne you would then set the engine at 92% for a climb at 2,000ft, and then take readings of the rpm, jet pipe temperature, fuel flow, fuel contents (mainly to check that the fuel balance system was working), altitude, OAT, etc. You would then take readings at 10,000ft intervals up to 40,000ft. Increase to maximum rpm to 45,000ft, check slams at 45,000ft, unless the 'creep' that you got from 20,000 to 40,000ft was incorrect. By 'creep', I mean the natural increase of 3%, which ideally increased the engine speed to 95% power at 40,000ft. If you got less than that, it was very likely you would have a very long slam time. You would open up the throttle and could sit there thinking, "It doesn't feel like starting today", and after a while it would wind up, but it might never get to maximum rpm. On the other hand, if you had a very high creep, then you would get a high flight idle. This meant there was a limit on how far you could throttle back, and you could tend to over-fuel during the slam and might go into surge. That would manifest itself as banging and rumbling in the intakes, and the jet pipe temperature starting to hurtle off the clock. Of course you would then have to throttle back very quickly. Only one engine would be done at a time, so you always had the other to rely on. Generally they were very good at re-lighting. We exercised shutting down one engine and re-lighting it. Again if it failed to re-light, you always had the other one to come back to base on.

Shutting one engine down during a loiter was certainly a practical requirement, if you were going to be at any altitude. If you operated off one engine, it meant that you were operating at a higher rpm, and if you were operating at a higher rpm it meant that you were nearer the design specific fuel consumption for the engine, therefore operating more efficiently. If you were on two engines, it is very likely you would have both engines at low rpm and they wouldn't be so efficient.

Having left Fleetlands to become Station Test Pilot at Yeovilton, I had probably not flown a Scimitar for some eighteen months when, in 1965, one arrived and needing ground running, taxiing and pre-flight checking. I climbed in and the whole cockpit came back to me, even though it had not been designed particularly ergonomically. Unlike the Sea Vixen, where everything was so illogical, and a six-week period away from the aircraft resulted in a quick trip back to the simulators to re-learn how to fly it, the Scimitar cockpit came back very easily.

I did not get back on the Scimitar until I was at RNAS Brawdy, Pembrokeshire, as Commanding Officer of the Maintenance Test Pilot School in 1966.

Would I agree that landing a Scimitar was almost a controlled crash? Ashore as afloat you would always fly the aircraft straight into the deck, on a 3° descent, but it was certainly controlled and definitely not a crash. The undercarriage was designed for it. On land you could rotate until your bumper was almost touching and use aerodynamic braking.

Did the number of hydraulic failures the Scimitar suffered from ever give me any cause for concern? No, there was duplex on two systems. I never had a hydraulic failure for real, although we practised it in the simulator. With the Scimitar it didn't really make much difference. If you had a hydraulic failure on the main services, you had duplication. If you had a flying control service failure, you had a duplication of that as well. There were four hydraulic pumps, two off each engine. A lot of my flying was test flying when we were not operating with worn components, except on acceptance. If you did get a double hydraulic failure, there was no way the aircraft would survive. You could not fly it in manual. But no, it never gave me any cause for concern.

Did I ever experience Inertia Roll Coupling? Yes, when doing flick rolls, mainly in aerobatics. As I've said you could do 540 degrees a second roll. The 'Twinkle Roll' was developed in formation aerobatics using this rate of roll. For a 20-ton jet to do that sort of manoeuvre is quite something. I found if you did a fast roll the thing would start to diverge. You could actually feel it diverge in yaw, unless you actually put in a boot of opposite rudder. It had super responsive controls.

What was my most dangerous moment flying the Scimitar? One of the most dangerous was the incident with the stick jamming that we have already mentioned. One nasty incident occurred whilst I was flying XD227 from Brawdy on 13 November 1967 when the windscreen cracked in a Mach Speed dive. I got this nasty chilled sensation. That feeling of security in front of you goes when this great crack appeared with a very loud bang. Fortunately it was only on the inner lamination and the external part was still complete. The temperature control valve on the compressor bleed blow, which was used as a demister, was not functioning. As I was at altitude, the differential in temperature was enough to cause a thermal crack.

On 1 August 1968 I was flying in XD322 when, immediately after take off from Brawdy and getting the undercarriage up, there was a great thump and the aircraft yawed, with the fire warning bells going off almost immediately afterwards. Having had that thump I knew very well it was not a spurious warning. I chopped the starboard throttle but the warnings continued, so I shut down the HP Cock. The warning was still there so I shut down the LP Cock. Again nothing. I pressing the fire extinguisher called a Mayday and, just as I was thinking of getting over the sea and leaving, it went out. I was then faced with the prospect of going back and doing a single-engine landing. Of course, we practised for such situations during our training and it landed perfectly all right. When I got back to dispersal at the repair unit (NASU), we could not get anyone up the jet pipe immediately as it was too hot. We then opened up a 'box' of small 'Tiffs', which we used for jet pipes, and sent one up when it was cool enough. He came back with a smudged face but with a very white complexion. Apparently there was an enormous hole all the way around the jet pipe, and it was all crusty and black inside - which we were not very surprised about. The explosion had almost completely severed the jet pipe, which had been blown in like the petals of a flower, sticking inwards where it had been torn by the blast. That is probably as near as I ever came to leaving a Scimitar.

An investigation revealed that the Number 3 bag-tank in between the two jet-pipes just aft of the engine bay had leaked into one of the jet pipe compartments. The heat of the jet pipe on take-off detonated this, the force of which almost completely severed the jet pipe. I, of course, had a fire warning. It was found that there was a one-inch black crust where the tank had nearly burnt through. The fuel tank had been assembled in Fleetlands without a gasket between the top flange of the tank and the tank bay. Every time it was pressure refuelled a bit of fuel leaked into the tank bay and eventually ignited.

That year at Brawdy, I performed at the Air Day and had 20,000 odd witnesses to the fact that the impossible happened on the aircraft. I could get either my nose wheel down with no main wheels, or my main wheels and no nose wheel down. In the end I had to throw away the high speed run, fly off to the islands west of Brawdy and pull 6g to shake the aircraft before I could get all three legs down, but without any cockpit indication. It just showed "three blacks". The tower confirmed that the legs were down but not guaranteed locked. In the middle of the Air Day I had to come in with another aircraft and do an emergency landing, the emergency services prepared just in case the undercarriage folded up. Luckily it held. My wife Rosemary had been in the crowd with our three little sons and was more than a little worried.

A basic rule with the Scimitar was if any of the undercarriage units could not be lowered, you ejected. If the nose wheel would not come down, it was very likely you would break the aircraft in half when you dropped the nose down from the main wheels. If the main wheels were not down you would hit the tail first because of the attitude, and break the aircraft that way.

Of the automatic things on board, probably the fuel balancing system needed the most watching. I think you had eight tanks, which all had to come down together. There were three speed pumps in each tank as a control system, so if one tank were a bit higher its pump would increase in speed until it had brought it down to the average level. The fuel from all the tanks went through the same fuel supply gallery.

It was an aircraft of contrast. Flying at low level the actual fuel consumption at maximum power was something in the order of 480lb per min. In 16 minutes you could end up with nothing in the tanks. Whereas on the other hand I've been up well over an hour, and certainly used to deliver aircraft from Lee to Lossiemouth, cruising at Mach 0.92 at altitude for 40 minutes. This was in a clean aircraft, and I still had enough fuel left to divert to Leuchars or Kinloss. Its altitude performance was pretty awful, and it was very sensitive at altitude.

I would consider that the best moment in flying a Scimitar was the ego bit of being able to throw it around in aerobatics; also the privilege of being able to fly the aircraft, when test flying, with a brand new finish on it and no external encumbrances: no tanks, weapons or pylons: absolutely clean. Its performance then was totally out of this world. It was a different aeroplane to when it was fully loaded.

Another was flying at maximum speed at low level, a formal requirement for a full test flight. I remember coming down the Solent on a very gusty day, having set up a level run at 645 knots, with the aircraft lurching. I thought it was just because it was very turbulent, but when I got back I found I had set up about five supersonic bangs. Although I hadn't exceeded the speed of sound on average, the gusts had just pushed me over, or been sufficient to cause a little 'pop' off the aircraft.

To finish off an air display, I would come in at 0.985 Mach and then do a 6g pull, hold the aircraft vertically and go around my own axis. If the conditions were slightly hazy, I could actually do a disappearing trick by going on up at full power and vanishing through my own vapour cloud, and finally falling out of the sky at about 30,000ft.

The Scimitar was stressed physically to 9g, but you were allowed to pull only 7.5g (of course most pilots would have blacked out by then). If you pushed it into a high speed 'pitch up' you would get this extra 1.5g imposed on the aircraft, which would take it up to its design limit, so the safety factor was there.

We had one aircraft at Fleetlands, where the wings were something like 13 minutes out of alignment, which showed up on the stall check at 25,000ft. The tolerance was ±15 minutes of arc, so it was within limits. Part of the test flight was to take the aircraft down to it lowest possible airspeed before it 'pitched up'. You could not actually stall the aircraft: you got to the position where the wing tips went into turbulent flow and lost all their lift, so the centre of pressure moved forward, at which critical point the aircraft pitched up.

This particular aircraft would flip on its back every time at 'pitch up', and we had to accept it in the end as being just a rogue aircraft with a Part 2 entry warning to aircrew. With most of them you had to let the speed trickle off at around one knot per second or less. Then you trimmed slightly forward and pulled the stick back with your fingertips until the thing ran away into 'pitch up'. Immediately you had to ease the stick forward to stop the nose rearing up. Very often you would have to let it fall out of the sky and build up indicated airspeed until you had enough grip on the air. If you tried to control it at too early a point you would not have enough airspeed and would be in a position where you might possibly go into a spin. I never did spin a Scimitar and I don't think I would have liked to have done so. I think that's when the fuselage length and the small wings would have been problematic.

*Lt Cdr P.M.Stevenson climbing aboard XD220 at RNAS Lee-on-Solent on 21 March 1968. This was the last Scimitar to leave RNAY Fleetlands. (P.M.Stevenson)*

How would I compare the Scimitar with other jet aircraft I flew? The only other advanced aircraft I flew was the Sea Vixen. I wasn't able to fly the Buccaneer or Phantom, so am unable to compare it. The Scimitar was a pilot's aircraft. At low level it was very responsive. It was not forgiving like a Sea Hawk (you could do the most appalling things with a Sea Hawk and it would let you off). The Scimitar had to be treated with respect all the time. At low level it would grip the air and would go around the most ridiculous corners, except of course when you got up to very high speed. In order to do a high-speed run for an Air Day at Lee, I would have to go around Gosport and the edge of Fareham to come into Lee again. It took that sort of circle before I could build up the speed and was like trying to run around a corner on oil. At altitude it was appalling. They reckoned if you went to 17 degrees of bank at 45,000ft it would stay in the air. If you went to 18, it would fall out of the sky. It was designed as a High Level Interceptor, but was found not to really work too well, whereas the Sea Vixen had a very large wing area and had very good performance at altitude. I remember one time at Brawdy being up in a Vixen, and chasing another of the Station Test Pilots, Simon Askins, who was in a Scimitar. I was at full throttle and could hardly keep up with him. His Scimitar had tanks on as well!

What developments do I think the Scimitar could have benefited from? If they had gone perhaps for finer lines, a thinner wing and possibly a twin crew, I could have seen advantages in the aircraft.

I cannot do a direct comparison with USN aircraft of the time, but it was rather too chunky an aeroplane to do the job efficiently, and as an operational aircraft it burned too much fuel. It certainly wasn't as fast as it should have been with that amount of power available, and it leaked like a sieve. The maximum speed I managed to get out of it was when I held it at Mach 1.3 in a dive.

With reference to the fuel leaks, the main trouble lay with the wing tanks. I came to grips with these when I was getting my Certificate of Competence as an AEO. There were not enough Scimitars for me to fly to do my conversion course with No.736 Sqn. The Squadron AEO, Lt Cdr Tony Griffin, said, "There's a Scimitar over there in the corner, you can have a couple of Tiffs, some Air Mechanics and a box of tools. If you can get it into working nick, I'll get the Senior Pilot (Jack Worth) to test fly it, and then you can use it for your conversion. At the same time we'll give you your Certificate of Competence". This was very fair, because it involved all the administration of getting the thing into the air, repairing it and physically working on it myself. An added incentive was that I was going to fly the thing afterwards. There was also an intensive oral exam too.

I spent two days on one intercostal in the wing. There was a wing tank into which we had to put some PRC sealant to stop it leaking. There was a little inspection hole, into which you could hardly get one hand, let alone both. This was the problem with the Scimitar: it was virtually unmaintainable. You had to have funny shaped people to work on it. On No.736 Sqn we had two Tiffs called Alfy and Dennis. Alfy was handy for jet pipes as he was small, about five feet, but very tough. He could nip down the jet pipe and lift it on his shoulders while we decoupled. Dennis was about six foot nineteen with articulated arms and long fingers, he was very handy for getting hold of things such as the ARC 52 and TACAN, and putting them up in the radio bay down the back end. We used to reckon these two characters were kept on a rack in the corner of the hangar and issued on Tool Control!

It took two days to get this intercostal in. In the end my wrists were bleeding and they had to be covered in Swarfega to get them in and out. It required an open-ended spanner on eight nuts and bolts, with washers, a twelfth of a turn a time, turning the spanner in my fingers, dropping it of course about every third time and having to find it again by feel.

If the Scimitar had been fitted with more advanced Nav-Aids and Weapon delivery, do I think it would have remained in service longer? No, I don't think it could because of its limited operational performance. As an aerobatic machine, as a pilot's machine, as a fun aircraft, something that would go fast and twiddle around in the air and be strong, something you could throw at anything and it would not break very easily, it was superb. It would actually carry quite a heavy load, and it had the Aden cannons, which were quite devastating. But one needed an aircraft that would stay airborne for some time. The only way this could be achieved was by hanging tanks on it, and in doing so you reduced its weapon-load. The Nav-Aids, for what they were, were actually not bad. I suppose you could have had more advanced Nav-Aids, but the TACAN was very good and gave you distance and bearing from any beacon in non-operational conditions. The *Blue Silk* Doppler Radar was very good if you had it set up properly. It worked off the normal instrument system, the radar radiated downwards and the Doppler reflections from which it would calculate its movement relative to the ground. As part of the test flight procedure from Lee, I normally set this up at zero to see how much error I'd got when I came back. Bear in mind that I'd been climbing, rolling and in inverted flight, this part of the test flight being of course, to make sure the engines kept on running whilst upside down. The aircraft was turned upside down and held there for 10 seconds and waited for the fuel pressure 'dolls eyes' to flicker. If they did you pulled hard, if they didn't you waited until the end of the 10 seconds and rolled out again and put a tick in the box.

On one occasion I had 405 miles registered on my *Blue Silk*, a total flight time of 35 minutes, and a zero error of something like one mile when I got back. So it was pretty accurate and reliable.

Also we tested the LABS system which was monitored by a cross-wire system rather like *Green Salad*. If you kept the needles in the centre of the instrument you would perform a 4G loop, automatically releasing the "bomb" at the right trajectory, rolling out on a reciprocal course.

The aircraft also had two radios: the ARC 52, which was very reliable, and a standby UHF, which was pretty good. I did actually fly a Scimitar which had been converted for Airwork use by Fleetlands, so it had an extra VHF. On this test flight from Lee, all the radios packed up and, as it was eight-eighths cloud below, I elected to go to Brawdy, which was going to be the eventual delivery point anyway. Southern Radar at Sopley suddenly saw this aircraft streaking across their screens, unaware of what it was and unable to make contact with it. I managed to come in and do a wing-waggle over the airfield at Brawdy for a green flare clearance to land, as I had no R/T at all, and got down safely.

On another occasion involving streaking across Southern England, we set up Simon Askins for a record flight from Brawdy to Yeovilton in a Scimitar. We received clearance at both ends and got him to take off and fly at 2,000ft with the throttle bent around the stops. I think he did it in something like less than 13 minutes from wheels roll to touchdown at Yeovilton. To prepare for this we had practised re-entries. There was no point in trying to run at 645 knots straight over the airfield to turn down wind, because you would finish up 7 or 8 miles away and be nowhere near the circuit. We briefed him to chop his throttles over Taunton, air-brakes out, and as soon as he got down to 300 knots put his undercarriage down, with the throttles right back, progressively lowering the flaps and then bringing the throttle on for the final landing. The record before had been about 17 minutes in a Hunter.

I also was able to claim to be the only person flying in the South of England, possibly the whole of the UK. In the winter of 1963 the big freeze arrived and one night it snowed continuously. The next morning I arrived at Flight Test at Lee to find that there was not a cloud in the sky. Furthermore Harry Simpson, the Head of ATC at Lee, had the forethought to call a friend at the then Army depot in Titchfield. This resulted in a jungle grader being loaned overnight. It went up and down the main 05/23 runway and the main perimeter track all night. The result was that the runway and the perimeter-tracks round to 781 and Flight Test were completely clear by the time we were ready for a check test flight. I took the Scimitar up into this deep blue cloudless sky. From 45000 ft I could see Lands End, the Channel and Cherbourg – the land pure white and the sea deep black; and one little strip of black opposite the Isle of Wight: the *Daedalus* runway. Sopley radar controllers were taking it in turns to control me, as there was no one else in the air. All other military and commercial airfields were closed, even Heathrow. Shortly afterwards 781 Squadron got airborne but I had my moment of glory in a Scimitar F.1.

If I could put the clock back, would I do it all over again? Too right I would, I loved every minute of it. "

### Captain W.A.Tofts CBE AFC

My first Scimitar unit was No.700X Squadron, the Intensive Flying Training Unit at RNAS Ford. I was with them from August 1957 until April 1958 as Senior Pilot. On the unfortunate death of the CO, Cdr T.G.Innes AFC, RN, I took over as acting CO. My next Scimitar outfit was No.807 Squadron, where I took over as CO on 19 September 1959 staying in the Squadron until December 1960.

I logged 370 hours in the aircraft including 30 at night. My thoughts on my first take-off were of being taken for a ride not quite in charge. The acceleration was very impressive. I had not any simulator experience as it was not introduced until after the IFTU. I never did a take-off with BLC off. Landings yes, you had to do a flatter approach and come in at a higher speed.

Regarding landings, it was a controlled approach to a touch down point and not 'almost a controlled crash'.

Hydraulic failures never gave me any cause for concern, as they were duplicated.

I would regard my most dangerous moment as the time I experienced vertigo (spatial disorientation) during a night on-board recovery.

My best moment I would describe as doing a maximum rate climb in a clean aircraft to 40,000ft. The clean aircraft was very impressive in climb and acceleration. Manoeuvrability at altitude left a lot to be desired. This shortcoming was somewhat reduced by the introduction of Sidewinder. It would have benefited by the introduction of a thinner wing.

*Lt Cdr Tofts, the CO of No.807 Squadron, taking off from HMS Ark Royal at anchor in Grand Harbour, Valletta on 12 November 1960. (FAA Museum)*

The tendency to 'pitch up' was not really a problem, but it did tend to restrict manoeuvrability at altitude. Compared to USN aircraft of that era, its acceleration and rate of climb was quite good, but as above again manoeuvrability was not too hot.

I do not think the Scimitar would have remained in service any longer if it had been fitted with more advanced Nav-aids or weapon delivery system as it was a strike fighter and the roles tended to vary. i.e., Buccaneer - strike; Vixen and Phantom - fighter.

The low speed handling could have been better if more positive, i.e., lushness. The high speed was OK.

Under different weapon configurations there was a marked difference in handling. A clean aircraft was very different from the aircraft carrying bombs or drop tanks. Weapons were not particularly clean in those days. The shape was still World War 2 vintage, and this tended to increase overall drag considerably. Also drop tanks were a permanent feature under the wings.

The Scimitar was the first of the heavy aircraft to enter service with the FAA, and on reflection it had its shortcomings. At the same time it was a great step forward. To operate 'heavies' from *Centaur* and *Hermes*, particularly in high ambient temperatures, was questionable. In many cases, therefore, the aircraft got the blame, when in actual fact the ship from which they operated was possibly the reason.

Most pilots I think were quite fond of the Scimitar. Few pilots would praise the Wyvern, but that was because they were apprehensive of it, not fully understanding the mechanics of it. Those who disliked the Scimitar I would put in the same category. Its fuel balancing and hydraulics were complicated, but nevertheless understandable.

A night catapult launch was an exciting experience, followed by a night recovery on board. The night launch was indeed the most difficult. The attitude of the aircraft when on the catapult was relatively steep (yet in actual degrees not too great). This attitude had to be maintained until adequate flying speed had been reached. On a dark night with no horizon this was quite difficult, since any increase in the attitude resulted in increased drag - the aircraft would sink, and yet with a reduction of attitude there would be a loss of lift resulting in sink, so you can see the pilot was working within very close limits. This could be judged by the movements of the elevator. This was verified by the rapid movements of the tail navigation light mounted on the bullet on the tailplane. It certainly moved up and down quite rapidly.

It must be remembered that the cockpit instrumentation was comparatively primitive by today's standards. In later aircraft such as the Buccaneer the launch problem was overcome by designing the 'hands off' launch technique. As a matter of interest, on 12 August 1960 my Senior Pilot and I actually did two night launches and recoveries to fulfil the night flying programme of No.890 Squadron Sea Vixens, none of which was serviceable. We flew the sorties from *Ark Royal* against the *Hermes* which was being inspected by FOAC.

How would I compare the Scimitar to other jet aircraft I have flown? A clean aircraft, very impressive in climb and acceleration. Manoeuvrability at altitude left a lot to be desired.

### Lt Cdr N.M.Tristram

After a spell at 738 Sqn, Lt Cdr Tristram went to 736 Sqn in January 1961 for Scimitar training, after which he joined 803 Sqn in June 1961 until October 1962. He subsequently undertook Buccaneer conversion with 809 Sqn, and his later career included a spell with the French Navy flying Etendards, nine months with the US Navy Test Pilot School at Patuxent River and then two years at Boscombe Down ending in January 1972. He logged a total of 259.35 hours on Scimitars.

Thoughts on first take-off? 'Good grief!'.

Would I agree that landing the Scimitar was almost a controlled crash? An *almost* controlled crash! In fact the Scimitar was the first RN aircraft to employ a no round-out landing technique, hence the "controlled crash" reputation. However all

*The damaged windscreen of Lt N.M.Tristram after landing safely on HMS Hermes following a large bird strike at 3,000ft over south-west Crete on 14 July 1962. (P.G.De Souza)*

subsequent Naval aircraft (Buccaneer, Phantom) employed the same technique, which no longer seems unusual.

How would you compare the Scimitar to other jet aircraft you have flown? Enjoyable to fly, but fell exactly half way between a fighter and an attack aircraft, so not particularly good at either role.

My most dangerous moment while flying the Scimitar was the time I forgot to switch the BLC off when carrying out a practice single engined landing at RAF Tengah. I got lower and lower with full power on the one engine. Finally I re-lit the second engine which 'caught' just in time to pull me over the tops of some palm trees - it was another two minutes before enough composure returned to allow me to figure out my mistake.

My best moment was my first deck landing. Owing to the Kuwait crisis this was postponed for over a week, which heightened the tension. Eventually I was launched with live ammunition (just in case) and was much relieved to carry out a reasonably competent recovery (after initially mistaking the planeguard destroyer as the carrier in the milk bowl conditions of the Gulf). The second deck landing was over ten days later, so we were not overburdened with flying practice.

During the Kuwait crisis we were issued with Browning pistols and an emergency kit containing, amongst other things, three gold sovereigns. These were to be used to bribe friendly Arabs not to castrate us. Confidence in the efficiency of this was weakened when it was found that the emergency kit was wrapped in a silk scarf bearing on one side a roughly printed map covering somewhat indifferently the area between Beirut and Bombay, whilst on the reverse we were exhorted to Remember the Russians our gallant allies treat them as such.

Another problem area on the Scimitar was the spurious fire warnings. Indeed the pilot I originally replaced in No.803 died from injuries received as a result of ejecting following what was almost certainly a spurious fire warning. However, with time we became used to the problem and aircraft were only abandoned if the fire was plainly visible. Nevertheless, a warning of fire certainly got the adrenaline going. I well remember the coolness with which the Senior Pilot (Colin Caspard) handled a double fire warning when we were half way to Lossiemouth from around the Lisbon area, disembarking after five months in the Med. He announced that he had "one of those lights on". Any mention of fire warning would have had the listening RAF Air Traffic Controllers in no end of panic. On being asked, "Is it port or starboard?", he coolly announced, "Both, but no need to curtail flight". Clearly diversion, with wives waiting at Lossiemouth, was out of the question. I spent the rest of the journey with my eyes glued to his tail pipes. They were spurious warnings.

❖❖❖❖❖❖❖❖❖❖❖❖❖❖❖❖❖❖❖❖❖❖❖❖

**Lieutenant P.A.A. 'Paddy' Waring**

During March and April 1966 the Aircraft Carrier HMS *Eagle* was on patrol off the coast of East Africa on what was to be known as the Beira Patrol. It was her job to stop oil tankers taking oil into Beira, and consequently denying oil to Rhodesia. How successful this was can be judged by the *Joanna V* episode. She waived two fingers at us and sailed on in.

Someone somewhere in the corridors of power decided that HMS *Eagle* should send one of her aircraft to photograph the sea front at Durban and then come all the way back to the ship. This would show those naughty Rhodesians the fantastic range of Naval aircraft and put the fear of God into them.

The following is what happened to the pilot of the Scimitar which was to be the tanker aircraft, in his own words.

"I took a Scimitar tanker out in a pair with a Sea Vixen. The Sea Vixen pilot was Alan Hickling and his Observer was Nick Childs. The three of us knew each other very well and had tanked often. We were going to do it as high as we could. We started tanking at 38,000ft, and when we actually finished we were at 43,000ft. Essentially we had tanked in the climb. We started at something like 140 and tanked right out to approximately 250 miles from the ship. I was in fact out of UHF range by that time, so at that height we must have been at least 250 miles from Mother.

When I had reached 40,000ft, I realised that there was something acutely wrong with the fuel system of the aircraft, because although the fuel tended to get into rather odd positions on the gauges in any in-flight refuelling that was heavy, this was definitely strange. I had four booster pump lights on. That meant that half of my booster pumps had stopped for one reason or another. Again, one used to have this happen with the wing tank, but with the fuel gauges and the lights off it all began to look a little strange.

I told Alan Hickling to get the hell out of it, but because of where he was fuelling, he was actually in my radio shadow and could not hear me. Realising that something was acutely wrong, I then slammed the emergency re-wind. As Alan came up alongside me he said, " What the hell is wrong?".

He had been sucking away quite happily and then suddenly 'Whoosh!', the hose had gone. It was quite a startling performance as it really came in on emergency. I told him to get the hell out of it, now that he could hear me, "On your way Buddy", I said, "There is nothing you can do to help me". I then put the aircraft in maximum rate turn and headed back for the ship. Half way around the turn I realised I was in real trouble because the In-Flight Refuelling Pod was filling up again. Therefore what little fuel I had left was going into the Pod, which it should not have been as the Pod was switched off. I knew then that I had a valve stuck and possibly would not get back to the ship. I pressed the 'Clear Wing' button and £38,000 worth of tank and pod came tumbling down from 43,000ft, which would have given somebody a headache.

I kept the turn going, tried to raise the ship and couldn't. What I did not know at this stage was for the first time in the commission the 984 Radar had gone on the blink, which turned out to be very nearly tragedy as far as I was concerned. As I got within radio range, which would have been about 190 miles from Mother, in my first call I said, "Scramble the tanker" and then told them I had very serious fuel problems.

Nigel Grier-Rees was actually in the ACRB at that moment having a coffee, and to his undying credit he was airborne 11 minutes later. This was a fantastic performance by him and the men of No.800B Sqdn. It was only when he got airborne that I realised that the ship did not know where I was. It was patently obvious when the Direction Officer came on the air that he had no idea where I was and could not see the aircraft on radar. Nobody had told me up to then that the 984 was not working.

At this stage I was trying to glide this brick-built aircraft with the engines at absolute optimum, which if I recall correctly was 250 knots. I did this for some 22 minutes. I then had to think how do I get Nigel to see me, as he was obviously going to climb to altitude. I then remembered that Alan Hickling and I had started trailing at 38,000ft, so instead of telling him to climb to my height (I was coming through 26,000ft), I told him to climb to 38,000ft and I would direct him on to me once I saw him. It now seemed apparent to me that the ship had no radar at all and we were going to have to do the whole thing visually.

I had quickly done my fuel calculations and it looked as if I was going to drop into the sea at well over 100 miles from the ship. It was a windy day, force 7 or 8 down below. I was upwind of the ship and therefore the helicopters were not going to be able to get to me. There was no way that they could take off at that range. I concluded that I was going to be sitting in a one man dinghy in shark infested seas which were pretty rough - a prospect I did not fancy at all. Therefore it was in my interest to do a first time successful tank.

Within four minutes Nigel was at 38,000ft and I saw him immediately he trailed. I then directed him in my 12 o'clock towards me until I could see him through the top of my cockpit. By then I was at 22,000ft. I then told him to spiral down and hopefully he would be in front of me, but I over cooked it. We had got to the same height and now I could not see him, nor him me. I thought that that was it. I had one booster pump left out of the eight. The gauges were in a pathetic state. I had fuel but could not get hold of it.

I do not know what made me, but I looked to my right and saw him in my four o'clock-clock as he was turning away from me about 3 miles away. I yelled at him and he then took up position to come up behind me.

What I had planned was that he should take up the tanking position ahead of me. I thought I might well run out of fuel before he got there, and if I did I was going to get him to dive with his air-brakes just out and hopefully he would have more drag than me as I was a clean aircraft. I would then use my air-brakes to control myself and tank in the dive and hope to relight my engine. This was the strategy I had in mind.

As Nigel creamed past me the last of my boosters pump lights came on, which showed I had no fuel left except that which was in the galleries. There was considerable difference of opinion between the engineers, some say that one engine would flame out at about the 30 second mark and the others say it could have been as much as 1 minute 34 seconds.

The thing was I had not actually done any in-flight refuelling for some considerable time. I had always been playing the tanker to someone else. Now it was a first shot or nothing situation. Nigel was as good as gold. I told him to shut up, and he did because I wanted absolute freedom. When I actually plugged in I let out a hell of a shout, which was terribly giggly, but I was a little up tight at the time. I was convinced that the first rush of fuel would only push air into the engine because the galleries would only be a quarter full or thereabouts. In fact both engines kept going and I received enough fuel to get me back to *Eagle*, on which I landed safely thanks to Nigel Grier-Rees's superb dash off of the deck. Had he been 30 seconds slower I would not have made it.

Later, after a thorough investigation, we found that corrosion had occurred behind the 494 switch. This switch connected pairs of tanks so if the booster pumps in one failed, you could then suck fuel out using the adjacent booster pump. As a result of this corrosion the interconnecting valves had been opening and closing throughout the flight as if there were no tomorrow. Of course they were not designed for this. They were designed to be either closed or open. Because of their continuous movement, one after another they had failed. Some failed closed, some open, others half and half. As a result I had inaccessible fuel all over the aircraft. This resulted in the situation just described and eventually I had the wonderful Christmas Tree of eight booster pump lights on at the same time. Probably the only Scimitar pilot to ever have that situation."

The crash at RAF Changi, Singapore:

On Monday September 20th 1965, Paddy Waring was detailed to test fly Scimitar XD223 of No.803 Sqdn operating off HMS *Ark Royal*. Selected because of his thorough knowledge of Scimitar emergency procedures and his above-average flying abilities, both of these qualities were to be put to the ultimate test, as he describes in his own words:

"The aircraft had a long history of being a 'Hangar Queen', being constantly robbed for spares and then re-assembled after many weeks, then going flying with an awful lot of changed parts, was never a good scene.

Apart from the initial delay in starting with the other engine running, therefore not hearing that one igniter was unserviceable, there was also the severe metal fatigue which led to the final failure of the auxiliaries on the live engine. I would say that the metal fatigue failure probably occurred one mile or so out from touch down, because I was actually on the Johore side of the creek on finals. I think it must have been in the order of 2,000 yards or more away. At that stage I had enough hydraulic pressure left and I thought I could get to the end of the runway.

I didn't actually know then what had happened, there had just been a big thump from the back end and I only had the one engine running. I then had a total electrical failure, followed by a double hydraulic failure. I suspect I was about 150ft, and I remember I had 152 knots on at that stage of the game. The aircraft was coming back onto the centre line as I was being directed by Air Traffic Control, then the stick went absolutely solid.

The first thing I realised, after a very quick calculation, was that with over 1,500ft per min accelerating rate of decent, and with one wing and the nose low, I would not live if I ejected. I therefore delayed the ejection, electing to stay with the aircraft until it impacted the ground when the rate of decent would be zero and I could get out, which also made the mathematics better.

I left the power where it was, let go of the control column and sat with both hands holding the face blind with it raised so that I could watch, my intention being to fire the seat within half a second of the ground, i.e. as impact occurred. The mathematics for a perfect ejection situation would pertain - wings level, aircraft horizontal, over 90 kts forward speed. The idea being that I made skywards before the aircraft fell to bits. As it was I got it slightly wrong! I pulled the handle a little late, because in horror I had realised that I was landing bang in the middle of the approach lights, fortunately between two rows of them. As a result of this fractional delay due to thinking time, the canopy went off at ground level and I had an interesting and exciting ride through the lights.

Amazingly in that half second or so I had time to register the following events:

a) The marked increase in noise as the very large canopy came off.
b) The 'bow-wave' of soft earth that came up either side of the cockpit.
c) The approach lights on their 'telegraph poles' of wood, frangible, I hoped.
d) The starboard main oleo, with full compression on the strut and with the tyre fully inflated, rising up in front of the cockpit.

e) The road with traffic stopped at the lights, and the thought that if I had dropped into that, I'd have had it.
f) The firing, impact of, and sight of the ejection sequence.

The seat functioned perfectly, the parachute deploying at about 50ft. When I say the seat worked perfectly, I do so with a wry grin *as one pin was still in!* The seat had been changed from a Mk.4A to a 4C. The difference being that the latter seat had a further explosive device - the drogue gun - which therefore meant that it had one more pin than the 4A. The Ejection Seat Pin Holder had not been changed when the seat was changed, so that when the all the holes were full there was still one pin left in the seat.

The result was that very quickly matters looked terminally grim. For the life of me I could not understand why I was going along head first, looking down on the heap that I had just vacated which now got airborne again and was flying inverted over the road. The penny dropped when there was a faint tug, which laid me in the correct position - fore-and-aft, but on my right side. At this stage I was descending in a shallow parabola and realised that the main parachute had not deployed!

As the angle of descent steepened I realised that I was going to hit the end of the runway and very permanently hard if nothing happened fairly smartly. It did. The main parachute expanded with a very hard jerk and a loud snapping noise. My body pendulumed (ugh!) fast forward, rotating around the centre of the parachute. This meant that I hit the ground at a relatively shallow angle, as witnessed by my jungle boots, the heels of which were abraded away. I estimate my forward momentum as in the order of 50mph, one of the car drivers watching from a perfect vantage point likened me to a landing Vulcan with it's tail chute out. My legs folded instantly, despite my efforts to use them. My backside then impacted with real force on the seat pack and the momentum of my carcass was still so great that I did a full forward somersault, parachute and all.

I was winded, lying flat on my back looking up at the bluest sky you ever saw. I moved one arm and then the other. I moved my legs gingerly, everything seemed OK so I sat up and saw the aircraft on fire about a hundred yards away - very theatrical with the one good engine blazing away out of the rear and a great ball of blue black smoke ascending against the vulgar green of tropical grass and trees, the white Headquarters building standing out behind the crash scene.

One of the things that had lessened the damage to me was the fact that I had not unclipped my Mae-West, hence the pack was snubbed tightly against my backside when I began my aerobatics without the aircraft. On arrival (with the ground) I apparently 'decimated' (the Armourer's word) the contents, reducing the survival goodies to shards, the high-grade top covering preventing any of the shards puncturing my buttocks. The last thing I remember before hitting the ground was the ejection seat hitting the ground in front of me and bouncing up again. In fact when I actually opened my eyes I was lying with my left hand on the seat, we had landed that close together. Had I still been in that seat I would not be here today.

The only people that I know of who actually saw me eject, apart from an RAF Sergeant who was in his car waiting to cross at the runway traffic lights, were some guys working on a Meteor. They came racing across, absolutely ashen-faced, and asked me to sit down. This was the last thing I wanted to do as I was now looking at my seat pack and the state it was in. I walked up to the remains of my Scimitar which was inverted and on fire. The fire crew were frantically trying to get in and at the cockpit to get me out. I saw this Group Captain stood watching and asked him what was going on. "We are trying to get the bloody pilot out of course. Who the hell are you?", he snapped. "Actually, I am the pilot", I told the poor chap.

The Sergeant I mentioned earlier who had been sat in his car recognised me over 12 years later. I was in Reading and this man rushed up to me and shook my hand. He was the man who likened my flight to a Vulcan, and was sat at the traffic lights waiting to cross when I, followed by my inverted Scimitar flew across in front of him.

❖❖❖❖❖❖❖❖❖❖❖❖❖❖❖❖❖❖❖❖❖❖❖❖

### Lt Cdr C.A. 'Chris' Wheal

After the usual training (Jet Provost T.3 and Vampire T.11 at Linton-on-Ouse, Hunter T.8 and GA.11 on No.738 Sqdn at Lossiemouth) I went through Strike OFT on No.736 Sqdn at Lossie from 1 October 1963 to 31 January 1964 before joining No.803 Sqdn in *Hermes* under Lt Cdr 'Freddie' Mills, Senior Pilot Lt Cdr Johnnie Johnson. I flew out to *Hermes* in the Channel and did my first ever real live deck landings on 6 Feb 1964. We had a relatively short embarked period (the ship was coming home after a fairly long cruise, probably to the Far East but I'm not sure) which nonetheless included an air defence exercise in the North Sea and a most enjoyable run ashore in Copenhagen. We disembarked to Lossie on 23 February, by which time I had a grand total of 7 cat shots and 12 deck landings in my log book. My ancillary duties in No.803, apart from the usual Divisional Officer obligations, were that I became the line book officer.

Freddie Mills was relieved by Pete Newman in mid-April and I stayed with No.803 flying disembarked at Lossie until the end of August 1964. We spent the time learning the finer points of low level strike operations and ACM tactics under the capable tuition of the squadron AWIs, Fred de Labilliere and Joe Billingham.

Fred and Joe also did their best to teach us the finer points of low level strike ingress. Thundering down the Loch Shin gap for a live strike at Tain or Rosehearty with three other Scimitars in battle formation at 420 knots and 250 feet - well, say 200 - well, maybe 150 - with one eye always out for the bounce was some of the most exhilarating flying I've ever done. Cranking up to 480 knots and sliding into an arrowhead low level strike formation during the run in and then moving across to echelon starboard for the pull-up and roll in on the target. We got to know the Scottish low level areas so well we hardly needed maps.

After one of these exercises that had culminated with a low level bombing attack at Tain, Johnny Flexman returned with fragmentation damage to his aircraft caused by a 25lb practice bomb. He was later heard to say: "I can't understand it. I just did my normal low level bombing attack, released the weapon and pulled up to miss the target".

At the end of August I was one of three No.803 Sqdn pilots selected to form 800B Flight under Lt (later Rear Admiral) Roger Dimmock. The other lucky pilot was Lt Paddy Meiklejohn. The original intent behind 800B was that we would be an adjunct to 800 Sqdn (Buccaneer 1s) providing experimental flight refuelling capabilities to all intents and purposes under the command of Chris Mather, the 800 CO, Roger, bless him, fought long, hard and in the end successfully to obtain virtually complete command autonomy, though in practice when we were embarked in *Eagle* we did most of our refuelling work with 800. Our usual configuration was four tanks, with a buddy pod on the starboard inner pylon.

There's an interesting story attached to the No.800B emblem, the foaming tankard that adorned the fins of our aircraft. When the flight first formed morale among the troops was pretty low. They came from all over the place - unlike us they weren't all ex-803 - most had been yanked out of secure billets where they were comfortable with their mates, but there were one or two real skates. We even had one who came to us straight from DQs. Guess whose division he ended up in. So, during the early weeks while everyone was feeling pretty disrupted and no-one knew what was to become of us, whether we would have an existence of our own or be forever subservient to Chris Mather's No.800 Squadron, morale among the troops was not good.

Then some brilliant fellow came up with the idea of the squadron emblem, which was immediately painted on the fins of our aircraft. It gave the sailors a sense of belonging and their spirit improved overnight. After a couple of days, however, Wings

*No.800B Flight personnel aboard HMS Eagle in May 1965. In the centre front are the three squadron pilots, left to right Lt Paddy Meiklejohn, Lt Roger Dimmock (CO) and Lt Chris Wheal. (C.A.Wheal).*

(whose name I have forgotten but who was considered rather a stuffy gentleman) decreed that the foaming tankard was unbecoming and ordered us to take it off. Morale plunged once more. As luck would have it there was a mess dinner the same week and in the course of the after dinner festivities, with my inhibitions loosened by alcohol, I happened to mention our problem to David Kirke, who was at that time the Captain of Lossiemouth. He, being the leader he was, saw straight away that the benefits far outweighed any slight irreverence and the next day countermanded Wings' order. So we got to keep our foaming tankard and the sailors loved it.

I spent my time in 800B as the squadron staff officer. At first there were just the three officers and 37 ratings with a senior CPO filling in as AEO. Later we gained a fourth pilot, Ian Frenz, and a real AEO, a SD Sub-Lieutenant whose name unfortunately escapes me. The atmosphere and morale in 800B were absolutely outstanding - it was like being in a small ship, quite unlike the largely impersonal atmosphere in a "normal" sized squadron where one hardly got to know any ratings outside one's division and the squadron senior rates.

We embarked in *Eagle* on 2 December 1964, just in time for Christmas, and immediately set off for the Far East. The ship was supposed to spend Christmas in Naples but "haven't you heard, it's all been changed," so we did a little flying off Aden and then went south for Christmas in Mombassa. After that it was a fairly standard Far East cruise - no flying on passage to Singapore, then disembarked to RAF Tengah in mid-January 1965 and led a relaxed existence working tropical routine until we went back to the ship on 28 January. While at Tengah we took part in something called Exercise *Iron Gate* and did our usual flight refuelling stuff with the Buccaneers and also with some Javelins from 65 Squadron. I have a photograph of a Javelin firmly plugged into the hose behind my Scimitar. I also remember incurring the mild displeasure of Wing Commander Flying for coming into the break at roughly 550 knots (or whatever the limiting speed was on the buddy pod, which I've forgotten) one day, just to show the Javelins who was boss.

We didn't do much variety of weaponry in *Eagle* - there wasn't a lot we could carry that was compatible with the four-tank configuration - but we did a fair amount of 30 mm strafing on the ship's splash target, which was great fun. Most of the time we just had a single gun loaded with ball ammunition, but in March 1965 we did a firepower demo called *Showpiece Malaysia* in which we had all four loaded with HE and simply hosed the target. I remember the feeling of astonishment as the aeroplane seemed to lose about 30 knots almost instantaneously as I pressed the trigger. It also provoked the typical Scimitar response of a hydraulic failure which was a pretty standard reaction to having four guns fired at once.

After Singapore we went to Subic Bay where we were very graciously hosted by the US Navy and had a guided tour (actually several guided tours) of Olongapo, then to Hong Kong and back to Singapore for another two weeks of shore-based operations, this time from RAF Changi. This was a much more relaxed period than the one at Tengah, in fact my logbook only shows three flights between transits to and from the airfield. However, I'm darned if I can remember much else of what we did apart from lying around the pool at, I think, Tamar and getting to know Bougis Street quite well.

*Eagle* returned to home waters and we disembarked to Lossie on 23 May 1965. We spent the summer doing the usual varieties of disembarked flying: weapons practice at Tain, shipping strikes, taking part in Lossie Air Day display and doing the odd session of MADDLs to keep our hands in. On one shipping strike while strafing the splash target I collected a 30mm ricochet down the port engine. The bullet lodged in the nose cone of the engine and stayed there for most of the flight home, but eventually fell out, stuck between two of the compressor stator blades and chewed up the first stage of the compressor rotor. That led to my first single-engine landing "in anger."

In August Pete McManus joined us from 803, so we were now up to four pilots, just in time to re-embark on 25 August and once again set sail for foreign parts, in this case the Med. September had us operating in the areas around Malta, but by October we had transited the canal and were heading for Mombassa again. Those were the days of the Rhodesian unilateral declaration of independence and after leaving Mombassa *Eagle* was scheduled to go on the Beira patrol. I was very glad that that was the moment to leave, as having South African connections I should have found it highly distasteful to take part in the blockade of a country with which I had strong sympathies. Paddy Waring joined in Mombassa as my relief and took over as the Staff Officer.

I flew a total of about 360 hours in the Scimitar. It was an impressive aeroplane and it was obviously in a different class from the Hunters that we had flown immediately before. I don't remember ever hearing it called "The Beast."

As Alan Goodenough wrote, the Scimitar conversion included an accelerate-stop up to about 70-100 kts before one's first flight, so the ground acceleration did not come as a surprise. But the airborne acceleration did and the feeling as the aircraft rushed up to the climbing speed of 500 kts was like barely hanging onto a runaway train. I couldn't believe the enormous nose-up attitude required to hold 500 kts, and 10,000 ft came up LONG before one was ready for it. One's brain was still on the runway. There just wasn't anything between the Naval Hunter with its one rather feeble 100-Series Avon and the Scimitar with its hairy-cheated pair of 200-Series engines. I later flew the RAF Hunters (6s and 9s) with 200-series engines and while not comparable with the Scimitar they would certainly have been a nice stepping stone. But then, we all apparently survived that first Scimitar take-off, so we probably didn't really need a stepping stone after all.

My most dangerous moment was unquestionably my one and only whispering bolter. I was young and cocky, had about 50 deck landings under my belt and thought I was invincible. I hadn't bolted in months, been catching 2 and 3 wires regularly and I was so (over) confident that I closed the throttle before I felt the wire. BIG mistake. Thank heavens the Scimitar didn't have fan engines or I wouldn't have made it. Wings (Duncan Lang) called me up to Flyco afterwards when I'd stopped shaking and he hardly said anything beyond "You won't do that again, will you?".

Best moment flying the Scimitar? It's hard to choose among them. Certainly taking part as a very junior squadron pilot in the giant Fleet Air Arm Anniversary flypast balbo at Yeovilton in 1964 was a thrill, as were the Navy Day flypasts, also at Yeovilton, in late June and early July. I suppose I thought I would never forget what Navy Day was. One occasion that sticks in my mind was a pre-dawn launch for a shipping strike in the South China Sea. It was still dark when we manned up and just barely getting light when we launched, but climbing up through a cloudless sky at about 20,000 feet I had my own sunrise. I am not usually a morning person, but it made the 0330 wake-up call and the groggy stumble down to the ACRB for a bacon sandwich all seem worthwhile.

Comparisons with other aircraft are a little difficult at this distance in time and I wish I had had a chance to fly the Scimitar again later in life when I had a more varied base to judge it against. However, I can certainly say that it was one of the most exhilarating aircraft I have ever flown and also one of the nicest handling. I would rank it in my personal top five, along with the Lightning, Harrier, Sea Fury and Spitfire.

The aircraft would have been transformed if some way could have been found to increase the internal fuel load. Eight thousand pounds internal fuel with those two thirsty Avons was somewhat ridiculous and of course led to the situation all too common with British aircraft where the only way to get any kind of range or endurance out of it was to fly with drop tanks, which immediately cut the number of useable weapon stations in half. Perhaps a centre-line tank would have been possible, though it would have screwed up the fuselage flaps.

Another thing that would have been interesting would have been to see if giving the aircraft a proper area rule configuration would lead to any gains in cruise performance. As it was, although the fuselage had a bit of a "coke bottle" squeeze amidships, it looked rather more cosmetic than scientific, and the transonic drag rise rather confirmed one's visual impressions.

It would have been fun with afterburners. Apart from giving it an even more shattering take-off and climb burners would have done something to rescue the high altitude turn performance, which was nothing to write home about between 20,000 and 30,000 ft and pretty well non-existent above 30,000. Burners would have made it a genuinely supersonic aircraft, though since its primary role was low level strike (despite the number of high level intercept exercises we used to fly in 803) it is doubtful whether that would have had any operational significance.

Whether the carrier cycle could have withstood the increased fuel consumption is another question. A more self-contained method of starting than low pressure air from a Palouste would have given it more flexibility in choice of diversion or cross-country fields. Possibilities might have been an internal electric starter (just about everywhere has power carts), the AVPIN starter that the RAF Hunters used (though AVPIN is nasty stuff and would probably have posed storage problems on board), or a small APU such as was fitted to the Harrier.

If memory serves, the Scimitar was operational when the USN was transitioning from earlier generations of aircraft like the F-9F and F-11F to the A-6, A-7, F-4, F-8, RA-5 and the like, with the A-4 being the fleet workhorse throughout the period. The climb and level flight performance of the non-afterburning US aircraft was probably inferior to the Scimitar, but apart from the A-4 and F-4 which used to carry even more external tanks than the Scimitar most of these aircraft had internal fuel capacities that at least gave them pretty respectable legs to start with, the A-6 and A-7 being particularly good in this respect. Then if the mission called for going even further, tanks gave them extra range.

"Almost a controlled crash" sounds emotive but in fact it is true of any correctly executed deck landing. The magic secret of the mirror landing sight (and its successor the projector sight) is that it is only by flying a constant descent angle right down to the deck with no flare at all that one can achieve the precision and consistency essential to operational flying. At 120 kts relative speed the rate of descent at touchdown is about 10 ft/sec which is a fair old thump but nothing to get upset about with a decent long stroke undercarriage, which the Scimitar certainly had. Naval aircraft are tested to much higher rates of descent than that during acceptance trials. I forget the exact numbers but it is certainly 25 ft/sec and may be as high as 30 ft/sec. That will really rattle your fillings.

Actually I always thought the Scimitar was a very easy aircraft to deck land. The approach speed was firmly on the back side of the drag curve and the excellent throttle response and longitudinal handling made it a lot easier than the Vixen which never had enough drag and also had a less than ideal longitudinal control system. In retrospect, after flying several other types to the deck, I could never understand why it wasn't allowed to night fly from the boat. The USN was flying single-seaters with no better handling (A-4, for example). I'd love to see the C Squadron test report(s) that led to that decision. Mind you, I would never have dreamed of querying it at the time, and however misguided the decision may have been from an operational point of view it at least allowed one to be a gentleman fighter pilot. Colin Morris had a good point when he said the best part of flying Scimitars was watching the Vixens night fly. I could add the Buccaneer 1s to that.

Would I do it again? Like a shot. I loved every minute of it.

**Captain J.L.Williams**

No.804 Squadron February to October 1960. Logged 111.05 hours.

Can I remember my thoughts on my first take-off, and did the acceleration surprise me? The aircraft had a very "urgent" feel, and very impressive acceleration/climb performance characteristics. Certainly a surprise in a brand new, clean Scimitar even after a Hunter conversion. But I had had one flight in a Sea Vixen observer's seat from Abbotsinch, so had some idea what to expect.

How would I compare the Scimitar to other jet aircraft I have flown? Fastest climb of all, good cockpit layout and comfort level, excellent engines, first class view and good gun fire power. The manoeuvrability (subsonic) at altitude was limited, (35-40,000 feet) also short on internal fuel.

What would I consider my best moment? Getting on to the tail of a Sea Vixen (for which I was the "AI target") flown by the CO of No.892, who had been my Senior Pilot in No.804 (Sea Hawk). Great.

What developments do I think the Scimitar could have benefited from? Nose wheel steering (fitted in the Sea Vixen) would have saved much brake, tyre and flight deck paint wear and simplified parking on deck. All other worthwhile improvements short of a major redesign (never on the cards with the Buccaneer coming along) were made while the aircraft was in service (e.g. introduction of air-to-air missile).

If the clock could be put back, would I do it all again? Of course.

Force of circumstances made the Scimitar an "interim" machine which I was lucky to have the opportunity to fly. Few aircraft types which actually entered squadron service failed to be developed to "Mark 2" standard, and often beyond, but that was the fate of the Scimitar because the Vixen had the superior air to air capability and the strike role was being assumed by the Buccaneer. I do not think the maintainers were sorry to see it go, but it was a fun machine for pilots.

### Captain J.Worth

From August 1959 until September 1960, I was the AWI on No.803 Squadron. Later, I became CO of No.736 Sqn from August 1964, then CO of No.803 Sqn from June 1965 until September 1966 when the squadron disbanded. I logged 650 hours flying the Scimitar.

My thoughts on my first take-off were that it was exhilarating. The acceleration was a surprise, but I had been well forewarned.

I agree that landing the Scimitar was almost a controlled crash. This was because landings were made at speeds on the wrong side of the drag curve; power was used to compensate for reduced lift.

Comparing the Scimitar to other jet aircraft I have flown, despite its limitations, in particular poor handling at high level and mediocre weapon load, the aircraft was extremely pleasant to fly. Its flying controls were exceptionally good for its era, remaining constant throughout the speed range 130-780 knots.

The tendency to pitch was no real problem. The aircraft really had to be abused to get into serious trouble, there were plenty of warning signs prior to 'departure' from normal flight.

Judged against US Navy aircraft of the time, it compared reasonably well with its main contemporary, the Skyhawk. While the Scimitar was relatively poor in payload/range and serviceability it was far superior in its handling, especially against an adversary; the A-4 was like a truck and poor in the dive/attack mode. The US A-6 Intruder was of course superior but this was the Buccaneer equivalent.

My most dangerous moment while flying the Scimitar was a deck landing in the Far Fast in no wind conditions at 38 degrees C in a single engine emergency; full power was needed to achieve a gentle turn straight and level, final line-up and glide-path adjustment left little margin for error. Not recommended for daily repetition.

My best moment was low-level flying in northern Norway through the fjords and mountains. In its day the Scimitar was incomparable low-level.

Due to the amount of hydraulic failures the Scimitar suffered from, did this ever give me cause for concern? Not really since there was a fairly comprehensive backup system, double failures were rare.

Did I ever night fly the Scimitar? Yes, including night weaponry under flare attacks. However the aircraft was a single seater and without radar, with very poor bolter characteristics on the deck. It was never a contender as a strike/attack vehicle.

If the clock could be put back, would I do it all again? Of course, no question.

### Lt Cdr M.Keighley R.N. (Rtd)

The Scimitar - A View from the Hangar

Mike Keighley served as the Assistant AEO (Air Engineer Officer) with No.807 from December 1960 until the Squadron disbanded in April 1962. During that time the squadron operated from *Ark Royal* and *Centaur*, with disembarked periods at Lossiemouth, Hal Far, Khormaksar and Tengah.

My first impression on confronting the Scimitar was how large it appeared compared with the previous generation of Naval jet aircraft such as the Sea Hawk and Sea Venom. There were a number of aeronautical features of the design not seen on RN aircraft before - a 45° swept back wing, blown flaps, a flying tailplane with 10° anhedral and an area-rule fuselage. All this seemed rather advanced at the time! With an all up weight of 43,500lbs, some 19.4 tons, man-handling the aircraft in and out of the hangar was now a thing of the past, as such movements could only be achieved safely with powered equipment - tractors ashore and specialised mechanical handlers at sea.

The propulsion was provided by two Rolls-Royce Avon RA.28 Mk 202 axial-flow gas turbines buried in the fuselage. Access to each engine was achieved by removing from the fuselage upper surface large panels secured by numerous countersunk screws, followed by the unbolting of portable half-frames at stations 12 and 14. An auxiliary gearbox mounted on top of each engine carried two hydraulic pumps and a 28 volt 6kw DC generator. An electrically operated valve, positioned on top of the compressor casing, ducted air for the blown flaps. In service these engines were quite reliable and gave little trouble, FOD (foreign object damage) to the first few rows of the compressor blades being perhaps one of the most frequent reasons for a non-routine engine change. If an engine failed to come up to performance on a test flight or a full-power tied-down run, there was little scope for rectification at front-line service level. An engine change was relatively straightforward although the replacement of the lower mounting bolts could be trying. The removal and replacement of the jet pipes was an awkward and frustrating job despite the provision of a portable rail assembly rig, these being designed to assist the inching of the pipes in and out of a somewhat confined space.

Starting the engines (port first), both ashore and afloat, was by LP air supplied from a ground starter rig, usually of the 'Palouste' type. Pressing the pilot's starter button sent a signal via a lead plugged into the aircraft causing a small centrifugal gas turbine in the starter rig to accelerate and a compressor bleed-valve to open, air then being ducted to the Avon engine starter mounted on front of the compressor. This system was remarkably effective considering the wear, tear and heavy handling involved and, apart from plug/socket damage and the occasional defective lead produced very few problems. I can only recall one instance when an Avon engine starter had to be changed.

Routine engine servicing was minimal but checking the engine oil levels could be difficult due to the arrangements for viewing the sight-glasses mounted on the right-hand side of each oil sump. On the starboard engine a panel had to be removed from the upper fuselage and the sight-glass viewed via a mirror located adjacent to the base of the engine, whilst for the port engine the level could be seen through a glass panel provided in top of the ammunition belt-link collector box. In the gloom of the hangar or at night the actual oil level could not always be readily determined.

The hydraulics system, or rather three hydraulic systems, were the veritable 'plumber's nightmare', with inaccessible components and yards of twisting small-bore pipe work, all pressurised to 4,000 psi. No.1 system, the primary, provided all the main services - flying controls, undercarriage, wingfold, wheel brakes etc; No.2 system flying controls only. Each system was pressurised by two hydraulic pumps (two-stage type, stage one gears; stage two seven piston radially displaced) one driven from each engine. In addition,

*No.803 Squadron pilots on board HMS Ark Royal in 1966. Left to right – seated Lt E.K.Somerville-Jones, Lt D.W.Moore, Sub-Lt G.M.Faulkner and Sub-Lt A.R.Dady; standing Lt M.J.Williams, Lt Cdr J.W.H.Purvis (Senior Pilot), Lt Cdr J.Worth (CO), Lt T.J.Notley, Lt P.G.De Souza and Lt R.J.Shercliff. (P.G.De Souza)*

No.1 system featured three air pressurised accumulators and both systems were provided with filters and hydraulic oil coolers, the heat transfer medium being fuel. The third system, described as the emergency system, consisted of a hydraulic motor/pump unit, powered by No.2 system which could be used to get down the undercarriage and deckhook (and flaps too, I think) in the event of a No.1 system failure.

The general functioning of the systems was good and in particular the Fairey flying controls and the various hydraulic jacks gave very little trouble, a non-routine replacement being rare. Nearly all the repair work, and there was plenty of it, resulted from leaks at joints and unions, split or fractured pipes, the latter being common. Failure of the No.1 system, due to a fractured pipe following firing of the 30mm Aden guns, occurred on a number of occasions. If this happened whilst at sea, the aircraft could be readily handled after an arrested precautionary landing (a pair of portable air/oil accumulators connected into quick-release couplings activated the wing-fold). Ashore it was a different matter as the wheel brakes were inoperative. This happened to Lieutenant Mike Griffin after landing at RAF Khormaksar with a gun-firing induced hydraulic failure. Unfortunately a 'Safe-Land' barrier was not available and XD282 ran off the end of the runway, bounced over a sand bund-wall and ended up in a salt water lagoon, rapidly settling up to its belly in rather foul and sticky mud. Despite the best efforts of the RAF Salvage Section with their tractors, the Scimitar would not budge and it subsequently took Squadron maintenance personnel working with the RAF almost two days to recover the aircraft. This involved disconnecting the undercarriage,

a most difficult job in extremely unpleasant conditions and resulted in considerable airframe damage before XD282 could be dragged into a position where it could be lifted. With a jury undercarriage fitted, the aircraft was later lightered back on board *Centaur*, eventually to be delivered to RNAY Fleetlands for a major repair. I remember seeing this aircraft some months later at Lee-on-Solent, just fresh out of the paint-shop, the Fleetlands fitters commenting on the amount of mud and seashells recovered from various apertures.

The cause of most of the non-routine maintenance work-load was undoubtedly the complex and often (or so it seemed) unreliable fuel system. This consisted of five fuselage tanks of the flexible self-sealing type and four integral wing tanks, two in each wing. These tanks provided a total capacity of 1,064 galls (8,512 lbs of AVCAT at 0.8sg). In addition, four external or 'drop' tanks could be fitted, one 150 gall outboard and one 200 gall inboard on each wing. With drop tanks installed the maximum full load was 1,764 galls (14,461 lbs) - almost 6.1 tons!

Each internal tank was provided with a booster pump (except Nos.3 & 4, which being inter-connected only had one), together with electrically operated in-line refuelling valves, non-return valves, high level and low level float switches and a means of measuring the fuel contents with tube-type capacitors. In addition, two air-pressurised recuperators fitted at the rear of No.5 tank could supply a total of 12 galls into the system when the aircraft inverted and the booster pumps lost suction. Each booster pump had three speeds below about 18,000 feet with a further two speeds above that altitude. Signals from the fuel contents capacitors in each tank were fed to a 'black box' which controlled the speed of each booster pump to ensure that the fuel in all the tanks emptied such that the aircraft trim (or balance) remained constant. If, say, the forward group of tanks were emptying too quickly, and the aircraft became tail heavy, then the 'black box' would cause the after group of pumps to speed up and the forward group to slow down until the balance was restored. To assist the pilot, a fuel balance gauging system was installed in the cockpit, the contents of each of the seven internal tanks (Nos.3 & 4 being treated as one tank) being indicated by a vertical strip of orange lights. As fuel was used these lights were extinguished in a horizontal line, indicating that fuel balance was being maintained. If for any reason a tank failed to empty, the lights for that tank would remain on. In this event the pilot could over-ride the system with the 'pilot select - nose heavy/tail heavy' switch and attempt to restore the balance manually.

In theory the system was admirable, being designed to reduce to a minimum the pilot's work-load in managing the fuel system; in practice it was rather different. 'Fuel balance U/S' was an all too frequent entry in the Form A700 and often resulted in many hours of work, both by the electrical and AE trades, to identify and rectify the fault. Access to components was restricted and care had to be taken not to over-tighten the fuel pipe couplings, which leaked all too readily, despite the use of special 'C' spanners. Perhaps the system component that was the most awkward to deal with was a device known as the fuel proportioner, basically a pump driven by a hydraulic motor (from No.1 hydraulic system) which took suction from the drop tanks and transferred the fuel into No.3 fuselage tank. Numerous fuel and hydraulic pipes had to be taken down to get at it, buried as it was in the centre of the fuselage forward of No.3 tank.

Changing a fuselage tank, particularly in the tropics, required considerable patience and stamina. Because the hangar of *Centaur* was situated over the boiler rooms, the temperature within the fuselage of the aircraft was often above 110°F, despite air being ducted into the tank bay to try and cool the air mechanic struggling to get the replacement tank unfolded and positioned to register the various flanges and couplings, together with the press-studs that located the tank within the bay. The high humidity experienced in the Persian Gulf during the 1961 Kuwait Crisis rendered a tank change an uncomfortable and sweaty operation. If an integral wing tank leaked (and most of them did), rectification at front-line level was rarely successful as the leak usually developed along a seam joint in the wing structure. Consequently large drip-trays had to be positioned beneath the wings whenever the aircraft was hangared. Fuel from a leaking wing-tank degraded the seal between the pylon fairing and the wing lower surface, transforming the seal material into a messy goo.

Towards the end of 1961 most of 807's aircraft had achieved between 300 to 500 flying hours and my 'AEO's Note-Book' records that there were some twenty items on the 'Black List', i.e., defects for which it was mandatory to raise a Defect Report - Form A.21. A number of these items related to skin or component cracking, particularly towards the rear of the aircraft, where acoustically induced panel cracking had given rise for concern on the development aircraft. It was said that the Scimitar was not only the largest, heaviest and most powerful day fighter the Royal Navy had acquired up to that time, but was also most certainly the noisiest! NDT (non destructive testing) procedures were just coming in for front line use and X-Ray examination of the internal structure at the base of the fin was one of the first areas where this technique was employed. However, although the Scimitar airframe was given a 1,000 hour fatigue life, it seems doubtful if more than a handful of the build run approached this figure.

Whether or not the Scimitar was successful for its intended purpose I shall have to leave to the aviators to comment, but observing the aircraft sink off the end of the catapult with only half fuel and a reduced weapon load in the high humidity and temperature of the Persian Gulf did cause me to wonder at the effectiveness of the design for carrier-borne operations, at least in the Middle Eastern theatre.

One factor perhaps not so widely appreciated was the effect on the morale of the ground-crews, especially those of the AE trades. Many of the most senior ratings, who had started their careers with the Sea Fury and had gone on to the Sea Hawk found the intimidating problems of trying to keep the Scimitar serviceable frustrating, particularly in view of the long hours involved and the disheartening degree of unreliability. In a cold Scottish hangar, with a diesel-driven hydraulic test rig coupled into each hydraulic system and a petrol 'Houchin' plugged in to provide electrical power, the levels of 'din', together with the exhaust fumes were not conducive to pleasant working conditions. 'Maintaining this type of aircraft just isn't fun any more', remarked one experienced mechanic, giving that as his reason as to why he would not be extending his period of service at the end of his 'twelve'. Maybe he was right, as with the advent of the Scimitar, the last aircraft to designed and built entirely by Supermarine, the days of the relatively cheap and simple likes of the Sea Fury and Sea Hawk had gone forever. And perhaps with it the fun too.

❖❖❖❖❖❖❖❖❖❖❖❖❖❖❖❖❖❖❖❖❖❖❖❖

**PO(El) Norman Eames**

Servicing the Scimitar

I may seem to be criticising an aircraft I thought most highly of, but I still think it would be a good match for anything we have flying today.

Being a new type of aircraft, engine life was very short, so changes became commonplace. On the electrical side it was easy: just a few connections, then to remain in attendance to help. The two main anchor points (one inboard and one outboard) had some peculiar way of being fitted to make a secure mounting. With the new engine still suspended from the crane, the manoeuvring required was very delicate indeed. The inboard connection had to be made first; sometimes this took a few minutes, other times it could be some hours: there was no set pattern no matter how good a fitter you were. Even I was allowed to have a go just to give the others a rest. Sometimes I did it easily, other times I didn't manage it at all. Once the inboard was fitted, one could see what had to be done to the other side, though it was just as difficult. From then on whoever was handy helped to finish off. Finally the top panel, with all of those screws, had to be put back. It was then moved out of the hangar for a run-up and power test.

The most annoying job for an electrician was the after-flight remedy of faulty 'Fuel Gauge' content readings. Seldom did one land on without such a problem. It was always the amplifiers situated in the wing root, situated under a panel some 2x3 ft held in place by approx 50 x 4BA screws, that were the cause of the problem. Next came the biggest of all headaches - The Master Reference Gyro; a large black unit found in the battery bay on the underside between the main undercarriage units. Again, once the fault became known (and it was nearly always the same) it was easy to change.

Even though it is some 25 years since I worked on the Scimitar, it still seems as though it was last week. The 1958 Farnborough Air Show I remember well, as it proved that we were all learning very fast. The achievement of keeping six aircraft flying for every one of the ten days was a record in itself. Cdr J.D. Russell, (our CO) made a point of thanking us for all our efforts.

Servicing the aircraft ashore on airfields other than our own could, and did, cause some problems at times. At one time No.803 Sqn operated from Hyères, a French airfield in the south of France. To us it looked more like a scrap yard, but did have a modern-looking tower. Each day a small party of us would be taken by bus from the ship, which was in Toulon, to the airfield. Due to the special fuel connectors on the aircraft we had to borrow a British European Airways fuel bowser from Nice airport to enable us to refuel the Scimitars. Having to adapt the one which the French had was very slow and often the pressure wasn't high enough to operate the inlet valves.

In order to refuel a Scimitar it was essential to have electrical power to enable the indicating and control systems to operate and to show when each tank was full. Whilst doing this an electrician would sit in the cockpit and do all the other between-flight checks, including helping out the pilot's Mate with air, oxygen etc.

On one of these occasions a Frenchman, using frantic sign language, tried to tell us the dangers of using electrics whilst fuelling at the same time. It was quite a task pacifying him, and he, having got the message, walked away into the hangar (full of various aircraft) used a lighter and begun puffing away at a cigarette. From that day on we put an extra 50 yards between us and that hangar. We knew *we* were safe but were not so sure about them.

On the occasion of Lt Maina shedding half of his jet pipe after take-off (XD237, 10.12.58), this meant for me my first flight in a helicopter. I was sent ashore to remove the MRG (Master Reference Gyro) from the aircraft at Hal Far where it had diverted to. Being a large, expensive and very delicate item, we needed all the spares we could lay our hands on. I had to ride back in the helicopter with this thing firmly clamped in my lap.

This Jet Pipe incident caused a great deal of work. A team from Rolls-Royce came out to the ship while we were still off Malta. We were split into teams to lift or remove anything which may have revealed a fault so that the Rolls-Royce men, armed with huge magnifying glasses, could inspect it. In the end the aircraft were cleared again for flying, but the Jet Pipe had to be removed for inspection after every 10 or 12 hours, and replaced with a new one after only 25 hours.

**John H. Stevens** [co-author]

Having joined the Royal Navy in 1962 as an Aircraft Handler, to me the Scimitar was the most aesthetically pleasing aircraft there was; it always reminded me of a shark, especially after being catapulted off, staying low-level and then hurtling skywards.

Aircraft Handler: The title speaks for itself. We were the guys who moved the aircraft around from one place to another, so that the Air Mechanics, Artificers and Armourers etc, could work on them. Not a terribly glamorous job, but a very important one nonetheless. Carried out with too much haste and slackness and it could result in the damage to an aircraft costing thousands of pounds. At night on a slippery, heaving deck, the movement of a 15 ton aircraft 700 or 800ft down the deck with no lights, and then parking it on a pre-arranged spot took quite a lot of skill. We were also the men who could, and did, rig the Emergency Barrier in less than 5 minutes; 20 or more men working as one. As such we were the men who were normally first on the scene in the event of a crash, even doing the actual rescue if needed and fighting the fire. We were also the men who chipped and painted the flight deck, the Island, the centre line, cleaned out the scuppers and scrubbed the deck. As I said, not a glamorous job but a very important one, and one which I loved.

My first view of a Scimitar gave me quite a shock. I had done my training on the Dummy Deck at RNAS Culdrose's School of Aircraft Handling, where the aircraft mainly in use was the dainty Sea Hawk which I had got used to working on and around.

The Scimitars were used on the Dummy Deck to give trainees some experience in moving large aircraft around confined spaces. As with the 508, they were also continually being subjected to close encounters with the hangar walls, each one having very dented tailplanes.

Each time I returned to the SAH for promotion courses, I would work with Scimitars. Two of them, the Type 544 prototypes WT854 and WT859, were no longer airworthy, but were there for us to train on. In one hangar the Type 508, minus its mainplanes, was used for tractor driver training. I always thought that it was an awful waste of such a rare aeroplane, gradually being battered to pieces by countless Naval Airmen bashing it against the hangar walls.

The actual simulated flying was still done by Sea Hawks, mostly 'piloted' by Petty Officer Aircraft Handlers.

I first encountered the type in actual service use whilst serving aboard HMS *Ark Royal* with 800 Squadron embarked (later meeting up with the type aboard HMS *Eagle*, though this time with No.800B Flight).

When I first witnessed Scimitars carrying out DLPs on *Ark Royal*, I watched them fly over and join the circuit for landing, getting nearer and increasingly bigger. Then, with one hell of a wham, thump and the loudest roar I had ever heard, it was gone again. I stood there in utter shock. About 15 tons of screaming jet aircraft had just shot past me at 135kts and less than 50ft away. This, then, was my introduction to Scimitar flight-deck operations.

On the flight deck the Scimitar was quite popular - that is, with the Aircraft Handlers. It had a wide wheelbase and good ground clearance, so seeing beneath it was easy. The drop tanks, however, did get in the way at times. Another aspect the Aircraft Handler liked about it was the position of the jet pipes, especially the Naval Airman who had the unenviable job of being hookman (I had this job myself for quite some time on *Ark Royal*'s deck in 1963 and *Eagle*'s in 1965/66). In the event of an arrester wire not dropping clear of the hook once the aircraft had landed, it had to be released manually by clambering underneath the jet pipes, with the engines still running, so enabling the aircraft to taxi clear of the landing area. Being quite high up, as long as you kept your head down while you were under the jet blast, you were okay. The best method was to run in under the trailing edge of the mainplane, crouch low and try to kick the wire free. If that failed you would then have to crawl right up to the hook, manhandle the wire off it and then get the hell out of it back to the deck edge to await the next aircraft. If that happened on a Sea Vixen it was a different story; one had to be a contortionist as the aircraft was so low. Every time one went in under one of those, you ran the very real risk of having your head blown or burnt off.

Moving a Scimitar around a hangar, or any aircraft for that matter, was a very skilful job. This of course was done purely by Aircraft Handlers. To move a Scimitar on or off the lift would take a team of four men: the Leading Hand, who would direct the move, and three Naval Airmen, one manning the steering arm on the nose wheel, another carrying the chocks on one side acting as a safety number, whilst the third would be the Mechanical Handler driver. This was a very powerful engine which would clamp around one main wheel and lock it against rollers, thus providing the power source to move the aircraft in and out of the hangar. Some moves could entail a distance of four or five aircraft lengths, which could be anything up to 200ft. The clearance on either side of the aircraft could be as little as one foot, which would require the squadron rating, sat in the cockpit (usually the Plane Captain), to be on the ball with the brakes, ensuring that he had sufficient brake pressure before the move was started.

When moving an aircraft in the Royal Navy, all orders are given relative to the tail. During a long hangar movement the poor Naval Airman on the steering arm would work up quite a sweat, depending very often on the speed at which he could whip the arm across, as the director shouted "Tail port; midships; tail starboard". The movement teams took great pride in their charges and in the event of a 'prang' the punishment metered out by the Squadron CO or AEO was nothing to the disgust they would feel within themselves.

The Squadron Handlers would always be in competition with their ship's company colleagues in this respect, although very often a movement team would consist of both squadron and ship's company men together.

One of the problems with moving the Scimitar in the confines of the hangar was the stores pylon on the underside of the outboard mainplane. Once the wings were folded, as they were whilst in the hangar, this pylon would stick out at right angles, which was not so

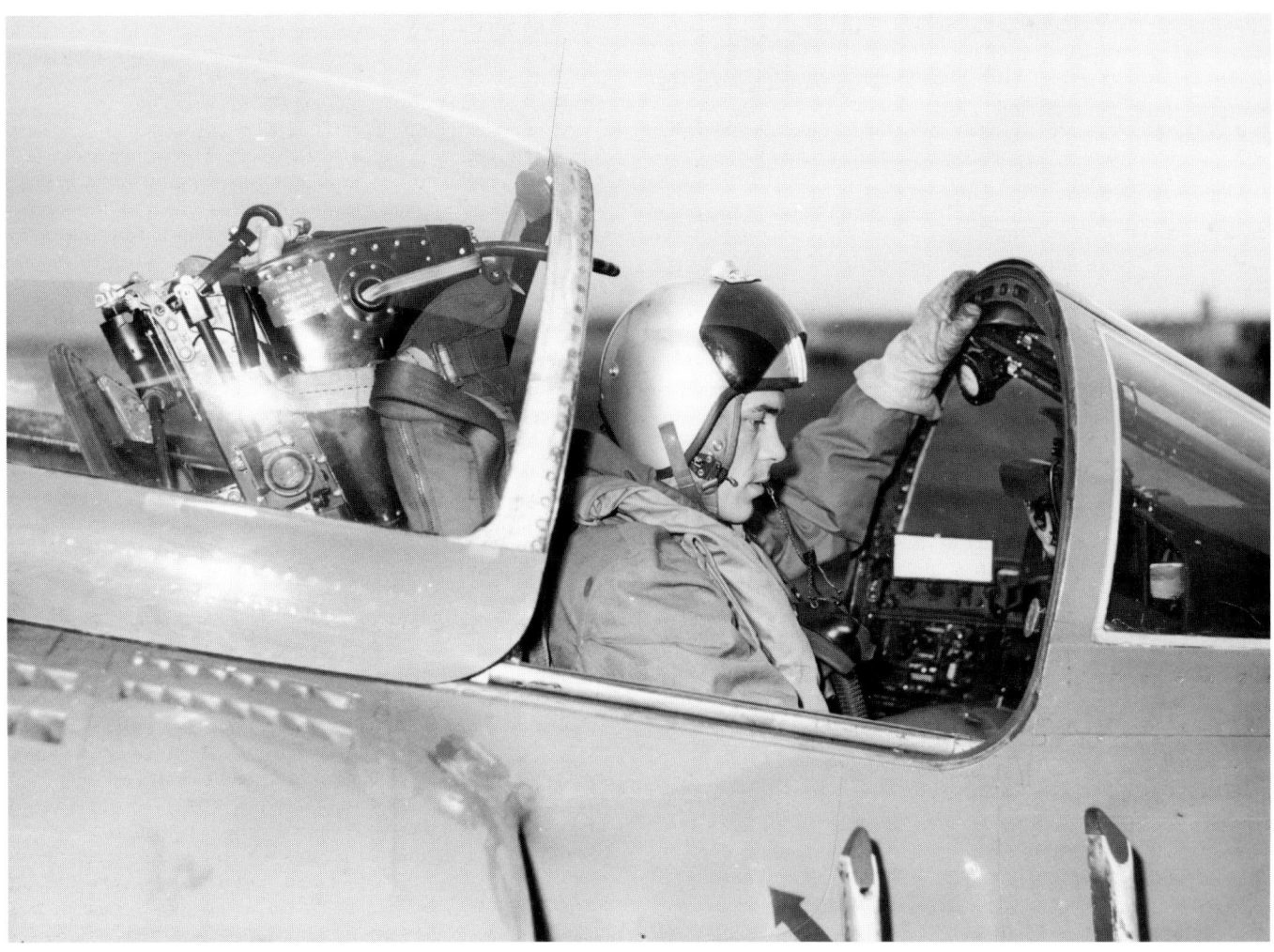

*Sub Lt C.D.Legg seated in the cockpit of a Scimitar at Lossiemouth in 1962. (RNAS Lossiemouth)*

much a problem for the side facing the centre of the hangar, but for the side against the bulkhead it sometimes caused some hairy moments.

There was one point during my time in *Ark Royal* that I can truly say was the only time I disliked the Scimitar. The aircraft would land and be directed forward to the area near the bow known as 'Fly One'. The pilots would remain in their cockpits with the engines running whilst the last aircraft was recovered. They would then, under their own power, be taxied out of 'Fly One', down the deck, around the aft lift and be re-spotted on the port side near the stern. During this operation we had to run alongside them carrying a pair of chocks which, in the event of a brake failure, you were meant to throw behind, or in front of, the wheel. This became known as doing the 'Tango'. The worst part was going around the after lift. One Naval Airman was lost that way when he slipped and the jet efflux from a Sea Vixen blew him over the side. He was never seen again. The practice was eventually done away with, finally being considered far too dangerous. It tended to keep you awake though. My heart would come up into my mouth every time I heard the pipe "Tango the aircraft in Fly One", at which point we would all try and hide somewhere.

During my time with *Ark Royal* in 1963 I once had a terrifying experience behind a Scimitar of No.800 Squadron. As a lowly Naval Airman of the flight deck party, my job on start-up was to man the chocks on the starboard mainwheel. This I did on a Scimitar in the range, but for some reason the aircraft went u/s and I, receiving no signal from the range director, remained lying on the chocks. The next aircraft, another Scimitar, was then taxied out of the range and, presuming that he would be directed up the deck towards the catapult, I braced myself for the jet blast which I knew would last for a couple of seconds as he turned. The aircraft moved out, turned as expected but then stopped. The pilot then proceeded to run up his engines, with the jet blast pointing directly on me. I could hardly breath or move, wrapping my arms around the oleo to stop myself from being blown over the ship's side which was only a matter of feet away. As the heat increased I then tried to climb up into the wheel bay, but by this time I was beginning to cook. I almost reached panic stations, with the bare areas of skin between my helmet and overalls feeling as if it was coming off, gasping for breath and feeling that I could not hold on for any longer, when it suddenly became calm, quiet and a lot cooler. CPO 'Dusty' Miller, who was the Captain of the Flight Deck, saw my predicament, rushed over, signalled to the pilot to shut down, came in and dragged me clear. That was the nearest I ever came to having an unscheduled swim with the compliments of a Scimitar.

Another hard-earned lesson, again on *Ark Royal* in 1963 (I was still very young and inexperienced), was the day I decided I wanted a photo of a Scimitar as it was tensioned on the catapult, and as it launched off the bow. For this shot I would need to get on top of FLYCO - "Officer country". I positioned myself thus, expecting to be told to clear off by the couple of young officers who were up there 'Goofing'. Nothing was said, but when the first Scimitar was ready on the starboard cat, they moved off. I had it all to myself, and so readied my camera. Up came the JBD, the FDO raised his flag and I was hit by the biggest blast of red hot air I had ever experienced in my short life. How I was not blown off FLYCO I do not know, but I still managed to press the button and I still have the photo. Each time I look at it I can still feel that blast.

I have never, of course, flown in a Scimitar, but at times I would be allowed to climb up and sit in the cockpit. I would sit there, grasp the stick and close my eyes, imagining I was at

20,000ft and screaming along at 600kts. I would envy the young pilots and greatly admired them - some not much older than myself. Therefore it was with great distress that while on watch one day, I watched one crash. Six Scimitars of No.800 Sqn had just taken off; two were overhead doing CAP, while the other four were attacking the splash target with rockets about 400 yards astern. The first three aircraft dived at the target, fired their rockets and climbed away. As the fourth one started his dive I said to myself, "My God, he's diving steep". The aircraft's angle of attack was much more acute than the previous three. He fired his rockets and immediately began to pull out, but it was too late. His downward momentum carried him on down and he hit the water belly first. There was an enormous splash, followed a split second later by a huge explosion. The impact area was marked by a circle of turquoise-coloured water - I can still see it now. In a matter of seconds the SAR Whirlwind was over the spot and the aircrew diver jumped out as it flew over, but it was all in vain, there being nothing left after such a huge explosion. I stood on the deck for quite some seconds in shock, not believing what I had just witnessed. That was the first time I had ever seen an aeroplane crash, and sadly it was not to be my last.

Whilst *Ark Royal* was exercising off Aden in May 1963, 800 Sqdn lost Scimitar XD239. The pilot, Sub Lt. Legg, had to bale out (his second ejection from a Scimitar at low level) over Aden Bay having almost made it to RAF Khormaksar where he was diverting to. The aircraft crashed in very shallow water and sustained very little damage. The water was only about 12ft deep and once the tide came in only the fin showed above the water – one time when a Scimitar really did look like a shark!

As well as my time in *Ark Royal* (1963/64) and *Eagle* (65/66), I also had the pleasure of serving aboard HMS *Hermes* (67/68), before once again returning to *Ark Royal* with 809 Buccaneer Squadron between 1969 and 1970.

The motto of the School of Aircraft Handling was *"Nostril In Minibus Tuti"*, which translated means *"Your life in their hands"*. This was very often true, particularly in the case of crash and rescue - ashore as well as afloat.

I am very proud to have been in that branch of the Royal Navy and, asked if the clock could be put back would I do it all again, my answer would be, "Yes Sir, I had a ball".

**Lt. Philip Mitchell RN (Rtd)**

In my 35 years service in the RN, during which I progressed from Junior Naval Airman AH3 to Warrant Officer and then to Commissioned Officer, I was fortunate enough to serve in a number of aircraft carriers, two of which operated the Scimitar.

My first ship, which I joined in 1962, was HMS *Hermes*, and part of its aircraft compliment was No.803 Squadron under the command of Lt Cdr N.J.P.Mills RN. I was a Junior Naval Airman 2nd Class AH3, drafted from RNAS Culdrose, where I had been trained on the dummy deck working with the Hawker Sea Hawk. As already stated there was an N.113D, WT854, in one of the Hangars and this would be wheeled out onto the dummy deck to give an idea of the size of the aircraft one could expect once on board an aircraft carrier. Working with one old N.113D compared to working around a fully operational squadron of Scimitars was, however, a different ball game. If you didn't keep your wits about you No.803 Squadron aircraft would, and could, bite you.

My everlasting memory of the Scimitar is of a moving leaking fuel tank. I had to lie on the chocks for start-up and more often than not there would be fuel dripping over me, or on to the deck around me, quickly soaking my overalls. The type was so well known as a mobile fuel leak that when being moved around the deck they always had a bucket tied underneath them to catch the principle fuel leakage, and when in the range this was replaced by a dustbin.

The noise from the Scimitar was indescribable and the power that the Rolls Royce Avons generated was awesome. As the Checkboard number my position for launch was situated between the catapults and I had to hold up a board which reminded the pilot that he should now have his "Cockpit Checked and Brakes Off". The pilot would indicate that this was done by giving a thumbs up, which would be relayed to the FDO who would then raise his green flag, giving the pilot permission to open the throttles to full power for take off. With Scimitars on both port and starboard catapults in the launch position, the noise was deafening. It seemed as if ones whole body was vibrating. With hands tightly pressed to ear defenders, and with teeth seemingly being loosened by the sheer voracity of it all, the noise level and vibration was almost unbearable.

In so modern and heavy a jet fighter, a peculiarity of the Scimitar was the absence of nosewheel steering, which sometimes resulted in the aircraft not getting lined up on the catapult correctly. To counteract this problem required the use of a "Soft Soap Number," and the task was given to the Aircraft Handler. This entailed him having a bucket, a small hand brush, and a quantity of soap, known throughout the service as "Pussers Hard". The AH would get his soap (it came in long hard blocks), half fill his bucket with water and then dissolve the soap to make a thick sludge. Positioned between the catapults he would rush in and slap a load of his soap mixture around the nosewheel tyre and on the deck when the aircraft was incorrectly aligned. This enabled it to be manhandled by the emergency party, i.e. pushed on the side of the nose where it would slide on the soap and be lined up for take off. I always thought it rather ironic that, with all the modern technology of the day, this nuclear bomber/jet fighter needed a naval airman with a bucket of soapy water to get it finally ready for its mission. This procedure was used in *Hermes* and *Ark Royal*, especially in the Far East when the flight deck was dry.

I look back with very fond memories of the days working on the flight deck with the aircraft of the 1960's, and unless the promise of the new carriers comes to fruition, the young men of today will never experience the excitement of a catapult launch or the arrested landing of a 20 ton aircraft onto a rolling and pitching deck. Not that I take anything away from the present day carriers and the Aircraft Handlers that man them: having served two commissions in *Invincible* I know from experience that they are exhilarating and dangerous places to work, and where the unexpected can happen at any moment.

A fully worked-up and operational flight deck on ships such as *Hermes*, *Eagle* and the others of that era was like watching a very fast, colourful, noisy and beautifully choreographed ballet. It is a great shame that we will probably not see the like again.

# SQUADRON AND UNIT HISTORIES

*Scimitar XD221 '512/FD' of No.700 Squadron ready for launch from the steam catapult of HMS Victorious around August-September 1958. Parked to one side are Scimitar F.1 XD220 '511/FD', Gannet AS.1 WN353 '504/FD' and Gannet AS.4 XG794 '503/FD' all of No.700 Squadron. (via Lee Howard)*

## No.700 SQUADRON

No.700 Squadron reformed on 18 August 1955 at RNAS Ford as a Trials and Requirements Unit with a variety of aircraft, including a Scimitar from March 1958 and, following the disbanding of 700X Flight, two more from May 1958. Further deck trials were carried out aboard HMS *Victorious* between 29 August and 4 September 1958 to test the ship's catapult at arrester gear prior to the embarkation of 803 Sqdn. The unit moved to RNAS Yeovilton on 19 September 1958 and finally relinquished its Scimitars in February 1959.

**Identification Markings**
Side codes *510-512* in black on a white nose panel, generally with fin code *FD* (sometimes sloping) and changed to *VL* in 9.58 when relocated to Yeovilton.

| Known Squadron Scimitar Pilots | |
|---|---|
| Cdr TG Innes AFC (CO) | 27.08.57 - 29.09.58 |
| Lt Cdr JW Ayres (Senior Pilot) | 17.06.57 - 30.6.58 |
| Lt Cdr RA Shilcock | 29.09.58 - 12.09.60 |

| Squadron aircraft | | |
|---|---|---|
| 510 | XD226 | 12.03.58 - 11.02.59 |
| 511 | XD220 | 29.05.58 - 20.02.59 |
| 512 | XD221 | 29.05.58 - 10.11.58 |

*XD221 '512/FD' of No.700 Squadron about to be launched from the steam catapult of HMS Victorious around August-September 1958. (via Lee Howard)*

*XD226 '510' of No.700 Squadron parked at Ford in 1958. (M.J.F.Bowyer)*

# No.700X SQUADRON

No.700X Squadron was formed as the Scimitar Intensive Flying Trials Unit on 27 August 1957 at RNAS Ford in Sussex under the command of Commander T.G.Innes AFC, RN, with Lt Cdr W.A.Tofts as the Senior Pilot. Its primary task was to ensure that the Scimitar entered front-line service capable of immediately performing, and sustaining its role over the longest period. The other original pilots were sent to Boscombe Down to fly swept wing Hawker Hunters as No.700X initially had no aircraft. The first few weeks were spent eagerly listening to reports on the progress of the first of the unit's Scimitars as they were put through the manufacturer's production testing. Meanwhile the squadron busied itself and on 4 September wet dinghy drill was carried out in the sea off nearby Clymping beach, to be completed by helicopter winching practice.

On its final check flight from South Marston XD221 suffered a bird strike, damaging one engine and, consequently, it was not until 10:10 on 25 September 1957 that Supermarine production test pilot Les Colquhoun delivered the aircraft to Ford as the unit's first Scimitar.

However progress came to an immediate halt as the aircraft became unserviceable and did not fly again until 30 September, when the CO carried out an air check, followed by familiarisation flights by Lt Cdr Tofts and Leece.

For each of the No.700X pilots the familiarisation flight was to be their first experience of an aircraft of the Scimitar's size and by 17 October all had completed their familiarisation programme using XD221 and XD220, which had been delivered six days earlier.

The Squadron would eventually have a complement of seven aircraft (with some being exchanged at various times) and the objectives of the Flight were:

(1) To check and evaluate the performance envelope of the aircraft, i.e. check that the pilots agreed with the Vickers figures.

(2) To prove the aircraft in its various roles, i.e. to evaluate its role as a fighting machine and establish basic guidelines for the operational squadrons, such as weapon delivery profiles, angles of dive, speeds at dive entry and weapon release, air to air combat at various heights including supersonic attacks above 40,000ft.

(3) To evaluate the maintainability of the aircraft as a whole, and to identify and eliminate as many potential problems as possible.

(4) To distribute the information gained so that action may be taken as appropriate.

*Members of No.700X Squadron. Left to right: back row Lt Pete Barber, Lt H.R.Jenkins, Lt Brian Davies, Lt Mike Gibson (electrical), Lt D.H.Pepper (Assistant AEO), Lt Lym Middleton (Assistant AWI) and unidentified (Gunner) ; front row Lt Cdr Tom Leech (AWI), unidentified (Instructor), Lt Cdr 'Jock' Tofts (Senior Pilot), Lt Cdr Donald Titford (AEO), Lt Cdr A.F.Mortimer (Electrical) and Lt Cdr John Checketts (AEO/Pilot). (E.B.Morgan archives)*

*XD230 '805/FD' and XD222 '802/FD' of No.700X Squadron undergoing maintenance in the hangar at RNAS Ford. (via R.C.Sturtivant)*

Resident with the Squadron was an additional pilot and two engineers, who were responsible for the development of the Scimitar simulator and cockpit procedure trainers.

From 24 October to 20 November all of the Scimitars were grounded due to the hydraulics becoming contaminated and consequently the systems had to be purged, and so it was not until 20 November that XD222 became the next aircraft to fly. On 25 April 1958 Lt Cdr Leece took a Scimitar to Wisley where he met H.R.H. Prince Philip who was inspecting the Scimitar aircraft on display, there being seven versions on show. The unit also had on its strength instructor Lt Cdr J.W.Bugler, whose job was performance reduction which included the plotting of normal range and endurance curves, and proving the optimum fighter and strike combat mission profiles. Apart from the flying trials, the Flight had to produce an engineering evaluation of the aircraft involving a period of continuous high-intensity flying, during which it was hoped to complete around 300 hours flying with one aircraft in six months. This kind of intensive flying uncovered the majority of defects and snags, so enabling them to be overcome before the aircraft entered squadron service. To demonstrate this point, one aircraft was flown on 44 sorties logging 35 hours in nine consecutive flying days. Another aspect of the unit's work was the evaluation of the aircraft's navigational and approach aids while performing let-downs on both one and two engines. The noise level of the Scimitar was by far above anything that had previously been heard at Ford. To reduce this level for ground running tests, Curran detuners were used with jet-pipe extensions to protect the tail skin and structure from noise damage. Each Scimitar had its own crew chief and ground crew as maintenance was carried out almost 24 hours a day, the unit being divided into two watches.

Tragically Commander Innes was killed in a car crash near Arundel on 20 March 1958, and the Senior Pilot, Lt Cdr Tofts, took over as CO temporarily until Commander J.D.Russell arrived and assumed command.

No.700X Sqn flew 982 sorties resulting in 935 flying hours and on 21 May 1958 four of the unit's aircraft, led by the CO, took off to carry out a 'low, fast and noisy' flypast of several 'places of historic interest', including Lee-on-Solent, Yeovilton, Bramcote, South Marston and Wisley prior to disbanding at Ford on 29 May 1958. Whilst some of the pilots and groundcrew stayed with No.700 Sqn when it transferred to Yeovilton to continue the deck trials aboard HMS *Victorious*, most were absorbed into the nucleus of No.803 Squadron along with the majority of the aircraft when it formed at Lossiemouth on 3 June 1958.

"We had a fairly easy time with regard to noise restrictions and supersonic bangs," Lt Cdr Leece recalled, "as such things were very new and we 'bent' the rules to our advantage at first, although later on we had to be more careful. I remember that Tom Innes was very keen that No.700X was seen to be doing its job and insisted that one of our aircraft took off at 0800 each morning as soon as the ATC team opened up the aerodrome. The local press went into print with a story about the Scimitar replacing the alarm clock". Sadly, though, the noise created by the intensive flying of Scimitars from Ford almost certainly precipitated the airfield's premature closure in late 1959.

*XD230 '805/FD' of No.700X Squadron RNAS Ford on 25 March 1958. (via R.C.Sturtivant)*

*XD220 '800/FD' and others of No.700X Squadron at the official presentation to the press at RNAS Ford on 25 March 1958. (MAP)*

| Identification Markings |
|---|
| Side codes *800-809* allocated to the Flight, though only *800-806* used by Scimitars (Vampire T.22 XG769 used code *809*). Applied on the nose in varied styles, generally with vertical or sloping fin code *FD*. |

| Squadron Officers | |
|---|---|
| Cdr TG Innes AFC (CO) | 27.08.57 - 21.02.58 |
| Lt Cdr WA Tofts AFC (SP & acting CO) | 27.08.57 - 17.04.58 |
| Lt Cdr DG Titford (AEO) | 27.08.57 - 29.05.58 |
| Lt Cdr JW Bugler (Instr) | 27.08.57 - 29.05.58 |
| Lt Cdr AF Mortimer AMIEE (ALO) | 27.08.57 - 29.05.58 |
| Lt DH Pepper (A/E) | 27.08.57 - 29.05.58 |
| Lt PJ Barber | 27.08.57 - 29.05.58 |
| Lt LE Middleton | 27.08.57 - 29.05.58 |
| Lt HR Jenkins | 27.08.57 - 27.01.58 |
| Lt B Davies | 27.08.57 - 27.01.58 |
| Lt CD Stimpson | 27.08.57 - 29.05.58 |
| Lt C Orpe BSc (A/E) | 03.09.57 - 29.05.58 |
| Lt Cdr TCS Leece (AWI) | 09.09.57 - 29.05.58 |
| Lt Cdr JT Checketts (SMP) | 27.08.57 - |
| Lt TFB Young | c13.12.57 - c03.05.58 |
| Lt ER Anson | 27.01.58 - 29.05.58 |
| Lt JG Beyfus | 27.01.58 - 29.05.58 |
| Lt AR Campbell | 10.02.58 - 07.03.58 |
| Lt MV Maina | 17.03.58 - 29.05.58 |
| Lt CS Casperd | 17.03.58 - 29.05.58 |
| Lt JW Beard | 17.03.58 - 29.05.58 |
| Lt CC Giles | 17.03.58 - 29.05.58 |
| Cdr JD Russell (CO) | 17.04.58 - 29.05.58 |
| Lt Cdr GR Higgs | 17.04.58 - 29.05.58 |

*Mike Lithgow looks on as Lt Cdr T.C.S.Leece of No.700X Squadron meets VIPs including His Royal Highness the Duke of Edinburgh at Wisley on 25 April 1958. In the background is Scimitar F.1 XD223 '803/FD'. Just in the picture on the left is Alan Clifton, the Chief Designer. (Vickers-Armstrongs)*

| Squadron aircraft | | |
|---|---|---|
| 800 | XD220 | 11.10.57 - 29.05.58 |
| 801 | XD221 | 25.09.57 - 29.05.58 |
| 802 | XD222 | 11.10.57 - 04.09.58 |
| 803 | XD223 | 23.10.57 - 29.05.58 |
| 804 | XD224 | 06.01.58 - 29.05.58 |
| 805 | XD225 | 06.01.58 - 07.03.58 |
| | XD230 | 26.02.58 - 09.09.58 |
| 806 | XD231 | 02.04.58 - 09.09.58 |
| (TIR) | XD226 | 28.02.58 - 12.03.58 |
| 809 Vampire T.22 | XG769 | |

| Chronology | |
|---|---|
| 27.08.57 | Unit formed at RNAS Ford, Sussex (HMS *Peregrine*) |
| 02.09.57 | Vampire Trainer XG769 transferred from parent station. |
| 25.09.57 | First Scimitar, XD221, delivered. |
| 11.10.57 | XD220 and XD222 delivered. |
| 18.10.57 | XD220 now totalled 3 sorties, 17 landings, 5 touchdowns, 9.40hrs. |
| | XD221 now 35 sorties, 43 landings, 56 touchdowns, 34.25hrs. |
| | XD222 Nil sorties, 6 landings, nil touchdowns, 3.50hrs. |
| 23.10.57 | XD223 delivered (4.15hrs) |
| 24.10.57 | XD222 first supersonic flight. All aircraft grounded due to contamination of the hydraulic systems. |
| 20.11.57 | Flying re-commenced with XD222. |
| 27.11.57 | XD222 successfully landed at Lee-on-Solent to establish the suitability of airfield for Scimitars operating from Fleetlands. XD222 put in 35.15 hrs, 44 sorties in 9 flying days. Engines 66 hour life. |
| 07.12.57 | XD220 stbd engine replaced. |
| 19.12.57 | XD222 FF after engine change. |
| 06.01.58 | XD224 and XD225 delivered. |
| 31.01.58 | Week ending, 282 sorties, 20.40 flying hours |
| 02.58 | Contract placed with Air Trainers Link Ltd. for two Flight Simulators for the N.113 to resemble XD220, the ninth aircraft built (the design having been frozen in January 1957 when the Ministry of Supply approved the final layout). |
| 26.02.58 | XD230 delivered as replacement for XD225. XD226 as the T.I.R. (15 sorties, 19.15 flying hours, 12,900 galls, 28 landings). |
| 11.03.58 | Director General Aircraft (Navy), Rear Admiral J.P.W.Furse visited the Flight. |
| 25.03.58 | XD223 first flown with P.R. nose fitted and photographic trials commenced. |
| 02.04.58 | XD231 delivered. |
| 25.04.58 | XD223 to V.A. Wisley to enable H.R.H. the Duke of Edinburgh to inspect an aircraft with a PR nose. |
| 30.04.58 | XD222 became first aircraft to attain 200 hrs. XD224 port engine changed. |
| 07.05.58 | XD220 first flight with an underwing store. |
| 08.05.58 | XD222 flown to V.A. Completed 209 sorties, 209.10 flying hours, 162,440 galls used, 219 landings. |
| 20.05.58 | First and only bombing sortie carried out, though no bombs dropped due to a blown fuse. |
| 21.05.58 | XD221 reached 200 flying hours. |
| 22.05.58 | XD221 transferred to 700 Sqdn. Completed 214 sorties, 200.00 flying hours, 166,129 galls, 226 landings. |
| 23.05.58 | XD220 transferred to 700 Sqdn. Completed 172 sorties, 161.00 flying hours, 159.060 galls, 187 landings. |
| 27.05.58 | Squadron disbanded. |

| Squadron aircraft statistics | | | | |
|---|---|---|---|---|
| AIRCRAFT | SORTIES | HOURS | GALLS | LANDINGS |
| XD221 | 214 | 200.00 | 166,120 | 226 |
| XD220 | 172 | 161.00 | 159,060 | 187 |
| XD222 | 209 | 209.10 | 162,440 | 219 |
| XD223* | 139 | 136.04 | 112,900 | 139 |
| XD224* | 139 | 144.15 | 135,400 | 149 |
| XD225 | 15 | 19.01 | 12,900 | 28 |
| XD230* | 47 | 47.00 | 55,000 | 54 |
| XD231* | 59 | 61.00 | 46,300 | 69 |
| TOTALS | 994 | 978.25 | 830,120 | 1,071 |
| *Up to 23.5.58 only. | | | | |

# No.736 SQUADRON

No.736 Squadron began re-equipment with six Scimitar F.1s in June 1959 for conversion courses and weapon training after a change of policy, this task having been originally intended for No.764 Squadron. Selected pupils were chosen for Scimitars after Sea Hawk training, the first course commencing in early July with just two students. The Interceptor Day Fighter (IDF) pipeline flowed along a seven-week cycle, the fourteen-week Scimitar OFS Part II Course being geared to this. Serviceability proved to be good, though spares tended to be in short supply. The last of the squadron's Sea Hawks went to No.738 Squadron in July 1960, and the number of Scimitars was increased to eight and later ten.

In June 1962 the squadron's instructors gave a demonstration for the School of Land Air Warfare, and three months later the squadron gave a flying display at that year's Farnborough Show, the five Scimitars being flown by the only five pilots then on the squadron. On 16 October the squadron flew over King Olaf of Norway's Royal Yacht at dawn as she steamed up the Firth of Forth for a visit to Edinburgh. In 1963 two Scimitars made a non-stop flight to Hyères in the south of France for a liaison visit with the French Navy. They were refuelled by a Valiant tanker on the way out, then arrived at their destination in a torrential downpour of tropical intensity and arctic temperature, this persisting throughout the two-day visit. The following year, in an exchange visit, Lieutenant Jacques Combry, F.N, was placed on the OFS course prior to joining No.803 Squadron, the reciprocation also involving a visit in March by four French Etendards. No.736 disbanded at Lossiemouth on 26 March 1965, its remnants becoming No.764B Squadron. On the same day the number 736, generally recognised as being used for the strike training squadron, was taken up by a new such unit equipped with Buccaneer S.1s.

*The short-lived XD222 '609/LM' of No.736 Squadron parked at Lossiemouth in 1960. (R.C.B.Ashworth)*

**Identification Markings**
Side codes *608-618*, initially in white on black panel on the nose, the last two digits being repeated in black on the nosewheel doors, with black fin code *LM*. By 9.60, white codes on a dark grey panel on the nose outlined in white, the last two digits of the code being repeated in black on the nosewheel doors and a small squadron badge on the nacelles, still with fin code *LM,* but now in white. By 1961 the white fin code was replaced by a blue lightning flash on a white fin.

**Squadron Officers**

| | |
|---|---|
| Lt(L) JH Webster BA | 06.01.58 - 10.11.59 |
| Lt Cdr JD Baker (CO) | 02.09.58 - 04.05.60 |
| Lt JA Carrodus (QFI) | 23.09.58 - 28.01.60 |
| Lt NE Lee RAN (QFI) (Senior Pilot from 21.2.59) | 23.09.58 - 17.09.60 |

**Squadron Officers continued**

| | |
|---|---|
| Lt A Stewart (TI) | 06.01.59 - 16.09.59 |
| Lt DP Mears (AWI) | 08.01.59 - 21.03.60 |
| Lt NL Dudgeon (TI) | 24.02.59 - 06.04.60 |
| Lt AT Atkinson (TI) | 28.04.59 - 15.08.60 |
| Lt J Worth (AWI) | 24.05.59 - 24.08.59 |
| Lt DJ Jenner (AEO) | 25.05.59 - 26.01.61 |
| Lt FE Esling (Asst ALO) | 10.05.59 - 10.06.60 |
| S/L RV Sabin (Asst AEO) | 25.05.59 - 29.09.60 |
| Lt JP Williams (AWI) | 27.07.59 - 15.08.60 |
| Lt H Rostokwsky (TI) | 01.09.59 - 20.10.59 |
| Lt CC Giles (Staff Officer) (TI) | 06.10.59 - 10.03.61 |
| Lt PMC Hessey (TI) | 20.10.59 - 12.12.59 |
| Lt CW Preston (ALO) | 03.11.59 - 24.04.61 |
| Lt BJ Bullivant (QFI) | 07.12.59 - 01.12.61 |

*XD223 '608' of No.736 Squadron parked at Lossiemouth around 1961. (via Philip Jarrett)*

*XD241 '614/LM' of No.736 Squadron landing at Lossiemouth during ADDLs in 1961. (B.J.Lowe)*

*XD246 '611' and others of No.736 Squadron lined up at Lossiemouth around 1961/2. (B.J.Lowe)*

| Squadron Officers continued | |
|---|---|
| Lt JA Sutton (AWI) | 11.01.60 - 01.08.60 |
| Lt MD Bristowe (TI) | 21.02.60 - 18.05.60 |
| Lt JRJ Rutherford (TI) | 21.02.60 - 20.08.60 |
| Lt Cdr A Mancais (CO) | 04.05.60 - 13.11.61 |
| S/L SA Lenton (Asst ALO) | 06.06.60 - 22.07.70 |
| Lt E Cope (Asst AWI) | 20.06.60 - 06.09.60 |
| Lt TM Tuke (Staff Officer) | 14.07.60 - 03.07.61 |
| Flt Lt M Farmer RAF | 15.08.60 - 22.06.61 |
| Lt(E) B Wallace (Asst AEO) | 29.09.60 - 04.05.61 |
| Lt PH Perks (Senior Pilot) | 07.10.60 - 22.01.62 |
| Lt PC Marshall (AWI) | 07.10.60 - 14.01.62 |
| S/L(E) RM Grove (Asst ALO) | 15.10.60 - 04.06.62 |
| Lt(E) JL Williams (Addl TI) | 22.11.60 - 14.01.61 |
| Lt Cdr(E) RA Griffin (AEO) | 24.01.61 - 24.11.62 |
| Lt(L) AAD Fellows (ALO) | 17.04.61 - 08.01.62 |
| Lt(L) KA Ryde (Asst ALO) | 17.04.61 - 06.05.62 |
| S/L(E) TJ Strong (Asst AEO) | 21.04.61 - 12.01.63 |
| Lt SC Creasy (Asst AWI) | 03.07.61 - 03.02.62 |
| S/L AHS Anderson (Staff Officer) | 14.08.61 - 08.10.62 |
| Lt Cdr PG Newman (CO) | 09.10.61 - 10.01.63 |
| Lt PG De Souza (QFI) | 20.11.61 - 21.08.63 |
| S/L(L) IGS Hamilton (ALO) | 16.12.61 - 10.04.64 |
| Lt RW Edward (AWI) | 12.01.62 - 20.12.62 |
| Lt JF Kennett (Senior Pilot) | 19.02.62 - 18.10.63 |
| Lt NB Taylor (Asst ALO) | 07.05.62 - 24.09.62 |
| Lt LA Wilkinson (Staff Officer) | 07.06.62 - 01.06.64 |
| Lt AMD de Labilliere (Asst AWI) | 01.07.62 - 06.08.62 |
| Lt MJ Doust (AWI) | 19.09.62 - 02.09.63 |
| Lt LG Scovell (AEO) | 20.11.62 - 31.07.64 |
| Lt VR Phillips (Asst AEO) | 11.12.62 - 19.12.63 |
| Lt JG Wood (AWI) | 07.01.63 - 31.07.64 |
| Lt T Millett (Asst ALO) | 08.01.63 - 02.11.63 |
| Lt Cdr JAD Ford (CO) | 10.01.63 - 01.06.64 |
| Flt Lt RN Davidson RAF (QFI) | 02.02.63 - 28.02.64 |
| Lt Cdr DA Vaughan (AEO) | 10.04.63 - 10.09.63 |
| Lt AS Park (Staff Officer) | 01.05.63 - 11.10.63 |
| Lt MT Hynett (AWI) | 29.07.63 - 15.01.64 |
| Lt JOF Billingham (AWI) | 29.07.63 - 14.03.64 |
| Lt DHT Dakin (Asst AEO) | 30.09.63 - 07.01.64 |
| Lt GR Roach (Asst AEO) | 07.10.63 - 01.12.63 |
| Lt PP Cardew (Senior Pilot) | 14.10.63 - 08.01.65 |
| Lt Cdr J Worth (CO) | 09.12.63 - 26.03.65 |
| Lt PJ Trudgett (QFI) | 06.01.64 - 26.03.65 |
| Lt R Newington (Asst AEO) | 14.01.64 - 18.11.64 |
| Lt J Shea (Asst AEO) | 14.01.64 - 30.05.64 |
| Lt G McBain (TI) | 04.02.64 - 08.06.64 |
| S/L JR Chicken (DAEO) | 06.05.64 - 26.03.65 |
| Lt PAA Waring (AWI/Simulator) | 11.06.64 - 26.03.65 |
| Lt ARD Monro-Davies (Staff Officer) | 22.06.64 - 31.08.64 |
| Lt Cdr DC Spragge (AEO) | 31.07.64 - 26.03.65 |
| S/L RC Chaffey (Asst AEO) | 18.11.64 - 26.03.65 |
| Lt AS Tuck (QFI) | 20.11.64 - 26.03.65 |
| Lt Cdr JWH Purvis (Senior Pilot) | 08.01.65 - 26.03.65 |
| Lt RA Highton (Asst AEO) | 17.03.65 - 26.03.65 |

| Known Trainee Pilots | |
|---|---|
| Lt JOF Billingham (72 OFS) | 15.06.59 - 28.08.59 |
| Lt TNF Skead (72 OFS) | 15.06.59 - 21.09.59 |
| Lt PM Stevenson (72 OFS) | 15.06.59 - 21.09.59 |
| Lt AG Claridge (73 OFS) | 14.07.59 - 23.09.59 |
| Lt NG Grier-Rees (73 OFS) | 20.07.59 - 26.10.59 |
| Mid RV Ponter (73 OFS) | 24.08.59 - 01.60 |
| S/L AHS Anderson (74 OFS) | 09.59 - 05.12.59 |
| S/L AT Poirrer (75 OFS) | 04.11.59 - 01.12.59 |
| Lt PG De Souza (75 OFS) | 04.11.59 - 03.60 |
| Lt MT Hynett (75 OFS) | 04.11.59 - 03.60 |
| S/L JGL Smith (75 OFS) | 04.11.59 - 03.60 |
| Lt MTH Styles (75 OFS) | 04.11.59 - 20.03.60 |
| Lt AJ Goodenough (76 OFS) | 09.12.59 - 12.04.60 |
| Lt PC Marshall (76 OFS) | 12.59 - 02.05.60 |
| Lt IB Macleod (76 OFS) | 25.01.60 - 13.04.60 |
| S/L NA Britton (77 OFS) | 04.03.60 - 16.06.60 |
| Lt MJM Brophy (78 OFS) | 27.03.60 - 12.07.60 |
| S/L JS Shepherd (78 OFS) | 27.03.60 - 02.05.60 |
| Lt AS Tuck (78 OFS) | 27.03.60 - 12.07.60 |
| Lt NJP Mills (additional) | 03.60 - 05.04.60 |
| S/L PJ Trudgett (79 OFS) | 05.60 - 28.08.60 |
| Lt JPE Faulkner (80 OFS) | 17.07.60 - 14.10.60 |
| S/L(E) MK Johnson (80 OFS) | 17.07.60 - 14.10.60 |
| Lt TJ Notley (80 OFS) | 17.07.60 - 14.10.60 |
| S/L AJ Stone (80 OFS) | 17.07.60 - 14.10.60 |
| Lt NJ Norris (81 OFS) | 05.09.60 - 16.11.60 |
| S/L MBV Moorhouse (81 OFS) | 05.09.60 - 16.11.60 |
| Lt GC Edwardes (82 OFS) | 17.10.60 - 19.02.61 |
| Lt PAA Waring (82 OFS) | 17.10.60 - 20.01.61 |
| S/L CJ Wilson (82 OFS) | 17.10.60 - 20.01.61 |
| Lt(E) MG Griffin (83 OFS) | 05.12.60 - 27.03.61 |
| Lt SE Askins (83 OFS) | 05.12.60 - 10.04.61 |
| Lt DS McIntyre (83 OFS) | 05.12.60 - 10.04.61 |
| Lt RDG Gray (84 OFS) | 26.01.61 - 05.05.61 |
| S/L Carver JL (84 OFS) | 26.01.61 - 05.05.61 |
| Lt NM Tristram (84 OFS) | 26.01.61 - 05.05.61 |
| S/L AM Hickling (85 OFS) | 23.03.61 - 10.07.61 |
| Mid CC Morris (85 OFS) | 23.03.61 - 10.07.61 |
| Lt JA (Manley 85 OFS) | 23.03.61 - 10.07.61 |
| Mid CA Bosworth (86 OFS) | 03.61 - 10.09.61 |
| Lt AG Ellis (86 OFS) | 17.04.61 - 28.07.61 |
| Lt TMH Laister (87 OFS) | 26.06.61 - 20.09.61 |
| S/L AD Alsop (87 OFS) | 26.06.61 - 09.10.61 |
| Lt CD Walkinshaw (87 OFS) | 26.06.61 - 09.10.61 |
| S/L GHR Wooff (88 OFS) | 11.09.61 - 22.01.62 |
| Lt LE Middleton (88 OFS) | 11.09.61 - 22.01.62 |
| S/L G McBain (89 OFS) | 25.10.61 - 19.02.62 |
| S/L CARP Wells (89 OFS) | 25.10.61 - 19.02.62 |
| Mid JS Flexman (90 OFS) | 12.61 - 07.05.62 |
| S/L L Ingham (90 OFS) | 12.61 - 07.05.62 |
| Lt PGJ (Murison 90/91 OFS) | 12.61 - 07.05.62 |
| Lt JPF Nichols (90 OFS) | 12.61 - 07.05.62 |
| S/L MJ Harwood (91 OFS) | 07.02.62 - 05.62 |
| Lt PP Cardew (Additional) | 05.03.62 - 14.03.62 |
| S/L CD Legg (93 OFS) | 04.62 - 27.07.62 |
| Lt JJR Tod (93 OFS) | 04.62 - 27.07.62 |
| S/L JM Heath (94 OFS) | 27.06.62 - 21.11.62 |
| Lt AG MacFie (95 OFS) | 09.62 - 21.01.63 |
| Lt IPF Meiklejohn (95 OFS) | 09.62 - 21.01.63 |
| Mid NHL Bowden (97 OFS) | 05.12.62 - 25.03.63 |
| Mid A McMeekan (97 OFS) | 05.12.62 - 25.03.63 |
| S/L RL Millett (97 OFS) | 05.12.62 - 25.03.63 |
| S/L RM Cockburn (99 OFS) | 07.03.63 - 30.06.63 |
| Mid IC Frenz (99 OFS) | 07.03.63 - 30.06.63 |
| S/L B Hutton (102 OFS) | 11.09.63 - 18.11.63 |
| Mid PJ McManus (103 OFS) | 18.09.63 - 27.01.64 |
| S/L CA Wheal (103 OFS) | 18.09.63 - 27.01.64 |
| Lt CJ Crowther (104 OFS) | 13.11.63 - 28.02.64 |
| S/L KB Owen (105 OFS) | 11.03.64 - 08.07.64 |
| Lt ARD Monro-Davies (106 OFS) | 02.03.64 - 22.06.64 |
| Also (109 OFS) | 31.08.64 - 18.11.64 |
| Lt EK Somerville-Jones (106 OFS) | 02.03.64 - 22.06.64 |
| Lt NE Rankin (109 OFS) | 20.07.64 - 09.11.64 |
| S/L PG Doughty (110 OFS) | 25.09.64 - 12.64 |
| S/L GM Faulkner (112 OFS) | 16.12.64 - 09.04.65 |
| S/L HW Thomas (112 OFS) | 18.11.64 - 24.03.65 |

*XD224 '614' and XD316 '612' of No.736 Squadron in formation at the SBAC Show at Farnborough in September 1962. (MAP)*

*Four Scimitar F.1s of No.736 Squadron inverted over Lossiemouth during an air display in 1961. (B.J.Lowe).*

*XD316 '612', XD220 '618', XD226 '615' and XD239 '613' of No.736 Squadron Lossiemouth in line astern in 1962. (FAA Museum)*

| Squadron aircraft | | | | Squadron aircraft continued | | |
|---|---|---|---|---|---|---|
| 608 | XD223 | 06.05.60 - 24.02.62 | | 613 | XD274 | 19.05.59 - 24.11.59 |
| 609 | XD222 | 12.04.60 - 16.11.60 | | | XD225 | 24.03.60 - 18.04.62 |
| | XD264 | 10.01.61 - 03.61 | | | XD239 | 26.04.62 - 07.12.62 |
| | XD231 | 15.08.61 - 04.04.62 | | | XD228 | 10.12.62 - 18.03.65 |
| 610 | XD226 | 12.05.59 - 27.07.60 | | | XD225 | 08.02.65 - 26.03.65 |
| | XD239 | 25.08.60 - 07.10.60 | | 614 | XD241 | 03.06.59 - 15.06.61 |
| | XD267 | 06.10.60 - 27.06.62 | | | XD212 | 05.07.61 - 20.09.61 |
| | XD282 | 11.10.62 - 23.11.62 | | | XD250 | 15.01.62 - 18.08.62 |
| 611 | XD272 | 11.05.59 - 29.10.59 | | | XD224 | 14.08.62 - 26.03.65 |
| | XD237 | 10.11.59 - 22.06.61 | | 615 | XD226 | 22.01.62 - 17.04.63 |
| | XD246 | 21.09.61 - 04.07.62 | | | XD227 | 23.05.63 - 26.03.65 |
| | XD265 | 20.06.62 - 15.11.62 | | 616 | XD234 | 15.10.59 - 03.08.60 |
| | XD232 | 29.11.62 - 10.06.64 | | | XD217 | 02.03.62 - 26.03.65 |
| | XD215 | 23.06.64 - 26.03.65 | | 617 | XD230 | 01.04.60 - 23.05.62 |
| 612 | XD273 | 12.05.59 - 16.11.59 | | | XD219 | 28.06.62 - 26.03.65 |
| | XD249 | 15.02.60 - 14.12.61 | | 618 | XD224 | 27.08.59 - 04.10.61 |
| | XD316 | 11.12.61 - 09.10.62 | | | XD220 | 15.02.62 - 26.03.65 |
| | XD332 | 11.01.63 - 26.03.65 | | - | XD244 | 25.08.60 - 20.10.60 (temp) |
| | | | | - | XD275 | 28.06.63 - 12.08.63 (temp) |

*Recovery action after Lt Cdr J.A.D.Ford in XD226 '615' of No.736 Squadron suffered a nose wheel collapse after landing at Lossiemouth on 9 April 1963. (via N.Parker).*

*XD217 '616' of No.736 Squadron being captured on film by an intrepid photographer in very inclement weather at Yeovilton in 1963. (N.D.Welch)*

## No.764 SQUADRON

No.764 Squadron at Lossiemouth was to have taken over the conversion task from No.807 Squadron, with XD226 arriving in February 1959. The remainder of the complement should have arrived in the latter half of May to begin conversion courses and weapon training for pilots going to Scimitar squadrons. However, the policy was changed, and No.736 Squadron would now be equipped with six Scimitars for this purpose. This was a major, disappointment to all in the squadron, and also the ratings who had joined for maintenance but now had to be redrafted to No.736, as was XD226. Instead, the squadron received the Hunter T.8, which in the event proved very popular.

| Squadron Commanders | |
|---|---|
| Lt Cdr DT McKeown | 02.59 - 19.04.59 |
| Lt Cdr RMP Carne | 20.04.59 - 05.59 |

*XD225 '620' of No.764B Squadron on approach to land at Lossiemouth with arrester hook down in 1965. (MAP)*

*XD215 '614', still in No.764B Squadron markings, aboard HMS Hermes at Devonport during pre-commission work-up deck handling in 1966. (MAP)*

*Having reached the end of their flying careers, Scimitars XD215 '614' and XD332 '616' ex No.764B Squadron Lossiemouth are seen here aboard aircraft lighter RNAIR54 in Plymouth Sound en route to HMS Hermes for work-up deck handling training in 1966 (FAA Museum)*

## No.764B SQUADRON

On 26 March 1965 No.764B Squadron was formed at Lossiemouth at flight strength from the remnants of No.736 Squadron, and was to continue exactly the same as before but with the intention of eventually absorbing the administration of the Scimitar training flight. It was proposed that Scimitar training would be conducted as a flight within 764 Squadron with as much common administration and servicing as possible, so as to achieve an immediate saving in manpower, with further savings when Regulating and Air Staff were combined. On 14 May it moved across the by now quite crowded airfield to share No.17 hangar with No.764 Squadron, leaving the main dispersal free for the growing Buccaneer force, No.800 Squadron taking its place in No.16 hangar on returning from HMS *Eagle* on 23 May. This ploy had the added advantage of disguising the fact that a new squadron had been formed, albeit for only a few months. It was given a variety of tasks in its short existence, including photography, Army co-operation and also HMS *Ark Royal*'s O.R.1 (Operational Readiness 1), aircraft being used to work up the ship, previously the task of the Fleet Requirements Unit. The squadron was to have participated in the Biggin Hill Air Fair that year, but its aircraft were grounded when someone removed the safety pins from the pylons. No.764 was, however, deployed to Yeovilton from 28 June to 8 July for the annual *Shop Window* exercise. The Squadron was also involved in several Air Days before disbanding on 23 November 1965 on completion of its task.

### Identification Markings
Side codes *614-617, 620-621* in white on the fuselage sides, immediately above the wings. Inherited from No.736 Sqn a blue lightning flash on a white fin.

| Squadron pilots: | |
|---|---|
| Lt Cdr J Worth (CO) | 26.03.65 - 14.06.65 |
| Lt Cdr JWH Purvis (Senior Pilot) | 26.03.65 - 17.05.65 |
| Lt PJ Trudgett (QFI) | 26.03.65 - 11.10.65 |
| Lt AS Tuck (AWI) (Senior Pilot from 17.5.65) | 26.03.65 - 11.10.65 |
| Lt PAA Waring (Simulator Officer) | 26.03.65 - 23.11.65 |
| Lt(E) JR Chicken (AEO) | 26.03.65 - 23.11.65 |
| Lt R C Chaffey (Asst AEO) | 26.03.65 - 23.11.65 |
| Lt Cdr PG Newman (CO) | 14.06.65 - 23.11.65 |
| **Pupils:** | |
| S/L AC Hill | 26.03.65 - 10.08.65 |
| Lt Cdr RF Shercliff (114 OFS) | 08.05.65 - 08.09.65 |
| Lt MJ Williams (114 OFS) | 08.05.65 - 08.09.65 |
| Lt TJ Notley [refresher flying] | 17.06.65 - 11.09.65 |
| S/L ZK Skrodzki (115 OFS) | 07.65 - 18.11.65 |
| Lt AR Dady (115 OFS) | 07.65 - 18.11.65 |

| Squadron aircraft | | |
|---|---|---|
| 614 | XD215 | 26.03.65 - 27.01.66 |
| | XD224 | 26.03.65 - 10.06.65 |
| 615 | XD227 | 26.03.65 - 29.11.65 |
| 616 | XD217 | 26.03.65 - 02.06.65 |
| | XD332 | 26.03.65 - 24.11.65 |
| 617 | XD219 | 26.03.65 - 17.05.65 |
| | XD246 | 07.05.65 - 12.08.65 |
| | XD267 | 20.07.65 - 01.12.65 |
| 620 | XD225 | 26.10.65 - 29.11.65 |
| 621 | XD220 | 26.03.65 - 02.10.65 |

*XD278 '102/R' and others of No.800 Squadron lined up in August 1959, soon after the squadron re-formed at Lossiemouth. (Vickers-Armstrongs)*

## No.800 SQUADRON

No.800 Squadron re-formed for the fifth time at RNAS Lossiemouth on 1 July 1959 under the command of Lt Cdr D.P.Norman AFC, RN, the Commissioning Warrant being read by the Flag Officer Reserve Aircraft, Rear Admiral A.J.Tyndale-Biscoe, CB, OBE. It was to remain at Lossiemouth for the remainder of the year and for the early part of 1960, undergoing intensive flying training until embarking in HMS *Ark Royal* on 3 March with six new Scimitar F.1s. During the short commission *Ark Royal* would take her air group to the Mediterranean (where at Hal Far, Malta, No.800 sent a detachment of four aircraft ashore), close to the ice shelf off Greenland, to New York and back again to the United Kingdom. One incident that took place during the visit to the Mediterranean was on 28 April, when Lt Peter Banfield was forced to land into the flight deck barrier as he was unable to lower his undercarriage fully. Banfield was unharmed but his aircraft, XD280, was badly damaged and had to be repaired at Fleetlands.

The squadron had disembarked from *Ark Royal* and returned to Lossiemouth on 27 February 1961. On 14 March, Lt M.Johnson was presented with the Kelly Memorial Prize by Her Majesty Queen Elizabeth the Queen Mother, this being awarded annually to the best General List Aviator qualifying for the award of pilot's wings. The squadron was chosen to appear on a number of public occasions as the Royal Naval Display Team. This was not a new thing for No.800 Sqn as they had performed at the SBAC Show at Farnborough in 1959, then flying the Sea Hawk. The main problem for the team, now named 'The Red Blades', was the very short time before the first show, not helped by the fact that only one of the pilots had any considerable experience of display flying. However, after many hours of practice, the team became very proficient. Four standard routines were worked out and practised for use in different weather conditions, therefore it was hoped that whatever the weather a display could be performed. The highlights of the season were appearances at the 24th Salon de l'Aeronautique (Paris Air Show) at Le Bourget in early June and the SBAC Show at Farnborough in September. In between these two displays there was the Lossiemouth Air Day on 22 July for which the team was led by the deputy leader, Lt Cdr J.A.D.Ford, as Lt Cdr Norman had a slight back injury, acquired while ejecting from XD264 after one main leg would not lower over the Moray Firth.

*XD280 '104/R' of No.800 Squadron after Lt P.E.H.Banfield came to grief whilst landing on HMS Ark Royal off Cyprus on 28 April 1960. (via J.H.Stevens)*

*XD280 '104/R' of No.800 Squadron's aerobatic team at Lossiemouth in 1961. (B.J.Lowe)*

Altogether the team displayed 19 times during the season, which was a tribute to the Squadron Maintenance Team as this kind of flying called for 100% serviceability most of the time. It was also with pride that the Squadron could say that it completed the season without any accidents or hair-raising incidents. In addition to Le Bourget and Farnborough, they had appeared at four RNAS Air Days, the first being on 17 June when they gave a restricted display at Yeovilton due to poor weather. Then both Brawdy and Culdrose on 15 July (being based at Brawdy), and then finally Lossiemouth. Seven days later they gave two displays on the same day despite poor weather. In addition to these they appeared at the Portsmouth Navy Day on 5, 6 and 7 August, again based at Yeovilton, as well as putting in appearances at the Rosyth Navy Day and also RAF Gaydon's Battle of Britain Day on 16 September when five aircraft were based at Yeovilton.

Therefore, after a very successful summer, No.800 Sqn returned to Lossiemouth, the complement being increased from six to twelve aircraft with effect from 15 September. It was here on 2 October 1961 that Lt Cdr. Norman handed over to the new Commanding Officer, Lt Cdr A.Mancais RN. The Squadron was now increased in strength to a total of twelve Scimitars by amalgamating the aircraft of No.800 and 807 Squadrons. All aircraft underwent a major modification programme at this time to equip them for Bullpup (Air to Ground) and Sidewinder (Air to Air Infra-Red) missiles, flying being severely restricted during this period. However, sufficient dummy MADDLs were achieved to enable three new pilots to carry out initial DLPs and for 10 aircraft to embark in HMS *Ark Royal* off Plymouth and proceed for work-up in the Mediterranean. The aircraft were now configured in the strike and reconnaissance role, and intensive live weaponry practice was carried out during this period, which was noteworthy for several highlights.

Lt Jack Smith, subsequently called 'Bomber' Smith, lobbed four 25lb Practice Bombs into the garden of Group Captain Bailey, Managing Director of Bailey Shipyards, Malta - finger or switch trouble!! Mike Faulkner experienced a tailplane 'lock' when flying at 620 knots, 50 feet on the Tarhuna LABS Weapons Range near USAF Wheelus Field. He recovered safely to Wheelus where a spanner was found to be lodged in the tailplane control run. Six elderly landing ships were demolished by VT-fused 1,000 lb bombs off Marsaxlokk with Dave Howard, Squadron AWI, suffering extensive damage to his aircraft due to an early 'cooker'. 'Bomber' Smith lobbed a 25 lb Practice Bomb into a Bedouin tent situated on the Tarhuna LABS Range. A goodwill visit from the CO, copious draughts of Arab tea, and the transfer of £5 soothed ruffled feelings, and apparently was enough to purchase or construct another tent shortly thereafter.

Squadron aircraft flew off from *Ark Royal* in the vicinity off Majorca on the morning of 10 January 1962, refuelling at Yeovilton en-route to Lossiemouth. Aircraft strength was increased to fourteen during the disembarked period and the squadron re-embarked in the Lyme Bay area on 10 March. The ship arrived in the Malta exercise area five days later, and after a short spell of flying against targets in Sicily and North Africa as well as other exercises, *Ark Royal* transited the Suez Canal on 23/24 March for a Far East deployment. Aden was reached on 27th, day and night flying exercises being undertaken in the area over the next four days, using RAF Khormaksar as a diversion airfield. The strength was increased to 14 aircraft with effect from 28 March, and on 31st the ship started the passage to the Straits of Malacca, intensive day and night flying then being carried out in the Penang area from 9th to 11th April, working in conjunction with the Royal Australian Air Force at Butterworth. Singapore Dockyard was reached on 12th and, after some self-maintenance

*XD265 '105/R' and five others of No.800 Squadron flying in formation over the town of Lossiemouth in 1961. (via Paddy Porter)*

*XD322 '106/R' and five others of No.800 Squadron flying in formation and making smoke during a display in 1961. (via Philip Jarrett)*

*HMS Ark Royal departing Singapore on 25 October 1962. On deck are 4 Scimitars of No.800 Squadron, 3 Sea Vixens of No.890 Squadron and the 4 Gannets of No.849C Flight. Parked aft are the vehicles and equipment of the 11th Sphinx Battery of 34 Light Anti-Aircraft of the Royal Artillery, being transported with the troops to Aden. (Royal Navy)*

*The 'Red Blades' aerobatic team, including XD322 '106/R', with hooks down, flying over a line of RAF Lightnings at Farnborough in September 1961.*
*(Vickers-Armstrongs)*

and repair to the ship, she sailed again on 24th for Exercise *Fantail*, working with No.2 Royal Marine Commando in Malaya, followed by Exercise *Sea Devil* in the South China Sea in conjunction with ships from the United States, Australian, Thai, New Zealand and Pakistan navies. This included round-the-clock air defence and strikes. Arriving in Manila Bay on 2 May, then on to Subic Bay three days later for exercises and cross-operations with the US Seventh Fleet. Leaving the Philippines on 16th, Hong Kong was reached the next day, the ship remaining there until 5 June when she headed for Japanese waters, putting in to Okinawa on 9th for maintenance, then sailing again seven days later to remain in the area for a few days. It was during Exercise *Rawfish* off Okinawa on 18 June that Lts Howard and Marshall, both AWIs, made history by firing the first Bullpup missiles by a RN front-line squadron. They hit the target, but had to divert from Torishima Range to the US Navy Base at Naha due to lack of fuel. Lt Entwisle was also forced to divert to Naha after a bird strike which burst his starboard drop tank.

On *Ark Royal*'s return to Singapore a detachment of five aircraft was sent ashore to RAF Tengah on 28 June. It was here on 3 July that Sub Lt Alsop had a very hairy landing after having hydraulic failure shortly after taking-off. No.800 were once again back in *Ark Royal* for Exercise *Fotex 62* from 12 July, then it was back to Tengah (six aircraft) on 26th. During a formation take-off on 1 August, Lt Ellis's aircraft, XD278, had the tread of his starboard wheel unwind; this caused damage to the brake lines and consequently during the landing he experienced partial brake failure and took the Safe-Land barrier at about 20 knots. The aircraft was extensively damaged and had to be left ashore at Tengah. During this period a four aircraft formation aerobatic team was formed, and led by the CO they performed at a number of air displays during the next four months.

The ship sailed on 6 August, but remained in the Singapore area for five days during Exercise *Showboat*, a demonstration designed to illustrate to civilian and service VIPs the day-to-day training carried out by operational units of the Royal Navy, and the state of efficiency and preparedness of the Far East Fleet. After this the carrier made its way south to Fremantle, Western Australia, the opportunity being taken en-route to carry out simulated tactical nuclear strikes on selected targets on the Australian mainland. Berthing alongside on 20th for a ten-day visit, six aircraft were detached to RAAF Pearce for continuation flying and to prepare replacement pilots for initial deck landings. Returning north, a further visit was made to Singapore on 13 September, sailing again on 28th to spend two days on *Pintail*, an army support exercise with elements of the 3rd Commando Brigade and the 17th Gurkha Division, this taking place on the Asahan Range and involving live firings. Further exercises were then carried out en-route to Hong Kong, the ship anchoring off Green Island on 5 October, to sail again seven days later for Singapore. Flying activities were restricted due to a faulty starboard catapult, but dummy attacks and RP sorties were carried out on wrecked tanks and vehicles on the Asahan Range during Exercise *Fantail 2*, this time involving 99 Brigade. Reaching Singapore on 19th, the ship sailed again five days later for home, a voyage that was to take nearly two months. Aden was visited 1-13 November and No.800 Sqn provided support for the RAF in combat air patrols in the Radfan area. It was during this period that the CO experienced a fire in his port jet pipe during a catapult launch with which he successfully coped and then proceeded single-engine to RAF Khormaksar. A brief visit was paid to Mombasa from 22nd to 26th November before heading for the Suez Canal, through which the ship passed on 5 December, reaching Gibraltar on 10th. The squadron disembarked off Plymouth on 14 December and flew to Lossiemouth for Christmas leave, the complement being then reduced from fourteen to twelve aircraft. On 19 February 1963, 'A' Flight re-embarked in *Ark Royal* in the English Channel for flying exercises in the South West Approaches, the ship returning to Devonport on 28th, sailing again seven days later for further flying exercises, culminating in Exercise *Dawn Breeze 8* from 9th to 14th March, the flight returning to Lossiemouth on 16th.

Lt Cdr Pete Newman was appointed Squadron CO, but was unable to take up the appointment due to a back injury. Lt Cdr Mills, the Senior Pilot was therefore appointed to relieve Lt Cdr Mancais who was then free to take up his new appointment as Chief Flying Instructor, Lossiemouth. By 5 March 1963 Lt Cdr Newman was fit enough to take up his appointment as the new Commanding Officer. No.800 Squadron remained at Lossiemouth until 4 May, when the complete squadron, consisting of 14 aircraft, left the United Kingdom to rejoin HMS *Ark Royal*. The ship had

*Lt C.D.Walkinshaw climbs out of the cockpit of XD321 '104/R' aboard HMS Ark Royal on 30 May 1963 after his port brake failed while taxying. The aircraft had swung to starboard, striking an anti-aircraft gun mounting. (Royal Navy)*

*XD317 '112/R' and another seen in a typical launch sequence on HMS Ark Royal in May 1963, with jet blast deflector raised behind the leading aircraft. (J.H.Stevens)*

*Having tried unsuccessfully to divert to RAF Khormaksar, XD239 '103/R' ditched in 6ft of water in Aden Harbour on 22 May 1963. The pilot, Sub-Lt C.D.Legg, was injured when he ejected. (Royal Navy via J.H.Stevens)*

*XD236 108/R suspended from a crane at Singapore in August 1963. (Royal Navy via J.H.Stevens)*

just left Gibraltar after a seven week refit in dry dock and was now steaming off the Balearic Islands in the western Mediterranean waiting for her Air Group to embark. All 14 of No.800 Squadron's Scimitars flew out from the U.K, being refuelled en-route by Valiant tankers of the RAF, except for one which experienced fuel transfer problems and instead landed at the French airfield at Orange to refuel. Three of the aircraft were flown out by ferry pilots (Lt Cope, Lt De Souza and Sub-Lt Morris) as three of the Squadron pilots were not yet deck qualified. All the ground crew were also embarked by air. *Ark Royal* made a fast passage to Aden, with a one night stop at Malta, transit of the Suez Canal being on 10 May. Off Aden two of the new boys were deck qualified. Sub Lt C.D.Legg had to divert to RAF Khormaksar but failed to make it, ejecting out of XD239 just before the aircraft landed in Aden Bay in about twelve feet of water; this was his second ejection from a Scimitar, and this time he sustained some back injury and therefore had to remain ashore for a while. Lt Walkinshaw was almost the cause of one of the flight deck directors having a heart attack on 31 May. He had just landed on and was taxying clear of the wires when his port brakes failed; despite frantic signals from the director to turn to port he continued straight ahead and smashed into an anti-aircraft gun on the starboard side just in front of the Island.

While *Ark Royal* and her ship's company enjoyed Mombasa, No.800 Squadron had a detachment of five aircraft ashore at Embakasi from 7 to 19 June. After re-embarking, the next thing was a small exercise and then passage to Singapore. It was after leaving Singapore and during *Fotex 63*, which lasted from 29 July to 9 August, that tragically one aircraft and its pilot were lost. On 31 July, Lt MacFie crashed into the sea astern of the ship while attacking the splash target.

From 7 to 29 August seven aircraft were detached ashore to RAF Tengah. It was here on 24th that Sub Lt McMeekan in XD221 had to abort a take-off and took the barrier; the aircraft was badly damaged and had to be left at Tengah. More flying exercises were carried out off Singapore and then a visit to Hong Kong from 6th to 12th September. Entry into Hong Kong was delayed by Typhoon *Faye*; *Ark Royal* sailed through the tail end of it, but that was bad enough. After Hong Kong there was Exercise *Dovetail* from 16th to 21st September, another short visit to Singapore, then a Flyex off Butterworth on 23rd, leaving the area on 26th. Four days later the ship passed from the limits of the Far East Station, to find itself engaged next day in a Middle East exercise. Khor al Fakkan, a beach resort at the northern end of the Gulf of Oman, was visited from 5th to 7th October, followed by the tri-service communications Exercise *Biltong* until 12th, this being in by far the

*XD333 '837' of the Airwork Fleet Requirements Unit parked at Hurn around 1969/70 (MAP)*

*XD214 departing Lee-on-Solent on 17 June 1966, piloted by legendary Shorts Ferry Pilot "Pancho" Brandt. Ross House, home of the air station's Captain, can be seen in the background. (Ivor Barnes)*

*With its outer wings shorn off, XD219 carries out wet runway breaking and aquaplaning trials at RAE Farnborough on 1 November 1971. (via Peter Cooper)*

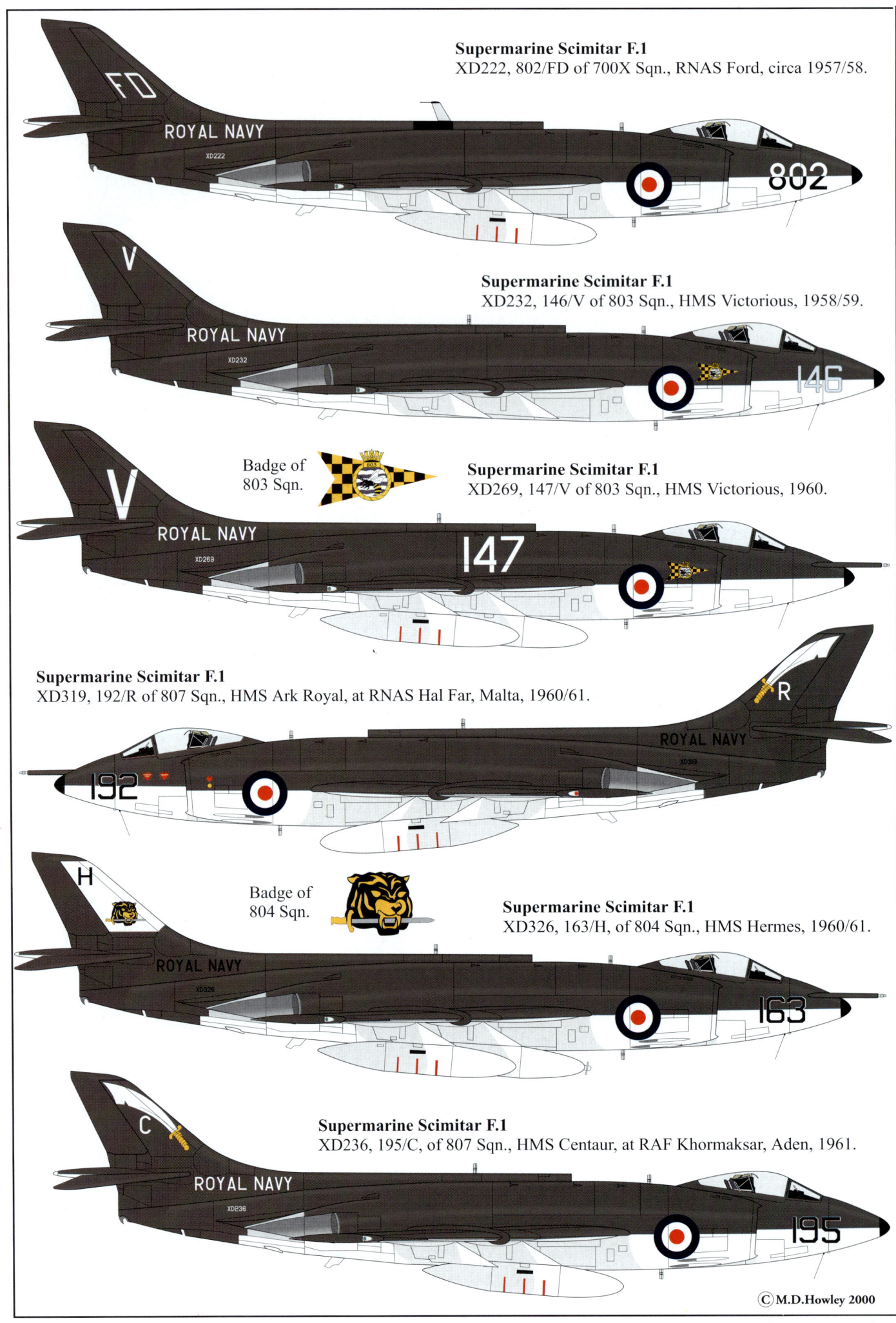

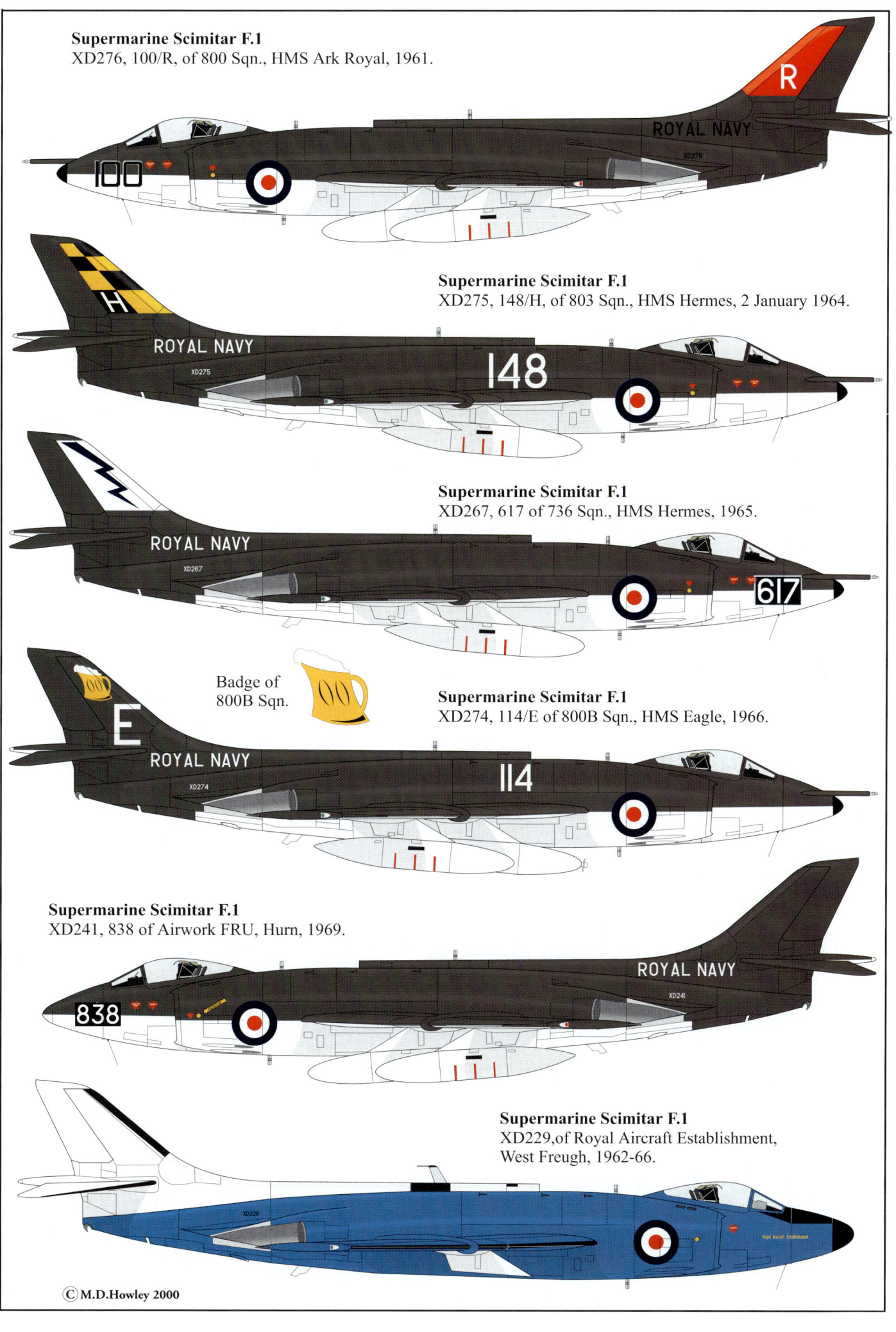

*XD235 on the Fleetlands Flight Test hardstanding at RNAS Lee-on-Solent in August 1966. Note the extremely high gloss finish. (Ivor Barnes)*

*XD236 '038' of the Airwork Fleet Requirements, Hurn flying south of the Isle of Wight in 1968. (MAP)*

*XD319 '192/R' of No.807 Squadron around 1959/60. (A.E.Hughes)*

*XD277 '101/R' of No.800 Squadron at the Paris Air Show in June 1961. (MAP)*

*XD219 '617' of No.736 Squadron Lossiemouth at Farnborough in 1962. (Philip Jarrett)*

*No.803 Squadron Scimitars on the flight deck of HMS Victorious around 1959, with No.893 Squadron Sea Vixens and No.849B Flight Skyraiders in the background. (via R.C.Sturtivant)*

*XD220 '618' of No.736 Squadron being refuelled by a Sea Vixen XJ580 '485/VL' of No.899 Squadron from Yeovilton in 1963. (via Tony Buttler)*

*XD275 117/E of No.800B Squadron about to take off from HMS Eagle around 1965/6, with a planeguard Wessex in attendance. (J.H.Stevens)*

*XD279 '159/R' of No.803 Squadron preparing to land on HMS Ark Royal in 1965. (MoD)*

*All-cream Supermarine 525 VX138 at the SBAC Show Farnborough in 1954.*

*Activity around the Scimitars of No.803 Squadron on the flight deck of HMS Victorious around 1959. (via R.C.Sturtivant)*

*XD221 '106/R' comes over the rounddown while landing on HMS Ark Royal in August 1963. (J.H.Stevens)*

hottest area yet visited. Opposition during the exercise was provided by RAF Canberras and ground forces on the Jebajib Range. After the Gulf it was a fast passage back to Mombasa, where a detachment of five aircraft once again went ashore to Embakasi, from 18 October until 1 November. On 9 November *Ark Royal* anchored some way off Karachi in company with the USS *Essex*, both carriers taking part in the CENTO Exercise *Midlink 6* from 14 to 23 November. Organised by the C-in-C Pakistan Navy, this exercise was very realistic, *Ark Royal* being continually attacked at very low-level by F-86 Sabres of the Pakistani Air Force. At one time four Sabres appeared over the ship and Lt Cdr Flying made a broadcast to the flight deck: "It's OK, those enemy Sabres have been shot down by our Scimitars". After the exercise, and while anchored off Karachi a short distance from the *Essex*, many of the Squadron personnel took the opportunity to visit her, as did many of her crew come over and visit *Ark*. The exchange visits were tragically and suddenly brought to a halt by the news of President Kennedy's assassination, that shocked the world on 22 November 1963. The next day the *Essex* had sailed.

*Ark Royal* and her squadrons sailed also from Karachi that day to begin a fast passage to Aden in order to participate on the 29th in an Air Day at Khormaksar, where the RAF onlookers were impressed by the "twinkle rolls" of the squadron's Scimitars. The ship then headed for Zanzibar, arriving there on 4 December. Her crew were to provide a Guard of Honour for HRH Prince Philip as he was the Queen's representative for Zanzibar's independence. After Zanzibar it was up to Mombasa on 11th to 14th for the independence celebrations of Kenya, then another quick visit to Aden on 18th for some last minute shopping. The Suez Canal was passed through on Christmas Eve, having been delayed for 24 hours by the Egyptians for some reason.

Arriving home, No.800 Squadron finally departed *Ark Royal* and returned to Lossiemouth on 31 December 1963. On 25 February 1964 the Squadron was disbanded, her Scimitars going to No.803 Squadron. Less than a month later No.800 would again re-form, but this time equipped with the Buccaneer S.1, leaving only one front-line squadron operating the Scimitar in its intended role.

| Squadron bases | |
|---|---|
| Lossiemouth | 1 Jul 1959 |
| HMS Ark Royal | 3 Mar 1960 |
| Lossiemouth | 30 Sep 1960 |
| HMS Ark Royal | 26 Oct 1960 |
| Hal Far (Dt4) | 4-24 Nov 1960 |
| Lossiemouth | 27 Feb 1961 |
| HMS Ark Royal | 13 Nov 1961 |
| Hal Far (Dt6) | 16 Dec 1961 |
| | to 2 Jan 1962 |
| Lossiemouth | 15 Jan 1962 |
| HMS Ark Royal | 10 Mar 1962 |
| Tengah (Dt5) | 28 Jun 1962 |
| | to 12 Jul 1962 |
| Tengah (Dt6) | 26 Jul 1962 |
| | to 6 Aug 1962 |
| Pearce (Dt6) | 19-30 Aug 1962 |
| Tengah (Dt8) | 13-28 Sep 1962 |
| Lossiemouth | 14 Dec 1962 |
| HMS Ark Royal ('A' Flight) | 19 Feb 1963 to 16 Mar 1963 |
| HMS Ark Royal | 4 May 1963 |
| Embakasi (Dt5) | 7-19 Jun 1963 |
| Tengah | 10 Jul 1963 |
| HMS Ark Royal | 25 Jul 1963 |
| Tengah (Dt7) | 7-29 Aug 1963 |
| Embakasi (Dt5) | 18 Oct 1963 |
| | to 1 Nov 1963 |
| Lossiemouth | 31 Dec 1963 |
| Squadron disbanded | 25 Feb 1964 |

**Identification Markings**
Black nose codes *100-113*, outlined in white. The last digit of the code repeated in black on the nose wheel door. White letter 'R' on a red fin.

*XD239 '103/R', on the flight deck of HMS Ark Royal at Karachi in November 1963. (J.H.Stevens)*

*XD272 '102/R' and another ready for launch from HMS Ark Royal. (J.H.Stevens)*

| Squadron Officers | |
|---|---|
| Lt Cdr DP Norman AFC (CO) | 01.07.59 - 02.10.61 |
| Lt NJP Mills (Senior Pilot) | 01.07.59 - 05.08.60 |
| (to Lt Cdr 12.2.60) | |
| Lt DH Pepper (A/E) | 01.07.59 - 14.10.60 |
| (to Lt Cdr 1.7.60) | |
| Lt(L) J Hickson | 01.07.59 - 03.07.61 |
| Lt RJ Noyes | 01.07.59 - 02.10.60 |
| Flt Lt GSC Mumford RAF | 01.07.59 - 19.11.59 |
| Lt WE Thorpe | 01.07.59 - 02.10.60 |
| Lt RW Edward | 01.07.59 - 11.05.60 |
| S/L WP Ryce (to Lt 13.8.59) | 01.07.59 - 11.01.61 |
| S/L(E) H Cunliffe | 01.07.59 - 04.11.61 |
| S/L(L) AJ Sell | 01.07.59 - 27.03.61 |
| S/L JB Cross | 01.07.59 - 30.10.59 |
| Lt(E) PEH Banfield | 20.10.59 - 13.09.61 |
| Lt AJ Goodenough | 15.05.60 - 13.11.61 |
| Lt GAI Johnston | 14.07.60 - 02.10.61 |
| Lt Cdr TFB Young (Senior Pilot) | 03.08.60 - 03.03.61 |
| Lt(E) MK Johnson | 01.10.60 - 13.09.61 |
| Lt Cdr MJ Hedges AFC | 03.10.60 - 07.06.61 |
| Lt Cdr WG Fairhead | 19.10.60 - 24.04.62 |
| S/L I Ellis | 20.03.61 - 03.01.63 |
| Lt TNF Skead | 30.03.61 - 20.09.61 |
| Lt NG Grier-Rees | 30.03.61 - 30.09.61 |
| Lt JL Carver | 05.03.61 - 20.06.62 |
| Lt Cdr JAD Ford (Senior Pilot) | 05.06.61 - 17.12.62 |
| Lt CC Giles | 05.06.61 - 16.12.61 |
| Lt AG Ellis | 24.07.61 - 17.11.62 |
| Lt Cdr DA Slater | 28.07.61 - 04.05.62 |
| S/L KR Entwisle (to Lt 20.9.62) | 08.08.61 - 14.12.62 |
| Lt JA Manley | 14.08.61 - 14.03.63 |
| S/L CC Morris | 14.08.61 - 06.05.63 |
| Lt JDHB Howard | 29.09.61 - 07.09.63 |
| Lt Cdr A Mancais (CO) | 02.10.61 - 24.03.63 |
| Lt JPE Faulkner | 02.10.61 - 09.03.62 |
| Lt AJ Stone | 02.10.61 - 09.03.62 |
| S/L JGL Smith (to Lt 16.12.62) | 02.10.61 - 19.04.62 |
| Lt CD Walkinshaw | 09.10.61 - 21.08.63 |
| Lt MJ Ebdon | 30.10.61 - 04.05.63 |
| Lt GHR Wooff | 12.02.62 - 04.04.63 |
| Lt AM Hickling | 12.02.62 - 07.09.63 |
| Lt G McBain | 12.02.62 - 31.12.63 |
| Lt PC Marshall | 27.02.62 - 21.10.63 |
| S/L AD Alsop | 27.02.62 - 14.12.62 |
| Lt JPF Nichols | 19.04.62 - 31.12.63 |
| Lt Cdr M Scadding | 27.04.62 - 29.11.63 |
| S/L L Ingham | 29.06.62 - 31.12.63 |
| Lt Cdr DF Mills (Senior Pilot) | 17.12.62 - 25.02.64 |
| (CO from 15.4.63) | |
| S/L(L) JR Chicken | 02.01.62 - 25.02.64 |
| Lt JJR Tod | 07.01.63 - 25.02.64 |
| Lt(E) R Hicks | 14.01.63 - 25.02.64 |
| Lt AG MacFie | 21.01.63 - 31.07.63 |
| Lt IPF Meiklejohn | 19.02.63 - 25.02.64 |
| S/L CD Legg | 19.02.63 - 22.05.63 |
| Lt Cdr PG Newman (CO) | 25.03.63 - 14.04.63 |
| Lt(L) LP Martin | 08.04.63 - 25.02.64 |
| S/L NHL Bowden | 08.04.63 - 25.02.64 |
| S/L A McMeekan | 08.04.63 - 25.02.64 |
| S/L IC Frenz | 22.08.63 - 25.02.64 |
| C de C MR Borney FN | 20.10.63 - 25.02.64 |
| Lt Cdr JF Kennett (Senior Pilot) | 25.10.63 - 25.02.64 |
| Lt Cdr MH Bolus | 20.11.63 - 25.02.64 |
| Lt MJ Doust | ? - ? |
| Lt Miles (AEO?) | ? - ? |

| Squadron aircraft | | |
|---|---|---|
| 100 | XD276 | 11.07.59 - 27.12.62 |
| | XD280 | 30.07.62 - 07.01.64 |
| 101 | XD277 | 03.07.59 - 09.03.61 |
| | | [and later?] |
| | XD221 | 21.02.62 - 17.07.62 |
| | XD231 | 05.01.63 - 05.02.64 |
| 102 | XD278 | 07.07.59 - 29.01.60 |
| | XD272 | 15.09.61 - 17.12.62 |
| | XD248 | 23.01.63 - 23.02.63 |
| 103 | XD279 | 13.07.59 - 18.11.60 |
| | XD330 | 23.10.62 - 10.12.62 |
| | XD239 | 23.01.63 - 22.05.63 |
| 104 | XD280 | 21.08.59 - 02.05.60 |
| | XD279 | 10.01.61 - 27.02.61 |
| | XD246 | 22.03.61 - 21.09.61 |
| | XD279 | 19.04.61 - 21.02.63 |
| | XD274 | 15.09.61 - 24.09.62 |
| | XD321 | 12.07.62 - 03.02.64 |
| 105 | XD265 | 18.05.61 - 18.09.61 |
| | XD325 | 13.09.61 - 14.03.63 |
| | XD271 | 27.03.63 - 26.02.64 |
| 106 | XD322 | 20.03.61 - @ 09.61 |
| | XD270 | 19.03.62 - 28.07.62 |
| | XD221 | 16.10.62 - 31.08.63 |
| | XD223 | 29.04.63 - 26.02.64 |
| 107 | XD250 | 25.03.61 - 28.11.61 |
| | XD277 | 22.03.61 - 22.10.62 |
| | XD270 | 02.05.63 - 13.02.64 |
| 108 | XD278 | 24.03.61 - 09.08.62 |
| | XD264 | 13.07.61 [5.61?] - 21.07.61 |
| | XD231 | 09.61 - 09.61 (loan) |
| | XD246 | 16.04.63 - 26.04.63 |
| | XD215 | 05.05.63 - 07.63 |
| | XD236 | 16.07.63 - 27.02.64 |
| 109 | XD239 | 23.08.61 - 12.09.61 (loan) |
| | XD322 | 04.63?-24.04.63 |
| | XD325 | 15.09.61 - 30.04.63 |
| 110 | XD267 | 09.61 - 09.61 (loan) |
| | XD324 | 13.09.61 - 19.02.63 |
| | XD320 | 12.07.62 - 26.02.63 |
| 111 | XD326 | 13.09.61 - 31.07.63 |
| | XD249 | 20.08.63 - 28.01.64 |
| 112 | XD322 | 10.62 - 01.63 |
| | XD317 | 14.01.63 - 27.02.64 |
| 113 | XD243 | 27.03.62 - 19.02.64 |
| ? | XD330 | 12.07.63 - 26.02.64 |
| - | XD234 | 16.10.61 - 26.10.61 (temp) |
| - | XD246 | 20.10.60 - 16.01.61 |
| (retained "150/V") | | |

*Aircraft of No.800 Squadron line up on the runway at Farnborough during the 1961 SBAC Show. The aerobatic team were given the name 'Red Blades' due to the colour of the fins. (E.B.Morgan archives)*

*'110/R' about to be launched from HMS Ark Royal. (B.J.Lowe)*

*'112/R' catches the wire on HMS Ark Royal. (B.J.Lowe)*

*XD268 '112/E' about to be launched from HMS Eagle around 1964/5, with the froth-laden tankard motif on its fin, symbolising the unit's close bond with Whitbread's brewery. (via Philip Jarrett)*

## No.800B FLIGHT

No.800B Flight formed on 9 September 1964 at Lossiemouth, associated with, but separate from, No.800 Squadron, for investigation into the operational techniques of air-to-air refuelling in the Royal Navy, with four Scimitar F.1s. Initially with three pilots, a fourth was appointed shortly before joining HMS *Eagle* on 2 December at full strength for a spell in the Far East, being the only Scimitar unit to embark in that carrier, which was on its first commission in its newly-modernised form. The Flight concentrated mainly on extending the operational range of the Buccaneer, working closely and successfully with No.800 Squadron, whose aircraft were consequently able to take off with a full bomb load from the carrier, being able to top up with fuel from a Scimitar tanker. The Scimitars were also able to refuel the Sea Vixens and many NATO aircraft as well as each other. Socially, the Flight had a friendly bond with Whitbreads brewery, which bore much enjoyable and alcoholic fruit both at home and in the Far East, a froth-laden beer tankard being painted on the fin of each aircraft.

*A Scimitar of No.800B in-flight refuelling Buccaneer S.1 XN963 '104/E' of No.800 Squadron. (B.J.Lowe)*

After sailing from Devonport, the ship sailed through the Suez Canal on 8 December, putting in to Aden seven days later to commence work-up. The ship arrived at Mombasa on 24 December and remained there until 4 January 1965 when she sailed for the Far East, arriving at Singapore on 13th for self-maintenance. Sailing again on 25th, work-up recommenced, the carrier arriving on 8 February at Subic Bay in the Phillipines, where work-up was completed by 21st. Reaching Hong Kong on 23rd for a further period of self-maintenance, *Eagle* left on 11 March to participate in Exercise *Fotex* from 15th, returning to Singapore on 26th to take part in Exercise *Seaday* the following day, followed by self-maintenance until 21 April. The ship then headed for the Middle East, putting in to Aden on 30th for three days. Passing through the Suez Canal on 5 May and reaching Beirut two days later.

The original life expectancy of the Flight had been nine months, but after returning to Lossiemouth on 7 May 1965 this was extended to two years, so it re-embarked in HMS *Eagle* eighteen days later for the second leg of her Far East commission. Serviceability, for both refuelling pods and aircraft, had been sufficiently high for the Flight to be no longer regarded as a trials unit, and it was now firmly planned into the operational set-up of the ship. So much so that it now provided the "insurance" during non-diversion flying with a tanker CAP, a dispenser going about his normal business and a third in Fly 4 at five minutes' notice. With only a CO, a Senior Pilot and a Junior Pilot, this put them on the limits. In addition to flight refuelling, some photography and strafing was undertaken, the latter marking obscure targets in desert terrain so that the Buccaneer pilots could see them on ADSL.

*Eagle* left Beirut on 10 May and sailed for Malta for a four-day stay from 15th to 19th May. By 21st she was off Gibraltar, to arrive at Devonport Dockyard on 24th. She was ready by 3 August when she commenced sea trials, returning to Devonport on 10th, to sail on 24th. By 28th she was off Gibraltar, and after putting in briefly, flying exercises were carried out south west of the Straits in flat, calm seas, reaching Malta on 4 September and taking part in Exercise *Emerald Green* from 14th to 17th September. The carrier sailed again on 23rd with orders to proceed to Aden due to

*Looking down into the hangars in HMS Eagle in 1966, giving a good idea of how closely the aircraft had to be stowed. No.800B Flight Scimitars (including XD270 '114/E') are in the upper hangar along with the Wessex of No.820 Squadron and the AEW Gannets of No.849D Flight, whilst below can be seen the Buccaneers of No.800 Squadron. (Royal Navy)*

political tensions in that area, passing through the Suez Canal and arriving off Aden at 0600 on 1 October. Flying exercises were then carried out before reaching Mombasa on 13th. Sailing again ten days later, nine days of flying operations were carried out during *Little Eastern*, a series of joint training exercises with many of the forces of Middle East Command, before heading east on 4 November. Eight days later the ship docked at Singapore, sailing again on 26th for flying exercises in the Singapore/Penang areas before steaming west to the Aden area. Arriving on 8 December, further flying exercises were undertaken before putting in to Bahrain on 20 December for the Christmas and New Year period.

The ship then sailed south, and on 10–11 January 1966 flying exercises were carried out off Mombasa, before heading north to remain in the Aden area from 15 January until 3 February. Then on 12 February *Eagle* returned to Singapore for maintenance. Leaving here on 28th, flying exercises were carried out in the Singapore/Penang areas until 4 March when the ship was ordered to sail at best speed for the Gan area. The ship was to participate in the British Government's embargo on oil to Southern Rhodesia, which would be enforced by a naval blockade of the Mozambique port of Beira. Arriving at Gan on 12th, from there she headed for the Mozambique Channel, to join the Beira Patrol, eventually leaving the area on 30 April, to be relieved by *Ark Royal*. By the time the ship arrived back at Singapore on 10 May, she had been continuously at sea for 71 days and steamed 30,000 miles – and got through 426,000 cans of beer! Her fixed-wing aircraft had flown 1,070 sorties totalling 2,000 hours and approximately 600,000 miles (equivalent to 27 times round the world). It was then that the Scimitar tanker really proved its worth.

*Eagle* sailed again on 1 June, putting in to Hong Kong six days later for a four-day stay. By 15 June she was in the Subic Bay area, spending ten days there before returning to Singapore for maintenance from 1-14 July. There then followed flying exercises in the Penang area from 15-18 July before heading for the Indian Ocean, Gan being reached on 22nd and Mombasa on 26th. Sailing again on the last day of the month, the ship then headed for home. Aden was reached on 3 August, and two days later she entered the Suez Canal, putting in to Malta on 9 August. Sailing again on 13th, No.800B Flight, along with the ship's Buccaneers and Sea Vixens, flew off next day from a position mid-way between Corsica and Majorca, all 24 aircraft landing safely at Yeovilton, where No.800B immediately disbanded. The ship, meanwhile, reached Gibraltar on 15th, leaving four days later to arrive back at Devonport on 22nd for a much needed refit.

**Identification Markings**

Side codes *111-117* in white on the fuselage sides above the wings. A large white letter 'E' on the fin, above it a stylised yellow tankard with white foam.

**Squadron bases**

| | |
|---|---|
| Lossiemouth | 9 Sep 1964 |
| HMS Eagle | 2 Dec 1964 |
| Lossiemouth | 23 May 1965 |
| HMS Eagle | 27 August 1965 |
| Changi (Dt2) | 11-20 Nov 1965 |
| Changi (Dt2) | 11-28 Feb 1966 |
| Changi (Dt1) | 1-12 Jul 1966 |
| Yeovilton - disbanded | 14 Aug 1966 |

**Squadron Officers**

| | |
|---|---|
| Lt RC Dimmock (CO) (to Lt Cdr 7.65) | 09.09.64 - 19.10.65 |
| Lt CA Wheal | 09.09.64 - 26.07.65 |
| S/L IC Frenz | 09.11.64 - 08.08.66 |
| Lt IPF Meiklejohn (Snr Pilot) | 02.12.64 - 24.05.65 |
| Lt PJ McManus | by 09.65 - 14.08.66 |
| Lt PAA Waring | 12.10.65 - 01.08.66 |
| Lt Cdr NG Grier-Rees (CO) | 20.10.65 - 14.08.66 |

**Squadron aircraft**

| | | |
|---|---|---|
| 111 | XD231 | 29.09.64 - 02.10.64 |
| | XD277 | 26.10.64 - 07.65 |
| 112 | XD268 | 15.09.64 - 15.07.65 |
| 113 | XD270 | 18.09.64 - 27.04.65 |
| | XD321 | 11.06.65 - 07.65 |
| 114 | XD274 | 02.09.64 - 02.08.66 |
| | XD271 | 08.07.66 - 14.08.66 |
| 115 | XD277 | 07.65 - 14.09.65 |
| | XD243 | 21.11.65 - 06.05.66 |
| | XD280 | 03.06.66 - 14.08.66 |
| 116 | XD321 | 07.65 - 03.03.66 |
| | XD321 | 23.05.66 - 14.08.66 |
| 117 | XD275 | 12.08.65 - 14.08.66 |
| - | XD244 | 16.03.66 - 04.05.66 (loan) |

*Classic portrait of a Scimitar in landing configuration: XD277 '111/E' on final approach to HMS Eagle with arrester hook down. (B.J.Lowe)*

*A spectacular shot of six No.803 Squadron Scimitars coming in low and fast at the SBAC Show at Farnborough in September 1958, each apparently wearing its own mini rain cloud. (Vickers-Armstrongs)*

## No.803 SQUADRON

No.803 Squadron was re-formed at Lossiemouth on 3 June 1958 under the command of Cdr J.D.Russell RN, the commissioning ceremony being attended by Rear Admiral D.R.F.Cambell, who was then Flag Officer Flying Training. The last type of aircraft flown by the squadron had been the Sea Hawk, but now they were equipped with an initial complement of eight of the Royal Navy's newest and largest aircraft. All the officers, and most of the ground crew, had previously been with No.700X Sqn, so all had a good knowledge of the Scimitar. The AEO (Air Engineering Officer) was Lt Cdr D.Titford RN.

The squadron soon commenced an intensive work up period in preparation for embarking in HMS *Victorious* and deployment to the Far East. On 21 June two aircraft flew down to RNAS Ford in Sussex to take part in the station's Air Day. These were piloted by Lts Anson and Middleton (both later to become Admirals).

The First Sea Lord paid a visit to Lossiemouth on 10 July and was very impressed by No.803 Sqn. Later a signal was received from him: "Even in so short a visit I could not fail to sense the enthusiasm and energy which are producing such good results in the Fighter School. I was very impressed with my escort and my brief look at the Scimitars. Thank you very much."

On 19 July the Senior Pilot took an aircraft to RNAS Eglinton and gave a flying demonstration that thrilled the crowd. For most it was the first time that they had seen the Navy's newest fighter, but unfortunately he could not land as there was no re-starting equipment. Next day, 20 July, was Lossiemouth's Air Day. This really would have given No.803 the chance to show off, but typical British weather played its part and the flying display had to be limited. Lt Middleton did, however, get in a low-level high speed run before it really clamped in.

By late August the team due to take part in the annual SBAC Show were down at RNAS Ford in Sussex and were busy rehearsing. As the eyes of the world would be on them they were determined to make every effort. On 27th, the full team in company with the Sea Hawks of No.800 Sqn were airborne for a full routine rehearsal. It was reported that many of the local residents were prepared to move house, and someone said that they had seen queues forming at telephone boxes. It was a fact that the station's switchboard was jammed with irate callers. The SBAC Show went off without any hitches, and the squadron felt that they had done a very good job, along with No.800 Sqn, in showing the aviation world the Navy's latest aircraft. This was confirmed by a signal received from the First Sea Lord saying:

*XD231 '152/V' at RNAS Ford in 1958. (via R.C.Sturtivant)*

*XD239 '151/V', XD235 '148/V', XD234 '147/V' and XD240 '145/V' fly overhead in box formation. (via M.J.Hooks)*

*Cdr JD Russell in XD240 '145/V' taxying out to join the newly modernised HMS Victorious steaming off the Isle of Wight on 25 September 1958. Unfortunately No.1 wire pulled out too far then parted, the aircraft ran over the end of the ship, and he was sadly drowned. (Royal Navy via N Parker)*

*XD242 '152/V' taxying at Lossiemouth in 1959. (MAP)*

*XD232 '146/V' aboard HMS Victorious in Grand Harbour, Valletta during the Home Fleet Spring Cruise in early 1959. (MAP)*

*An atmospheric shot of a No.803 Squadron Scimitar being prepared for launch from HMS Victorious around 1958/9 (via Lee Howard)*

"Please convey my hearty congratulations to No.803 and 800 Squadrons on their first class display at Farnborough. It was a great pleasure to see the fastest operational aircraft on view wearing Royal Naval insignia".

After the successful Farnborough display, all the aircraft were back at Lossiemouth by 11 September, most aircraft having had engine changes and been fitted with stores pylons in preparation for intensive weapon training which was carried out until 22nd. The squadron departed Lossiemouth at 1100 hours on 23 September and headed for RNAS Yeovilton where, one hour later, the last of the eight aircraft landed. Two days later the squadron left Yeovilton to embark in pairs in HMS *Victorious* which was steaming off the Isle of Wight. The flight deck was clear and all were eagerly awaiting the arrival of the first Scimitar Squadron to join an operational carrier. The CO was the first to land on; after a perfect approach he engaged number one wire. Tragically, as the aircraft slowed, the end of the wires pulled out, then parted; the CO's aircraft carried on up the deck, over the angle and into the sea. The SAR Whirlwind was on the scene in seconds, and although flown superbly, enabling the rescue aircrewman to actually sit astride the cockpit while being lowered from the helicopter, it was too late. Cdr Russell was unable to get out of the cockpit and sank with the aircraft. The rest of the aircraft were sent back to Yeovilton. The cause of the wire failure was quickly discovered, and this enabled Commander Air of *Victorious*, Cdr Richardson, to make the decision to allow the rest of the squadron to land on, which they did without further incident. This was a very sad day for the squadron, Cdr Russell being a much respected and well liked CO. That evening a memorial service was held in the ship's chapel, it being full to overflowing. The Senior Pilot, Lt Cdr G.R.Higgs, took over as CO.

The squadron remained in *Victorious*, sailing for the Mediterranean on 28 September, to commence work-up. Whilst off Gibraltar on 6-8 October, Scimitars and Sea Venoms were exercising, including two pre-planned simulated strikes against the Rock, when a signal was received from Sir Winston Churchill in the yacht *Christina*, as he was about to fly home from North Front, stating that he would be delighted to see aircraft from the ship before his departure, and the Scimitars duly obliged by beating up the aerodrome. The carrier arrived at Malta on 13th, but put to see again next day to commence working up. A visit was made on 24th to Toulon, which the ship left on 1 November to arrive in the Malta area six days later, but on 8th No.803 was put ashore due to catapult problems on the ship. The squadron re-embarked on 10 December, but that day Lt Maina, in XD237, lost half of his port jet pipe, and had to divert to Hal Far, landing safely ashore. After this all Scimitars were grounded as the jet pipes had to be removed for crack detection tests.

The ship sailed on 2 January 1959 to return to the UK, calling at Gibraltar on 9th-10th, and half the squadron personnel disembarked to Lossiemouth on 13th, the remainder staying

*XD264 '154/V' and '147/V' on the flight deck of HMS Victorious around 1959/60. (Cyril Peckham/RAF Museum)*

*XD236 '150/V' and '145/V ready for launch from HMS Victorious around 1958/9*

aboard ship. All rejoined to sail again on 21 February back to Gibraltar, arriving there four days later and departing next day for flying exercises in the Western Mediterranean. *Victorious* returned once again to Gibraltar on 6 March for seven days of self-maintenance, after which she participated in Exercise *Dawn Breeze 4* until docking at Portsmouth on 24th. On 20th, Lt Westlake had the distinction of carrying out the first ever Scimitar flight deck barrier landing, due to his hook failing to lower.

Meanwhile, No.803 returned to Lossiemouth on 23 March, but on 30 April the main party of ratings left for Portsmouth and the following day ten squadron aircraft flew south to Yeovilton, from where they re-embarked three days later. Three of the aircraft had to turn back to Yeovilton, but after refuelling they were finally embarked by 19.00. Next day the ship proceeded to Plymouth Sound to embark stores, and the ground party joined from Yeovilton. The ship next visited Spithead for a *Shop Window* display from 25th to 29th May. Then came a visit to Rosyth for self-maintenance from 31 May until sailing on 8 June for Exercise *Fairwind*. Following this, Aarhus in Denmark was visited from 13th to 16th June, then Oslo from 17th to 20th, King Olaf of Norway visiting the ship on 18th June, after which she returned to Portsmouth on 22nd. This was followed by a visit to the USA,

*HMS Victorious at sea in the murky weather, with No.803 Squadron Scimitars, No.893 Sea Venoms and No.849B Flight Skyraider parked on the flight deck, possibly during Exercise Bar Frost off the Norwegian coast 23-28 September 1959. (via Lee Howard)*

leaving Portsmouth on 30 June and arriving at Norfolk (Virginia) on 10 July for a four-day stay. Then came participation in Exercise *Riptide* from 15th to 20th July, returning to Norfolk on 21st and sailing again next day. Boston (Massachusetts) was visited from 25th to 29th July and New York from 30 July to 3 August, after which the ship sailed home. The strength had been increased to twelve aircraft prior to this visit, which included cross-operations with USS *Saratoga*. When the ship returned to the UK, the Squadron disembarked on 9 August to Lossiemouth for some leave.

Re-embarking in *Victorious* from Yeovilton on 15 September with twelve aircraft for Exercise *Bar Frost*, this taking place from 23rd to 28th September off the coast of Norway in the Bardufoss area. Disembarking to Lossiemouth on 30 September, the Squadron re-embarked on 31 October 1959 and sailed for Gibraltar, where the ship remained from 6-11 November. Then came Exercise *Longhaul* from 19-21 November, this being a joint RN/6th US Fleet exercise, mainly involving mock attacks on USS *Saratoga*, the last day being a joint defence for the two navies against attacks by high-flying RAF Canberras. On 19 November, Lt J.B.Cross was very lucky when the arrester wire parted just after he had hooked on; his aircraft, XD266 went over the angle and into the sea, but fortunately he was able to abandon the sinking aircraft in the water and was picked up unharmed by the SAR helicopter. The ship visited Malta (27-30 November) and Marseilles (3-8 December), before calling in at Gibraltar on 10 December on her way home. The Squadron returned to Lossiemouth on 14 December, Lt Cdr A.J.Leahy MBE, DSC, RN then taking over as CO.

Much of 1960 was spent ashore at Lossiemouth, but the Squadron re-embarked eleven aircraft in *Victorious* off Ailsa Craig on 2 February for flying exercises. On 9th a Scimitar piloted by Lt Worth made the first Dart Target snatch from the deck, the target being dropped ashore before returning to the ship, and a second trial was carried out with a Mk 2 target. A visit was made to Hamburg on 14th, the ship sailing up the ice-packed River Elbe. Departing on 19th, the Scimitars flew off to Lossiemouth on 25 February, the ship then proceeding to Portsmouth for a refit. February was a bad month for the Squadron, which lost two aircraft, one pilot being killed. Another aircraft was lost on 14 May, Lt Macleod being seriously injured in a crash at Yeovilton as he attempted to do a single-engined overshoot of the airfield in XD242 on arrival from Lossiemouth. During the period ashore two aircraft were loaned to HMS *Hermes* from 27 August to 1 October,

four to HMS *Ark Royal* for the NATO Exercise *Swordthrust* in the Northern hemisphere from 19 September to 1 October, and two to HMS *Victorious* for wire pulling from 24 to 30 September, all returning to Lossiemouth by 8 October. The Squadron embarked with eight aircraft in HMS *Victorious* on 19th October, sailing in 21st for the Mediterranean, where they visited Gibraltar (24-26 October), Malta (4-25 November) and Naples (25-29 November) and took part in Exercises *Royal Flush* on 1 December and then *Pink Gin*. Another aircraft, XD329, was lost on 9 December when it ditched after being catapulted off, the pilot, Lt J.Purvis, being picked up unharmed. The ship then returned to the UK and No.803 disembarked to Lossiemouth on 18 December for Christmas, Lt Cdr T.C.S.Leece then taking over as CO.

The Squadron re-embarked in HMS *Victorious* in Lyme Bay with nine aircraft on 20 January 1961, firing practice being carried out on the Aberporth range from 22nd to 27th. The ship then sailed for a ten-month Far East deployment, arriving on 30th at Gibraltar and sailing south two days later via Gambia to Cape Town to arrive on 17 February for eleven days self-maintenance, during which a 'Shop Window' was given to VIPs. Thence a visit to Aden (11-18 March) and flying exercises in the area, reaching Singapore on 4 April. Departing on 17th, a short visit to Pulau Tioman followed on 23 April for SEATO Exercise *Pony Express*, one more Scimitar, XD273, being lost on 28th. Lt G.C.Edwards was recovered with a broken leg, but unfortunately his condition deteriorated and he died five days later in Changi Hospital. The ship arrived that day at Balambangan Island off the north-west coast of Borneo, then sailed again the following day. On 8 May the Scimitars disembarked to RAAF Butterworth whilst the ship was in dock at Singapore. Re-embarking on 19 June for an intended visit to Hong Kong, this was cancelled at the last minute as the political situation in the Persian Gulf had deteriorated, and HMS *Victorious* was ordered to make full speed for the area, the ship entering the Gulf on 8 July and appearing off Kuwait the next day. Very soon No.803's Scimitars were to be seen on the airfield at Almadi and the more forward one at Farwania. One aircraft, XD269, was lost while patrolling off Kuwait on 9th in a freak accident; Lt McIntyre had landed on and as he taxied clear of the wires he had starboard brake failure. Unable to do anything about it, he taxied over the ship's side. Fortunately he was picked up by the SAR helicopter none the worse, although very wet.

*XD268 '156/V' on the runway during the SBAC Show at Farnborough in 1960. (Air-Britain)*

*A worm's-eye view of XD236 '150/V' and '145/V' about to be launched from HMS Victorious around 1958/9, with 'goofers' on the bridge. (via Lee Howard)*

*XD242 '152/V' ready for take-off from HMS Victorious with a planeguard Dragonfly off the port bow. (via Lee Howard)*

*The launching bridle drops away from XD264 '154/V' as it leaves HMS Victorious around 1959/60. (via R.C.Sturtivant)*

While cruising off Kuwait, a great deal of trouble was caused with the Scimitars due to sand getting in the micro-switches of the undercarriage and wing fold: it was always dangerous flying around the Gulf, due to the limited visibility from driving sand. The sand haze could sometimes extend 100 miles into the Gulf and up to 20,000ft. On 31 July *Victorious* withdrew, being relieved by HMS *Centaur*, then visiting Mombasa (8-20 August). Heading back to the Gulf, Aden was visited from 29 August to 2 September before sailing east again. On 12 September, Lt Askins successfully completed the squadron's 3,000th Scimitar deck landing.

Returning to Singapore the Squadron disembarked to RAF Tengah two days later, to re-embark on 5 October for the postponed visit to Hong Kong (17-25 October). Next to Subic Bay in the Philippines (27-31 October) for cross-operations with the USS *Ticonderoga* during Exercise *Cross Tie*, this presenting some problems as the American catapults employed rigid hold-backs with a very limited number of settings, which meant the Scimitars had to be forced into the launching attitude on the catapult by means of a plank placed under the nose wheel, before the hold back could be fitted. Following a brief return to the Singapore area from 4th to 14th November, during which the squadrons remained on board, the voyage back to the UK was interrupted by a mercy mission to Mombasa to assist with flood relief. Then north to Aden (26-28 November) and, via the Suez Canal on 2 December, to the Mediterranean, participating in Exercise *Solinos* off Malta, and flying off on 9 December, when the ship was off Sardinia, via Yeovilton to its base at Lossiemouth for Christmas.

The Squadron re-embarked for the last time in HMS *Victorious* on 5 February 1962 for flying exercises, followed by a visit to Brest (15-19 February) and thence to Gibraltar from 11th to 13th March for self-maintenance. A visit was made to Vigo in Spain (17-22 March), then followed Exercise *Dawn Breeze* from 26th to 30th March on the return passage to the UK, the squadron then disembarking to Lossiemouth on 30 March. During the commission in HMS *Victorious* No.803 had carried out 2,604 sorties and made 2,038 deck landings in a total of 2,207 flying hours, with the loss of eight aircraft and sadly the lives of two pilots.

The Squadron carried out deck trials in HMS *Hermes* in April

*XD268 '156/V' parked during the SBAC Show at Farnborough in September 1960. It was a photographic aircraft previously used during Bullpup trials, and an underslung camera is visible under the belly and in front of the starboard undercarriage leg. (B.J.Lowe)*

*XD268 '156/V' taking off at Farnborough during the 1960 SBAC Show. The aircraft, attached to RAE Weapons Flight, opened the show by photographing the airfield, landing, having the film and pictures developed and then presented to Mr Roy Dobson the SBAC President, in the President's Tent before the end of the show.*

prior to embarking on 25 May with 10 aircraft, and the ship sailed for the Mediterranean six days later, calling at Gibraltar before proceeding to Malta for work-up. Arriving on 4 June, seven Scimitars went ashore to Hal Far from 12th to 27th whilst the ship undertook self-maintenance before continuing work-up. The relatively short runway at Hal Far, combined with the summer heat, made stopping a Scimitar quite difficult, especially if landed heavy with unused fuel. This would make engaging the arrester a necessity, as more than one pilot would testify. Whilst there, a great deal of Scimitar-to-Scimitar refuelling practice took place using the Mk.20 pod. In the course of this so many drogues and probes were lost into the sea that FOAC said that that Navy could not afford it and it had to stop. From then all in-flight refuelling was to be done from the Sea Vixens using the Mk.20A pod. Beirut was visited from 5th to 9th July, after which the carrier returned to the Malta area until 20th. While returning from a sortie on 14 July, Lt N.M.Tristram had a bird strike in XD213 whilst flying at 3,000 feet over south-west Crete; the bird passed through the front windscreen, hitting Lt Tristram in the face. Luckily he was only slightly injured, one deep cut on the forehead and numerous small cuts on his face and eyeballs, his cornea fortunately escaping damage. Despite the howling slipstream in the cockpit, and the fact he had only partial eyesight and never saw the ship or mirror until the last 100 yards, Lt Tristram managed to land back on board. Throughout the incident Sub Lt Bosworth in another aircraft was observing him and continued to give him help and advice. Without this help Lt Tristram would have been forced to eject. After he was talked down to a landing, he was made to taxi out of the wires as normal. When he was clear of the wires he immediately shut down his engines. "*This,* (in Lt. Tristram's own words) *caused a bit of consternation. The director, who I could not see at all was wanting me to be taxied up into Fly 1. No way was I going to allow that, not being able to see. Also there were aircraft behind to waiting to land on.*

"*Once it was seen that I was obviously in quite a lot of distress, it was decided to get me out of the cockpit there and then. This was achieved with quite a lot of difficulty owing to the damage done by the bird's impact. In fact a crowbar had to be used to open the cockpit. I was finally extracted and placed in a Neal Robertson stretcher.*

"*It had been decided by the powers that be to use this incident as a good opportunity to exercise the getting of a casualty down to the Sickbay. This they intended to do by putting me, in my stretcher, onto one of the bomb-lifts and then having the bomb-lift stop off at the Sick-Bay where I would be taken off and interned. Unfortunately there were aircraft parked over the bomb-lift, and they could not be re-spotted until the other aircraft airborne had been landed on. While all this was going on I was meant to lay docile on this Neal Roberson Stretcher. After laying there for quite some considerable time, and as I had a face full of perspex and bird entrails I said 'bugger this', got them to release me from the stretcher and walked down to the Sickbay on my own.*"

No one in FLYCO realised the true extent of the problem. It was thought he had some slight damage to the windscreen that restricted his vision. Little did they realise that he had no windscreen, and that the whole interior was bloodstained by the bird which further restricted his vision; also he had dozens of slivers of perspex embedded in his eyeball. Lt Tristram told his CO later that, after the impact, the bird's remains hit him in the face (he did not have his visor down at the time) and he could see nothing. He put his hands up to his face and could feel the bird's entrails, which he at first thought was his own brains. He was on the verge of ejecting when his wing man took over and started the long process of talking him back to the ship.

As a result of staying with his aircraft and landing it back on the ship, Lt. N.M.Tristram was awarded the Queens Commendation for Brave Conduct.

On 27th, *Hermes* put into Gibraltar and eight No.803 Squadron aircraft went

*XD239 '151/V' ready for launch from HMS Hermes in late 1960. (FAA Museum)*

*Lt J.W.H. Purvis ejecting at low level from XD329 '154/V' on 9 December 1960 after staggering into the air from HMS Victorious in a nose-up attitude from a catapult launch with 1,000 bombs and drop tanks on during Exercise Decex off Aden. (Royal Navy)*

*The tail of XD329 '154/V' is just visible in the spray as Lt J.W.H. Purvis completes a successful low-level ejection, his parachute being visible on the left of the picture. (Royal Navy)*

ashore to North Front, Lt Cdr N.J.P.Mills RN taking over as CO from 1 August. Re-embarking on 9 August, the ship left to sail west for Exercise *Riptide III* with USS *Enterprise* and USS *Forrestal*. On 13 August the Senior Pilot, Lt Cdr B Willson, had to eject from XD331, being picked up by HMS *Scarborough*'s sea boat. Another aircraft was badly damaged after it went into the catwalk after landing off-centre. Next came visits to Lisbon (16-18 August) and Palma (23-27 August), before returning to Malta with Exercise *Alfex* in co-operation with the French Navy en route, followed by self-maintenance from 6th to 18th September during which seven Scimitars went ashore to Hal Far. Then came seven days of flying exercises followed by Exercise *Falltrap* from 25th to 28th September. While flying was taking place east of Gibraltar the after lift stuck, so the aircraft landed ashore at North Front.

On 2 October the ship sailed for home, but shortly after sailing the Scimitars were flown off to return to Lossiemouth for one month. The complement was reduced from eleven to nine aircraft on 5th, on which date *Hermes* arrived at Portsmouth for self-maintenance until 12 November. No.803 re-embarked next day for another deployment to the Far East, exercising off Gibraltar before participating in Exercise *Poker Hand* with the Americans. Then heading for the eastern Mediterranean, the ship proceeded through the Suez Canal on 4 December before briefly stopping at Aden on 8-9 September. Finally on to Singapore for Christmas, arriving on 21st September.

HMS *Hermes* sailed on 6 January 1963, with the complement reduced from ten to nine aircraft, for exercises with USS *Ranger* and visits to Subic Bay (13-16 January), Hong Kong (24 January to 14 February) and Baem Bangan (18-19 February), returning to Singapore on 22nd. Sailing again on 27th for the Commonwealth Exercise *Jet 63*, which lasted from 5th to 18th March. The CO had a nasty experience on 9 March when he landed on *Hermes* and caught No 5 wire, but at the wire's maximum pull-out it parted down in the machinery room. Luckily he managed to stop the aircraft with his brakes, his aircraft suffering complete electrical failure due to the operation of inertia switches, the fire extinguishers also operating. The Squadron disembarked to Tengah on 18 March, the ship then going into dock at Singapore for six days. Re-embarked on 24 April for SEATO Exercise *Sea Serpent*, this ended on 8 May when Manila was reached. Leaving here two days later, a return visit was paid to Hong Kong for self-maintenance from 14th to 17th May, then heading for Japanese waters, the ship was off Okinawa from 30 May to 5 June, followed by Yokosuka until 10th.

On 13 June *Hermes* arrived once more at Singapore, for repairs and further docking, leaving on 16th for flying exercises in the Pulau Tioman area until 4th, followed by more flying exercises in the Butterworth area from 6th to 10th July. After this the ship started to gradually head for home, mail being picked up at Gan en route. Self-maintenance was carried out at Mombasa from 20th to 30th July, after which fourteen days was spent in the Aden area from 4 August. Passing through the Suez Canal on 22nd, the ship arrived at Portsmouth on 29th, the aircraft remaining aboard. Flying exercises were carried out from 5th to 9th September, followed until 11th by a rehearsal for Exercise *Unison*.

Returning to Portsmouth on 12th for 14 days, five squadron aircraft were put ashore to Yeovilton from 11th. On 20th, Sub Lt Middleton was forced to abandon XD213, but he ejected safely and his aircraft crashed into the hills near Weymouth, where he had the indignity of landing amongst a herd of cows, being consequently avoided for weeks by the other squadron pilots.

The ship sailed again on 26th for Exercise *Unison*, and No.803 flew aboard next day, returning to the Mediterranean for Exercise *Triple West* off Tobruk on 3-8 October and Exercise *Poker Hand* on 10-11 October. A visit was paid to Barcelona (14th-18th) on the return journey to UK before disembarking to Lossiemouth on 22 October, the ship reaching Portsmouth next day. Re-embarking on 30 November for Exercise *Lime Jug*, which commenced on 2 December, thence to Lossiemouth on 12 December for Christmas. *Hermes*, meanwhile, returned to Portsmouth on 14th. During 1964 the squadron moved between Lossiemouth, Yeovilton and spells aboard HMS *Hermes*. Lt Cdr G.A.I.Johnson engaged the barrier on 2 January after damaging his hook while attempting to land on a heaving deck. No.803 re-embarked for flying assessors on 16 January with nine Scimitars and commenced Exercise *Phoenix* six days later, this lasting until 30th, the ship returning to Portsmouth on 1 February. Two days later she sailed for a visit to Copenhagen (18-22 February), and on 23rd No.803 left the ship for the last time, to head home for Lossiemouth. Two days later it took over the remnants of the

*XD235 '149/V' about to land on HMS Victorious in 1962. (B.J.Lowe)*

*XD331 '145/V' ready for launch from HMS Victorious around 1960/1. (B.J.Lowe)*

*XD215 '150/V' just airborne at RAAF Butterworth in 1961 in fighter-like fashion, with gear just tucking up. (Richard Ward)*

*XD333 '147/H' and '149/H' on HMS Hermes with the ship's crew lining the flight deck as she sails into Grand Harbour, Valletta around 1962. (C.J. D'Amato)*

*XD215 '150/H' having run off into the catwalk aboard HMS Hermes on 24 July 1962. (B.J.Lowe)*

*XD244 '151/H', XD213 '152/H', '147/H' and another lined up at RAAF Butterworth around 1962/3. (B.J.Lowe)*

disbanding No.800 Squadron to be increased to sixteen aircraft. On 6 March, Lt N.E.Rankin was presented with the Kelly Memorial Prize, awarded annually to the best General List Aviator qualifying for the award of pilot's wings. Lt Cdr P.G.Newman took over as CO from 4 May 1964, and No.803 participated in the Fleet Air Arm Jubilee Review at Yeovilton on 28 May. During the summer there were ADA trials on board HMS *Eagle and* air displays at the RN Air Stations, then the SBAC Show at Farnborough in September, and deck landing practice on board HMS *Ark Royal* from 8th to 11th December, keeping the Squadron busy until Christmas.

When the Squadron embarked in HMS *Ark Royal* in the Moray Firth on 23 January 1965 to commence work-up, it was made up of a hotchpotch of aircraft from various previous squadrons, the intention being to make it fully versatile with four aircraft configured for nuclear strike, eight aircraft for conventional attack and four aircraft as in-flight refuellers. A good idea theoretically, but a disaster in practice, especially as the aircraft all had different modification states and were in very poor shape fatigue-wise, as events were to prove. The enlarged squadron compounded the difficult maintenance problems suffered by the aircraft, especially as *Ark Royal* was itself in poor shape and in need of a major overhaul and modernisation of its facilities.

A visit was made to Brest on 27 January, sailing again on 1 February to arrive back in the Moray Firth three days later. The carrier went into Rosyth on 13th, but returned to the Moray Firth on 25th, then back to Rosyth again on 3rd March, only to sail again next day for the NATO Exercise *Pilot Light* in northern waters before visiting Bergen from 10th to 15th the returning to Rosyth on 16th, No.803 then disembarking to Lossiemouth.

It was a fairly happy ship and squadron that sailed for the Far East on 17 June, when No.803's ground party joined at Plymouth and the aircraft re-embarked as she sailed. Lt Cdr J.Worth was 'pierhead jumped' as the CO, Lt Cdr Newman having a back problem which prevented him from embarking. Flying assessments were carried out en route to Gibraltar, which was reached on 22nd, and the Suez Canal was negotiated on 28th, the ship arriving at Aden on 2 July and proceeding on 7th to Singapore to relieve HMS *Victorious*, flying exercises being carried out en route in the Penang area from 12th to 17th. On reaching Singapore on 19th a detachment of eight aircraft went ashore to RAF Changi, where they remained until 7 August when they re-embarked for further flying exercises. The first loss took place on 30 August when Lt N.Rankin had to land into the flight deck barrier; he was unharmed, but the aircraft (XD328) was eventually written-off. Then followed Exercise *Guardrail* from 16 August to 4 September, cross-deck operations taking place with the USS *Hancock* off Subic Bay in the Philippines. The ship returned to Singapore on 4 September, but the aircraft remained aboard, being involved in flying exercises from 18th to 24th. *Ark Royal* then visited Hong Kong from 29 September to 12 October, after which she sailed again for the Phillipines, arriving at Subic Bay on 13th until 18th. On returning to Singapore the squadron went ashore to RAF Changi on 19-20 October, moving to RAAF Butterworth on 10 November to gain experience of flying over Malaysia, returning to Changi on 22 November. During this time an aircraft was lost while attempting to land at Changi, the pilot ejecting safely. The squadron re-embarked eleven aircraft from Changi on 7 December. The next visit was to Hong Kong, and after that *Ark Royal* headed south to spend Christmas in Fremantle, Australia. Another

*An impressive view of XD214 '146/H' just after catching a wire on HMS Hermes around 1962/3. (B.J.Lowe)*

Scimitar, XD318, was lost on New Years Eve, Lt Williams ejecting downwind from the ship as he suffered a double flame-out, but fortunately he was quickly picked up safely by the SAR helicopter.

The ship returned to the Singapore area in the New Year 1966 and disembarked the Squadrons to Changi for a short spell. Between 2 January and 17 February three more aircraft were lost or written off, all piloted by Sub Lt Z.K.Skrodski. The first (XD279) involved a deck accident on 2 January caused by the slippery deck and the ship heeling. The others were ejections, one on finals to land (XD316) and the other (XD265) some distance from the ship following a fire between the jet pipes. On each occasion the pilot ejected safely. Over the next few months all the aircraft had to have their collector boxes (fuel traps beneath the engines) removed and repaired as well as No.5 tanks re-built. It was these three problem areas that were to cause the disastrous fires between the jet pipes, and made the fire extinguishers totally inadequate to cope with the problem. The fires were so intense that the CO watched on two occasions the airbrake's flaps melt and fall away. He was airborne at the time and had closed up alongside to inspect them when the fire warnings occurred. He told the pilots on both occasions to eject, but neither heard due to the din of the fire warnings bells. As fast as the pilots cancelled the warning bells and hit the fire extinguisher, the bells came on again.

Mombasa was visited in late February 1966, and then it was back to Singapore, with a spell on the Beira Patrol on the way. Lt Notley, on 7 March, had to land into the barrier as he was unable to lower his hook. The aircraft, XD325, was a write-off but he was unhurt. Once at Singapore the squadron went ashore to RAF Changi for a rest, but two more Scimitars were lost: XD277 piloted by Lt P.G De Souza who ejected off the coast near Changi and the other, XD323, by Lt Monro-Davies, whose aircraft was so badly damaged after the nosewheel collapsed on landing at Changi that it had to be written-off.

*XD250 '147/H' flies overhead fully bombed-up around 1963/4. (via Philip Jarrett)*

Lt De Souza's crash in XD277 on 6 April 1966 occurred just after take-off from Changi. After his fire warning, and knowing he would have to eject, he stayed with his aircraft until it was safely heading out to sea. After ejecting he landed in very shallow water near the beach. As he waded in he met a schoolgirl and towed her in his dinghy. She was most surprised to meet this pilot who had descended from the sky as she was having a swim. Next day there were headlines in the papers: "*Beautiful blonde saves naval pilot*". No mention of his risk in taking the aircraft to a safe area before ejecting.

*Ark Royal* returned to the Beira Patrol to relieve HMS *Eagle* (*Eagle* having been at sea for 72 days by the time she returned to Singapore), and was herself relieved by HMS *Victorious* on 25 May 1966. On her way home *Ark Royal* called into Aden, the last time a Royal Navy carrier would call there. The Suez Canal was passed through on 4 June and No.803 Squadron was back at Lossiemouth eight days later, having flown off whilst the ship was passing through the Mediterranean. During the commission the squadron lost nine aircraft, but none of its pilots.

The Squadron re-embarked on 2 August with 10 aircraft to participate in Exercise *Straight Laced* off the Norwegian Coast, interspersed with a short visit to Oslo and finally a visit to Portsmouth for Navy Days. This was followed by a visit by the Queen Mother on 20 September, the Squadron disembarking and disbanding on 1 October, marking the end of the Scimitar as a front line aircraft after just over eight years service with the fleet.

*XD275 '148/H' in the barrier after its hook struck the rounddown whilst landing on HMS Hermes on 22 January 1964. (B.J.Lowe)*

On 1 October 1966 the following signal was received by Lt Cdr J.Worth:
"From FOAC (FLAG) to the Commanding Officer No.803 Squadron.
 1. In saying goodbye to a fine and spirited squadron I am conscious that this is a sad occasion. The SCIMITAR is leaving the Fleet and the squadron disbanding.
 2. No.803 is to be congratulated on the manner in which it has met and tackled some particularly testing situations. I have been particularly impressed to see in these last months how well you have managed to get these old aircraft working probably better than ever before.
 3. Good luck to you all. I shall personally miss the black and yellow chequers very much."

*[Our grateful thanks to Captain J.Worth RN, Lt Cdr T.C.S.Leece RN (Rtd) and Lt Cdr J.W.H.Purvis RN (Rtd) for their help and contributions to this brief history]*

*XD271 '155' parked at Lossiemouth in 1964. (R.C.B.Ashworth)*

*XD330 '159/R' is the nearest aircraft in the line-up at Lossiemouth in 1964. (FAA Museum)*

*XD323 '157/R' catches a wire as it lands on HMS Ark Royal in 1965. (B.J.Lowe)*

*The pilot climbs into XD235 '149/V' aboard HMS Victorious around 1965. (B.J.Lowe)*

**Identification Markings**
Initially yellow/gold codes thinly edged in black in range *143-159* on the nose, and a large white letter 'V' on the fin; some aircraft also with a small squadron badge pierced by a black and yellow checked arrowhead on the forward engine nacelle. Later white codes on engine cowlings above the wings with large sloping 'V' or 'H' on fin. From 4.62, no nacelle badge, black and yellow checks on fin with small white letter 'H' on bottom black check, the latter being replaced by a white letter 'R' in 5.64. From 7.65, white fuselage codes changed to *015-017, 020-027 and 030-034*, retaining white letter 'R'.

**Squadron bases**

| | | |
|---|---|---|
| Lossiemouth | | 3 Jun 1958 |
| HMS Victorious | | 25 Sep 1958 |
| Hal Far (Dt2) | | 18-22 Oct 1958 |
| Hyères (Dt4) | | 24 Oct 1958 |
| | to | 3 Nov 1958 |
| Hal Far | | 8 Nov 1958 |
| HMS Victorious | | 10 Dec 1958 |
| Lossiemouth | | 13 Jan 1959 |
| HMS Victorious | | 21 Feb 1959 |
| Lossiemouth | | 23 Mar 1959 |
| Yeovilton | | 1 May 1959 |
| HMS Victorious | | 4 May 1959 |
| Lossiemouth | | 9 Aug 1959 |
| Yeovilton | | 14 Sep 1959 |
| HMS Victorious | | 15 Sep 1959 |
| Lossiemouth | | 30 Sep 1959 |
| HMS Victorious | | 31 Oct 1959 |
| Lossiemouth | | 14 Dec 1959 |
| HMS Victorious | | 2 Feb 1960 |
| Lossiemouth | | 28 Feb 1960 |

**Squadron bases** continued

| | | |
|---|---|---|
| HMS Hermes (Dt2) | | 27 Aug 1960 |
| | to | 1 Oct 1960 |
| HMS Victorious | | 19 Oct 1960 |
| Hal Far | | 5 Nov 1960 |
| HMS Victorious | | 15 Nov 1960 |
| Lossiemouth | | 19 Dec 1960 |
| HMS Victorious | | 20 Jan 1961 |
| Tengah | | 28 Mar 1961 |
| HMS Victorious | | 12 Apr 1961 |
| Butterworth | | 8 May 1961 |
| HMS Victorious | | 16 Jun 1961 |
| Tengah | | 14 Sep 1961 |
| HMS Victorious | | 5 Oct 1961 |
| Yeovilton | | 8 Dec 1961 |
| Lossiemouth | | 9 Dec 1961 |
| HMS Victorious | | 5 Feb 1962 |
| Lossiemouth | | 30 Mar 1962 |
| HMS Hermes | | 25 May 1962 |
| Hal Far (Dt7) | | 12-27 Jun 1962 |
| North Front (Dt8) | | 27 Jul 1962 |
| | to | 9 Aug 1962 |
| Hal Far (Dt7) | | 5-18 Sep 1962 |
| Yeovilton (transit) | | 2 Oct 1962 |
| Lossiemouth | | 2 Oct 1962 |
| HMS Hermes | | 13 Nov 1962 |
| Tengah (Dt6) | | 20 Dec 1962 |
| | to | 7 Jan 1963 |
| Tengah (Dt7) | | 18 Mar 1963 |
| | to | 24 Apr 1963 |
| Yeovilton (Dt5) | | 11-27 Sep 1963 |
| Lossiemouth | | 22 Oct 1963 |
| HMS Hermes | | 30 Nov 1963 |

| Squadron bases continued | |
|---|---|
| Lossiemouth | 12 Dec 1963 |
| HMS Hermes | 16 Jan 1964 |
| Lossiemouth | 23 Feb 1964 |
| Yeovilton | 24 Jun 1964 |
| Lossiemouth | 3 Jul 1964 |
| Yeovilton | 30 Aug 1964 |
| Lossiemouth | 21 Sep 1964 |
| Yeovilton(Dt2-DLP) | 6-7 Nov 1964 |
| HMS Ark Royal | 8 Dec 1964 |
| Lossiemouth | 11 Dec 1964 |
| HMS Ark Royal | 23 Jan 1965 |
| Lossiemouth | 16 Mar 1965 |
| HMS Ark Royal | 17 Jun 1965 |
| Changi (Dt8) | 19 Jul 1965 |
| to | 7 Aug 1965 |
| Changi | 20 Oct 1965 |
| Butterworth | 10 Nov 1965 |
| Changi | 22 Nov 1965 |
| HMS Ark Royal | 7 Dec 1965 |
| Changi | 6 Jan 1966 |
| HMS Ark Royal | 27 Jan 1966 |
| Changi | 15 Mar 1966 |
| HMS Ark Royal | 24 Mar 1966 |
| Lossiemouth | 12 Jun 1966 |
| HMS Ark Royal | 2 Aug 1966 |
| Lossiemouth | 1 Oct 1966 |
| - Sqdn disbanded | |

*Sub-Lt Z.K.Skrodski in XD279 '034/E' had landed on HMS Ark Royal in the Far East on New Year's Day 1966 and was taxying out of the wires when the ship heaved. His aircraft slid along slippery deck and the nose wheel ran off into catwalk by the starboard Howdah. (via R.C.Sturtivant)*

*XD278 '145/R' just after taking off from HMS Ark Royal around 1964/5. (E.B.Morgan archives)*

| Squadron Officers | |
|---|---|
| Cdr JD Russell (CO) | 03.06.58 - 23.09.58 |
| Lt Cdr DG Titford (AE) | 03.06.58 - 22.12.58 |
| Lt Cdr GR Higgs (Senior Pilot) (became CO 25.9.58) | 03.06.58 - 14.12.59 |
| Lt Cdr(L) AF Mortimer | 03.06.58 - 14.12.59 |
| Lt ER Anson (Senior Pilot from 25.9.58) | 03.06.58 - 09.08.59 |
| Lt CS Casperd | 03.06.58 - 11.58 |
| Lt JG Beyfus | 03.06.58 - 30.04.59 |
| Lt JW Beard | 03.06.58 - 14.12.59 |
| Lt C Orpe (A/E) | 03.06.58 - 09.08.59 |
| Lt CC Giles | 03.06.58 - 01.10.59 |
| Lt LE Middleton | 03.06.58 - 09.08.59 |
| Lt MV Maina | 03.06.58 - 01.10.59 |
| S/L(S) GT Anderson | 03.06.58 - 01.09.58 |
| S/L(L) CS Drake | 04.09.58 - 30.03.60 |
| Lt Cdr A Greenhalgh (A/E) | 22.12.58 - 28.03.60 |
| Lt B Davies | 13.02.59 - 10.01.60 |
| Lt MD Bristowe | 13.02.59 - 21.03.60 |
| S/L RWD Westlake | 13.02.59 - 07.02.60 |
| Lt JRJ Rutherford | 20.04.59 - 21.03.60 |
| Lt AMD de Labilliere | 04.06.59 - 20.12.60 |
| Lt Cdr PS Davis DSC (Senior Pilot) | 24.08.59 - 09.11.60 |
| Lt DGM Wilkie (A/E) | 24.08.59 - 25.08.60 |

| Squadron officers continued | |
|---|---|
| Lt J Worth | 24.08.59 - 14.10.60 |
| Lt JOF Billingham | 28.08.59 - 13.03.61 |
| S/L JB Cross | 02.10.59 - 20.12.60 |
| Lt AG Claridge | 26.10.59 - 15.07.60 |
| Lt Cdr TFB Young | 09.11.59 - 28.07.60 |
| Lt Cdr(L) LP Watkinson | 14.12.59 - 15.05.61 |
| Lt Cdr AJ Leahy MBE DSC (CO) | 14.12.59 - 18.12.60 |
| Lt JWH Purvis | 04.01.60 - 16.06.61 |
| S/L AHS Anderson | 12.01.60 - 25.07.61 |
| S/L(L) FG Allford | 23.03.60 - 25.07.61 |
| Lt Cdr CW Preston | 28.03.60 - 19.12.61 |
| Lt IB Macleod | 02.06.60 - 17.05.60 |
| Lt AS Tuck | 12.07.60 - 19.12.61 |
| Lt MJM Brophy | 12.07.60 - 19.12.61 |
| S/L RA Routledge (A/E) | 22.08.60 - 07.04.62 |
| Lt E Cope | 04.10.60 - 20.01.62 |
| Lt Cdr CS Casperd (Senior Pilot) | 10.11.60 - 09.04.62 |
| S/L JG Wood | 28.12.60 - 31.07.62 |
| Lt Cdr TCS Leece (CO) | 18.12.60 - 01.08.62 |
| Lt PAA Waring | 20.01.61 - 10.04.62 |
| S/L CJ Wilson | 20.01.61 - 31.07.62 |
| Lt GC Edwardes | 24.03.61 - 10.05.61 |
| Lt DS McIntyre | 15.04.61 - 16.09.61 |
| Lt SE Askins | 15.04.61 - 25.05.62 |
| Lt(E)(L) APD Ouvry | 13.05.61 - 24.03.63 |
| Lt NM Tristram | 26.06.61 - 05.10.62 |
| S/L CA Bosworth | 05.10.61 - 30.08.63 |
| Lt EO Tonkin (A/E) (to Lt Cdr 1.10.62) | 21.12.61 - 20.06.63 |
| Lt SC Creasy | 20.01.62 - 16.09.63 |
| Lt AJ Middleton | 05.02.62 - 22.10.63 |
| Lt B Willson | 02.04.62 - 16.12.63 |
| Lt MJM Railton (EngM)(A/E) | 03.04.62 - 14.01.64 |
| Lt PP Cardew | 06.04.62 - 12.09.63 |
| Lt RV Ponter | 21.05.62 - 22.12.64 |
| S/L JS Flexman | 21.05.62 - 04.08.64 |
| S/L CARP Wells | 22.07.62 - 08.08.62 |
| S/L MJ Harwood | 24.07.62 - 26.07.63 |
| Lt Cdr NJP Mills (CO) | 01.08.62 - 07.05.64 |
| Lt AMD de Labilliere | 08.08.62 - 05.10.62 |
| Lt AHS Anderson | 08.10.62 - 22.02.64 |
| Lt(E)(L) C Cooper (A/E) | 17.03.63 - 26.02.64 |
| Lt Cdr(E)(M) A Reynolds (A/E) | 13.06.63 - 29.01.65 |
| Lt AMD de Labilliere | 16.09.63 - 03.02.65 |
| Lt R Wren (QFI) | 04.11.63 - 25.10.65 |
| S/L JM Heath | 11.11.63 - 25.10.65 |
| Lt Cdr GAI Johnston (Senior Pilot) | 16.12.63 - 23.05.65 |
| Lt RC Dimmock | 06.01.64 - 09.09.64 |
| Lt GHJ Daykin (EngM)(A/E) | 06.01.64 - 16.06.65 |
| Lt CA Wheal | 02.02.64 - 09.09.64 |
| S/L PJ McManus | 02.02.64 - 06.11.65 |
| Flt Lt RN Davidson RAF | 02.03.64 - 15.04.65 |

*XD328 '015/R' being lifted clear of the deck by "Jumbo", the flight deck mobile crane, after Hydraulic 1 failure prior to landing on 30 August 1965. The port wheel remained retracted after use of the emergency system, and Lt N.E. Rankin, who was unhurt, made an emergency landing, catching No.1 wire and engaging HMS Ark Royal's barrier.*

| Squadron officers continued | |
|---|---|
| Lt JOF Billingham | 01.04.64 - 15.04.65 |
| Lt IPF Meiklejohn | 01.04.64 - 09.09.64 |
| S/L JC Frenz | 01.04.64 - 12.11.64 |
| S/L A McMeekan | 01.04.64 - 08.10.64 |
| Lt CJ Crowther | 01.04.64 - 05.09.64 |
| Lt Cdr PG Newman (CO) | 04.05.64 - 14.06.65 |
| S/L KB Owen | 08.07.64 - 20.02.65 |
| Lt J Comby FN | 13.07.64 - 16.06.65 |
| Lt NE Rankin | 03.11.64 - 12.06.66 |
| Lt ARD Monro-Davies | 22.11.64 - 12.06.66 |
| Lt Cdr(E)(M) A Wormell (A/E) | 14.12.64 - 07.10.66 |
| Lt BP Marindin | 11.01.65 - 25.03.66 |
| Flt Lt TG Gilroy RAF | 24.02.65 - 27.11.65 |
| Lt EK Somerville-Jones | 24.02.65 - 07.10.66 |
| Lt HW Thomas | 24.02.65 - 25.04.66 |
| Lt Cdr NG Grier-Rees | 03.05.65 - 10.09.65 |
| S/L GM Faulkner | 03.05.65 - 07.10.66 |
| S/L DW Moore (to Lt 23.8.66) | 03.05.65 - 07.10.66 |
| Lt Cdr JWH Purvis (Senior Pilot) | 22.05.65 - 07.10.66 |
| Lt Cdr CJ Worth (CO) | 14.06.65 - 07.10.66 |
| S/L DJL Arnold | 16.06.65 - 07.10.66 |
| Lt PAA Waring | 17.06.65 - 10.10.65 |
| Lt TJ Notley (AWI) | 11.09.65 - 07.10.66 |
| (to Lt Cdr 16.9.66) | |
| Lt RF Shercliff | 12.09.65 - 07.10.66 |
| Lt MJ Williams | 12.09.65 - 07.10.66 |
| Lt PG De Souza (QFI) | 18.10.65 - 07.10.66 |
| Lt ZK Skrodzki | 18.11.65 - 07.04.66 |
| S/L AR Dady | 18.11.65 - 07.10.66 |
| Lt(L) JR Chicken | 25.11.65 - 07.10.66 |
| Lt(L) DG Withers | 23.01.66 - 07.10.66 |

| Squadron aircraft | | |
|---|---|---|
| 143 | XD279 | 08.64 - 65 |
| 144 | XD248 | 23.02.63 - 06.08.64 |
| | XD328 | 06.08.64 - 07.65 |
| 145 | XD230 | 27.05.58 - 09.09.58 |
| | XD240 | 25.07.58 - 25.09.58 |
| | XD238 | 23.10.58 - 06.02.60 |
| | XD331 | 18.10.60 - 13.08.62 |
| | XD278 | 03.02.64 - 07.65 |
| 146 | XD232 | 06.06.58 - 12.04.60 |
| | XD275 | 12.07.60 - 30.03.62 |
| | XD214 | 17.04.62 - 12.01.65 |
| | XD276 | 25.10.64 - 07.65 |
| 147 | XD234 | 30.05.58 - 09.10.59 |
| | XD243 | 21.09.59 - 26.02.60 |
| | XD269 | 08.04.60 - 25.07.60 |
| | XD333 | 18.01.61 - 19.12.63 |
| | XD250 | 31.10.63 - 08.64 |
| | XD225 | 08.64 - 01.65 |
| | XD332 | 15.01.65 - 07.65 |
| 148 | XD235 | 07.06.58 - 26.08.60 |
| | XD330 | 19.10.60 - 08.02.61 |
| | XD327 | 16.03.61 - 20.09.63 |
| | XD275 | 20.09.63 - 03.02.64 |
| | XD320 | 26.02.63 - 15.10.64 |
| | XD280 | 04.11.64 - 07.65 |
| 149 | XD237 | 12.07.58 - 14.01.59 |
| | XD270 | 11.02.59 - 12.12.59 |
| | XD271 | 09.05.60 - 18.12.61 |
| | XD235 | 19.01.62 - 25.02.65 |
| | XD272 | 14.12.64 - 07.65 |
| 150 | XD236 | 31.05.58 - 26.03.59 |

*XD324 '033/R' refuelling XD278 '016/R' in flight around 1965/6.*

*XD274 '024/E' of No.803 Squadron parked at Yeovilton in 1966 still retains its No.800B Flight tail fin markings. (B.J.Lowe)*

*A crowd of "goofers" on HMS Ark Royal's bridge watch Lt T.J.Notley in XD325 '024/R' engage the barrier whilst on Beira patrol off East Africa on 7 March 1966, when the nose wheel would not lower.*

| Squadron aircraft continued | | |
|---|---|---|
| 150 | XD271 | 27.04.59 - 22.01.60 |
| | XD244 | 16.01.60 - 25.08.60 |
| | XD250 | 08.10.60 - 11.01.61 |
| | XD215 | 01.02.61 - 02.10.62 |
| | XD241 | 07.08.62 - 12.05.65 |
| | XD333 | 11.05.65 -    07.65 |
| 151 | XD239 | 23.07.58 - 25.08.60 |
| | XD248 | 24.08.60 - 26.01.61 |
| | XD214 | 16.12.60 - 26.01.61 |
| | XD269 | 24.04.61 - 09.07.61 |
| | XD244 | 01.10.61 - 30.10.63 |
| | XD267 | 04.11.63 - 09.02.65 |
| | XD325 | 08.02.65 -    07.65 |
| 152 | XD231 | 20.05.58 - 09.09.58 |
| | XD242 | 07.08.58 - 12.07.60 |
| | XD273 | 15.08.60 - 27.04.61 |
| | XD213 | 30.06.61 - 20.09.63 |
| | XD246 | 26.09.63 -    04.65 |
| | XD318 | 03.05.65 -    07.65 |
| 153 | XD246 | 05.02.59 - 04.04.60 |
| | XD328 | 26.07.60 - 08.11.62 |
| | XD234 | 27.04.62 - 11.05.65 |
| | XD244 | 07.05.65 -    07.65 |
| 154 | XD264 | 06.02.59 - 12.04.60 |
| | XD329 | 25.07.60 - 09.12.60 |
| | XD318 | 01.02.61 - 23.10.63 |
| | XD225 | 31.10.63 -    08.64 |
| | XD250 | 08.64 -    07.65 |
| 155 | XD266 | 12.04.59 - 19.11.59 |
| | XD267 | 01.09.60 - 06.10.60 |
| | XD271 | 26.02.64 -    07.65 |
| 156 | XD269 | 29.06.59 - 18.12.59 |
| | XD268 | 21.06.60 - 27.10.60 |
| | XD223 | 26.02.64 -    07.65 |
| 157 | XD269 | 24.04.61 - 09.07.61 |
| | XD230 | 27.02.64 - 28.09.64 |
| | XD323 | 14.12.64 -    07.65 |

| Squadron aircraft continued | | |
|---|---|---|
| 158 | XD236 | 01.04.63 - 05.03.65 |
| | XD324 | 19.01.65 -    07.65 |
| 159 | XD330 | 26.02.64 - 03.07.64 |
| | XD279 | @ 05.65 -    07.65 |
| - | XD223 | 29.05.58 - 12.09.58 ["803"] |
| ? | XD224 | 03.06.58 - 17.07.58 |
| ? | XD225 | 03.06.58 - 13.07.58 |
| [153, 155 or 156?]? | XD245 | 15.01.60 - 07.02.60 |
| ? | XD250 | 27.01.60 - 24.03.60 |
| ? | XD269 | 10.04.59 - 30.04.59 |
| ? | XD330 | 10.12.62 - 21.02.63 |
| From 7.65 | | |
| 015 | XD328 | 07.65 - 16.09.65 |
| | XD316 | 18.08.65 - 28.01.66 |
| | XD320 | 12.04.66 - 01.10.66 |
| 016 | XD278 | 07.65 - 01.10.66 |
| 017 | XD276 | 07.65 - 01.10.66 |
| 020 | XD322 | 07.65 - 01.10.66 |
| 021 | XD280 | 07.65 - 24.06.66 |
| 022 | XD272 | 07.65 - 01.10.66 |
| 023 | XD333 | 07.65 - 01.10.66 |
| 024 | XD325 | 07.65 - 07.03.66 |
| | XD274 | 06.05.66 - 02.08.66 |
| 025 | XD318 | 07.65 - 31.12.65 |
| | XD221 | 19.01.66 - 21.04.66 |
| | XD243 | 06.05.66 - 24.08.66 |
| 026 | XD244 | 07.65 - 03.10.66 |
| 027 | XD250 | 07.65 - 17.02.66 |
| 030 | XD271 | 07.65 - 27.04.66 |
| 031 | XD223 | 07.65 - 20.09.65 |
| | XD327 | 27.09.65 - 01.10.66 |
| 032 | XD323 | 07.65 - 18.04.66 |
| 033 | XD324 | 07.65 - 01.10.66 |
| 034 | XD279 | 07.65 - 27.01.66 |
| | XD330 | 20.01.66 - 01.10.66 |
| "115/" | XD277 | 31.03.66 - 06.04.66 |

*XD272 '166/H' with the Fleetlands Flight Test section at RNAS Lee-on-Solent on 12 May 1960, shortly before being despatched to rejoin No.804 Squadron. (A.W.M.Groth)*

## No.804 SQUADRON

No.804 Squadron was re-formed at RNAS Lossiemouth on 1 March 1960 under the command of Lt Cdr T.V.G.Binney, equipped with six Scimitar F.1s.

On the day of the commissioning ceremony, which was performed by Admiral Sir Martin Dunbar Nasmith, none of the squadron pilots had actually flown a Scimitar, so Lt Cdr Binney took up the only serviceable aircraft. The pilots on commissioning were: the CO; Lt Cdr B.G.Young, the Senior Pilot; Lts D.F.Mills, J.L.Williams, D.P.Mears and M.T.Hynett; Sub Lt J.G.L.Smith and Flt Lt M.J. Webb RAF. Lt J.P.E.Faulkener and Sub Lt A.J.Stone were to join later.

Directly after the commissioning the Squadron embarked on a very intensive work-up period at Lossiemouth, including a brief spell of deck landing practice in HMS *Hermes* in May. On 1 June the CO had a Hydraulic 1 failure, and a total loss of brake pressure; he landed hook down and engaged the airfield arrester gear. On the same day Lt Mills had a 1,000lb bomb hang up which would not release even after using the jettison button. He eventually landed with the bomb still hung up. It was found that there was a fault in the jettison gear.

By 6 July the work-up was complete and everyone was ready to embark in HMS *Hermes*, which they did without incident and then sailed for the Mediterranean, reaching the Malta area on 11 July. Lt Williams had to divert to Hal Far after experiencing a Hydraulic 1 failure on 18 July. A visit was made to Messina from 22nd to 25th July, returning to Malta on 29th, and on 18th August some American officers came on board and witnessed four Scimitars being scrambled. The aircraft were all launched within four minutes, carried out their interceptions and returned to the ship, all landing on again within four minutes, including one overshoot. The Americans were very impressed. The following day Sub Lt Smith performed a stunt for a film company; he made a late overshoot, hook down, over a raised barrier, and was afterwards heard to remark "It's just routine". At one time while in the Mediterranean one of the Squadron pilots, Lt A.J.Goodenough, on loan from Lossiemouth, came as near to disaster as one could possibly get. He made such a low pass over the splash target being towed astern of *Hermes*, that he scraped the hydraulic drain pipe on the underside of the fuselage (known as the donkey's plonk) on the sea at about 400kt.

Algiers was visited on 18 August, then four days later the ship sailed for home, arriving at Rosyth on 5 September for self-maintenance. On 1 September three aircraft had to divert to Lossiemouth. One was Sub Lt Smith, who had to do a single-engined landing due to the fact that his throttle jammed open. He flamed out the starboard engine by using the LP cock. On returning to the ship the next day he had the same problem. This time, however, he landed on board at the third attempt.

Sailing again on 15th, the carrier steamed back under the Forth Bridge to take part in the NATO Exercise *Swordthrust* in northern waters. This commenced on 21st off Norway and included mock nuclear strikes as well as Combat Air Patrols. The second part of the exercise commenced on 26th under the name *Cooltime* in which strikes consisted of flying to *Ark Royal* to refuel all four drop tanks to take advantage of her stronger catapult, so giving a maximum sortie range against troops on shore. This exercise ended on 29th.

Returning home, No.804 Sqn was then shore-based at

*XD272 '166/H' after rejoining No.804 Squadron. (via Philip Spencer)*

*XD274 '164/H' on board HMS Hermes during the Navy Day at Portsmouth Dockyard in 1961. (via Philip Jarrett)*

Lossiemouth until 28 November, when they then flew out to RAF North Front at Gibraltar to rejoin HMS *Hermes*, which they did the next day, ground personnel being flown out from Heathrow Airport. Exercise *Royal Flush* then followed off Malta, after which the ship sailed for the Suez Canal, which was navigated on 6 December. Arriving at Aden on 8 December she relieved HMS *Albion*, then sailed to spend Christmas at Colombo (Ceylon), which was reached on 23rd. Departing on 26th, Singapore was reached on New Year's Eve, the squadron going ashore to RAF Tengah whilst *Hermes* went into the Naval dockyard for self-maintenance. Re-embarking on 12 January 1961, the ship sailed for exercises off the Philippines, arriving at Subic Bay six days later, leaving after two days to arrive at Hong Kong on 23rd. While in the Hong Kong area, two of the Squadron pilots made themselves unpopular with the residents of Hong Kong and Kowloon when they made a sonic dive in that direction. Shop windows were broken and many Chinese were frightened by the resulting bangs. The two pilots concerned were Lt Hynett and Sub Lt Smith (the latter eventually becoming an airline captain in Hong Kong with Cathay Pacific).

Sailing on 1 February, the ship arrived back at Singapore six days later for further self-maintenance, leaving for a leisurely return home on 18th. A short stop was made at Trincomalee from 24th before departing on 27th, the ship participating in Exercise *Jet 61* until 9 March, eventually arriving at Aden on 17th. Passing through the Suez Canal on 24th, Malta was reached on 27th. Bombing practice was then carried out over the Filfla LABS range, the CO successfully dropping a 'SHAPE'. The Senior Pilot was less fortunate, his 'SHAPE' remaining hung up after two attempts to drop. Departing on 4 April, a visit was paid to Naples from 8th, after which the ship sailed on 12th for Gibraltar, eventually arriving at Portsmouth on 18 April, the Scimitars being then flown off to Lossiemouth.

The Squadron flew from their Scottish base on 29 May to rejoin HMS *Hermes* at Spithead for flying exercises in the English Channel. 4 June saw Lt Mears complete the Squadron's 1000th deck landing, after which the ship took part in Exercise *Shopwindow* off Portsmouth from 7th to 9th June. A visit was paid to Falmouth on 10th, then next day *Hermes* sailed north for Lossiemouth harbour, arriving on 17th. Two days later they were at sea again for *Fairwind IV*, an air defence exercise in the North Sea area, arriving back at Portsmouth on 22nd. It was then intended to visit America, sailing on 30th for Norfolk, Virginia, but events intervened. General Kassim, the Iraqi president, was making threats to Kuwait, warranting the immediate deployment of ships and troops to the Persian Gulf. *Hermes* was ordered to Gibraltar, which she reached on 4 July, and took the opportunity to re-store. The atmosphere in the Middle East gradually cooled down, and the ship sailed for Portsmouth on 21st, arriving three days later, but kept her Air Group on board. In the meantime, on 1 July 1961, the CO had been selected for promotion to Commander.

Exercise *Bismark* took place at the end of July. Waves of Vulcan bombers closed on the ship at midday on 27 July. No.804 Squadron Scimitars, being kept at Condition One, were scrambled seven times, during which four kills were claimed on the Vulcans, the rest being missed because of their height. On 9 August *Hermes* sailed for Oslo, arriving on 15th for a four-day visit before reaching Portsmouth once more on 25th, the CO being then launched off to reconnoitre the Farnborough area. While he was away the weather deteriorated considerably to a cloud base of about 200ft. On returning to the ship he made two attempts to land on, but finally diverted to Thorney Island, where he landed on a closed airfield in visibility of less than half a cable, his engines cutting as he braked to a halt due to lack of fuel.

On 10 September 1961, 804 Squadron disembarked from HMS *Hermes* for the last time, for a non-stop flight to Lossiemouth which included a pass over the SBAC Show at Farnborough. The wind had dropped 6kts before the launch, so the aircraft had to burn off 1,760lb of fuel. The subsequent delay caused some anxious moments but they managed to arrive over Farnborough with about 15 seconds to spare. Unfortunately, on arrival at Lossiemouth, all the Squadron baggage was searched by Customs officers very thoroughly, as a large sum of money had gone missing on *Hermes*. It must be added that it was not found. This was not quite the reception they had anticipated.

Five days later, on 15 September, the Squadron was disbanded after just over 18 months of flying the Scimitar. In this time, up until 7 July, they had achieved 1,077 sorties flown, totalling 1,367 hours, 1,075 catapult launches, 1,150 deck landings, 1,090 3in RPs and 7,020 rounds of 30mm ammunition fired. The Squadron was also able to return to Lossiemouth with all its aircraft and pilots, not one being lost during the commission, a fact the CO was justly proud of.

*Postscript. There was one incident that marred the almost perfect record. Sub Lt J.G.L.Smith was recovered on 25 August 1960 onto Hermes with a red light indicated on the nose wheel, which collapsed on landing. Sub Lt Smith was unharmed. Another episode worthy of mention, which almost grounded the complete squadron was when FOAC Admiral Sir Richard Smeeton (an ex-CO of 804) personally engaged the entire air group aircrew in the after-dinner Wardroom games. He practically decimated the lot, being very big and strong. Next day there was hardly a pilot fit to fly.*

**Identification Markings**
Black nose codes *161-166*, outlined in white with the last digit repeated on the nose wheel door. White fin panel bearing the central motif of the squadron badge, consisting of a yellow and black tiger's face holding in its mouth a dagger, and above it a small black letter 'H'.

| Squadron bases | |
|---|---|
| Lossiemouth | 1 Mar 1960 |
| HMS Hermes | 6 Jul 1960 |
| Lossiemouth | 1 Oct 1960 |
| North Front | 28 Nov 1960 |
| HMS Hermes | 29 Nov 1960 |
| Tengah | 29 Dec 1960 |
| HMS Hermes | 12 Jan 1961 |
| Lossiemouth | 18 Apr 1961 |
| HMS Hermes | 29 May 1961 |
| Lossiemouth | 10 Sep 1961 |
| Squadron disbanded | 15 Sep 1961 |

| Squadron officers | |
|---|---|
| Lt Cdr TVG Binney (CO) | 01.03.60 - 15.09.61 |
| Lt Cdr BG Young (SP) | 01.03.60 - 15.09.61 |
| Lt Cdr(E) R Baker (A/E) | 01.03.60 - 15.09.61 |
| Lt Cdr(L) CJ Jackson | 01.03.60 - 15.09.61 |
| Lt JL Williams (A/E) | 01.03.60 - 30.09.60 |
| Lt DP Mears | 01.03.60 - 15.09.61 |
| Flt Lt MJ Webb RAF | 01.03.60 - 15.09.61 |
| Lt MT Hynett | 01.03.60 - 15.09.61 |
| S/L AJ Gerry | 01.03.60 - 24.08.61 |
| S/L JGL Smith | 01.03.60 - 15.09.61 |
| S/L(E) L Carter | 07.03.60 - 15.09.61 |
| Lt DF Mills | 05.04.60 - 26.08.60 |
| Lt JPE Faulkner | 19.10.60 - 15.09.61 |
| S/L AJ Stone | 24.10.60 - 15.09.61 |

| Squadron aircraft | | |
|---|---|---|
| 161 | XD324 | 01.03.60 - 13.09.61 |
| 162 | XD323 | 01.03.60 - 13.09.61 |
| 163 | XD326 | 09.05.60 - 13.09.61 |
| 164 | XD267 | 01.03.60 - 05.05.60 |
|  | XD274 | 07.05.60 - 15.09.61 |
| 165 | XD268 | 01.03.60 - 14.05.60 |
|  | XD325 | 18.05.60 - 15.09.61 |
| 166 | XD272 | 18.03.60 - 15.09.61 |
| ? | XD327 | 05.12.60 - 16.03.61 |
| ? | XD332 | 21.11.60 - 06.12.60 |

*XD267 '193/R', XD243 '190/R', XD248 '195/R' and XD250 '197/R' in box formation in June 1959. (via M.J.Hooks)*

## No.807 SQUADRON

No.807 Squadron re-formed under the command of Lt Cdr K.A.Leppard RN at RNAS Lossiemouth in Scotland on 1 October 1958, the Flag Officer Flying Training, Rear-Admiral D.R.F.Cambell, DSC, arriving from Yeovilton to present him with the Commissioning Warrant. Fairey Fulmar G-AIBE was flown into Lossiemouth for the occasion, kindly loaned by the Fairey Company to represent the type of aircraft which equipped the Squadron when it was originally formed in September 1940. The first two Scimtars, XD243 and XD244, had been delivered two days earlier, to be followed in due course by XD245 to XD250. On that date one flight was made by the Senior Pilot, Lt Cdr T.C.S.Leece, this being an acceptance and re-familiarisation flight. A third aircraft (XD245) arrived on the 4th.

Two weeks after the commissioning, from 16th to 18th October, still only equipped with four aircraft, No.807 Sqn, in company with aircraft of Fighter Command RAF, became part of the defending side during *Sunbeam*, an annual major Defence of Great Britain exercise. It was thought unique that a squadron should act in this type of exercise only fifteen days after forming. Tragically, the first aircraft and pilot were lost on 19 November when Lt C.R.Cresswell died from his injuries after inadvertently being ejected from his aircraft following an explosion in mid-air. A Board of Enquiry was held on 24th, moving to Dingwall the following day to interview civilian witnesses. All Scimitars, Hunter T.8s and Sea Vixens were grounded pending an inquiry on the ejection seats. On 26 November the Sea Vixens and Hunter T.8s were allowed to fly again, followed on 3 December by the Scimitars. However, the Scimitars were again grounded on 12th following an accident to an aircraft of another squadron while landing on *Victorious*. Due to this, from 15th to 19th, the squadron aircrew took the opportunity to visit the Vickers airfield at Wisley and then went to Whale Island, Portsmouth, for a lecture on the LABS technique. Fortunately in the meantime, on 16th, the CO, on a visit to the Admiralty, was informed that the grounding order had been lifted.

Flying training continued, and on 19 January 1959 a record number of Scimitar sorties was achieved: 20 in one day with a flying time of 12 hours and 10 minutes. From 27th to 29th January the squadron ground party was detached to West Freugh. The Squadron remained at Lossiemouth for most of 1959, but the CO and part of the squadron were detached to Yeovilton for flying from 9th to 12th June, and from 7th to 9th July two aircraft went to West Freugh for Profile trials. The squadron flew down to Culdrose on 25 June to participate in a flying display, returning to Lossiemouth the next day. Then from 2nd to 15th September they moved temporarily to Farnborough to display at the annual SBAC

*XD249 '196/R, XD243 '190/R', XD268 '194/R' and XD245 '192/R' inverted in formation over the Moray Firth in August 1959. Below can be seen the disused airfield of Banff. (Vickers-Armstrongs)*

Show. They were a great success, bringing the crowds to their feet with spectacular aerobatics. The CO was invited to appear on the BBC programme *'What's My Line'* in which he succeeded in beating the panel. After this very successful Farnborough Show, all agreed it had been a most enjoyable week, spent amongst interesting aircraft and people.

On 18 September, after returning to Lossiemouth, the squadron received the Sandison Trophy for the outstanding achievement in a Strike Squadron by Lt Paul Perks for his work as Air Warfare Instructor to the squadron and LABS expert to the Royal Navy. Four days later, Lt Cdr Leppard handed over command of the Squadron to Lt Cdr W.A.Tofts RN. Flying training continued up until Christmas Leave, participating in Exercise *Kingpin* on 15 October and Exercise *Scramble*, an ECM practice against Valiants, on 5 November. Unfortunately XD281 was lost when Lt N.Grier-Rees was forced to bale out after his controls locked 26,000 ft over the Highlands on 19 November. Whilst the aircraft crashed into hill country near Aberfoyle, Perthshire, Grier-Rees parachuted safely down on to the snow-covered Ben Bhreac (2,300 ft), and subsequently had to walk for several days before reaching a farmhouse at Callander from where he was eventually picked up. This was the first successful ejection from a Scimitar.

From 3rd to 6th January 1960 the Squadron pilots were on an Atomic Course at HMS *Excellent*, Portsmouth. Then from 20th to 23rd January 1960, two aircraft were embarked in HMS *Victorious* for deck landing practice, being flown on board by the CO and Lt G.Hoddinott via Yeovilton. Lts Skead and Aitcheson also went aboard, embarking by Sea Venom and Skyraider. Just over a week later, on 2 February, the CO and Lt D.Pentreath went aboard HMS *Ark Royal* for deck wire-pulling trials, calling in at Boscombe Down en-route. 3rd March saw the whole squadron embarked in *Ark Royal*, which sailed from Devonport that day for work-up in the Mediterranean with all her fixed wing and helicopter squadrons on board. The Scimitars, having being seen off by No.803's ground crew, had departed Lossiemouth in pairs at half-hour intervals starting at 1235. Landing conditions on *Ark Royal* were fairly good, although there was no time for any DLPs, which caught the less experienced pilots a little off their guard, but all hooked on safely.

*Ark Royal* also embarked No.800 Squadron Scimitars under the command of Lt Cdr D.P.Norman: the only time two Scimitar squadrons would operate together on the same ship. By 6 March the Senior Pilot (Lt F.Hefford), Lts Perks and De Souza had carried out their deck qualification landings with one incident: the Senior Pilot developed a rate of sink on the approach and hit the round-down, fortunately bouncing into and catching the wire.

*XD267 '193/R', XD243 '190/R' and XD249 '196/R' in a near vertical dive over Scotland. (via M.J.Hooks)*

*The 807 Squadron Scimitar display team led by Lt Cdr Keith Leppard, lined up on their new Triumph Jaguar mounts at the SBAC Show Farnborough in September 1959. (Vickers-Armstrongs)*

*XD249 '196/R', XD243 190/R, XD268 '194/R', XD250 '197/R' and XD267 '193/R lined up at Lossiemouth. (via Philip Jarrett)*

*XD248 '195/R' displays its twenty-four 3-inch rocket projectiles in 1959. (via Derek Collier Webb)*

Gibraltar was reached on 7 March, and the ship sailed two days later for Malta, where she arrived in Grand Harbour on 11th. Work-up was commenced in the Malta area on 14th, and on 18th *Ark Royal* flew 50 fixed wing sorties, of which 15 were credited to No.807 Sqn. The ship sailed again on 19th for further work-up off Marsaxlokk, a visit being made to Palermo in Sicily from 25th to 28th. The ship returned to Marsaxlokk on 3 April, and serviceability and turn-round time on deck was very much improved, this being shown again on 4 April when No.807 flew 18 sorties totalling 20 hours 30 minutes flying time. *Ark Royal* had by now built up great confidence in her two Scimitar squadrons which worked well together.

A detachment went ashore to Hal Far from 8th to 18th April, then a practice strike was carried out on *Centaur* on 20th, followed on 27-28 April by Exercise *Fawley* before going to the western Cyprus area on 28th to participate next day in an Army co-operation exercise named *Pink Gin*, 19 sorties being flown by No.807, all at low-level from Condition One. Returning briefly to the Malta area on 2 May, the ship continued to Gibraltar for docking from 5th to 20th May, six aircraft of No.807 Squadron being disembarked to Hal Far on 1 May. The ship arrived back at Marsaxlokk on 22nd, and four days later the detachment re-embarked there. *Ark Royal* then headed for the west coast of Sardinia to rendezvous with the US Sixth Fleet to take part in Exercise *Royal Flush I*. This was an air defence exercise on 26th controlled by *Ark Royal* in the area between Sardinia and Majorca, ending the same evening. The carrier then put in to Toulon on 28th, leaving there on 30th to participate in Exercise *Junex I* starting on 1 June, practice strikes being made on *Ark Royal* by the Sixth Fleet on the second day. After anchoring off Barcelona from 3rd to 8th June, flying exercises followed in the western Mediterranean. On 10 June the day was devoted to private flying, so a competition was arranged between the Scimitar squadrons for RP firing at the splash target. After a bad start, the weather conditions improved and some very good runs were made by both squadrons. No.800 ended up with the better average radial (i.e. more on a line near the centre), beating No.807 by one yard; however Lt Hoddinott won for No.807 the trophy for the best individual sortie. On 11th, six French Navy Aquilons (French-built Sea Venoms) were embarked for deck landing practice, these disembarking two days later, sadly with the death of one pilot when his aircraft crashed off the port bow.

*XD322 '190/R' on the steam catapult of the ice-covered HMS Ark Royal during Arctic trials in September 1960. (FAA Museum)*

*Birds-eye view of XD270 '191/C' on the flight deck of HMS Ark Royal around 1960/1. (B.J.Lowe)*

*XD236 '195/C' off down HMS Ark Royal's steam catapult in 1961. (J.A.Pike)*

*Scimitar XD236 '195/C' and Sea Vixens of No.890 Squadron surrounded by spray and steam on the flight deck of HMS Ark Royal around 1961/2. (J.A.Pike)*

*XD316 '194/C' on the tarmac at Lossiemouth around 1960/1. (B.J.Lowe)*

Exercise *Royal Flush II* took place from 15th to 17th June with cross-control of aircraft, then the ship went back to Gibraltar on 20th for self-maintenance until 4 July, two Scimitars being disembarked until 5th. Another exercise, *Pink Gin II*, commenced on 11th in the Cyprus area, following which the ship put in to Athens on 19th for four days.

Practice strikes were made against HMS *Tiger* on 24th, and on 28th the squadron engaged in defence of the ship against Canberra bombers, five aircraft then disembarking to Hal Far when the ship arrived back at Malta on 29th. Two days later the Senior Pilot received his half stripe. The shore detachment re-embarked on 9 August and the ship sailed next day, the squadron carrying out practice strike on *Hermes* and *Ark Royal* on 12th. On 15-16 August, Exercise *Royal Flush* took place, then the ship anchored off Palma (Majorca) on 19th, leaving on 22nd August to sail home, arriving in the Moray Firth area on 29th before going in to Rosyth from 5th to 15th September for self-maintenance.

Following this she headed north for Arctic trials, participating in Part I of Exercise *Swordthrust* from 22 September, the ship steaming between the Shetland Isles and Iceland. Strikes were flown to the west coast of Norway, and the Senior Pilot flew a total of 650nm on one strike, this being the furthest strike of the day. At one time *Ark Royal* sailed very close to the ice shelf off Greenland, the first British carrier to do so. Flying from the ship in the kind of conditions experienced in that area called for the very best in airmanship. It was a great trial for the aircrew and the flight deck crews, but one which they all came through with flying colours.

On 30 September 1960 *Ark Royal* flew off all her fixed wing aircraft (making her 500 tons lighter), Nos.800 and 807 Squadrons returning to Lossiemouth. All 16 Scimitars from both squadrons were launched from *Ark Royal* in 8 minutes and 20 seconds, showing the efficiency of her catapult and flight deck crews and a tribute to the maintenance crews of the squadrons. The latter were disembarked in the Clyde two days later for Lossiemouth.

By 26 October the squadrons were back in *Ark Royal*, which sailed from Devonport that day heading for the Mediterranean once again, to arrive at Gibraltar on 30th for a two-day stay. The squadron went ashore to Hal Far on arrival at Malta on 4 November. While at anchor in Grand Harbour, Malta, it was decided that two more Scimitars were required ashore at Hal Far. The Senior Pilot did all the calculations and it was agreed that it was possible to launch the Scimitars off the ship while at anchor. History was therefore made by 807 Squadron on 12 November when Lt Cdr Tofts and Lt Cdr Hefford were launched; the wind was from red 025 at 10 knots and each aircraft carried 3,500lb of fuel, both landing at Hal Far a few minutes later. This was the first time a jet aircraft had been launched from a carrier while anchored in harbour.

No.807 Squadron was the only Scimitar squadron to carry out night flying operations from a ship in earnest. Two-thirds of the pilots were night qualified. During November, Lts Skead and De Souza reached 20 hours night flying, and on the same night Lt

*XD282 '193/C' after Lt(E) M.G.Griffin suffered hydraulic failure while landing on the 2,800yd runway at RAF Khormaksar on 14 September 1961. The brakes failed and he ran off into deep mud at the edge of the sea just below high water mark. The aircraft was eventually freed from the mud by MARTSU, then shipped home aboard HMS Centaur at Aden to be repaired at RNAY Fleetlands.*
*(via Philip Jarrett)*

Hessey, much to his embarrassment, attempted to land his Scimitar at Hal Far on his drop tanks and fuselage flaps. Fortunately he was able to apply full power in time and go around again, this time to land on his wheels (it is not recorded what the CO had to say to him!). Eventually all the Squadron pilots would be night qualified, but in the event most of the night flying fell to the CO and Senior Pilot.

The squadron re-embarked on 14 November, the ship participating in Exercise *Royal Flush IV* on 5 December, this being followed by Exercise *Pink Gin III* which commenced on 5 December. It was quickly followed by Exercise *Deux* on 9th and 10th, a large scale exercise involving RAF Canberra bombers and maritime reconnaissance Shackletons from Malta, the aim being to pass *Ark Royal* and other ships through the Sicilian narrows under a simulated atomic and submarine threat. Gibraltar was visited from 13th to 15th December. Eight aircraft disembarked to Hal Far from 17th to 19th, then squadron personnel went ashore to Malta for Christmas, returning to the ship after the New Year festivities.

On 10 January 1961 the ship took part in Exercise *Mixit* east of Malta, then sailed for the west coast of Spain as well as paying a five-day visit to Lisbon from 18th to 23rd January, following which she continued north via the Davis Strait and Baffin Island for arctic trials, many icebergs being seen. After turning south, she anchored off Block Island on 16-17 February, a visit then being made to Pier 90, New York, from 18th to 22nd February before heading east across the Atlantic. No.807 Sqn left *Ark Royal* for the last time, returning to Lossiemouth on 27 February, the complement being now reduced from nine to six aircraft. The carrier entered Devonport on 28th and the squadron then proceeded on leave.

Lt Cdr G.A.Rowan-Thompson took over as CO from 1 March at Lossiemouth, and on 5 April a group of three squadron aircraft went aboard *Centaur* for wire-pulling trials. The remainder of No.807 joined them off Lossiemouth on 10 April, and the ship reached the Gibraltar area three days later. Arriving off Malta on 19th, the ship commenced its first working-up period, eventually putting into Grand Harbour on 29th for a short period of self-maintenance, No.807 being disembarked to Hal Far. A second period of working-up started on 8 May when the squadron re-embarked, and Operation *Mainscrub* commenced next day, after which exercises were carried out in the Malta area and Marsaxlokk.

The carrier put in at Messina on 19th for a three-day stay, arriving back off Malta on 25th for a third and final period of work-up. On 27th the ship left Marsaxlokk for Exercise *Cantcop*, the setting for this being a local war in the Mediterranean with the ship under mock attack from aircraft of the 6th US Fleet, the exercise ending on 30th. Next day the carrier sailed for Spain with units of the Mediterranean Fleet, paying a visit to Barcelona from 2nd to 7th June. She then sailed for the Toulon area for flying exercises in the western Mediterranean until putting into Gibraltar on 14th, the aircraft being disembarked to North Front. A long-awaited visit to the USA and Canada was cancelled when a crisis in Kuwait intervened, *Centaur* and her air-group being ordered to proceed to the Persian Gulf at high speed. The Scimitars re-embarked on 30th and the carrier put to sea again. Sailing via the Suez Canal, the ship reached Aden on 9 July and two Scimitars were put ashore. Four days later, XD282 suffered brake failure on landing at RAF Khormaksar, and ran into deep mud in the over-shoot, causing quite severe damage. *Centaur* sailed on 21st and eventually entered the Persian Gulf, to relieve HMS *Victorious* in the Kuwait area on 31st. The first two weeks in August were then spent in

*XD236 '195/C' on the runway at Khormaksar, Aden in 1961.*
*(via A.S.Thomas)*

*807 Squadron personnel pose for the camera in front of XD243 '191/C' aboard HMS Centaur around 1962/2. (J.A.Pike)*

very hot conditions, No.807 Sqn Scimitars being seen landing at the forward airfield at Farwania. *Centaur* remained off Kuwait for only a short period, before returning to Aden, where XD282 was hoisted aboard from a lighter on arrival on 20 August. Next day the ship sailed for the Mediterranean, passing through the Suez Canal, and Port Said on 20-21 August, the Scimitars flying off to Hal Far on 27th. The aircraft then flew from Hal Far back to Lossiemouth on 31 August, apart from XD282 which was taken back home in the ship, to be repaired at Fleetlands. The carrier arrived in Plymouth Sound on 1 September, with the retard squadron party then leaving for Lossiemouth.

The squadron was once again back in *Centaur* on 20 October 1961, embarking in Lyme Bay, the ship then sailing to Aberporth for a spell of guided weapons training. Leaving Cardigan Bay on 29th, she sailed rather leisurely for the Far East. Arriving at Gibraltar on the last day of the month, the ship sailed again next day, putting in to Toulon on 3 November, leaving there on 7th for flying exercises, arriving at Marsaxlokk on 12th. After operating in the Malta area for the next two days, No.807 Sqn went ashore to Hal Far on 15th, squadron members rejoining the ship on 25th to be ready for the aircraft re-embarking two days later after the ship left Grand Harbour to continue the voyage east. Transit of the Suez Canal was carried out on 1 December, and fourteen days later the carrier put into Kilindini Harbour, Mombasa for a period of self-maintenance, during which Christmas was spent there. Sailing again on 27th, New Year's Eve was spent at Aden where some flying was carried out in the northern Arabian Sea area, the ship then heading east to arrive at Hong Kong on 17th.

The ship sailed again on 24th, taking part in Exercise *Talisman* with the Army on 29th-30th, close flying support being provided to the 17th Gurkha Infantry Division in Malaya. Four aircraft were flown off on 31st to RAF Tengah, where they were to be left behind to provide a pool of fully modified aircraft in the Far East, being replaced by aircraft in an older modified state to take back to the UK. The ship put in to Singapore for maintenance next day, the remainder of No.807 then disembarking to Tengah, where

the Senior Pilot, Lt J.W.Moore, proved the effectiveness of the Safeland Barrier on 7th after hydraulic failure in one of the replacement aircraft, XD248. Returning towards the Mediterranean for the homeward leg, Singapore was left behind on 19th, with Trincomalee being reached on 26th, Flag Officer Second in Command Far East Fleet Rear Admiral J.B.Frewen CB and his staff being embarked for the forthcoming Exercise *Jet 62* involving air, surface and underwater attacks. Sailing again on 2 March, *Centaur* then participated in this for the next eight days, a mock attack being carried out on RAAF Butterworth on 6th. The most spectacular incident of the commission took place off Aden on 7 March, when Sub Lt A.D.Alsop in XD319, missed the wires and attempted a bolter, but unfortunately failed to gain height and ditched into the sea just forward of the ship. Much to the surprise and relief of the flight deck crew he escaped unharmed, and was picked up by the SAR Whirlwind. The fleet arrived at Pulau Langkawi on 10th, and Rear Admiral Frewen transferred his flag to

*XD319 '192/C' making a rather alarming-looking landing on HMS Centaur around 1961/2. (J.A.Pike)*

*Another view of XD319 '192/C', this time after it ran off the runway into mud at Gibraltar around December 1960. (via J.A.Pike)*

*XD321 '194/C' receiving attention aboard HMS Centaur in 1961. (via J.A.Pike)*

*XD248 '190/C' being hoisted aboard HMS Centaur on 13 February 1962 for return to the UK after Lt JW Moore suffered hydraulic failure on a test flight and engaged the Safeland barrier at Tengah six days earlier. (via J.A.Pike)*

*Belfast*. Sailing again two days later, *Centaur* arrived off Aden on 23rd, when No.807 was put ashore at RAF Khormaksar where, with the other squadrons, they participated in a flying display on 30th as the climax to Aden Forces' Week. The aircraft re-embarked on 31st and the ship then left Aden, anchoring in Suez Bay on 3 April to await the north-bound convoy to proceed through the canal next day to the Mediterranean, where a visit was made to Istanbul from 7th to 11th April. From 12th to 16th the ship was on passage to Tripoli for *Meniscus III*, an Army support exercise with the 1st Battalion, Royal Scots. Then on 18 April the ship sailed into Grand Harbour, Malta for self-maintenance, and the remaining Scimitars flew ashore for the last time, landing at Hal Far after a flypast in echelon formation, the ground parties being put ashore. On 26 April four aircraft flew home direct to Lossiemouth, the remainder of the squadron re-embarking on the last day of the month. The ship left Grand Harbour on 3 May to commence the ships' Exercise *Centex*, reaching Gibraltar on 9 May and leaving there two days later to arrive back at Spithead on 15th. There No.807 Sqn officially disbanded, those on board being joined by the CO and pilots who had flown home from Malta. At 1515 there was an impressive de-commissioning ceremony during which they were addressed by the Captain, the finale being the cutting up of a large iced cake bearing the squadron's battle honours and all the trade badges in red and blue icing.

In the three years and five months that the squadron operated the Scimitar three of its aircraft had been lost and written off, one of these with the life of the pilot. Some other aircraft were damaged but all were repairable and flown again.

| Identification Markings |
|---|
| Gold/Bronze nose codes *190-198* thinly edged in black, with the last digit repeated in black on the nose wheel door. Nose codes later black, usually edged in white. On the fin a white letter 'R' (changing to 'C' in 3.61), with above it a gold-handled white-bladed scimitar hilt-down. |

| Squadron bases | |
|---|---|
| Lossiemouth | 1 Oct 1958 |
| Yeovilton (dett) | 9-12 Jun 1959 |
| West Freugh (Dt2) | 7-9 Jul 1959 |
| Culdrose (detd) | 25 Jul 1959 |
| Lossiemouth | 26 Jul 1959 |
| Farnborough | 2 Sep 1959 |
| Lossiemouth | 15 Sep 1959 |
| HMS Victorious (DLP) | 20-23 Jan 1960 |
| HMS Ark Royal (Dt) | 3-8 Feb 1960 |
| HMS Ark Royal | 3 Mar 1960 |

| Squadron bases continued | |
|---|---|
| Hal Far (Dt) | 8-18 Apr 1960 |
| Hal Far (Dt6) | 1-23 May 1960 |
| North Front (Dt2) | 20 Jun 1960 |
| to | 5 Jul 1960 |
| Hal Far (Dt5) | 29 Jul 1960 |
| to | 9 Aug 1960 |
| Lossiemouth | 30 Sep 1960 |
| HMS Ark Royal | 26 Oct 1960 |
| Hal Far | 4 Nov 1960 |
| HMS Ark Royal | 24 Nov 1960 |
| Hal Far | 17 Dec 1960 |
| HMS Ark Royal | 19 Dec 1960 |
| Lossiemouth | 27 Feb 1961 |
| HMS Centaur (Dt3) | 5-10 Apr 1961 |
| HMS Centaur | 10 Apr 1961 |
| Hal Far | 29 Apr 1961 |
| HMS Centaur | 8 May 1961 |
| North Front | 15 Jun 1961 |
| HMS Centaur | 30 Jun 1961 |
| Khormaksar (Dt2) | 9 Jul 1961 |
| to | 1 Jul 1961 |
| Hal Far | 27 Aug 1961 |
| Lossiemouth | 1 Sep 1961 |
| HMS Centaur | 20 Oct 1961 |
| Hal Far | 15 Nov 1961 |
| HMS Centaur | 27 Nov 1961 |
| Hal Far | 18 Apr 1962 |
| Lossiemouth (Dt4) | 26 Apr 1962 |
| to | 14 May 1962 |
| HMS Centaur | 30 Apr 1962 |
| Lossiemouth | 14 May 1962 |
| Squadron disbanded | 15 May 1962 |

| Squadron Officers | |
|---|---|
| Lt Cdr KA Leppard (CO) | 01.10.58 - 22.09.59 |
| Lt Cdr TCS Leece (Snr Pilot) | 01.10.58 - 03.11.59 |
| Lt Cdr JT Checketts (AEO) | 01.10.58 - 24.07.60 |
| Lt PH Perks | 01.10.58 - 03.10.60 |
| Lt B Davies | 01.10.58 - 13.02.60 |
| Lt PJ Lovick | 01.10.58 - 05.01.60 |
| Lt Cdr MJ Gibson | 01.10.58 - 04.07.60 |
| Lt GB Hoddinott | 01.10.58 - 03.10.60 |
| Lt MD Bristowe | 01.10.58 - 13.02.60 |
| Lt DJ Jenner (A/AEO) | 01.10.58 - 05.06.59 |
| Lt D Pentreath | 21.10.58 - 08.06.60 |
| S/L CR Cresswell | 04.11.58 - 19.11.58 |
| Lt CS Casperd | 17.11.58 - 04.02.60 |
| Lt JRJ Rutherford | 25.11.58 - 10.04.59 |
| S/L AMD de Labilliere | 06.01.59 - 15.05.59 |
| S/L A Smith (A/ALO) | 20.01.59 - 20.03.61 |
| S/L IMB Aitchison | 09.05.59 - 03.10.60 |
| Lt J Fleetwood (A/AEO) | 01.06.59 - 22.12.60 |
| Lt TNF Skead | 16.09.59 - 20.03.61 |
| Lt Cdr WA Tofts AFC (CO) | 22.09.59 - 14.03.61 |
| Lt NG Grier-Rees | 27.10.59 - 20.03.61 |
| Lt F Hefford (Senior Pilot) | 03.11.59 - 27.06.61 |
| Lt PG De Souza | 11.02.60 - 16.06.61 |
| Lt Cdr PJ Flynn (AEO) | 22.06.60 - 26.11.61 |
| Lt Cdr J Northam (ALO) | 22.06.60 - 17.05.62 |
| S/L NA Britton | 22.06.60 - 24.03.62 |
| Lt JRJ Rutherford | 29.08.60 - 10.10.60 |
| S/L PJ Trudgett | 29.08.60 - 20.10.61 |
| Lt PMC Hessey | 03.10.60 - 24.01.62 |
| Lt TJ Notley | 10.10.60 - 17.05.62 |
| Lt M Keighley (A/AEO) | 21.12.60 - 17.05.62 |
| S/L G Pike (A/ALO) | 12.03.61 - 17.05.62 |
| Lt Cdr GA Rowan-Thomson (CO) | 15.03.61 - 17.05.62 |
| Lt(E) MG Griffin | 27.03.61 - 11.11.61 |
| Lt JW Moore (Senior Pilot) | 26.06.61 - 17.05.62 |
| Lt RDG Gray | 26.06.61 - 17.05.62 |
| Lt Cdr DA Vaughan (AEO) | 23.11.61 - 17.05.62 |
| S/L AD Alsop | 23.11.61 - 27.03.62 |
| Lt PC Marshall | 22.01.62 - 27.03.62 |

*S/L A.D.Alsop in XD319 '192/C' (1) attempting to accelerate and go round again after missing the wires and bolting on HMS Centaur in the Gulf of Aden on 7 March 1962, and (2) dropping below deck level after he failed to gain height, to ditch 200yds ahead of the ship, from where he was picked up unharmed by the SAR helicopter, to be known henceforth as "The famous Scimitar Hydroplane Experimentalist". (Royal Navy)*

| Squadron aircraft | | |
|---|---|---|
| 190 | XD243 | 01.10.58 - 07.59 |
| | XD281 | 24.09.59 - 10.11.59 |
| | XD322 | 26.02.60 - 14.04.60 |
| | XD322 | 02.07.60 - 20.03.61 |
| | XD330 | 18.04.61 - 31.01.62 |
| | XD248 | 01.02.62 - 13.02.62 |
| 191 | XD244 | 01.10.58 - 16.01.60 |
| | XD318 | 14.01.60 - 14.03.60 |
| | XD270 | 14.04.60 - 27.08.61 |
| | XD243 | 26.08.61 - 27.03.62 |
| 192 | XD245 | 04.10.58 - 15.01.60 |
| | XD319 | 04.12.59 - 07.03.62 |
| 193 | XD246 | 17.11.58 - 10.12.58 |
| | XD267 | 13.03.59 - 09.10.59 |
| | XD282 | 07.10.59 - 14.07.61 |
| | XD320 | 30.08.61 - 31.01.62 |
| | XD232 | 01.02.62 - 26.04.62 |

| Squadron aircraft continued | | |
|---|---|---|
| 194 | XD247 | 04.11.58 - 19.11.58 |
| | XD268 | 04.03.59 - 09.10.59 |
| | XD316 | 04.11.59 - 28.08.61 |
| | XD321 | 26.08.61 - 31.01.62 |
| | XD332 | 08.02.62 - 26.04.62 |
| 195 | XD248 | 13.01.59 - 01.02.60 |
| | XD320 | 15.01.60 - 20.12.60 |
| | XD269 | 13.06.59 - 29.06.59 |
| | XD236 | 23.06.61 - 31.01.62 |
| | XD317 | 12.02.62 - 26.04.62 |
| 196 | XD249 | 14.10.58 - 15.02.60 |
| | XD321 | 30.01.60 - 10.03.61 |
| 197 | XD250 | 10.12.58 - 27.01.60 |
| | XD317 | 23.02.60 - 23.06.61 |
| 198 | XD274 | 09.59 - 09.59 (temp) |
| - | XD267 | 11.02.60 - 23.02.60 |

*XD228 outside 'F' Shop at RNAY Fleetlands in March 1958. (© Crown Copyright/MOD. Reproduced with the permission of Her Majesty's Stationery Office)*

# RNAY FLEETLANDS

By the mid 1950s, with the planned introduction into the Fleet Air Arm of not one, but two new types of aircraft which would eventually take the form of the Scimitar and Sea Vixen, thoughts turned to the infrastructure required to carry out deep maintenance, overhaul and modification of the aircraft.

Created by the Admiralty soon after the outbreak of the Second World War, the network of Royal Naval Aircraft Repair Yards provided all such facilities at strategic locations around the World at relatively low cost, and allowed the aircraft factories to concentrate on priority production rather than repair work. With the end of hostilities, production requirements began to drop and aircraft companies started taking on some of the repair work, resulting in the number of Yards world-wide reducing substantially. By the end of the 1950s there remained just two main overhaul and repair sites – RNAY Sydenham in Belfast, Northern Ireland, and RNAY Fleetlands in Gosport, Hampshire.

With an envisaged production run of 148 Sea Vixens and 100 Scimitars it was obvious that, even allowing for the reduction of the Scimitar contract to 76 aircraft, one site would not be able to accommodate both types. As a result the decision was made to allocate the Sea Vixens to Sydenham, with Scimitars going to Fleetlands.

Situated adjacent to Portsmouth Harbour RNAY Fleetlands had, being a non-airfield site, always seemed an odd place to carry out fixed-wing aircraft work, and indeed in this respect was quite unique. Sydenham, by comparison, was an airfield site and as a bonus was built next to the Harland & Wolff shipyard, providing easy access to aircraft carriers and lighters.

From its inception in 1940, a whole range of Fleet Air Arm types had been overhauled at Fleetlands, being flown into and air tested from nearby RAF Gosport, and transported to and from there along a specially-constructed towing route. With the imminent closure of what had by now become RNAS Gosport in the mid 1950s, all flight test operations were relocated to nearby RNAS Lee-on-Solent – a much more suitable airfield for the operation of the first-generation jet types which were entering service and which would soon be processed through the Yard.

However more suitable Lee was for the operation of small jet aircraft, the Scimitar posed an altogether different story. With a main runway of just 4,294 ft length, the airfield was not an ideal location to land this large and heavy aircraft in anything but the best conditions. It was in such suitably inclement weather that, on 11 November 1957, the Commanding Officer of 700X Sqdn, Cdr Tom Innes, flew XD222 in from its base at RNAS Ford in a joint exercise that would both assess the feasibility of operating the Scimitar in and out of Lee and also formally present the aircraft to the national press.

But getting the aircraft in and out of Lee-on-Solent was only one part of the equation; the Scimitar represented a substantial technological advance over the Yard's current major commitment – the diminutive Sea Hawk – and, together with new ground support equipment, jigs and facilities, training on the advanced structures and systems to be found on the aircraft was also required. In order to begin preparation for acceptance of the first aircraft, the very able chargehand whose job it was to oversee the flight testing of fixed wing types from Fleetlands, Ron Holbrow, was sent to RNAS Ford for a short period to familiarise himself with the Scimitar. It would not be until the overhaul and repair programme was in full swing a few years later that other members of the flight test team and a select few of the general maintenance workforce were sent on proper courses at South Marston.

In February 1958 XD228, fresh from the production line, was flown direct from South Marston to Lee-on-Solent and from there became the first of the type to be towed along the newly constructed larger towing route to RNAY Fleetlands. The exact reasoning for the aircraft's delivery is not quite known, but it seems reasonable to assume that it was used to test the route and hangar facilities. Its stay was brief for, the following month, it departed Lee for the A&AEE at Boscombe Down.

*XD228 at RNAY Fleetlands Flight Test section, RNAS Lee-on-Solent, in March 1958. (© Crown Copyright/MOD. Reproduced with the permission of Her Majesty's Stationery Office)*

*XD322 '190'R' ex No.807 Squadron arriving at RNAS Lee-on-Solent for RNAY Fleetlands on 14 April 1960.
(A.W.M.Groth)*

*XD268 undergoing maintenance in 'F' Shop, RNAY Fleetlands, in November 1959. (© Crown Copyright/MOD. Reproduced with the permission of Her Majesty's Stationery Office)*

*XD274 '613' with the Fleetlands Flight Test section at RNAS Lee-on-Solent on 2 May 1960.
(A.W.M.Groth)*

*Scimitars being worked on at RNAY Fleetlands around 1960.
(© Crown Copyright/MOD. Reproduced with the permission of Her Majesty's Stationery Office)*

*XD213 in its protective cocoon being towed at Fleetlands prior to being shipped to the Far East, April 1961. (© Crown Copyright/MOD. Reproduced with the permission of H.M. Stationery Office)*

*XD244 cocooned for shipment to the Far East, at RNAY Fleetlands in August 1961. (© Crown Copyright/MOD. Reproduced with the permission of Her Majesty's Stationery Office)*

*XD320 '195/R' still in No.807 Squadron markings at Fleetlands Flight Test at Lee on 23 August 1961 before despatch to AHU Lossiemouth. (A.W.M.Groth)*

*A very shiny XD282 with the Fleetlands Test Flight section in the 'C' Squadron hangar at A&AEE Boscombe Down in 1962.
(MAP)*

*Lt Cdr A.R.Campbell, Fleetlands MTP, standing in the cockpit of XD322 '190/R' at Lee-on-Solent in June 1960. (A.R.Campbell via L. Howard)*

Maintenance Test Pilots (MTP), Lt AHP 'Freddie' Firth was killed whilst test flying a Sea Hawk over the Solent. With the first of the overhauled Scimitars soon to be finished, and no other suitably qualified MTP in residence at Fleetlands, Lt Cdr Alistair Campbell was urgently re-draughted from the Aircraft Holding Unit at Lossiemouth to take up the post. Having briefly served with No.700X Sqdn at Ford between February and March 1958 before taking up the MTP job at Lossiemouth, Campbell was an ideal choice for the job.

In February 1960 Scimitars began emerging from Fleetlands at the rate of approximately two a month, having each taken in the region of 20,000 man-hours to complete. Whilst the Sea Hawks and Sea Venoms had previously enjoyed the use of nearby Ford as a diversionary airfield in the event of an emergency, its premature closure in late 1959 meant another suitable location had to be found. Flag Officer Air (Home), with its base also at Lee, arranged for Fleetlands to make use of Boscombe Down as and when required. With its huge runway it offered the safety margin that Lee could not provide and was closer than Yeovilton - the next largest airfield with a naval contingent. The latter, though, remained as a diversion.

The take-off at Lee was always exciting: with tyre pressures reduced due to the low LCN runway, a fuel load of 2,000 – 2,200lb and the required 5kts of headwind recommended by the Air Safety Board, the aircraft would be run up to 92% power, at which point the lightly-loaded Scimitar would start to slide on locked wheels. With brakes released the acceleration was huge and the aircraft would be airborne within two thirds of the runway.

*An anonymous Scimitar in the ground running pen at RNAY Fleetlands. Note how the aircraft is secured in position using the arrester hook attached to a substantial bracket bolted to the ground. (via Graham Cooper)*

By the middle of 1959 the residents of Stubbington and Lee-on-Solent were regularly having their peace and quiet shattered as the first of the Scimitars began arriving at Lee. Sadly, on 24 September of that year, the first of the Scimitar-qualified -

*XD213, piloted by the Fleetlands Maintenance Test Pilot, Lt Cdr P.M.Stevenson, crosses Marine Parade West on approach to Runway 05 at RNAS Lee-on-Solent for RNAY Fleetlands in March 1962. (A.W.M.Groth)*

Landing the aircraft and, more importantly, stopping safely within the airfield confines, were the main concerns. As a result two sets of CHAG arrester gear, one at either end of Runway 05-23, were installed. The gear consisted of two arrester wires being strung across the runway, raised off the surface by crescents of old tyres, and attached to many tons of heavy chain link looped in such a way as to play out progressively when pulled. Rudimentary but very effective. Although used a few times, this was the exception rather than the norm.

However, noise posed a great problem. On several occasions during the years of operations from Lee, the MTPs were sent memos from HMS *Ariel* (as it was from 1959 until 1965 before reverting to HMS *Daedalus*) urging them to make less commotion on take-off as it was disturbing the Captain's wife in Ross House, situated directly adjacent to the end of Runway 23. Sometimes, with the wind blowing away from the house, the noise level was dissipated sufficiently for the Captain to congratulate the pilots on quietening down operations!

*XD275 in 'F' Shop at RNAY Fleetlands around March 1964. (© Crown Copyright/MOD. Reproduced with the permission of Her Majesty's Stationery Office)*

*XD220, piloted by Lt Cdr P.M.Stevenson, departing Lee-on-Solent for NASU Brawdy on 21 March 1968. Note the CHAG arrester gear in the foreground. (via L.Howard)*

Indeed on one occasion an urgently required Scimitar being ground run on a Sunday morning succeeded in drowning out the service at Stubbington's Holyrood Church. Such was the level of local outrage that questions were asked in the Houses of Parliament soon afterwards.

At Boscombe, a corner of the 'C' (RN Test) Sqdn hangar was set aside for the flight test crew. A team from Lee, led by Ron Holbrow, would make the journey by road with the ground equipment remaining at Boscombe. If the air test was prolonged, Campbell would sometimes also commute by car, though often in the FOA(H) Sea Hawk XE390.

The Maintenance Test Flight usually took between fifty minutes and one hour and would include the following:

i) A straight timed climb to 45,000 ft with turns at that altitude to check manoeuvrability.
ii) Timed level acceleration at about 35,000 ft (depending on temperature) from 0.7M to 0.93M.
iii) A full power diving Mach run over the sea supersonically off Portland (trying to avoid the danger areas where Naval ships were firing and exercising).
iv) Testing the navigational equipment by homing on Yeovilton.
v) Stalling the aircraft, both clean and with gear, hook and flaps down.
vi) Check the fuel balancing system in the fuel tanks.
vii) Check the relight on each engine.
viii) Invert the aircraft to shake any odd spanners left in the cockpit or elsewhere!

*The remains of XD214 in the scrap compound at RNAY Fleetlands on 13 June 1970. The rear fuselage has been crudely cut off and the wings are in the foreground. (A.W.M.Groth)*

The average of two or three test flights required on each aircraft bore testament to the high standard of work carried out at Fleetlands, with many claiming that the finished product was as good, if not better than, the original manufacture.

On completion the aircraft would normally be collected by the civilian pilots from the Rochester-based Shorts Ferry Flight who would deliver them to either the user units or AHU Lossiemouth (in later years NASU Brawdy).

With the completion of the Sea Hawk programme in 1961, the Scimitar became the last operational fixed-wing type to be worked on in the Yard. In October 1965 XD246 arrived for conversion for Fleet Requirement Unit duties with Airwork at Hurn and, by the time the contract was completed just over two years later, some sixteen aircraft had been thus modified.

In 1967 the changes in British military aircraft maintenance procedures brought about by the recommendations of the Templar Report, saw the Royal Air Force being given sole responsibility for the overhaul and repair of all three of the service's fixed-wing aircraft. Similarly the Royal Navy were tasked with undertaking all such work on rotary wing types, thus signalling the end of Fleetland's involvement with conventional aircraft.

With the general run-down in operations by Fleetlands from Lee it was felt unnecessary to keep a full-time fixed-wing MTP on the Yard's books, and so for the final few aircraft Lt Cdr Paul Stevenson, himself a former Fleetlands MTP and now the commanding officer of the MTP School at Brawdy, was brought in as and when required to test the aircraft.

It was therefore without fanfare or publicity, on a cold and sunny 21 March 1968, that Stevenson climbed aboard XD220 to make the last Fleetlands-generated, jet movement from Lee. As the aircraft roared off the runway and set a course for Brawdy, no doubt the local residents breathed an audible sigh of relief at seeing the end of the Scimitar!

| Fleetlands Scimitar-qualified Maintenance Test Pilots (in order of service) | |
|---|---|
| Lt(AE) AHP Firth | by 08.59 - 24.09.59 |
| Lt Cdr AR Campbell | by 12.60 - 10.61 |
| Lt Cdr PM Stevenson | 11.61 - 12.63 |
| Lt(E) MG Griffin | 12.63 - 04.66 |
| Lt Cdr JT Spafford | |
| Lt Cdr CR Newnes | by 06.67 |
| Lt Cdr PM Stevenson (from MTPS Brawdy) | - 21.03.68 |

# SHORTS FERRY FLIGHT

In November 1950 Short Brothers of Rochester were awarded the Admiralty contract to supply ferry pilots to the Fleet Air Arm (not to be confused with a similar ferry unit set up by Airwork Services at Hurn who specialised in deliveries to foreign governments).

Flying all manner of aircraft, in varying states of serviceability, from locations as far afield as Lossiemouth and Hal Far, these ex-military fliers led a charmed and strange existence, spending as they did half their time in the air and half on trains transiting from one base to another. Originally having to travel in full flying gear with their parachutes, many were known to abandon the latter due to its cumbersome proportions and elect, instead, to sit in the aircraft on their suitcases or grips.

Probably the longest serving, and arguably the most noteworthy of this motley band of veteran airmen, was 'Pancho' Brandt. Squadron Leader Jack Brandt, DFC, MBE, RAF (Ret'd), also held the rank of Lt Cdr RNVR and was a legend in his own lifetime, due in no small part to the seemingly cavalier fashion in which he approached flying.

With his trademark battered trilby hat, which would remain in place until he was strapped in and ready to start (at which point it would be removed and stuffed behind the ejector seat), 'Pancho', so called because of his swarthy looks and pencil moustache, would frequently carry with him a chrome-plated aircrew urine receptacle which he had been presented with by the Flight Test crew at Lee. With its tube welded over and a spring clip riveted to the back, it would be clipped to the aircraft's control column and used as an ashtray for the relatively long flights to Lossiemouth!

However colourful the characters who made up the Short's Ferry Unit were, their ability to fly several different types of aircraft during the course of one day demonstrated a rare talent, though frequently they would be observed taxying out whilst still furiously thumbing through a set of Pilot's Notes!

Brandt's last known Scimitar flight took place on 21 June 1966 when he flew XD214 from RNAS Lee-on-Solent to NASU Brawdy, shortly after which, it is thought, the Admiralty contract expired.

| Shorts ferry pilots known to have flown Scimitars | |
|---|---|
| Lt Cdr J Brandt MBE DFC RNR | by 12.60 - 06.66 |
| Mr DR Skinner | by 06.61 |
| Mr KB Owen | by 1965 |

# AHU LOSSIEMOUTH

Once the Scimitars had completed their initial manufacturer's production test flying programme, they were flown (usually by Shorts) to the Aircraft Holding Unit at RNAS Lossiemouth in Scotland.

The function of the AHU was twofold: firstly to receive and store Naval aircraft prior to being issued to the Fleet, and secondly to accept new day fighters from the manufacturers.

The Scimitars began arriving from South Marston in April 1958 at the rate of one or two a month. Having been given an acceptance test flight by the resident MTP, they then received maintenance checks before the MF700 series of log book and log cards were raised and naval records introduced. The daily and other inspection cycles were then started, before the aircraft were towed around to the waiting squadron.

| Aircraft Holding Unit, RNAS Lossiemouth | | |
|---|---|---|
| Lt AR Campbell | by | 03.58 - 11.59 |
| Lt Cdr BEN Neave | by | 11.59 - 61 |

*XD329 with the Aircraft Holding Unit at Lossiemouth, seen during an Air Day in 1960. This was the aircraft from which Lt Purvis later ejected. (R.C.B.Ashworth)*

*XD241 with the Aircraft Holding Unit Abbotsinch in the Static Park at a rather wet Navy Day in 1961. (N.D.Welch)*

*XD234 '025' of the Airwork Fleet Requirements Unit, Hurn, visiting RNAS Yeovilton around 1968. (Royal Navy)*

# AIRWORK FLEET REQUIREMENTS UNIT

Based at Hurn (Bournemouth Airport) and operated by Airwork Ltd with civilian pilots and military aircraft, the Fleet Requirements Unit had for many years provided gunnery tracking, ship's radar/radio calibration and simulated strike attack training facilities for naval vessels operating out of southern ports.

In 1964, with the requirement for a faster, more representative aircraft type to replace the diminutive Sea Hawks, the Scimitar was proffered to take up the role. The choice was not a popular one; the Sea Hawk had been a much-loved mount for FRU pilots and those who had experience of the Scimitar in front-line service had misgivings about its suitability.

To enable the aircraft to carry out the tasks assigned to it, a comprehensive modification and overhaul programme was initiated at RNAY Fleetlands beginning with XD246 in October 1965. Operational support was provided by NASU Brawdy and Airwork themselves. No.764B Sqdn at RNAS Lossiemouth carried out the training of FRU pilots during 1965 and upon completion in November of that year one of its aircraft, XD267, was flown to Hurn to provide continuation and familiarisation training until the arrival of XD246 in June 1966.

The original Scimitar flight simulator was installed at Hurn and Hunter T.8s of the Naval Flying Standards Flight from Yeovilton provided the swept-wing check-outs for the Scimitar pilots.

Peter de Souza, formerly Lt Cdr (QFI) of No.803 Sqdn, describes his experiences with the Fleet Requirement Unit:

"September of 1968 found me well and truly 'on the beach', having resigned my commission in the Royal Navy and, after fourteen years nestling under the safe umbrella of the Services, as a civilian.

Although armed with an ATPL (endorsed with something really useful like a Beagle 206!), I then joined the ranks of the unemployed and, at the age of 31, felt dubious about my flying career. Since I was returning to my home town of Bournemouth, I thought I would contact Airwork, the Fleet Requirements Unit at Hurn Airport, on the off chance that they might have a vacancy. Fortunately I had experience on all the types they operated and was still a current QFI/IRI on the Meteor and Hunter. As for the Scimitar, their recently acquired equipment, I had two frontline tours and training experience under my belt, so hoped the lack of potential training costs might weigh in my favour. As it transpired they were short of one staff pilot. So in October 1968 I arrived at Hurn by the Chapple Gate to join Airwork Limited.

The Fleet Requirements Unit was an ideal, non-traumatic way to transition into civilian life. One still flew military equipment, continued to enjoy the comradeship of squadron life, and yet free of the shackles of military discipline and extraneous duties. Airwork was a pleasant company to work for, relaxed yet efficient, didn't

*XD267 seen still in No.764B Squadron markings whilst on loan to the Airwork Fleet Requirements Unit at Hurn for familiarisation on the type. The onlooker is no doubt admiring the complex-looking wing-fold mechanism. (MAP)*

*Scimitars of the Airwork Fleet Requirements Unit lined up at Hurn around 1968. (MAP)*

pay much, but full of nice chaps. The FRU was a veritable melting pot of individuals. There were only about ten or so pilots of which three were ex-Navy and the remainder ex-Air Force or civilian lineage.

The little squadron had its own little enclave of a couple of old hangars and a World War 2-vintage group of blockhouses which served as accommodation. There was the old Scimitar simulator that I had abused in the 1950s and the use of the BAC canteen, where meat and two veg could be acquired for four bob, commensurate with our salaries and lifestyle (still somewhat of a shock after the luxuries of Mess life). The staff pilots were generally senior in years and many had accrued thousands of flying hours on fighter types, making my personal log book entries seem relatively pitiful. Duty hours were usually nine to five weekdays, seldom any night work, and if weather precluded flying and the rampant 'card school' did not require your participation, one usually finished early.

I had flown most of the Scimitars on the FRU inventory before. My preconception that the type was an outrageously bad choice for civilian operations was to be tempered by the fact that the serviceability rate was far better than I ever experienced in the Service. This was partly due to the operating techniques adopted.

In the services, fighters were always flown close to their limits – 'firewall the throttles and pull as much G as the hangover would allow' – and engine changes after 100 hours were the order of the day. Deck landings would loosen the staunchest of hydraulic couplings (let alone one's bowels!). As a civilian operator, accountants had major inputs, and although it was still in the days of cheap fuel, the 'kick the tyres' syndrome was to a large extent eradicated. The aircraft had undergone comprehensive overhaul before delivery and much unnecessary equipment like LABS gear and *Blue Silk* (latterly highly confidential) had been removed. Harley lights were fitted in the nose on most. The cockpits seemed fairly spartan, now being devoid of extraneous switchery. Never having had much in the way of NAV gear, there now seemed even less: a TACAN for use with Royal Navy ships, UHF and VHF radios and possibly an NDB, but not much else. The Mark-One eyeball and back-of-the-fag-packet DR augmented local knowledge, but even those resulted in one fatality.

Although Hurn airport actually boasted GCA facilities on their super-colossal 1,830 metre East-West runway, and landing was no major problem, the mind was concentrated on those wet and windy winter days. The no cut/no flare technique of carrier landing was used ashore to good effect, but one was conscious that in nominal

*XD241 '838' of the Airwork Fleet Requirements Unit at Hurn in 1969.*

*XD317 '833' of the Airwork Fleet Requirements Unit at Hurn in 1969. (MAP)*

landing weights immediate brake application at normal touchdown speed would result in burn-out prior to stopping. So a technique involving some aerodynamic braking was used.

Operationally the FRU configured the aircraft with two inboard 200-gallon drop tanks and two 150-gallon tanks outboard. This presented no problems for take-off, being grossly over-thrusted, and a small derate was possible. General cruising to and from exercise areas was at a sedate 360 or 420 knots (625 available if late for tea). With prudent throttle handling a very reasonable fuel consumption and on-station sortie times of an hour or more could be achieved even at low level. Most sorties involved straight and level flight, e.g. ship's radar/radio calibration, gunnery tracking and simulated attacks on the fleet, so the aircraft were in no way stressed as in frontline service. This led to much higher serviceability rates and decidedly fewer hydraulic problems. I forever take my hat off to those remarkable chaps who serviced the Scimitar, as it remained the technical nightmare to work on until the end.

As someone who has had his share of frights courtesy of Messrs Vickers Supermarine, and as one of the many ejectees from the Scimitar in earlier days, I felt surprisingly confident and at ease with the aircraft in its swansong. Great credit must go to Airwork for what they achieved, both operationally and with servicing.

Although not a great success operationally, and very few were built, it has its place in British Aviation history. Ask any ex-Scimitar pilot for his recollections of the type and, although they may not be too complimentary, all will agree: 'Lad, it went like s**t off a shovel!'."

The Scimitars began to be withdrawn from FRU use in late 1969 and early 1970. Most aircraft were sold to the Ministry of Technology and were flown to Southend Airport, from where they were roaded to P&EE Shoeburyness to act as targets for ordnance trials – an ironic fate considering the type's role with the FRU.

The last ever flight of a Scimitar was made on 12 February 1971 when XD244, the reserve aircraft, was itself ferried to Southend to await the same ignominious fate.

**Identification Markings**
White nose codes in the range *025-038* on a black panel, changing in 1.69 to the range *830-839*.

*During the Scimitar service with the FRU the idea of carrying unit insignia on the fin was resurrected (a similar plan having being made many years beforehand for the unit's Firefly TT.4s). Although designs were made, consisting of the Airwork emblem made from Scimitar swords and a dagger, the idea was sadly never implemented.*

**Airwork Scimitar pilots**

| | |
|---|---|
| Mr C Butt (Senior Pilot) | 1967 |
| Mr PG De Souza | 1968/9 |
| Mr J Duncan | 1967/9 |
| Mr TE Hill | killed 26.6.68 |
| Mr RV Lacey | 1967 |
| Mr RC Minton | 1969 |
| Mr JV Mullins | 1967 |
| Mr J Rees | 1965 |
| Mr Saunders | 1969 |
| Mr KG Wilson | 1965 |

**Scimitar aircraft**

| | | | |
|---|---|---|---|
| 025 | XD234 | 07.04.67 - 03.69 | (code applied by 10.67) |
| 029 | XD225 | 21.11.66 - 08.01.69 | (code not carried) |
| 030 | XD214 | 17.10.66 - 03.69 | (code applied by 10.67) |
| 031 | XD232 | 12.01.67 - 03.69 | (code applied by 10.67) |
| 032 | XD235 | 11.11.66 - 12.68 | (code applied by 10.67) |
| | XD241 | 15.11.68 - 12.68 | (code not carried) |
| 033 | XD317 | 02.11.66 - 03.69 | (code applied by 10.67) |
| 034 | XD267 | 01.12.65 - 21.11.66 | (not applied. Retained '617') |
| | XD267 | 18.09.68 - 12.68 | (FRU code not applied) |
| 035 | XD246 | 28.06.66 - 20.08.68 | (code applied by 10.67) |
| 036 | XD227 | 27.11.67 - 12.68 | (code not carried) |
| 037 | XD333 | 03.11.67 - 24.11.67 | (FRU code not applied) |
| 038 | XD236 | 15.12.66 - 26.06.68 | (coded by 10.67) |
| - | XD227 | 06.02.67 - 06.04.67 | (FRU code not applied) |
| - | XD327 | 06.04.67 - 04.06.69 | (remained uncoded) * |
| - | XD219 | 02.03.67 – 06.03.67 | (incorrect mod state) |

\* Aircraft carried black rectangular background on nose with no code.

From 12.68

| | | | |
|---|---|---|---|
| 830 | XD214 | Recoded 03.69 - 28.05.69 | |
| 831 | XD232 | Recoded 03.69 - 05.12.69 | |
| 832 | XD235 | Recoded 12.68 - 30.01.70 | |
| 833 | XD317 | Recoded 03.69 - 04.08.69 | |
| 834 | XD234 | Recoded 03.69 - 30.11.70 | |
| 835 | XD267 | Recoded 12.68 - 11.09.69 | |
| 836 | XD227 | Recoded 12.68 - 15.03.69 | (code not carried) |
| 837 | XD333 | Recoded 02.69 - 20.01.71 | |
| 838 | XD241 | 15.11.68 - 02.12.70 | (coded by 12.68) |
| 839 | XD322 | 11.12.68 - 02.12.70 | |
| - | XD327 | 06.04.67 - 04.06.69 | (remained uncoded) |

XD244 flown from NASU Brawdy to FRU Hurn 3.9.70 and held in open storage as reserve aircraft. Not flown by the unit. Made last Scimitar flight when delivered to Southend 12.2.71.

*With the closure of RNAS Brawdy, XD244 was transferred to open storage at Hurn, where it is seen around 1970. Never used by the FRU, on 12 February 1971 it became the last Scimitar to fly when it was delivered to Southend Airport for onward transportation to P&EE Shoeburyness. (MAP)*

*XD216 of the Aeroplane & Armament Experimental Establishment aboard HMS Victorious in the English Channel in October 1959 for armament and catapult trials. (via Lee Howard)*

## OTHER SCIMITAR PILOTS

| A&AEE, Boscombe Down (including 'C' Naval Test Sqdn) | |
|---|---|
| Lt Cdr PJ Barber RN | by 31.03.60 |
| Cdr PCS Chilton AFC RN | by 04.58 |
| Lt DF Fieldhouse RN | by 07.60 |
| Lt GB Hoddinott RN | 04.04.61 - 07.62 |
| Lt Cdr HG Julian DSC AMIMechE RN | |
| Cdr CM Little RN | by 04.56 |
| Lt Cdr DP Norman RN | 56 - 57 |
| Cdr SG Orr DSC AFC RN | |
| Lt Cdr TA Rickell RN | killed 05.07.55 |
| Lt Cdr DF Robbins RN | 57 - 58 |
| Lt JT Spafford RN | 61 |
| Lt Cdr DJ Whitehead RN | by 08.57 |

| Vickers-Armstrongs (Supermarine), South Marston and Wisley |
|---|
| Lt Cdr HJD Abraham RN (seconded from Royal Navy) |
| LR Colquhoun GM DFC DFM |
| WD Jarvis AFC |
| WR Judge |
| MJ Lithgow OBE (Chief Test Pilot) |
| DW Morgan MBE |
| Lt Cdr SG Orr DSC AFC RN (seconded from Royal Navy) |
| EB Trubshaw MVO |

| Maintenance Test Pilots School, RNAS Brawdy |
|---|
| Lt Cdr SE Askins RN |
| Cdr PM Stevenson RN |

| Royal Aircraft Establishment |
|---|
| F/Lt DL Bywater RAF (ETPS) |
| Lt Cdr TC Evans AFC RN (CO Experimental Flying) |
| F/Lt JF Farley RAF (ETPS) |
| F/Lt BL Gartner RCAF (ETPS) |
| F/Lt AJ Hawkes RAF (ETPS) |
| Lt Cdr GR Higgs RN (CO Naval Test Flt, Bedford) |
| Lt Cdr MT Hynett RN (incl. Weapons Flt) |
| Lt Cdr P Millett DSC RN (RAE Bedford) |
| Lt Cdr PI Normand RN (RAE Bedford) |
| F/Lt AW Picking RAF |
| Capt WR Pogue USAF (Weapons Flt) |
| JP Skyrud USN (ETPS) |
| Lt Cdr JT Spafford RN (RAE Bedford) |
| F/Lt NR Williams RAF (Weapons Flt, Farnborough/West Freugh) |

*As the only Scimitar not to sport a standard Royal Navy colour scheme, XD229 of RAE Weapons Flight is seen taxying at West Freugh around 1964/5. The aircraft is painted in a powder blue, white and black scheme. (MAP)*

*XD268 '156/V' (ex No.803 Squadron) with the Aeroplane and Armament Experimental Establishment's Weapons Flight at West Freugh in 1962. (MAP)*

*XD248 of RAE West Freugh on 8 March 1968 during bomb trials. (via Peter Cooper)*

*XD231 of RAE Bedford taxying straight into the hangar on arrival at Fairford in August 1966 from Oklahoma after completion of storm turbulence trials with NASA. The title 'RAE BEDFORD' is applied to the fin in black, along with a 'Stormform' badge. (Ray Deacon)*

*Wingless XD219 after coming off the runway into mud during wet runway braking and aquaplaning trials at RAE Farnborough on 9 January 1973. Having struck a runway light, the nose wheel was ripped off and the aircraft's back broken in the subsequent heavy impact with the ground. (via Peter Cooper)*

*XD219 of the Maintenance Test Pilot's School lands at its base at RNAS Brawdy circa 1967/8 where it was used to teach pilot engineers modern test flying methods for advanced aircraft types.*

*XD220 being delivered by Lt Cdr P.E.H.Banfield into storage at RNAS Lee-on-Solent for the Fleet Air Arm Museum on 23 July 1970. This was to be the last flight of a Scimitar in naval hands. (A.W.M.Groth)*

*A2590 (ex XD324 '033/R' of No.803 Squadron), A2587 (ex XD275 '117/E' of No.800B Flight) and another awaiting their fate at RNAS Lee-on-Solent around 1969/70 after retirement from the Air Engineering School.*

*A2588 (ex XD243 '025/E' of No.803 Squadron) with the Air Engineering School at Lee-on-Solent around 1969.*

*A2574 (ex XD332 '616' of No.764B Squadron) with the School of Aircraft Handling, Culdrose in 1965.*

*XD322 (ex '839' of the Airwork FRU, Hurn) having arrived at Southend Airport on 2 December 1970, en route to the nearby Proof and Experimental Establishment at Shoeburyness. (MAP)*

## PROOF & EXPERIMENTAL ESTABLISHMENT SHOEBURYNESS

Situated on the bleak, remote north-east corner of Foulness Island near Southend, Essex, the Proof and Experimental Establishment outstation at Shoeburyness was, for many years, an aviation graveyard, littered with the corpses of innumerable aircraft, several of which having once been unique prototypes. It was here that the hulks of once-elegant aircraft were subjected to trials of gunfire to both assess the effectiveness of the ballistics and to determine the resistance of modern airframe structures to battle damage. Famous aircraft such as the TSR-2, Bristol 188 and Fairey Delta all succumbed to this ignominious fate.

In early 1969, with the imminent retirement of the Scimitar from FRU service, the Ministry of Technology (MinTech) at Farnborough expressed an interest in acquiring the type to take part in 'Vulnerability Trials'. In their opinion the aircraft's robust construction made it the most 'reasonable representative' of Russian aircraft types. In a memo to P&EE dated 1 April, MinTech detailed the procurement of three Scimitars and four obsolescent Buccaneer S.1s. which also fell into this category. One Scimitar would be used in the trials of 35mm HE shells against aircraft structures, with the other two becoming targets for bullets, shells and direct-hitting warheads. The planned delivery by road to P&EE, the memo concluded, would occur between June and July of that year.

Aircraft began to appear gradually and by 16 March 1970, when XD235 flew to Southend Airport, the nearest airfield to Shoeburyness, five Scimitars had been transported to the 'Damage to Aircraft Trials' (DAT) Battery within the establishment. The transportation of XD235 by road from the airport had to be planned carefully and included the negotiation of a 14ft overhead bridge. As roads would have to be closed, the move was carried out during the night, beginning on 19 March and being completed by 23rd.

On 30 November 1970, the Ministry of Aviation Supply (previously the MinTech), notified P&EE that the last five Scimitars in use at Hurn would become surplus at the beginning of December 1970 and would be delivered fully serviceable to P&EE via Southend in accordance with the wishes of MoD (Navy) who had been impressed by the efficient manner in which XD235 had been delivered. Such a method negated the high dismantling

*A wing of XD228 at the Proof and Experimental Establishment at Shoeburyness around 1990. (R.C.Sturtivant)*

*The partial remains of XD235, XD215 and XD267 at the Proof and Experimental Establishment at Shoeburyness around 1990. (via N.Parker)*

costs and reduced to a minimum the road haulage fees.

Once all five aircraft (XD234, XD241, XD244, XD322 and XD333) had arrived at Southend, it was planned that a working party from Airwork would be sent to defuel and de-arm the aircraft and remove the wing pylons and fuel tanks in preparation for the road move (the latter, presumably, to aid internal inspection of structures when fired upon).

Upon arriving at P&EE, the aircraft were towed from the Headway in the Central area across the Sands via the 'Broomway' to the DAT area – the normal route for large and heavy loads. It was here, for the next twenty years, that the majority of the aircraft would languish at the mercy of the British climate and ordnance test engineers. By 1978 a specialist unit dealing with the inspection and investigation of various types of battle damage was in operation at 71MU, RAF Abingdon, and on occasion some of the Scimitar hulks were noted being roaded to and from the Oxfordshire base. Airframes were also supplied by Shoeburyness to other weapon testing ranges around the country including Aberporth and Pendine.

By the late 1980s only a handful of airframes remained at Shoeburyness in the 'Half-Way' and 'White City' areas, and in late 1990 a mass purge of the redundant carcasses began. The remains were purchased by the Mayer and Perry scrapyard and removal of the airframes took place in April 1991.

Although in poor condition, a few of the cockpit sections of the remaining aircraft were saved and, through Parkhouse Aviation, were sold to private collectors around the country.

It is ironic that, having been earmarked for destructive testing, the allotment of aircraft to P&EE ensured the survival of a handful of Scimitars for future preservation.

*The battered remains of XD322 at the Proof and Experimental Establishment at Shoeburyness around 1990. (R.C.Sturtivant)*

*Supermarine Type 525 VX138 at the Aeroplane and Armament Experimental Establishment, Boscombe Down on 26 April 1954.*
*(via B.J.Lowe)*

# INDIVIDUAL AIRCRAFT HISTORIES

## SUPERMARINE 508

**3 SUPERMARINE 508 prototypes ordered 13.11.47 to Cont No 6/Acft/1508/CB.7b under Spec N.9/47 and numbered VX133, VX136 and VX138. (Two 6,500shp Rolls-Royce Avon R.A.3)**

VX133  Completed as Type 508 in the Experimental Dept, Hursley Park. First flown at Boscombe Down, then to VA Chilbolton 31.8.51. Farnborough for display at SBAC Show 11.9.51. VA Chilbolton 17.9.51. A&AEE trials 11.51. Violent shaking at low altitude, wheels unlocked and opened, accelerometer registered 11G, damaged Cat 3 5.12.51 (MJ Lithgow), cause established as being aileron flutter. VA Chilbolton to 9.4.52 (arresting trials prior to deck trials). RAE Bedford 29.4.52 (arresting trials). VA Chilbolton 2.5.52. To RAE Farnborough, then returned to Chilbolton en-route for deck trials based at Ford 17.5.52. *Eagle* 28.5.52 (arresting trials). VA Chilbolton 29.5.52. Participated in Lee-on-Solent 'At Home' air display but damaged by severe vibration in flight 12.7.52. Measurement of loads during arrested landings at RAE Farnborough 15.4.53. RAE Farnborough 13.7.53 (measurement of loads during arrested landings). RAE Bedford 22.8.55. Aboard *Bulwark* for trials 31.10.55. RAE Bedford 14.11.55. HM Dockyard Devonport for trials on *Centaur* to test hangar deck strength 24.9.56. RAE Bedford 28.11.56 (resumed arrester gear development). Loan extended to permanent basis 18.9.59. Released by NAD/RAE Bedford 29.3.63. First noted at MARTSU Lee-on-Solent 26.11.63 and still there 25.12.63. To SAH Culdrose by road for tractor driver training. Became GI Class II *A2529* 7.1.64. To Predannack for firefighting by 1.8.70, gone by 1984.

VX136  Completed with minor mods as Type 529 in Experimental Dept, Hursley Park. FF Chilbolton 29.8.52. SBAC Farnborough 31.8.52. VA Chilbolton 8.9.52. RAE Farnborough 20.4.53 (tail down landing trials). FL at Farnborough 5.5.53. VA Chilbolton 8.5.53 (survey and repair). RAE Farnborough 22.6.53 (acceleration trials). VA 10.7.53 (resume contractors development trials). Work-up for deck trials at RAE 1.10.53. RAE Farnborough c.9.10.53 (deck trials on *Eagle* 3-4.11.53). Allotted RAE Farnborough, acceptance ex contract on return 18.11.53. VA Chilbolton 19.11.53 (resumption of contractors development). Emergency landing with port undercarriage only in down position, Cat.4 damage, starboard wingtip, flaps, chassis door and aileron distorted and buckled, port chassis door buckled and torn from hinges, Chilbolton 2.12.53 (Lt Perkins). Allotted VA 13.1.54 (temp storage). Authority to SOC 27.10.54. Fuselage and wings arr P&EE Shoebury-ness by road ex VA Chilbolton as ballistic trials target 30.7.56, engine to RAE Bedford. Nose and cockpit section to Farnborough 12.58. Rest scrapped Shoeburyness 9.61.

VX138  Completed as Type 525 at Experimental Dept, Hursley Park. Roaded to A&AEE Boscombe Down 25.4.54. FF Boscombe Down 27.4.54 (MJ Lithgow). VA Chilbolton 6.5.54. SBAC Show Farnborough 7-12.9.54. To VA Chilbolton 13.9.54. To Hursley Park by road for installation of flap blowing system early 1955. Roaded to VA Chilbolton. A&AEE Boscombe Down 4.7.55 (trials). 20min after take-off, spun in from 3,000ft 2m SSE of airfield, Cat 5(S) 5.7.55 (L/C TA Rickell DoI). Wreckage to Chilbolton. SOC 30.1.56. [64:20hrs]

# SUPERMARINE SCIMITAR

**Two Supermarine Type 544 Scimitar prototypes ordered 29.3.51 under Cont No 6/Acft/6579/CB.7(b) to Spec N.113D and numbered WT854 and WT859. (Two Avon RA.23)**

WT854 Constructed at Experimental Dept, Hursley Park. To Boscombe Down by road 14.1.56. FF Boscombe Down for 10 minutes 19.1.56 (MJ Lithgow). VA Chilbolton 30.1.56. VA Wisley 25.2.56. RAE Bedford 6.3.56. VA Chilbolton 10.3.56. A&AEE Boscombe Down 22.3.56. *Ark Royal* 5.4.56 (deck landing trials on *Ark Royal* by MJ Lithgow, first deck landing of RN aircraft of over 25,000lbs). Took off from *Ark Royal* with handbrake on, landed back safely for wheel change 9.4.56 (L/C CM Little). VA Chilbolton 12.4.56. VA Wisley 16.4.56 (Mods to wings and tailplane after handling problems). Nosewheel failed to lower, landed at Wisley with nose wheel retracted, nose probe bent, slight damage to external skins 20.8.56 (MJ Lithgow). At SBAC Show Farnborough 4-7.9.56. A&AEE Boscombe Down 17.10.56 (trials of mods). VA [Wisley?] 27.10.56. Intended to carry out tests, d/d 26.11.56 ((a) - test with a special nose incorporating a dummy flight refuelling probe. (b) - preliminary fuel jettison tests using water). Fence variations, nose portions only, tests with one pylon, Wisley 1.1.57. Valiant as tanker on flight refuelling refuelling tests as drogue differed from one to be used, flight refuelling Canberra to be available, d/d 2.1.57. Flown 116hrs 20min by 23.1.57. Dummy nose offered up unsuccessfully, nose to Eastleigh for modification, d/d 5.2.57. Nose offered up at Wisley, now OK, returned to Eastleigh for completion 12.2.57. Measured take-offs by MJ Lithgow 11.3.57. ADDLs on 21.3.57, 24.3.57, 2.4.57 and 4.4.57 totalling 2hrs 5min. Embarked *Ark Royal* 5.4.57 (9th and 10th deck landings - RA.28 engines, dorsal ventilation intakes). Flown on autostabiliser tests 11.4.57. Reported lateral rocking with the latest aileron configuration appeared to be more satisfactory, d/d 24.4.57. A&AEE temp, on firm's charge 26.4.57 [until when?]. Reported unstable oscillations at high speed, initial trials with flight refuelling nose satisfactory, d/d 6.5.57. Instrument tests on fuel jettisoning deferred pending MoS reconsideration of need for it, d/d 15.5.57. Flow successfully behind another Scimitar up to 550K IAS 16.5.57. Modified jet exit fairings being fitted 6.6.57. A&AEE 23.8.57. VA Wisley 17.9.57. Nose probe to be fitted to XD218, d/d 1.4.58. Engines inhibited and disposal instructions awaited 21.5.58. Reported unsuitable for ETPS 22.7.58. RAE Bedford 8.12.58 (general naval development work, not including flying, associated with B.S.4 catapult, Mk.13 arrester gear, jet blast, deflector bridle catching, possibly to be tested to destruction). Blackburn, Holme-on-Spalding Moor 28.10.59 (arrester gear trials - water squeezey). NAD/RAE Bedford 16.12.59 (General development work associated with BS4 catapult, Mk.13 arrester gear, jet blast deflectors, bridal catching, possibly to destruction, also from 8.1.60 continue barrier trials). Allocated to Class II GI at AES Arbroath 25.10.60. Allocation cancelled. Released by NAD/RAE Bedford 10.8.64. SOC 6.11.64. Transported to SAH Culdrose. Removed to P&EE Shoeburyness 1967.

WT859 Constructed at Experimental Dept, Hursley Park. To Boscombe Down by road, FF 26.6.56 by MJ Lithgow. Returned VA Wisley [when?]. A&AEE 28.8.56. VA Wisley 30.8.56. Converted to Avon 20201 with flap blowing, at Wisley 8.10.56, continued at Hursley Park by 10.12.56. Transported by road to A&AEE for re-assembly and test flights 27.12.56. Break away of port engine jet efflux fairing 3m S of Selsey Bill, damaged arrester, Cat HC 17.6.57 (Mr DW Morgan). Burst hydraulic pipes, brakes inoperative, landed safely Boscombe Down, Cat LC 13.7.57 (Mr JWR Judge). A&AEE 21.3.58 (C(A) release trials). VA Wisley 23.5.58 (C(A) release trials under Cont No KC/A/01/CB.5(a)). A&AEE 9.6.58 (temp for roll/yaw handling trials for C(A) release). RAE Bedford on permanent C(A) charge 23.7.58 (general catapult and arrester gear development - non-flying, may be tested to destruction). Allotted RNAY Fleetlands on C(A) charge for instructional purposes 25.7.60. SAH Culdrose via Vickers, arr 29.10.60. WOC 29.11.60 as GI *A2499*. In Air Command Driving School, Culdrose by 1971 until to P&EE Shoeburyness 25.11.71 and 1.12.71. Used for trials 3.83. Derelict by 3.88. Fuselage and rear end to Mayer and Perry scrapyard, Snailwell, Cambs 4.91 and scrapped. Nose section to The Vampire Collection, Ruislip 25.4.91, passing on loan to Brooklands Museum 18.7.91 and extant.

**1 Supermarine Scimitar prototype ordered 12.6.51 under Cont No 6/Acft/6579/CB.7(b) to Spec N.113D and numbered WW134. (Two Avon RA.24)**

WW134 Constructed at Experimental Dept, Hursley Park. To Boscombe Down by road, FF 10.10.56 (MJ Lithgow) and retd Wisley for handling trials (fitted with flap blowing, in operation during flight). A&AEE 24.10.56. VA Wisley 2.11.56. RAE Bedford 26.11.56. VA Wisley 12.56. A&AEE 10.12.56 (catapult take-off trials). ADDLs 18.12.56. Proving trials *Ark Royal* 2.1.57 (carrier trials). VA Wisley 7.1.57. ADDLs 1.2.57. VA South Marston 7.2.57 (further development work and C(A) release under Cont No 6/Acft/14390/CB.5(a)). VA Wisley by 6.57. Naval Sqn A&AEE 2.7.57 (handling trials for C(A) release). DL trials on *Ark Royal* 15.7.57. Measured take-offs and landings at Boscombe Down, port brake overheated, resulting in wheel fire at 33,000lbs, Cat LX 7.8.57 (L/C DJ Whitehead). Handling under intensive flying conditions, loud explosion, sheet flame from port engine on opening up for take-off at Boscombe Down, compressor failure, Cat HX 19.8.57 (L/C DJ Whitehead). Aircraft grounded for repairs. VA South Marston 17.9.57 (further C(A) release trials). 'C' Sqn Boscombe Down, tail skid hooked into a runway light on arrival, Cat LX 10.4.58 (Cdr PCS Chilton). Authority for drop-in at RAE Bedford for OE measurements 4.7.58. VA Wisley, bird strike, panels of windscreen broken over Bedford airfield, engine damaged 9.7.58 (MJ Lithgow). RAE Bedford 22.9.58. A&AEE 4.2.59 (spinning trials). VA South Marston 5.5.59 (LR Colquhoun) (de-instrumentation prior to disposal against Cont No KC/A/044/CB.5(a)). Also determination of runway characteristics under Cont No KC/A/075/CB.5(a) 28.7.59). VA Wisley 9.10.59 (rough runway trials in connection with TSR-2 contract). VA South Marston/Weybridge 14.10.60 (landings at varying vertical velocities, angles of bank and rates of drift, also drag parachute landing). VA Wisley to VA South Marston 15.3.62 (preparation for Anglo-French underwater sink-rate trials under Cont KC/2/015/CB.5(a). To Trials Officer MoA, St.Mandrier, Toulon, France 17.6.62 (Anglo-French underwater sink rate trials). Engines removed and catapulted off *Centaur* in Mediterranean as part of trials, but failed to give expected results (now on sea bed 24.10.62). SOC 2.11.62.

**100 Supermarine Scimitar F.1 production ordered in 1956 under Cont No 6/Acft/8812/CB.5(b) Vickers-Armstrong, South Marston and numbered XD212 to XD250, XD264 to XD282 and XD316 to XD357. Only 76 built, Cancelled from XD334. (2 Rolls-Royce Avon 202)**

XD212 FF VA South Marston 11.1.57 (MJ Lithgow). Retained by VA South Marston. To VA Wisley on C(A) charge for C(A) release 17.4.57. Returned VA South Marston by 15.5.57.

Loaned Mkrs for participation in Paris Air Show 31.5.57 - 3.6.57. Flown VA South Marston – VA Wisley 5.6.57 (LR Colquhoun). Flight refuelling trials as receiver from 9.10.57. Take-off abandoned when pilot experienced no response to longitudinal control, control column locked up at point of lift-off, engines cut but brakes burnt out before end of runway, aircraft overran, crossed airfield boundary road, entered field, hit lighting pole, nose wheel torn off, mainplane leading edge damaged, Wisley, Cat 4 14.10.57 (L/C HJD Abraham) *[Partial seizure of the tailplane control had occurred due to the ingestion of FOD in the hydraulic system, caused by disintegrating filters, which caused excessive wear in the tailplane hydro booster valve].* To RN charge at VA 4.6.58. Free loan for flight refuelling trials, to be used as a receiver 30.6.59 (continued until 31.3.61). VA Wisley on MoS charge 8.10.59. Probe nozzle broke off during flight refuelling test flight 11.11.59. RAE Bedford 7.4.60 (MJ Lithgow) (mod - production pylons under catapulting and arresting loads). VA Wisley c.19.4.60. A&AEE Boscombe Down 13.5.60 (MJ Lithgow) (flight refuelling pod ground trials in blower tunnel). VA Wisley 16.5.60 (MJ Lithgow). Port flap and aileron struck treetop on landing, flap trailing edge slightly bent, Boscombe Down 1.6.60. ROS, still at A&AEE 10.6.60. Flight refuelling hose failure, drogue left impaled on probe, fuel over windscreen 17.6.60 (MJ Lithgow). Flight refuelling hose severed, drogue broke away and dropped near Lewes, Sussex, 21.7.60 (MJ Lithgow). VA Wisley to VA South Marston 12.8.60. VA Wisley 31.8.60. Flight refuelling exercise with XD227, hose severed causing slight damaged to rudder and tailplane 27.9.60. VA South Marston to VA Wisley 10.11.60 (LR Colquhoun). A&AEE 22.11.60 (DW Morgan). VA South Marston 23.2.61 (trials of streamlined flight refuelling probe under Cont No 6/Acft/13619/CB.5(a). Removal of instrumentation prior to return to RN authorised 30.3.61. Flight refuelling trials as receiver VA 4.61. AHU Lossiemouth on RN charge 12.5.61. 736 Sqn Lossiemouth ('614') 5.7.61. Bird strike starboard leading edge after low-level sortie 400ft, Cat LQ 14.9.61 (Lt PC Marshall). Spun in from low height while orbiting contact point army co-operation exercise, crashed in field Raich Hill, nr Forgie, 6m ENE of Huntly, Aberdeenshire, Cat ZZ 20.9.61 (Lt TMH Laister killed). [170.20hrs by 5.7.61]

*XD212 '614' of No.736 Squadron Lossiemouth with everything down in 1959. (MAP)*

XD213　Retained VA Wisley 21.5.57 (trials for C(A) release). Le Bourget for Paris Show 31.5.57 and demonstrated there by MJ Lithgow 1 & 2.6.57. VA Wisley 3.6.57 (detd A&AEE for 3-4 days, authorised 21.6.57). Farnborough Show 9.57. 'C' Sqn A&AEE Boscombe Down 25.4.58 (C(A) release trials - gun firing). Slight mishap due to wrong labelling of pitot lnes 12.8.58. RAE Bedford 21.11.58 (trials to assess suitability of Scimitar launching bridle retaining device). VA South Marston 16.2.59 (TI of ammunition tank and feed chute, also mod of canopy jettison and seat ejection systems). A&AEE 22.4.59 (butt firing tests). VA South Marston 28.10.59 (to RN charge for conversion and modernisation under Cont No KG/G/017/CB.24 (b) to post-31st aircraft production standard). To Lee-on-Solent 6.4.61 and cocooned by MARTSU. Shipped to Far East (via RNAY Fleetlands). Arr AHU Tengah 17.5.61. 803 Sqn ('152/V') 30.6.61. Starboard engine malfunction on start-up *Victorious*, Cat SS 23.2.62 (L/C TCS Leece). RNAY Fleetlands 30.3.62. Towed to Lee-on-Solent by 17.4.62 and departed to 803 Sqn ('152/H') 24.4.62. *Hermes*, probe damaged whilst flight refuelling off Malta, Cat LX 27.6.62 (S/L CA Bosworth). Large bird strike at 3,000ft over SW Crete, landed safely *Hermes*, Cat LQ 14.7.62 (Lt NM Tristram). Drop tank burst during pressure refuelling *Hermes*, Cat SS 27.9.62. Bird strike on low level Navex, Cat LQ 3.1.63 (S/L CA Bosworth). Hydraulic 1 failure after take-off from *Hermes*, port leg failed to lower on approach to Yeovilton, and aircraft was overweight for a safe landing, unable to steer aircraft out to sea, pilot ejected safely, aircraft crashed in field nr East Chaldon, nr Weymouth, Dorset, Cat ZZ 20.9.63 (S/L AJ Middleton landed safely among herd of cows - Ejection No.740). Wreckage to AIU Lee-on-Solent, then to RNAY Fleetlands by 19.12.63 to at least 17.9.64. [483.25hrs]

XD214　FF 31.5.57 VA South Marston. VA Wisley to VA South Marston 13.6.57. To VA Wisley and TOC RN 20.7.57 (LR Colquhoun). To C(A) charge at VA Wisley 29.7.57 (trials for C(A) release) (LR Colquhoun). A&AEE by 9.57. VA Wisley by 4.58. Naval Test Sqn A&AEE Boscombe Down 9.6.58 (preparation and checks for tropical trials). Hot weather trials at Bahrein 7.58 [also El Adem?]. A&AEE 8.9.58. VA Wisley 24.9.58 (flight trials of anti-icing system, also flight trials and ground tests of air conditioning system if necessary, Cont No KC/A/043/CB.15(a)). VA South Marston 24.7.59. Ex C(A) to RN charge for conv to post-31st aircraft production standard 29.10.59. AHU Lossiemouth 1.12.60 (urgent ferry flight by Fleetlands MTP L/C AR Campbell). 803 Sqn ('151/V') 16.12.60. While parked, hit by Sea Vixen XJ586 making night landing *Victorious*, Cat HY 25.1.61. RNAY Fleetlands 26.1.61. Towed to Lee-on-Solent 8.2.61. VA South Marston 11.2.61. AHU Lossiemouth 7.11.61. MoA Air Fleet at VA South Marston 8.1.62 (free loan for TI of LABS recording facility under Cont No KC/2/017/CB.5(a). loan extended 26.1.62 for embodiment of photographic marking facility against KC/A/018/CB.5(a). Released 6.3.62). AHU Lossiemouth 30.3.62 (mods). 803 Sqn ('146/V') 17.4.62. MoA Air Fleet at VA South Marston 30.5.62 (TI of Bullpup marking facility and tone transmission of ejection, Cont Nos KC/A/0145 and KC/2/030/CB.5(a)). Stn Flt Lossiemouth 20.7.62. 803 Sqn (via Culdrose) ('146/H') 8.8.62. False fire warning, diverted to St.Mawgan, Cat SS 18.11.62 (S/L CA Bosworth). Bird strike, normal landing *Hermes*, Cat LQ 28.12.62 (S/L MJ Harwood). On *Hermes*, port throttle jammed in RP attack, Cat SW 22.1.63 (L/C NJP Mills). Slippery deck, nose wheel fairing damaged when ship rolled, *Hermes*, Cat LQ 3.8.63. Starboard hood rail partially detached at start of climb, *Hermes*, Cat LQ 25.1.64 (Lt AMD de Labilliere). Took off from *Hermes*, fuel transfer problem, diverted to Yeovilton, Cat SS 7.2.64 (Lt R Wren). Undercarriage failed to lock down, used emergency system, landed Boscombe Down, Cat LQ 22.5.64 (S/L PJ McManus). Bird strike at 900ft, Cat LC 17.6.64 (L/C GAI Johnston). Flaps failed in night landing, emergency selection made, Lossiemouth, Cat LQ 9.11.64 (L/C JOF Billingham). Hydraulic leak while taxying, Cat LQ 16.11.64 (Lt NE Rankin). Fuel system malfunction, landed safely, Cat LQ 26.11.64 (S/L KB Owen). Code change 12.64 ('146/R'). To Lee-on-Solent 12.1.65 (now coded '-/R') and towed to RNAY Fleetlands (modernisation). Towed back to Lee-on-Solent 25.3.66. NASU Brawdy 21.6.66 (Lt Cdr J Brandt). Airwork FRU Hurn 17.10.66. Coded by 10.67 ('030'), recoded 12.68 and applied 3.69 ('830'). Nose wheel collapsed landing Yeovilton, Cat HY 28.5.69 (Mr RC Minton). To MARTSU Lee-on-Solent 17 or 19.6.69. SOC 23.6.69. RSP 1.7.69. Still at Lee-on-Solent 26.7.69. Removed to RNAY Fleetlands late 1969. Still on Fleetlands dump 13.6.70. [909.45hrs]

XD215 FF c 6.57 VA South Marston. To C(A) loan at VA South Marston and to Boscombe Down 10.7.57 (LR Colquhoun) (trials for C(A) release against Cont No 6/Acft/14390/CB.5(a)). 'C' Sqn A&AEE 10.7.57 (acceptance trials and Bullpup missile trials). DL trials on *Ark Royal* 15.7.57. VA South Marston 26.7.57 (continue trials for C(A) release). VA Wisley 30.9.57. Catapult programme 12-18.2.58. RAE Bedford 23.2.59 (catapult launches/deck gear trials with dart target towing mod until 9.7.59). A&AEE 27.2.59 (snatching trials). VA Wisley 28.4.59 (daily visit to A&AEE as necessary). VA South Marston - VA Wisley 15.5.59 (DW Morgan). NAD/RAE Bedford 26.6.59 (part evaluation of specialities). A&AEE 29.6.59 (continue part evaluation of specialities). VA Wisley 13.7.59. VA South Marston 28.10.59 [12.8.59?] (instrumentation removed, converted and modernised to post 31st aircraft production standard). Tested at South Marston 21.1.61. 803 Sqn ('150/V') 1.2.61. Port compressor blades found damaged *Victorious*, Cat LY 9.11.61. Brake failure landing, engaged airfield arrester wire Yeovilton, Cat LQ 15.3.62 (L/C CS Casperd). Code change 4.62 ('150/H'). Drifted to port, engaged No.3 wire, port and nosewheel in catwalk, Cat HY 24.7.62 (S/L CARP Wells). Shipped to Portsmouth 2.10.62. Lightered to RNAY Fleetlands for MARTSU and to VA South Marston 8.11.62. 800 Sqn ('108/R') 5.5.63. Bird strike on port engine 11.6.63. AHU Lossiemouth 5.2.64. 736 Sqn Lossiemouth ('611') 23.6.64. Bird strike at 400ft, Cat LQ 29.7.64 (Lt IPF Meiklejohn). Ricochet debris damage on Tain range, Cat LQ 30.9.64 (L/C PP Cardew). Fuel pump problem, landed safely, Cat SS 12.10.64 (Lt NE Rankin). Hydraulic problem landing, emergency selection, touched down safely, Cat LQ 23.10.64 (L/C PP Cardew). Bird strike on radome, West Freugh, Cat LQ 28.10.64 (Lt BP Marindin). Defective undercarriage warning light, normal landing, Cat LQ 4.11.64 (L/C J Worth). Hydraulic failure, emergency landing, Cat LQ 16.2.65 (L/C JWH Purvis). Access panel lost in flight, Cat LQ 22.3.65 (S/L GM Faulkner). 764B Sqn ('614') 29.3.65. UHF failure, landed safely, Cat LQ 20.5.65 (Lt RF Shercliff). False undercarriage warning light, landed safely, Cat LQ 21.5.65 (Lt MJ Williams). Faulty compass, Cat LQ 27.5.65 (Lt PJ Trudgett). Starboard engine light warning after take-off, single-engined landing, Cat SS 7.7.65 (Lt RF Shercliff). Lee-on-Solent 27.1.66 (last flight). RNAY Fleetlands 28.1.66. To *Hermes* 21.5.66 (deck handling training aboard after refit). Lee-on-Solent LTS by MARTSU 31.7.66 (open storage). Dismantled at Lee-on-Solent 2.10.67 and by road to SAH Culdrose 6-9.10.67 as GI Class II *A2573* (engine Nos *E4584/4585*). Code 'SAH-18' allocated but not applied 29.11.67 (used by Culdrose Fire Section but not burnt). To P&EE Shoeburyness 25.11.71 and 1.12.71 (gunfire assessment 7.72 to 8.77). Cockpit canopy to RAE Farnborough 24.5.78. Became part of Lot 5 in MoD surplus sale at Shoeburyness. Rear fuselage to Mayer & Perry yard, Snailwell, Cambs and scrapped 22-26.4.91 along with other Scimitar remnants. Cockpit section bought by Barry Parkhouse/Parkhouse Aviation, Ottershaw, Surrey 25.4.91. Bought by Nick Parker, Cheltenham for restoration 19.2.94. Extant. [796.05hrs]

XD216 Production test VA South Marston 25.5.57 (LR Colquhoun). To C(A) charge at VA Wisley 27.5.57 (trials for C(A) release). A&AEE 13.6.57 (preliminary handling trials). VA Wisley 16.6.57. A&AEE 12.8.57 (trials for C(A) release). VA Wisley 5.9.57 (trials for C(A) release; later flight refuelling trials as receiver, Bullpup missiles, dummy TMB, two 200 plus two 150-gallon drop tanks and four 1,000-lb bombs; performance measurement). Extended pitot head fitted c1.4.58. A&AEE 15.4.58 (authorised to complete preview of handling with inboard drop tanks). VA Wisley 28.4.58. RAE Farnborough to VA Wisley 18.8.58. 4-store programme by 10.9.58. Tail cone became disengaged during flight causing loss of cone and anti-spin parachute whilst over Lasham 22.10.58. Bird strike with seagull, Cat 1 9.1.59. VA South Marston by 14.1.59 (repair). A&AEE 27.1.59 (store handling preview). VA Wisley 26.2.59. Air test after long sojourn in hangar 8.5.59 (MJ Lithgow). A&AEE 1.7.59 (measurement of pilot error) (DW Morgan). RAE Farnborough 28.8.59 (weapons test). Improved-view nose fitted 10.9.59. VA Wisley to NAD Bedford 23.9.59 (proofing of prototype redesigned pylons prior to carrier trials, also check of revised audio pattern for specialities equipment). A&AEE 30.9.59 (for carrier trials). To *Victorious* in English Channel 13.10.59 (4–stores and specialities/Ferranti altitude indicator). A&AEE 19.10.59. VA Wisley 22.10.59 (re-instrumentation for continuation of flight trials - final measurement of performance, pilot errors and flight resonance and subsequent instrumentation for spinning trials, Cont No KC/A/044/CB.5(a)). A&AEE 27.11.59 (check measurement of performance and pilot error). VA Wisley. A&AEE 30.12.59 (DW Morgan). Spinning trials with large tailplane 18.2-7.3.60. A&AEE Boscombe Down 24.3.60 (handling assessment of four 200-gallon drop tanks configuration). During proofing trials with Mod 5072 pylons and all external stores, pitch- up followed by spin, shedding drop tanks, both outboard and one inboard pylon torn off, pitot head strut torn off, underside of mainplanes holed, four small craters and kerosene damage to crops Dorchester, Cat SS 31.3.60 (Lt PJ Barber). Mkrs South Marston 5.4.60 [or accident 5.4.60 and to VASM 13.4.60?] (repair damage, maincheck 5, embodiment of static vents for investigation of altimeter errors, to Cont Nos KC/2/010/CB.5(a) and KC/A/77/CB.5(a)). To permanent C(A) charge on repayment terms 14.6.60. Remained VA South Marston 14.10.60 - 8.61 (engine relight trials against Cont No KC/A/098/CB.5(a) and flight handling Bullpup and Sidewinder on Cont No KC/A/091/CB.5(a)). Air-test post repair 14.11.60 (LR Colquhoun). Bullpup and Sidewinder trials from 17.11.60. Top forward and rear sections of tail parachute canister lost in flight 3.2.61. Add pressure error trials against Cont No KC/A/077/CB.5(a) 25.4.61. Task amended to pressure error trials, TI of tone transmission in ejection and LABS work against Cont No KC/A/077/CB.5(a) 9.10.61. NAD/RAE Bedford [when from?] until 20.12.61. VA South Marston 7.5.62 (preparation for ETPS on Cont No KK/G/0389/CB.24(b)). ETPS Farnborough ('22') 28.6.63 (student training, also lift boundary investigation). Turning test at 30,000ft, during spin complete electrical failure initiated by operation of crash inertia switches in violent manoeuvre, pilot recovered at 14,000ft, but starboard engine then port engine surged and flamed out, pilot ejected over coast at 1,500ft and 200knots but remained attached to seat by leg restraint cords, aircraft crashed in sea ½m off West Wittering, Sussex, Cat ZZ 16.7.64 (F/Lt BL Gartner RCAF waded ashore - Ejection No.871). Wreck salvaged. Fuselage and fin remains noted in Sale Pound at RNAY Fleetlands 7.67. SOC 19.10.67 [19.10.64 per MoD(PE) card]

*NOTE. In the book 'Learn to Test: Test to Learn', Flt Lt David Bywater gives a good description of what happened: "One of the exercises for which the Scimitar was used was to investigate lift boundaries, for this aircraft had a very distinctive buffet followed by pitch-up, followed by a wing drop. On 16 July [1964] I got the first exercise on it and I hit this particular phenomenon at about 1.3 Mach, pulling through the buffet and the aircraft did something quite extraordinary at about 30,000ft and I sort of blacked out at the time. When I came to at about 23,000ft the manoeuvre had been completed and that was that. I tried to diagnose what had happened whilst the second student, RCAF Flt Lt Barry Gartner, took off for the South Coast to complete the same exercise. He had the same sort of problem but in his case, when he came to, the aircraft seemed to be semi-closed down electrically. In fact we later found out that what had happened was that the 'g' reversal from quite a large positive 'g' in the pitch up to quite a large negative 'g' and then back around 1 'g' in the wing drop had actually thrown the crash switches and he was left with little or no electrics, engines in a stall condition because he had no booster pumps, and so on. Eventually he ejected at low level just off West Wittering but, having strapped in incorrectly, his leg restraint held him to the seat and he went into five feet of water, just four hundred yards offshore. By taking a deep breath and bending down he undid himself from the seat and waded ashore to cheers from the holiday-makers. That was the end of the Scimitar.*

XD217   FF 19.5.57, Retained for manufacturer's test flying and trials work. To C(A) charge at VA South Marston 16.8.57 (trials for C(A) release). VA Wisley to 'C' Sqn A&AEE Boscombe Down 20.9.57. Assessment by US Navy test pilots until 27.9.57, supersonic investigation, handling at high Mach numbers, climbed to 45,000ft, following two supersonic dives, abrupt thump heard and large yaw felt, at 600 knots at 4,000ft, precautionary landing, slight damage to fin and rudder, Cat LQ 18.9.57 (Capt M Debencourt USMC) *[found that fin had failed due to flutter induced by loss of aerodynamic damping]*. VA Wisley 4.10.57 (continuation of C(A) release trials against Cont No 6/Acft/14390/CB.5(a)). 'C' Sqn A&AEE 23.12.57 (continuation of C(A) release trials). Violent airframe vibration, exceeded 0.90 IMN below 10,000ft, rudder etc damaged, Cat LX 21.5.58 (L/C DF Robbins). VA Wisley 8.7.58. VA South Marston 24.4.59 (MJ Lithgow). Air test and to A&AEE 10.5.59 (LR Colquhoun) (evaluation of UHF against Cont No 6/Acft/14079/CB.5(a)). VA South Marston 25.6.59 (Maincheck 3. Later TI of *Violet Picture* against Cont No KC/A/073/CB.5(a) authorised 17.8.59. Fin flutter tests (27.8.59) and measurement of misc flight temperatures against Cont No KC/A/057/CB.5(a)) (authorised 5.1.60). VA Wisley 21.12.59. A&AEE 18.3.60 (evaluation of *Violet Picture* UHF homer, also final evaluation of radio altimeter Mk.5). Main and nose wheels reported down, port wheel light remained red, Cat SS 4.4.60 (Lt PJ Barber). VA South Marston 31.5.60 (removal of instrumentation against Cont No KC/2/014/CB.5(a), also modernisation and refurbishment to operational standard on Cont No KK.G/017/CB.245(c)). Delivered AHU Lossiemouth 28.2.62 (STS). 736 Sqn Lossiemouth ('616') 2.3.62. Fuel vapour in cockpit, precautionary landing, Cat LQ 23.7.62 (Lt JJR Tod). Port undercarriage problem, retd base, Cat LQ 20.8.62 (S/L JM Heath). Large fuel leak after landing, tank ruptured, Cat LQ 2.10.62 (Lt IPF Meiklejohn). Bird strike on pull-out from dive bombing attack Rosehearty Range, Cat LX 12.7.63 (F/Lt RN Davidson). Bird entered starboard intake on take-off, sortie terminated, Cat HY 11.5.64 (Lt LA Wilkinson). Oxygen hose problem at 20,000ft, landed safely, Cat SS 27.7.64 (Lt NE Rankin). Faulty switch, RP fell in sea off Tain Range, Cat SS 18.3.65 (L/C JWH Purvis). 764B Sqn Lossiemouth('616') 29.3.65. Hydraulic failure on MADDLs touch-down, stayed down, Cat LQ 30.3.65 (Lt DW Moore). Fuel control problem during night descent, landed safely, Cat SS 13.5.65 (S/L AC Hill). Undercarriage warning light malfunction, Cat LQ 24.5.65 (Lt PJ Trudgett). To Lee-on-Solent 1.6.65 and to RNAY Fleetlands 2.6.65 (overhaul). Towed to Lee-on-Solent 20.3.67 and departed 16.6.67. 'C' Sqn Boscombe Down 19.6.67 (flight trials of carrier bomb triple ejector (TER). Later airborne photographic trial of FGS Mk.7 (low level) camera in connection with clearance of installation in Harrier, Phantom and F.111K (in place of crashed Javelin FAW.9 XH891), concurrently with TER trials, authorised 11.12.67. Also trials of 50-gallon tank from TER and added commitments = 1,000-lb, 1,000-lb retracted bomb, twin suspension Lepus flare). NASU Brawdy 27.3.68 (LTS). ADW 13.5.59. SOC and RSP 4.9.69. [787.40hrs]

XD218   FF c 5.57 VA South Marston. To C(A) charge at VA Wisley 28.6.57. SBAC Show Farnborough 1.9.57. VA Wisley 9.9.57. From permanent to temp C(A) charge in exchange for XD229 at RAE Bedford 28.10.58 (catapult trials). VA Wisley 31.10.58. 'C' Sqn A&AEE by 5.59 (deck landing, dummy TMB, two 200 plus two 150 gallon drop tanks and four 1,000-lb bomb trials). RAE West Freugh 2.6.59 (authority given to land at West Freugh on a daily basis as and when needed 1-20.6.59 and 9-22.7.59) (DW Morgan). VA Wisley 2.6.59. RAE West Freugh 18.6.59 (DW Morgan). VA Wisley 19.6.59 (DW Morgan). To/from West Freugh 30.6.59 and 3.7.59 (DW Morgan). Air test after Main Check 3 12.10.59 (MJ Lithgow). Authorised 11.1.60 to visit A&AEE for 2 days on drop-in basis for purpose of position error (also authorised 25.4.60 for further 1 month when necessary). VA Wisley to A&AEE and return 29.1.60. Purchased on repayment terms 29.3.60. Air test from VA South Marston 22.4.60 (LR Colquhoun). VA Wisley 25.4.60 (MJ Lithgow). Authorised 23.5.60 to transfer to RAE West Freugh for approx 3 months armament trials. To permanent C(A) charge 14.6.60. To permanent C(A) charge on repayment terms 1.7.60. RAE Bedford [no date]. Authorised to RAE West Freugh from 14 days wef approx 1.11.60 (trials of 2,000-lb MC bomb). Authorised to RAE Bedford on drop-in basis for approx 4 days wef 30.11.60 (catapulting clearance of TMB vibration store), also 1 more day 8.12.60. Authorised to West Freugh for approx 1 week wef 13.2.61 (25lb practice bomb ballistic trials on Cont No KC/A/0109/CB.5(a)), extended for further week wef 20.2.61. Authorised temp transfer to RAE Farnborough and/or West Freugh as and when needed during 6 month period from 10.7.61 (general armament and development clearance trials on same contract). RAE Farnborough 5.8.61 [8.8.61?] (EB Trubshaw). RAE West Freugh 1.12.61. VA Wisley 27.12.61 (MJ Lithgow). Temp RAE West Freugh 15-31.1.62 (armament trials on Cont No KC/A/0130/CB.5(a)). RAE Farnborough to VA Wisley 6.2.62. Temp RAE Farnborough 12-15.2.62 (DW Morgan). Temp RAE West Freugh 19.2.62 - 16.3.62 and 9-16.4.62. VA South Marston to Hyères 19.6.62. C(A) Wisley by 12.7.62 (air test after Main Check that day - MJ Lithgow). Temp to RAE Farnborough 17.8.62 (MJ Lithgow). RAE Farnborough 11.9.62. VA Wisley 13.9.62. Temp RAE West Freugh 18.9.62 - 26.10.62 (armament trials, still on same contract) (DW Morgan). VA, temp transfer to RAE Farnborough or West Freugh on drop-in basis during period 5-21.12.62 (armament). RAE Farnborough to VA Wisley 21.12.62. RAE Farnborough 1.1.63. VA 18.1.63. RAE Farnborough 11.2.63 [15.2.63?]. Fire warning light in starboard engine, force landed Tangmere 18.2.63 (DW Morgan). [VA to RAE Farnborough 11.3.63??]. RAE West Freugh 22.4.63. VA 17.5.63. RAE Farnborough or West Freugh 20.5.63 (armament trials, same contract). VA 11.8.63. RAE Farnborough or West Freugh 19.8.63 (armament trials). [Reported at Wisley 9.63]. VA South Marston 25.10.63 [temp transfer on drop-in basis RAE Farnborough or West Freugh 1.1.64 - 1.7.64]. Undershot runway on landing, minor damage 30.4.64. VA South Marston to Weapons Flight RAE Farnborough 26.11.64 (general armament development trials). To RAE West Freugh, bird strike on port engine, Cat LX 3.2.65 (Capt WR Pogue USAF). To be retd to RN charge from permanent MoA charge in exchange for XD228 18.11.66. Damaged during refuelling, Cat 5 early 1967. RNAY Fleetlands by road, arr 20/21.4.67 (LTS). Allocated scrap 20.7.67. SOC 6.9.67 and BU 25.10.67. [453.30hrs]

XD219   Production test VA South Marston 15.8.57 (LR Colquhoun). To C(A) charge at VA South Marston 16.8.57 (trials for C(A) release). A&AEE Boscombe Down 17.8.57 (LR Colquhoun) (trials for C(A) release). Roaded to VA Hursley Park 22.8.57 (continuation of C(A) release trials against Cont No 6/Acft/14390/CB.5(a) included firing trials of Aden cannon installation, 20,033 rounds being fired up to 3.2.58).

A&AEE 4.12.57 (gunnery trials). VA Wisley 24.2.58 (continuation of C(A) release trials on Cont No KC/A/01/CB.5(a)). RAE Bedford 23.6.58 (C(A) release - arrester gear/catapult trials). VA Wisley 21.8.58 (Lt Cdr PI Normand - preparation for ground engine strain gauge test and for and flight trials of TI *Blue Silk* on Cont No 6/Acft/14439/CB.5(a)) (Strain gauge work carried out by Rolls-Royce team on one engine at South Marston early 1959). A&AEE 28.4.59 (*Blue Silk* trials) (WD Jarvis). VA South Marston 22.7.59 (LR Colquhoun) (TI and flight trials of night fighter sight against Con No KC/A/068/CB.5(a) and TI and flight trials of roller maps on KC/A/067/CB.5(a)). A&AEE 26.11.59 (assessment of improved vision night fighter sight and *Spector* camera recorder). Canopy came off shortly after take-off while accelerating to climbing speed, landed safely, Cat LQ 7.7.60 (Lt DF Fieldhouse). VA Wisley 28.7.60. VA South Marston 5.8.60 (brought up to production standard, instrumentation removed against Cont No KC/2/014/CB.5(a)). AHU Lossiemouth 24.5.62. 736 Sqn Lossiemouth ('617') 28.6.62. Severe slipstream on 10G turn, Cat LQ 24.9.62 (S/L JM Heath). Undercarriage indicator malfunction, Cat SS 18.12.62 (Mid NHL Bowden). Starboard oleo warning light malfunction landing, Cat SS 9.9.63 (Lt AMD de Labilliere). Starboard oleo warning light malfunction, Cat SS 19.9.63 (Lt PEH Banfield). Hydraulic failure, landed safely, Cat LQ 31.7.64 (Lt NE Rankin). Flap malfunction at 20,000ft, landed safely, Cat LQ 27.1.65 (S/L GM Faulkner). False instrument readings in RP dives, Cat LQ 12.3.65 (Lt AS Tuck). Cat SS 18.3.65. RP fired in dispersal, faulty switch, 764B Sqn Lossiemouth ('617') 29.3.65. To Lee-on-Solent and roaded to RNAY Fleetlands 17.5.65. Roaded to Lee-on-Solent 15.12.66, departed 27.2.67. Airwork FRU Hurn 2.3.67 (found to be in incorrect mod state for use with FRU). MTPS Brawdy 6.3.67. Stn Flt Lossiemouth for static display 9.9.67. Stn Flt Brawdy 11.9.67. NASU Brawdy 9.1.68. RAE West Freugh 16.2.68. Stn Flt Brawdy 24.5.68. To permanent Ministry of Technology charge at RAE Farnborough 7.11.68 and flown Brawdy-Farnborough 16.12.68 (Lt Cdr PM Stevenson). Wings cropped for wet runway braking/aquaplaning trials with Western Squadron by 3.71. Ran off runway during a high speed run and wrecked 9.1.73. Fuselage (with broken back) and engines to P&EE Shoeburyness 21.7.75. Trials 7.84 to 1.86. Fuselage less rear section to Yeovilton fire dump by road for CRT practice 1.11.90. Scrapped 15.3.94. Tail section was part of Lot 5 of MoD sale at Shoeburyness by 4.12.90. Scrapped c.4.91.

XD220 Force landed at Boscombe Down with ASI and hydraulic trouble on test flight 12.8.57 (LR Colquhoun). Boscombe Down to VA South Marston 13.8.57 (LR Colquhoun). Delivered 700X Flt Ford ('800/FD') 11.10.57 (Mr DW Morgan). Engine fire while attempting to relight port engine, fire extinguisher worked perfectly, landed safely, Cat SS 13.12.57 (Lt TFB Young). High tailplane column forces experienced, Cat SS 6.3.58 (Cdr TG Innes). To 700 Sqn Ford ('511/FD') 5.58 (deck trials on *Victorious* in English Channel 1958). 700 Sqn Yeovilton (511/VL') 17.9.58. RNAY Fleetlands 20.2.59. Towed to Lee-on-Solent flight test 31.1.62 and departed 13.2.62. 736 Sqn Lossiemouth ('618') 15.2.62. Port engine warning light on at top of dive Tain Range, retd base, Cat SS 7.3.62. Hydraulic failure while strafing Tain Range, landed safely, Cat LQ 16.3.62 (both Mid JS Flexman). Bird strike on low level sortie, Cat LQ 9.4.62 (Lt AHS Anderson). Hydraulic failure, landed safely, Cat SS 16.10.62 (Lt RW Edward). Hydraulic failure, emergency landing, Cat LQ 13.5.63 (F/Lt RN Davidson). Undercarriage problem landing, Cat LQ 20.5.63 (F/Lt RN Davidson RAF). Nosewheel collapsed on start-up, Cat LQ 20.6.63 (S/L RM Cockburn). Hydraulic failure, precautionary landing, Cat SS 27.11.63 (F/Lt RN Davidson RAF). R/T failure, Cat SS 10.1.64 (F/Lt RN Davidson RAF). Hydraulic failure, emergency landing, Cat SS 22.1.64 (Lt MT Hynett). Hydraulic failure, precautionary landing, Cat LQ 28.2.64 (F/Lt RN Davidson RAF). Undercarriage hydraulic failure, port leg freed by positive and negative G, Cat LQ 4.6.64 (L/C J Worth). Hydraulic failure landing, Cat LQ 4.8.64 (Lt PJ Trudgett). Undercarriage warning light defect, landed safely, Cat LQ 10.11.64 (S/L PG Doughty). Bird strike on starboard intake, Cat HY 18.1.65 (L/C JWH Purvis). 764B Sqn Lossiemouth ('621') by 6.65. White smoke from drop tank, landed safely, Cat SS 21.9.65 (L/C CC Giles). Undercarriage warning light failure, landed safely Cat LQ 8.10.65 (Mr J Rees of Airwork). Bomb fell off on landing, Cat SS 12.10.65 (S/L ZK Skrodzki). To Lee-on-Solent 27.10.65. Towed back to Lee-on-Solent 25.1.68 (abortive take-off 27.2.68, braked and arrested with CHAG gear). NASU Brawdy LTS 21.3.68 (Lt Cdr PM Stevenson). Flown to MARTSU Lee 22.7.70 for FAA Museum storage (Lt Cdr PEH Banfield). Dismantled and transported by road to RNAY Wroughton 14.3.73 (further storage). Exchanged by the FAA Museum for a former US Marine Corps F-4. Loaded aboard RFA *Olna* at Portsmouth by 7.6.86 and shipped to USA for display on board USS *Intrepid* in New York Harbour. Current, undergoing refurbishment 1999.

XD221 Production test VA South Marston 30.8.57 (LR Colquhoun). Suffered bird strike during test flight, engine damaged, South Marston 21.9.57 (LR Colquhoun). Delivered 700X Flt Ford ('801/FD') 25.9.57 (LR Colquhoun). 700 Sqn Ford ('512/FD') 29.5.58. Temp C(A) charge at A&AEE 11.8.58 (evaluation, setting up, calibration and pilot familiarisation of AII and A55U prior to carrier trials). Returned 700 Sqn Ford ('512/FD') 4.9.58. 700 Sqn Yeovilton ('512/VL') 17.9.58. To Lee-on-Solent 10.11.58 and towed to RNAY Fleetlands. Towed back to Lee-on-Solent by 3.2.61 (test flew 8.2.61 – possibly to/from Boscombe Down in natural metal finish) and departed to 800 Sqn Lossiemouth ('101/R') 21.2.62. Port ammunition tank panel detached on take-off, Cat LQ 2.3.62 (Lt CD Walkinshaw). Probe damaged when tanker-hose failed to reel in at 30,000ft, *Ark Royal*, Cat LQ 17.6.62 (L/C JAD Ford). *Ark Royal*, two greens and three reds on selecting up button on undercarriage after take-off, then Hydraulic 1, unable to change the configuration with the emergencies, flaps would not come down, only the port drop tank would jettison, which did so over the sea, flapless landing on foam-prepared runway, nose wheel collapsed, starboard drop tank burst, Tengah, Cat HC 3.7.62 (S/L AD Alsop). AHU Tengah 17.7.62. 800 Sqn ('106') 16.10.62. Port tyre burst landing Lossiemouth, Cat LQ 6.3.63 (Lt GHR Wooff). While parked, hit by Gannet XP229 taxying, Cat LQ 28.5.63. Aborted take-off after rudder malfunction, engaged Tengah barrier at 135knots, Cat LC 24.8.63 (S/L A McMeekan). AHU Changi 31.8.63. 803 Sqn ('025/R') 19.1.66. Crashed Malaya 21.4.66. NASU Changi 4.4.66 (sic) [486.55hrs]. SOC RSP 6.6.66. Left Changi for spares in 1966. Fuselage dumped Sembawang 1.67.

XD222 Production test VA South Marston 29.9.57 (LR Colquhoun). Delivered 700X Flt Ford ('802/FD') 11.10.57 (Mr JWR Judge). Presentation to the Royal Navy at Lee-on-Solent 11.11.57 (Cdr TG Innes). VA Wisley 7.5.58 (overhaul and prep for simulated cold chamber Arctic trials). Minor damage on transfer by road to Weybridge 2.6.58. In cold chamber Weybridge 5.6.58. Engine runs carried out post cold chamber trials 3.7.58. VA Wisley to VA South Marston 24.12.58 (less engine, brought up to production standard). Air tested from 19.2.60. AHU Lossiemouth 25.3.60. 736 Sqn Lossiemouth ('609/LM') 12.4.60. After ground power checks starboard ECU, found to have extensive compressor blade damage, Cat SS 21.9.60. Crashed on low level Navex, Bridge of Cally, 6m N of Blairgowrie, Perthshire, Cat ZZ 16.11.60 (Lt NJ Norris killed) [216.30hrs by 12.4.60]. Wreckage to AIU Lee-on-Solent 1.12.60.

XD223 Production test VA South Marston 23.10.57 (LR Colquhoun) and delivered 700X Flt Ford ('803/FD') 23.10.57 (Mr MJ Lithgow). Being lowered on jacks, port jack slipped, Cat L 28.11.57. 803 Sqn Lossiemouth (still marked "803") 29.5.58. AHU Lossiemouth 12.9.58. VA

South Marston 26.2.59 (brought up to production standard). Air tested 3-28.3.60 (LR Colquhoun). AHU Lossiemouth 11.3.60. 736 Sqn Lossiemouth ('608/LM') 6.5.60. Starboard engine damaged by bird strike, Cat SS 16.6.60 (L/C NE Lee RAN). Hydraulic 1 failure during RP practice, precautionary landing base, engaged wire, Cat SS 15.2.61 (Lt DS McIntyre). Nosewheel light remained red even after bouncing the aircraft on the runway, nosewheel collapsed after landing, Cat LQ 28.3.61 (L/C PH Perks). Windscreen hit by bird at 2,000ft during live 18-lb HE GP attack, Cat LQ 25.5.61 (Lt BJ Bullivant). Brake binding after landing, port wheel caught fire in dispersal, Cat LQ 21.11.61 (S/L G McBain). Tailpipe fire on light-up, Cat SS 10.1.62 (S/L L Ingham). RNAY Fleetlands 21.2.62 (modernisation). Roaded to Lee-on-Solent by 6.4.63 and last test flight 18.4.63 (during which period flown in natural metal finish with oversize roundels and serials crudely applied due to busy Dope Shop). AHU Lossiemouth 18.4.63. 800 Sqn ('106/R') 29.4.63. *Ark Royal*, fuel flow problem, diverted to Port Reitz, Cat SS 22.6.63 (Lt PC Marshall). Fuel flow problem, *Ark Royal*, Cat SS 5.11.63 (L/C JF Kennett). 803 Sqn ('156/H') 26.2.64. Bird strike on take-off, Cat LQ 23.3.64 (Lt JOF Billingham). RNAY Fleetlands 5.6.64 (for minor repair). Towed back to Lee-on-Solent by 7.7.64 and departed Lee-on-Solent 22.8.64. 803 Sqn ('156/R') 22.8.64. Starboard oil pressure warning, single-engined landing Lossiemouth, Cat HY 9.12.64 (S/L PG Doughty). Port tyre burst on MADDL touchdown, landed safely Lossiemouth, Cat LQ 8.1.65 (L/C NJP Mills). Hood came off during catapult launch, *Ark Royal*, Cat LQ 2.3.65 (Lt BP Marindin). Recoded 7.65 ('031/R'). Mast inadvertently raised into trailing edge of tailplane, *Ark Royal*, Cat LQ 13.7.65. Test flight, crashed on final approach during diversion following engine problem, pilot ejected, RAF Changi, Cat ZZ 20.9.65 (Lt PAA Waring slightly injured - Ejection No.1095). Allocated for fire fighting 30.10.65. Wreck to Sembawang by 1966. [1047.20hrs]

*NOTE. Extract from 'Cockpit' magazine - "Took off from HMS Ark Royal on a test fight, the pilot being specially selected because of his thorough knowledge of Scimitar emergencies and his above-average flying ability. The relight systems on the engines were tested at 20,000ft. Port engine failed to relight at 300kts. Further attempt at 400kts was unsuccessful. The ship was informed and he was diverted to Changi for a single-engined landing. Half a mile from touch-down there was a hydraulic failure followed by a total control lock. The stick was solid and the pilot decided to eject 300yds from the runway. Whilst ejecting the aircraft struck the ground nose down, one wheel was torn off and the machine burst into flames. The pilot, Lt PA Waring RN, landed safely."*

*XD223 '156/V' ready for take-off. (MAP)*

XD224   [VA South Marston 5.9.57]. Production test VA South Marston 26.10.57 (LR Colquhoun). Delivered 700X Flt Ford ('804/FD') 6.1.58 (Mr MJ Lithgow). Compressor blade failure in starboard engine, Cat SS 3.3.58 (Lt PJ Barber). 803 Sqn Lossiemouth 3.6.58. AHU Lossiemouth 17.7.58 (STS). 736 Sqn Lossiemouth ('618/LM') 27.8.59. Take-off aborted, jet pipe temperature too high, Cat SS 23.11.59 (S/L AHS Anderson). Starboard fuse box panel became detached in flight and some portion passed through the starboard engine, Cat LX 30.1.60 (Lt JA Sutton). Recoded by 6.60 ('615/LM'). Hydraulic failure, services lowered emergency system, hook prevented from lowering, Cat LX 23.8.60 (Lt JPE Faulkner). VA South Marston 4.10.60. VA Wisley 5.11.60. AHU Lossiemouth 18.7.62. 736 Sqn Lossiemouth ('614') 14.8.62. Undercarriage lights malfunction, landed safely, Cat LQ 23.11.62 (L/C DF Mills). Hydraulic failure, landed safely, Cat LQ 26.11.62. Altimeter and ASI over-reading, made formation landing, Cat SS 2.2.63 (Mid NHL Bowden). Fire warning in starboard engine, single-engined landing in company, Cat SS 7.5.63 (S/L A McMeekan). Taxied into XD227, Cat SS 6.8.63 (Cdr WGB Black). False fire warning, single-engined landing, Cat LQ 23.10.63 (S/L CA Wheal). [Dave Morgan made a test flight against this aircraft at South Marston 5.3.64]. False undercarriage warning light, Cat LQ 5.10.64 (Lt BP Marindin). Instrument failure on approach, formation landing, Cat LQ 5.10.64 (Lt BP Marindin). Undercarriage problem on take-off, normal landing, Cat LQ 7.10.64 (L/C MJ Hedges). Undercarriage problem on take-off, normal landing, Cat LQ 9.10.64 (S/L PG Doughty). Hydraulic failure on take-off, burnt off fuel, selected emergency flap and hook, landed safely, Cat SS 24.10.64 (L/C PP Cardew). 764B Sqn Lossiemouth ('614') 29.3.65. Heavy vibration from port engine, landed safely, Cat SS 7.4.65 (L/C JWH Purvis). To Lee-on-Solent and towed to RNAY Fleetlands 10.6.65 (modernisation). Towed back to Lee-on-Solent 19.7.67, but returned to Fleetlands c10.67 (lightered to *Victorious* via Fleetlands 31.10.67 for deck handling trials prior to planned Mediterranean carrier trials. Plan subsequently cancelled.) [BUT noted XD224 retd Fleetlands from Lee-on-Solent 8.11.67 – flight test complete]. Returned RNAY Fleetlands via MARTSU 8.1.68, before returning to Lee-on-Solent and departing To NASU Brawdy 22.1.68. 'C' Sqn A&AEE Boscombe Down 30.4.68 (armament trials, also photographic work for D.A.Nav). Released by C(A) wef 16.7.69 (possible carrier trials in Med cancelled). Sold to Ministry of Technology for P&EE 12.9.69. At Lee-on-Solent 1970. Arr P&EE Shoeburyness 23.1.70. Trials 4.75 to 10.79. Wingless fuselage still at Shoeburyness 3.88. Believed scrapped soon afterwards.

XD225   Production test VA South Marston 29.11.57 (LR Colquhoun). Delivered 700X Flt Ford ('805/FD') 6.1.58 (Mr JWR Judge). RAE Bedford 7.3.58 (Lt E Anson) (up-rating trials of Mk.13 arrester gear, also proofing Scimitar to higher engine speeds). Accident, damage to airframe, hydraulics and airframe skin, Cat 3 17.5.58. 803 Sqn Lossiemouth 3.6.58. Landing accident 23.6.58. VA South Marston by road 13/14.7.58 (Cat 4 repair. refurbishment and systems updating to production standard). Air tested 29.1.60 - 15.2.60. AHU Lossiemouth 10.3.60 (STS). 736 Sqn Lossiemouth ('613/LM') 24.3.60. Port undercarriage warning light, precautionary landing, Cat SS 17.2.61 (S/L JL Carver). Hydraulic failure after dive bombing sortie, Cat LX 9.3.61 (Lt RDG Gray). Airframe overstressed after dummy dive bombing attack Tain Range, Cat LQ 14.3.61 (Lt DS McIntyre). Undercarriage hydraulic problem, landed safely, engaged wires, Cat LQ 25.4.61 (Lt NG Grier-Rees). After formation landing, overran XD240 lead aircraft, port wing damaged, Cat LQ 17.11.61 (S/L AJ Middleton). Low oil pressure warning starboard engine, Cat SS 21.11.61 (L/C DG Halliday). RNAY Fleetlands 18.4.62 (modernisation). Towed back to Lee-on-Solent by 31.5.63 and last test there 18.6.63. AHU Lossiemouth 20.6.63. 803 Sqn ('154/H') 31.10.63. Foreign body in engine en route Lossiemouth to *Ark Royal*, Cat SS 30.11.63 (Lt R Wren). Bird strike on drop tank on low level Navex at 200ft, Cat LQ 10.1.64 (S/L JS

Flexman). Code change by 28.5.64 ('154/R') and 8.64 ('147/R'). Windscreen broke up during LABS run at 400ft, Cat LQ 15.10.64 (L/C JOF Billingham). Skidded and nose struck island after landing *Ark Royal*, Cat LQ 20.1.65 (Lt CJ Crowther). AHU Lossiemouth 1.65. 736 Sqn Lossiemouth ('613') 8.2.65. 764B Sqn Lossiemouth ('620') 29.3.65. Hydraulic problem, emergency landing, Cat LQ 5.4.65 (L/C J Worth). Port engine problem during night descent, single-engined landing, Cat LQ 15.5.65 (L/C J Worth). Port oil pressure warning light, single-engined landing, Cat SS 4.8.65 (S/L AR Dady). To Lee-on-Solent 23.11.65 (skidded on to grass following brake failure – Lt Cdr J Brandt). Towed to RNAY Fleetlands 29.11.65 (modernisation). Towed back to Lee-on-Solent 17.8.66. NASU Brawdy 31.8.66 (mod). Airwork FRU Hurn 21.11.66. Not coded in FRU service (c/s '029' allocated c11.67). To Lee-on-Solent 8.1.69 (arrested landing) to await disposal. RAE Farnborough on permanent Ministry of Technology charge 3.2.69. Sold to Ministry of Technology for P&EE 14.5.69. By road to RNAY Fleetlands by 1.9.69 for spares recovery. To P&EE Shoeburyness 1.70. Fuselage to Larkhill artillery ranges as a target 8.10.70 to at least 5.71. [1259.55hrs]

XD226 Production test VA South Marston 20.12.57 (LR Colquhoun). To C(A) at Vickers 6.1.58 (TI of target towing mod under Cont No 6/Acft/14079/CB.5(a)). A&AEE 20.1.58 (Target Towing trials). Ford 28.2.58. 700 Sqn Ford ('510/FD') 12.3.58 (on C(A) charge 11.7.58 - 8.8.58). A&AEE 7.8.58 (evaluation, setting up, calibration and pilot familiarisation of AII and A55U prior to carrier trials). Returned 700 Sqn Ford 4.9.58. 700 Sqn Yeovilton ('510/VL') 19.9.58. 764 Sqn Lossiemouth 11.2.59. 736 Sqn Lossiemouth ('610/LM') 12.5.59. RNAY Fleetlands 13.7.59. Depart Lee-on-Solent 29.7.59. Returned 736 Sqn ('610/LM') 31.7.59. Starboard brake failure, overshot, ended in ditch, Cat HX 4.9.59 (Lt AG Claridge). AHU Lossiemouth 27.7.60 (modernisation). VA South Marston 23.8.60 (brought up to production standard). AHU Lossiemouth 3.11.61. Air test 12.61 (LR Colquhoun). 736 Sqn Lossiemouth ('615') 22.1.62. Windscreen panel shattered in climb at 7,000ft 5m NE of Elgin, Cat LQ 24.1.62 (Lt AHS Anderson). Port aileron touched runway on GCA and mirror landing in gusty conditions, Cat LQ 15.2.62 (S/L MJ Harwood). Power loss on MADDLs overshoot, Cat SS 23.1.63 (S/L CD Legg). Nosewheel collapsed after landing, Cat HX 9.4.63 (L/C JAD Ford). AHU Lossiemouth 17.4.63. C(A) loan at VA South Marston 11.11.63 (TI of Mod 1119) against Cont No KC/A/164/CB.5(a)). AHU Lossiemouth 11.3.64 (NAMM). RAF Handling Sqn Boscombe Down 22.6.64. AHU Lossiemouth 12.8.64. A&AEE loan 19.7.64 (canopy jettison trials). AHU Lossiemouth 12.8.64. To AES Arbroath as Class I GI 7.1.65. Downgraded to Class II as *A2562* 27.7.67 (engine Nos *E4572/4573*). Downgraded to Class III 6.69. To Farnborough by road 24.6.70. [570.10hrs]

XD227 Production test VA South Marston 23.12.57 (LR Colquhoun). To C(A) charge at VA 1.1.58. RY 4.1.58. RAF Handling Sqn Boscombe Down 8.1.58. VA Wisley 19.3.58. VA South Marston 2.4.58 (fuel system improve-ments, flight refuelling trials as tanker aircraft and PR nose, some trials being conducted jointly with 'C' Sqn A&AEE Boscombe Down). Tail cones disintegrated in flight on two inboard drop tanks 4.3.59. RAF Handling Sqn Boscombe Down 1.5.59 (engineering assessment of flight refuelling system and engineering assessment/evaluation of camera nose installation) (DW Morgan). VA Wisley 20.7.59 (preparation for final phase of flight refuelling trials). VA South Marston 12.8.60 (DW Morgan). Armament safety break plug inserted causing drop tanks to jettison, Cat SS 29.8.60 (LR Colquhoun). Hose severed during refuelling exercise causing slight damage to XD212 27.9.60. A&AEE 22.11.60 (flight refuelling trials, Cat 2 damage to buddy pod) (EB Trubshaw). Hose inadvertently jettisoned during test of flight refuelling fitments, Cat LX 12.1.61 (Lt JT Spafford). Hydraulic failure while refuelling Sea Vixen from Hatfield 35,000ft over Sussex, successful emergency landing, Cat LQ 23.1.61 (Lt JT Spafford). VA South Marston 23.2.61 (trial of streamlined flight refuelling pod). Take-off abandoned causing substantial damage to 200-gallon drop tank and wheel brakes, also minor damage to Mk.20 refuelling pod and contamination from foam spray, Cat 2 15.3.61. Pilot unable to wind in refuelling hose, jettisoned it on firm's airfield, refuelling hose and drogue damaged 18.4.61. A&AEE 28.4.61 (trials of PR nose). VA South Marston 17.5.61 (instrumentation removed on Cont No KC/2/014/CB.5(a), then modernised and brought up to production standard from 9.6.61). Free loan for trials of PR nose 26.4.62. VA South Marston 18.5.62. Delivered AHU Lossiemouth on RN charge 2.4.63. 736 Sqn Lossiemouth ('615') 23.5.63. 25-lb practice bomb fell 2m SW Rosehearty Range without pilot's knowledge, Cat SS 20 6.63 (Capitaine de Corvette MR Borney, French Navy). Taxied into by XD224, Cat SS 6.8.63. Starboard engine fire warning light after take-off, jettisoned drop tanks and landed safely, Cat LX 13.9.63 (L/C JF Kennett). Bird strike on ATC exercise at Banff, Cat LX 22.11.63 (S/L PJ McManus). Bird strike on port wing turning at 500ft after low level flight, Cat LQ 28.1.64 (Lt BP Marindin). False nosewheel warning light landing, Cat SS 3.4.64 (Lt MJM Brophy). Damaged during flight refuelling with XD232, Cat LQ 5.6.64. Flap problem, safe flapless landing, Cat LQ 9.6.64 (S/L KB Owen). ASI failure on take-off, pairs landing, Cat SS 23.7.64 (Lt JG Wood). Port brake failure on moving off at night, swung to starboard and nose slightly struck next aircraft in line, Cat LQ 2.11.64 (Lt ARD Monro-Davies). Windscreen cracked during GCA approach in heavy rain, Cat LQ 2.12.64 (S/L PG Doughty). Bird strike on port intake, Cat HY 8.1.65 (S/L HW Thomas). Bird strike on nose at 300ft over sea, Cat LQ 4.3.65 (S/L GM Faulkner). Bird strike on port outer leading edge flap, Cat LQ 6.3.65 (Lt AS Tuck). 764B Sqn Lossiemouth ('615') 29.3.65. Refuelling hose problem, precautionary landing, Cat SS 24.6.65 (Lt CA Wheal). Starboard engine warning light, single-engined landing, Cat LQ 8.7.65 (Lt PJ Trudgett). Starboard wingtip struck lorry taxying, Cat LQ 14.7.65 (Lt PJ Trudgett). Hydraulic leak, landed safely, Cat LQ 24.7.65 (Lt AS Tuck). Port flap problem, landed safely, Cat LQ 18.9.65 (Lt PG De Souza). To Lee-on-Solent (with XD225/620) 23.11.65 and to RNAY Fleetlands 29.11.65 (modernisation). NASU Brawdy 15.3.66 (storage). Airwork FRU Hurn 6.2.67. NASU Brawdy 6.4.67. Windscreen cracked during air test 13.11.67. Airwork FRU 27.11.67. Remained uncoded in FRU service (allocated c/s '036' 12.67 and '836' 12.68). Retired from use 15.3.69. By road to Ministry of Technology Farnborough 29/30.7.69 and used as an instructional airframe at the Apprentices School. SOC and dismantled for P&EE Foulness 15.9.69. Transported to Shoeburyness 12.11.69. Trials 8.70. Fuselage to Larkhill ranges 18.12.70 to at least 5.71

XD228 Production test VA South Marston 31.12.57 (LR Colquhoun). Delivered VA South Marston to Lee-on-Solent 14.2.58 and roaded to RNAY Fleetlands (LR Colquhoun). A&AEE 20.3.58 (free loan for C(A) release trials with 24x3-inch rocket packs and inboard-facing cine cameras fitted under wingtips to record live firings). To 700X Sqdn 24.3.58 (Lt Cdr Norman), and later noted with fin code 'FD'. RAE Bedford 16.6.58 (proving of external stores under catapulting and arresting loads). Returned A&AEE 26.6.58. Grounded awaiting replacement engine 30.7.58. VA Wisley 29.10.58 (fitment of modifications to improve handling characteristics). A&AEE 26.8.59 (armament trials and handling checks). VA Wisley 14.10.59 (fitting Mod 5072 pylons and instrumentation for armament trials, flight handling checks 4 x 200gall drop tanks). VA South Marston 4.11.59 (installation of camera pods and prod swept pylons). West Freugh by 23.1.60 (TMB trials). 'C' Sqn A&AEE 26.1.60 (C(A) armament trials and handling checks). Failure of No.1 hydraulic system due to fractured pipe, Cat 2

26.1.61). VA South Marston 13.3.61 (removal of instrumentation, then refurbished to operational standards on Cont No KC/2/014/CB.5(a)). A&AEE to VA South Marston 3.5.61. Flown at A&AEE 16.5.61 (MJ Lithgow). AHU Lossiemouth 20.11.62. 736 Sqn Lossiemouth ('613') 10.12.62. Outer PBCs jettisoned without pilot's knowledge, Cat SS 31.1.63 (Lt LA Wilkinson). Piece of arrester gear lost on Rosehearty Range, Cat LQ 27.2.63 (F/Lt RN Davidson RAF). Debris struck canopy pulling out from RP attack Tain Range, Cat LQ 18.7.63 (L/C JF Kennett). Undercarriage light malfunction, Cat SS 14.10.63 (S/L B Hutton). Bird strike on high level formation sortie, Cat SS 21.11.63 (Lt JG Wood). Fire warning in port engine in climb, single-engined landing, Cat LQ 24.2.64 (Lt DB Knowles). Radio failure in flight, Cat SS 12.3.64 (Lt JG Wood). Bird strike on flap on low level sortie, Cat LQ 21.7.64 (Lt PJ Trudgett). Heavy landing, tyre burst, swung off to starboard, Cat LQ 13.10.64 (Lt PG Doughty). A&AEE 18.3.65 (free loan C(A) for TI of NGR1901, clearance of napalm stores). RAE Bedford 23.4.65 (catapult arrester gear and instrumentation development for naval aircraft). To permanent MoA charge 18.11.66. Non-flying hack from 15.2.67 (same task). Released 31.3.70. RAE Farnborough 22.6.70 and SOC as a GEV. In derelict state 3.76. Parts to P&EE Shoeburyness 9, 23 and 31.9.75. Trials from 7.84. Mid fuselage and engines to P&EE Pendine Ranges, Dyfed 6.7.83. Wings and part fuselage dumped separately 3.88. Wings formed part of Lots 6 & 7 in MoD surplus sale at Shoeburyness by 4.12.90. Scrapped 4.91.

XD229 To C(A) charge at VA Wisley 28.6.57 (*Red Beard* (OR.1127) trials against Cont No 6/Acft/15220/CB.5(a)). A&AEE 13.3.58 (C(A) release trials - drop tank handling. LABS manoeuvres). VA Wisley 10.4.58 (TMB and LABS trials against Cont No 6/Acft/15220/CB.5(a)). Weapons Flight, RAE Farnborough 26.6.58 (*Red Beard* development. trials with TMB using LABS. two 200 plus two 150 gallon drop tanks and four 1,000-lb bombs. For part of the trials it was based RAE West Freugh - also at RAE Bedford). Transferred from temp to permanent C(A) charge in exchange for XD218 as quota aircraft. Starboard aileron damaged, Cat 2 12.11.58. Development trials of conventional armament for Scimitar aircraft from 17.11.59. "Attention getters" flashed during take-off, no central warning panel indication, take-off abandoned, damaged nosewheel door, spine fairing, pitot head, leading edge flaps, seized brakes, Farnborough, Cat HC 27.5.60 (F/Lt AW Picking RAF). Bird strike, starboard lower fuselage flap and stiffener damaged, flap jack strained, Cat 2 25.9.61. No.2 Hydraulic system failed 15min after take-off due to inadequate clipping of pipe, Cat 1 17.10.61. Loss of control due to rudder pedals unlocking in flight, Cat 1 24.11.61. Flap failure due to broken cable 24.5.62. Instrument failure due to failure of supply from Nos.1 and 2 inverters 22.10.62. A&AEE loan 1962, then retd Weapons Flt RAE (Painted in non-standard colour scheme whilst with Weapons Flight of powder blue with white fin with black leading edge and anti-dazzle panel). RAE West Freugh to VA South Marston 15.1.65 (mods and preparation for trials). RAE West Freugh 3.6.65 (weapons development trials). Weapons Flight RAE 10.6.65. RAE West Freugh, damaged landing 8.65. Ground hydraulics accident during ground trials work 8.66. SOC as source of spares for other MoA Scimitars 12.10.66. On dump by 3.71 to at least 5.75, being removed for scrap in 6.76. Parts eventually to RNEC Manadon.

XD230 Production test VA South Marston 21.1.58 (LR Colquhoun). VA South Marston 28.1.58 (gun firing mods). Delivered 700X Flt Ford ('805/FD') 26.2.58 (Lt AR Campbell). Bird strike, seagull in port engine during formation take-off, Cat SS 3.3.58 (Lt TFB Young). Jet pipe fire following attempted relight of starboard engine at 21,000ft near South Marston, successfully extinguished and landed back at Ford 13.3.58 (Lt PJ Barber). 803 Sqn ('145/V') 27.5.58. AHU Lossiemouth 9.9.58 (STS). VA South Marston 3.2.59 (brought up to production standard). Air tested 3-23.2.60. AHU Lossiemouth 18.3.60. 736 Sqn Lossiemouth ('617/LM') 1.4.60. Tain Range, vibration and drop in rpm, emergency landing, Cat SS 6.5.60 (Lt JRJ Rutherford). Bird strike, port engine compressor blades damaged, Cat LX 27.5.60 (Lt MJM Brophy). Port engine damaged by bird strike, Cat SS 16.6.60 (S/L JGL Smith). Engine fire warning light, engine shut down and extinguisher fired, single engine landing, Cat LQ 30.8.60 (F/Lt M Farmer RAF). Starboard engine throttled back after severe vibration, landed safely with engine throttled back, Cat SS 28.9.60 (F/Lt M Farmer RAF). Intermittent hydraulic failure, Cat SS 11.10.61 (S/L GHR Wooff). RNAY Fleetlands 23.5.62 (modernisation began 7.6.62). To Lee-on-Solent Dope Shop by 13.9.63 and flew Lee-on-Solent to Boscombe Down 29.7.63 and return 2.8.63. Last air test 21.8.63 and departed Lee-on-Solent to AHU Lossiemouth 30.9.63. 803 Sqn ('154/H') 27.2.64 and recoded 5.64 ('154/R'). Fuel transfer problem after flight refuelling, diverted to Sumburgh, Cat LQ 23.9.64 (L/C GAI Johnston). Hydraulic 1 failure whilst acting as tanker, ditched after port leg would not lower after several minutes of trying to dislodge it, pilot gained height and ejected into Moray Firth off Lossiemouth, Cat ZZ 28.9.64 (S/L PJ McManus recovered injured from sea by helicopter - Ejection No.920). Airframe recovered, eventually to West Freugh where still in use as GI airframe 1969. [530.15hrs]

XD231 Production test VA South Marston 27.1.58 (LR Colquhoun). Delivered 700X Sqn Ford ('806/FD') 1.4.58 (LR Colquhoun). 803 Sqn ('152/V') 20.5.58. AHU Lossiemouth 9.9.58 (STS). RNAY Fleetlands (via Yeovilton) 13.11.58. Towed to Lee 14.7.61. Air test to Boscombe Down 20.7.61. Air tested there until 31.7.61. 736 Sqn Lossiemouth ('609/LM') 15.8.61. 800 Sqn loan to RAE Farnborough for trials of airfield friction brake arrester, wire pulled out, A-frame distorted, Cat LX 21.8.61 (S/L KR Entwisle). Loaned to 800 Sqn as '108/R' for SBAC Show 9.61. Returned 736 Sqn Lossiemouth ('609/LM') 9.61. VHF failure above cloud, landed safely standby UHF Channel Guard, Cat SS 19.9.61 (L/C A Mancais). Ricochet damage to starboard wing Tain Range, Cat HX 6.11.61 (S/L GHR Wooff). Undercarriage malfunction, landed safely, Cat SS 1.2.62 (L/C PG Newman). Port ammunition tank detached on take-off, Cat SS 21.3.62 (S/L L Ingham). To Lee-on-Solent 3.4.62 (acceptance test flight same day) and to RNAY Fleetlands 4.4.62. Towed to Lee-on-Solent 25.7.62, flew Lee-on-Solent to Boscombe Down 15.8.62, thence to-AHU Lossiemouth 16.8.62. 800 Sqn ('101/R') 5.1.63. Starboard intake struck by tailplane of XD323 being manoeuvred in hangar, Lossiemouth, Cat LX 5.2.63. Fuel flow problem, Cat SS 27.7.63 (Lt IPF Meiklejohn). Foreign body snagged elevator controls, normal landing, *Ark Royal*, Cat LQ 27.11.63 (Lt IPF Meiklejohn). Nosewheel warning light problem, Cat SS 14.1.64 (CdeC MR Borney, French Navy). Defective altimeter, Cat SS 24.1.64 (Lt IPF Meiklejohn). Fuel leak, emergency landing, Cat LQ 28.1.64 (CdeC MR Borney, French Navy). AHU Lossiemouth 5.2.64. 800B Flt Lossiemouth ('111/E') 29.9.64. AHU Lossiemouth 2.10.64. RNAY Fleetlands 26.10.64 (Cat 4 rectification). RAE Bedford.64 (demonstration flight). To RNAY Fleetlands c.12.64 (fitment of instrumentation for turbulence tests). Allotted RAE Bedford 12.2.65 (study of aircraft behaviour in severe storms). Shipped to Oklahoma 3.65 (storm turbulence tests with NASA for MoA). On return to VA South Marston 31.8.66 (located RAF Fairford for weapon development trials, carrying title "*Stormform*" on tail fin). To RAE Farnborough/West Freugh (with Aero Flight 8.66). NASU Brawdy by 7.67. Weapons Flt RAE Farnborough 2.8.67 [ex Fairford]. Returned Farnborough to be scrapped 25.3.69. Allocated for effect of ERU ejection forces on aircraft structure 21.8.69. SOC as a Ground Engineering Vehicle 17.6.70. Allocated P&EE Shoeburyness 16.6.70, but still intact at Farnborough 7.71 and later in hangar there for 'static trials' 9.74. Almost complete in sections to P&EE

Shoeburyness 4.7.75, 16.7.25, 31.7.25 and 22.9.75. Rear fuselage and jet pipes to Pending Ranges, Dyfed 6.7.83.

XD232  Production test VA South Marston 19.2.58 (LR Colquhoun). Delivered AHU Lossiemouth 23.4.58 (acceptance test flight). Fire in port engine, precautionary landing Leuchars, Cat LX 7.5.58 (Lt AR Campbell). 803 Sqn ('146/V') 6.6.58. Collided with jet blast deflector while taxying *Victorious*, Cat LX 3.1.59 (Lt ER Anson). Hit by XD264 *Victorious*, Cat LY 20.3.59. Hold back ring entered starboard catapult *Victorious*, Cat SS 7.5.59. Airbrakes and undercarriage selected, hydraulic failure Lossiemouth, Cat LQ 10.9.59 (S/L RWD Westlake). Hydraulic system failure *Victorious*, Cat SS 21.9.59 (Lt B Davies). After landing, no response from port brake, hook lowered and arrester wires engaged Lossiemouth, Cat SS 25.1.60 (L/C AJ Leahy). To Lee-on-Solent 12.4.60 and to RNAY Fleetlands (modernisation). Towed back to Lee-on-Solent by 20.6.61 and air test from Lee to Boscombe Down 26.6.61. Last air test 11.7.61. To AHU Lossiemouth. To C(A) at VA South Marston on free loan 20.7.61 (catapult trials with various stores to check CofG positions). A&AEE 6.9.61. AHU Lossiemouth 9.10.61. To Lee-on-Solent for MARTSU 20.10.61 (preparation for shipment). Shipped to Far East aboard SS *Benarty* from Southampton 11.11.61, arriving AHU Tengah 13.12.61. 807 Sqn ('193/C') 1.2.62. Stn Flt Lossiemouth 26.4.62. To Lee-on-Solent 15.5.62 and towed to RNAY Fleetlands. Towed back to Lee-on-Solent by 21.11.62 and last air test there 26.11.62. Hydraulic failure while ferrying, landed safely Lossiemouth, Cat SS 28.11.62 (Mr DR Skinner). 736 Sqn Lossiemouth ('611') 29.11.62. Port brake failed landing, swung to starboard on to grass, Cat LQ 19.3.63 (L/C JAD Ford). False undercarriage warning light, Cat LQ 14.5.63 (S/L CD Legg). RNAY Fleetlands 5.6.63. 736 Sqn Lossiemouth ('611') 10.7.63. Hydraulic failure, precautionary landing, Cat LQ 25.7.63 (Lt D Richardson). Hydraulic failure at 40,000ft, Cat LQ 3.10.63 (L/C JAD Ford). Hydraulic failure on GCA recovery, Cat SS 4.11.63 (Lt R Wren). Damaged during flight refuelling with XD227, Cat HY 5.6.64 (S/L KB Owen). To Lee-on-Solent 10.6.64 (noted in Flight Test hangar, Lee, 19.7.64) and to RNAY Fleetlands (repair and FRU conversion). Towed back to Lee-on-Solent 10.1.66 and departed c2.66. RAE Bedford 17.3.66 (DAX.1 arrester gear intensive trials). NASU Brawdy 12.10.66. Airwork FRU Hurn 11.1.67. Coded c10.67 ('031'). New code allocated 12.68 and applied 3.69 ('831'). Sold to Ministry of Technology for P&EE Foulness 11.9.69. Ministry of Technology at RAE Farnborough for scrapping 5.12.69. P&EE Shoeburyness by road 16-18.6.70 (overnight at Everley's Yard, Hayes). Believed finally left Shoeburyness 2.11.83. [1011.50hrs]

XD233  Retained by makers as static test airframe, repeated loading cycles being applied to airframe to represent a typical low-level sortie and to prove that the aircraft would be good for a fatigue life of 1,000hrs, believed at Vickers Flight Test Centre, Wisley.

XD234  Production test VA South Marston 14.4.58 (LR Colquhoun). Delivered South Marston to AHU Lossiemouth 2.5.58 (acceptance test flight that day). 803 Sqn ('147/V') 30.5.58. Hydraulic failure while selecting wheels up *Victorious*, Cat LX 2.7.59 (Lt LE Middleton). Failure of No.1 hydraulic system, landed safely *Victorious*, Cat SS 17.7.59 (Lt ER Anson). Technical fault ashore UK 9.9.59. RNAY Fleetlands (via Lee) 9.10.59. 736 Sqn Lossiemouth ('616/LM') 15.10.59. High frequency vibration port ECU, engine shut down, single-engined landing, Cat SS 22.7.60 (Lt CC Giles). RNAY Fleetlands 3.8.60 (modernisation). Air tested Lee-on-Solent to Boscombe Down 23-24.8.61. AHU Lossiemouth 1.9.61. 800 Sqn *Ark Royal* 16.10.61. After landing, fire damage found in starboard dive brake bay, Lossiemouth, Cat LY 17.10.61 (Lt CC Giles). AHU Lossiemouth 22.10.61. RNAY Fleetlands 3.11.61. Back to Lee-on-Solent by 21.3.62 and departed 18.4.61. 803 Sqn ('153/H') 27.4.62. During heavy weather at night, tailplane tip hit by XD318, *Hermes*, Cat LQ 13.8.62. Port outer bomb carrier fell off at 35,000ft, Cat SS 29.11.62 (S/L JS Flexman). Hydraulic problem, landed safely, Cat SS 28.5.63 (Lt AHS Anderson). To AHU Tengah 5.63. Returned 803 Sqn ('153/H') 6.63 and recoded 5.64 (153/R'). Hydraulic failure, landed safely, Cat LQ 11.1.65 (Lt JM Heath). False engine fire warning, landed safely *Ark Royal* Cat SS 8.3.65 (Lt BP Marindin). Starboard brake failure, landed safely Lossiemouth, Cat SS 1.4.65 (F/Lt TG Gilroy RAF). To Lee-on-Solent (with XD219) 17.5.65 and to RNAY Fleetlands (modernisation and conversion for FRU duties). Towed back to Lee-on-Solent 22.2.67 and departed 21.4.67. Airwork FRU Hurn 7.4.67. Coded c10.67 ('025'). New code allocated 12.68 and applied 3.69 ('834'). Hydraulic leak, landed Yeovilton, lost brake pressure, ran slowly off side of runway, Cat LQ 6.2.69 (Mr J Duncan). Sold to Ministry of Technology for Foulness 30.11.70. Flown from Hurn to Southend 20.1.71. Complete to P&EE Shoeburyness by road 14-15.2.71. Almost complete to RAE Farnborough dump (North side) 16.5.74. Left by road at some time, but later retd. Remains derelict by 1977. [1316.40hrs]

XD235  Production test VA South Marston 25.4.58 (LR Colquhoun). Delivered AHU Lossiemouth 30.4.58. Acceptance test flight 6.6.58. 803 Sqn Lossiemouth ('148/V') 7.6.58. All pressure instruments failed after take-off Lee-on-Solent, Cat SS 27.8.59 (Lt AHP Firth). To Lee-on-Solent 1.9.60 and to RNAY Fleetlands (modernisation). Back to Lee-on-Solent by 15.1.62 and departed 16.1.62. 803 Sqn ('149/V') 19.1.62 and recoded 4.62 ('149/H'). NARIU Lee-on-Solent 29.4.62. RNAY Fleetlands 16.8.62. First air test and departed Lee-on-Solent c27.9.62. 803 Sqn ('149/H') 18.10.62. Unable to release live 1,000-lb bomb, landed safely, Cat SS 1.11.62 (S/L CA Bosworth). Tail skid dragged on catapulting *Hermes*, Cat LC 18.12.62 (Lt SC Creasy). Slow response from engine during landing problem, *Hermes* in Lyme Bay, Cat SS 17.1.64 (Lt RC Dimmock). Recoded 5.64 ('149/R'). ASI problem in fast descent in cloud, formation landing, Cat LQ 24.9.64 (Lt CJ Crowther). Starboard engine failure during steep turn, single-engined landing, Cat LY 28.10.64 (L/C PG Newman). Flew with code '235/R' applied during 1-2.65. Hydraulic failure after inverted flight, Cat LQ 12.1.65 (L/C JOF Billingham). Altimeter problem during descent, formation landing, Lee-on-Solent 23.2.65. RNAY Fleetlands 25.2.65 (modernisation and conversion for FRU duties). Towed to Lee-on-Solent 11.7.66. NASU Brawdy 31.8.66 (mods). Airwork FRU Hurn 11.11.66. Fuel problem, landed safely, Cat SS 26.4.67 (Mr J Duncan). Coded c10.67 ('032') and recoded 12.68 ('832'). RAE Farnborough, sold to Ministry of Technology for Foulness 30.1.70. Flown from Hurn to Southend 16.3.70. P&EE Shoeburyness by road 19-23.3.70. Believed to Larkhill Ranges c.4.71 [doubtful?]. Used for trials 10.74 to 9.83. To Abingdon (where a small team inspecting various types for battle-damage was in operation) 12.10.77. Fuselage less engines retd Shoeburyness 25-27.4.78. Became part of Lot 5 of MoD surplus sale at Shoeburyness by 4.12.90. Fuselage remains finally scrapped by Mayer and Perry scrapyard, Snailwell, Cambs 4.91. Cockpit section acquired by Jeff King and by 1997 at No.424 Sqn ATC Southampton/Hall of Aviation. To Dave Thomas, Welshpool, Powys, 20.2.99. [1434.25hrs]

XD236  Production test VA South Marston 22.4.58 (LR Colquhoun). Delivered AHU Lossiemouth 8.5.58. Acceptance test flight 9.5.58. 803 Sqn ('150/V') 31.5.58. No 1 hydraulic system failure *Victorious*, Cat LX 9.10.58 (L/C GR Higgs). Unable to lower hook, arrested by emergency barrier *Victorious*, Cat HY 20.3.59 (S/L RWD Westlake) [the first operational barrier landing by a Scimitar]. RNAY Fleetlands 26.3.59 (repair). Air tested Lee to Boscombe Down 9.6.61 until 19.6.61. 807 Sqn ('195/C') 23.6.61. ERU inadvertently fired during ground testing Lossiemouth, Cat SS 28.9.61. AHU Tengah 31.1.62. Hood jettisoned inadvertently in hangar, Cat LX 28.5.62. 803 Sqn ('158/H') 1.4.63. Both engines flamed out taxying into dispersal RAAF Butterworth, Cat SS 8.4.63 (S/L AJ Middleton). AHU Tengah 27.6.63. 800 Sqn ('108') 16.7.63. 803 Sqdn ('158/H') 27.2.64 and recoded 5.64 ('154/R'). Bird strike at low level, Cat LQ 12.10.64 (L/C GAI Johnston). Bird strike when flew through flock of birds on low level trial sortie, Cat LQ 24.10.64 (L/C GAI Johnston). Drogue and hose became detached on selection of flight refuelling, Cat SS 30.10.64 (S/L IC Frenz). Bird ingested in engine at 200ft, Cat HY 11.1.65 (Lt J Comby, French Navy). To Lee-on-Solent 5.3.65 and towed to RNAY Fleetlands (modernised and converted to FRU duties). Towed back to Lee-on-Solent 7.9.66 and air tested to Boscombe Down 16.12.66. Airwork FRU Hurn 15.12.66 [sic]. Hydraulic failure, landed safely, Cat SS 9.6.67 (Mr C Butt). Hydraulic leak at 21,000ft, landed safely, Cat LQ 14.6.67 (Mr JF Mullins). Coded c10.67 ('038'). Undercarriage hydraulics problem, diverted safely to Yeovilton, Cat LQ 27.11.67 (Mr RV Lacey). Radio altimeter failure while flying in bad visibility as 'target' for the Fleet radar picket *Corrunna*, flew into high ground St.Catherines Down, 300 yds north of the St.Catherine Pt, Isle of Wight, Cat ZZ 26.6.68 (Mr TE Hill killed). Remains to AIU Lee for investigation by 1.7.68. SOC at RNAY Fleetlands 19.3.69 (extant 8.69), scrapped. [722.45hrs]

*XD236 '195/C' of No.807 Squadron and a Sea Vixen surrounded by spray and steam on the flight deck of HMS Centaur. (J.A.Pike)*

XD237   Production test VA South Marston 22.4.58 (LR Colquhoun). Delivered AHU Lossiemouth 20.6.58. Acceptance test flight 7.7.58. 803 Sqn ('149/V') 12.7.58. Flying from *Victorious*, rear of port jet pipe detached and damaged airframe, emergency landing Hal Far, Cat LC 10.12.58 (Lt MV Maina). RNAY Fleetlands 22.1.59 (repair). Lee-on-Solent to Boscombe Down 27.10.59, air tested 28.10.59. Lossiemouth 4.11.59. 736 Sqn Lossiemouth ('611/LM') 10.11.59. Tain Range, after release of bombs port wing was found to be damaged on inspection, Cat LQ 20.10.60 (Lt CC Giles). Starboard tyre burst landing, Cat LQ 5.6.61 (L/C PH Perks). Lost height slowly while orbiting after dive attack during army co-operation exercise, hit ground at shallow angle, BU, Stripeside Grange Farm, 2nm E of Keith, Banffshire, Cat ZZ 22.6.61 (F/Lt M Farmer RAF killed - suspected limited cockpit distraction due to generator failure warning). WOC 2.7.63.

XD238   Production test VA South Marston 25.4.58 (LR Colquhoun). Delivered AHU Lossiemouth 20.6.58. Acceptance test flight 30.9.58. 803 Sqn *Victorious* ('145/V') 23.10.58. Rocket adapters and rails jettisoned in error Lossiemouth, Cat SS 21.4.59 (Lt MD Bristowe). Hold-back ring entered starboard catapult *Victorious*, Cat SS 7.5.59. Starboard tyre burst after brake fire Lossiemouth, Cat LQ 14.10.59 (Lt MD Bristowe). On taxying, tail was swung and touched a bowser refuelling adjacent aircraft Lossiemouth, Cat LQ 12.1.60 (L/C AJ Leahy). Flying from *Victorious*, fuel leak, rapid fuel loss, engine flamed out on final approach, pilot ejected, aircraft crashed on road near Lossiemouth Golf Course on airfield boundary, Cat ZZ 6.2.60 (L/C PS Davis slightly injured - Ejection No.337). SOC 31.8.60. Wreckage on western boundary of Lossiemouth airfield 6.64 but gone by 1.7.64.

XD239   Production test VA South Marston 23.5.58 (LR Colquhoun). To C(A) charge at VA South Marston. Delivered AHU Lossiemouth 1.7.58. Acceptance test flights 3.7.58 and 19.7.58. 803 Sqn ('151/V') 23.7.58. Hydraulic failure and engine fire start up, Lossiemouth, Cat SS 12.9.59 (Lt JW Beard). Fire in port engine after relight, single-engined landing Bristol, Cat SS 14.9.59 (Lt MD Bristowe). Tugmaster skidded wet deck when ship rolled and hit starboard flap of aircraft, *Victorious*, Cat LQ 11.2.60. 736 Sqn Lossiemouth ('610/LM') 25.8.60 (fitted VHF). RNAY Fleetlands 7.10.60 (modernisation). Towed to Lee 14.7.61 and departed 31.7.61. AHU Lossiemouth 17.8.61. 800 Sqn ('109/R') loan aerobatic team for 1961 SBAC Show 23.8.61. AHU Lossiemouth 12.9.61. RNAY Fleetlands 12.12.61. Controls jammed on air test at Lee 17.4.62 (Lt Cdr PM Stevenson). Departed Lee-on-Solent 26.4.62. 736 Sqn Lossiemouth ('613') 26.4.62. Port tyre burst taxying, Cat LX 20.6.62 (Lt AMD de Labilliere). Hydraulic failure, precautionary landing, Cat LQ 29.6.62 (L/C PG Newman). Hook missed runway arrester wire, Cat SS 22.11.62 (Lt AG MacFie). To Lee-on-Solent 7.12.62 (acceptance test flight) and departed Lee-on-Solent 21.1.63. 800 Sqn ('103/R') 23.1.63. Drogue hit nose during flight refuelling, Cat LQ 10.4.63 (S/L NHL Bowden). Undercarriage hydraulic failure, Cat SS 13.5.63 (L/C DF Mills). *Ark Royal*, diverted to RAF Khormaksar with radio and Hydraulic 1 intermittent failure after making four failed deck passes, failed on first attempt at runway due to poor visibility, lost height in turn, ejected, aircraft ditched in 6ft of water, Aden Harbour, Cat HZ 22.5.63 (S/L CD Legg injured - Ejection No.690). Wreckage shipped to UK for repair, arr RNAY Fleetlands 12.7.63 (Cat. 4 work commenced 22.7.63). Stripped to bare airframe but repair abandoned as not funded, items being set aside for the rebuild of XD328. SOC 23.9.64. Remains held at Fleetlands as a spares source for XD220 until moved to dump 28.4.66. Scrapped by Birmingham Unimetal 3.67. [673hrs].

XD240   Production test VA South Marston 23.5.58 (LR Colquhoun). Delivered AHU Lossiemouth 10.7.58. Acceptance test flight 24.7.58. 803 Sqn ('145/V') 25.7.58. Displayed at SBAC Show Farnborough 9.58. Sqn CO leading the first Scimitar squadron aboard the newly modernised *Victorious* steaming off the Isle of Wight, caught No.1 wire, which pulled out too far then parted, aircraft carried on up deck and ran over angle at walking pace into sea ahead of ship 50°24.5'N 0°52.5'W, Cat ZZ 25.9.58 (Cdr JD Russell trapped in cockpit and sank with aircraft, drowned). SOC 30.10.58. Nose section salvaged four weeks later from a depth of 220ft by the *Barfoss* and *Barbastel*, L/C M Paynter (CO), S/L EWJ Smith and Lt WD Barrington being diving officers in charge of operations aboard HMS *Reclaim*. Cockpit section to AIU Lee-on-Solent by MARTSU.

*[This episode took place before the national press, and embarrassingly front-page pictures appeared before the pilot's family had been informed. The SAR Whirlwind had been over the spot in seconds and the rescue crewman was actually astride the cockpit as it sank, but was just too late. Later the cause of the wire failure was discovered, and about 3 hrs afterwards L/C GR Higgs led the squadron on board in staggered flights, all landing safely]*

XD241   Production test VA South Marston 30.6.58 (LR Colquhoun). Taken on C(A) charge at VA South Marston for trials 1.7.58 (to substantiate the complete, fully modified MRG system and check flight performance on Cont No KC/A/045/CB.9(a)). VA Weybridge 18.7.58. A&AEE 5.9.58 (full substantiation of performance and reliability of fully modified MRG system and RC-8A and RC-8B inverters). RAE Bedford 15.9.58 (catapult arrester and MRG trials). A&AEE 21.11.58. AHU Lossiemouth 5.3.59. Acceptance test flight 1.6.59. 736 Sqn Lossiemouth ('614/LM') 3.6.59. [A&AEE 5.9.59, retd 736 Sqn?]. Flew through large flock of birds, one hit nose and entered starboard intake causing vibration, Milltown, Cat SS 19.8.60 (Lt JRJ Rutherford). Engine compressor found to be damaged by foreign body, Cat SS 16.11.60 (Lt CC Giles). No 1 hydraulic failure occurred as aircraft joined landing circuit, landed with hook down and caught wires, Cat LX 1.12.60 (S/L CJ Wilson). Indications of hydraulic failure, precautionary landing, Cat LY 27.2.61 (Lt(E) MG Griffin). Bird entered starboard intake while landing, Cat SS 24.5.61 (Lt MV Maina). To Lee-on-Solent 15.6.61 (still as '614/LM') and to RNAY Fleetlands (modernisation). Back to Lee-on-Solent by 13.4.62 and flown Lee-on-Solent to Boscombe Down 18.4.62. RAF Handling Sqn Boscombe Down 25.4.62. AHU Lossiemouth 11.5.62. 803 Sqn ('150/H') 7.8.62 (via Culdrose). Starboard engine flamed out in tailchase, relit, Lossiemouth, Cat SS 29.10.62 (S/L MJ Harwood). Starboard engine lost rpm in flight from *Hermes*, landed safely Tengah, Cat SS 27.12.62 (S/L JS Flexman). Compressor failure on catapult, single engine landing *Hermes*, Cat SS 8.1.63 (S/L AJ Middleton). Nozzle damage during flight refuelling by Sea Vixen XJ586, Cat LQ 15.1.63 (S/L CA Bosworth). Panel lost in flight, Cat LQ 4.10.63 (Lt RV Ponter). Bomb fragments damaged wing root, Garvie Island Range, Cat LQ 20.11.63 (S/L JS Flexman). Recoded 5.64 ('150/R'). Windscreen started to break up on take-off, Cat LQ 3.11.64 (Lt CJ Crowther). Windscreen cracked in flight, Cat LQ 9.11.64 (L/C JOF Billingham). Flap damaged in practice dog fight, Cat LX 24.11.64 (Lt NE Rankin). Port engine vibration, single-engined landing Lossiemouth, Cat SS 6.4.65 (S/L T Thomas). AHU Lossiemouth 12.5.65. To Lee-on-Solent 5.11.65 and noted with MARTSU 15.11.65. Towed to RNAY Fleetlands 22.12.65 (modernisation and conversion for FRU duties). Towed back to Lee-on-Solent 24.1.68 and departed during first test flight to NASU Brawdy 22.2.68 (Lt Cdr PM Stevenson). Airwork FRU Hurn 15.11.68. Coded 12.68 ('838'). Hydraulic leak, precautionary landing Yeovilton, Cat LQ 25.8.69 (Mr RC Minton). Transferred to MinTech (Farnborough) charge and flown to Southend 2.12.70. Then by road to P&EE Shoeburyness 21.12.70. SOC 19.1.71. Used for trials 11.73 – 1.74. Rear fuselage and jet pipes to P&EE Pendine Ranges, Dyfed 6.7.83. Wing only at Shoeburyness by 1990, these forming part of Lots 6 and 7 of an MoD surplus sale at Foulness by 4.12.90 and apparently scrapped by 4.91. [1140.35hrs]

XD242  Production test VA South Marston 18.6.58 (LR Colquhoun). Delivered AHU Lossiemouth 24.7.58. Acceptance test flight 25.7.58. 803 Sqn ('152/V') 7.8.58. Touched down wires and both tyres burst *Victorious*, Cat LQ 6.1.59 (Lt PJ Barber). Panel detached during take-off Lossiemouth, Cat SS 20.2.59 (Lt GB Hoddinott). Bird strike, undercarriage problems Lossiemouth, Cat LQ 1.9.59 (Lt CC Giles). Returning after DLPs on *Hermes*, shut down one engine to conserve fuel for the last stage, attempted single-engined landing, overshot from a too close final approach, failed to gain height or speed and crashed in wheels-up landing on airfield, Yeovilton, Cat HZ 14.5.60 (Lt IB Macleod severe spinal injuries). Aircraft transported by road to RNAY Fleetlands 24.6.60 (en-route became stuck in corner of Quay Street/East Street, Fareham, and blocked the traffic for several hours). Loaded aboard lighter at Foxbury Point and shipped to Scotland. Fuselage arrived at AES Arbroath by 12.7.60 as GI Class II airframe (no number allocated) to at least 9.64. At MARTSU Lee-on-Solent 1.65 to 5.65. Wreckage to Aberporth by 9.67 for missile blast-effect ground tests.

XD243  Production Test VA South Marston 4.7.58 (LR Colquhoun). Delivered AHU Lossiemouth 1.9.58. Acceptance test flight 26.9.58. 807 Sqn ('190/R') 30.9.58. Counter weight crane hit starboard air intake Lossiemouth, Cat HC 10.12.58. Fire warning system operated, relight abandoned Lossiemouth, Cat SS 14.3.59 (Cdr JD Treacher). To Lee-on-Solent by 31.7.59 and repainted by RNAY Fleetlands at Lee. 803 Sqn ('147/V') 21.9.59. Being moved on deck during refuelling operations, ship rolled, aircraft slid on deck, dragging Tugmaster with it, coming to rest with main wheels in catwalk *Victorious*, Cat HY 3.2.60. RNAY Fleetlands 26.2.60. VA South Marston 11.4.60 (Cat 4 repair and mod programme). RNAY Fleetlands 19.6.61. Towed back to Lee-on-Solent 7.7.61. Air test from Lee-on-Solent to Boscombe Down 8.7.61 and air tested there until flown back to Lee 28.7.61. To AHU Lossiemouth. 807 Sqn ('191/C') 26.8.61. All pressure instruments failed after orbiting for 5 min in cloud, landed in formation with shepherd aircraft, Cat SS 6.10.61 (Lt(E) MG Griffin). 800 Sqn ('113/R') 27.3.62. Undercarriage malfunction, landed safely *Ark Royal* 60m SSE of Hong Kong, Cat SS 29.5.62 (L/C JAD Ford). Speared wire on landing *Ark Royal*, Cat SS 11.9.62 (S/L AD Alsop). Flames from port exhaust after catapult launch *Ark Royal*, diverted to Khormaksar, single-engined landing, Cat SS 17.11.62 (L/C A Mancais). Nose-probe broke off during flight refuelling, Cat LQ 7.3.63 (S/L CD Legg). Foreign body entered port engine, normal landing Lossiemouth, Cat SS 11.4.63 (Lt E Cope). Bird strike over Dornoch Firth, Tain Range, Cat LQ 18.4.63 (S/L A McMeekan). Hood blew off in climb, landed safely Lossiemouth, Cat LQ 1.5.63 (Lt JPF Nichols). Port engine flamed out landing Embakasi, Nairobi, Cat SS 2.10.63 (S/L NHL Bowden). Hydraulic problem during maintenance, Culdrose, Cat LQ 30.1.64. To Lee-on-Solent 20.2.64 and to RNAY Fleetlands (modernisation). Towed back to Lee-on-Solent 21.5.65 and prepared by MARTSU for shipment. To Far East in *Bacchus* 28.7.65. NASU Changi 10.9.65. 800B Flt ('115/E') 21.11.65. Hose parted during flight refuelling at 30,000ft over Red Sea, *Eagle*, Cat SS 20.1.66 (Lt PAA Waring). Drop tank problem after launch, then hydraulic failure, landed safely, *Eagle*, Cat SS 16.3.66 (Lt PJ McManus). Met severe turbulence, hail and icing at 40,000ft in cloud, landed safely *Eagle*, Cat LQ 15.4.66 (Lt PJ McManus). Flight refuelling problem 200 miles from ship in Mozambique Channel, retd safely, *Eagle*, Cat SS 17.4.66 (Lt PAA Waring). 803 Sqn ('025/E') 6.5.66. Tailplane damaged by ricochet during practice strafing, Cat LQ 15.7.66 (Lt PG De Souza). Cat SS 26.7.66 (Lt MJ Williams). To GI Class I at AES Lee-on-Solent 24.8.66. Downgraded to GI Class II as A2588 27.2.68 (Engine Nos E4606/4607). To RNAY Fleetlands for de-instrumentation 22.9.70. By road to P&EE Shoeburyness 15-17.9.70 and used for trials 10.72 to 2.80. Port wing to Farnborough 30.6.76, retd from 71 MU 18.11.76. Rear fuselage and jet pipes to P&EE Pendine Ranges, Dyfed 6.7.83 and current 3.94. [880.20hrs]

XD244  Production Test VA South Marston 7.7.58 to 20.8.58. Delivered AHU Lossiemouth 25.8.58. Acceptance test flights 15 & 16.9.58. 807 Sqn ('191/R') 29.9.58. Practising LABS manoeuvres on Tain Range, on return, nose wheel retracted or unlocked and collapsed, Lossiemouth, Cat HC 29.1.59 (Lt PH Perks). 803 Sqn ('150/V') 16.1.60 (fitted VHF). 736 Sqn Lossiemouth (uncoded) 25.8.60. To Lee-on-Solent 25.10.60 (coded '-/LM') and to RNAY Fleetlands 20.10.60. Air tested to Boscombe Down 27.7.61 until 1.8.61. Prepared for sea transit at Fleetlands and departed via MARTSU for Far East 17.8.61. Arr AHU Tengah 18.9.61. 803 Sqn ('151/V') 1.10.61. Port engine compressor blades damaged by foreign body *Victorious*, Cat LY 3.12.61. To Lee-on-Solent 18.12.61 and to RNAY Fleetlands (port ECU change). ECU check test and departed Lee-on-Solent 13.1.62. 803 Sqn ('151/V') 13.1.62. Fuselage hit by tailplane of XD328 during deck move *Victorious*, Cat LQ 27.3.62. Recoded 4.62 ('151/H'). Port tyre burst taxying onto catapult, swung to starboard, *Hermes*, Cat LQ 14.11.62 (S/L MJ Harwood). Smoke from PR nose taxying Tengah, Cat LQ 1.1.63 (S/L MJ Harwood). Probe damage during flight refuelling, Cat LQ 21.2.63 (L/C B Willson). Bird strike on Navex from *Hermes* in South Malaya low flying areas, Cat LQ 19.3.63 (Lt RV Ponter). Damaged on deck by Sea Vixen XJ514 8.10.63. RNAY Fleetlands 30.10.63 (Maincheck 2 and Cat 4 repair). Depart Lee-on-Solent 24.4.65. AHU Lossiemouth 26.4.65. 803 Sqn ('153/R') 7.5.65. Starboard engine fluctuation, single-engined landing, Cat LQ 26.5.65 (Lt R Wren). Recoded 7.65 ('026/R'). Hose broke off at 1,000ft after refuelling 4 aircraft, Cat SS 31.8.65 (F/Lt TG Gilroy RAF). Flight refuelling hose parted on withdrawal from probe of XD278, Cat SS 24.9.65 (Lt JM Heath). Fire shortly after take-off, successful single-engined landing, *Ark Royal*, HY 31.12.65 (Lt NE Rankin). Fire warning port engine, landed safely Changi, Cat SS 28.1.66 (Lt BP Merindin). Port engine fire warning, single-engined landing, *Ark Royal*, Cat SS 7.3.66 (S/L AR Dady). Loaned 800B Flt 16.3.66. Returned 803 Sqn ('026/R') 4.5.66. Bird strike on starboard engine, Cat SS 22.7.66 (Lt EK Somerville-Jones). From *Ark Royal*, hit power cable at 250ft over Astfyorden Fjord, diverted to Oerland airfield, landed safely, Cat LX 16.8.66 (S/L GM Faulkner). NASU Brawdy 3.10.66. Air brake problem, landed safely, Cat LC 6.10.66 (L/C PM Stevenson). On closure of RNAS Brawdy to Airwork FRU Hurn as reserve aircraft in open storage 3.9.70 (not flown). Flown to Southend 12.2.71 (last flight of a Scimitar), then by road to Shoeburyness 15.2.71. Sold to Ministry of Technology for AWRE/P&EE 24.2.71. Starboard wing to RARDE Fort Halstead 23.1.74. Used for trials 10.74 – 11.82. Fuselage and port wing to RAE Farnborough 30.6.76, wing retd from 71 MU 18.11.76 and fuselage 12.10.77. Fuselage remains finally scrapped by Mayer & Perry scrapyard, Snailwell, Cambs 4.91, parts going to Parkhouse Aviation, Ottershaw. [918.30hrs]

XD245 Production Test VA South Marston 18.7.58 to 27.8.58. Delivered AHU Lossiemouth 29.8.58. Acceptance test flight 3.10.58. 807 Sqn Lossiemouth ('192/R') 4.10.58. Nose oleo collapsed starting port engine, Cat LC 19.8.59 (Lt GB Hoddinott). 803 Sqn (code unknown - could be '155' or '156') 15.1.60. *Victorious* in Moray Firth, DLP, No.1 Hydraulic failure, undercarriage lowered but unable to lower hook, emergency hook selector failed to operate hook, unsuccessfully bounced on deck to try and free hook, low fuel state, with wheels and flaps down was out of rage of diversion, emergency barrier rigged but by then down to 300lbs fuel, pilot climbed and ejected at 2,000ft, 1m on port beam of ship, aircraft went into sea, Cat ZZ 7.2.60 (Lt RWD Westlake killed when parachute remained attached to seat and failed to deploy, body not found) [236.35hrs]

XD246 Production test VA South Marston 29.8.58 (LR Colquhoun). Delivered AHU Lossiemouth 25.9.58. 807 Sqn Lossiemouth ('193/R') 17.11.58. Fire warning light, single-engined landing, Cat SS 19.11.58 (Lt MD Bristowe). RNAY Fleetlands (via Yeovilton and Lee-on-Solent) 10.12.58. 'C' Sqn A&AEE 19.1.59 (C(A) clearance of 25lb practice bomb in the LABS manoeuvre). 803 Sqn 5.2.59. Slipped out of chocks and hit XD264, *Victorious*, Cat LY 20.3.59. RNAY Fleetlands 24.3.59. 803 Sqn Lossiemouth ('153/V') 23.4.59. Skin flaps damaged after bombing at RAE West Freugh, Cat LX 27.4.59 (Lt B Davies). To Lee-on-Solent 4.4.60 and to RNAY Fleetlands (flown Lee-on-Solent to Boscombe Down 8.9.60 and air tested there 9.9.60). AHU Lossiemouth 21.9.60. 800 Sqn ('150/V') 20.10.60. *Ark Royal*, windscreen shattered during LABS manoeuvre Tarhua Range, Libya (32°25'N 13°15'E), Cat LQ 12.1.61 (Lt AJ Goodenough). AHU Hal Far 16.1.61. To Lee-on-Solent 8.3.61 (coded '-/R') and to RNAY Fleetlands. Air tested from Lee on delivery to Yeovilton 20.3.61. 800 Sqn ('104/R') 22.3.61. 736 Sqn Lossiemouth ('611/LM') 21.9.61. Partial instrument failure, landed safely led in by Vampire, Cat SS 29.9.61 (Lt PH Perks). Undercarriage indicator malfunction, Cat LQ 21.3.62 (Lt AHS Anderson). RNAY Fleetlands 4.7.62 (maintenance and refurbishing). Back to Lee-on-Solent by 3.4.63 and last test there/departed to AHU Lossiemouth 5.4.63. 800 Sqn ('108/R') 16.4.63. AHU Lossiemouth 26.4.63. 803 Sqn ('152/H') 26.9.63. Damaged by bomb debris on Tain Range, Cat LQ 11.3.64 (S/L JS Flexman). Recoded 5.64 ('152/R'). Debris damage during low strafing sortie, Tain Range, Cat LC 11.11.64 (L/C GAI Johnston). Flaps damaged on folding wings after landing, Cat LX 27.2.65 (Lt ARD Monro-Davies). To AHU Lossiemouth 4.65. 764B Sqn ('617') 7.5.65. Port engine problem, single-engined landing, Cat SS 29.6.65 (L/C PP Cardew). Hydraulic problem, normal GCA, Cat LQ 29.7.65 (Lt AR Dady). Nosewheel problem after take-off, landed safely, Cat SS 3.8.65 (Lt MJ Williams). AHU Lossiemouth 12.8.65. NARIU Lee-on-Solent 29.10.65 (trial conversion for Airwork FRU). Airwork FRU Hurn 28.6.66. Coded 10.67 ('035'). AHU Brawdy 29.11.66 (repair). Airwork FRU ('035') 12.12.66. To Lee-on-Solent 20.8.68 in open storage. By MARTSU to RNAY Fleetlands by 29.8.68. To permanent Ministry of Technology charge (RAE Farnborough) and transported to P&EE Shoeburyness 8.5.69 (noted in Everley's Transport Yard, Dawley Rd, Hayes 8-11.5.69), arriving 12.5.69. Used for trials 5.70. Transported to Larkhill Ranges as target 5.71. [1220.05hrs]

XD247 Production Test VA South Marston 26.8.58 to 24.9.58. Delivered AHU Lossiemouth 25.9.58. Acceptance test flight 6.10.58. 807 Sqn Lossiemouth ('194/R') 4.11.58. Mid-air explosion, pilot ejected but seat did not separate, aircraft crashed Cullicudden, Black Isle, Ross & Cromarty, Cat ZZ 19.11.58 (S/L CR Cresswell RN DoI 20.11.58). Aircraft had only flown 33.45 hours.
*NB. All Scimitars grounded for several weeks following this incident with a suspected fault in the ejection seat mechanism. It was later proved that the ejection seat had not been fired by the cables or by movement of the seat on its rails. It seems the hood time delay mechanism must have been displaced by the explosive force. The pilot was subject to an inadvertent ejection with little or no delay after the hood fired.*

XD248 Production test VA South Marston 29.9.58 (LR Colquhoun). Delivered AHU Lossiemouth 31.10.58. Acceptance test flight 18.12.58. 807 Sqn ('195/R') 13.1.59. Loud bang followed by port engine failure Lossiemouth, Cat LQ 12.2.59 (L/C KA Leppard). Undercarriage problems, greens main undercarriage by bumping, Lossiemouth, Cat SS 2.7.59 (L/C KA Leppard). Asymmetric braking landing run Lossiemouth, Cat SS 3.11.59 (L/C WA Tofts). To Lee-on-Solent 29.1.60 and to RNAY Fleetlands 1.2.60. Flown Lee-on-Solent to Boscombe Down 16.8.60 and air tested there 21.8.60. 803 Sqn Lossiemouth ('151/V') 24.8.60. On *Victorious*, hydraulic failure, diverted to Yeovilton, Cat SS 20.10.60 (Lt AS Tuck). Bird entered starboard engine air intake during night landing Lossiemouth, Cat LQ 13.1.61 (S/L AHS Anderson). Bridle-catching trials, *Victorious*, 24.1.61 with 803 Sqn. AHU Lossiemouth 26.1.61. Lost R/T contact on GCA, overshot Yeovilton and landed Henstridge, damaged flaps on fence posts on runway, Cat LX 12.6.61 (Mr DR Skinner ferry pilot). RNAY Fleetlands 12.6.61. Air tested from Lee 19.9.61, then shipped to Far East. Loaded by MARTSU aboard SS *Coromandel* at Southampton (cocooned). AHU Tengah 6.11.61. 807 Sqn ('190/C') 1.2.62. *Centaur*, hydraulic failure on test flight, engaged Safeland barrier Tengah 7.2.62 (Lt JW Moore). Hoisted aboard *Centaur* for return to UK 13.2.62. Stn Flt Lossiemouth 26.4.62. Hood inadvertently jettisoned in hangar, rating injured, Cat LX 18.5.62. To Lee-on-Solent 8.6.62 and shipped back to Tengah 8.62. Back to RNAY Fleetlands. Air test at Lee-on-Solent 4.12.62 & 5.12.62 and departed to AHU Lossiemouth 6.12.62. 800 Sqn ('102/R') 23.1.63. Bird strike on port outer pylon fairing over Dornoch Firth, Cat LQ 30.1.63 (Lt L Ingham). Starboard pylon fairing lost in flight, Cat SS 16.2.63 (Lt AM Hickling). False hydraulic warning on take-off Lossiemouth, Cat SS 19.2.63 (Lt AM Hickling). 803 Sqn ('144/(H)') 23.2.63. Undercarriage hydraulic failure on take-off, emergency landing

Lossiemouth, Cat SS 3.4.63 (Lt GHR Wooff). Undercarriage hydraulic problem, emergency landing Lossiemouth, Cat SS 10.4.63 (Lt PC Marshall). Foreign body damaged engine, *Ark Royal*, Cat SS 24.6.63. At Lossiemouth, hood came off at 32,000ft, Cat LQ 17.1.64. Recoded 5.64 '144/R'). To Lee-on-Solent 6.8.64 and to RNAY Fleetlands (modernisation). Towed back to Lee-on-Solent 14.12.65. Experienced technical malfunction over Isle of Man during ferry flight Lee-on-Solent to Lossiemouth, refused permission to land on Isle of Man and diverted back to Lee, 23.2.66 (Lt Cdr J Brandt). Departed Lee-on-Solent again 7.3.66. Flew back to Lee-on-Solent 11.3.66 (with four underwing pylons reportedly for 'bombing trials' carried out from Lee-on-Solent 4.4, 6.4 and 22.4.66). C(A) loan 27.4.66. RNAY Fleetlands (via Lee) to RAE Weapons Flight West Freugh 12.5.66 (development and proving trials of No.907 fuse, No.947 fuse, 1,000lb retarded bomb and 28lb retarded practice bomb). Suspected brake failure, diverted to Lossiemouth, Cat LQ 19.1.67 (Lt MT Hynett). [Braking trials aircraft at Farnborough circa 1967 until delivered to NASU?]. NASU Brawdy 17.4.68 (removal of instrumentation). Airwork FRU late 1968 but rejected as sub-standard and returned NASU Brawdy by 22.12.68 (open storage). SOC RSP 8.7.69. Scrapped there 5.70. [639.40hrs]

*XD248 '190/C' about to be launched from HMS Centaur in 1962. (J.A.Pike)*

XD249 Production test VA South Marston 19.9.58 (LR Colquhoun). Delivered AHU Lossiemouth 30.9.58. Acceptance test flight 14.10.58. 807 Sqn Lossiemouth ('196/R') 14.10.58. Bird strike on take-off, Cat SS 12.11.58 (Lt PJ Lovick). 736 Sqn Lossiemouth ('612/LM') 15.2.60. Tain Range, bird hit starboard intake on a low level strike, Cat LQ 20.9.60 (S/L AJ Stone). C(A) free loan for relight tests MoA, authorised 27.2.61 [at Lossiemouth?]. Returned 736 Sqn Lossiemouth ('612/LM') 25.3.61. Ricochet damage in RP attack Tain Range, Cat HX 17.5.61 (Lt GB Hoddinott). Hydraulic failure, landed safely, Cat SS 16.6.61 (Lt JA Manley). False fire warning light during formation aerobatics, Cat SS 12.7.61 (L/C JAD Ford). Failure of undercarriage warning light, landed safely, Cat SS 4.9.61 (Lt JDHB Howard). Swung to starboard after landing wet runway, Cat LQ 3.10.61 (S/L GHR Wooff). Lead aircraft in formation landing, overrun by XD225, starboard wing damaged 17.11.61 (S/L AJ Middleton). Ricochet damage, Tain Range, Cat LQ 23.11.61 (L/C PG Newman). To Lee-on-Solent 14.12.61 (air test 15.12.62 & 18.12.62) and on to RNAY Fleetlands. Flew Lee-on-Solent to Boscombe Down 20.9.62, returned Lee-on-Solent 24.9.62 and final test there 3.10.62. To Far East in SS *Ben Wyvis* 6.11.62. AHU Tengah 18.12.62. 800 Sqn ('111/R') 20.8.63. Ferrying from Yeovilton, shortage of fuel, ditched in Moray Firth off Lossiemouth after Hydraulic 1 failure resulted in partial lowering of starboard undercarriage which pilot unable to lock on emergency, Cat ZZ 28.1.64 (Lt PEH Banfield ejected, injured, picked up by SAR Helicopter - Ejection No.794). SOC 6.2.64.

XD250 Production Tests VA South Marston 30.9.58 (LR Colquhoun). Delivered AHU Lossiemouth 28.10.58. Acceptance test flight 9.12.58. 807 Sqn Lossiemouth ('197/R') 10.12.58. Hydraulic system failure, Cat SS 6.2.59 (S/L RWD Westlake). 803 Sqn 27.1.60. Temp C(A) loan to MoA 24.3.60 (test flying by Rolls Royce pilot at Lossiemouth to assess relight characteristics of Avon 202 to post and pre Mod 1990/2262). To Lee-on-Solent 14.4.60 and to RNAY Fleetlands on RN charge 14.4.60. Towed back to Lee-on-Solent by 4.10.60 and flown Lee-on-Solent to Boscombe Down 10.10.60 and air tested there 11.10.60. 803 Sqn ('150/V') 18.10.60. AHU Lossiemouth 11.1.61. 800 Sqn ('107/R') 25.3.61. RNAY Fleetlands 3.5.61. Air tested Lee then delivered Yeovilton 15.5.61. 800 Sqn ('107/R') 16.5.61. AHU Lossiemouth 28.11.61. 736 Sqn Lossiemouth ('614') 15.1.62. Fire on starting port engine, Cat LQ 27.2.62 (Lt PGJ Murison). To Lee-on-Solent 17.8.62 and on to RNAY Fleetlands (modernisation began 22.11.62). Flew Lee-on-Solent to Boscombe Down 2.8.63 and 6.8.63, returning 7.8.63. Depart Lee-on-Solent to AHU Lossiemouth 10.9.63. 803 Sqn ('147/H') 31.10.63. Sidewinder missile fell off at 4,000ft, Cat SS 3.12.63 (Lt MT Hynett). Recoded 5.64 ('147/R'). Port engine vibration on take-off, single-engined landing, Cat SS 26.6.64 (Lt JOF Billingham). Recoded 8.64 ('154/R') and 7.65 ('027/R'). Hydraulic failure, fire in aircraft, rolled to starboard due to involuntary lowering of flaps and dive brakes, violent trim changes and fire warning lights, ditched in Indian Ocean 30m from *Ark Royal*, 90m E of Mombasa, Cat ZZ 17.2.66 (S/L ZK Skrodzki picked up unhurt by 815 Sqn Wessex - Ejection No.1219). [977.45hrs]

XD264 Production test VA South Marston 28.10.58 (LR Colquhoun). Delivered AHU Lossiemouth 11.58. Acceptance test flight 6.12.58. RNAY Fleetlands 11.12.58. 803 Sqn ('154/V') 6.2.59. Defective brakes, collided with XD232 *Victorious*, Cat LY 20.3.59. Hit by XD246 *Victorious*, Cat LY 20.3.59. RNAY Fleetlands 25.3.59. 803 Sqn ('154/V') 23.4.59. Vibration and thud from starboard engine, closed down Ince Bay, Cat SS 27.4.59 (Lt LE Middleton). RNAY Fleetlands 13.5.59 until departure from Lee-on-Solent 21.5.59. 803 Sqn Lossiemouth ('154/V') 15.6.59. Cartridge fired and hood jettisoned *Victorious*, Cat SS 22.7.59 (L/C GR Higgs). Canopy blew off West Freugh, Cat LX 28.8.59 (Lt MD Bristowe). RNAY Fleetlands 12.4.60. Flown Lee to Boscombe Down 20.12.60 and air tested there 3.1.61. 736 Sqn Lossiemouth ('609/LM') 10.1.61. To Lee-on-Solent 28.3.61 and to Fleetlands. Air tested from Lee-on-Solent then to Boscombe Down 17.4.61 (now repainted, uncoded but with red fin for 800 Sqdn). Hydraulic failure taxying for take-off at RAE Bedford, Cat SS 11.7.61 (S/L CA Bosworth). Warning lights came on when selecting undercarriage down, landed safely, Cat SS 12.7.61 (S/L CA Bosworth). 800 Sqn ('108/R') 13.7.61. Hydraulic failure during aerobatic sortie, starboard leg remained retracted, pilot ejected at 8,000ft 6m out over sea, aircraft turned about and crashed in wood 5m S of Cullen, Morayshire, Cat ZZ 21.7.61 (L/C DP Norman minor back injuries). Written off as uneconomical to repair 24.7.61. Wreckage to AHU Lossiemouth, then to Staravia dump at Fleet 12.63. Finally disposed of 12.65.

XD265 Production test VA South Marston 20.11.58 (LR Colquhoun). To C(A) charge at VA South Marston 19.12.58 (fit UHF Mod 266 *Blue Silk*). Returned RN at VA charge 6.59 (brought up to RN standard). Delivered AHU Lossiemouth 31.7.59. Acceptance test flight 24.8.59. 800 Sqn ('105/R') 26.8.59. Fire warning relighting port engine, Leuchars, Cat SS 19.9.59 (Lt RW Edward). No 1 hydraulic system failure, Lossiemouth, Cat SS 15.12.59 (Lt RJ Noyes). AHU Lossiemouth 3.5.61. 800 Sqn ('105/R') 18.5.61. To Lee-on-Solent 18.9.61 and on to RNAY Fleetlands(modernisation). AHU Lossiemouth 25.4.62. 736 Sqn Lossiemouth ('611') 20.6.62. During simulated DLP, bird ingested into starboard engine during overwater flight at 420 knots and 400ft, engine caught fire, crashed in Moray

*An early photograph of XD267 '193/R' at Lossiemouth in 1959. (J.A.Pike)*

Firth nr Milltown, Cat ZZ 15.11.62 (L/C JF Kennett injured during ejection at 400ft and recovered by RAF Leuchars SAR helicopter a few minutes after hitting water - Ejection No.624). Wreckage dumped Arbroath and scrapped early/mid 1963. [445.50hrs]

XD266 Production Test VA South Marston 14.12.58 – 19.2.59. Delivered AHU Lossiemouth 19.2.59. Acceptance test flight 23.2.59. 803 Sqn ('155/V') 12.4.59. AHU Lossiemouth 29.5.49. 803 Sqn ('155/V') 20.6.59. VA South Marston on C(A) charge 1.10.59 (prepare for night deck landing assessment against Cont No KC/A/044/CB.5(a)). A&AEE 5.10.59 (check of cockpit lighting, flight checks of ASSU and instrumentation required for night deck landing trials). a 803 Sqn ('155/V') 10.59. Night catapult launch, load left aircraft at RAE Bedford, Cat LQ 15.10.59 (Lt GR Higgs). Fifth aircraft to land, caught No.1 wire which pulled out and parted, carried on up deckover angle into sea *Victorious*, Cat ZZ 19.11.59 (Lt JB Cross quickly escaped unhurt, picked up by SAR Dragonfly VX598 Lt Dobree-Carey/LACMN Crispin).

XD267 Production test VA South Marston 12.12.58 (LR Colquhoun). Delivered AHU Lossiemouth 11.2.59. Acceptance test flight 5.3.59. 807 Sqn (193/R') 13.3.59. RNAY Fleetlands 9.10.59. Flown Lee-on-Solent to Boscombe Down 4.2.60, last air test there 8.2.60. 807 Sqn (uncoded) 11.2.60. 804 Sqn ('164/H') 23.2.60. AHU Lossiemouth 5.5.60. Temp 803 Sqn Lossiemouth ('155/V') 1.9.60. 736 Sqn Lossiemouth ('610/LM') 6.10.60 (relight tests on C(A) free loan 3.2.61 - 25.3.61). RNAY Fleetlands 29.3.61. Air tested at Lee 18.4.61. 736 Sqn Lossiemouth ('610/LM') 18.4.61. Ricochet damage in dive bombing attack Tain Range, Cat HX 18.5.61 (F/Lt M Farmer RAF). Impact damage to tailplane, Cat LQ 23.1.62 (S/L L Ingham). Hydraulic system failure while strafing on Tain Range, Cat LQ 5.4.62 (Lt JF Kennett). To Lee-on-Solent 2.7.62 and to RNAY Fleetlands (modernisation). Back to Lee-on-Solent by 21.4.63. Flew Lee-on-Solent to Boscombe Down 1.5.63 and last test/departed Lee-on-Solent to AHU Lossiemouth 3.5.63. 803 Sqn Lossiemouth ('151/H') 4.11.63. Inboard half pylon fairing found missing on landing, Cat SS 12.11.63 (S/L JS Flexman). Flight refuelling problem, *Hermes*, Cat SS 6.12.63 (Lt RV Ponter). Throttle problem in inverted flight at 20,000ft, Cat SS 8.1.64 (S/L JS Flexman). Recoded 5.64 '151/R'). Panel fell off on take-off, Cat LQ 16.7.64 (S/L A McMeekan). Canopy lost over sea after take-off, landed safely, Cat LQ 21.9.64 (S/L KB Owen). Night dive bombing sortie, ammunition panel lost, Cat LQ 12.11.64 (L/C GAI Johnston). ASI problem in wire-pulling trials off Portland Bill, Cat LQ 30.11.64 (L/C JOF Billingham). AHU Lossiemouth 9.2.65. 764B Sqn Lossiemouth ('617') 20.7.65. Undercarriage warning light malfunction, Cat SS 9.9.65 (Mr KG Wilson, Airwork). Two 25-lb practice bombs fell off outer pylon on landing, Cat LQ 22.9.65 (S/L AR Dady). Probe head broke off during flight refuelling, Cat LQ 13.10.65 (S/L AR Dady). Airwork FRU Hurn 1.12.65 (for pilot familiarisation on type, still in 764B markings). NASU Brawdy 21.11.66. Airwork FRU Hurn 18.9.68. Coded 12.68 ('835'). Warning light after take-off, wing tanks jettisoned in sea, landed safely, Cat SS 6.2.69 (Mr JF Mullins). Sold to Ministry of Technology for AWRE Foulness 11.9.69. RAE Farnborough for apprentice training 17.10.69. To Proof & Experimental Establishment Shoeburyness 15/16.6.70. Used for trials 5.71 to 7.84. Part of port inner wing to Shellmex Stanlow 8.6.71. Port outer wing to RARDE Poton Island 17.5.71. [1100.45hrs]

XD268 Production test VA South Marston 19.12.58 (LR Colquhoun). Delivered AHU Lossiemouth 17.2.59. Acceptance test flight 19.2.59. 807 Sqn ('194/R') 4.3.59. To Lee-on-Solent 11.6.59. On 15.7.59, Cdr IHF Martin set up the fastest overall time of 43min 11 sec for a self-piloted aircraft in the Daily Mail Paris to London Bleriot Anniversary Race [car Arc de Triomphe to Issy, Whirlwind to Villacoublay, Scimitar to Wisley, Whirlwind to Chelsea Reach, boat and motor cycle to Marble Arch]. RNAY Fleetlands 9.10.59. Air test from Lee-on-Solent to Boscombe Down 23.2.60. 804 Sqn ('165/H') 27.2.60. AHU Lossiemouth 14.5.60. 803 Sqn ('156/V') 21.6.60 (LABS aircraft, bridle catching trials). VA South Marston on free loan 27.10.60 (TI of Bullpup and Sidewinder armament against Cont No KC/A/091/CB.5(a)). A&AEE 21.3.61 (Bullpup and Sidewinder C(A) release trials). VA South Marston 10.5.61 (installation of specialities airstream direction detector against Cont No KC/A/091/5(a). To Boscombe Down 21.5.61 (LR Colquhoun) and on to RAE Bedford 29.5.61 (catapult trials with Sidewinder). To South Marston 30.6.61 (LR Colquhoun). A&AEE 11.7.61 (Sidewinder alignment trials). VA South Marston 17.7.61 (Check 3 and ECU.). A&AEE 30.8.61 (LR Colquhoun) (Bullpup trials). VA South Marston 27.9.62 (TI of emergency braking system and removal of instrumentation). RNAY Fleetlands 21.11.62 (modernisation began 27.5.63). To Lee-on-Solent Dope Shop by 31.1.64 (presumably returned to Fleetlands again) and departed Lee-on-Solent 8.9.64. AHU Lossiemouth 15.9.64. 800B Flt ('112/E')

15.9.64. ASI failure on night take-off, landed safely, Cat SS 5.11.64 (Lt IPF Meiklejohn). Single-engined practice circuit at Lossiemouth, port engine shut down and on first circuit aircraft turned from down wind, airspeed decayed to such a degree that when bank applied the pilot encountered longitudinal instability, aggravated in the turn by wing drop and the aircraft pitched up, insufficient thrust available to accelerate the aircraft out of trouble, crashed 2m short of runway in field nr Duffus, Aberfoyle, Perthshire, Cat ZZ 15.7.65 (S/L AC Hill ejected with minor injuries - Ejection No.1046). Aircraft totally destroyed, narrowly missed herd of prize-winning cows, some of which were slightly burnt. Remains sold to Messrs Gordon Wilkinson, Elgin, Morayshire 26.1.66. SOC 10.2.66. [501.40hrs]

XD269 Production test VA South Marston 22.12.58 - 22.2.59. Delivered AHU Lossiemouth 4.3.59. Acceptance test flight 6.3.59. 803 Sqn (uncoded?) 10.4.59. AHU Lossiemouth 30.4.59. 807 Sqn ('195/R') 13.6.59. Panel detached in flight, Cat SS 26.6.59 (Lt AR Campbell). 803 Sqn ('156/V' to at least 9.59) 29.6.59. RNAY Fleetlands 18.12.59 (mods and refurbishment). Airtested from Boscombe Down 31.3-7.4.60. 803 Sqn 8.4.60. Recoded by 5.60 ('147/V'). To Lee-on-Solent 25.7.60 and towed to RNAY Fleetlands (mods). Flown Lee-on-Solent to Boscombe Down 26.10.60 and air tested there until 8.11.60 when flown to Yeovilton (allotment to 803 Sqn 8.11.60 cancelled – LABS aircraft, fitted with *Blue Silk*). Hal Far 15.11.60. Tengah 30.12.60. 803 Sqn ('151/V') 24.4.61. Starboard brake failure as taxied out of wires, aircraft carried on up deck and over port side of the angle into sea, hitting water nose first and upside down, *Victorious* off Kuwait, Cat ZZ 9.7.61 (Lt DS McIntyre rescued unhurt from sinking aircraft by SAR). [278.15hrs]

XD270 Production Test VA South Marston 4.12.58 - 26.1.59. Delivered AHU Lossiemouth 8.2.59. Acceptance test flight 10.2.59. 803 Sqn ( '149/V') 11.2.59. Hydraulic failure, landed safely North Front, Cat LQ 10.11.59 (Lt B Davies). RNAY Fleetlands 12.12.59. Flew Lee-on-Solent to Boscombe Down and air tested there 7.4.60. 807 Sqn ('191/C') 14.4.60. Fire in starboard engine indicated, single-engined landing, engaged airfield arrester gear Hal Far, Cat SS 5.8.60 (S/L NA Britton). Undercarriage not lowered on GCA approach, landed safely after undercarriage check Hal Far, Cat LQ 17.11.60 (Lt PMC Hessey). Leading edge flap damaged by ricochet of 30mm round during strafing Tain Range, Cat LQ 24.3.61 (L/C F Hefford). To Lee-on-Solent 28.8.61 (arrested landing) and to RNAY Fleetlands 27.8.61. Back to Lee-on-Solent by 9.3.62, flew Lee-on-Solent to Boscombe Down 12.3.62 (return Lee-on-Solent same day). Depart Lee-on-Solent to Yeovilton 15.3.62. 800 Sqn ('106/R') 19.3.62. Bird strike at 80ft, diverted ashore to AF Base Naha, Okinawa, Cat HY 7.6.62 (Lt KR Entwisle). *Ark Royal*, damaged by ricochet on China Rock Range, Cat HY 24.7.62 (Lt JPF Nichols). AHU Tengah 28.7.62. Shipped to UK. VA South Marston by road 15.11.62. 800 Sqn ('107/R') 2.5.63. Bird strike in starboard engine en route Lossiemouth to *Ark Royal*, Cat SS 4.5.63 (Lt L Ingham). Starboard Sidewinder missile came off on landing *Ark Royal*, Cat SS 6.7.63 (Lt L Ingham). Struck bush while recovering from dummy dive on to target, Ulu Tiram range, Cat LQ 21.8.63 (S/L NHL Bowden). AHU Lossiemouth 13.2.64. 800B Flt ('113/E') 18.9.64. Hydraulic failure, emergency landing, Cat LQ 6.11.64 (Lt IPF Meiklejohn). Undercarriage warning light failure, Cat LQ 17.11.64 (Lt CA Wheal). Crashed after double flame-out, *Eagle* in Aden area, 12°6'N 45°24'E, Cat ZZ 27.4.65 (Lt IPF Meiklejohn ejected safely). [623.00hrs]

XD271 Production test VA South Marston 23.2.59 (LR Colquhoun). Delivered AHU Lossiemouth 13.3.59. Acceptance test flight 16.3.59. 803 Sqn ('150/V') 27.4.59. Ammunition tank cover detached in flight Lossiemouth, Cat SS 21.10.59 (Lt JB Cross). RNAY Fleetlands 22.1.60. Flown Lee to Boscombe Down 4.5.60 and air tested there 6.5.60. 803 Sqn ('149/V') 9.5.60. Starboard practice bomb carrier found missing on landing Lossiemouth, Cat SS 28.6.60 (Lt JOF Billingham). To Lee-on-Solent 25.7.60 and to RNAY Fleetlands (mods). Flown Lee to Boscombe Down and air tested en route 18.10.60. 803 Sqn ('149/V') 18.10.60. Precautionary landing after failure of ASI Gibraltar, Cat SS 26.10.60 (S/L AHS Anderson). Port brake failure while parking, swung into XD328, *Victorious* in Gulf of Aden, Cat LQ 28.8.61 (Lt JG Wood). By lighter from *Victorious* in Portsmouth Harbour, then to RNAY Fleetlands 18.12.61 (modernisation). Back to Lee-on-Solent by 25.2.63 and last test there 27.2.63. AHU Lossiemouth 24.3.63. 800 Sqn ('105/R') 27.3.63. Electrical leak, bomb and drop tank misfired, Garvie Island, Cat SS 22.4.63 (Lt AG MacFie). From *Ark Royal*, port engine problem, single-engined landing Khormaksar, Cat SS 14.5.63 (Lt L Ingham). 803 Sqn ('155/R') 26.2.64. Hydraulic failure in circuit, used emergency system, landed safely, Cat LQ 15.10.64 (S/L IC Frenz). Nosewheel problem, landed safely, Cat LQ 3.11.64 (F/Lt RN Davidson RAF). Code change 7.65 ('030/R'). Part of port drop tank dropped off on catapult launch, Cat SS 5.8.65 (L/C JWH Purvis). NASU Changi 12.8.65. 803 Sqn ('030/R') 17.9.65. Smoke in cockpit after take-off, tanks jettisoned, landed safely, Changi, Cat LQ 22.4.66 (Lt MJ Williams). NASU Changi 27.4.66. 800B Flt ('114/E') 8.7.66. Yeovilton 15.8.66. To Class I GI airframe at Lee-on-Solent 14.9.66. Downgraded to Class II as *A2589* 27.2.68 (Engine Nos *E4608/4609*). Placed on Field Gun Track as an advertisement for forthcoming Air Day 7.69. RNAY Fleetlands 14.9.70 (de-instrumentation). Transferred to MoD(Air) and by road to P&EE Shoeburyness 24/25.9.70. Fuselage to P&EE Pendine Ranges, Dyfed 15.9.71. Remainder used for trials 1.72 to 9.84, then scrapped. [703.30hrs]

XD272 Production test VA South Marston 23.1.59 (LR Colquhoun). Delivered AHU Lossiemouth 25.3.59. Acceptance test flight 13.4.59. 736 Sqn Lossiemouth ('611/LM') 11.5.59. Bird strike after take-off, Cat LX 22.7.59 (Lt J Worth). RNAY Fleetlands 29.10.59. Towed back to Lee-on-Solent by 29.2.60, flown Lee to Boscombe Down 2.3.60 and air tested there 8.3.60. 804 Sqn ('166/H') 18.3.60. RNAY Fleetlands 11.4.60. Flown Lee to Boscombe Down 16.5.60 (air test there same day). 804 Sqn ('166/H') 18.5.60. Collided with Sea Vixen XJ556 while taxying *Hermes*, Cat SS 17.8.60 (F/Lt MJ Webb RAF). RNAY Fleetlands 1.5.61. 804 Sqn ('166/H').61. Foreign body found to have entered starboard compressor during ground check *Hermes*, Cat LY 10.8.61. 800 Sqn ('102/R') 15.9.61. Drop tanks failed to transfer en-route NAS Naha, Okinawa, Cat SS 18.6.62 (Lt JDHB Howard). To Lee-on-Solent and to RNAY Fleetlands 28.1.63 (modernisation). Towed back to Lee-on-Solent and last noted 17.6.64. AHU Lossiemouth 26.6.64. 803 Sqn ('149/R') 14.12.64 (miniature beer tankards on yellow fin checks 6.66 suggest loan to 800B Flt). Port engine flamed out on overshoot, Cat SS 12.1.65 (Lt CJ Crowther). Starboard fire warning light after inverted flight, landed safely, Cat LQ 13.1.65 (Lt R Wren). Port engine vibration, landed safely, Cat SS 5.3.65 (Lt EK Somerville-Jones). False engine fire warning at Tain Range, precautionary landing, Cat LQ 26.3.65 (F/Lt TG Gilroy RAF). Erratic ASI and Machmeter readings, formation landing, Cat LQ 12.4.65 (Lt EK Somerville-Jones). Code change 7.65 ('022/R'). Nosewheel retraction problem, Cat LQ 8.3.66 (Lt EK Somerville-Jones). Bombs released prematurely, Tain Range, Cat SS 10.8.66 (S/L DW Moore). AHU Lossiemouth 1.10.66. RAE Bedford 10.66 (arrester gear trials). To GI Class I at AES Arbroath 8.11.66. Downgraded to Class II as *A2585* 5.3.68 (Engine Nos *E4600/4601*). Downgraded to Class III 6.69. Presumably scrapped when Arbroath closed 31.3.71. [884.40hrs]

XD273 Production test VA South Marston 27.2.59 (LR Colquhoun). Delivered AHU Lossiemouth 19.3.59. Acceptance test flight, panel detached in flight, Cat SS 20.3.59 (Lt AR Campbell). 736 Sqn Lossiemouth ('612/LM') 12.5.59. Port undercarriage fairing detached during undercarriage retraction, Cat LX 21.9.59 (Lt AG Claridge). Starter disintegrated, fuel lines severed, fire Yeovilton, Cat HY 22.10.59 (Lt JB Cross). RNAY Fleetlands 16.11.59 (Cat 4 repairs 2.5.60) [but reported to Lee-on-Solent 29.2.60]. Flown Lee-on-Solent to Boscombe Down and air tested there same day 15.8.60. 803 Sqn ('152/V') 15.8.60. Foreign body in intake during ground run *Victorious*, Cat SS 9.2.61. ERU inadvertently fired while being removed at night *Victorious*, Cat SS 22.3.61. Joint exercises with US Pacific Fleet, fire warning after pulling out of strafing dive, unable to cancel, climbed to 4,000ft and ejected at 300kts, nr North Borneo 7°7'N 117°2'E, Cat ZZ 27.4.61 (Lt GC Edwardes injured in ejection, died in Changi hospital 3.5.61).

XD274 Production test VA South Marston 19.3.59 (LR Colquhoun). Delivered AHU Lossiemouth 1.4.59. Acceptance test flight 13.4.59. 736 Sqn Lossiemouth ('613/LM') 19.5.59. Temp loan to 807 Sqn ('198/R') for the SBAC Show 9.59. RNAY Fleetlands 24.11.59; Lee-on-Solent 28.4.60. Flown Lee to Boscombe Down 2.5.60 and air tested there to 3.5.60. 804 Sqn by ferry ('164/H') 7.5.60. Starboard throttle jammed at 94%, diverted to Lossiemouth, single-engined landing 1.9.60 (S/L JGL Smith). Receipt check, port engine second stage blades damaged, starboard engine first and second stage damaged, Cat SS 9.5.60 (Mr Judd). Both main wheel tyres burst landing *Hermes*, Cat LQ 18.9.60 (L/C BG Young). Cover plate flew off starboard engine during ground run *Hermes*, Cat LQ 16.2.61. To Lee-on-Solent 1.5.61 and to RNAY Fleetlands. Depart Lee-on-Solent 30.6.61. 800 Sqn ('104/R') 15.9.61. Smoke from forward nosewheel, Cat HY 27.6.62. AHU Tengah 25.7.62. To Lee-on-Solent 24.9.62 and to RNAY Fleetlands (repairs and Mod ZN1 started 10.6.63). Depart Lee-on-Solent to AHU Lossiemouth 20.3.64. 800B Flt ('114/E') 2.9.64. Electrical problem, landed safely, Cat LQ 4.11.64 (Lt RC Dimmock). From *Eagle*, hose separated from POD during flight refuelling and struck Buccaneer XN953, Cat SS 20.1.65 (S/L IC Frenz). Hose defect after flight refuelling, *Eagle*, Cat SS 3.2.65 (Lt CA Wheal). Port inboard drop tank failed to jettison, port aileron hit arrester wire landing *Eagle*, Cat LQ 18.3.65 (Lt IPF Meiklejohn). Hose parted while refuelling with Buccaneer, Cat SS 20.5.65 (Lt CA Wheal). Starboard outer drop tank lost in flight, Cat SS 11.11.65 (L/C NG Grier-Rees). Flight refuelling hose lost in flight, Cat SS 9.3.66 (Lt PJ McManus). 803 Sqn ("024/EMPTY") 6.5.66. Nosewheel locking failure, recovered safely into wires, *Ark Royal*, Cat SS 1.6.66 (Lt RF Shercliff). Hydraulic failure during dummy strafing dive on Tain Range, Cat LQ 15.7.66 (Lt PG De Souza). landed safely Lossiemouth, To Class I GI at AES Arbroath 2.8.66. Downgraded to Class II as *A2584* 5.3.68 (Engine Nos *E4598/4599*). Presumed scrapped there when Arbroath closed 31.3.71. [707.35hrs]

XD275 VA South Marston 10.7.59. Production test VA South Marston 20.7.59 (LR Colquhoun). To C(A) charge 15.7.59. Delivered to A&AEE 20.7.59 (pre-tropical trials). Tropical trials in RAF Idris during 8 & 9.59. VA South Marston 24.9.59 (manufacturer's examination of tropical mods, minor TIs as agreed with RTO, removal of instrumentation and preparation for return to RN). Delivered AHU Lossiemouth 1.2.60 (LABS aircraft, fitted with *Blue Silk*). 803 Sqn ('146/V') 12.7.60. During Exercise *Swordthrust*, hook struck round down and rebounded up, *Hermes*, Cat HC 26.9.60 (S/L AHS Anderson). A&AEE Boscombe Down 7.10.60 (awaiting collection for RNAY Fleetlands). To Lee-on-Solent 27.10.60 and to RNAY Fleetlands 28.10.60 (Cat 4 repairs). Flown Lee to Boscombe Down for air test 4.1.61. 803 Sqn ('146/V') 11.1.61. Severe starboard engine vibration, single-engined landing. Returned RNAY Fleetlands, then air tested from Lee before delivery to Yeovilton 10.5.61. *Victorious* in Lyme Bay, minor incident, Cat SS 6.2.62 (Lt PAA Waring). Bomb carriers self-jettisoned taxying after landing *Victorious*, Cat SS 15.3.62 (S/L CJ Wilson). RNAY Fleetlands 30.3.62 (modernisation). Back to Lee-on-Solent by 21.2.63 and departed 22.2.63. AHU Lossiemouth 25.2.63. VA South Marston on free loan to C(A) 2.4.63 (TI of mod 1211 against Cont N0 KC/A/0145/CB.5(a)). AHU Lossiemouth 28.5.63. 736 Sqn Lossiemouth temp 28.6.63. Undercarriage warning light malfunction, Cat LQ 25.7.63 (Lt PG De Souza). Noise suppressor trials at Yeovilton 7.63-8.63. AHU Lossiemouth 12.8.63. 803 Sqn ('148/H') 20.9.63. Hydraulic problem, Yeovilton, Cat LQ 20.9.63 (Mr DR Skinner). Exercise *Phoenix*, landing on from Fayid, into barrier *Hermes* 2.1.64. Hook struck roundown landing, into barrier, *Hermes*, Cat HY 22.1.64. RNAY Fleetlands 3.2.64 (repair). 803 Sqn, Hydraulic failure in flight, landed successfully Lossiemouth, Cat LQ 6.1.65 (L/C PG Newman). RNAY Fleetlands.65; Towed to Lee-on-Solent 5.7.65. Brake failure whilst taxying after landing 14.7.65. Departed Lee 11.8.65. 800B Flt ('117/E') 12.8.65. Hose and drogue failed to rewind, Flight refuelling pod jettisoned prior to landing on *Eagle*, Cat SS 27.3.66 (L/C NG Grier-Rees). Yeovilton 15.8.66. To AES Lee-on-Solent as GI as Class I. Downgraded to Class II as *A2587* 22.8.67 (Engine Nos *E4604/4605*). SOC 27.2.68. RNAY Fleetlands by road 21.9.70 (de-instrumentation). Transferred to MoD(Air) and to P&EE Shoeburyness by road 9.9.70 (trials from 5.73). On West Freugh dump by c.1972 [544.25hrs]

XD276 Production test VA South Marston 28.5.59 (LR Colquhoun). Delivered AHU Lossiemouth 30.6.59. 800 Sqn ('100/R') 11.7.59. Skidded on spilt kerosene while taxying deck, nose of aircraft struck island *Ark Royal*, Cat LQ 29.8.60 (Lt AJ Goodenough). RNAY Fleetlands 28.4.61. 800 Sqn ('100/R') 11.5.61. Probe damaged drogue during flight refuelling nr Lossiemouth, Cat SS 12.8.61 (L/C JAD Ford). Flap damage *Ark Royal*, Cat LX 13.12.61. Flight refuelling POD failure, Cat SS 3.9.62 (Lt CD Walkinshaw). To Lee-on-Solent 21.12.62 and to RNAY Fleetlands 27.12.62 (modernisation began 9.5.63). To Lee-on-Solent by 20.12.63 and following test flight, swung to port after engaging airfield arrester gear, bogged down in soft grass, Lee-on-Solent, Cat SS 28.1.64 (Lt(E) MG Griffin). AHU Lossiemouth 5.2.64. 803 Sqn ('146/R') 25.10.64. At Lossiemouth, trim problem after take-off, drop tanks jettisoned in sea, landed safely Yeovilton, Cat LQ 9.12.64 (L/C PG Newman). Code change 7.65 ('017/R'). Port engine vibration, normal landing, Cat SS 7.8.65 (S/L HW Thomas). Engine panel blown overboard by wind while securing on deck of *Ark Royal*, Cat SS 12.10.65. Bird strike on windscreen, Cat LQ 12.11.65 (F/Lt TG Gilroy RAF). Starboard brake failed landing, ran off port side of runway, Butterworth, Cat LQ 12.11.65 (F/Lt TG Gilroy RAF). Yeovilton 1.10.66 (last operational Scimitar flight, from *Ark Royal* to Yeovilton, Lt PG De Souza). To GI Class I at Lee-on-Solent 21.10.66. Downgraded to Class II as *A2591* 27.2.68 (*Engine Nos E4612/4613*). RNAY Fleetlands by road 23.9.70 (sic) (de-instrumentation). Transferred to MoD(Air) and to P&EE Shoeburyness by road 21.9.70. To P&EE Pendine Ranges, Dyfed 18.8.71. Fuselage remains scrapped [at Shoeburyness?] by 5.94. [759.00hrs]

XD277 VA Wisley by 2.59; Production test VA South Marston 29.5.59 (LR Colquhoun). A&AEE by 5.69 - 6.69. Delivered AHU Lossiemouth 24.6.59. Acceptance test flight 25.6.59. 800 Sqn Lossiemouth ('101/R') 3.7.59. Nose wheel collapsed after taxying to dispersal Cottesmore, Cat LQ 19.9.59 (Lt NJP Mills). Damaged when spilt fuel ignited on second relight attempt West Freugh, Cat HX 19.10.59 (Lt WP Ryce). RNAY Fleetlands 29.1.60. 800 Sqn ('101/R') 4.3.60. To Lee-on-Solent 8.3.61 (coded '-/R') and to RNAY Fleetlands 9.3.61. Air tested Lee-on-Solent then delivered Yeovilton 21.3.61. 800 Sqn ('101/R') 22.3.61. Controls partly jammed after inverted flight 5m NE of airfield, flapless landing, engaged wires, Cat LQ 17.5.61 (Lt NG Grier-Rees). 25-lb practice bomb came off during dive bombing Munxar Range, landed close to house on outskirts of Marsaxlokk, Cat SS 18.12.61 (Lt JGL Smith). Undercarriage light malfunction Lossiemouth, Cat SS 7.2.62 (Lt JGL Smith). Hydraulic pressure loss, precautionary landing Lossiemouth, Cat SS 27.2.62 (S/L CC Morris). Reportedly recoded during 1962 ('107/R'). A/c rolled and yawed on take-off *Ark Royal*, Cat LQ 15.5.62 (L/C A Mancais). Nose wheel went over side manoeuvring on deck, *Ark Royal*, Cat HY 17.10.62. AHU Tengah 22.10.62. Shipped to UK. RNAY Fleetlands 7.1.63 (Cat 4 repair and Mod ZN1 began 18.7.63). Depart Lee-on-Solent to AHU Lossiemouth 19.8.64. 800B Flt ('111/E') 26.10.64. Starboard engine fire warning, emergency landing Tengah, Cat LQ 21.1.65 (S/L IC Frenz). Code change 7.65 ('115/E'). Starboard engine vibration, single-engined landing Lossiemouth, Cat SS 28.7.65 (Lt CA Wheal). Dropped rapidly on night approach, tail skid hit boundary fence, Cat SS 10.8.65 (L/C RC Dimmock). Hook struck rounddown, caught No.2 wire, *Eagle*, Cat LY 2.9.65 (Lt PJ McManus). To Lee-on-Solent 14.9.65 and to RNAY Fleetlands until 27.9.65. To AHU Lossiemouth 1.10.65. A&AEE 5.10.65 (for EMC trials, but found aircraft not in good enough condition). To MARTSU Lee-on-Solent 15.10.65 (prepared for shipment 3.11.65). Shipped to Far East 15.11.65. Arr NASU Changi 12.65. 803 Sqn ('115/E') 31.3.66. Partial hydraulic failure and fire warnings after take-off from Changi, first starboard, then port engine, aircraft headed seawards and pilot ejected, aircraft crashed in sea in flames, Cat ZZ 6.4.66 (Lt PG De Souza rescued injured about 100yds from coast by helicopter - Ejection No.1270). SOC 11.5.66 [780.05hrs]. Large portions salvaged by Chinese using oil drums and tidal lift, then taken to Singapore and sold to scrap merchants, thus hindering AIU investigations.

XD278  Production test VA South Marston 15.6.59 (LR Colquhoun). (Fitted UHF) Delivered AHU Lossiemouth 26.6.59. Acceptance test flight 6.7.59. 800 Sqn ('102/R') 7.7.59. RNAY Fleetlands 29.2.60. Flown Lee to Boscombe Down and air tested there same day 1.3.60. 800 Sqn ('102/R') 4.3.60. Abbotsinch 7.3.61. 800 Sqn ('108/R') 24.3.61. En route Yeovilton to Orange, hydraulic system failure over France, retd Yeovilton, Cat LX 22.11.61 (Lt CC Giles). Port outer ERU fired during practice bomber carrier check, Cat SS 14.2.62. Towing tractor damaged underside of aircraft on lift, Cat LC 28.6.62. *Ark Royal*, tread stripped from starboard tyre on take-off, damaging wing flap, engaged Mk.6 Safeland barrier Tengah, Cat HC 1.8.62 (Lt AG Ellis). AHU Tengah 9.8.62. RNAY Fleetlands 24.9.62 (repairs, modernisation and mods started 18.2.63). Flew Lee-Boscombe Down 1.11.63 and return 8.11.63 (in Lee-on-Solent Dope Shop by 15.11.63). Depart Lee-on-Solent 2.12.63. AHU Lossiemouth 4.12.63. 803 Sqn ('145/H') 3.2.64. Undercarriage warning light failure, Cat SS 15.5.64 (L/C PG Newman). Code change mid 1964 ('145/R'). Undercarriage hydraulic failure, locked down on emergency, landed safely, Cat LQ 14.7.64 (F/Lt RN Davidson RAF). From *Hermes*, ASI and Machmeter faulty, diverted to Yeovilton, successful formation landing, Cat SS 12.2.64 (S/L PJ McManus). ASU fell to zero in barrel roll, landed safely, Cat SS 11.1.65 (F/Lt R Davidson RAF). Feel simulator magnetic indicator showed white in flight, Cat LQ 5.4.65 (Lt EK Somerville-Jones). Code change 7.65 ('016/R'). A/c hit by flight refuelling hose and drogue which parted from XD244 after withdrawal, Cat LQ 24.9.65 (Lt ARD Monro-Davies). Hose broke away after flight refuelling, Cat SS 8.3.66 (Lt NE Rankin). AHU Lossiemouth 3.10.66. To GI Class I at AES Arbroath 3.11.66. Downgraded to GI Class II as *A2586* 5.3.68 (*Engine Nos E4602/4603*). Presumably scrapped when Arbroath closed 31.3.71. [984.35hrs].

XD279  Production test VA South Marston 22.6.59 (LR Colquhoun). Delivered AHU Lossiemouth 3.7.59. Acceptance test flight 11.7.59. 800 Sqn ('103/R') 13.7.59. *Ark Royal*, outboard drop tanks self jettisoned in straight and level flight, Cat SS 23.4.60 (Lt WE Thorpe). Lowering aircraft off jacks, port jack collapsed prematurely, damaged fuselage forward of jacking point Hal Far, Cat LY 8.11.60. Ferried back to UK 18.11.60. To Lee-on-Solent 1.12.60 and to RNAY Fleetlands. Flown Lee-on-Solent to Boscombe Down 4.1.61 and air tested there 6.1.61. 800 Sqn ('104/R') 10.1.61. Windscreen shattered, parts went down both engine intakes 12.1.61 (Lt AJ Goodenough). VA South Marston 27.2.61 (proof installation of smoke making equipment against Cont No KC/A/087/CB.5(a)). 800 Sqn ('104/R') 19.4.61. Wing flap failure, flapless landing, Cat SS 26.9.61 (Lt AJ Goodenough). Nose damaged by another Scimitar's tailplane while manoeuvring in deck park *Ark Royal* 13.11.62. Sidewinder missile dropped in sea on launch, *Ark Royal*, Cat SS 7.12.62. Undercarriage hydraulic problem landing, Cat LQ 24.1.63 (Lt JJR Tod). RNAY Fleetlands 21.2.63 (modernisation began 3.7.63). Depart Lee-on-Solent to AHU Lossiemouth 14.4.64. 803 Sqn ('143/R') 10.8.64. Hydraulic leak during taxying, Cat LQ 16.11.64 (Lt JM Heath). Difficulty winding in flight refuelling hose, landed safely, Lossiemouth, Cat SS 7.12.64 (L/C GAI Johnston). Code change by 5.65 ('159/R') and 7.65 ('034/R'). Landed *Ark Royal* in Far East, taxying out of wires when ship heaved, aircraft slid along slippery deck, nosewheel ran off into catwalk by starboard Howdah, Cat HY 1.1.66 (S/L ZK Skrodski unhurt). NASU Changi 27.1.66. RSP. SOC 6.6.66. Wreckage dumped at Sembawang. [938.15hrs]

XD280  Production Test VA South Marston 5.7.59 - 11.7.59. Delivered AHU Lossiemouth 23.7.59. Acceptance test flight 20.8.59. 800 Sqn ('104/R') 21.8.59. Ammunition tank panel detached take-off Lossiemouth, Cat SS 15.12.59 (Lt NJP Mills). Cyprus exercise area, main wheels failed to lock fully down, caught wire and entered barrier, small fire in port engine *Ark Royal*, Cat HY 28.4.60 (Lt PEH Banfield). AHU Hal Far 2.5.60. RNAY Fleetlands 29.7.60 (air tested Lee 17.4.61). [Also reported Yeovilton to Lee-on-Solent 1.12.60]. Returned to RNAY Fleetlands, and noted there on 13.4.62 (repairs). Flew Lee-on-Solent to Boscombe Down 15.5.62, last test 18.5.62 and departed to AHU Lossiemouth 24.5.62. Returned to RNAY Fleetlands Flight Test section, Lee, by 8.6.62 (prepared for shipment by MARTSU). Arr Far East 29.7.62. 800 Sqn ('100/R') 30.7.62. Drop tanks failed to transfer, jettisoned for landing *Ark Royal*, Cat SS 30.8.62 (L/C JAD Ford). Starboard intake blister damaged by debris after strafing attack on Army support exercise, Asahan Range, Cat LQ 18.10.62 (Lt JDHB Howard). Fuel transfer failure *Ark Royal*, Cat SS 9.11.62 (S/L CC Morris). Fuel transfer failure *Ark Royal*, Cat SS 30.11.62 (Lt PC Marshall). Starboard nose panel came loose landing Lossiemouth, Cat SS 15.2.63 (L/C A Mancais). Flight refuelling hose problem, POD jettisoned, *Ark Royal*, Cat SS 4.6.63 (Lt CD Walkinshaw). Bird strike off Penang, Cat SS 10.7.63 (Lt AG MacFie). AHU Lossiemouth 7.1.64. 803 Sqn ('148/R') 4.11.64. Brake light problem in circuit, landed safely, Cat LQ 1.12.64 (Lt CJ Crowther). Code change 7.65 ('021/R'). Undercarriage hydraulic failure, emergency landing *Ark Royal*, Cat LQ 17.7.65 (S/L GM Faulkner). NASU Changi 26.4.66. 800B Flt ('115/E') 3.6.66. AHU Lossiemouth 14.8.66. To GI Class I at AES Arbroath 3.10.66. Downgraded to GI Class II as *A2583* 14.2.68 (*Engine Nos E4596/4597*). Downgraded to Class III at Arbroath 19.3.69. Presumably scrapped when Arbroath closed 31.3.71 [660.00hrs]

XD281  Production Test VA South Marston 21.8.59 - 28.8.59. Delivered AHU Lossiemouth 8.9.59. Acceptance test flight 18.9.59. 807 Sqn ('190/R') 24.9.59. Hydraulic failure returning from tactical reconnaissance exercise, controls locked, abandoned at 26,000ft, aircraft crashed in hilly country in Loch Carn/Ben Volich area, nr Aberfoyle, Perthshire, Cat ZZ 10.11.59 (Lt NG Grier-Rees came down safely on the 2,300ft snow-covered Ben Bhreac, then over several days walked 13 miles before reaching a farmhouse at Callander, Perthshire). Wreckage recovered by helicopter for analysis by AIU Lee-on-Solent.

XD282  Production test VA South Marston 16.9.59 (LR Colquhoun). Delivered AHU Lossiemouth 2.10.59. Acceptance test flight 6.10.59. 807 Sqn ('193/R') 7.10.59. Starboard throttle jammed after take-off Lossiemouth, Cat SS 10.12.59 (L/C WA Tofts). Test flights of Avon Mod 1990 by Rolls Royce test pilot 15.12.59. No.1 hydraulic system failure, landed safely, inspection tail skid had disintegrated *Ark Royal*, Cat LQ 30.11.60 (Lt TNF Skead). Code change 3.61 ('193/C'). Hydraulic failure landing on 2,800yd runway, brakes failed, ran off into deep mud edge of sea just below high water mark, RAF Khormaksar, Cat HZ 14.7.61 (Lt(E) MG Griffin). Later recovered from beach by MARTSU. Left at Aden until ship returned from Kuwait area. Hoisted aboard *Centaur* at Aden 20.8.61 for UK. RNAY Fleetlands 14.9.61 (repair and mods). Back to Lee-on-Solent by 24.7.62 and demonstrated at Lee-on-Solent Air Day 11.8.62 (Lt Cdr PM Stevenson). AHU Lossiemouth (via Lee) 25.8.62. 736 Sqn Lossiemouth ('610') 11.10.62. Control difficulties on MADDL approach following bird strike, ditched 2m E of Milltown airfield, Cat ZZ 23.11.62 (S/L CD Legg ejected at 100ft, landed safely in soft muddy ground - Ejection No.626). Wreckage and to AIU Lee-on-Solent 30.11.62. RNAY Fleetlands for disposal as scrap 8.7.63.

XD316  Production test VA South Marston 25.9.59 – 1.10.59 (LR Colquhoun). Delivered AHU Lossiemouth 19.10.59. 807 Sqn ('194/R') 4.11.59. Code change 3.61 ('194/C'). False fire warning, successful single-engined landing on *Centaur* off Gibraltar, Cat HX 17.4.61 (Lt PG De Souza). AHU Lossiemouth 28.8.61. False fire warning while inverted, successful single-engined landing, Cat SS 30.8.61 (Lt GJ Edwards). 736 Sqn Lossiemouth ('612/LM', later just '612') 11.12.61. Undercarriage hydraulic warning system failure, successful precautionary landing, Cat LQ 15.12.61 (Lt PGJ Murison). Undercarriage red warning light on incorrectly, Cat SS 10.1.62 (S/L AM Hickling). Undercarriage malfunction, Cat LQ 23.1.62 (Mid JS Flexman). Bird strike, Cat LQ 7.2.62 (Lt PGJ Murison). Wheels locked on touchdown, Cat LQ 11.5.62 (Lt TNF Skead). Undercarriage light malfunction, Cat LQ 20.6.62 (Lt PG De Souza). Hydraulic failure, landed safely, Cat LQ 4.10.62 (S/L JM Heath). RNAY Fleetlands 9.10.62 (modernisation began 27.11.62). Back to Lee-on-Solent by 22.7.63 and last test 9.9.63. AHU Lossiemouth 27.8.63 [sic]. Starboard engine vibration, Cat SS 18.11.63 (L/C CR Newnes). Port mainplane hit by boundary metal gate while being towed in high wind Lee-on-Solent, Cat LX 21.11.63. RNAY Fleetlands 22.11.63 (prepared for shipment in SS *Benarty*) [actually loaded by MARTSU aboard SS *Flintshire* in cocoon bag]. AHU Tengah LTS 16.1.64. AHU Sembawang LTS by 8.64. 803 Sqn ('015/R') 18.8.65. Flying from *Ark Royal*, pitched up on final approach, unable to recover, pilot ejected at 300ft, aircraft ditched in South China Sea, Cat ZZ 28.1.66 (S/L ZK Skrodzki picked up unhurt by SAR helicopter - Ejection No.1206). SOC 31.1.66. [598.20hrs]

XD317  Production test VA South Marston 6-14.10.59. Delivered AHU Lossiemouth 11.11.59. 807 Sqn ('197/R') 23.2.60. Code change 3.61 ('197/C'). AHU Lossiemouth 23.6.61. To Lee-on-Solent 20.10.61. Shipped to Far East aboard SS *Benarty* from Southampton 11.11.61. Arr AHU Tengah. 807 Sqn ('195/C') 12.2.62. Port aileron tip damaged by crane Trincomalee, Cat LQ 28.2.62. Mid-air collision with XD332 off Malta in formation flypast, Cat LQ 18.4.62 (Lt TJ Notley). AHU Lossiemouth 26.4.62. RNAY Fleetlands 16.5.62. Back to Lee-on-Solent by 13.11.62 and last test 30.11.62. 736 Sqn Lossiemouth for 800 Sqn 28.11.62 [sic]. 800 Sqn ('113/R') 14.1.63. Bird strike on finals Lossiemouth, Cat LQ 8.4.63 (Lt AM Hickling). Bird strike, Cat LQ 15.4.63 (Lt PC Marshall). Probe broke in flight refuelling with a Valiant, Cat LQ 24.10.63 (Lt AM Hickling). To Lee-on-Solent 27.2.64 and to RNAY Fleetlands (modernisation). Towed to Lee-on-Solent 7.10.65 and departed 22.11.65 (developed hydraulic problems en-route and diverted to Boscombe Down) Returned to Lee-on-Solent 26.11.65. Depart Lee-on-Solent to RAE Bedford 6.1.66 (DAX.1 arrester gear intensive trials). On C(A) loan from 24.1.66. RAE Farnborough 10.3.66 (limited flight trials of TER and two store carriers). RAE Bedford 1.4.66. NASU Brawdy 27.7.66. Airwork FRU Hurn (initially uncoded) 2.11.66. Coded by 10.67 ('033') and recoded 3.69 ('833'). Hydraulic problem landed Yeovilton, Cat LQ (Mr Saunders). To RAE Farnborough 4.8.69. Then to FAA Museum Yeovilton by road 8.69 for preservation and display. Officially SOC 18.9.69. Standing in open 12.69, then put on display as "112/R". Later moved inside new museum buildings and by 1994 had become part of the 'Carrier' display. Current in 2000.

XD318  Production test VA South Marston 29.10.59 – 16.11.59 (LR Colquhoun). Delivered AHU Lossiemouth 5.1.60. 807 Sqn ('191/R') 14.1.60. Excessive rate of descent, struck round-down before engaging No.5 wire *Ark Royal*, Cat HY 6.3.60 (Lt F Hefford). AHU Hal Far 14.3.60. Shipped to UK. To Lee-on-Solent 1.12.60 and to RNAY Fleetlands 2.12.60. Flown Lee to Boscombe Down 23.1.61 and air tested there 25.1.61. 803 Sqn ('154/V') 1.2.61. Port tailplane hit by shrapnel after live practice rocket attack in Aden Protectorate, Cat LQ 17.3.61 (S/L AHS Anderson). Struck by practice bomb carrier inadvertently fired from XD331, *Victorious*, Cat LQ 21.3.61. Loss of engine power, landed safely *Victorious*, Cat HY 22.6.61 (Lt PAA Waring). Starboard brake failed taxying *Victorious* in Gulf of Aden, Cat SS 28.8.61 (Lt SE Askins). Port compressor blades damaged by foreign body *Victorious*, Cat LY 3.12.61. Recoded 4.62 ('154/H'). During heavy weather at night, slid across wet deck and hit XD234, *Hermes*, Cat LQ 13.8.62. To Lee-on-Solent 13.9.62 (acceptance test flight 14.9.62) and to RNAY Fleetlands (Main Check 5). Back to Lee-on-Solent by 18.11.62 and flown Lee-on-Solent to Boscombe Down, returning 19.11.62. Departed Lee-on-Solent to Yeovilton 20.11.62 to 803 Sqn ('154/H'). To Lee-on-Solent 24.10.63. Stored in Flight Test hangar, Lee-on-Solent c15-29.11.63 and to RNAY Fleetlands (modernisation began 15.7.64 and trial of polyurethane paint finish) Re-coded during repaint ('152/R'). Depart Lee-on-Solent to AHU Lossiemouth 30.3.65. 803 Sqn ('152/R') 3.5.65. Recoded 7.65 ('025/R'). After in-flight refuelling, low pressure fuel warning, waved off once, bolted once, then both engines failed whilst downwind for a third attempt, aircraft ditched, pilot ejected, recovered by SAR helicopter, *Ark Royal* in Far East, Cat ZZ 31.12.65 (Lt MJ Williams picked up unhurt by SAR). Wreckage to Sembawang. [505.36hrs by 3.5.65]

XD319  Production test 16.10.59 - 26.11.59. Delivered AHU Lossiemouth 27.11.59. 807 Sqn Lossiemouth ('192/R') 4.12.59. Leading edge flap damaged by weapon fragments/debris on firing range Garvie Island, Cat LQ 10.2.60 (Lt F Hefford). Tugmaster being moved on deck and struck port trailing edge flap of aircraft, *Ark Royal*, Cat LQ 26.4.60. AHU Lossiemouth 14.1.61. 807 Sqn ('192/C') 10.3.61. Canopy flew off during catapult launch *Centaur*, Cat LQ 8.7.61 (Lt(E) MG Griffin). From *Centaur*, damaged by XD330 when touched during refuelling 20,000ft, 60m off Lisbon, Cat SS 30.10.61 (Lt(E) MG Griffin). Missed wires, attempted to go round again, failed to gain height, ditched 200yds ahead of *Centaur* in Gulf of Aden, Cat ZZ 7.3.62 (S/L AD Alsop picked up unharmed by SAR Helicopter). [462.40hrs] [The aircraft had been due to go to 800 Sqn]

XD320  Production Test 11.11.59 - 10.12.59. Delivered to AHU Lossiemouth 15.12.59. 807 Sqn ('195/R') 15.1.60. Flown off *Ark Royal* in the Mediterranean direct to Yeovilton 20.12.60. AHU Lossiemouth 22.12.60. RNAY Fleetlands 19.6.61. Air tested from Lee-on-Solent 23.8.61 and departed 26.8.61. AHU Lossiemouth 28.8.61. 807 Sqn ('193/C') 30.8.61. AHU Tengah 31.1.62. 800 Sqn ('110/R') 12.7.62. Rating injured fitting loaded ERU, *Ark Royal*, Cat SS 8.8.62. Low power due to foreign body in engine, sortie abandoned, retd *Ark Royal*, Cat HY 7.5.63 (Lt PC Marshall). 803 Sqn ('148/H') 26.2.63. 800 Sqn, Hydraulic failure, landed safely Lossiemouth, Cat SS 30.1.64 (S/L A McMeekan). Recoded .64 ('148/R'). Engine problem, landed safely, Cat LY 18.5.64 (Lt RC Dimmock). Control problem pulling out,

*A dramatic view of XD318 '154/H' as she leaves the angled deck on take-off from HMS Hermes around 1963. (B.J.Lowe)*

of dive, landed safely, Cat LQ 1.9.64 (S/L PJ McManus). To Lee-on-Solent 16.10.64 and to RNAY Fleetlands (modernisation). Towed back to Lee-on-Solent 7.1.66. Embalmed for shipment by MARTSU 18.2.66. Shipped to Far East 2.66. NASU Changi 30.3.66. 803 Sqn ('015/R') 12.4.66. AHU Lossiemouth 1.10.66. NASU Brawdy 3.10.66 in open storage. ADW 19.11.69. SOC 6.2.70 and scrapped Brawdy 5.70. [832.05hrs]

XD321 Production Test 26.11.59 - 31.12.59. Delivered AHU Lossiemouth 25.1.60. 807 Sqn ('196/R') 30.1.60. Post of A-frame bay pierced by jack 16.9.60. AHU Lossiemouth 10.3.61. RNAY Fleetlands 18.5.61 until 15.6.61. Air tested from Lee-on-Solent to Boscombe Down 20.6.61 and air tested there 23.6.61. AHU Lossiemouth 23.6.61. 807 Sqn ('194/C') 26.8.61. Drop tanks inadvertently jettisoned in hangar Lossiemouth, Cat SS 27.9.61. AHU Tengah 31.1.62. 800 Sqn ('104/R') 12.7.62. Nose glass of Sidewinder missile broke off in heavy rain at 9,000ft, Cat SS 18.9.62 (Lt JPF Nichols). Sank on approach, tail skid hit rounddown heavily, *Ark Royal*, Cat HC 13.11.62 (Lt PC Marshall). RNAY Fleetlands 3.2.63. Back to Lee-on-Solent by 4.2.63 and departed to AHU Lossiemouth 13.2.63. 800 Sqn 13.2.63. Port elevator struck by port tail fin of Sea Vixen XN708 being manoeuvred on forward lift *Ark Royal* 28.5.63. Port brake failed taxying after landing, swung to starboard and struck gun mounting, *Ark Royal*, Cat LQ 30.5.63 (Lt CD Walkinshaw). To Lee-on-Solent 3.2.64 and to RNAY Fleetlands (modernisation). Depart Lee-on-Solent 5.1.65. Returned to Lee-on-Solent 7.4.65 and departed again to AHU Lossiemouth 17.5.65. 800B Flt ('113/E') 11.6.65. Access panel lost in flight, Cat LQ 21.6.65 (Lt CA Wheal).

Recoded 7.65 ('116/E'). Fuel system malfunction, emergency landing *Eagle*, Cat LQ 3.9.65 (L/C RC Dimmock). Starboard tailplane tip hit hangar door while being moved on *Eagle*, Cat LQ 10.9.65. Bird strike in steep turn at 1,000ft, arrested safely on landing *Eagle*, Cat LY 10.1.66 (Lt PAA Waring). Hydraulic failure on flight refuelling pod, landed with hose trailed, Changi, Cat SS 24.2.66 (Lt PJ McManus). From *Eagle*, fuel tank emptied in 3G turn, diverted to Changi, Cat LX 3.3.66 (Lt PJ McManus). NASU Changi 3.3.66 (repair). 803 Sqn ('142/R') 12.4.66. NASU Changi 27.4.66. 800B Flt ('116/E') 23.5.66. From *Eagle*, fuel leak, diverted to Butterworth, 15.7.66 (Lt PJ McManus). Brawdy 14.8.66. NASU Brawdy 11.10.66, placed in open storage. ADW 19.11.69. SOC, RSP 30.1.70. Scrapped 5.70 (reported to P&EE Shoeburyness). [967.20hrs]

XD322 Production test VA South Marston 15.12.59 (LR Colquhoun). Delivered AHU Lossiemouth 6.1.60. 807 Sqn ('190/R') 26.2.60. After attempted relights, fire indicated in port engine, warning went out, single-engined landing board *Ark Royal*, Cat LY 6.4.60 (Lt PH Perks). To Lee-on-Solent 14.4.60 and to RNAY Fleetlands 25.4.60. Flown Lee to Boscombe Down 17.6.60 and air tested there 20.6.60. Via Yeovilton and North Front to 807 Sqn ('190/R') 2.7.60. Foreign body in intake *Ark Royal*, Cat SS 5.12.60 (L/C F Hefford). 800 Sqn ('106/R') 20.3.61. Port engine flamed out during refuelling 17,000ft 15m SE of Lossiemouth, single-engined landing, Cat SS 28.7.61 (Lt JL Carver). Hose refuelling POD broke while reeling in 10m N of Daventry, Cat LQ 1.9.61 (S/L KR Entwisle). Engine vibration 5 min after launch, landed safely *Ark Royal* 30m SW of Malta, Cat

SS 22.11.61 (S/L KR Entwisle). *Centaur*, fire warning light port engine while 30m W of Penang, diverted to Butterworth, Cat LQ 9.4.62 (Lt JL Carver). Hydraulic failure, landed *Ark Royal* 60m SSE of Hong Kong, Cat SS 29.5.62 (Lt JPF Nichols). Starboard engine cut, single-engined landing *Ark Royal*, Cat SS 18.6.62 (L/C JAD Ford). Flaps failed to raise after take-off from *Ark Royal* 70m E of Singapore Island, landed Changi, Cat SS 13.7.62 (Lt G McBain). Hydraulic failure, landed safely *Ark Royal* 100m W of Butterworth, Cat SS 11.9.62. Recoded by 11.62 ('112/R'). Warning light malfunction after take-off Lossiemouth, Cat SS 11.1.63 (Lt CD Walkinshaw). Foreign body damaged starboard engine compressor, Cat SS 20.2.63 (L/C DF Mills). Recoded by 4.63 ('107/R'). Hydraulic failure landing, Cat LQ 9.4.63 (L/C PG Newman). AHU Lossiemouth 24.4.63. Recoded by late 1963 ('109/R'). VA South Marston 22.5.63 (modernisation). AHU Lossiemouth 14.7.64. To C(A) at A&AEE 15.9.64 (Radhaz/EMC trials). AHU Lossiemouth 6.10.64. 803 Sqn ('147/R') 15.1.65. Recoded 7.65 ('020/R'). Starboard engine fire warning after take-off from *Ark Royal*, landed safely Changi, Cat LX 27.1.66 (Lt EK Somerville-Jones). NASU Brawdy 1.10.66. Stn Flt Brawdy 3.10.66. NASU Brawdy 28.2.67. To Lee-on-Solent 9.3.67 and to RNAY Fleetlands by 15.3.67. Lightered to *Eagle* (via Foxbury Jetty, Fleetlands) for deck trials 22.3.67. Back to Lee-on-Solent by MARTSU by 11.7.67 and departed to NASU Brawdy 27.7.67 (Lt Cdr PM Stevenson). Severe fire while on engine test 1.8.68 (Lt Cdr PM Stevenson). Airwork FRU Hurn 11.12.68 (with letters 'BY' crudely painted in starboard side of fin). Code allotted in 12.68 and applied 3.69 ('839'). Flown to Southend Airport 2.12.70. By road to P&EE Shoeburyness 21.12.70 [Officially disposed out of service to RAE Farnborough 19.1.71]. Used for trials 8.73 to 9.81. Engines to RAE Farnborough 21.6.76. Fuselage remains scrapped on site by Mayer & Perry scrapyard, Snailwell, Cambs 4.91. [1085.10hrs]

XD323   Production test VA South Marston 18.1.60 – 23.2.60 (LR Colquhoun). Delivered AHU Lossiemouth 23.2.60. 804 Sqn ('162/H') 29.2.60. Tain range, port mainplane damaged by ricochet of direct hit on tank target, Garvie Island Range, Cat HX 28.3.60 (F/Lt MJ Webb RAF). No 1 hydraulic system failure, ineffective braking, engaged runway arrester wires Lossiemouth, Cat LQ 1.6.60 [16.9.60?] (L/C TVG Binney). Port brake failure landing Lossiemouth (Lt MT Hynett). Foreign body found to have damaged starboard engine compressor, *Hermes*, Cat SS 13.4.61. Hydraulic problem, landed safely, Cat SS 5.5.61 (Lt PEH Banfield). Port tailplane struck wing of parked Sea Vixen while being manoeuvred at night in *Hermes* hangar, Cat LQ 8.7.61. 800 Sqn ('105/R') 13.9.61. Drop tanks failed to transfer, jettisoned for landing, Sidewinder missile lost in sea landing *Ark Royal*, Cat SS 13.8.62 (S/L AD Alsop). Bird strike at 500ft over jungle, Kota Tinggin, South Malaya, Cat LQ 20.9.62 (Lt JDHB Howard). Hydraulic failure landing Lossiemouth, Cat SS 9.1.63 (Lt JPF Nichols). Rudder trim problem on take-off Lossiemouth, Cat SS 22.1.63 (Lt JJR Tod). Tailplane hit starboard intake of XD231 while being manoeuvred in hangar, Lossiemouth, Cat LX 5.2.63. VA South Marston 14.3.63 (modernisation). AHU Lossiemouth 6.4.64. 803 Sqn (157/R') 14.12.64. Flight refuelling POD ERU inadvertently fired on start-up, *Ark Royal*, Cat SS 16.3.65 (Lt NE Rankin). Recoded 7.65 ('032/R'). Brake problem landing *Ark Royal*, Cat LQ 9.12.65 (Lt HW Thomas). Hose parted in withdrawal from pod, Cat SS 21.12.65 (Lt EK Somerville-Jones). Hose problem, landed safely, Cat SS 22.12.65 (S/L GM Faulkner). Hydraulic failure, nosewheel collapsed landing Changi, severely damaged, Cat HY 18.4.66 (Lt ARD Monro-Davies). Was to be retd to RNAY Fleetlands for repair (but NTU). To NASU Changi for RSP. SOC 6.6.66. Wreckage at Sembawang 1966/67.

XD324   Production test VA South Marston 4-10.2.60 (LR Colquhoun). Delivered AHU Lossiemouth 29.2.60. 804 Sqn ('161/H') 29.2.60. Port ammunition tank panel became detached from aircraft take-off Lossiemouth, Cat SS 21.6.60 (F/Lt MJ Webb RAF). Port tyre burst as aircraft returned to dispersal after normal landing Lossiemouth, Cat LX 18.11.60 (L/C TVG Binney). Port inboard drop tank struck barrier stanchion while being taxied on deck *Hermes*, Cat LQ 20.2.61. Arrester centre span parted, pilot stopped aircraft with brakes *Hermes*, Cat SS 23.2.61 (Lt JPE Faulkner). Light stores carrier outboard pylons self-jettisoned in air, *Hermes*, Cat SS 27.2.61 (L/C BG Young). Drop tanks self-jettisoned *Hermes*, Cat SS 17.3.61 (Lt JPE Faulkner). AHU Lossiemouth 18.4.61. 804 Sqn ('161/H') 28.4.61. Undercarriage hydraulic problem, landed safely, Cat SS 11.5.61 (L/C TVG Binney). 800 Sqn ('110/R') 13.9.61. *Ark Royal*, practice bomb released inadvertently Tarhuna Range, Cat SS 4.1.62 (Lt JGL Smith). *Ark Royal*, damaged by fragmentation in dive bombing practice Filfla, landed safely Luqa, Cat LX 7.1.62 (Lt JDHB Howard). Hydraulic failure on Tain Range, landed safely Lossiemouth, Cat LQ 13.2.62 (Lt JGL Smith). Fragmentation damage Garvie Island Range, Cat LC 27.2.62 (Lt KR Entwisle). Flew through flock of birds on low level bombing attack Torr-Shina, landed safely *Ark Royal*, Cat LX 7.6.62 (Lt JA Manley). Drop tanks failed to transfer, jettisoned for landing on *Ark Royal*, Cat SS 14.8.62 (S/L L Ingham). Drop tanks jettisoned, fuel transfer failure *Ark Royal*, Cat SS 2.10.62 (Lt KR Entwisle). Sparks from engine pipe running up *Eagle*, Cat SS 8.11.62. Hydraulic failure on finals, Cat SS 31.1.63 (Lt L Ingham). En-route Lossiemouth-Lee, cabin pressure failure at top of climb, diverted to Yeovilton, Cat SS 20.2.63 (Mr DR Skinner). To Lee-on-Solent 20.2.63 and noted being towed to RNAY Fleetlands 19.7.63 (modernisation began 30.9.63). Depart Lee-on-Solent to AHU Lossiemouth 9.10.64. 803 Sqn ('158/R') 19.1.65. 2-inch rocket POD inadvertently jettisoned on deck, *Ark Royal*, Cat SS 2.2.65 (L/C GAI Johnston). RP ricochet damage to starboard flap, Tain Range, Cat LQ 9.2.65 (Lt R Wren). Bird strike on starboard inner pylon on low level sortie, Cat LQ 7.4.65 (Lt J Comby, French Navy). MRG and compass failure in cloud, Cat SS 26.5.65 (L/C NG Grier-Rees). Recoded 7.65 ('033/R'). From *Ark Royal*, port engine warning light at 20,000ft in climb, single-engined landing Labuan, Cat LX 18.10.65 (Lt RF Shercliff). From *Ark Royal*, hydraulic failure, landed safely Yeovilton, Cat LQ 29.9.66 (S/L AR Dady). To Lee-on-Solent 14.10.66 and became GI Class I 23.8.66. Downgraded to GI Class II as A2590 27.2.68 (*Engine Nos E4610/4611*). To MARTSU by 20.7.70 and to RNAY Fleetlands by road 21.9.70 (de-instrumentation), then to P&EE Shoeburyness 23.9.70. Transferred to MoD(Air) and to Dowty-Rotol Ltd, Staverton for development of fuel systems for MRCA (later to become Tornado) in sections 17.5.71, 8.6.71 & 23.8.71. Returned P&EE Shoeburyness 8 & 14.1.75. Used there for trials 2.75 to 1.82. Last noted 8.82, presumably then scrapped. [945.40hrs]

XD325   Production test VA South Marston 14-15.3.60 (LR Colquhoun). To C(A) charge at VA South Marston 28.3.60 (proof installation of Mod 478 *(Violet Picture))*. Delivered AHU Lossiemouth 11.5.60. 804 Sqn ('165/H') 18.5.60. On landing, bird entered starboard intake, Lossiemouth, Cat SS 1.6.60 (L/C BG Young). Starboard braking not available landing, hook lowered, engaged runway wires Hal Far, Cat LQ 3.8.60 (L/C TVG Binney). Fuel shortage, nose wheel light red, collapsed during arrested landing *Hermes*, Cat LX 26.8.60 (S/L JGL Smith). Tailplane hit obstruction taxying *Hermes*, Cat LQ 20.1.61 (F/Lt MJ Webb RAF). Starboard outer pylon hit seagull crossing coast 300ft during low level Navex, Cat LX 17.5.61 (S/L JGL Smith). AHU Lossiemouth 28.4.61. 804 Sqn ('165/H') 12.5.61. Starboard tailplane damaged in practice dive bombing attack in Persian Gulf, *Victorious*, Cat LQ 28.7.61 (Lt JG Wood). 800 Sqn ('109/R') 15.9.61. Canopy disintegrated and damaged starboard engine, *Ark Royal* 30m SW of Malta, Cat LX 22.11.61 (L/C JAD Ford). Starboard aileron damaged in low level bombing Tain Range, Cat LQ 15.2.62 (Lt KR Entwisle). Hydraulic failure pulling out of dive, West Freugh Range, Cat LQ 22.2.62 (Lt JDHB Howard). Fuel spillage damage on flight-refuelling at 35,000ft, precautionary landing Lossiemouth, Cat LQ 23.2.62 (L/C PH Perks). Undercarriage hydraulic failure after an overshoot Lossiemouth, Cat SS 9.1.63 (S/L AD Alsop). Hydraulic failure, emergency landing, Cat SS 8.4.63 (Lt AG MacFie). Drop tank disintegrated on Tain Range, Cat LQ 18.4.63 (Lt G McBain). To AHU Lossiemouth 30.4.63. To Lee-on-Solent 7.5.63 and towed to RNAY Fleetlands 7.6.63 (reportedly no serials under wings, but large serial on fuselage side outlined in white). Lightered to *Victorious* in Portsmouth Harbour 1.7.63 (deck handling post-refit and static display). Lightered back to RNAY Fleetlands 8.8.63 (modernisation began 3.12.63 and complete refinish). Lee-on-Solent to AHU Lossiemouth 6.10.64. 803 Sqn ('151/R') 8.2.65. Hydraulic failure in circuit, landed safely, Cat LQ 30.3.65 (L/C JOF Billingham). Bird strike on port outer pylon, Cat LQ 5.4.65 (Lt EK Somerville-Jones). Hydraulic failure in circuit, precautionary landing, Lossiemouth, Cat LQ 12.4.65 (S/L HW Thomas). Hook bounced and missed wires, rear fuselage damaged, Cat LY 28.6.65 (Lt R Wren). Recoded 7.65 ('024/R'). NASU Changi 22.9.65. 803 Sqn ('024/R') 3.11.64. *Ark Royal* on Beira patrol off East Africa, nosewheel would not lower, entered barrier landing, nosewheel forced through forward fuselage, fuselage ripped open, Cat HY 7.3.66 (Lt TJ Notley unhurt). To NASU Changi. RSP 21.4.66. SOC 27.4.66. Wreckage Sembawang by 1.67. [795.15hrs]

XD326 Production test VA South Marston 15.3.60 - 20.4.60 (LR Colquhoun). Delivered AHU Lossiemouth 2.5.60. 804 Sqn Lossiemouth ('163/H') 9.5.60. Garvie Island range, bombs failed to drop by normal selection, port bomb dropped by means of jettison button, Cat SS 1.6.60 (Lt DF Mills). Starboard engine seized on start-up *Hermes*, Cat SS 19.2.61. AHU Lossiemouth 19.4.61. 804 Sqn ('163/H') 8.5.61. Windscreen panel cracked 6,000ft 500 knots, Cat LQ 25.5.61 (Lt JPE Faulkner). 800 Sqn ('111/R') 13.9.61. *Ark Royal*, partial elevator failure, successful emergency landing USAF Wheelus, Tripoli, Cat LQ 13.12.61 (Lt JPE Faulkner). Canopy detached on catapulting *Ark Royal* 40m S of Malta, Cat LQ 19.3.62 (L/C A Mancais). Nose-wheel collapsed landing *Ark Royal*, Cat LQ 25.4.62 (L/C JAD Ford). Hydraulic failure 60m S of Hong Kong, flapless landing Kai Tak, Cat LQ 29.5.62 (L/C A Mancais). Top of rudder damaged moving aircraft in hangar *Ark Royal*, Cat LQ 18.6.62. Hydraulic problem landing Lossiemouth, Cat SS 4.2.63 (Lt PC Marshall). Nose-wheel failed to lift, aborted, overshot, Cat LX 11.6.63 (Lt AM Hickling). Low level RP attack on splash target, attempted to recover too late, hit sea in almost level attitude astern *Ark Royal* in FE 2°01'N 104°35'E, Cat ZZ 31.7.63 (Lt AG MacFie killed).

XD327 Allocated VA South Marston 30.3.60. Production test VA South Marston 10-24.5.60 (LR Colquhoun and MJ Lithgow) (1,000lb Mk.10 bombing trials - E.L and V.T. fusing, also 25lb practice bombs - 45 and 100 degree LABS manoeuvres). To C(A) charge at VA 2.6.60. A&AEE 8.6.60 (preparation for bombing trials at El Adem). VA South Marston 28.7.60 (removal of instrumentation). Delivered AHU Lossiemouth 13.9.60. Collected by 804 Sqn Crew and delivered to Malta 21.11.60. AHU Hal Far 23.11.60. 804 Sqn 5.12.60. 803 Sqn ('148/V') 16.3.61. False fire warning, single-engined landing *Victorious* off North Borneo, Cat SS 3.5.61 (S/L AHS Anderson). Starboard wingtip hit radome of Sea Vixen XJ519 while being marshalled for launch *Victorious* in Bay of Bengal, 10.9.61 (Lt PAA Waring). Recoded 4.62 ('148/H'). Starboard engine shut down after take-off, single-engined landing *Victorious* in Penang area, Cat SS 15.11.61 (Lt PAA Waring). Dusk DLP, 6 ratings received minor injuries from arrester wire, Cat SS 7.3.63 (L/C NJP Mills). To Lee-on-Solent 20.9.63 and to RNAY Fleetlands (modernisation began 18.7.63). Depart Lee-on-Solent to AHU Lossiemouth 25.2.65. To Lee-on-Solent 7.4.65 (preparation for shipment). During night tow from naval base to AHU Changi, edge of Durban Road collapsed and starboard wheel sank 2ft into soft ground, Cat LQ 16.6.65. 803 Sqn ('031/R') 27.9.65. Flight refuelling hose lost turning to land, Cat SS 29.1.66 (Lt EK Somerville-Jones). NASU Brawdy 3.10.66. Airwork FRU Hurn 6.4.67 (remaining uncoded in FRU service). Wfu 14.6.68 due to problems with port wing hinge. Used as source of spares at Hurn. To RNAY Fleetlands by road 4.9.68. SOC and sold as scrap 7.1.69. [870.10hrs]

XD328 Production Test VA South Marston 27.5.60 - 11.7.60. Delivered AHU Lossiemouth 13.7.60 (tropicalised and fitted UHF). 803 Sqn ('153/V') 26.7.60 (LABS aircraft). AHU Lossiemouth 3.10.60. 803 Sqn ('153/V') 13.10.60. No 1 hydraulic system failure when undercarriage was locking down, landed using emergency system, *Victorious*, Cat SS 22.11.60 (Lt E Cope). Nose hit by XD271 parking *Victorious* 28.8.61. Engine vibration, emergency landing *Victorious* off Aden, Cat SS 29.8.61 (Lt PAA Waring). Tailplane hit fuselage of XD244 during deck move *Victorious* 27.3.62. Flight refuelling probe damaged starboard rudder of Sea Vixen taxying *Hermes*, Cat LQ 27.9.62 (Lt RV Ponter). To Lee-on-Solent c10.62 and to RNAY Fleetlands 8.11.62 (modernisation – began 2.4.63). AHU Lossiemouth 1.1.64. 803 Sqn ('144/R') 6.8.64. ASI and Machmeter failure in combat formation, landed safely, Lossiemouth, Cat LQ 18.3.65 (Lt ARD Monro-Davies). Hydraulic failure, landed safely, Cat LQ 2.4.65 (F/Lt TG Gilroy RAF). Rating injured during servicing, Lossiemouth, Cat SS 11.6.65 (AA2/C MR Hoskins injured). Recoded 7.65 ('015/R'). Severe starboard engine vibration, Cat LQ 9.8.65 (F/Lt TG Gilroy RAF). Hydraulic 1 failure prior to landing, port wheel remained retracted after use of emergency system, emergency landing, caught No.1 wire, engaged barrier, *Ark Royal*, Cat HY 30.8.65 (Lt NE Rankin unhurt). AHU Sembawang 16.9.65. RNAY Fleetlands 15.11.65 (repair). Intended to be last aircraft on Scimitar programme at Fleetlands, but replaced by XD220. ADW 19.4.66. Stripped of useable parts 23.6.66. SOC, RSP 26.7.66 and hulk in scrap compound by 25.8.66. [642.05hrs]

XD329 Production test VA South Marston 27.6.60 - 6.7.60 (LR Colquhoun). Delivered AHU Lossiemouth 15.7.60 (tropicalised and fitted UHF). 803 Sqn ('154/V') 25.7.60. *Victorious* in Exercise *Decex* off Aden, staggered into the air in nose-up attitude after catapult launch with 1,000 bombs and drop tanks on, pilot unable to maintain control, ejected at low level, parachute opened as hit water, Cat ZZ 9.12.60 (Lt JWH Purvis rescued unhurt by SAR - Ejection No.404).

XD330 Production test VA South Marston 13.7.60 - 12.8.60 (LR Colquhoun). Delivered AHU Lossiemouth 16.8.60. 803 Sqn *Victorious* ('148/V') 19.10.60 for 803 Sqn (acceptance flight en-route to *Victorious*). Struck by a Sea Vixen while embarked 25.1.61. MARTSU Lee-on-Solent 8.2.61. Transported by MARTSU by road to VA South Marston 15.2.61. Test flown 30.3.61 VA South Marston (LR Colquhoun). RNAY Fleetlands (via Lee) 12.4.61. 807 Sqn ('190/C') 18.4.61. From *Centaur*, undamaged when touched XD319 during refuelling 20,000ft, 60m off Lisbon, Cat SS 30.10.61 (L/C GA Rowan-Thomson). False fire warning at 18,000ft, single-engined landing, Cat SS 11.12.61 (S/L NA Britton). AHU Tengah 31.1.62. 800 Sqn ('103/R') 23.10.62. 803 Sqn 10.12.62. AHU Tengah 21.2.63. 800 Sqn 12.7.63. 803 Sqn ('159/R') 26.2.64. To Lee-on-Solent 3.7.64 and to RNAY Fleetlands (modernisation). Towed to Lee-on-Solent 1.9.65 and handed over to MARTSU Lee-on-Solent for preparation for shipment 26.10.65. Shipped to Far East, arr NASU Changi 4.11.65. 803 Sqn ('034/R') 20.1.66. NASU Changi 6.66. Returned to UK. NASU Brawdy 1.10.66. RSP 17.11.69. SOC 20.1.70 and scrapped Brawdy 5.70. [656.55hrs]

XD331   Production test VA South Marston 17.8.60 - 31.8.60 (LR Colquhoun and MJ Lithgow). Delivered AHU Lossiemouth 16.9.60. 803 Sqn *Victorious* ('145/V') 18.10.60 (acceptance flight en-route ship). Injested foreign object into intake while engine running *Victorious*, 3.11.60. Parhuna Range, No 1 hydraulic system failure, precautionary landing, Cat SS 21.11.60 (Lt AMD de Labilliere). Canopy jettisoned in flight during dive, Cat LQ 2.12.60 (Lt AS Tuck). Ship rolled on touchdown, port outer drop tank hit deck *Victorious*, Cat LQ 24.1.61 (Lt MJM Brophy). Foreign body damaged engine blades *Victorious*, Cat SS 7.3.61 (L/C TCS Leece). Practice bomb carrier inadvertently fired and struck XD318, *Victorious* 21.3.61. Foreign body entered intake ground run RAF Tengah, Cat SS 8.4.61. Starboard compressor blades damaged by foreign body during ground run *Victorious*, Cat LY 25.11.61. Recoded 4.62 ('145/H'). Probe broke while flight refuelling, Cat LQ 22.6.62 (Lt PP Cardew). Drop tank burst during pressure refuelling by bowser Hal Far, Cat SS 26.6.62. *Hermes* in Mediterranean Exercise *Rip Tide III*, fuel starvation and resultant double flame-out at 37,000ft, glided until over escort HMS *Scarborough* at 8,000ft, then ejected, aircraft ditched 41°34'N 12°9'W, Cat ZZ 13.8.62 (L/C B Willson picked up slightly injured by escort's sea-boat - Ejection No.595). SOC 14.8.63. [289.10hrs]

XD332   Production test VA South Marston 15.9.60 - 21.9.60 (LR Colquhoun). Last air test 31.10.60 (LR Colquhoun). To AHU Lossiemouth 4.11.60. 804 Sqn (uncoded?) 21.11.60. To Far East in *Hermes* 6.12.60. AHU Tengah 30.12.60. 807 Sqn ('194/C') 8.2.62. *Centaur* 40m NNW of Singapore, bird strike at 500ft on low level Navex, landed safely Tengah, Cat SS 9.2.62 (Lt JM Moore). Mid-air collision with XD317 off Malta in formation flypast, Cat LQ 18.4.62 (Lt RDG Gray). AHU Lossiemouth 26.4.62. En-route to Lee-on-Solent diverted to Thorney Island 24.5.62. To Lee-on-Solent 25.5.62 and to RNAY Fleetlands (Main Check 4). Flown Lee-on-Solent to Boscombe Down 8.12.62 (possibly returning 19.12.62), last test and departed Lee-on-Solent 21.12.62. 736 Sqn Lossiemouth ('612') 11.1.63. To Lee-on-Solent 5.6.63 and to RNAY Fleetlands by 21.6.63 (Maincheck 4). Depart Lee-on-Solent to 736 Sqn Lossiemouth 10.7.63. Starboard ammunition bay panel detached on take-off RAE Bedford, Cat SS 11.12.63 (S/L PJ McManus). Flight refuelling, probe damaged, Cat LQ 10.2.64 (Lt LA Wilkinson). Bird strike on starboard intake on take-off, Cat SS 24.2.64 (Lt LA Wilkinson). Tyre burst landing, Cat LQ 28.2.64 (F/Lt TG Gilroy RAF). Nosewheel light failure, Cat SS 2.6.64 (S/L KB Owen). Bird strike at 2,000ft in circuit, Cat LQ 5.6.64 (Lt J Comby, French Navy). Heavy landing checks 13.10.64. Starboard oil pressure problem, single-engined landing, Cat SS 5.2.65 (Lt AS Tuck). Part of hook frame lost in flight, Cat LQ 11.3.65 (S/L GM Faulkner). 764B Sqn Lossiemouth ('616') 26.3.65. Faulty aircraft warning light landing, Cat LQ 17.6.65 (Lt PJ Trudgett). Starboard engine problem, single-engined landing, Cat LQ 17.6.65 (Lt PJ Trudgett). 25-lb practice bomb dropped off on touch-down, Cat SS 6.8.65 (Lt MJ Williams). Brawdy, temp for Maintenance Test Pilots course 24.11.65. To Lee-on-Solent 17.2.66 and on to RNAY Fleetlands (modernisation). *Hermes* (for deck handling training at Plymouth including XD215) 24.5.66. Lightered to MARTSU Lee-on-Solent 31.7.66 (open storage). To GI Class II at SAH Culdrose as *A2574* 6.10.67 (Engine Nos *E4586/4587*), allocated code 'SAH-19' but not applied. Downgraded to Class GI III 5.10.71, used by RN Driving School. Towed to Cornwall Aeronautical Park, Helston 6.7.76 and repainted in 736 Sqdn marks coded "612/-". Repainted as "194/C" by 9.91 (now known as Flambards Village Theme Park). To Southampton Hall of Aviation by road 10.3.99. Currently in open storage in museum car park.

XD333   Production test VA South Marston 22.12.60 (LR Colquhoun). Delivered AHU Lossiemouth 10.1.61. 803 Sqn ('147/V') 18.1.61. Port ammunition bay panel became detached on take-off, Cat LQ 18.4.61 (Lt AS Tuck). Recoded 4.62 ('147/H'). From *Hermes*, Sidewinder missile fell off in turn at 28,000ft, Cat SS 28.5.63 (S/L MJ Harwood). Hook hit rounddown and damaged tail *Hermes*, Cat LQ 11.5.63 (Lt SC Creasy). To Lee-on-Solent 18.12.63 and to RNAY Fleetlands some time after 31.1.64 (modernisation). Towed back to Lee-on-Solent 31.3.65 and departed to AHU Lossiemouth 30.4.65. Shipped to the Far East. 803 Sqn ('023/R') 11.5.65. Hose broke away after flight refuelling with Sea Vixen, Cat SS 7.3.66 (Lt BP Marindin). Practice bombs came off prior to launch from *Ark Royal* off Lossiemouth, Cat SS 9.8.66 (S/L GM Faulkner). Tailskid oleo collapsed during launch from *Ark Royal*, hook stuck to catapult track, diverted safely to Lossiemouth, Cat LY 20.9.66 (Lt EK Somerville-Jones). NASU Brawdy 3.10.66. Airwork FRU 3.11.67 but returned to Brawdy 24.11.67. Returned Airwork FRU Hurn ('837') 26.6.68 (Lt Cdr PM Stevenson). RAE Farnborough 20.1.71. Flown to Southend 20.1.71. To P&EE Shoeburyness by road 15.2.71. SOC RN 26.1.71. Used for trials 8.73 to 1.74. Gone by 12.89.

**UNIDENTIFIED**
No date   Cocooned Scimitar loaded by MARTSU aboard SS *Benalbanach* at Berth 47 [location?] for Seletar.
24.2.65   2 wings and 2 tailplanes from 2 Scimitars arrived P&EE Shoeburyness ex Bicester/RAE Bedford.
3.3.65    Fuselage with cockpit and engines arrived P&EE Shoeburyness ex Bicester/RAE Bedford.

**SURVIVORS**
WT859   Brooklands Museum, Weybridge, Surrey (cockpit section only).
XD215   Nick Parker, Cheltenham, Surrey (cockpit section only).
XD220   USS *Intrepid* Air and Space Museum, New York, USA (Fleet Air Arm Museum loan).
XD235   Dave Thomas, Welshpool, Powys (cockpit section only).
XD317   Fleet Air Arm Museum, Yeovilton, Somerset.
XD332   Southampton Hall of Aviation.
--------   Simulator, City of Norwich Aviation Museum, Norwich Airport, (cockpit section mock-up, synthetic procedures trainer).

*A close-up of the tail of XD243 adorned with the tankard motif when flown by No.800B Flight as '115/E'.*

*XD248 '195/R' of No.807 Squadron does a low flypast during the SBAC Show at Farnborough in September 1959. The extension on the normal arrester hook is the pick-up hook for the Dart Target. (Vickers-Armstrongs)*

# A DESCRIPTION

## CONSTRUCTION

The all-metal fuselage was of oval sections except for the front and rear portions and was built up of frames, longerons, intercostals and light alloy plating. The front section accommodated the pilot in a pressurised cockpit just ahead of the engine air intakes and was provided with a superb all-round view, despite the high cockpit coamings and windscreen frames which, in keeping with the rest of the aircraft, were substantial. The cockpit itself was comfortable and roomy, and the general layout was good with all controls coming readily to hand. The jettisonable canopy slid electrically rearward and a Martin-Baker Type 4C ejector seat was installed with a Duplex drogue, a single combined parachute-and-seat-harness release box, and an 80 ft/sec ejection gun. Forward of the pressurised section the fuselage nose could be folded to aid storage whilst embarked.

The semi-monocoque fuselage was markedly waisted aft of the wing leading edge, suggestive of area ruling. This resulted from a selection of a wing-fuselage junction which minimised peak suctions and maintained the sweep of the pressure isobars over the wing surfaces, thus delaying the drag rise.

Pioneering engineering practices used on the Scimitar included high strength steel spars and members in areas of high stress in the wing and tail structure, the use of titanium for lower stressed areas where heat resistance was essential, and the use of chemical etching to remove surplus metal from wing and tail panels, a method not used before in Britain and one more accurate in terms of determining panel thickness with the added bonus of being quicker and cheaper than conventional machining.

The Scimitar was not only the largest, heaviest and the most powerful fighter the Royal Navy had acquired up to that time, but was also certainly the noisiest. During early operational use it was found that acoustic waves set up by the engine noise on the structure aft of the jet pipes were resulting in cases of skin cracking. By using thicker skins, replacing light alloy ribs with steel ones and employing synthetic resin bonding backed by foam filling, the problem was sufficiently overcome to enable a fatigue life of 1,000 hours to be achieved.

*Rear view of a Scimitar F.1 at RNAS Abbotsinch, showing the petal-type air brakes. (via N.Parker)*

*A Scimitar cockpit photographed on 25 March 1958. (Vickers-Armstrongs)*

The mainplanes were of all metal construction with forward, main and aft spars and were swept back at an angle of 45 degrees. Hydraulically-powered outer mainplane folding was provided, reducing the overall width of the aircraft to between 20ft 6½in and 26ft 9½in dependant on modification state and configuration. Trailing edge flaps were fitted to both inner mainplanes, and leading edge flaps were fitted to both mainplanes.

Hydraulically-operated air brakes were provided and comprised six small flaps (mounted three either side of the fuselage) installed just forward of the jet pipe outlets. Aft of these outlets, the fuselage became circular and merged into an empennage. The empennage structure consisted of the swept-back fin, the tailplane and its hydraulic actuator, the tail skid, deck arrester hook and the hold-back gear, the latter two items being hydraulically retractable.

## FLYING CONTROLS

Flying controls were hydraulically operated and were controlled by a conventional column and rudder bar. The tailplane and ailerons were powered by dual hydraulic systems (four hydraulic pumps, two per engine) running at an unusually high pressure of 4,000lb/sq in with no provision for manual reversion in the event of failure. The rudder, on the other hand, was operated by one system only and could revert to manual control if required. Hydraulic 'feel' simulation was provided for the tailplane and rudder control, and 'spring' feel for the ailerons. Electrically operated actuators for trimming were fitted – aileron and elevator controls being adjusted with a four-way thumb switch on the control column, and the rudder from a switch on the left console behind the throttles. The slab-type tailplane, a feature necessary in aircraft operating beyond 0.85 – 0.9M, was originally fitted with ten degrees of dihedral, but early investigations into the aircraft's tendency to pitch-up in the turn showed that by lowering the tailplane tips into the wake of the mainplane, this effect was markedly reduced. As a result the whole assembly was redesigned and refitted with 10 degrees of anhedral. The unit was interconnected with the trailing edge flaps to compensate for trim changes on flap deployment.

## FUEL SYSTEM

Fuel was carried in five bag tanks in the fuselage and four integral tanks in the mainplanes. Provision was made for carriage of four jettisonable pylon-mounted drop tanks beneath the mainplanes. The fuel system was pressurised and a complex and often troublesome balance system regulated the supply from individual internal tanks. A fuel proportioner controlled the supply from the jettisonable drop tanks. Two recuperators maintained a supply of fuel to the engine for a limited period when the aircraft was subjected to negative 'g' condition.

The total nominal internal fuel capacity of the Scimitar was 1,065 Imperial gallons made up as follows:

*A close-up of the Maxaret Brake System used on the Scimitar for trials. (RAE)*

| | |
|---|---|
| No.1 Fuselage Tank | 93 gallons |
| No.2 Fuselage Tank | 253 gallons |
| No.3 & 4 Fuselage Tanks | 171 gallons |
| No.5 Fuselage Tank | 206 gallons |
| Inner Wing Tank | 122 gallons |
| Outer Wing Tank | 208 gallons |
| Fuel in Recuperator | 12 gallons |

*The 30mm Aden gun being installed into second production Scimitar F.1 XD213. (Vickers-Armstrongs)*

*The hinged nose of the Scimitar in the open position. This nose is the Photo pack version, housing up to three F.95 cameras for photo reconnaissance duties. (Vickers-Armstrongs)*

## ELECTRICAL SYSTEM

The electrical system consisted of a 28V DC single-pole earth return system, powered by two engine-driven 28 volt 6 kW wide speed generators. AC power for instruments, radio etc was supplied by two 115V 3 phase inverters which employed an automatic change-over circuit giving standby facilities. Radio services included VHF communications and homing systems, telebriefing, radio altimeter, navigation and operational aids.

## ARMAMENT

Conventional armament consisted of four 30mm Aden Mk.4 cannon, mounted in pairs in the inverted position under each engine bay. Gun access panels were situated between frames 14 and 16 at the root end of the mainplane. Two smaller panels, forward of the gun bay on each side of the aircraft, gave access to the front mountings and barrel supports of the outboard guns, and barrel supports only, of the inboard guns.

Ventilation was provided by a scavenger scoop mounted on the underside of the aircraft forward of the gun bay. When the trigger was operated, the scoop was lowered and the gun bays were automatically purged by ram air. The blast tubes were situated below and aft of the air intakes. Blast deflectors were fitted in each tube to prevent nose down change in pitch when the guns were fired. The nominal rate of fire of the Aden gun was 1,200 rounds per minute, eight seconds being taken for a four gun fire-out.

*XE214 '146/H' of No.803 Squadron firing a Bullpup missile in 1962. (B.J.Lowe)*

To effect gun installation and removal the units were raised and lowered by means of cables which ran through pivoted pulleys mounted on frames. During hoisting or lowering operations the cables were connected to attachment points on each side of the gun cradles and the other end connected to a Type 'C' hoist suspended from an attachment on the underside of the fuselage forward of the gun bay. During flight the pulleys had to be locked in the "UP" position and the cables secured by elastic cords in the gun bay.

The ammunition tanks were built into the root ends of the mainplanes in which a full load of 160 rounds per gun could be carried, including the ammunition in the feed chute. A link collecting tank was fitted in the fuselage midway between the gun bays.

The electrical gun firing installation was fitted with the X1154 firing unit. The guns were operated by a trigger-type firing button mounted on the front of the control column which had a safety catch incorporated.

### Bullpup

The American-supplied Bullpup was an air-to-ground radio-link command-guided powered bomb. Following modifications, which included the fitting of a Hussenot recorder in the port gun bay and a forward-facing camera in the nose to record the firings, the Scimitar was able to carry four of these weapons weighing some 570lbs each, 10.5 feet long and with a maximum diameter of just over three feet. The missile came in three parts: the front section housing the guidance systems, the centre section containing the 250lbs warhead, and the after section with the propellant including two parasite flares which were used for tracking purposes. On this section were mounted the four wings.

Jettison was achieved either by firing the missile unarmed and unguided or by forcing the missile from the launcher in a rearward direction, by an electrically operated cartridge situated in the rear of the launcher, in a method known as 'Kick-Back'.

On being cleared for Service use it was recommended by the A&AEE that for carriage the maximum IAS was 625 knots or Mach 1.1. and a maximum of 5G in rolling pullouts, with no rapid rates of roll. Maximum launch speed of the missile was Mach 0.95 at dive angles of up to 45°.

When the weapon was fired in the guided mode the pilot controlled it using a switch mounted on the port side of the cockpit. Only the four cardinal commands of up, down, left and right could be given, and only one at a time. After firing the pilot endeavoured to keep the flares aligned with the target by use of the missile control switch, and after impact he was free to break away.

*XD248 '195/R' of No.807 Squadron makes a practice rocket attack. (via Philip Jarrett)*

A Hussenot recorder was fitted in the port gun bay and, if required, a forward-facing camera was placed in the nose to record the firings for later analysis.

The increased accuracy of this missile meant that the number of weapons and aircraft needed to deal with any one target was considerably reduced.

### Sidewinder

Sidewinder, a passive infra-red homing missile weighing 160lbs and just over 9ft long with a maximum diameter of 22 inches, was another American weapon supplied to the Fleet Air Arm. The missile was reasonably simple (compared to the *Firestreak*, fitted to the Sea Vixen), reliable and effective, required the minimum of testing was very easy to assemble and was treated as a further round of ammunition. As a result a simulator was not used and pilots quickly became accustomed to its use.

Powered by a 5-inch Air-to-Ground standard American rocket motor, guidance was given by a control system on the nose of the missile which contained a gyro-stabilised homing eye. The 25lb fragmenting explosive warhead could be detonated either by contact or by a proximity fuse and was effective out to some thirty feet. If the missile missed its designated target it would self-destroy after twenty four seconds.

An acquisition round was used which gave the pilot all the actual reactions of a live weapon, thus enabling him to see what the missile could do without the expense of actually firing a live version.

After Service clearance trials at the A&AEE in early 1963 it was recommended that the missile could be launched or jettisoned from the aircraft at any speed and with a 'G' limit of between −1.5 and +40 at a maximum dive angle of −65 degrees. Fitted on the cockpit coaming to aid operation of the missile were an angle of attack and accelerometer indicators, along with a missile selection switch.

Before flight a member of the ground crew would shine a torch on the missile eye to replicate an infra-red source; if all was well, the pilot would hear a 'growl' in his earphones – exactly as he would when locked on to a target during an interception. Firings were made only after a visual sighting of the target by the pilot.

### L.A.B.S

Equipment changes carried out during conversion for LABS operation included the removal of the Mk VIII gyro gunsight, all four Aden cannons and associated ammunition feed, empty link and cartridge case ejector chutes and both gun blast tubes. These would be replaced by a light fighter sight, LABS control switch boxes, roller map display, tracking unit (mounted in the starboard gun bay) and ballast weights to compensate for the removed cannons.

*XD277 '111/E' of No.800B Squadron from HMS Eagle refuelling an RAF Gloster Javelin FAW.9 XH895 'G' all-weather fighter of No.64 Squadron Seletar (Singapore) in 1965. (E.B.Morgan archives)*

*An Avon 20201 production engine received at Wisley from Rolls-Royce on 28 November 1956 for fitment in one of the Scimitar prototypes. (Rolls-Royce)*

*Lt Jack Worth (now Captain Rtd) in XD246 '153/V' of No.803 Squadron does a pick-up of the Dart Target from the deck of HMS Victorious in February 1960 with the aid of an extended hook. This made it impossible to land on board. It was proved that the aircraft could tow the Dart Target and in fact did so up to 40,000 feet and at speeds in excess of Mach 1. However, it was not feasible to use the Scimitar in this role. (FAA Museum)*

### T.M.B

The tactical nuclear weapon assigned for use with the Scimitar (and eventually the Buccaneer) was the 25 kiloton device codenamed *Red Beard*. In an attempt to disguise its real identity and purpose it was given the extremely vague reference of 'Target Marker Bomb' (TMB – sometimes also referred to as TV.11).

Although exact details of the device are not fully known, it is understood to have been a relatively crude first-generation nuclear weapon of quite large physical proportions which had to be handled with extreme caution. Inadvertent dropping or even scraping of the assembly could result in it exploding with a force of up to 1 kiloton. Unlike the Buccaneer, which could accommodate the device in its capacious rotating bomb bay out of harm's way, the Scimitar had to carry it on one of the underwing pylons. As a result of its potentially volatile nature, and vulnerable position, proposed deck landings with a *Red Beard* fitted were prohibited and Scimitars would be diverted to a land base.

The bulk of the TV.11 trials were carried out using XD218 with the final such flights being made by Dave Morgan on 19 and 20 September 1963.

### TANKER ROLE

In addition to the capability to refuel from tanker aircraft, the Scimitar was required to operate as a tanker itself in what became known as the 'Buddy Refuelling' role. The Mk.20A flight refuelling pod was fitted on the starboard inner pylon and a control panel replaced the armament control in the cockpit.

The pod itself carried 145 gallons of fuel but this was replenished from the aircraft's fuel and any amount could be transferred.

There were two problem areas in the development of the system: The early drogue was a rigid metal cone and, unless contact was made right in the centre, it would topple. The hose was of composite construction; wire-wound and canvas covered. This tended to become unstable in slight turbulence particularly above around 250 knots.

The risk of failure to connect was high and some breakages of both the nozzle and hose were experienced. The answers were found in the form of the 'collapsible' drogue and the 'black rubber' hose. The former resembled the frame of an umbrella, hinged on the casing of the refuelling socket, with the ends of the spines joining by a circular drogue which spread the whole assembly into a cone when it was streamed from the pod. If contact was made off-centre this drogue remained stable and allowed the probe to slide into the socket.

The 'black rubber' hose was much less prone to instability (otherwise known as 'crank-shafting') and contacts were made up to 300 knots IAS at low levels and 0.8 IMN at 30,000 feet. Contacts could be made up to higher speeds in both cases, but the hose tended to become too lively and consequently hese were seldom done.

### TARGET TOWING ROLE

To allow the Scimitar to be employed for target towing duties, using the 'Dart' target, special extended 'A' frame members were attached to the existing arrester hook assembly, at the end of which a forked hook was fixed with a special jettison mechanism. Target release could be effected by pressing the camera button on the control column.

## POWERPLANTS

The Scimitar was powered by two Rolls-Royce Avon R.A.202 15-stage axial-flow turbo-jets, mounted side-by-side in the fuselage. The nominal static thrust at sea level of these units was given as 11,250lbs at 8,000rpm.

## SUPERMARINE SCIMITAR F.1 GENERAL DATA

Dimensions: Span 37 ft 2 in. Length 55 ft 4 in. Height 17 ft 4 in. Span folded 20 ft 6.5 in. Wing area 485 sq. ft.

Weights: Empty, 23,962lb. Loaded, 34,200lb.

Performance: Maximum speed, 710 mph at sea level, Mach 0.97 at altitude. Rate of climb, 12,000 ft/min. Range, 1,422 miles. Service ceiling, 46,000 ft

*XD239 '144/R' of No.803 Squadron seen with a dummy Red Beard TMB mounted on the port inner pylon during the Leuchars Battle of Britain day in September 1964. (A.Carlaw)*

*XD322 '839' of Airwork Fleet Requirements Unit, Hurn with the letters 'BY' crudely painted on the fin. (J.D.R.Rawlings)*

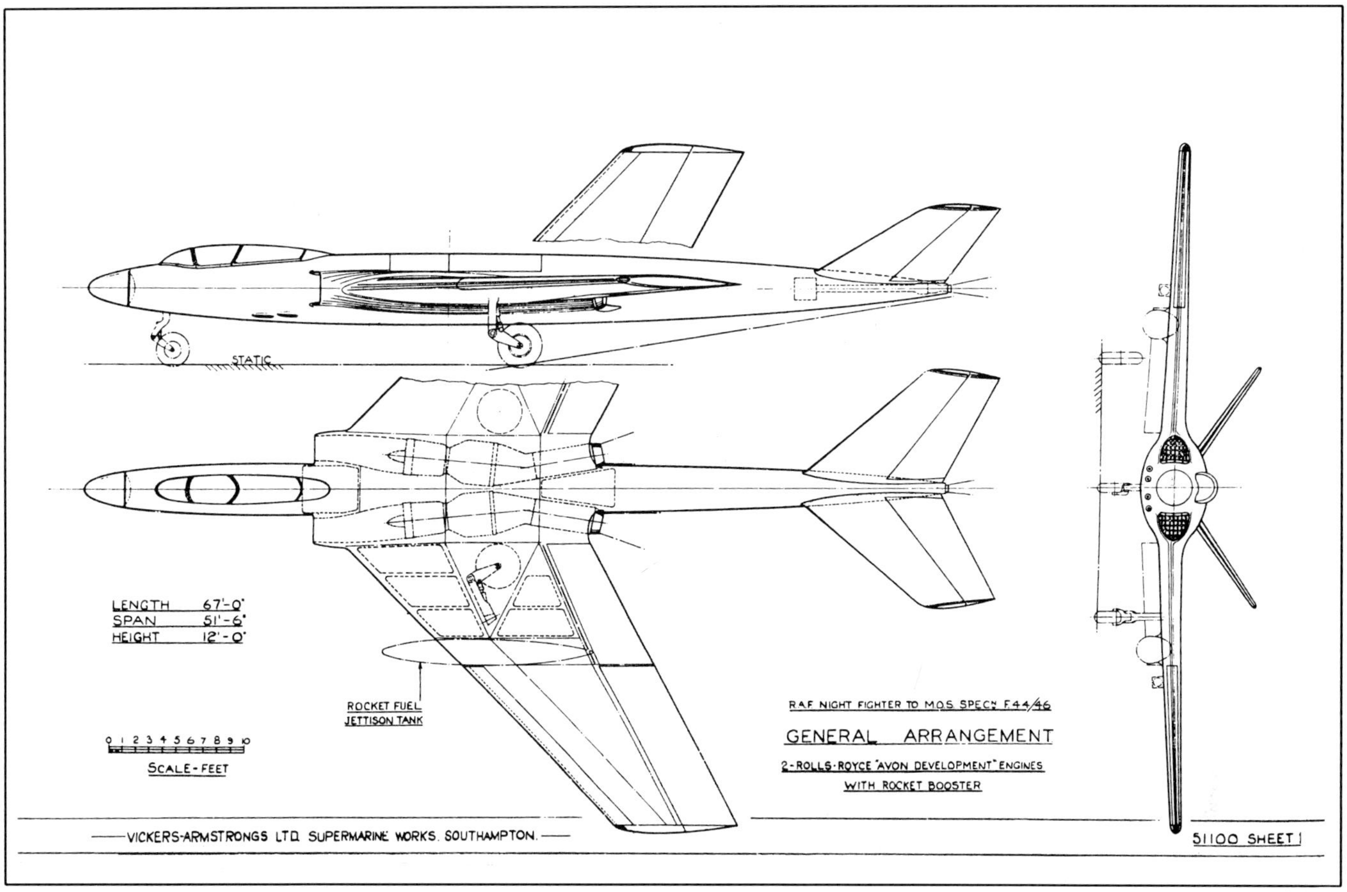

*Type 511. Drawing No.51100 Sheet 1. Swept wing. General arrangement with rocket booster.*

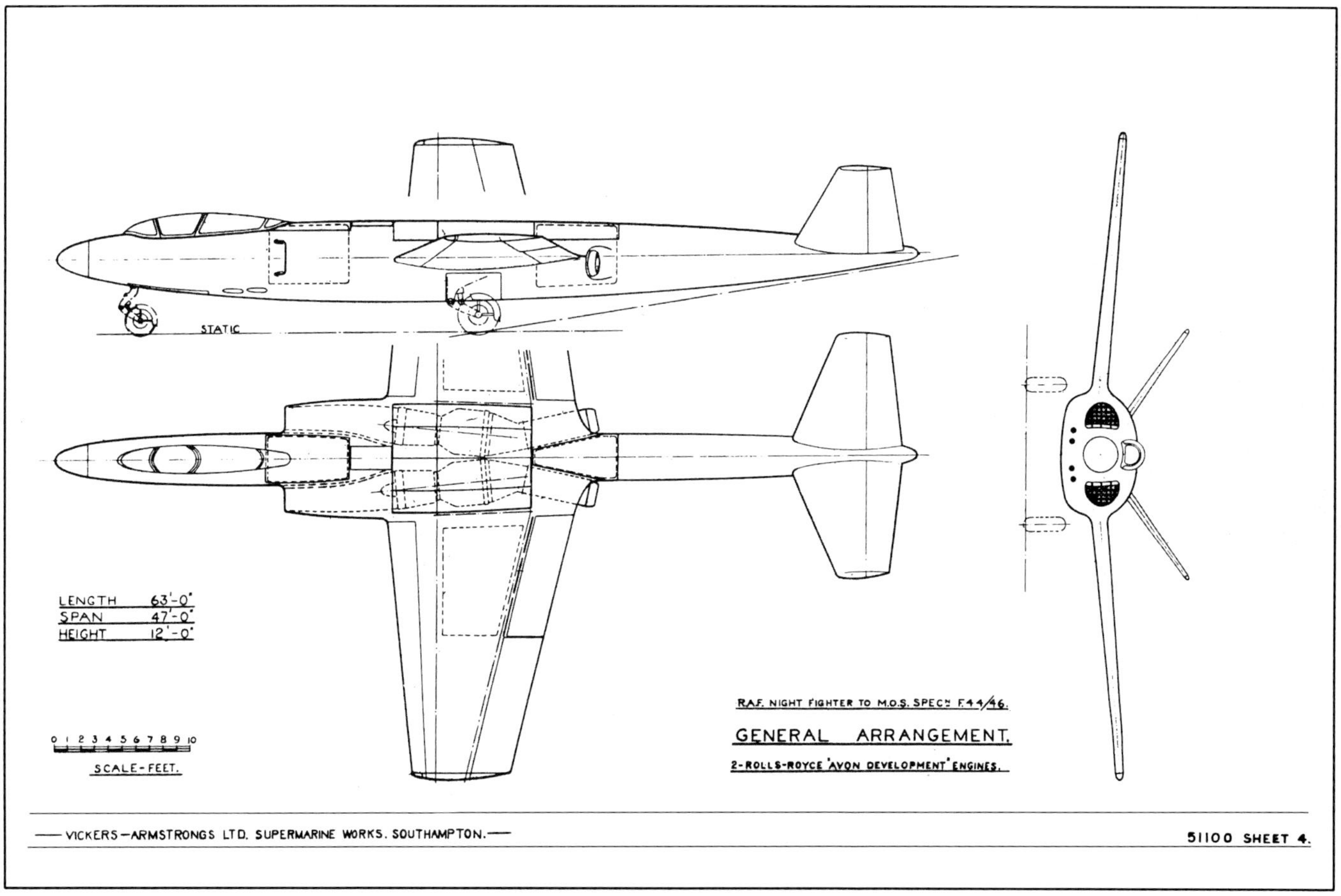

*Type 511. Drawing No.51100 Sheet 4. Straight wing. General arrangement.*

# VARIATIONS ON A THEME

## TYPE 511

The Supermarine Specification 505, Type 511, was submitted to the MoS Specification F.44/46 for an RAF night fighter, being one of a number of Scimitar variant projects.

Alternative designs were considered, with respectively swept-back wings and straight surfaces. The former had the advantage of a 50-knot higher speed at the given operational height, but it required a rocket booster in order to meet the climb requirement. The straight wing aeroplane met the climb requirement without the rocket engine by virtue of its lighter weight, and just met the speed requirement. The main undercarriage of the swept back design was housed within the wings, whereas in the straight wing it retracted into the fuselage because the wings were not thick enough.

In other respects the designs were similar, having twin Rolls-Royce Avon engines and four 30mm guns. A pressure cabin seated a crew of two in tandem, and a 'V' tail was adopted. The difficulties associated with a wing having a large amount of sweepback were well known, the most serious being the provision of stability and control at the stall. There seemed to be three probable ways of rendering a back-swept wing satisfactory: by fitting leading edge slats over the outer portion of the wing, by sucking off the boundary layer towards the tips, or by reducing the spanwise drift of the boundary layer by keeping the aspect ratio down to about 3.60. In this design Supermarine provided automatic leading edge slats over the outer wing, but by keeping the aspect ratio down to 3.56 it was hoped to be able to ultimately dispense with slats. As a further step to making the stall gentle an aerofoil profile with a large leading edge radius was chosen.

Stability in pitch and yaw was provided by swept back surfaces arranged in the form of a vee tail. Longitudinal control was achieved by means of elevators, these being moved differentially to give directional control. Dive recovery brakes were fitted to the under surface as a precautionary measure and air brakes which could be operated up to the maximum diving speed of the aeroplane were installed. These took the form of spoilers which protruded from the upper surface of the wing at 70% of the chord together with the landing flap which was deflected by 12 degrees. The nose flap extended throughout the complete span and was deflected downwards through 25 degrees. A plain flap of 25% mean chord and having 60 degrees deflection was fitted to the trailing edge over the inner part of the span. The slotted ailerons were arranged to droop by 10 degrees when the trailing edge flaps were lowered.

On the straight wing version, stability in pitch and yaw was provided by surfaces arranged in the form of a V tail. This arrangement had been chosen to keep the interference effects to a minimum. Longitudinal control was achieved by altering the incidence and camber of the whole surface whilst for directional control the trailing edge flaps were moved differentially.

### Design data

|  | Swept Wing | Straight Wing |
| --- | --- | --- |
| Span | 51.5 ft | 47 ft |
| Length | 67 ft | 63 ft |
| Height | 12 ft | 12 ft |
| Basic operational weight | 23,454 lb | 20,786 lb |
| Maximum speed at sea level | 583 kts | 562 kts |
| Climb to 45,000 ft | 8.6 min | 9.92 min |
| Range with drop tank | 1,320 miles (2 x 300 gal tanks) | 1,445 miles (2 x 270 gal tanks) |
| Service ceiling | 48,000 ft | 49,300 ft |

---

*DRAWINGS (page 191)*

*51100 Sheet 1. Swept wing. General arrangement with rocket booster.*
*51100 Sheet 4. Straight wing. General arrangement.*

---

Other tenders to Specification F.44/46 were the D.H.100, a modified EEC Canberra B.8, the Gloster P.228, the Gloster Meteor T.7 converted to NF.11 (which was selected for production) and the Hawker P.1056.

## TYPE 522

Supermarine Specification 514, Type 522, was a proposed conversion of the N.9/47 single-seat interceptor to Naval Staff Requirement NR/A.19 for a single-seat twin-engined strike aircraft.

The conversion brochure on Type 522 was supplied in accordance with MoS letters dated 7 July and 4 October 1948. The document showed that a certain amount of space was available in the underside of the fuselage between the power plants and the removal of the gun armament had made available a little more, allowing weapons to be partially housed into this recess and enclosed by bomb doors which, when closed, would form a shallow blister fairing on the underside of the fuselage.

These were the main alterations before the aircraft could be converted from an interceptor to a strike aircraft. The stores to be carried included the following; one 2,000lb AP or two 1,000lb MC bombs and lesser combinations up to 2,000lb, two AM Type 6 or four A Mk.8 mines, two 1,050lb *Red Angel* rockets or eight 60lb conventional warheads.

The investigations were not straightforward, however, as some of the established stores required to be carried were undergoing a dimensional metamorphosis, while those of others still in the design stage had not yet been stabilised. Two of these were ASR and 'Window' dispensing apparatus.

In addition to use in the strike role the aircraft was required for reconnaissance duties. In this role the fuel would have taken priority and the Type 522 could be made to carry 600 gallons internally, two 200 gallon drop tanks and two 100 gallon fuel tanks in the bomb cells, giving a total capacity of 1,200 gallons.

---

*DRAWINGS (page 193)*

*52200 Sheet 1. General arrangement of N.9/47 conversion to meet Naval Staff Requirement NR/A19.*
*52200 Sheet 22. Possible alternative installations of 'Blue Sky'.*

---

## TYPE 523

A second planned conversion of N.9/47 formed Supermarine Specification No.516, Type 523 - a swept wing variant of the Type 522. At this point the Scimitar lineage began to emerge.

"This proposed conversion of N.9/47 by the incorporation of sweepback results in a most attractive interceptor fighter of exceptionally high performance with supersonic potentialities", the Supermarine brochure stated. Attention throughout was given to the RAF F.31/48 Specification, the requirements of which were met. The internal fuel capacity was in excess of the specification even when using reheat. The estimated performance with two Rolls-Royce Avons was calculated to be:

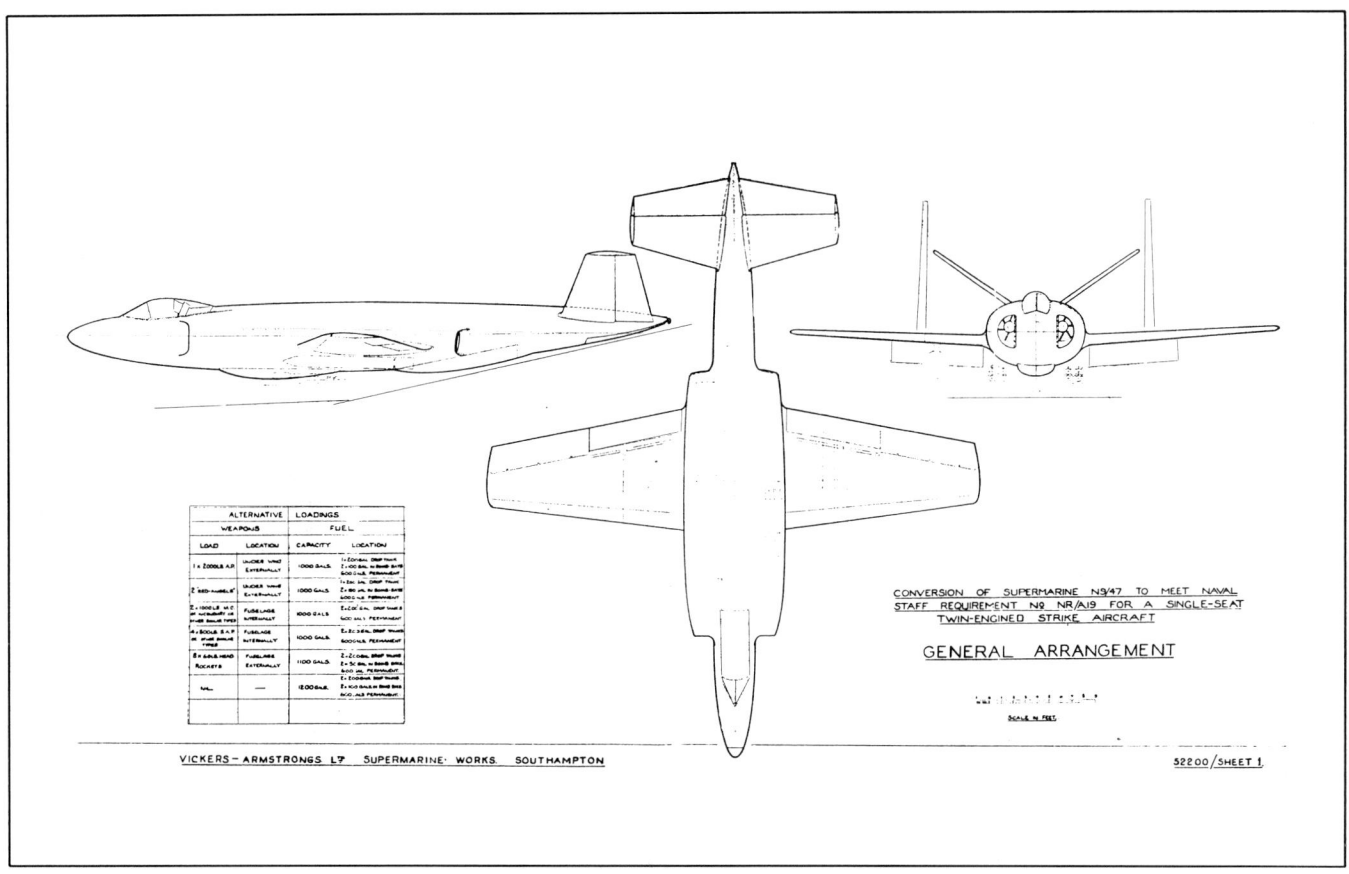

*Type 522. Drawing No.52200 Sheet 1. General arrangement of N.9/47 conversion to meet Naval Staff Requirement NR/A19.*

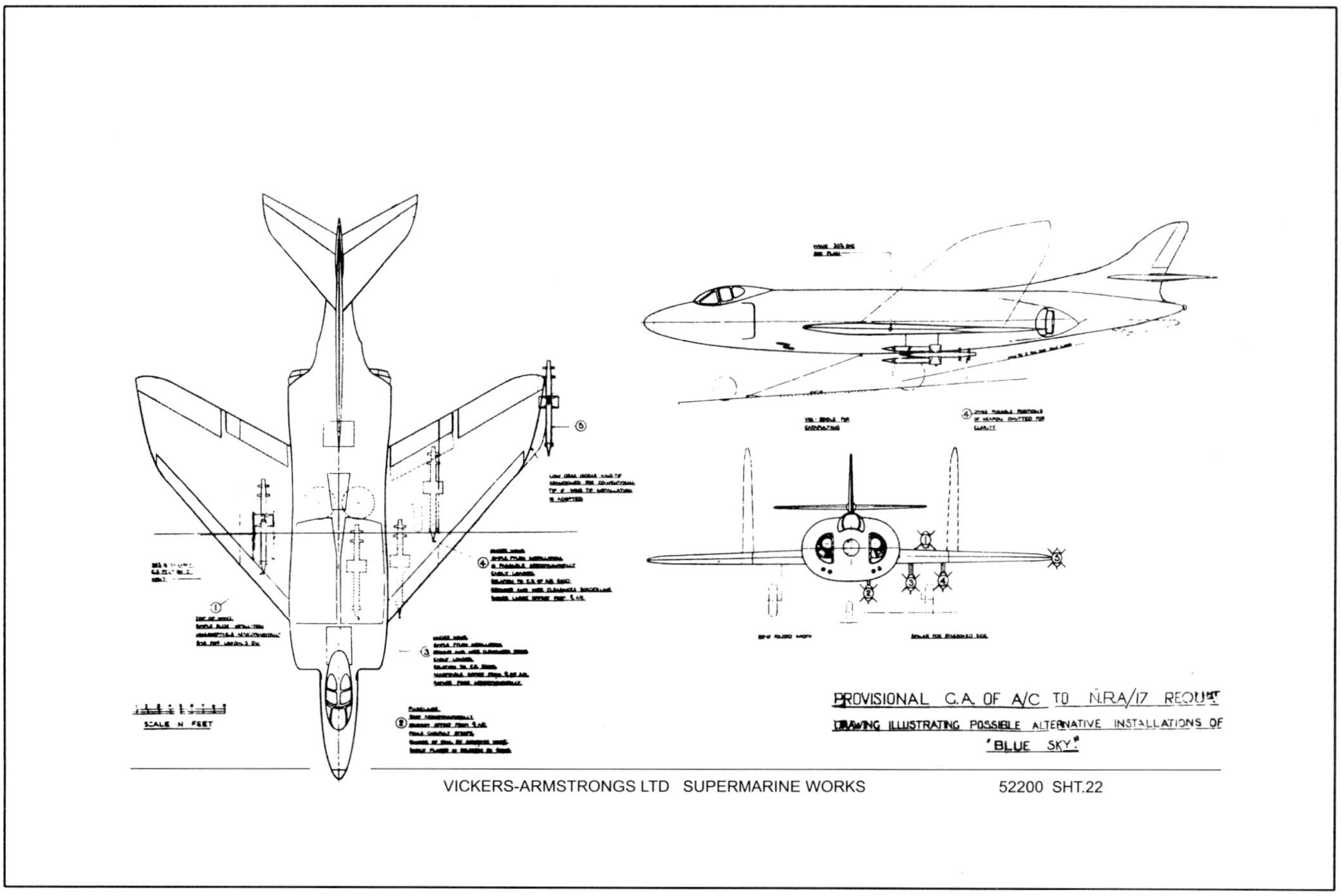

*Type 522. Drawing No.52200 Sheet 22. Possible alternative installations of 'Blue Sky'.*

|  | Without reheat | With reheat |
|---|---|---|
| Take-off weight | 18,000 lb | 19,100 lb |
| Fuel carried | 350 gal | 440 gal |
| Maximum speed | 595 kts | 617 kts |
| Speed at 45,000 ft | 536 kts | 558 kts |

The lifting surfaces were sweptback and of low aspect ratio and were designed to be attached to the existing N.9/47 fuselage which was substantially unaltered. The undercarriage was retained, but could be removed with a resulting improvement in climb and manoeuverability at altitude had the Air Staff decided that the 'Carpet' landing technique could be applied to RAF types. Installation of the Avon engines was identical to N.9/47 but an investigation had been made into the installation of two Armstrong-Siddeley Sapphires. The wing had a sweepback of 45 degrees and conventional ailerons operated by means of a power booster. Leading edge slats were fitted to the outer half of the wing which could be locked from the cockpit. Trailing edge flaps were NACA double slotted types.

A 'V' tail was proposed with surfaces swept back through 45 degrees. Four 20mm Hispano V guns were fitted with 200rpg, but provision was made for six 20/30mm. General dimensions, wing span 37ft, length 52ft 6in, height 11ft 6in.

## TYPE 526

The Type 526 was to have been an interceptor to Air Ministry specification F.3/48, replacing the Type 523, and was considered to be the RAF version of the Type 525. Deletion of folding wings, arrester gear, catapult hooks and other specialised equipment together with a reduced fuel requirement resulted in a reduced wing area. This was done simply by clipping the wing tips.

In 1950 the Royal Navy called for a strike version of N.9/47 (Type 525) with a single seat and two engines, to meet specification NR/A.19. Supermarine decided to submit the revised Type 525 because detail design of the prototype N.9/47 was still 'fairly fluid'. All the offensive loads were to be housed internally and the weight of the strike aircraft was little more than that of the interceptor. No guns were fitted, space allowance only being provided, but eight 60lb-head RPs could be carried externally under the inner wing sections. 530 gallons of fuel allowed a combat envelope of climb to 30,000ft and 330 sea miles at the most economical speed at the same height, followed by 90 miles at full power at sea level. If required, the sea level dash could be substituted by 20 minutes loiter.

For reconnaissance duties a 200 gallon tank plus 215 gallon wing tip drop tanks would increase the total to 1,260 gallons.

One major modification would have been a completely new swept-back tail unit complete with folding piece of the fuselage on which it was mounted. The incidence of the tailplane was adjustable in flight to counter compressibility effects and to facilitate the trimming of the aeroplane at approach speeds.

Technical data: Length 52ft, span 35ft 6in, height 15ft 3in. Sweepback 45 degrees. Normal AUW 18,000lb (20,000lb).

With two Avon engines and provision for reheat the performance would have been: (a) At sea level 595kts (617kts with reheat); At 20,000ft 574kts (591kts with reheat); At 45,000ft 536kts (538kts with reheat); Time to 45,000ft (includes 1.2min for starting, taking-off and accelerating) 6.45min (4.65min with reheat).

## TYPE 537

Following on from the Type 522, and to the same specification, was the projected swept-back version Type 537, raised in response to a request from the MoS dated 10 January 1950.

As with the Type 526, the fluidity of the design led to Supermarine deciding that it was possible to improve very considerably on the earlier proposal, and it had been a relatively simple matter to ensure that the design would be suitable for adaptation to strike duties. *Red Angels*, the 2,000lb AP bomb, and even the mine A No.9 were now housed internally.

The weight of the strike aeroplane was little more than that of the fighter. Modification to the fuselage was confined to the underside with the installation of the engines being unaffected. The overall length was retained within 50ft by folding the nose.

The undercarriage of the fighter aircraft was arranged so that a detail modification would permit the wheels in the retracted position to be drawn apart sufficiently to provide width for a bomb cell in between. Instead of the two separate cells of the N.9/47 proposal, one long cell was obtained from frame 14 to frame 34, and the various weapons could be disposed near the aircraft C.G. where their release would entail minimum change of trim. The alternative 8 x 60lb-head rocket load was carried externally.

Weights: AUW 23,950lb. Performance: 589kts at sea level (clean), 495kts with drop tanks.

> *DRAWINGS (page 194)*
>
> *53700 Sheet 1. General arrangement of N.9/47 swept-back conversion.*
> *53700 Sheet 2. Fuselage layout.*

## TYPE 539

This specification was raised in accordance with a request contained in a letter from RDN.2 dated 2 March 1949 to Supermarine. The swept-back variant was used for the investigation, though the straight-wing N.9/47 could have been used. Standard Naval Staff requirements for Trainer conversions had not been formulated but it was understood that the requirements were:

Cockpits - arrangement of front cockpit (trainee) to be as near identical as possible with that of the single-seat aircraft and the instructor's cockpit should be similar and contain duplicate flying controls.

Ejection seats - required in each cockpit and both cockpits to be pressurised. Only two guns were required with Radar Ranging.

In the arrangement, drawing 53900 sheet 1, a periscope is used to give the instructor the necessary view for gunnery training. The cabin top slides was designed in sections for access to the cockpits.

The conversion of the aircraft into the trainer role entailed the removal of equipment from the aircraft nose and the front cockpit moved slightly forward. Space for the rear cockpit was obtained by removing No.1 fuel tank. No.5 tank was also removed for balance purposes and the internal fuel was thereby reduced to 400 gallons, which with normal drop tank fuel (430 gallons) provided an endurance of well over 2 hours at sea level.

Even with these modifications the dimensions would not have changed and the weight of the aircraft would have been approximately 1,500lb less than that of the fighter, so that no strengthening of structure would have been required.

In the event, no two-seat trainer was produced.

> *DRAWING (page 196)*
>
> *53900 Sheet 1. Trainer fuselage layout.*

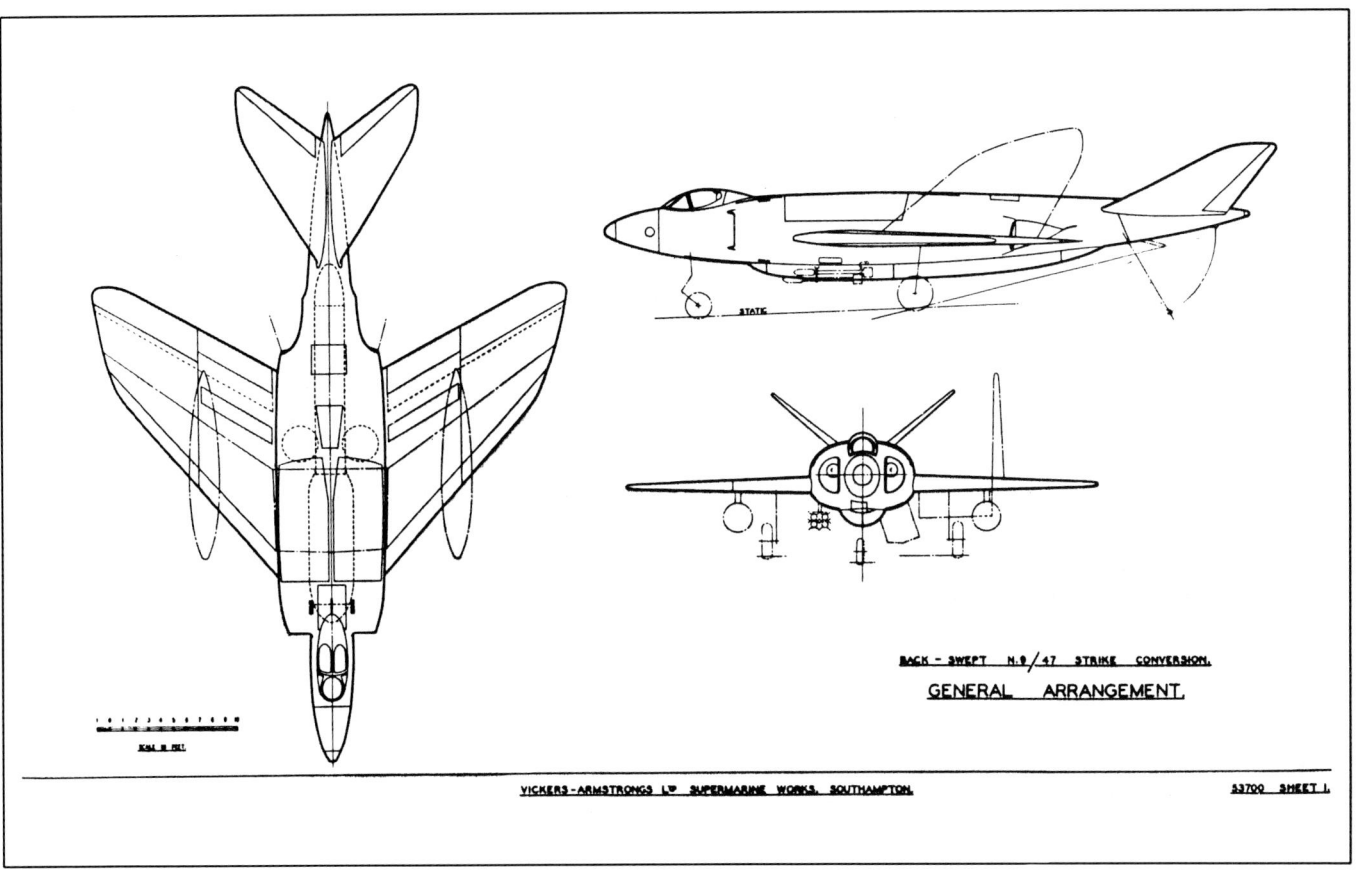

Type 537. Drawing No.53700 Sheet 1. General arrangement of N.9/47 swept-back wing conversion.

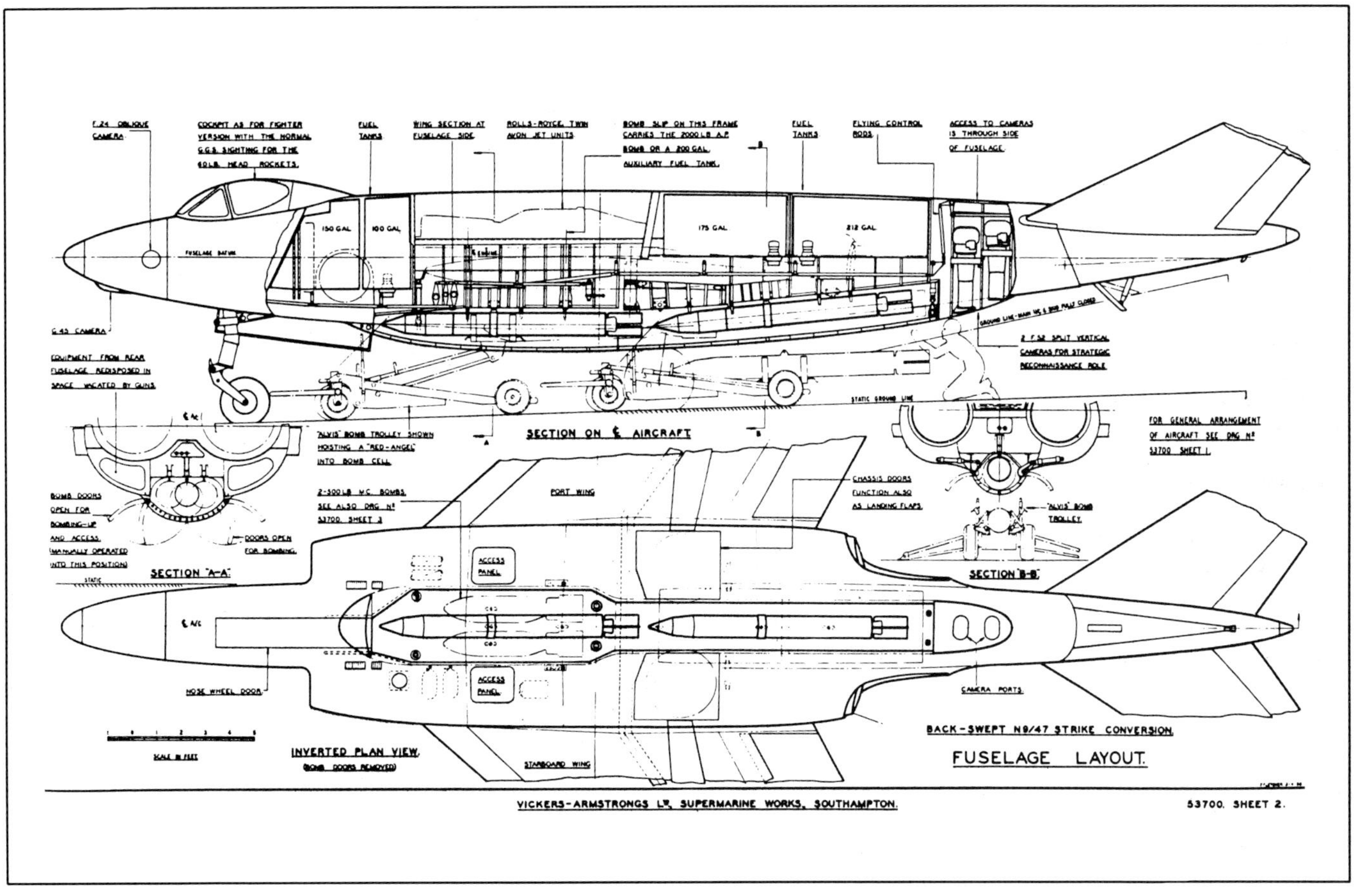

Type 537. Drawing No.53700 Sheet 2. Fuselage layout.

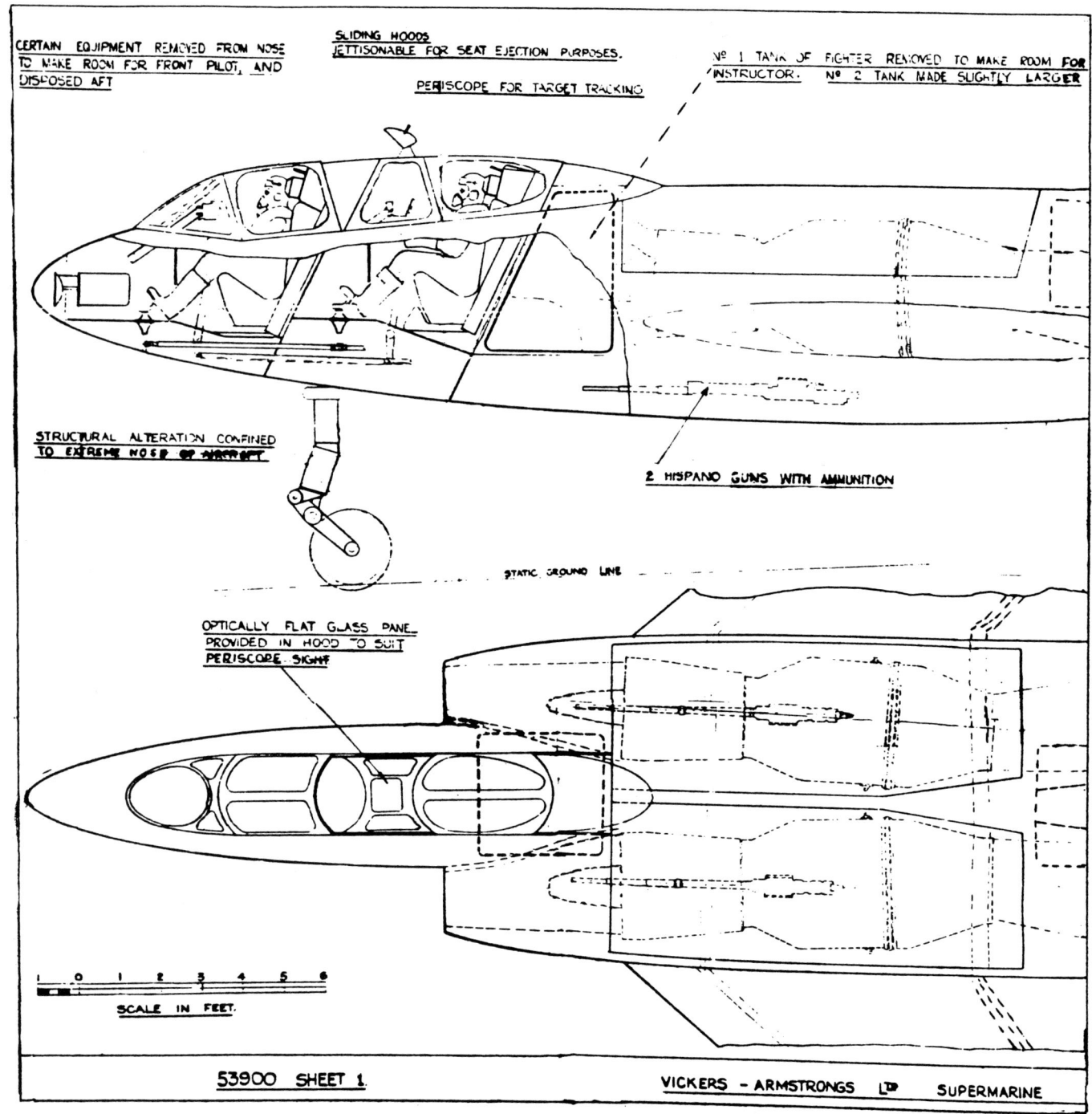

*Type 539. Drawing No.53900 Sheet 1. N.9/47 and variants – trainer fuselage layout.*

## TYPE 543

A final design for an undercarriage-less supersonic fighter with the associated handling equipment was submitted to the Ministry of Supply. This proposed a twin-engine side-by-side installation using Bristol BE.15 engines of 9,000lb st, though developments of the Rolls-Royce Avon and Armstrong-Siddeley Sapphire AS.Sa.50 and the Napier E.143 were also investigated. The specification performance was to reach 45,000ft in 3 minutes and to have an endurance of one hour in addition to 10 minutes combat at that height with a top speed of more than 1,000mph (Mach 1.52). Armament was to be four 30mm Aden or two Aden and 20 recoilless 50mm guns each firing a spin stabilised rocket. Catapult take-off and carpet landing would be utilised. The specification went on to say, "Until the carpet has been tried out, there are no fundamentally new problems to be solved in order to operate the undercarriage-less type of aeroplane," and that, "So far as operating technique is concerned, a modification of existing practice is all that is necessary."

To help their case Supermarine reiterated that an undercarriage represented an addition of approximately 65% to the military load carried and that without it the 'same' aircraft could thus be some 35% smaller and lighter.

Both single- and twin-engined aircraft were both considered, each with the same military load requirements, but only the latter was considered as having the better performance.

The death knell for the type most probably sounded as a result of the following paragraph: "It will be appreciated that to operate aircraft of this type some modifications to existing catapult and arresting equipment would be necessary. Further, an increase in

*An artists impression of the proposed Type 543 undercarriageless fighter.*

length of lifts would also be required. It is probable that existing ships could be refitted to provide the necessary characteristics."

The Royal Navy would certainly not want one of their carriers out of commission for modifications for what was, to them, an as-yet untried system.

The selection of the power units was based on thrust per sq ft of frontal area and it was decided to employ the largest available axial jet with the highest possible degree of reheat.

In the case of the single-engined version, the frontal area of the pilot and his cockpit and the engine intake area were together much greater than the engine frontal area, making it impossible to take full advantage of the slender power plant in the single-engined type. The supersonic requirements necessitated intakes in the nose, and the jet pipes were led aft to the extreme end of the fuselage. In the twin-engine layout the horizontal arrangement was selected because it gave a lower total drag than a fuselage housing the engines vertically when the gross wing area was constant. The maximum lift developed was the same in both cases and so the minimum drag arrangement was chosen. In addition, the efficiency of the intakes was considered to be higher resulting in an increase of approx. 1,000lb st at the maximum speed condition. A fuel metering system would be employed for CofG balancing purposes.

To ensure the lowest possible landing speed, a droop-nose type high lift device extending along the whole of the leading edge was proposed, with double slotted flaps being fitted from the wing fold to the side of the fuselage. A cruciform tail with variable incidence was also incorporated.

With knowledge of supersonics as it was in the late 1940s, Supermarine was keen to avoid over-ambitious steps in the aerodynamic field and to take only reasonable, and what seemed to them to be logical, steps from their existing knowledge, based on both model and full scale research. At that time there was only one supersonic wind tunnel available in the country, this being the 3ft x 3ft Ministry of Supply facility at Farnborough, and only supersonic model tests using a Vickers transonic rocket had so far taken place.

198

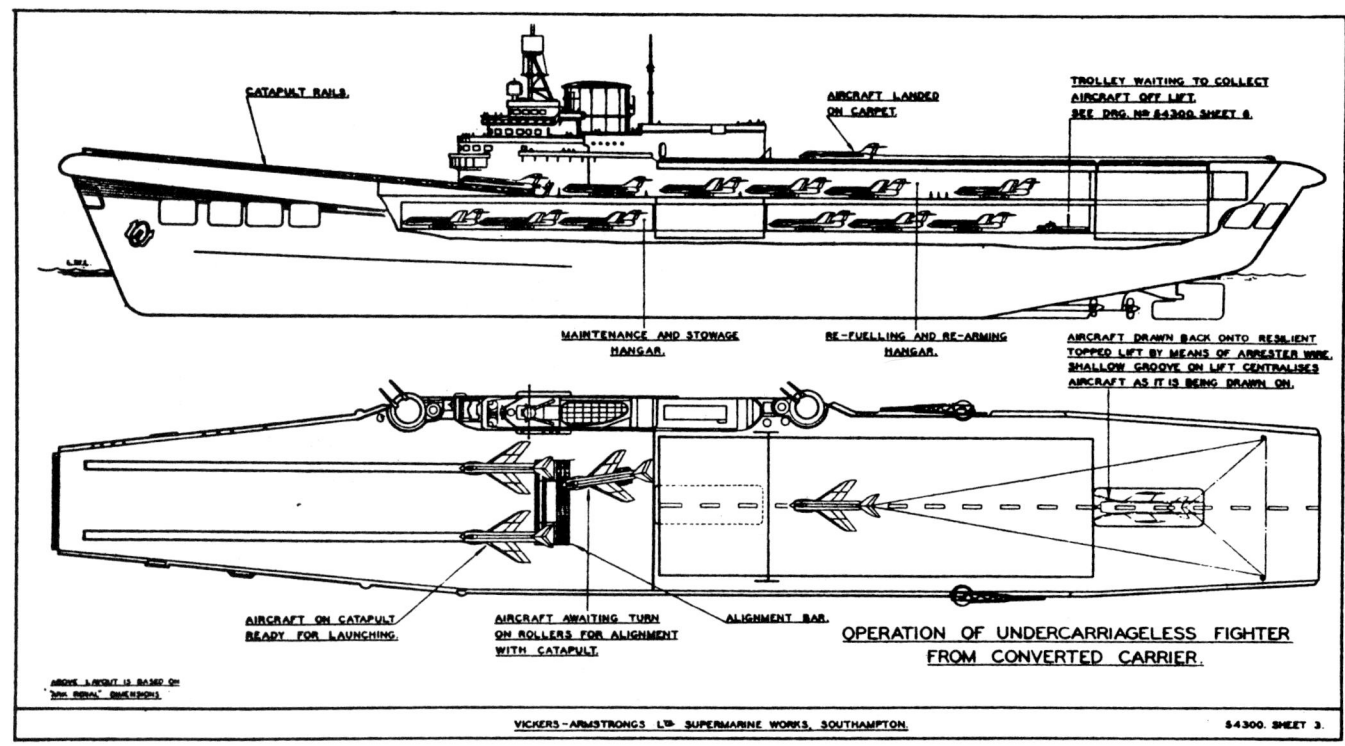

*Type 543. Drawing No.54300 Sheet.3. Operation of undercarriageless fighter from converted carrier.*

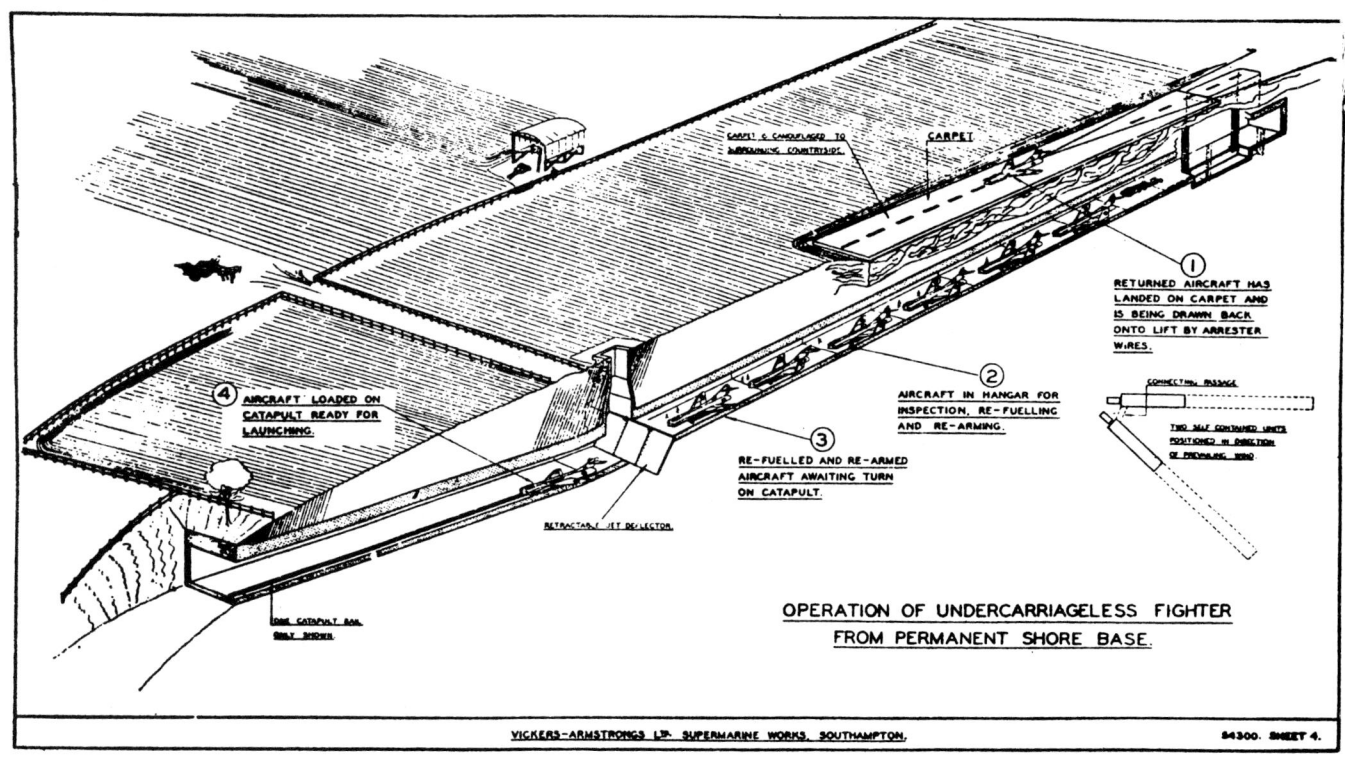

*Type 543. Drawing No.54300 Sheet 4. Operation of undercarriageless fighter from permanent shore base.*

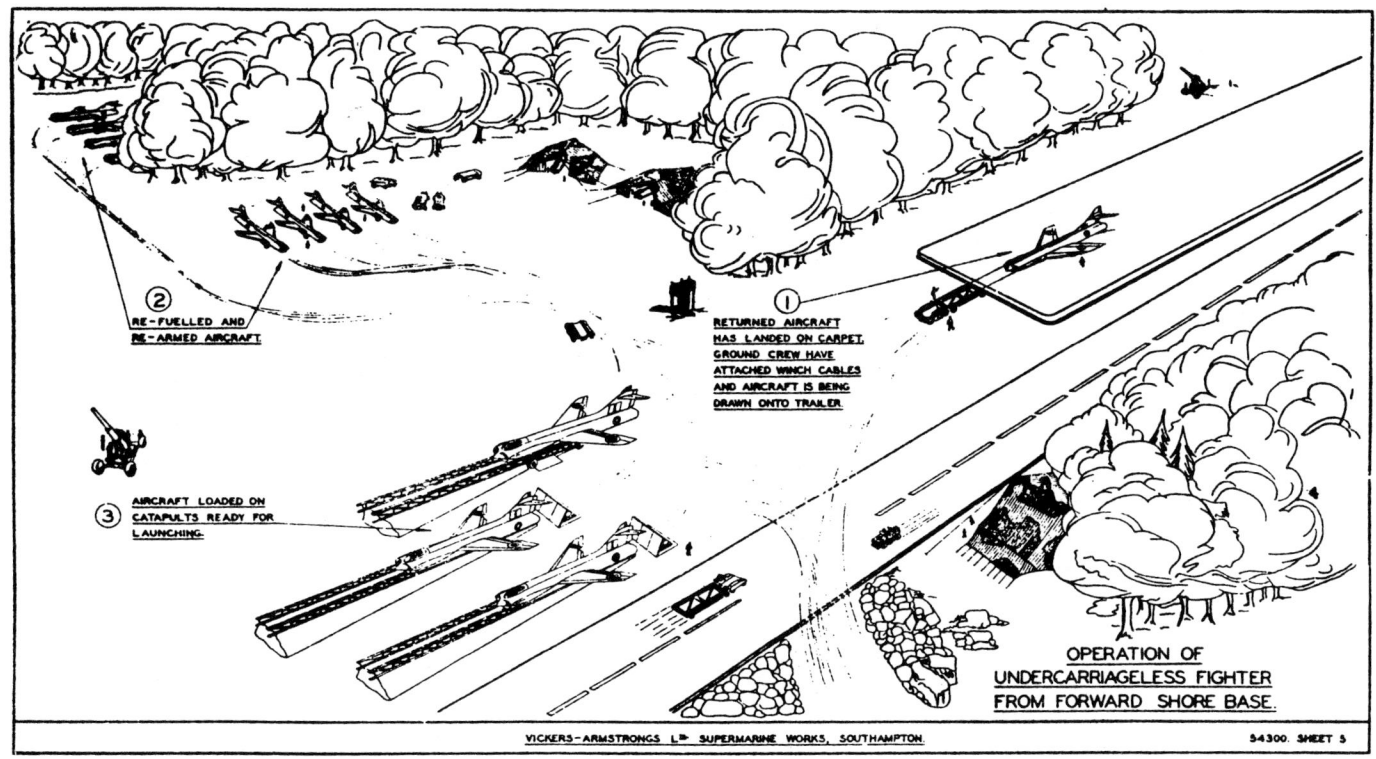

*Type 543. Drawing No.54300 Sheet.5. Operation of undercarriageless fighter from forward shore base.*

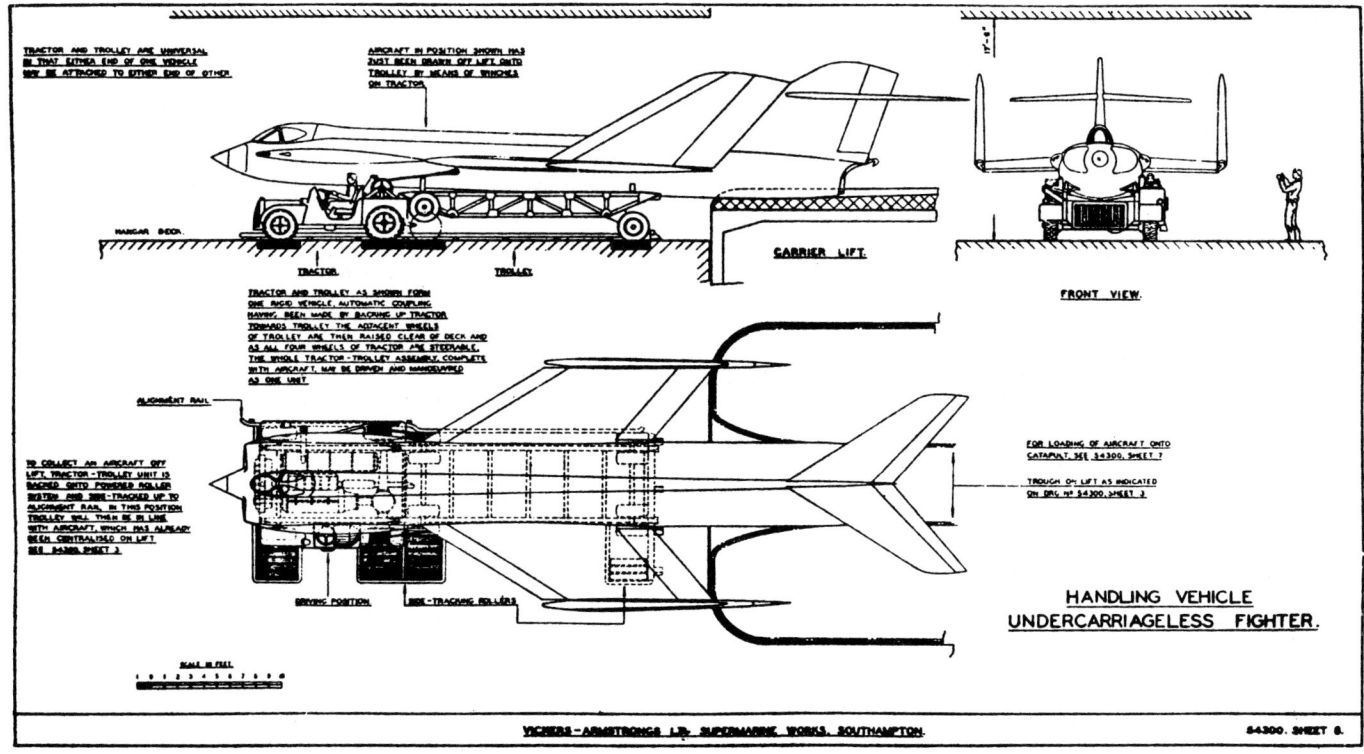

*Type 543. Drawing No.54300 Sheet 6. Modified tractor and carrier lift for handling undercarriageless fighter.*

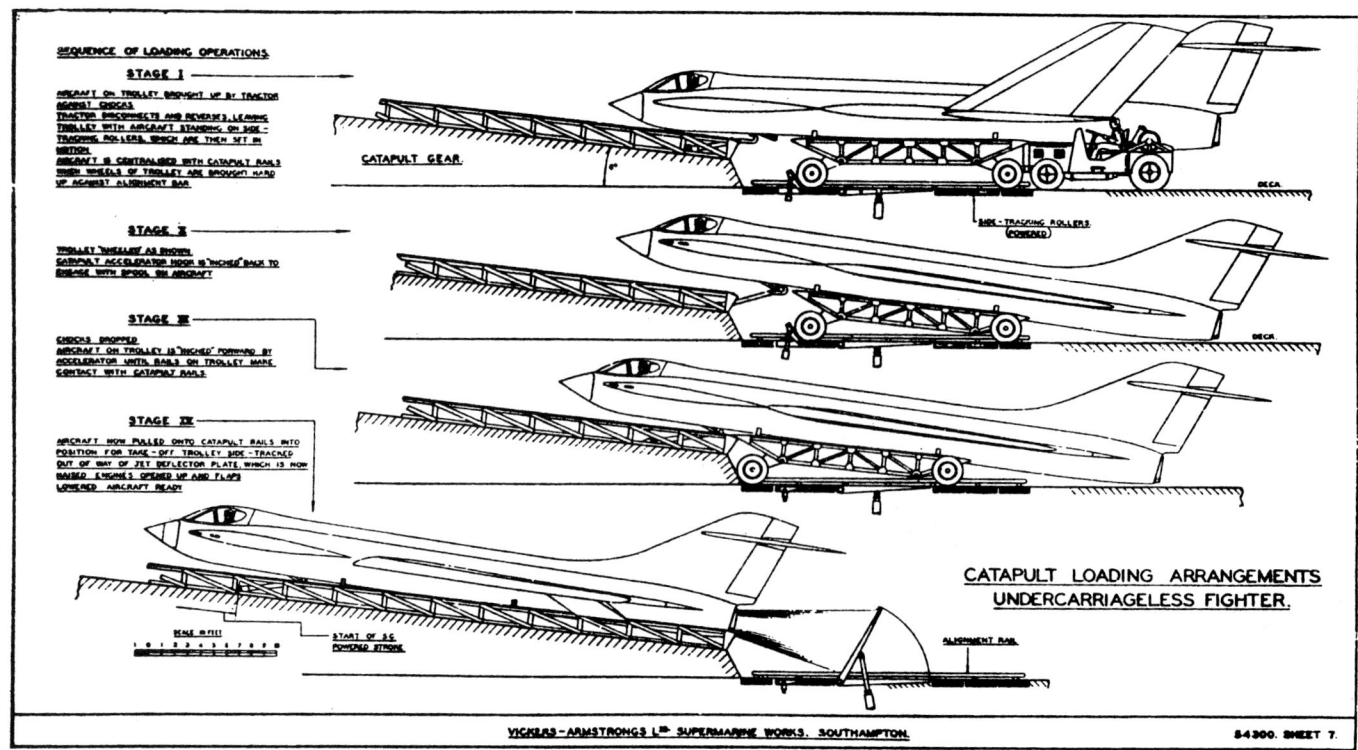

*Drawing No.54300 Sheet 7. Method of loading undercarriageless fighter on to catapult.*

*DRAWINGS (pages 198 to 200)*

*54300 Sheet 3. Operation of undercarriageless fighter from converted carrier.*
*54300 Sheet 4. Operation from permanent shore base.*
*54300 Sheet 5. Operation from forward shore base*
*54300 Sheet 6. Modified tractor and carrier lift.*
*54300 Sheet 7. Method of loading on to catapult.*

**The Handling Problem.**

Handling of the aircraft on the ground proved to be the major problem envisaged. Drawings showed the landed aircraft being drawn off the carpet backwards by the arrester wire into a shallow groove centralising the aircraft. Also shown were the roller system for alignment on the catapult, modified tractor and carrier lifts and the method that could be used for loading onto the catapult.

The concept of an undercarriage-less carrier-borne aircraft proved to require too much extra work to be feasible, and also precluded the converted vessels from operating conventional types. The idea was eventually dropped.

Dimensions: Length 58.5ft; Span spread 32.5ft, folded 20ft; Height 11ft; Sweep back on quarter chord 55 degrees.

Weight: Normal AUW 30,300lb.

Performance: Maximum speed at sea level 766kts (M = 1.16), at 36,000ft 880kts (M = 1.53), both with reheat. Without reheat 685kts and 655kts respectively.

**TYPE 556**

This type was also submitted to Specification N.139 to which de Havilland submitted their navalised DH.110. However on 23 September 1954 one aircraft, XH451, was ordered as a Developed Scimitar to Specification NA/38 from Vickers under contract 6/Air/11268/CB.5(b) to become the two-seat strike version for evaluation only. Two months later, on 26 November, Supermarine compared the navalised DH.110 against their Type 556 as follows (DH.110 in brackets): Weights: Tare 25,857lb (22,629), Basic 27,698lb (24,470). Operating 28,170lb (24,942), Landing 32,374lb (28,338), Take-off 38,993lb (33,938).

The figures showed that the Type 556 would have been heavier than the DH.110 but the aircraft had a number of additional features, including a higher maximum diving speed, installation of reheat and flap blow, side-by-side seating arrangement, a complex fuel tank layout (mostly in fuselage), and higher weights of fuel.

A mock-up was constructed of the forward section of the Type 556's fuselage but work on it was suspended on 27 April 1955 when it was officially cancelled, the pre-production order having gone to the DH.110 in February of that year.

The project was not quite forgotten however because on 9 July 1956 the brochure was dusted off and the design was looked at again, only this time fitted with two Vickers *Red Dean* semi-active homing air-to-air missiles. The weight of these would have been 1,780lb plus 1,750lb of fittings, compared to the 850lb of two *Blue Jay*. Only the quickest of summaries was possible however, as *Red Dean* was itself cancelled in the same month.

Technical details: Engines - two Rolls-Royce RA.24 with reheat in lieu of RA.23.

Dimensions: Length 58.5ft, folded 51ft. Span 37.17ft, folded 20ft. Height 14.9ft, folded 15.2ft. Tailplane: Span 15.83ft, Sweepback 40 deg.

Weights: Normal take-off 36,230lb.

Aircraft weapons: Fighter four guns 33,195lb; Fighter two guns & two *Blue Jay* 35,272lb; Fighter two guns & four *Blue Jay* 35,981lb at Combat weight.

Fighter long range: four guns 38,271lb; two guns & two *Blue Jay* 38,348lb; two guns & four *Blue Jay* 39,057lb. Extra long range: four guns 41,775lb; two guns & two *Blue Jay* 41,852lb.

Performance: Climb at sea level 43,000ft/min (21,100ft/min without reheat), at 40,000ft 7,100ft/min (2,800ft/min without reheat). Service ceiling 52,150ft (45,800ft without reheat). Endurance 1.75 hours at 40,000ft (reserves not included) with 1,215 gallons fuel.

*DRAWING (page 201)*

*55600 Sheet 1. General arrangement of 2-seater all-weather naval fighter.*

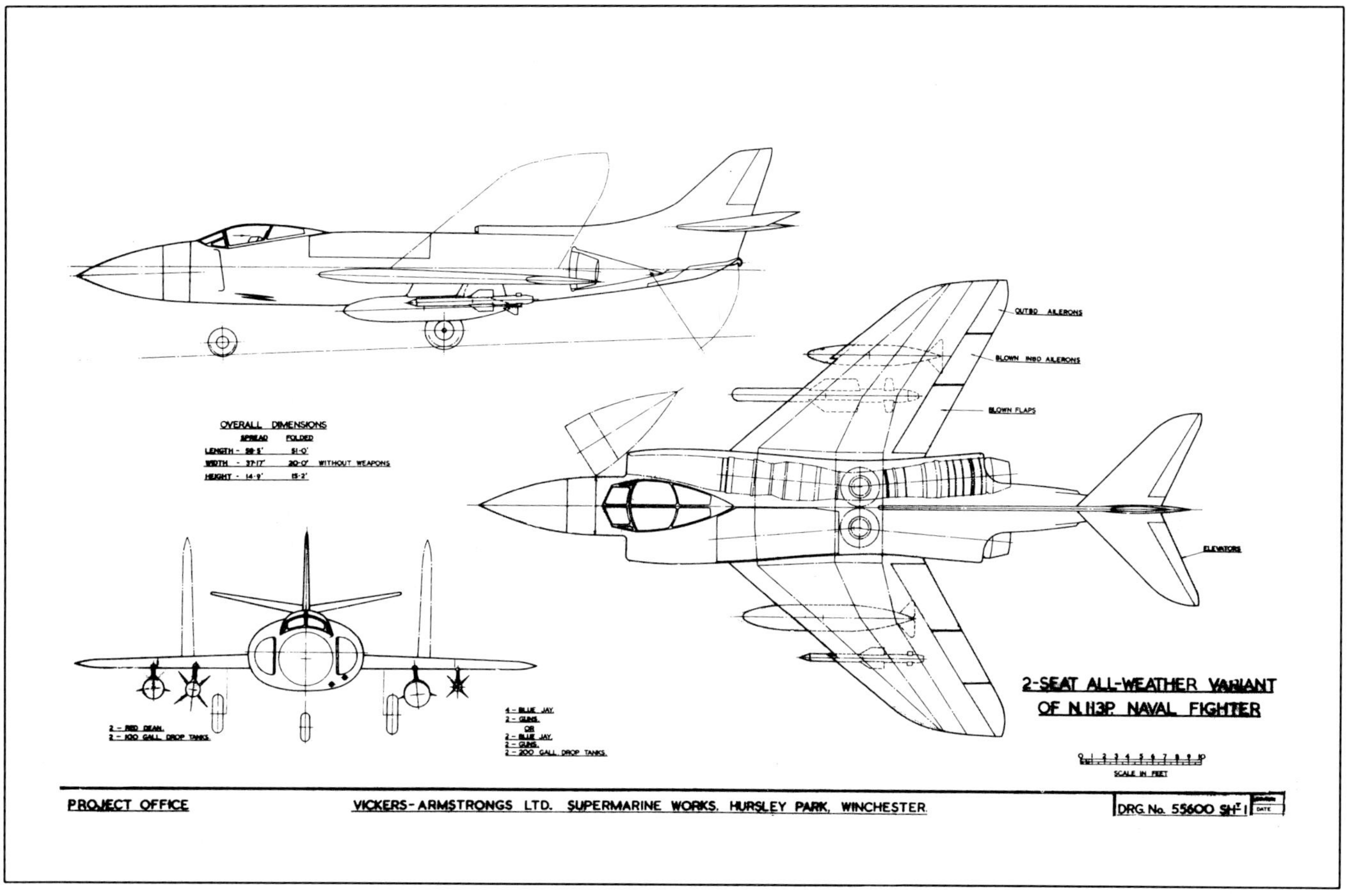

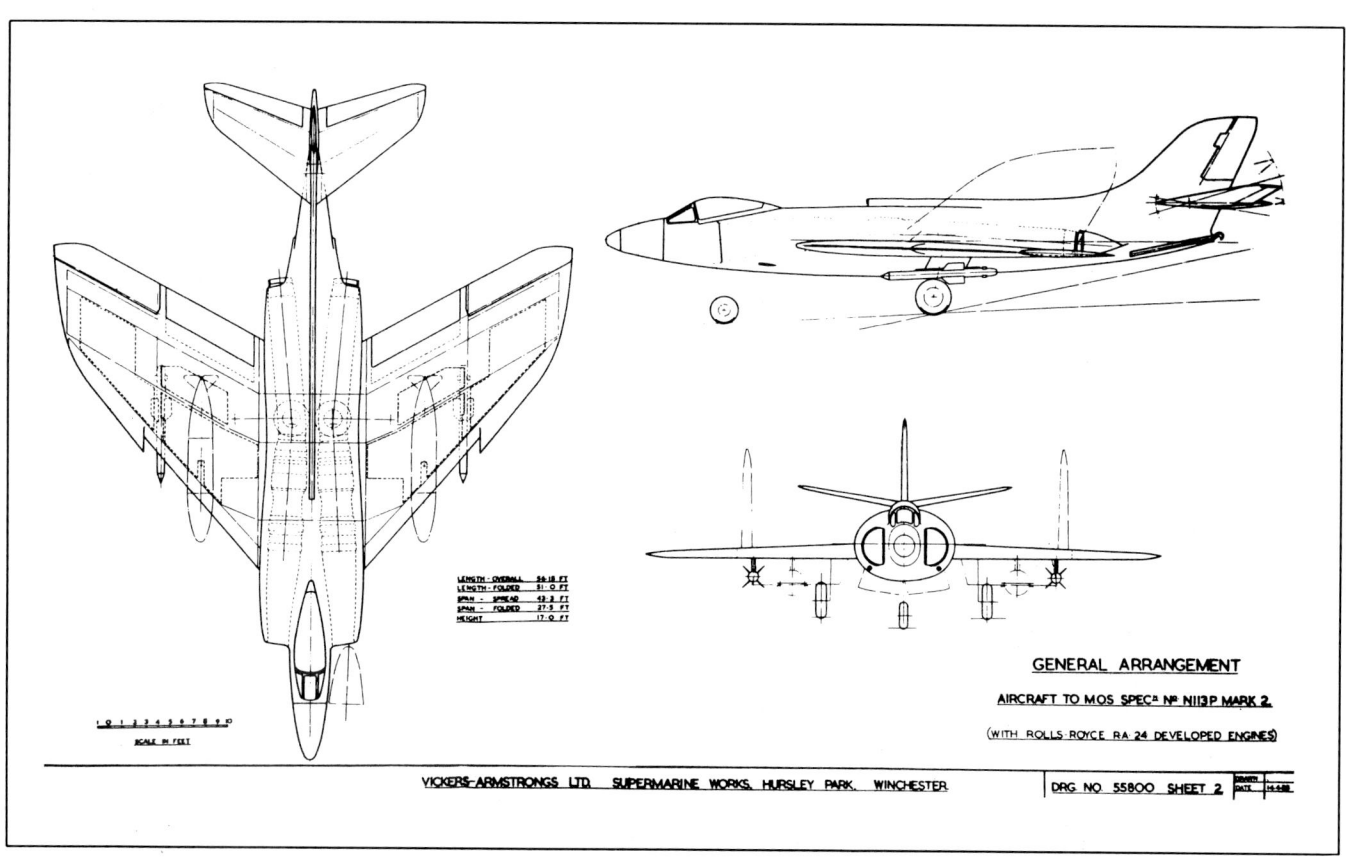

*Drawing No.55600 Sheet 1. General arrangement of 2-seater all-weather naval fighter variant of N.113P.*

*Drawing No.55800 Sheet 2. General arrangement of N.113P Mark 2.*

## TYPE 558

The Type 558 was a proposed Mark 2 version of the N.113P, designed to meet the additional requirements for a high altitude interceptor armed with *Blue Jay* guided weapons.

The conflicting requirements of the high and low altitude duties could not easily be reconciled in one aircraft. The situation was discussed at some length during meetings between DAW, DMARD(RN) and Vickers on 7th and 16th March 1955 and DAW made certain concessions.

The basic difference between the Mark 2 aircraft and the basic Mark 1 was an increase in wing area from 478sq ft to 650sq ft.

It had originally been thought that the loss in performance brought about by the increase in weight of the Mark 2 aircraft would be more than made good at higher altitudes by the addition of reheat and at landing by blown flaps. Both of these devices, however, involved serious weight penalties and it was found extremely difficult, if not impossible, to employ them to meet the manoeuvre and landing requirements specified by DAW without exceeding the limit placed on take-off weight.

Finally Vickers were asked to examine the possibilities of an aircraft with Avon engines without reheat, but having increased wing area, a maximum speed of 660 kt, and a normal armament of Two Aden guns and two *Blue Jay* weapons.

Reheat and blown flaps were accordingly discarded in favour of increased wing area and higher powered engines without reheat, which were of value throughout the height range and consequently more economical from the weight standpoint.

A proposal on these lines powered by Rolls-Royce R.A.24 engines, with increased mass flow and sea level static thrust without reheat raised to 13,400lb st, was prepared and discussed with DAW and DMARD(RN) at a meeting on 15 April 1955.

In deciding on the form of the larger wing, considerable importance was attached to the flight experience already obtained with the Type 525 aircraft (the wing of which was essentially the same as that of the N.113D Mark 1). It was decided for this reason to retain all the geometrical characteristics of the Mark 1 wing by merely stepping up the scale.

Advantage was taken of DAW's relaxation on folded width of aircraft to move the fold line further outboard and the folding part of the new wing was substantially the same size as that of the Mark 1 wing. No weight was therefore lost on the fold and all stores were mounted on the fixed centre section.

Normal armament was assumed to be two Aden guns with 160 rpg plus two *Blue Jay* and Radar Ranging Mark 3. Facilities to be provided for a change-over to the alternative four Aden gun armament were also detailed.

In accordance with the recent ruling of DAW, the two guns of the normal armament would be carried symmetrically one port and one starboard and the *Blue Jay* black boxes transferred from their original crated position in the starboard gun bays to the wing roots, where they could be housed in the empty ammunition tanks of the two absent guns. The ammunition tanks would be specially adapted with a removable wall for this purpose.

The possibility of a third alternative four *Blue Jay* arrangement was discussed.

Dimensions: Length 56.15ft, folded 51ft; Span 43.33ft, folded 27.5ft; Height 17ft folded and spread. Sweepback 45 deg; Tailplane: Span 18.4ft. Sweepback 34 deg; Dihedral 10 deg.

Weights: Normal AUW 37,200lb.

Performance: Initial rate of climb at sea level 22,750ft/min, at 45,000ft 2,890ft/min; Max. level speed at sea level 635 knots, at 45,000ft 548 knots. Patrol endurance 1.5 hours (not including reserves). Service ceiling 49,450ft.

---

*DRAWING (page 201)*

55800 Sheet 2. General arrangement of N.113P Mk.2.

---

## TYPE 560

Early in 1957 the Swiss Government began looking for a fighter to supersede the ageing Vampires and Venoms of their Air Force as a temporary respite before the planned quantity-production of their own jet fighter, the FFA P-1604, was due to begin in late 1958. A copy of the brochure detailing the Type 560, a de-navalised version of the Scimitar, was duly forwarded to them in February 1957.

In the event, however, the Swiss did not build any production P-1604s but instead opted for licence-built French Mirages.

Three-view drawings are not shown as the aircraft would have appeared exactly like the Type 544 Scimitar.

## TYPE 561

First thoughts on this type resulted in a proposed improvement of the Type 558 and took the form of a de-navalised, high speed, low level atomic strike development of the N.113 Mark 2 for the RAF.

The aircraft would have had a range of 500 miles and could have cruised at 500ft at Mach 0.95 (625 knots) carrying an atomic weapon.

The Air Staff showed a lot of interest but were not satisfied with the range, so Supermarine increased the fuel tankage to a total of 500 gallons. This would give the Type 561 a range of 800 miles at a speed of 550 knots, or a reduction to Mach 0.84.

A meeting, held on 26 April 1956, of principal members of Supermarine, discussed delivery dates as this de-navalised aircraft could have been in service by the end of 1958 with negligible modifications. However, due to the fact that Supermarine were moving their experimental design department from Hursley Park to South Marston between June 1956 and the end of 1957, it was thought difficult to put an exact date on completion.

At a further meeting held by Supermarine on 10 May 1956 the work required for de-navalisation was gone into in depth. The mainplane modification meant a new wing box from root rib to tip with blow deleted but with plain flaps, taking an estimated 640 man hours. The fuselage would have been altered from Frame 25 to the stern, including removal of catapult fittings, tail skid, etc requiring another 435 man hours and with flying control modifications and others coming to 94 man hours. Total time required for the conversion, therefore, was given as approximately 1640 man hours.

A brief discussion on 26 June between Supermarine and Henry Gardner of Vickers-Armstrongs (Aircraft) concerned the possibility of installing the Vickers *Red Dean* on the 561. However major alterations would have been required and, with the cancellation of the thin-wing Javelin fitted with *Red Dean,* the missile project was cancelled later that month.

In July the whole question of the best method of delivering tactical atomic bombs was still under review and the Air Staff were not convinced that the low level sortie was the right answer. The navigation problem was very great and they were not convinced either that it could be resolved by *Blue Silk.*

Also in July, a 500-gallon drop tank was designed, resulting in the 561 taking off at 44,500lb with two 500-gallon tanks plus TMB and a 200-gallon tank. This was disliked on principle, because the external fuel exceeded the internal fuel.

An oversight, whilst producing the Type 561 brochure, gave the best range height as 30,000ft; this was true, but the fact that the aircraft was designed to cruise at 45,000ft was omitted. Tactically, 30,000ft was the perfect height for GCI interceptions with a minimum of ground control as condensation trails could normally be relied upon to disclose the position of an aircraft. Finally, on 26 July, during a discussion at Hursley Park, Group Captain Wheeler of the Air Ministry, forcibly expressed his views on the requirements for a single-seat, low-level, high-speed, tactical atom bomber. Wheeler stated that the weapon should be dropped within a radius of 1,200 yards from the centre of the target, a requirement

*An artists impression of the proposed Type 562*

which implied navigation to within a similar limit of accuracy even allowing for the use of LABS.

The Air Staff view seemed to be that the problem of pilot navigation to such close limits in a sortie of some 400 miles radius at low level was so great that it could rule out the concept of a single-seat aircraft for this role, and that a two-seater aircraft carrying side-looking radar with a map-matching system operated by a navigator in the second seat might be the only practical solution.

In a letter from Quill to the Chief Designer, Alan Clifton, on 15 August, he wrote:

"Therefore, if our 561 proposal is to receive continued consideration this fundamental problem must be fully studied and it can be available within the time-scale proposed for the Type 561." Quill went on to outline some observations and recommendations that were put forward for consideration. These included the incorporation of a moving map display which would be tested in a Swift and the results then linked in with the ongoing work with *Blue Silk* development.

On 27 September, Quill met with Air Commodore Kirkpatrick, DOR(A), to discuss the type of atomic strike aircraft to enter service in 1964. The following aircraft characteristics were 'desirable':

(1) Radius of actions. Cruise at low level at M 0.9 600nm. High-Lo-High sortie. 1,000nm.
(2) Maximum speed. Capable of short bursts at sea level of M 1.2 to M 1.3.
(3) Armament. Tactical Atom Bomb, with alternative HE and Rocket capability.
(4) Crew. Pilot and Radar Navigator.
(5) Navigation Equipment. Side looking radar and map matching (this meant moving map with automatic feed from a radar equipment).
(6) Cameras. FR cameras. F.95 - or developments for low level FR (up to 5,000ft).

At the end of the meeting it was made clear that the Air Staff regarded the Type 561 as the only current possible interim solution.

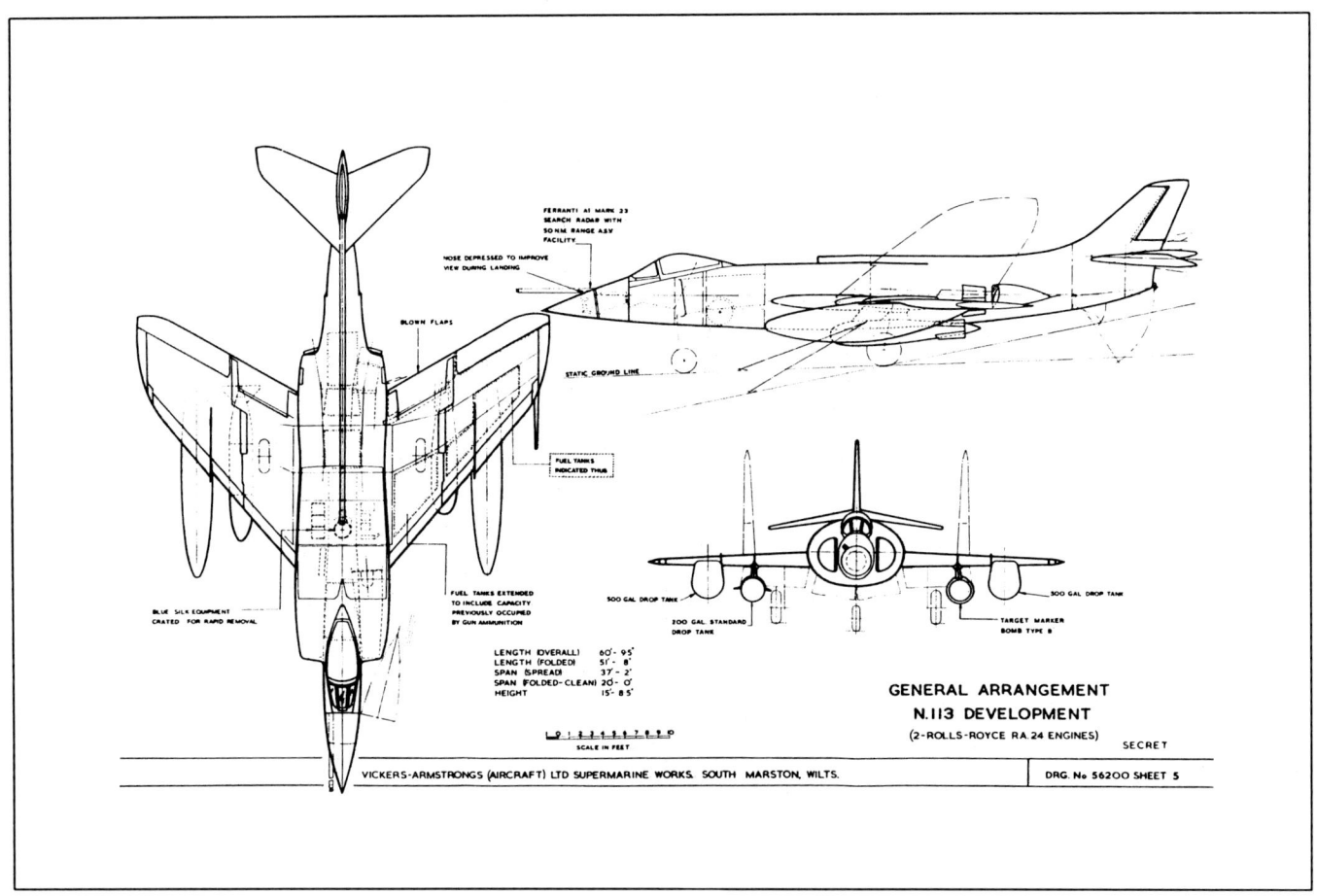

*Drawing No.56200 Sheet 5. General arrangement of Type 562 N.113 development.*

## TYPE 562

The first reference to the Type 562, a direct descendant of the Type 544 fitted with radar and RATOG but without guns, appeared on 19 January 1956 when the initial brochure was circulated to concerned personnel. The document was quite comprehensive, giving details of the powerplant (two Rolls-Royce R.A.24 engines), nose flaps, landing flaps and the different roles it could be used for. These ranging from the basic single-seat fighter fitted with *Blue Jay* missiles, which would have been similar to the Swift installation already tested, though the American *Sparrow II* missile was smaller and a cleaner weapon. With these would be two 500-gallon drop tanks on the outer pylons giving an increase in radius of action of 350nm. It was proposed to fit the *Blue Jays* initially with subsequent conversions to *Sparrows* after 1959.

In the strike role the aircraft would have had one TMB on the port inboard pylon, one 200-gallon standard drop tank on the starboard inboard pylon, and one 150-gallon standard drop tank on each outboard pylon.

For reconnaissance an alternative nose containing the camera installation could be fitted in lieu of the normal nose containing the AI.23 radar installation.

In the ground attack configuration the aircraft could carry four 1,000lb bombs, four 500lb bombs or four RP clusters or a combination of any of these with external fuel. Provision for in-flight refuelling would also be fitted.

RATO gear was not a requirement at this stage but Supermarine had it under constant examination.

The development was an effort to improve the operational efficiency of the N.113, both in radius of action and in navigational and search facilities. For the latter the Ferranti AI Mark 23 radar with a 50nm range ASV was proposed. To increase radius of action two 500-gallon nacelle-type wing mounted drop tanks would have been installed in place of the normal 150-gallon pylon mounted units. Internal tanks would be enlarged to include the volume previously occupied by the guns and ammunition making a total fuel capacity of 2,360 gallons.

Strikes over heavily-defended territory would be carried out at low level at all times. Optimum cruising speed would be normal up to 50 miles from the predicted target, with the run in and out at 550 knots. The landing weight of the Type 562 was less than that of the N.113 and it would need only 17 knots headwind when using the undeveloped Mk.13 arrester gear. At the all-up weight it could be catapulted into a 28 knot wind over the deck by using 18 standard rockets. As an alternative to rocket assisted take-off at all-up weight, flight refuelling could take place immediately after take-off.

On 15 March 1956 a meeting was held between Commander Mungo RN and Mr Maliphant representing the Royal Navy and Alan Clifton and his deputy, George Henson, of Supermarine to discuss the types of weapons on offer, including *Blue Vesta*, *Red Hebe*, *Sparrow II* and *III* and *Falcon IA* and *IC*, the *Blue Vesta* at 730lb a pair, and *Sparrow* II 900lb plus *Red Duster* (basically ground-to air) at 2,000lb a pair were considered further. *Blue Vesta* and *Falcon IA* were infra-red, *Sparrow III* was fully active radar, the remainder were semi-active.

Such were the possibilities in the fighter role. In the strike and PR roles it was simpler. First - remove all the guns and ammunition permanently. Then in the strike role install a navigational aid, *Blue Silk* or *Yellow Lemon*. In the PR role, either add PR nose (satisfactory for short sorties), or add PR nose and install navigation equipment.

The RTO (Resident Technical Officer) requested details of the Type 562 in June 1956, this time carrying the Vickers *Red Dean* missile controlled by a computer for an instantaneous collision course. The aeroplane was designed for combat air patrol at 100

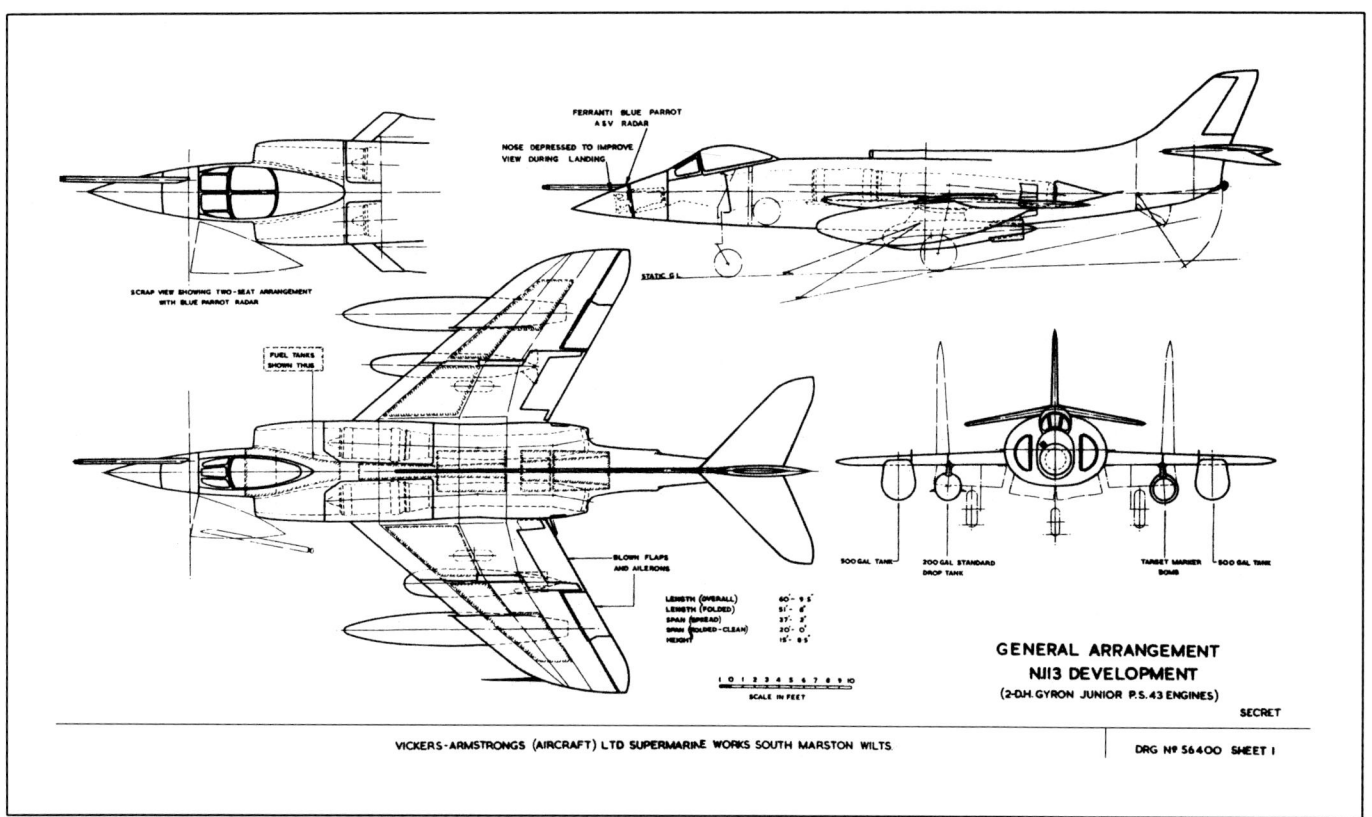

*Drawing No.56400 Sheet 1. General arrangement of Type 564 N.113 development.*

nautical miles from a carrier task force. Maximum early warning range available on a 50,000ft altitude target was 250 miles, achieved by using radar. The dual role was kept in mind and as an interceptor the aeroplane could carry the *Blue Jay* Mark II passive infra-red or the *Sparrow II* fully active radar homer. In the strike role, a nuclear TMB weapon was specified with the AI Mk.23 radar used in the simple ASV mode. Once airborne the pilot would check his track by means of *Blue Silk* equipment and the special charts provided with it. A number of engines were considered, including the Rolls-Royce RA.24/29 non-reheat but with a rocket, the same engine with reheat and no rocket, the Rolls-Royce Conway 31 plus rocket non-reheat, two Armstrong-Siddeley Sapphire 10R with reheat or one DH Gyron Junior PS.78 plus rocket and reheat.

On 18 September 1956 the decision was taken to start work on the mock-up with a scheduled completion time of six weeks.

At another conference on 16 October, the project was further discussed when types of radar, guidance and jamming were brought up. The two radars available were AI Mk.18 requiring an operator and AI Mk.23 for pilot operation.

During 1957, development was at its peak and new designs, schemes and philosophies were looked at and especially with regard to power. The engines considered for the project were:

(1) RR Conway.
(2) RR RA24/29 with and without reheat.
(3) AS Sapphire with reheat.
(4) DH Gyron Junior with reheat.
(5) 8,000lb st. rocket engine.

In their submission to the Air Ministry Supermarine claimed that the Type 562 could be delivered to Service during 1959, if production had proceeded from the 101st production Scimitar (the original order for 100 aircraft having not yet been reduced to 76).

*DRAWING (page 204)*

*56200 Sheet 5. Type 562 general arrangement.*

## TYPE 563

Following on from the Type 560, the Type 563 was to have been a two-seat variant of the Type 562 fitted with Rolls-Royce RA.24 Avon engines, again for the Swiss Air Force. Had the production line continued, this would have been the 141st aircraft to be built.

When the brochure was raised on 17 January 1957 it was described as a de-navalised version of the Type 544 with internal fuel of 1,142 gallons and fitted with twin 500-gallon wing drop tanks. The take-off weight was estimated at 32,854lb as a four-gun fighter. Two 2,000lb pylons, two 200-gallon drop tanks and two 500-gallon drop tanks would have raised the take-off weight to 45,369lb. With the *Blue Silk* doppler navigation equipment, guns and ammunition, the weight was 31,644lb. With the same radar and guns, plus additional external fuel amounting to 1,200 gallons the weight would have risen to 44,122lb.

## TYPE 564

The Type 564 was a revision of the Type 562 with provision being made for the installation of the de Havilland Gyron Junior engine in place of the developed version of the Avon in the Type 562 resulting in a weight increase to 48,764lb. There was also provision for carrying the American *Sparrow Mark II* and *III* air-to-air missiles.

This version would increase still further the radius of action and with a better specific fuel consumption this engine looked very promising. The Gyron Junior DGJ.1 began test-bed running in August 1955 and the first 150 hours were completed by September 1956. The engine had a static thrust of 7,000lb (3,180kg). Shortly after this brochure was submitted the Gyron Junior was first flown in modified Canberra WF909 on 28 May 1957. Changes made to the design included the substitution of Gyron Juniors for the original Avon RA.24 engines, the addition of extra fuel in the space saved and the extension of 'blow' over half the ailerons.

The landing weight would be reduced by over 2,100lb, and the wind over the deck for landing would be 11 knots with the take-off

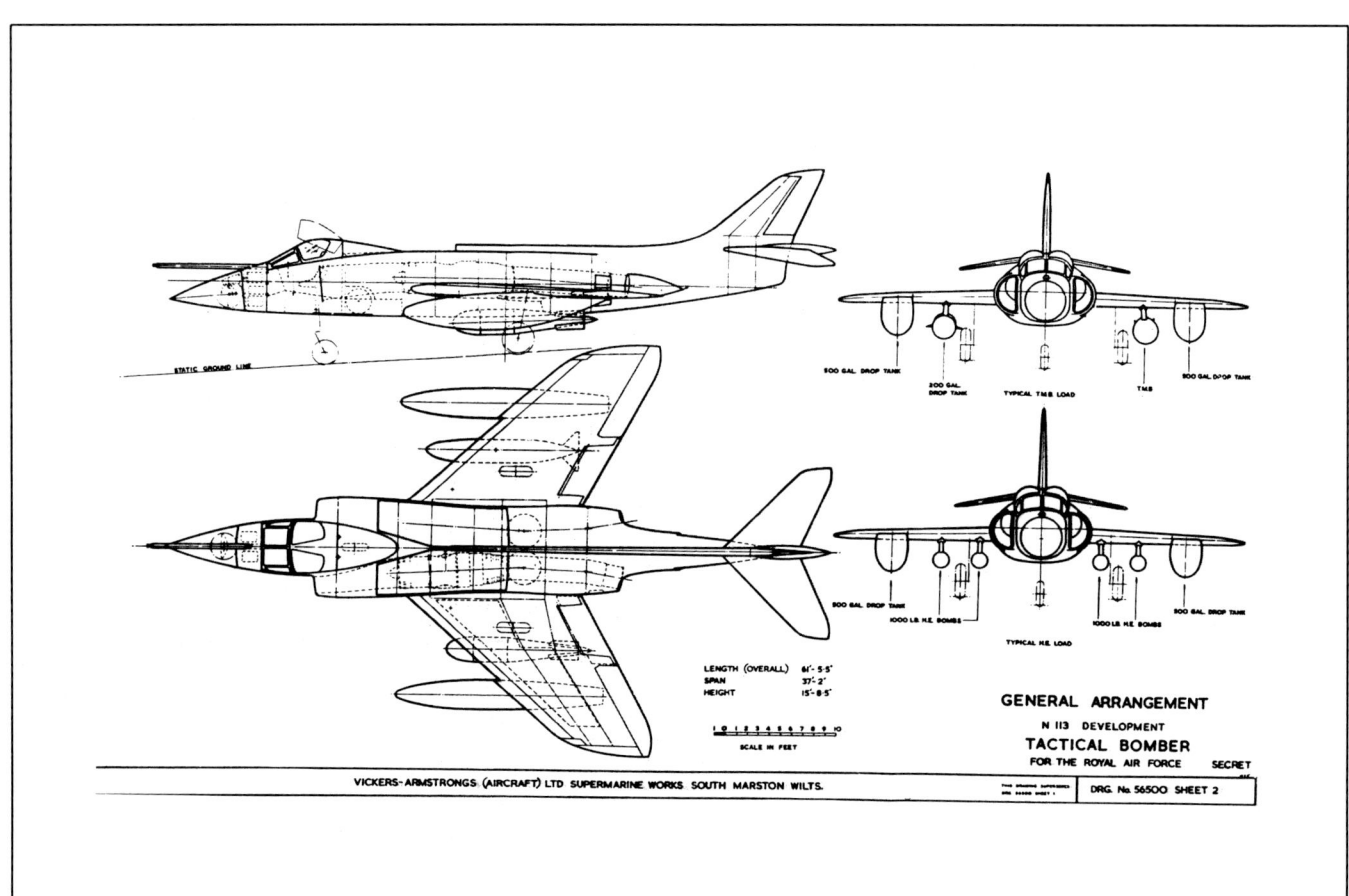

*Drawing No.56500 Sheet 2. General arrangement of Type 565 N.113 development tactical bomber.*

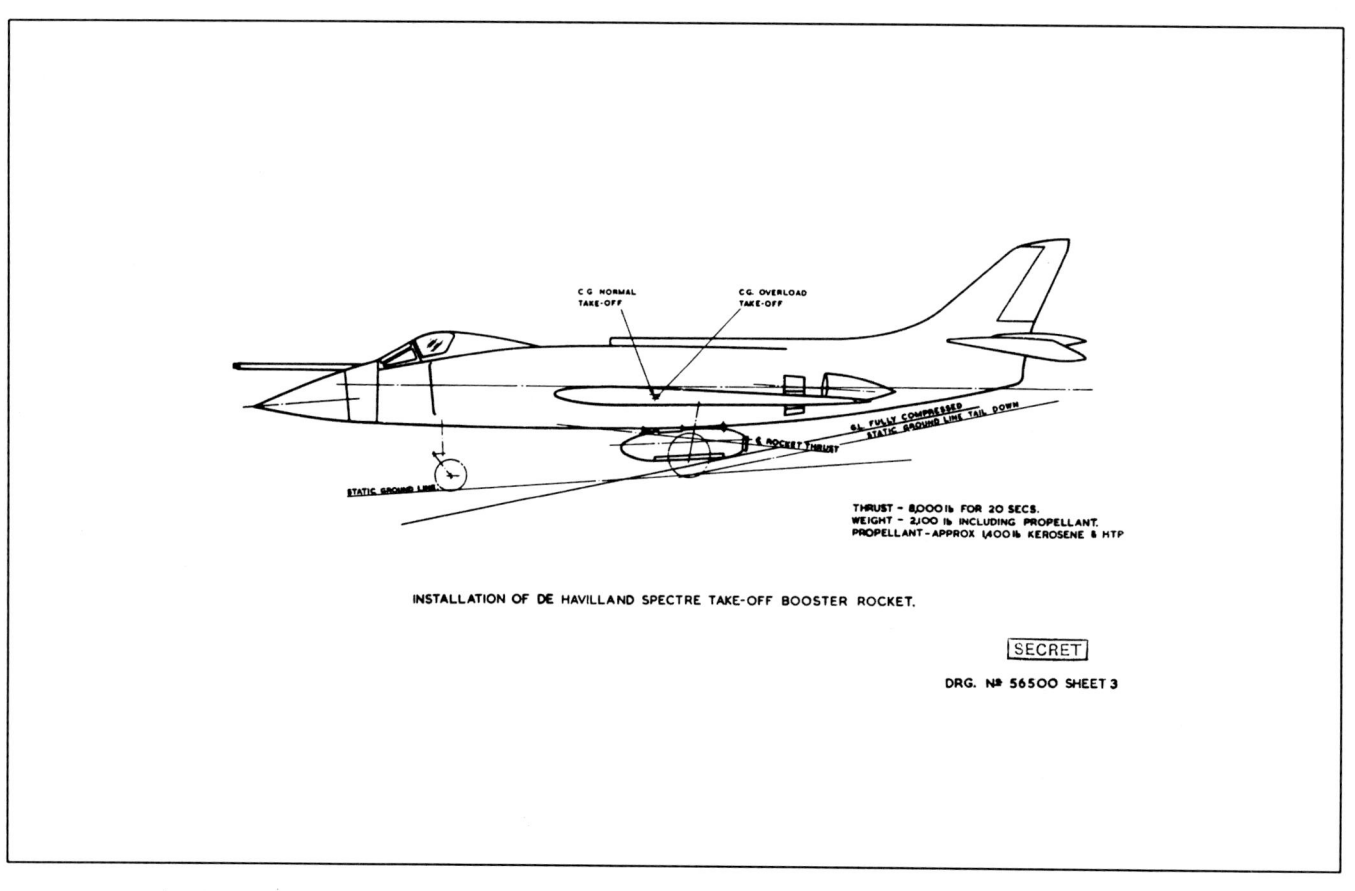

*Drawing No.56500 Sheet 3. Type 565, installation of de Havilland Spectre take-off booster rocket.*

weight being increased by 1,300lb. This would be compensated by extending the 'blow' over half the aileron and the take-off capabilities would remain as described as for the RA.24 version.

The types of sorties envisaged were: High passage, low-level strike with radius of action of 940nm; Low-level strike with radius of action of 630nm; and Ferry or Photo-Reconnaissance with a 2,540nm range.

The slightly later time scale of the Gyron Junior version, envisaged as coming into service in 1961, would have permitted the introduction of *Yellow Lemon* and the single-seat version of *Blue Parrot*, replacing *Blue Silk* and AI Mk.23 respectively.

A study was made of the possibility of linking *Blue Silk* (or *Yellow Lemon*) to the engine throttle to obtain a constant ground speed and of linking AI Mk.23 (or *Blue Parrot*) to the Auto pilot and LAB system. This appeared technically feasible and a realistic assessment of the desirability of doing so could have been made during evaluation on the N.113 of the delivery of the ballistic TMB.

---
*DRAWING (page 205)*

56400 Sheet 1. Type 564 general arrangement.

---

## TYPE 565

Following on from the Type 564, where different engine types were evaluated with the HI/LO sortie profile, the 565 studies brought in the concept of an increase in the number of pylons for stores carriage in a study for the Royal Air Force as a Tactical Bomber.

By utilising integral tanks within the fuselage, in line with recent official recommendations, it was found possible to increase the internal fuel capacity by approximately 200 gallons. A lower fuel consumption also resulted in a change in nozzle guide vanes by Rolls-Royce.

To meet an increased emphasis on the importance of HE stores and rockets, additional pylon stations were proposed, one port and one starboard, inboard and forward of the undercarriages. It thus enabled the Scimitar to carry either 6 x 1,000lb stores with full internal fuel or other combinations.

Flight refuelling was also included to increase the range. To improve the take-off performance, especially in the overloaded case, a DH Spectre take-off rocket pack was proposed to assist (instead of the two-Sprite pack previously assumed). The Spectre liquid rocket motor gave 8,000lb of thrust for 20 seconds.

Take-off weight with full internal fuel and offensive weapon load was 48,570lb. At this weight it was too heavy for the carrier, and the lifts and catapults would have to be re-designed to take them. Until now aircraft up to 45,000lb had only been thought about but not used. At this take-off weight the maximum range in a low passage sortie would be 670nm or up to 950nm in a HI-LO sortie. However, the reinforcing range with one flight refuelling, and allowances for 2 minutes take-off and 20 minutes single-engine loiter at 10,000ft over base, was 3,390nm. The dimensions were; Length (over probe) 62ft 2in (61ft 5.5in on two-seat); Span 37ft 2in; Height 15ft 8.5in.

In a further study the Type 565 was considered as a single-seat aircraft carrying a multitude of drop tank permutations, together with several different types of weapon loads. The only dimensional difference brought about by this concerned the length which was reduced to 57ft 0in.

---
*DRAWINGS (page 206)*

56500 Sheet 2. Type 565 tactical bomber.
56500 Sheet 3. Spectre take-off booster rocket installation.

---

## TYPE 566

This type number introduced an internal modification only and proposed: "To develop and obtain flight experience with a Sperry Integrated Flying Control System fitted to a prototype N.113 aircraft".

Investigations by Supermarine for future aircraft had led, over the previous two years, to the conclusion that an integrated control system would be required for current aircraft types and more advanced strike or fighter aircraft. To this end it was considered that installation and flight testing of the existing Sperry integrated control system would be an excellent first step in such a programme.

The system was originally designed for another aircraft and was at that time on a ground test simulator rig. It was found that a reasonable installation could be effected in a selected prototype N.113 aircraft, using the majority of equipment already existing It was proposed that the first prototype N.113 should be made available for this work [drawing at bottom of page 208]. The Sperry system was considered particularly suitable for the first stage as it did not rely completely on electrical signalling, having provision for automatic reversion to orthodox mechanical signalling in the event of malfunctioning or failures in the electrical signalling system. This approach had also the advantage that it would lead to a production form available to match the time scale of proposed N.113 developments.

In order to obtain maximum value from this work, flight testing was recommended to commence within approximately 12 months of the specification being submitted.

This however came to nothing on this aircraft though it was later developed more fully for the Type 571 which would eventually develop into the TSR-2.

## TYPE 567

Another progression of the N.113 line resulted in a pproposed single-seat or two-seat strike fighter for the Royal Navy fitted with Flight Refuelling and known as the Type 567. The type's design progressed through 17 September 1957 for a single or twin-seat tactical bomber for the Royal Navy. On 1 October wing tip tanks were proposed to increase the range, whilst a later proposed solution saw the bag tanks being changed for integral ones. The bomb load could have been typical of the following:

(a) Typical TMB load at 50,578lb all-up weight. One Target Marker Bomb (TMB) with one 200gall and two 500gall drop tanks.

(b) Typical HE load at 50,964lb all-up weight. Four 1,000lb HE bombs and two 500gall drop tanks

Dimensions would have been: Length overall 61ft (61ft 10.5in 2-seat); Length folded 51ft 8in; Span spread 37ft 2in; Span folded - clean 20ft; Height 15ft 8.25in.

## TYPE 572

This was to have been the Scimitar in the tactical teconnaissance role. At a meeting in the Chief Designer's office on 4 February, 1958, the Scimitar was considered as a Swift replacement for the 2nd Tactical Air Force in Germany; the latter, it was envisaged, being life-expired (at 400 hours) by 1960. The requirements were not clear except that:

(1) The radius of action must be 500nm.
(2) Alterations to the aeroplane must be kept to a minimum. Simple de-navalisation acceptable but no major redesign is possible. The aeroplanes must be delivered off the production line in about two years. Further, TAF were likely to require that:
(3) The sortie be at low level all the way (under 1,000ft)
(4) *Blue Silk* and the Roller Map be fitted.

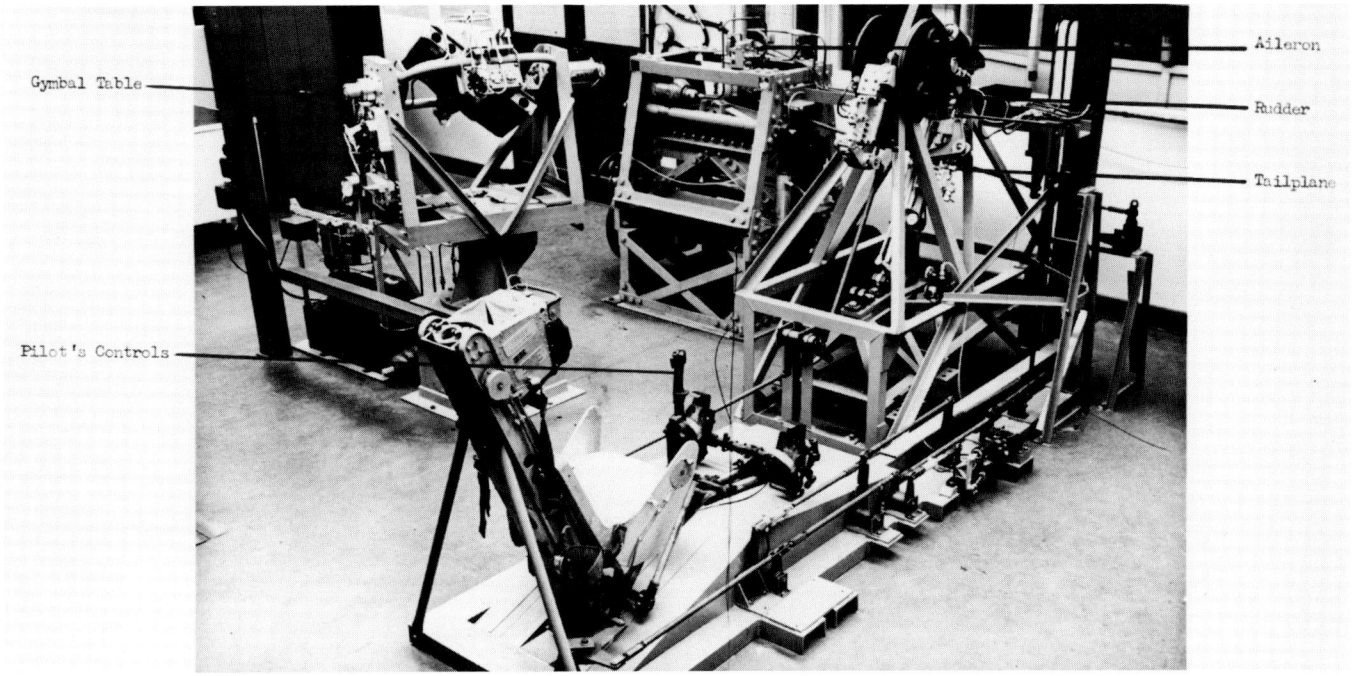

*Integrated control system simulator: mechanical components.*

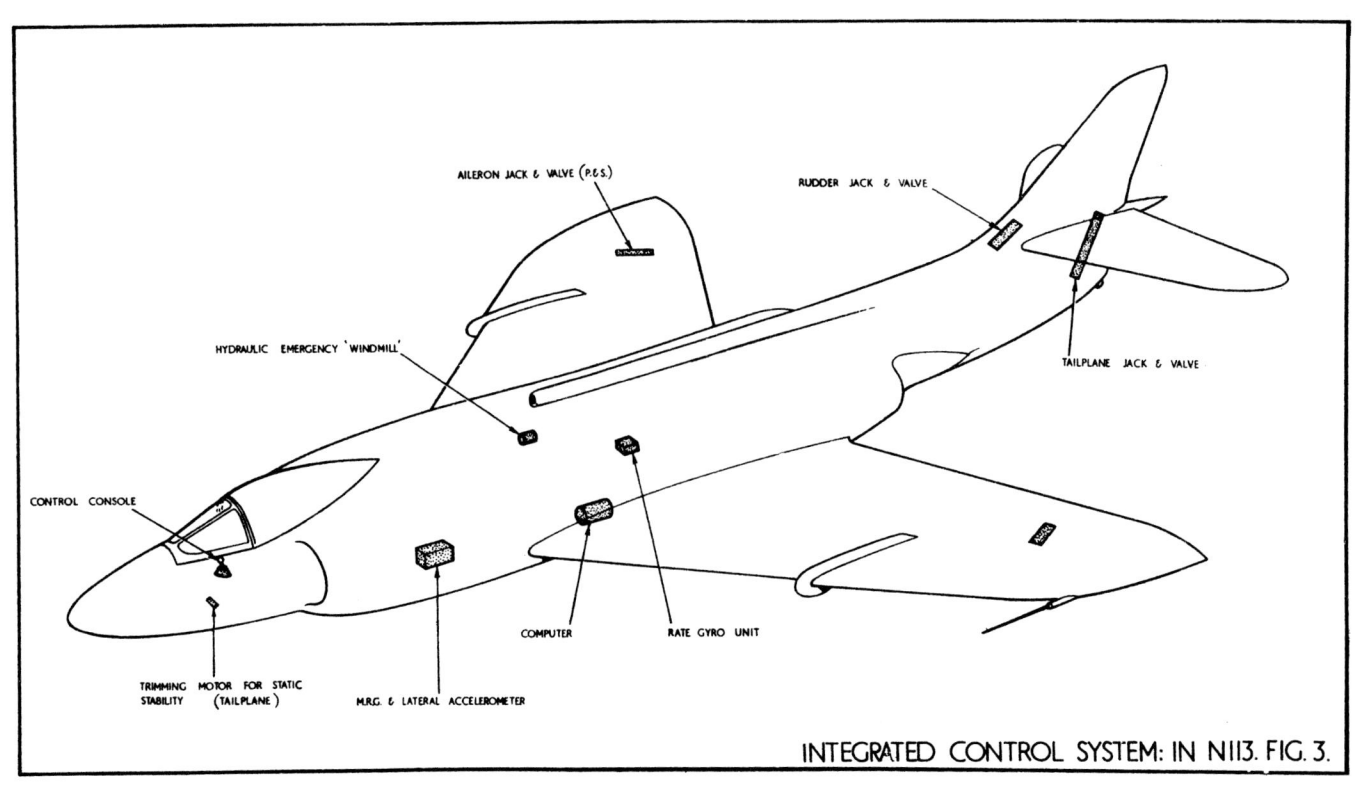

*Proposed integrated control system in N.113 prototype.*

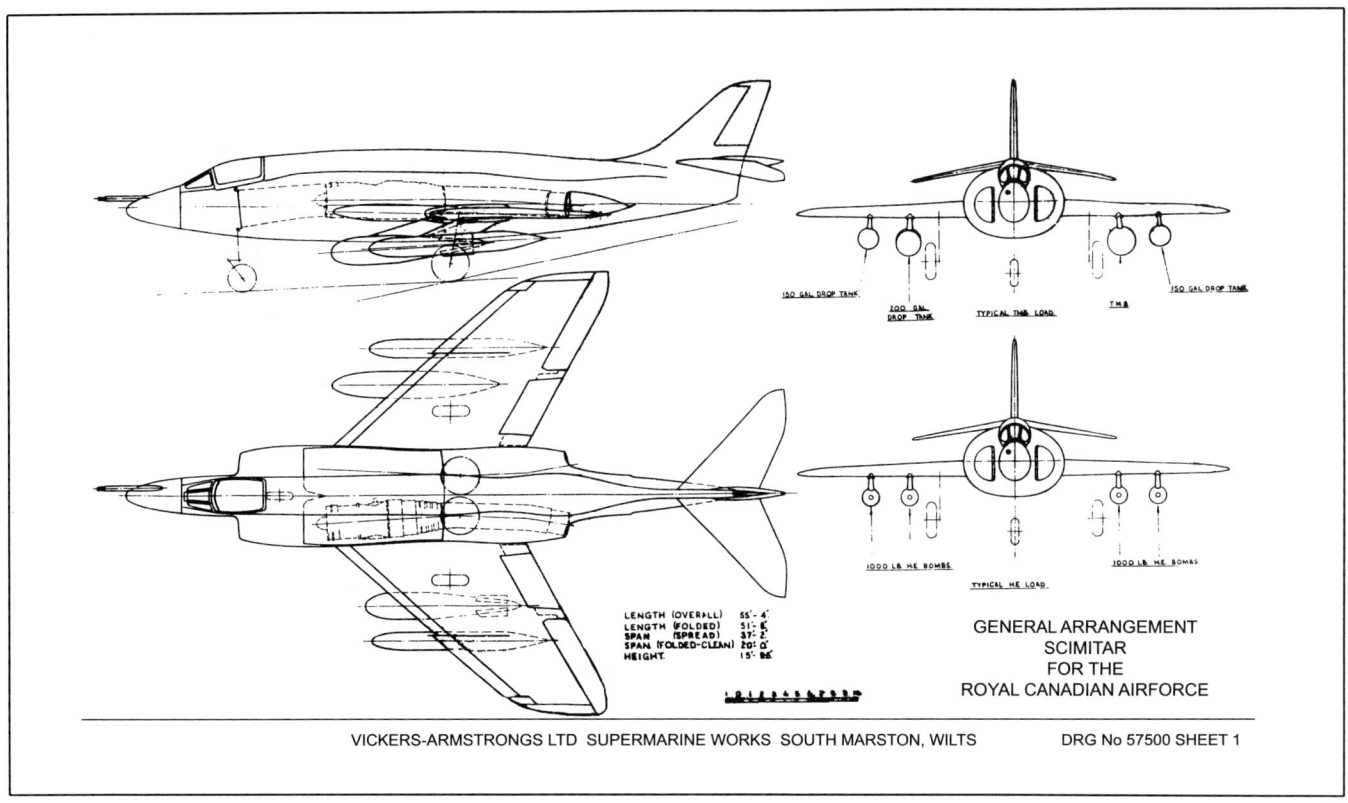

*Drawing No.57500 Sheet 1. General arrangement of a proposed Type 575 Scimitar for the Royal Canadian Air Force.*

(5) The photographic equipment is at least up to Swift standard.
(6) Take-off shall be 2,800 metres to 50ft.
(7) Gun armament may be deleted but provision should be made for alternative load of RPs or Rocket Batteries (reduction in range accepted) together with a suitable sight (suggest Ferranti Fighter Sight).

Much of the work required to cover this application of the Scimitar had already been done in the course of the production of the series of 544 development brochures.

In order to meet the fuel capacity requirements, every available space was considered to house tanks, including moving the forward by 2.3 ft, extending the camera nose by 2 ft and placing fuel in the gun barrel, wing fold jack space and arrester gear bays. The possibility of fitting a fuselage blister tank outside the intakes underneath the wing was also considered but found to be impractical.

By 17 February, however, the Air Ministry had confirmed the decision to have Hunter F.6s for tactical reconnaissance following their issue of Specification FR.164D to Hawker in 1957, the first Hunter F.6 flying in this guise on 7 November 1958.

However the development of the project continued and, by 21 February, Supermarine proposed an aircraft having fuel for 500nm at low level under tropical conditions and in addition carriage of Recce Radar (sideways looking) and terrain-clearance radar.

To cater for these new requirements 815 man weeks design time was estimated to introduce them as a 'paper exercise'.

## TYPE 576

Although a direct development of the Scimitar, the Type 576 was to produce a dramatic alteration to the aircraft's profile and came in two main versions, one of which sported liquid rocket motors in fixed pods at each wing tip. The fuselage was bulky, being enlarged with additional structure aft of the cockpit. Maximum all up weight was 50,964lb. The underwing fuel tanks fed into the main tanks in the fuselage. The Ferranti Airpass I search radar system replaced the Radar Ranging Mk.I and the GGS Mk.8. For navigation over land a Kelvin-Hughes Roller Map monitored by the *Blue Silk* Doppler was incorporated.

A Rolls-Royce RB.146 engine, an RA.24 development, was the proposed powerplant. With an extra stage at the front of the compressor the thrust available was 13,220lb. The wings had super-circulation as standard. Maximum strike radius with one TMB was 520 miles. A two-seat development was submitted to Specification M.148B with *Blue Silk* and Roller Map and *Airpass II* radar. 600 gallons of fuel was stored behind the two-seat cockpit in the bulged portion of the fuselage and two, 1,000lb bombs were stowed internally. The twin de Havilland rocket motors at the wing tips, fed by fuel also stored in fuselage dorsal tanks, would have provided 10,000lb thrust for 1.75 minutes and they were capable of being throttled in order to prolong a longer duration.

A typical attack profile would be location of the enemy target at 45,000ft at Mach 0.95. The rocket engine would then be ignited accelerating the aircraft to Mach 1.4 and climbing to 55,000ft. A target flying at Mach 2 at 65,000ft would involve a weapon with 15,000ft of jump-up capability. The de Havilland *Firestreak* and *Red Top* both had that capability. In bad weather the attack would be made in a similar manner but instead of guided a rocket battery would be employed. The American *Sparrow* semi-homer was considered to be an effective weapon and the company was prepared to license produce the missile for the Mark.III version.

To reduce the drag of the tip mounted rocket motor pods, room could be made for a twin unit in the rear fuselage with fuel supplied from dorsal tanks. Extended wing tips and a larger fin or a ventral strake were proposed. All the proposed modifications could be retro-fitted to service Scimitars and the new aeroplanes were scheduled for Royal Navy service in 1962.

*DRAWINGS (page 210)*

*57600 Sheet 1. Type 576 general arrangement.*
*57600 Sheet 4. General arrangement with wing tip rockets.*

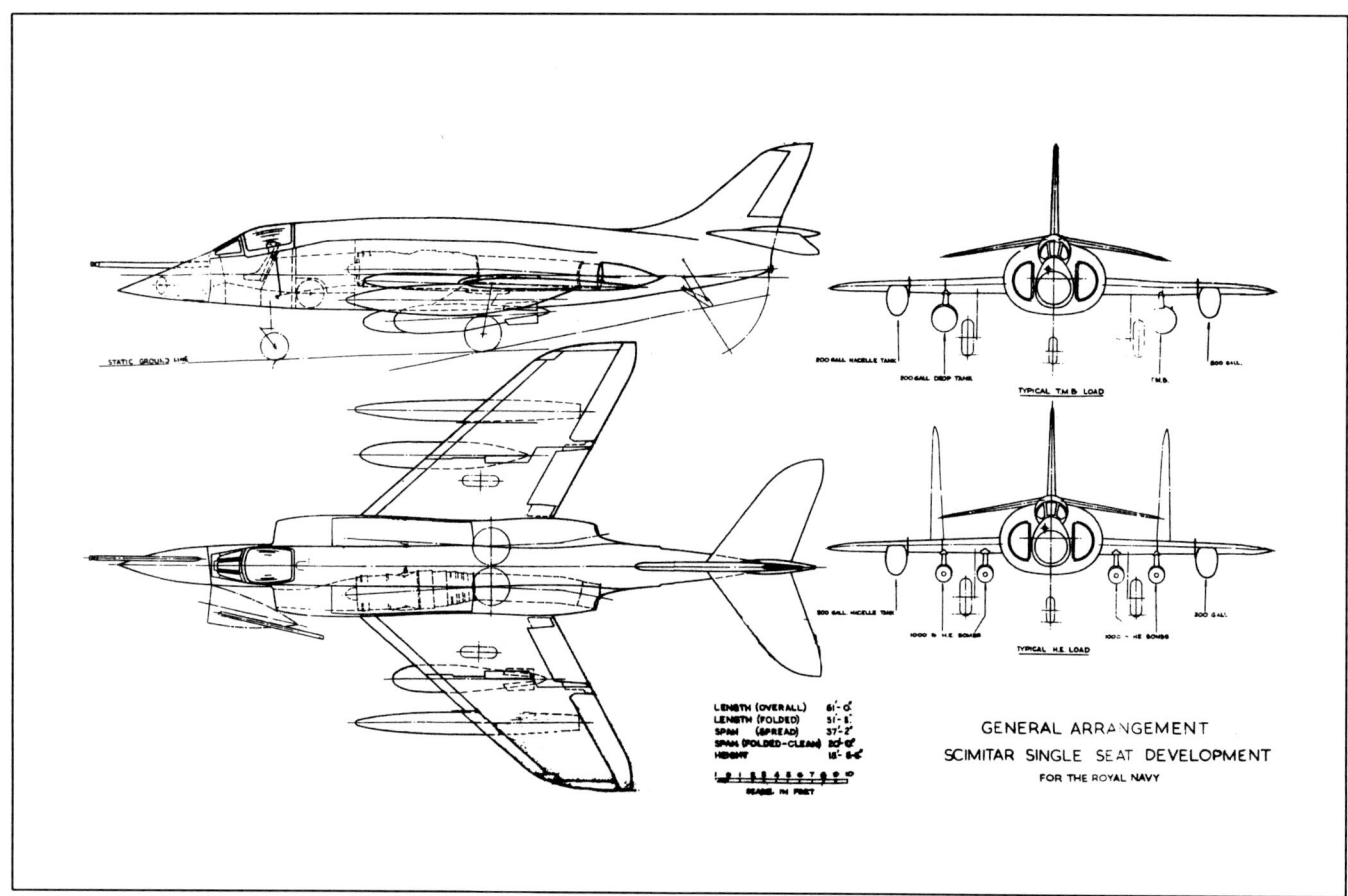

Drawing No.57600 Sheet 1. General arrangement arrangement of the Type 576 single-seat Scimitar development for the Royal Navy.

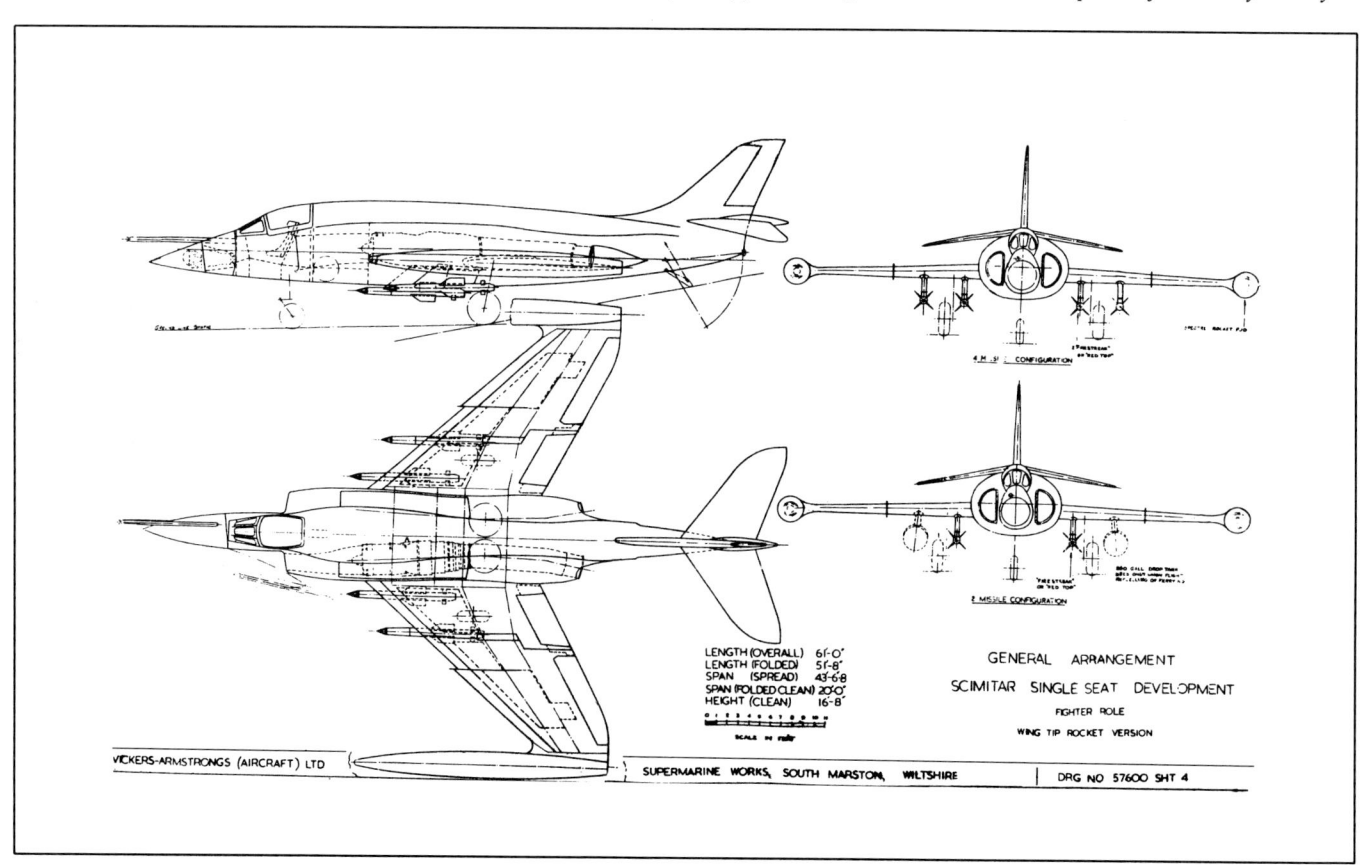

Drawing No.57600 Sheet 4. Type 576 general arrangement with wing tip rockets.

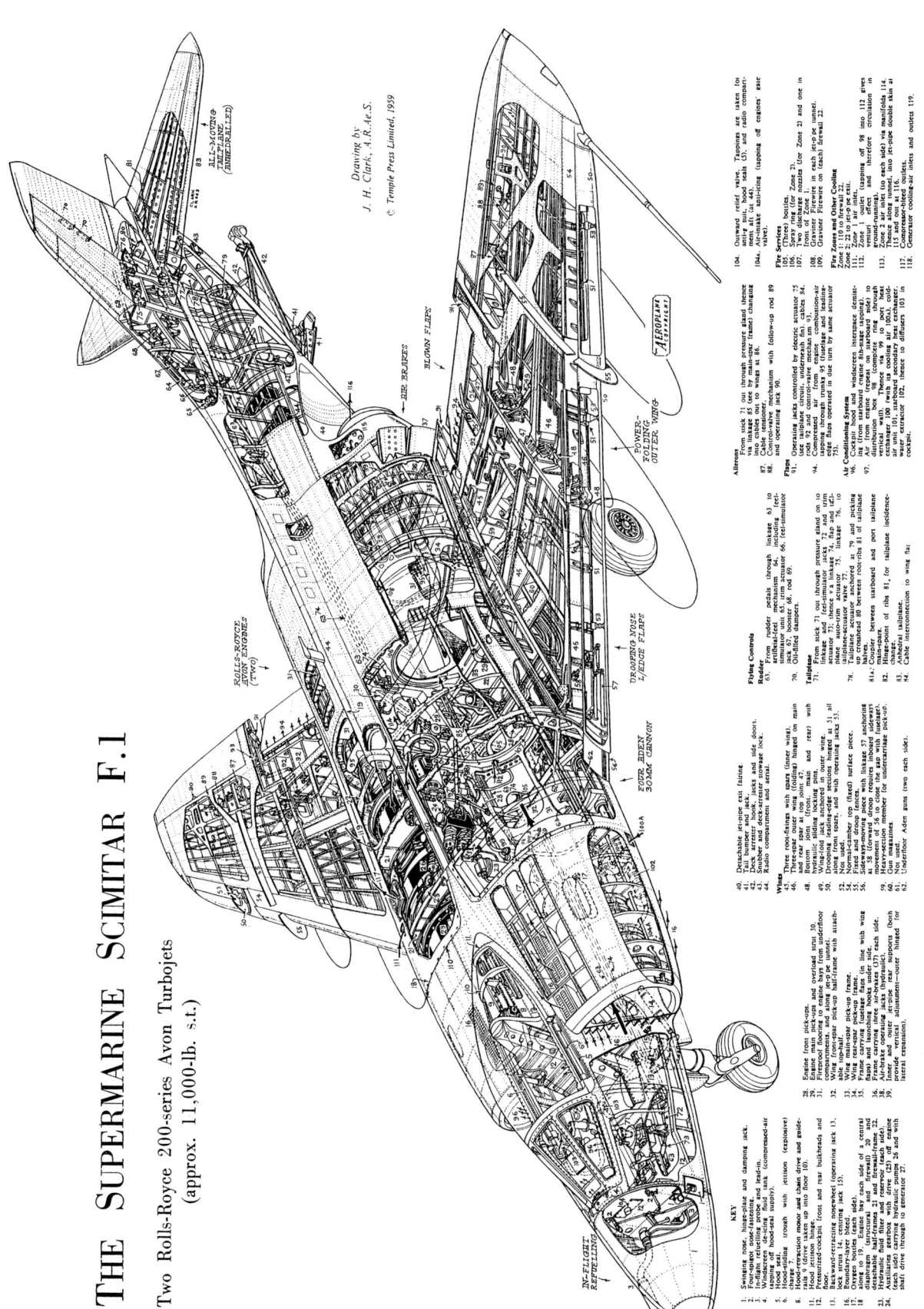

Cut-away drawing of Scimitar F.1. (by kind permission of the Editor of 'Aeroplane' magazine)

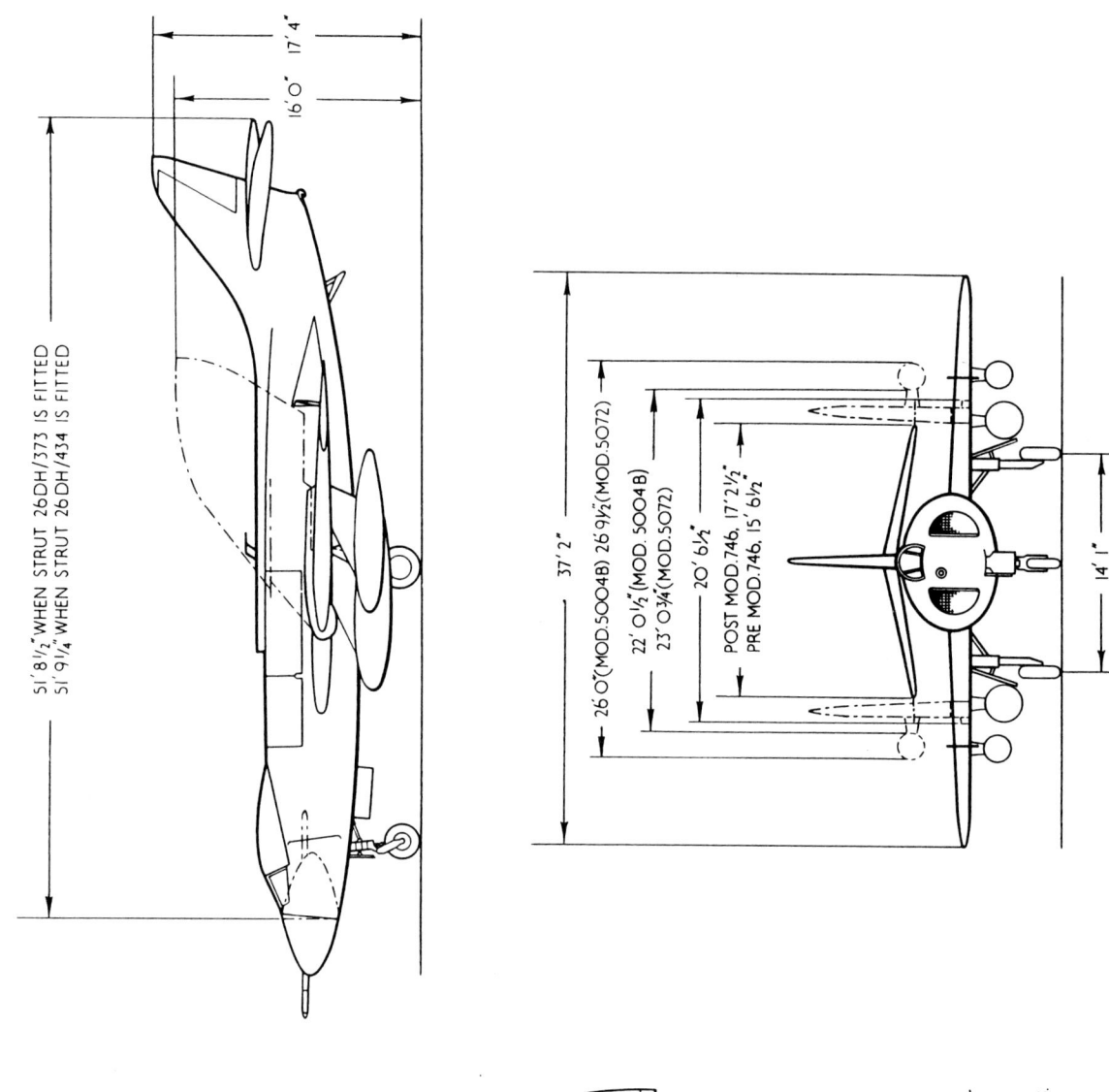

General arrangement of Scimitar F.1

213

## KEY

- (2) 1 HYDRAULIC-FLUID PIPE CONNECTION TO RESERVOIR
- (1) 2 HYDRAULIC-FLUID RESERVOIR PIPE CONNECTION
- (45) 3 ENGINE-STARTER AIR DUCT CONNECTION (ENGINE)
- 4 ENGINE STARTER
- (42) 5 FUEL MAIN-FEED PIPE (ENGINE)
- *6 COMPRESSOR-BLEED OUTLET FLANGE
- (46) 7 STARTER ELECTRICAL-LEAD SOCKET (ENGINE)(P)
- (37) 8 ENGINE SUSPENSION LINKS FWD MOUNTING (2 OFF)
- (49) 9 ANTI-ICING SYSTEM PIPE CONNECTION (ENGINE)
- (50)*10 WHEELCASE BREATHER PIPE CONNECTION (ENGINE)
- (31)*11 AIR SUPPLY PIPE CONNECTION TO DISTRIBUTION BOX (ENGINE)
- 12 ENGINE SLING
- 13 BLOWN FLAPS ELBOW DUCT PRESSURE TAPPING TO FUEL CONTROL UNIT
- 14 COMBUSTION CHAMBER ELBOW DUCT
- *15 FIREWALL-SEAL AND ADAPTOR FLANGE (ENGINE)
- 16 ENGINE AFT BEARING COOLING-AIR DISCHARGE DUCT
- (61) 17 TRUNNION SOCKETS, ENGINE AFT MOUNTINGS (2 OFF)
- 18 COVER PLATE, JET PIPE CONNECTOR (2 OFF)
- 19 JET PIPE
- (60)*20 EXHAUST-UNIT DRAIN CONNECTION (ENGINE)
- (59)*21 COMBUSTION-TUBES DRAIN CONNECTION (ENGINE)
- (58)*22 FLOW CONTROL-UNIT DRAIN CONNECTION (ENGINE)
- (56) 23 OUTBOARD IGNITER-LEAD CONNECTION (ENGINE)
- (55) 24 THROTTLE-CONTROL ROD CONNECTION (ENGINE)(P)
- (54)*25 FUEL PRESSURIZING-AIR PIPE ADAPTER (ENGINE) (P)
- (53)*26 OIL-COOLER DRAIN PIPE CONNECTION (ENGINE)
- 27 FIREWALL
- (47)*28 COMPRESSOR-SEAL VENT OUTLET (ENGINE)
- 29 INBOARD FIREWIRE CONNECTION (BAY)
- (48) 30 ENGINE ELECTRICAL SERVICES SOCKETS (P)
- (11) 31 AIR SUPPLY PIPE CONNECTION TO DISTRIBUTION BOX (BAY)
- 32 GENERATOR GEARBOX SUPPORT-ROD ATTACHMENT BRACKET (BAY)
- 33 GENERATOR AIR-EXTRACTOR PIPE CONNECTION (BAY)
- 34 GENERATOR LEADS TO TERMINAL BOX
- 35 GEARBOX DRIVE-SHAFT, QUICK-RELEASE COUPLING (BAY)
- 36 GENERATOR GEARBOX OIL PIPE CONNECTIONS (BAY)
- (8) 37 ENGINE SUSPENSION LINKS (BAY)

*Installation of the port Rolls-Royce Avon 20201 engine change unit.*

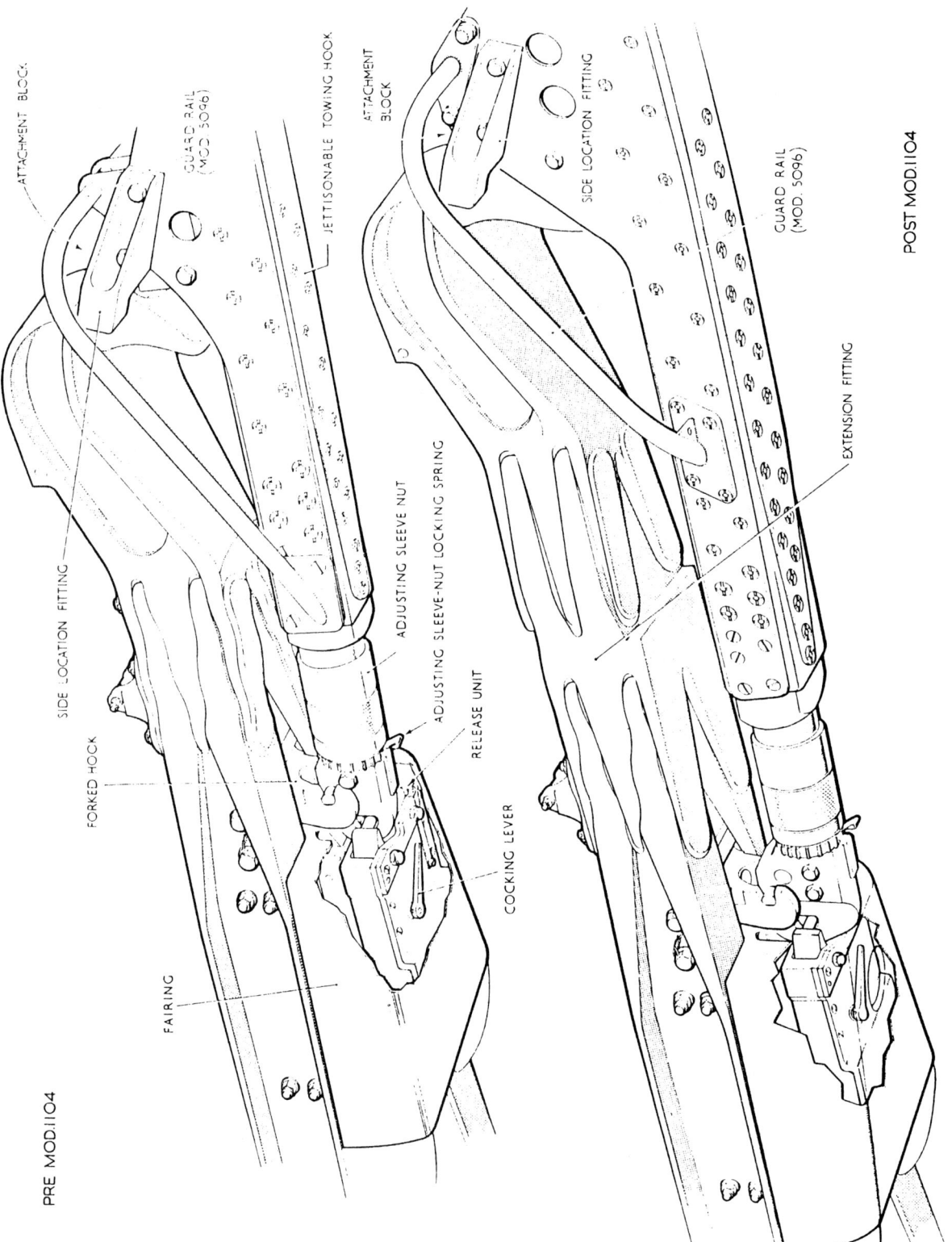

*View showing the extended hook assembly for towing the Dart target.*

# INDEX OF NAMES

Abraham Lt Cdr HJD, 41, 156, 161
Aitchison S/L IMB, 68, 146
Allford S/L(L) FG, 131
Alsop S/L AD, 103, 114, 144, 146, 147, 166, 172, 180, 181,182
Anderson Lt AHS, 58, 73, 103, 131, 166, 167, 168,170, 173, 174, 176, 177, 179, 182
Anderson S/L(S) GT, 131
Andon Lt W, 13
Anson Vice Admiral Sir Edward, 55, 100, 131, 170
Arbuthnott J, 69
Arnold S/L DJL, 132
Askins Lt Cdr SE, 103, 131, 156, 179
Atkinson Lt AT, 101
Ayres Lt Cdr JW, 96

Baker Lt Cdr JD, 101
Baker Lt Cdr R, 137
Ballington Mr F, 23
Banfield Lt Cdr PEH, 55, 56, 108, 114, 166, 174, 178, 181
Barber Lt Cdr PJ, 49, 55, 98, 100, 156, 164, 165, 169, 172
Barrington Lt WD, 172
Beard Lt JW, 100, 131, 171
Bell Gp Capt, 59
Beyfus Lt JG, 100, 131
Billingham Lt JOF, 87, 103, 131, 132, 163, 167, 168, 170, 172, 174, 175, 176, 182
Binney Cdr TVG, 56, 137, 181, 182
Black Cdr WGB, 167
Bolus Lt Cdr MH, 114
Borney C de C MR (FN), 114, 168, 170
Bosworth S/L CA, 103, 131, 163, 170, 172, 175
Bowden S/L NHL, 103, 114, 166, 167, 171, 172, 176
Brandt Lt Cdr J, 152, 168, 174
Bristowe Lt MD, 103, 131, 146, 171, 173, 174
Britton S/L NA, 103, 146, 176, 183
Brophy Lt MJM, 103, 131, 168, 169, 183
Brown Lt Cdr EM, 12, 13
Bugler Lt Cdr JW, 99, 100
Bullivant Lt BJ, 101, 167
Burnet Mr C, 26
Butt Mr C, 155, 171
Bywater F/Lt DL, 156, 164


Cambell Rear Admiral DRF, 118

Campbell Lt Cdr AR, 100, 151, 152, 163, 169, 170, 176, 177
Campbell Cdr I, 55
Cardew Lt Cdr PP, 55-56, 103, 131, 164, 167, 173, 183
Carne Lt Cdr RMP, 106
Carrodus Lt JA, 101
Carter S/L L, 137
Carter Lt Cdr WJ, 53-54
Carver Lt JL, 55, 103, 114, 168, 181
Casperd Lt Cdr CS, 73, 100, 131, 146, 164
Chaffey Lt RC, 103, 107
Checketts Lt Cdr JT, 98, 100, 146
Chicken Lt JR, 103, 107, 114, 132
Childs Lt, 85
Chilton Cdr PCS, 32, 33, 37, 156
Claridge Lt AG, 103, 131, 168, 177
Clifton Mr A, 14, 27, 33, 43, 100
Cockburn S/L RM, 103, 166
Colquhoun Mr LR, 37, 47, 48, 49, 50, 52, 156, 163, 164, 165, 166, 167, 168, 169, 170, 171, 172, 173, 174, 176, 177, 178, 179, 181, 182, 183
Comby Lt J (FN), 132, 171, 181, 183
Cooper Lt C, 131
Cope Lt E, 73, 103, 112, 131, 172, 182
Creasy Lt SC, 103, 131, 170, 183
Cresswell S/L CR, 138, 146
Crispin LAcmn, 175
Cross Lt JB, 114, 122, 131, 173, 176, 177
Crowther Lt CJ, 103, 132, 168, 170, 172, 177, 179
Cunliffe S/L H, 114

Dady Lt AR, 91, 107, 132, 168, 173, 175
Dakin Lt DHT, 103
Davidson Flt Lt RN, 103, 132, 165, 166, 169, 176, 178
Davies Lt B, 98, 100, 131, 146, 170, 173, 176
Davis Lt Cdr PS, 131, 171
Daykin Lt GHJ, 131
Debencourt Capt M (USMC), 39, 165
de Labilliere Cdr AMD, 57-60, 87, 103, 131, 146, 163, 166, 171, 183
De Souza Lt Cdr PG, 58, 60-63, 91, 103, 112, 128, 132, 137, 139, 146, 153-155, 168, 172, 178, 179
Dimmock Rear Admiral RC, 87, 88, 117, 131, 170, 177, 178, 180, 181
Dobree-Carey Lt RdeH, 175
Doughty S/L PG 103, 166, 167, 168, 169
Doust Lt MJ, 103, 114

Drake S/L CS, 131
Dudgeon Lt NL, 101
Duncan Mr J, 155, 170

Eames PO, 92-93
Ebdon Lt MJ, 114
Edward Lt RW, 58, 103, 114, 166, 175
Edwards Lt GJ, 179
Edwardes Lt GC, 103, 122, 131, 177
Ellis Lt AG, 70, 103, 114, 178
Ellis S/L I, 114
Entwisle S/L KR, 114, 169, 176, 181, 182
Esling Lt FE, 101
Evans Lt Cdr TC, 63, 156

Fairhead Lt Cdr WG, 55, 114
Farley F/Lt JF, 156
Farmer Flt Lt M, 103, 169, 171, 175
Faulkner S/L GM, 91, 103, 132, 164, 166, 168, 173, 179, 181, 183
Faulkner Lt JPE, 103, 114, 135, 137, 167, 181, 182
Fellows Lt AAD, 103
Fieldhouse Lt DF, 156, 166
Firth Lt AHP, 150, 151, 170
Fleetwood Lt J, 146
Flexman S/L JS, 103, 131, 166, 168, 170, 172, 173, 175, 179
Flynn Lt Cdr PJ, 146
Ford Lt Cdr JAD, 55, 103, 105, 108, 114, 166, 168, 170, 172, 174, 177, 178, 181, 182
Frenz S/L IC, 103, 114, 117, 132, 171, 176, 177, 178
Furse Rear Admiral JPW, 100

Gartner F/Lt BL (RCAF), 156, 164
Genders Flt Lt GEC, 13
Gerry S/L AJ, 137
Gibson Capt D, 69
Gibson Lt Cdr MJ, 98, 146
Giles Cdr CC, 55, 64-65, 100, 101, 131, 114, 166, 170, 171, 172, 178
Gilroy Flt Lt TG, 132, 170, 173, 177, 178, 182, 183
Goodenough Lt Cdr AJ, 55, 103, 114, 135, 173, 177, 178
Gray Lt RDG, 103, 146, 168, 183
Greenhalgh Lt Cdr A, 131
Grier-Rees Lt Cdr NG, 103, 114, 117, 132, 139, 146, 168, 177, 178, 179, 181
Griffin Lt MG, 172, 177, 179, 180
Griffin Lt Cdr RA, 91, 103, 146, 151
Grove S/L RM, 103
Halliday Lt Cdr DG, 168

Hamilton S/L IGS, 103
Hargraves Cdr CF, 33
Harris Lt BH, 13
Harwood S/L MJ, 103, 131, 168, 172, 173, 183
Hawkes F/Lt AJ, 156
Heath S/L JM, 103, 131, 165, 166, 170, 173, 178, 170
Hedges Lt Cdr MJ, 114, 167
Hefford Capt F, 65-66, 139, 142, 146, 176, 179, 180, 181
Henson Mr G, 27
Hessey Lt PMC, 101, 146, 176
Hickling Lt AM, 85, 103, 114, 174, 179, 182
Hicks S/L R, 114
Hickson Lt J, 114
Higgs Cdr GR, 37, 64, 66-67, 100, 121, 131, 156, 171, 172, 174, 175
Highton Lt RA, 103
Hill S/L AC, 107, 165, 176
Hill Mr TE, 155, 171
Hill-Norton Capt, 66
Hoddinott Lt Cdr GB, 67-68, 146, 156, 172, 173
Horne Lt GJ, 13
Hoskins AA2/C MR, 182
Howard Cdr JDHB, 11, 68-70, 114, 174, 177, 178, 181, 182
Hughes Mr S, 14
Hutton S/L B, 103, 169
Hynett Lt Cdr MT, 70-72, 103, 135, 137, 156, 166, 174, 181

Ingham Lt L, 98, 99, 103, 114, 148, 167, 169, 174, 175, 176, 181
Innes Cdr TG, 83, 96, 100, 166

Jackson Lt Cdr CJ, 137
Jarvis Mr WD, 156, 166
Jenkins Lt HR, 98, 100
Jenner Lt DJ, 101, 146
Johnson Lt MK, 87, 103, 108, 114
Johnston Lt Cdr GAI, 55, 114, 126, 131, 163, 169, 171, 173, 175, 178, 181
Judd Mr, 177
Judge Mr JWR, 37, 42, 51, 156, 166, 167
Julian Lt Cdr HG, 37, 156

Keighley Lt Cdr M, 90-92, 146
Kennett Lt Cdr JF, 58, 103, 114, 167, 168, 169, 175
Kirke Capt DW, 88
Knowles Lt DB, 169
Lacey Mr RV, 155, 171
Laister Lt TMH, 103, 163

Leahy Capt AJ, 57, 66, 72, 122, 131, 170, 171
Lee Lt NE, 101, 167
Leece Lt Cdr TCS, 68, 73-74, 98, 99, 100, 112, 122, 131, 146, 163, 183
Legg S/L CD, 94, 103, 112, 114, 168, 170, 171, 172, 179
Lenton S/L SA, 103
Leppard Lt Cdr KA, 57, 68, 138-140, 146, 173, 174
Lithgow Mr MJ, 17, 23, 26, 27, 30, 32, 33, 36, 37, 39, 42, 43, 156, 161, 163, 165, 167, 169, 182, 183
Little Cdr CM, 29, 30, 156, 162
Lovick Lt PJ, 146

MacFie Lt AG, 103, 114, 171, 176, 179, 182
Macleod Lt IB, 103, 122, 131, 172
Maina Lt MV, 93, 100, 131, 171, 172
Mancais Lt Cdr A, 68, 103, 109, 114, 172, 178, 179, 182
Manley Lt JA, 55, 103, 114, 174, 181
Marindin Lt BP, 132, 164, 167, 168, 170, 173, 183
Marshall Lt PC, 70, 103, 111, 114, 146, 167, 174, 179, 180, 182
Martin Cdr IHF, 53-54, 73, 176
Martin Lt LP, 114
McBain Lt G, 103, 114, 167, 181, 182
McFie Mr R, 43, 45
McIntyre Lt DS, 75, 103, 122, 131, 167, 168, 176
McKeown Lt Cdr DT, 106
McManus Lt PJ, 103, 117, 131, 163, 168, 169, 172, 178, 180, 181, 183
McMeekan S/L A, 103, 112, 114, 132, 166, 167, 172, 175, 180
Mears Lt DP, 101, 135, 137
Meiklejohn Lt IPF, 87, 88, 103, 114, 117, 132, 164, 165, 170, 176, 176, 177
Middleton Lt AJ, 126, 131, 163, 168, 171, 172, 174
Middleton Rear Admiral LE, 74, 98, 100, 103, 131, 170, 174
Miles Lt, 114
Millett S/L RL, 103
Millett Lt T, 103
Millett Lt Cdr P, 45, 156
Mills Lt Cdr DF, 114, 135, 137, 167, 171, 181, 182
Mills Lt Cdr NJP, 57, 74-75, 87, 95, 103, 111, 114, 126, 131, 163, 167, 178, 182
Minton Mr RC, 155, 164, 172
Mitchell Lt P, 95
Mitchell Mr RJ, 27
Monro-Davies Lt ARD, 103, 128, 132, 168, 173, 178, 181, 182
Moore S/L DW, 91, 132, 177

Moore Lt JW, 144, 146, 174
Moorhouse S/L MBV, 103
Morgan Mr DW, 26, 31, 33, 37, 42, 43, 45, 48, 49, 51, 156, 163, 164, 165, 166, 167, 168
Morris Lt CC, 55, 75, 103, 112, 114, 178, 179
Mortimer Lt Cdr AF, 98, 100, 131
Mullins Mr JF, 155, 171, 175
Mumford Flt Lt GSC, 114
Murison Lt PGJ, 103, 174, 179

Nasmith Admiral Sir Martin Dunbar, 135
Neave Lt Cdr BEN, 152
Newington Lt R, 103
Newman Lt Cdr PG, 57, 58, 87, 103, 107, 111, 114, 128, 132, 169, 170, 171, 174, 177, 178, 181
Newnes Lt Cdr CR, 151, 179
Nichols Lt JPF, 103, 114, 172, 176, 180, 181
Norman Cdr DP, 37, 55, 63, 66, 68, 75-76, 108, 109, 114, 156, 169, 175
Normand Lt Cdr PI, 156, 166
Norris Lt NJ, 103, 167
Northam Lt Cdr J, 146
Notley Lt TJ, 91, 103, 107, 132, 146, 179, 182
Noyes Lt RJ, 114, 175

Orpe Lt C, 100, 131
Orr Cdr SG, 30, 156
Ouvry Lt APD, 131
Owen Lt KB, 76, 103, 132, 152, 163, 168, 170, 175, 183

Park Lt AS, 103
Paynter Lt Cdr M, 172
Pentreath Cdre D, 68, 77, 146
Pepper Lt DH, 98, 100, 114
Perkins Lt, 161
Perks Lt PH, 68, 103, 139, 146, 167, 171, 173, 181, 182
Phillips Lt VR, 103
Picking F/Lt AW, 156, 169
Pike S/L G, 146
Plews Lt WN, 13
Pogue Capt WR (USAF), 156, 166
Poirrer S/L AT, 103
Ponter Lt RV, 103, 131, 172, 173, 175, 182
Preston Lt Cdr C, 101, 131
Purvis Lt Cdr JWH, 73, 77-78, 91, 103, 107, 122, 126, 131, 132, 164, 165, 166, 167, 176, 183

Railton Lt MJM, 131
Randall Mr B, 51
Rankin Lt NE, 103, 128, 132, 163, 164, 165, 166,

172, 173, 181, 182
Rees Mr J, 155, 166
Reynolds Lt Cdr A, 66, 131
Richardson Lt D, 170
Rickell Lt Cdr TA, 91, 156
Roach Lt GR, 103
Robbins Capt DF, 78, 156, 165
Rostokwsky Lt H, 101
Routledge S/L RA, 131
Rowan-Thomson Lt Cdr GA, 143, 146, 183
Russell Cdr JD, 99, 100, 118, 121, 131, 172
Rutherford Lt JRJ, 103, 131, 146, 169, 172
Ryce Lt WP, 78-79, 114, 178
Ryde Lt KA, 103

Sabin S/L RV, 101
Saunders Mr, 155, 217
Scadding Lt Cdr M, 114
Scovell Lt LG, 103
Sell S/L AJ, 114
Shea Lt J, 103
Shepherd S/L JS, 103
Shercliff Lt Cdr RF, 91, 107, 132, 137, 164, 177, 182
Shilcock Lt Cdr RA, 96
Shirvall Mr A, 16
Skead Lt TNF, 55, 103, 114, 146, 179
Skinner Mr DR, 152, 170, 174, 177, 181
Skrodzki Lt ZK, 107, 128, 132, 166, 174, 178, 179
Skyrud JP (USN), 156
Slater Lt Cdr DA, 114
Slattery Rear Admiral Matthew, 17
Smith S/L A, 146
Smith S/L EWJ, 172
Smith Mr J, 16, 23, 27
Smith Lt JGL, 79-80, 103, 108, 114, 135, 137, 169, 177, 178, 181, 182
Somerville-Jones Lt EK, 91, 103, 132, 173, 177, 178, 181, 182, 183
Spafford Lt Cdr JT, 151, 156, 168
Spragge Lt Cdr DC, 103
Stevens JH, 93-95
Stevenson Cdr PM, 80-83, 103, 151, 156, 166, 171, 172, 173, 179, 181, 183
Stewart Lt A, 101
Stimpson Lt CD, 100
Stone Lt AJ, 103, 114, 135, 137, 174
Strong S/L TJ, 103
Styles Lt MTH, 103
Sutton Lt JA, 103, 167

Taylor Lt NB, 103
Thomas Lt HW, 103, 132, 168, 181, 182
Thomas Lt Cdr JE (USN), 13

Thomas S/L T, 172
Thorpe Lt WE, 114, 178
Titford Lt Cdr DG, 98, 100, 118, 131
Tod Lt JJR, 103, 114, 165, 178, 181
Tofts Capt WA, 66, 83-84, 98-100, 139, 142, 146, 174, 179
Tonkin Lt EO, 131
Treacher Cdr JD, 172
Trim Mr VD, 33, 45
Tristram Lt Cdr NM, 84-85, 103, 125, 131
Trubshaw Mr EB, 156, 168
Trudgett Lt PJ, 103, 107, 146, 164, 165, 166, 168, 169, 183
Tuck Lt AS, 103, 107, 131, 166, 168, 173, 183
Tuke Lt TM, 103
Tyndale-Biscoe Rear Admiral AJ, 108

Vaughan Lt Cdr DA, 103, 112, 146

Wailes Lt, 54
Walkinshaw Lt CD, 103, 114, 166, 177, 179, 180, 181
Wallace Lt B, 103
Waring Lt PAA, 85-87, 88, 103, 107, 117, 131, 132, 167, 172, 177, 179, 181, 182
Watkinson Lt Cdr LP, 131
Webb Flt Lt MJ, 135, 137, 181, 182
Webster Lt JH, 101
Wells S/L CARP, 103, 131, 164
Westlake S/L RWD, 131, 170, 171, 173, 174
Wheal Lt Cdr CA, 87-89, 103, 117, 131, 168, 176, 177, 178, 180
Whitehead Lt Cdr DJ, 30, 32, 37, 156
Wilkie Lt DGM, 131
Wilkinson Lt LA, 103, 165, 169, 183
Williams Capt JL, 89-90, 103, 135, 137
Williams Lt JP, 101
Williams Lt MJ, 91, 107, 132, 137, 164, 173, 176, 180, 183
Williams F/Lt NR, 156
Willson Lt Cdr B, 131, 173, 183
Wilson S/L CJ, 103, 131, 172, 177
Wilson Mr KG, 155, 175
Wilson Lt Cdr PS, 13
Withers Lt DG, 132
Wood Lt JG, 73, 103, 131, 168, 169, 176, 182
Wooff Lt GHR, 103, 114, 166, 169, 174
Wormell Lt Cdr A, 132
Worth Capt J, 90, 91, 101, 103, 107, 122, 128, 131, 132, 164, 166, 168, 176
Wren Lt R, 131, 163, 168, 170, 173, 177, 181, 182
Young Lt Cdr BG, 135, 137, 177, 181, 182
Young Lt Cdr TFB, 100, 114, 131, 166, 169

# PHOTO MISCELLANY

*XD317 with NASU Brawdy in 1966. (MAP)*

*XD223 '156/R' parked in the Far East around 1964/5. (A.Pearcy)*

*A Scimitar F.1 undergoing arrester trials at RAE Bedford. (E.B.Morgan archives)*

*XD332 '616', formerly of No.764B Squadron, aboard a lighter in 1966. (MAP)*

*A dummy Scimitar just after engaging a test barrier. The barrier straps are wrapped around the dummy, the port wing of which has been knocked off by the edge ropes.*

*Having been damaged in a ground hydraulics accident in August 1966, XD229 was retired from service and is seen here on the dump at West Freugh in 1972. (MAP)*

# OTHER NAVAL AVIATION TITLES PUBLISHED BY AIR-BRITAIN

## THE SQUADRONS OF THE FLEET AIR ARM
(ISBN 0 85130 223 8)

### Ray Sturtivant and Theo Ballance

A completely revised and updated edition of this standard reference work. The original book, published in 1984, was based on many years of research into British naval aviation history. The format is changed to 480 A4-size pages. Fully illustrated with 600 photographs, few of which appeared in the original edition. The co-author for this edition is a serving officer, Lt-Cdr Theo Ballance of RNAS Yeovilton, who has undertaken much of the research on updating entries to cover the period since 1984 as well as various other aspects. In all, there are many hundreds of new and amended entries throughout the book.

Every past and present first and second-line squadron is listed, including Australian, Canadian and Dutch naval squadrons where their unit numbering makes them relevant. The coverage for each squadron comprises a concise narrative history, the squadron badge (if any), photos of representative aircraft in most instances, detailed tables of aircraft types flown with dates and examples, lists of commanding officers and lists of bases including detachments of all sizes. In addition the new edition includes a brief summary of the different types of identification marking carried over the years by squadron aircraft, and also lists battle honours awarded. Detailed indexes cover aircraft equipment, UK and overseas locations, ships names mentioned in the lists, plus a new index of commanding officers names.

Detailed appendices, all updated, cover Boyd Trophy awards, ships names of FAA stations, FAA bases at home and overseas, aircraft carriers, Mac-ships, helicopter-carrying ships, pre-war FAA numbered flights and miscellaneous FAA units. New appendices list FAA Flag Officers and major WW2 warships fitted with catapults. The latter, and also the lists of carriers and helicopter-carrying ships, now include tables of relevant squadrons and flights, with dates and aircraft types with examples. As a cross-reference, there are lists of the identity numbers allocated in recent years to Wasp, Wessex and Lynx flights. There is also a list of naval aircraft currently held by the Yeovilton and Nowra museums.

The whole range of side markings carried on naval aircraft since 1933 is covered in a series of detailed appendices, now revised and updated. Much new information has come to light, especially on wartime markings, and allocations under the current system have been brought right up to date. By reference to these lists and the accompanying general explanation, in conjunction with the information given for each squadron, it should be possible to identify the unit of most naval aircraft bearing a full side marking.

## FLEET AIR ARM AIRCRAFT, UNITS AND SHIPS 1920 TO 1939
(ISBN 0 85130 271 8)

### Ray Sturtivant with Dick Cronin

The first detailed work on the Fleet Air Arm between the wars. Full histories of flights and squadrons, including movements, aircraft types and COs; detailed individual aircraft histories with many aircrew names; detailed histories of FAA and coastal prototypes (N127 to N256 and others); comprehensive details of the complicated and colourful system of code markings and carrier bands; names of pupil Pilots, Observers and TAGs on courses up to the end of 1939; 3,000 name index; detailed movements of 12 aircraft carriers and seaplane carriers, and 60 seaplane-carrying battleships, cruisers and a submarine with a photograph of each ship. Hardback, 448 A4-size pages, including 16 full colour pages illustrating aircraft markings of the period, with 509 photographs.

## ROYAL NAVY SHIPBOARD AIRCRAFT DEVELOPMENTS 1912 TO 1931
(ISBN 0 85130 165 7)

### Dick Cronin

This work covers in detail one of the many interesting aspects of early British naval aviation, and complements 'Royal Navy Aircraft Serials and Units 1911 to 1919'. It has been the subject of numerous enthusiastic reviews in the aeronautical and naval press, both at home and in America. The book deals in depth with a variety of early British naval air operations before flight from aircraft carriers became the normal method of operating.

Coverage includes activities in the North Sea, East Africa, the Eastern Mediterranean and South Russia. The book tells an enthralling story which includes the destruction of two Zeppelins over the North Sea, one by an aircraft from a lighter towed behind a ship, and the other by a machine launched from a platform mounted above a ship's gun turret. There is coverage of such episodes as the vital part played by the RNAS in the destruction of the German cruiser Konigsberg lurking up an East African river, putting spies ashore in Turkish-occupied territory, and the post-war trials of an air-to-surface missile, initially carried out from a warship before being transferred to the Iraqi desert. The book runs to 384 pages and is illustrated by nearly 500 illustrations, including many rare photographs of ships and aircraft as well as maps and side-view drawings of aircraft.

## THE HORNET FILE
(ISBN 0 85130 202 5)

Lewis G. Cooper

A comprehensive record of this beautiful aircraft which recounts its history with Fighter Command. All the aircraft have detailed individual histories and there is a full account of its activities in the squadrons. Includes 49 pages devoted to the Sea Hornet. Naval development from the RAF's Hornet. Squadron and support unit histories with details of individual aircraft flown and squadron pilots. Detailed individual aircraft histories. 148 pages, 116 black and white photographs, six pages of drawings.

## ROYAL NAVY INSTRUCTIONAL AIRFRAMES
(ISBN 0 85130 263 7)

Ray Sturtivant and Rod Burden

Detailed histories of British naval aircraft relegated to ground training tasks and given A2000-series numbers over the last 40 years, plus available information on earlier allocations, also relevant RAF 'M' serials. Previous service identities, code markings, locations etc. Detailed guide to units involved. Comprehensive cross-index. 128 pages, 74 black and white photos. Laminated full colour cover.

## THE HOVERFLY FILE
(ISBN 0 85130 262 9)

Eric Myall

The Sikorsky R-4 Hoverfly was the first practical helicopter and most important forerunner of the world's civil and military rotary wing aircraft. Details the part played by the Royal Navy and the Royal Air Force in its introduction and subsequent development into the Hoverfly II. Detailed individual histories. Hardback, 108 pages, 120 photos, some in colour. Line drawings, 2 pages of full colour graphics.

## ROYAL NAVY AIRCRAFT SERIALS AND UNITS 1911 TO 1919
(ISBN 0 85130 191 6)

Ray Sturtivant and Gordon Page

Probably the most ambitious project of its nature ever attempted, this work provides complete or near complete histories of over 15,000 aircraft flown by the Royal Naval Air Service from 1911 and by successor units of the Royal Air Force from 1 April 1918 until the end of 1919. It also lists their squadrons, units and bases.

During many years of research the authors examined nearly 3,000 files and ships logs in the Public Record Office, as well as numerous documents and photographs in various other archives including the Fleet Air Arm Museum, the Royal Air Force Museum, the Imperial War Museum, the National Maritime Museum and the Liddle Collection at Leeds University. The resulting book runs to 480 pages and contains 321 photographs illustrating the majority of aircraft types flown, including prototypes. Sixteen pages of drawings include plans of over 80 U.K. land and marine bases, as well as location maps of aerodromes and place names in France and Belgium. A comprehensive index details around 4,000 individual names referred to in the lists.

The lists cover aircraft operated in such diverse locations as United Kingdom coastal waters, the North Sea, the Western Front, East Africa, the Eastern Mediterranean, the Dardanelles, the Aegean, Mesopotamia, post-war Russia and training stations at home and in France, as well as aboard ships ranging from impressed paddle-steamers up to battleships. There is detailed coverage of successes and losses on the Western Front. All known operational and non-operational casualties are listed, both fatal and otherwise, in most cases with brief information on the incident and the individual aircraft involved.

There are details of numerous attempts by coastal aircraft to bomb U-boats around the coast of Britain, and of land-based naval aircraft making hazardous night flights to help stem the Zeppelin menace. The many individual incidents include Major Barker's dramatic fight in October 1918 when, despite his Sopwith Snipe being riddled with bullets as he came down, he managed to account for four enemy aircraft before making a crash landing from which he and his aircraft survived, for which unique exploit he was awarded a well merited Victoria Cross.

## AIR-BRITAIN - THE INTERNATIONAL ASSOCIATION OF AVIATION HISTORIANS - FOUNDED 1948

Since 1948, Air-Britain has recorded aviation events as they have happened, because today's events are tomorrow's history. In addition, considerable research into the past has been undertaken to provide historians with the background to aviation history. Well over 17,000 members have contributed to our aims and efforts in that time and many have become accepted authorities in their own fields.

Every month, AIR-BRITAIN NEWS covers the current civil and military scene. Quarterly, each member receives AIR-BRITAIN DIGEST which is a fully-illustrated quality journal containing articles on various subjects, both past and present.

For those interested in military aviation history, there is the quarterly AEROMILITARIA which is designed to delve more deeply into the background of, mainly, British and Commonwealth military aviation than is possible in commercial publications and whose format permits it to be used as components of a filing system which suits the readers' requirements. This publication is responsible for the production of the present volume and other monographs on military subjects.

Also published quarterly is ARCHIVE, produced in a similar format but covering civil aviation history in depth on a world-wide basis. Both magazines are well-illustrated by photographs and drawings.

In addition to these regular publications, there are monographs covering type histories, both military and civil, airline fleets, Royal Air Force registers, squadron histories and the civil registers of a large number of countries. Although our publications are available to non-members, prices are considerably lower for Air-Britain members, who have priority over non-members when availability is limited. Normally, the accumulated price discounts for which members qualify when buying monographs far exceed the annual subscription rates.

A large team of aviation experts is available to answer members' queries on most aspects of aviation. If you have made a study of any particular subject, you may be able to expand your knowledge by joining those with similar interests. Also available to members are libraries of colour slides and photographs which supply slides and prints at prices considerably lower than those charged by commercial firms.

There are local branches of the Association in Blackpool, Bournemouth & District, Central Scotland, Heston, London, Luton, Manchester, Merseyside, North-East England, Rugby, Severnside, Sheffield, Solent, South-West Essex, Stansted, West Cornwall and West Midlands. Overseas in France and the Netherlands.

If you would like to receive samples of Air-Britain magazines, please write to the following address enclosing 50p and stating your particular interests. If you would like only a brochure, please send a stamped self-addressed envelope to the same address (preferably 230mm by 160mm or over) - Air-Britain Membership Enquiries (Mil), 1 Rose Cottages, 179 Penn Road, Hazlemere, High Wycombe, Bucks., HP15 7NE.

### MILITARY AVIATION PUBLICATIONS

Royal Air Force Aircraft series: (prices are for members/non-members and are post-free)

| | | | | | |
|---|---|---|---|---|---|
| J1-J9999 | (£8.00/£10.00) | K1000-K9999 | see The K-File | L1000-N9999† | (£12.00/£15.00) |
| P1000-R9999† | (£11.00/£14.00) | T1000-V9999† | (£12.00/£15.00) | W1000-Z9999† | (£13.00/£16.50) |
| AA100-AZ999† | Reprinting* | BA100-BZ999 | (£6.00/£7.50) | DA100-DZ999 | (£5.00/£6.00) |
| EA100-EZ999 | (£5.00/£6.00) | FA100-FZ999 | (£5.00/£6.00) | HA100-HZ999 | (£6.00/£7.50) |
| JA100-JZ999 | (£6.00/£7.50) | KA100-KZ999 | (£6.00/£7.50) | LA100-LZ999 | (£7.00/£8.50) |
| MA199-MZ999 | (£8.00/£10.00) | NA100-NZ999 | (£8.00/£10.00) | PA100-RZ999 | (£10.00/£12.50) |
| | | SA100-VZ999 (£6.00/£7.50) * | | WA100-WZ999 (£5.00/£7.50)* | |

#### Type Histories

| | | | | | |
|---|---|---|---|---|---|
| The Anson File | (£10.00) * | The Battle File | (£20.00/£25.00) | The Beaufort File | (£10.00/£12.50) |
| The Camel File | (£13.00/£16.00) | The Defiant File | (£12.50/£16.00) | The DH4/DH9 File | (£24.00/£30.00) |
| The Halifax File | (£6.00/£9.00)* | The Hampden File | (£11.00/£13.50) | The Harvard File | (£7.00/£8.50) |
| The Hornet File | (£9.00/£11.00) | The Hoverfly File | (£16.50/£19.50) | The Lancaster File | (£8.00/£12.00)* |
| The Martinsyde File | (£24.00/£30.00) | The Norman Thompson File | (£13.50/£17.00) | The Oxford File | (in preparation) |
| The S.E.5 File | (£16.00/£20.00) | The Stirling File | (£6.00/£9.00)* | The Typhoon File | (£4.00/£6.00)* |
| The Washington File | (£2.00/£3.00)* | The Whitley File | (£4.50/£6.75)* | | |

#### Hardbacks

The Squadrons of the Royal Air Force and Commonwealth† (£15.00/£15.00)*
The Squadrons of the Fleet Air Arm† (£24.00/£30.00)

Both the above cover the histories of all squadrons with precise tables of movements and equipment. Squadron badges are included and both are profusely illustrated.

Royal Navy Shipboard Aircraft Developments 1912 - 1931 (£10.00)
Royal Navy Aircraft Serials and Units 1911 - 1919 (£10.00)
Fleet Air Arm Aircraft, Units and Ships 1920 - 1939 (£26.00/£32.50)
Fleet Air Arm Aircraft 1939 - 1945 (£24.00 /£30.00)*
Royal Navy Instructional Airframes (£14.00/£17.50)
Central American and Caribbean Air Forces (£12.50/£15.50)*
The British Aircraft Specifications File (£20.00/£25.00)
The K-File (the RAF of the 1930s) (£23.00/£30.00)
Aviation in Cornwall (£14.00/£17.50)
Royal Air Force Flying Training & Support Units (£20.00/£25.00)*
Broken Wings – Post-War RAF accidents (£21.00/£26.00)

#### Individual Squadron Histories

With Courage and Faith - The History of No.18 Squadron, Royal Air Force (£5.00/£7.50)
Hawks Rising – the History of No.25 Squadron, Royal Air Force (in preparation)
United in Effort - The Story of No.53 Squadron, Royal Air Force (£15.00/£19.00)
Strike True - The History of No.80 Squadron, Royal Air Force (£4.00/£6.00)*
Scorpions Sting - The Story of No.84 Squadron, Royal Air Force (£11.00/£16.50)
Always Prepared – The History of No.207 Squadron, Royal Air Force (£22.00/£27.50)
The Hornet Strikes - The Story of No.213 Squadron, Royal Air Force (£20.00/£25.00)
Rise from the East - The History of No.247 Squadron, Royal Air Force (£13.00/£16.50)

Except where out of print (marked *), the above are available from Air-Britain Sales Department, 19 Kent Rd, Grays, Essex RM17 6DE.
Visa, Mastercard, Delta/Visa, accepted with number and expiry date, also Switch (with Issue No.also ).
† - completely revised editions.